Turbo Pascal® Tutor

A Self-Study Guide to Turbo Pascal on the Macintosh™

Borland International
4585 Scotts Valley Drive
Scotts Valley, CA 95066
U.S.A.

Printed in the U.S.A.

10 9 8 7 6 5 4 3 2 1

Table of Contents

Part 2 A PROGRAMMER'S GUIDE TO TURBO PASCAL

Appendixes

Welcome to Turbo Tutor, the tutorial for Borland's Turbo Pascal for the Macintosh. This book, in tandem with the sample programs on the disk, teaches you how to write programs on the Macintosh in Turbo Pascal.

How to Use this Book

This book is really two books in one: a textbook on Turbo Pascal and a textbook on writing Macintosh programs in that language. The first three sections describe how to use Macintosh Turbo Pascal to write "standard" Pascal programs; that is, programs that run on the Macintosh pretty much as they would run on a standard personal computer such as an IBM PC.

You won't get into Macintosh-specific material until Part 4, "Using the Power of the Macintosh." If you already know standard Pascal (perhaps you've used the IBM PC version of Turbo Pascal), you may choose to skim these first three sections and plow right into the Macintosh material. But be warned: True Macintosh programming requires a good grasp of the language, particularly of pointers and data typing.

If you're a novice computer user or programmer, begin with Part 1, "Turbo Pascal for the Absolute Novice." It introduces basic information about computers and programming. There's also a simple Pascal program example that you learn to compile and execute.

If you're a more experienced programmer, you may want to glance over the first part and then plunge into Part 2, "A Programmer's Guide to Turbo Pascal." This section provides the basic elements of programming in Pascal, moving step by step through the different aspects of Pascal in general and

Turbo Pascal in particular. You'll see how easy Turbo Pascal makes it to move existing standard Pascal programs over to the Macintosh.

Initially, you'll write simple programs. As you progress, you'll tackle increasingly sophisticated code. Part 3, "Advanced Topics in Turbo Pascal," introduces such subjects as nonlinear data structures, linked lists, stacks, typed constants, and writing large programs.

Part 4, "Using the Power of the Macintosh," provides an overview of the remarkable Macintosh computer—the hardware and software features that make it so different from conventional personal computers.

Part 5, "Programming the Macintosh," digs into the Macintosh/Pascal relationship, working through the major components of the software Toolbox. By the end of Part 5, you'll have seen the insides of a true double-clickable Macintosh application.

Appendices provide reference information. Appendix A is a synopsis of the key Toolbox procedures and functions built into the Macintosh, B gives the answers to the exercises sprinkled within the book, and C provides answers to common questions about Turbo Pascal. Appendix D lists and explains the system error codes, while E is a chart of the Macintosh character set.

Following the appendices are a suggested references list, a glossary of technical terms, and an index.

What this Book Isn't

This book is intended to complement, not replace, the *Turbo Pascal Reference Manual*. It will help you grasp basic Pascal principles and apply them to the Macintosh programming environment. The reference manual can then be used to give exact definitions of the Turbo Pascal implementation. In other words, read this book from beginning to end, then use the reference manual like a dictionary when specific questions come up.

The Disk

The disk that accompanies this package contains the source form of all the the programs discussed in the book. The disk also contains an application called Turbo Tutor—see the next chapter for the complete list of the disk's contents and an explanation of how to use Turbo Tutor.

Typographical Conventions

All typefaces used in this manual were produced by Borland's Sprint: The Professional Word Processor. Remember that any boldface type in this book within program code is for clarity only: Turbo Pascal itself does not recognize or care about such special type treatment of words.

Roman	The body is set in normal, roman type.
Keycaps	This typeface is used for keys on the computer keyboard, such as *Return* and *Options*.
Monospace	Program code is in `typewriter-like` type.
Italics	*Italics* emphasize certain concepts—identifiers, units, types, procedures, and functions.
	Terms that may be unfamiliar are also italicized when first mentioned.
Boldface	**Boldface** type highlights reserved Pascal keywords like **begin** and **end**. (What's a keyword? Stay tuned.)

A Note on Terminology

You may find references in this manual to the *Command* and *Backspace* keys. On the Macintosh SE and II, Apple has renamed these keys *Apple* and *Delete*, respectively. Some keyboards have both the Apple and cloverleaf symbols on the *Command* key.

The functions and uses of these keys haven't changed; only their names have.

What You'll Need

Besides this tutorial and the *Turbo Pascal Reference Manual*, you'll need a few other things. First and foremost, you'll need a Macintosh. This is very much a hands-on course: The best way to learn Pascal is to actually do the things we tell you to do as you work through this book. Only by actually writing Turbo Pascal programs can you gain an appreciation for the language.

You'll also need a supply of blank disks, unless your computer has a hard disk, in addition to the Turbo Pascal program disk and the disk that came with this book.

It will be helpful to have a printer connected to your computer. Bugs are often easier to spot on paper than on the screen.

Contacting Borland

The best way to contact Borland for any assistance is to log on to Borland's forum on CompuServe: Type GO BOR from the main CompuServe menu and select ENTER LANGUAGE PRODUCTS FORUM from Borland's main menu. Leave your questions and comments for the support staff here.

If you prefer, write a letter describing your problem in detail and address it to Technical Support Department, Borland International, 4585 Scotts Valley Drive, Scotts Valley, CA 95066, USA.

As a last resort, you can telephone Technical Support. Please have the following information handy before you call:

- the product name and version number
- your computer make and model number
- your operating system and version number

Now find a comfortable and quiet place, preferably with a large work area so that you can spread out your work and keep everything handy. If there's a phone nearby, unplug it. Take a deep breath, and enjoy your exploration of Turbo Pascal.

TURBO PASCAL FOR THE ABSOLUTE NOVICE

1

Getting Started with Turbo Pascal

There is no easy way to learn a "foreign" language. Going through the material in this book will take time and effort. But when you finish, you'll have acquired the skills necessary to use what many consider to be the most elegant and powerful programming language available today: Turbo Pascal.

We don't know how much you already know about computers. So we'll assume that you're like most people when they get their first computer and consider programming it: a bit overwhelmed, maybe even intimidated by all the jargon attendant to programming.

We further assume a basic level of Macintosh competence. You should already know how to turn the machine on, insert and eject disks, point and click, choose from pull-down menus, start up applications, and manipulate files (copy, delete, rename). If you would like to review these procedures before beginning, your Macintosh owner's manual is a gold mine of information.

If you've spent some time with MacWrite or another word-processing program, you'll find that the Turbo Pascal editor works similarly.

The Macintosh is the most sophisticated personal computer to date, yet it's the simplest to learn to use. Turbo Pascal for the Macintosh is one of the most sophisticated program development systems available on any computer, at any price; it, too, is relatively straightforward to learn. Its fast compilation, windowing editor, and integrated design make it an ideal choice for anyone considering Macintosh programming: professional developer, hobbyist, or student.

Information Resources

Successful programming depends less on having a Vulcan-like memory than in knowing where to find answers. Programmers work best with a few key references within easy reach, and we hope Turbo Tutor becomes that sort of resource for you. Later in your studies, it will be helpful to have access to the set of technical manuals known as *Inside Macintosh*, which provides the detailed information necessary to write complex Macintosh applications. *Inside Macintosh* supplements the information presented in Part 5 of this book.

People are good resources, too. The dealer who sold you your Macintosh is a potential information source. If you don't have a helpful dealer or Macintosh-knowledgeable friend, a local Macintosh users' group can be invaluable. You can find out about such groups in computer magazines or by asking around at computer stores.

Files on the Disk

The disk contains a variety of programs that you can study and adapt for your own purposes. There's an interactive tutorial program called Turbo Tutor: It lets you peruse the source code of several programs, each demonstrating a particular aspect of Pascal and its output. These exercises come complete with quizzes to test your understanding. Turbo Tutor is explained more fully in Chapter 4.

The following table contains a brief description of the disk's contents.

Table 1.1: Files on the Distribution Disk

Readme	This file contains any information more current than that in this manual. To read it, double-click its icon.
Turbo Tutor	A tutorial program that teaches Turbo Pascal concepts on the Macintosh.
Tutor.Pas	The source-code form of the Turbo Tutor program. It requires a number of *include* files (ending in the extension .Inc) for compilation.
Tutor.R	Resource source file for Turbo Tutor program (that is, the RMaker input file).
Tutor.Rsrc	Output of the RMaker program (resource compiler) given in the file Tutor.R. Must be

present to run Turbo Tutor from within Turbo Pascal.

Typist

Typist.Pas	A typing game using standard (non-Macintosh) terminal input/output.
Typist.Data	The data file for the game, containing the words to be typed out.
TypistHelper.Pas	Source code for unit TypistHelper.
TypistHelper	The object form of unit TypistHelper (a UnitMover document).

MacTypist

MacTypist.Pas	The same typing game as a true Mac application.
MacTypist.R	The RMaker input file.
MacTypist.Rsrc	The RMaker output file.
Background.Data	MacPaint file needed by MacTypist.

Lessons contains sample procedures for Turbo Tutor. These procedures are included automatically when you compile the Turbo Tutor program. You can also compile each .Inc file separately by following the instructions at the end of each file:

Arrays1.Inc	Recursion.Inc
Arrays2.Inc	RepeatUntil.Inc
Chars.Inc	Scalars.Inc
ForDo.Inc	Sets1.Inc
IfCase.Inc	Sets2.Inc
Integers.Inc	Strings1.Inc
Pointers.Inc	Strings2.Inc
RandomFiles.Inc	WhileDo.Inc
ReadText.Inc	WriteText.Inc
Reals.Inc	

Miscellaneous

Manual.Pas	has all the source code examples shown in this book. Take advantage of it if you don't want to type in a long example.
Animals.Pas	uses binary trees and artificial intelligence to play a guessing game.
EventWorkbench.Pas	demonstrates event processing.
WindowDemo.Pas	demonstrates window management.

Control Demo

ControlDemo.Pas	demonstrates control processing.
ControlDemo.R	The RMaker input file.
ControlDemo.Rsrc	The RMaker output file.

Dialog Demo

DialogDemo.Pas	demonstrates dialog processing.

| DialogDemo.R | The RMaker input file. |
| DialogDemo.Rsrc | The RMaker output file. |

File Demo

FileDemo.Pas	illustrates choosing and reading files.
FileDemo.R	The RMaker input file.
FileDemo.Rsrc	The RMaker output file.

Menu Demo

MenuDemo.Pas	shows menu and desk accessory processing.
MenuDemo.R	The RMaker input file.
MenuDemo.Rsrc	The RMaker output file.

| **QuickDraw Examples** | contains .Pas files demonstrating QuickDraw calls. |

Now, let's begin by briefly discussing computers in general—the myths surrounding them, their capabilities and limitations, and some hardware and software basics.

2

Computer Basics

"Things are always at their best in their beginning."
　　　—Blaise Pascal, *Lettres Provinciales*, No. 4

There are serious misconceptions about what computers are and what they can do—so many that we're going to devote the first part of this chapter to myth debunking. We'll then look at some basic properties of computers: hardware, digital information, software, and characters.

Myth versus Reality

If you are new to computers, you may have some unrealistic expectations based on movies or science-fiction books. Authors tend to give computers powers beyond those of mere machines, such as true intelligence and human emotions.

So what are computers *really* like? Well, beyond the misconceptions lie three basic properties shared by all modern computers:

- Computers are fast.
- Computers are stupid.
- Computers are literal.

Computers Are Fast

Computers are incredibly fast at certain simple, repetitive, usually numeric tasks—like adding numbers. For instance, a Turbo Pascal program that counts from zero to a million by ones would finish the job in six seconds. (If *you* were to count a number every second, you would take eleven and a half days to reach a million.)

Computers Are Stupid

Computers are stupid in the extreme: They cannot do *anything* without being told explicitly to do so.

Every single action a computer takes is based on an instruction given to it. The actual, physical *hardware* is useless without *software*; that is, without the necessary commands to make it do useful work. If you turn on a Macintosh without built-in software, it does absolutely nothing. It doesn't know how to display characters on the screen or accept characters from the keyboard. This is why the Macintosh, like all modern computers, has startup software built into its electronic circuits—enough to display an opening screen and to read other programs (like the Finder) from disk.

Computers Are Literal

Computers take every instruction they are given literally. They do exactly what they are told—no more, no less. Even if you tell it to do something unreasonable, the computer blindly follows your orders. For example, if you were to write a program that told the Macintosh to count from zero to a trillion by zeros, it would count 0...0...0... very quickly, and potentially forever, until you stopped it. A human being would quickly see that counting by zeros accomplishes nothing and give up; the computer has no such wisdom.

The bottom line is that computers aren't magic. They don't do *everything* well.

All that said, there is a certain fascination in making that mass of wire and silicon do what you want it to. Be forewarned: you may find yourself spending countless hours hunched over your keyboard, adding just one more feature or removing one last bug.

Just keep in mind that you must tell your computer exactly what you want it to do, and when and how you want it to do the task. Fortunately, this process is now much simpler than it used to be—as you shall see in the next sections.

Computer Hardware

Hardware refers to the physical equipment that makes up a computer system. A Macintosh consists of the following components:

- Central Processing Unit (CPU)
- Memory: Random-Access Memory (RAM) and Read-Only Memory (ROM)
- Mass storage device(s): floppy disks or hard disk drive
- Input devices (keyboard, mouse)
- Output devices (screen, printer)

Central Processing Unit

The CPU is the "brain" of the computer. (Brain may be too strong a word, because the CPU isn't very smart—it is capable of executing only very simple instructions.) The CPU can do such things as retrieve a number stored in a memory location, get another number, add the two numbers, and store the result in yet another memory location.

The CPU type determines the kinds of programs your computer can run. Some popular CPUs (also known as *microprocessors*) are the 8080 and Z-80 (which are used in computers running the CP/M operating system) and the 8086 family (used in IBM PCs and compatibles to run MS-DOS). Macintoshes use processors made by Motorola, the 68000 (in the Plus and SE) and the 68020 (in the Macintosh II).

Memory

Every Macintosh has read/write, *random-access memory* (RAM), which stores programs and information while the machine is turned on. It's called "random-access" because its microprocessor can read or write any part at any time, rather than having to access things in a particular order. You can change what's stored in RAM very quickly: It takes the processor on the order of a millionth of a second (0.000001 seconds) to read or write a single data item in RAM. A Macintosh contains anywhere from 128,000 to over 4,000,000 memory cells of RAM.

There's also *read-only memory* (or ROM). ROM stores the instructions (programs) permanently built into the computer and is just as "random-access" as RAM. The Macintosh has hundreds of subroutines built into ROM that are available for use by programs you write; you'll learn how to use them in Part 5 of this book. ROM also has a startup routine that is automatically executed every time you flip on the power switch; it performs a self test, displays the familiar "Welcome to Macintosh" screen, and loads and runs the Finder. Most Macintoshes currently contain 128K of ROM.

The Macintosh Plus is extremely difficult to take apart (the process requires two tools not often found outside an Apple repair depot or a well-equipped surgical suite), but the Macintosh II and SE aren't. If you look inside a Mac, you'll see the *logic board* nestled at the bottom of the case. On this board are the ROM, RAM, and CPU chips that form the heart of the Macintosh. The various connectors on the back of the machine tie directly into the logic board; the screen and disk drive are connected by cables.

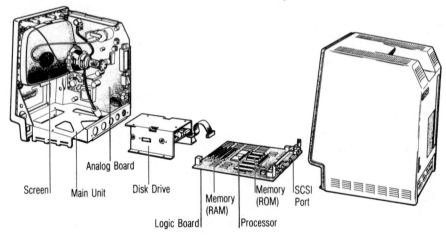

Figure 2.1: The Insides of a Macintosh

Mass Storage

Computers have a limited amount of RAM. (A rule of thumb holds that at any given time a personal computer has about half as much RAM as its owner would like.)

RAM has room for a relatively small amount of information at any one time, certainly not all the programs and data you would prefer to have available. Another limitation is that for most types of RAM, including that used in the Macintosh, turning off the power for even a fraction of a second causes everything stored in RAM to be lost.

The solution to RAM's limitations is *mass storage*. Also called secondary storage to differentiate it from primary storage (memory), these peripheral devices store large amounts of data with or without the power turned on. Macintosh mass storage takes the form of one or more disk drives. Every Macintosh has a built-in 3 1/2-inch drive. Even though there isn't anything flexible about the hard shell that encases a Macintosh disk, for historical reasons removable disks of this type are called *floppy disks*. (They *are* floppy inside the shell.)

You may also have an external floppy drive (which doubles your storage) or, on an SE or II, two internal floppy drives. If you're lucky, you have a *hard disk*. It not only stores huge amounts of data, it also works with that data many times faster than a floppy disk drive does.

For this book's purposes, we refer to mass storage as a *disk drive* unless it is important to distinguish between a floppy disk and a hard disk.

Input and Output Devices

An input device *sends* data to the computer. The Macintosh's input devices are its mouse and keyboard. The mouse sends position information whenever it is moved and button status information (pressed or not) continuously. The keyboard transmits data whenever a key is pressed.

An output device *receives* data from the computer. The Macintosh's primary output device is the screen. A less important output mechanism is the speaker. Other output devices include printers and modems.

Digital Data

Your Macintosh's memory (RAM and ROM) can be thought of as a huge wall of switches. Each switch has only two positions, on and off. When a switch is on, it lets electricity flow to another part of the computer; when it's off, electricity can't flow. Let's call the *on* state of the switch *1* and the *off* state *0*.

A single switch controls (or represents) only a single *bit* (binary digit) of information. If you arrange two switches side by side, four different things can be controlled or represented, as shown here:

Switch A		Switch B		Number Represented
OFF	0	OFF	0	0
ON	1	OFF	0	1
OFF	0	ON	1	2
ON	1	ON	1	3

And, if you have eight switches arranged next to one another, you can control or represent 256 different things. Each switch you add doubles the number of possible states. This system of representing quantities by 0s and 1s is called the *binary system* (or base 2). The system of numbers you're most familiar with is the *decimal system* (base 10).

Now let's look at how the computer's memory stores instructions and information. For the moment, think of RAM as a group of switches arranged in a matrix of 8 columns by *n* rows. For a 64K memory, 65536 rows of switches are required. (In the context of programming, 1K equals 1024, so 64K = 64 * 1024 = 65536.) Each row can store an 8-bit code representing a number, a character, or an instruction that the CPU understands. The CPU is "told" what operation to perform via such a coded instruction from memory.

As it turns out, 8 bits is an especially handy number of bits for computers to work with, so a group of 8 bits is given a special name: a *byte*. If your system contains 512K of RAM, it has the equivalent of 8 columns by 524288 rows of switches.

The switches that make up RAM are microscopic electronic circuits capable of controlling the flow of electricity. They are contained in small (though not microscopic) packages called *integrated circuits*, or *chips*, that are mounted on the logic board along with the processor and other components.

Addresses

Each byte of memory has a unique *address*: in a 128K system, addresses range from 0 to 131071; in a 512K system, from 0 to 524287; and so on. The processor uses this address to access a particular byte of memory, similar to the way the telephone network uses phone numbers to access individual phones out of millions.

The CPU retrieves instructions stored in RAM by requesting ("dialing") the contents of a particular address in memory. The binary code (1s and 0s) contained in memory passes over wires (or printed circuits) to the CPU. CPU instructions are numeric codes that instruct the CPU to move data from one location to another; add, subtract, multiply, and divide data; and perform other basic operations. This binary code is called *machine language*.

If the instruction retrieved by the CPU happens to require additional data, the instruction tells the CPU to go to a particular memory address and get that data. If the instruction creates new data (say, the result of adding two numbers), it instructs the CPU to place the new data in a vacant memory location.

The individual operations that a CPU can perform are surprisingly limited—reading and writing memory and basic arithmetic. The processor may have a small repertoire, but it can perform that repertoire at the rate of hundreds of thousands of instructions per second; this allows elaborate operations to be built up by combining simple ones.

Computer Software

So far, we've tried to restrict our discussion to computer hardware. This is difficult, however, because software is so closely related to hardware. One without the other is useless. Computer *software* refers to instructions that the computer can read to make it perform some function. Software that is permanently encoded in ROM is called *firmware*—a semantic compromise between hardware and software.

In general, computer software can be divided into two broad categories: system software (or operating systems) and application software.

System Software

When you program, you don't want to have to continually tell the computer how to perform certain basic tasks—such as accept characters from the keyboard, display characters on the screen, send characters to the printer in the correct format, write a byte of data to the disk, read a byte of data from the disk, or create and delete files. Indeed, if you had to tell the computer how to do all these things, you'd never get around to the original problem you set out to solve: Not only are these functions menial, they're exceptionally hard to program.

Such tasks are handled by a program that is already written, usually by the computer's manufacturer. It's called the *operating system*. An operating system performs basic functions in response to commands that your programs issue. This frees you to concentrate on the bigger issues of your task, rather than the fine details of keyboard and disk hardware.

On the Macintosh, the role of the operating system has been expanded far beyond that available on previous personal computers. There are some 600 separate operations that the Macintosh operating system will do for you (including the utilities in the Macintosh Toolbox). When you have advanced a bit in your studies, you'll realize that about 80 percent of Macintosh programming is learning to use these Toolbox routines properly.

Application Software

Application software consists of task-specific programs. Some of these programs may come with your computer; others are available for purchase. Application software can be written also by you, your friends, or your company to solve a particular problem. Examples of application software are word processors like MacWrite and Microsoft Word, spreadsheets like Excel, database managers like Reflex, and communications programs like SideKick's MacTerm.

Assemblers, compilers, and *interpreters* are programmers' applications—a special class of software used in the development process to translate programs written in a computer language, such as Pascal or BASIC, into a form your computer can run. For example, Turbo Pascal was written using an assembler and is itself a compiler. We'll talk more about this in the next chapter.

Characters

In the processor's world, everything is a number. Circuits inside the keyboard convert the action of a finger pressed against a key into numbers sent down the curly cable to the logic board; circuits in an ImageWriter convert numbers sent down the printer cable into alphanumeric ink-on-paper images that mean something to human beings.

To a programmer, the term *character* refers to the letters, numbers, and punctuation marks displayed by your computer's screen or printer and depicted on its keyboard. This definition of a character also includes certain nonprinting *control characters* that are used to send commands (for example, *Tab* and *Return*) rather than to represent a printable form. So characters are divided into two groups: the printing characters, which have a visual equivalent, and the control characters, which don't.

The printing characters are on the Macintosh keyboard. They include the 26 letters of the alphabet (in both uppercase and lowercase), the digits 0 through 9, and various punctuation symbols (,./?!#&, and so forth). Spaces (the gap between words produced by pressing the space bar) are considered characters in their own right. Additional printing characters can be produced by using the *Option* key as a second "shift." The Key Caps Desk Accessory that comes on your Macintosh system disk provides software key caps to describe what keys to press to get these additional characters. For example, *Option-G* produces ©, the copyright symbol.

Characters aren't represented pictorially in memory; instead, numeric codes stand for the characters. For example, internally the Macintosh represents a question mark (?) with a code value of 63; *A* is code 65; a space is code 32.

It would be very confusing if different computer manufacturers used their own codes for representing characters. Fortunately, most follow a standard called the American Standard Code for Information Interchange, ASCII (pronounced *as'-key*) for short.

The ASCII character set (shown in Figure 2.2) is nothing more than an agreement that associates a number between 0 and 127, inclusive, with 128 common printable and non-printable control characters. With the adoption of ASCII in the 1960s, it became possible for Manufacturer X to hook his printer up to Manufacturer Y's computer and have both machines agree on the code that represents *A*.

DEC	HEX	CHAR	DEC	HEX	CHAR	DEC	HEX	CHAR
0	00		43	2B	+	86	56	V
1	01		44	2C	,	87	57	W
2	02		45	2D	-	88	58	X
3	03	ETX	46	2E	.	89	59	Y
4	04		47	2F	/	90	5A	Z
5	05		48	30	0	91	5B	[
6	06		49	31	1	92	5C	\
7	07		50	32	2	93	5D	]
8	08	BS	51	33	3	94	5E	^
9	09	TAB	52	34	4	95	5F	_
10	0A		53	35	5	96	60	`
11	0B		54	36	6	97	61	a
12	0C		55	37	7	98	62	b
13	0D	CR	56	38	8	99	63	c
14	0E		57	39	9	100	64	d
15	0F		58	3A	:	101	65	e
16	10		59	3B	;	102	66	f
17	11		60	3C	<	103	67	g
18	12		61	3D	=	104	68	h
19	13		62	3E	>	105	69	i
20	14		63	3F	?	106	6A	j
21	15		64	40	@	107	6B	k
22	16		65	41	A	108	6C	l
23	17		66	42	B	109	6D	m
24	18		67	43	C	110	6E	n
25	19		68	44	D	111	6F	o
26	1A		69	45	E	112	70	p
27	1B	ESC	70	46	F	113	71	q
28	1C	FS	71	47	G	114	72	r
29	1D	GS	72	48	H	115	73	s
30	1E	RS	73	49	I	116	74	t
31	1F	US	74	4A	J	117	75	u
32	20	*space*	75	4B	K	118	76	v
33	21	!	76	4C	L	119	77	w
34	22	"	77	4D	M	120	78	x
35	23	#	78	4E	N	121	79	y
36	24	$	79	4F	O	122	7A	z
37	25	%	80	50	P	123	7B	{
38	26	&	81	51	Q	124	7C	|
39	27	'	82	52	R	125	7D	}
40	28	(	83	53	S	126	7E	~
41	29	)	84	54	T	127	7F	DEL
42	2A	*	85	55	U			

Figure 2.2: Partial Character Set (Standard ASCII Only)

Examine this chart for a few minutes. Note that each lowercase letter's code is exactly 32 greater than its uppercase equivalent. *A* is ASCII code 65, *a* is code 97; *B* is 66, *b* is 98. This means that you can convert a lowercase letter to uppercase by subtracting 32 from its ASCII code (or, to do the reverse, by adding 32). Note also that the codes for the decimal digits can be translated into their numeric value by subtracting 48. For example, the ASCII code for *2* is 50; 50 minus 48 equals 2. This sort of translation comes in handy.

The characters you can create with the *Option* key have code values above 127 and aren't part of the ASCII standard. They result from Apple's engineers taking a fresh look at ASCII's omissions. The copyright symbol © has code value 169, which means you'll never see a copyright symbol in a text file that originated with a standard ASCII computer. It also means that if you send an Option key character to a non-Macintosh computer, it won't know what to do with it.

Review

A modern microcomputer consists of a central processing unit (CPU), random-access memory (RAM), read-only memory (ROM), a mass storage device (disk drive), a keyboard, and a screen. An operating system provides you with a base of low-level subroutines that can be accessed by application programs. ASCII is a near-universal method of representing textual information by converting letters, numbers, and punctuation symbols into numeric form the computer can understand.

Let's now discuss programming languages in general, and Pascal in particular.

3

A Brief History of Programming

While you don't have to know the history of computer programming to use Turbo Pascal, this chapter will give you an appreciation of just how far computer technology has come in a short period of time. (If you need to start programming in Pascal right away, skip ahead to Chapter 4 and save this one for later.)

In the Beginning

In the early days of computers (about 40 years ago), there were no programming languages. Programs were created by physically connecting wires inside bulky machines. Wires were moved and suddenly a computer could calculate 10-inch cannon projectile trajectories instead of 8-inch trajectories. Then someone (probably a wirecutter, *er*, programmer) had the marvelous idea of installing switches in the place of the wires. To this day, many computers have such switches for entering small programs.

To program by flipping switches, you had to convert everything to a binary number: The switch was on for *1* and off for *0*. (We referred to this in Chapter 2 as a binary, or base 2, system.) You would set an instruction by flipping as many as 64 switches (representing one number or code), press another switch to enter the instruction, then repeat this process to enter the next instruction. A series of lights corresponding to each switch indicated the contents of the instruction entered. In many cases, the result of running a program was simply a display of lights that had to be converted into a meaningful number. The programmer was in big trouble if a bulb burned out.

Let's say you wanted the computer to calculate the result of 2 + 2. You would have to convert these numbers to binary form (*0000000000000010 + 0000000000000010*), enter them, and then enter the binary code to add the contents of the two memory locations holding those numbers (perhaps a code such as *0001100011010001*). You'd then press the Run button, the lights would blink, and the answer would be displayed as a row of lights. In this case, the correct answer is *0000000000000100*, which is the binary representation of the decimal number 4. If, instead, the answer presented was *1*, you probably set a switch that told the computer to divide rather than add. You can imagine the complications of dealing with negative numbers and fractions.

Programming Shorthand

The practice of entering instructions as binary numbers, called machine language, was tedious and prone to error. Frustrated programmers soon devised ways to make the computers themselves perform this chore, using an English-like method of representing instructions. This shorthand is *assembly language.*

Using assembly language, programmers can enter a line such as MOVE (16),(211) to move the contents of memory location 16 to memory location 211. The computer does the dirty work of converting the programmer's shorthand into binary machine code. The program that performs the conversion is called an *assembler.*

Assemblers are still widely used today—in fact, Turbo Pascal itself was written in assembly language. Work in assembly language requires an assembler designed specifically for the CPU in your computer and a solid understanding of your computer's hardware. It also helps to have an inexhaustible supply of patience and a cyborg-like brain.

The one-to-one relationship between assembly language and the target CPU's instruction set allows a programmer to create the smallest, fastest programs possible for a given machine—which is why Turbo Pascal is written in assembly language. However, both the assembler and the assembly-language programs written for it can only be used with one particular CPU type. If you spend many months and thousands of dollars writing an assembly-language program for a particular computer, you'll have to spend even more time and dollars to rewrite it for another computer with a different CPU and assembly language. This is one reason high-level programming languages, such as Pascal, were invented.

High-Level Languages

In a high-level language, a single line of programming code may implement ten or more lines of assembly language. In theory, high-level languages allow one programmer do the work of ten assembly-language programmers. The trade-off is that the programs produced by a high-level language aren't as fast or conservative of memory as an equivalent assembly-language effort.

A high-level language also makes it unnecessary for the programmer to know many of the machine's technical details. By and large, high-level languages "look" the same to the programmer, no matter what computer is being used. The programmer need only be familiar with the language. For example, a program written in Turbo Pascal for the IBM PC usually requires only minor modifications to run on the Macintosh.

There are several prominent high-level languages. When the United States Department of Defense decided that it wanted to run its programs on many kinds of machines, it chose the **CO**mmon **B**usiness **O**riented **L**anguage, or COBOL for short. (It has since switched to Ada, a Pascal-like language.) When scientists learned that computers could help in their calculations, they invented a language specifically designed to process scientific formulas called **FOR**mula **TRAN**slator (FORTRAN). FORTRAN is still widely used today due to IBM's adoption of it as the "official" language for its mainframe computers.

Other languages—such as PROLOG, C, BASIC, ALGOL, APL, and LISP—have also appeared on the scene. Each has special features for a particular kind of work. PROLOG, for example, is used in artificial intelligence (AI) research, and APL is suited to scientific and statistical work.

Programming Languages and Microcomputers

When the microcomputer came along in the mid-seventies, it had very little memory and ran much slower than its larger cousins. Languages like

FORTRAN and COBOL stretched the microcomputer's resources in addition to being too complex for the average microcomputer user to learn.

A simpler language was needed, and the language that most microcomputer manufacturers chose was BASIC (**B**eginner's **A**ll-purpose **S**ymbolic **I**nstruction **C**ode). BASIC is relatively easy to learn and is still an excellent choice for solving simple problems. However, it's difficult to divide a BASIC program into many small parts and construct each part separately, so it can be less appropriate for sophisticated applications. Pascal was developed as one educator's divide-and-conquer approach to programming.

And Finally...Pascal

Pascal is a relatively young programming language. It was developed by a distinguished computer scientist named Niklaus Wirth in Zurich, Switzerland, in the early seventies. Wirth based some of Pascal's concepts on some other languages he helped develop, PL/1 and ALGOL. (If there was a Programming Languages Hall of Fame, Wirth's bust would be in a place of honor.)

Professor Wirth designed Pascal to teach his students how to program effectively. Good programming starts with accurately defining the problem, breaking it down into small parts, and then writing commands that solve each of these smaller problems (which may need further subdivision). Pascal is said to be a "structured" language: You write programs in small chunks, following predefined steps. Certain parts must be placed in specific locations within a program and must follow certain rules.

You'll find that the statements in a Pascal program read much like English sentences. In a well-written Pascal program, the definition of a problem, the smaller parts that make it up, and the ways in which the smaller problems are solved are easy to see.

Interpreters and Compilers

Regardless of which high-level language you use, something has to translate the English-like words of the program into the binary *1*s and *0*s (machine language) that the computer's CPU understands. The programs that perform this translation can be divided into two categories: *interpreters* and *compilers*. Turbo Pascal and most other high-level languages are compiled.

The difference between interpreting and compiling concerns how programs are executed.

An interpreter translates your instructions *during* execution. You run the interpreter program every time you want to execute your program. The interpreter then reads each statement of the program one at a time, figures out the operation being requested, and then performs the necessary acts.

By contrast, a compiler translates your entire program into machine (or some other low-level) language *before* the program begins to run. Once translation is finished, the compiler is no longer needed—the application program can run on its own. Because the translation isn't performed at run time, a compiled program almost always runs faster than one that must be interpreted.

Which of these two approaches is best? It depends on your requirements. A large program written with an interpreter tends to require less memory than an equivalent compiled program, but may execute as much as 10 to 50 times more slowly. Programs compiled with a powerful, efficient compiler can approach the size and speed of assembly language; however, the program must be recompiled each time a change is made. This means the speed with which you can test your program, find errors, fix those errors, and retest the program is greatly reduced.

An interpreted language is most efficient during the process of testing and modifying your program. There is no need to wait for the program to recompile—you can give the interpreter the Run command and road test your program at any time.

With traditional compilers, you must write your application program using a stand-alone text editor, then start up the compiler and give it the name of the file you want to compile. Most compilers take several minutes to compile a moderately complex program. Then, when you return to execute your program, you'll probably find mistakes (commonly referred to as *bugs*). So you'll have to restart your editor, reload the original program, and try to figure out what went wrong (known as *debugging*). Then, you must recompile the program and test it again. You usually have to repeat this edit-compile-test cycle many times to produce a program that works the way you want it to.

Ideally, then, one would like a compiler that is so fast that using it is like using an interpreter. And that's exactly what Turbo Pascal for the Macintosh is: It's a compiled language that's as convenient to use as an interpreted language.

The Turbo Pascal Advantage

Turbo Pascal is a compiler, but it doesn't put you through the grueling cycle just described. You can perform all the functions necessary to write a program without leaving the Turbo Pascal environment. And the compiler is so fast you can compile most programs in a matter of seconds instead of minutes. Once compiled, you can run your program to test it without leaving the Turbo Pascal environment. Finally, when errors are found, Turbo Pascal shows you the line of the program that caused the error.

Turbo Pascal's edit/compile/test cycle is so fast that, in most cases, there is virtually no distinction between it and an interpretive language—except that your programs execute 10 to 50 times faster. In the next chapter, you'll learn how to prepare your computer for Turbo Pascal.

4

Getting Ready to Use Turbo Pascal

Before using Turbo Pascal, you should make working copies of your master disks (both Turbo Pascal and Turbo Tutor). This chapter explains how to make these backups. It also describes how to use the Macintosh Turbo Tutor teaching program that came with this book.

Backing Up: Why and How to

Although the Macintosh's shirt-pocket-sized disks are better than their 5 1/4-inch ancestors in this regard, they can still be rendered unreadable by many things—coffee, dogs, two-year-olds, magnetic fields, heat, and the most pernicious of all: accidental erasure due to operator error.

At some point most of us fall prey to one or more of these disk-destroying perils. Losing an occasional disk is a fact of computer life. Losing work doesn't have to be, *if you back up your work*. There are two types of backups, corresponding to the two types of files you work with.

Some files never change. For example, the RMaker program on the Turbo Pascal Utilities & Sample Programs disk never changes, no matter how many thousands of times you use it. So it only needs to be backed up once.

Other files change daily. When working with Turbo Pascal, the most dynamic files are the text files you create and edit. These files need to be backed up whenever you have more work in them than you can afford to lose. Given that it takes only a minute or two to protect yourself, most people should probably back up every few hours.

To back up your master Turbo Pascal and Turbo Tutor disks, follow the instructions below that describe your configuration (single drive, two drive, and hard disk).

NOTE: Turbo Pascal is shipped on two 400K floppies. The disk labeled *Program Disk* is a bootable disk and contains the compiler itself (the file Turbo, with the checkered flag icon). Also on this disk is a System file and the Finder program. The disk labeled *Utilities & Sample Programs* contains various auxiliary programs (RMaker, Font+DA Mover), and a number of example programs in source form.

For safety's sake, write-protect your originals before beginning the copy procedure. A disk is write-protected by sliding *open* the tab in the upper right-hand corner (look at the back of the disk). If you can see light through the hole, the disk is said to be write-protected, and any attempt to alter its contents will fail. (You can still zap a disk by leaving it on the dashboard of a black car in Houston, Texas, in August, for example, so backing up is essential.)

Single-Drive Machines

1. Insert the Turbo Pascal Program Disk and turn the Macintosh on.

2. Select the disk's icon (put the pointer on it and click) and choose Eject from the File menu. Note that this is *not* the same as dragging it to the trash. The Program Disk's icon is dimmed as the disk is ejected from the drive.

3. Insert a blank disk (or a disk whose contents you don't need any more). If it needs formatting, this operation takes place automatically. If you have a double-sided (800K) drive, you'll be asked if you want to format the disk as single or double sided. Assuming you inserted a disk certified for double-sided use, choose double sided.

4. Select the dimmed icon of the Turbo Pascal system disk and drag it on top of the blank disk's icon.

5. The Finder then asks if you want to replace the entire contents of the blank disk with the contents of the Turbo Pascal Program disk. Click OK.

6. When the copy completes (several swaps are necessary), the formerly blank disk will be identical to the Turbo Pascal Program distribution disk, although it will have a different name. You can name your new backup disk by clicking in the area under the disk icon and typing a new name, such as TP Work Disk.

7. Repeat this process with the Utilities & Sample Programs and the Turbo Tutor disks.

Two-Drive Machines

1. Boot with the Turbo Pascal system disk in the internal drive.
2. Insert a blank disk into the external drive. If it needs formatting, that takes place automatically: If you have a double-sided drive, click on Two-sided when asked by the Finder.
3. Select the icon of the Turbo Pascal system disk and drag it on top of the blank disk's icon.
4. The Finder will ask if you want to replace the entire contents of the blank disk with the contents of the Turbo Pascal system disk. Click OK.
5. When the copy operation is finished, the formerly blank disk is identical to the Turbo Pascal program distribution disk, although it will have a different name. You can name your new backup disk by clicking on the area under the disk icon and typing a new name, such as TP Work Disk.
6. Repeat this process with the Utilities & Sample Programs and Turbo Tutor disks.

Once you have created your backup copies of the Turbo Pascal and Turbo Tutor disks, we suggest that you place your originals in a safe place, to be used only if something happens to the copies of the program disks.

Hard Disk Users

Create a new folder named Turbo Pascal in the root window (highest level) of your hard disk's file system. Into this folder, copy everything from both distribution disks *except the System folder from the program disk*. You have a System file and Finder on your hard disk already; you don't need another set.

Finally, store the originals in a safe place.

Using Turbo Tutor

You'll find a tutorial program named Turbo Tutor on your distribution disk. Designed to demonstrate various Pascal topics, this program is provided in source form and must be compiled before you run it. You'll find that we refer you to the appropriate sample Turbo Tutor program throughout this book. Chapter 1 lists the sample procedures in "Files on the Disk."

Double-click the Turbo Tutor folder to open it. Then, double-click file Tutor.Pas. This launches Turbo Pascal. Turbo Tutor makes extensive use of the $I(nclude) compiler directive to access the source code for each topic—the same text that appears when you run the program and choose that topic.

To run the Tutor program, choose Run from the Compile menu. Once the program begins, you'll see two windows. The upper one shows the output generated when running one of the sample procedures; the lower window displays its source code.

(If you're running off a 400K disk, Tutor.Pas won't compile correctly. An error box will come up; dismiss the error message and follow the instructions you find there.)

After first choosing a topic with the File menu's Open command, the source code demonstrating that topic is loaded from disk (from the Lessons folder) and displayed in the source window. You're then free to peruse—but not edit—the source code for that topic's procedure, using standard Macintosh scrolling techniques. At any time, you can choose Run from the File menu to execute this code, causing its output to appear in the upper window.

Click the mouse button at any time to terminate the run. This program demonstrates, among other things, techniques involved in mixing and matching code from a traditional personal computer (such as the IBM PC) and the Macintosh User Interface.

The Test Option

Try out your knowledge of the subject by choosing Test from the File menu. This brings up a series of questions on the selected topic; choose the Hint option under the File menu if you get stuck.

Modifying the Examples

Once you've studied an example using the Tutor program, you can make changes to the example procedure in order to master its material. Here's how you'd modify and test the code in example *Array1*, for example:

Using the Finder's Duplicate option, make a copy of Array1.Inc. The resulting file (Copy of Array1.Inc) serves as a backup. Now start up Turbo Pascal and edit file Array1.Inc in any way you see fit. You can't compile this file directly (it holds a procedure, not a program), so after first saving your changes, Open and Compile Tutor.Pas. When you execute the resulting program and Open lesson file Array1.Inc, you'll see the result of your change in the source and execution windows.

Each sample procedure contains instructions that tell you how to run it.

In the next chapter, you'll learn how to start Turbo Pascal; use the editor to create, look at, and modify programs; and use menu selections to compile and run a program.

5

Using Turbo Pascal

In this chapter, you'll sit down at your Macintosh and go through the steps required to write, compile, and run a simple program. Have your original Turbo Pascal disks filed safely away and working copies ready to go. You may want some paper and a pencil so you can take notes. Ready? Let's begin.

Starting Turbo Pascal

Boot your system on your Turbo Pascal work disk (the one we labeled TP Work Disk in the previous chapter) or, for hard-disk users, boot up like always. When the Finder appears, find the checkered-flag icon labeled Turbo that represents the Turbo Pascal application. Although dozens of files are included on the two disks shipped with Turbo Pascal, this single file *is* Turbo Pascal. It contains everything you need to write programs.

Turbo

Figure 5.1: The Turbo Pascal Icon

Start up Turbo Pascal by double-clicking on its icon. After a few seconds, the main screen appears (see Figure 5.2).

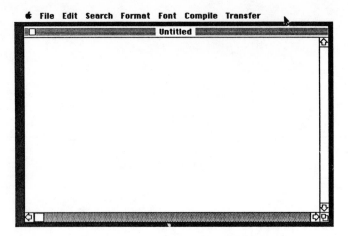

Figure 5.2: The Turbo Pascal Main Screen

Turbo's main screen resembles that of many Macintosh applications. There's a menu bar at the top, and beneath it a large, empty window named "Untitled."

The Menu Bar

The menu bar contains eight menu options, with the various commands that you'll use to run Turbo Pascal: Apple, File, Edit, Search, Format, Font, Compile, and Transfer. We'll go over these menus individually later in this chapter.

The empty window under the menu bar is for creating and working with Pascal source programs. It's the "text editor" part of Turbo Pascal. Working in this window is very much like using MacWrite or some other Macintosh word-processing program. Unlike MacWrite, however, you can have as many as eight windows (corresponding to eight separate programs) open at one time.

The Editor Window

Experiment with the editor: press a few keys, type your name. (Heck, go ahead—type Philippe Kahn's name.) The default font is 9-point Monaco.

While not one of the most beautiful fonts around, Monaco has an important virtue: Each character has the same width.

Most fonts are proportionally spaced; for instance, *i*'s are narrower than *m*'s. Monaco's fixed spacing makes it easy to neatly line up groups of statements, and, in Pascal, neatness counts. The 9-point size was chosen to get as many characters on a line as possible while still being readable. In any case, you can change both the size and font.

Editing Text

You can edit text that you've entered in the window with various standard Macintosh techniques. First, let's review some terminology and shortcuts. When you move the pointer into the editing window, it changes from an arrow to a shape known as the *I-beam cursor*. The I-beam shape is ideal for pointing operations related to working with text. Move it out of the window, and it changes back to an arrow.

Use the mouse to move the I-beam cursor between any two characters (can you see why the I-beam shape is preferable to the arrow?) and click the button. A flashing vertical line called the *insertion point* appears. This places anything you type between the characters bracketing the insertion point.

You can select a word by double clicking on that word. Furthermore, if you double click and drag, the selection proceeds a word at a time rather than a character at a time. This shortcut saves keystrokes, so remember it.

If you're new to Macintosh editing, you may be surprised to learn that Macintosh editors have no overstrike mode; that is, you can't type over existing text. New characters are always inserted, pushing existing text to the right and down, as necessary.

Highlighting Lines

In working with program text, you'll often highlight whole lines at a time. The best way to select one or more entire lines is *not* to drag from left to right across the full width of the window, but rather to manipulate the I-beam at the left edge of the screen. Click and hold just before the first character on a line; then drag straight down. With some practice, you'll find that you can highlight lines with a minimum of motion.

Deleting Text

Pressing *Backspace* moves the insertion point one position to the left, deleting one character in the process. To delete several characters at once, use the dragging technique to highlight (in reverse video) the text that you want deleted.

This is a two-step process; first highlight, then delete. To highlight, move the pointer to the beginning of the text to be deleted and then *press and hold* the mouse button. Now move the pointer to the last character to be deleted, keeping the button pressed; this is called *dragging*. Keep cool if the black background spills into areas you don't want highlighted; nothing happens as long as you keep the button down. When you've highlighted what you want, release the button. Now relax. It stays highlighted until your next move.

Highlighting text is a precursor to performing an operation on it. It's a key Macintosh user-interface concept: Select (highlight) something, then perform an action on what's selected. In this case, you want to delete the selected text.

Selected text is deleted by pressing *Backspace*. If no text is selected, pressing *Backspace* deletes only one character to the left of the cursor. If text (up to thousands of characters) is selected, then pressing *Backspace* deletes every character in the highlighted range.

If text is highlighted and you type any character, say, *A*, then the text is deleted and *A* is substituted.

Edit Menu Commands

There are several particularly handy commands under the Edit Menu. These are Undo, Cut, Copy, and Paste.

The Undo Option

One of the under-praised advances of the Macintosh is the ungrammatical first option of the Edit menu, *Undo*. Well-bred Macintosh applications support Undo, a sort of universal "oops" eraser. For example, if you accidentally backspace across more characters than you mean to delete, choosing Undo restores the characters.

Undo can't fix every editing mishap, especially if you don't choose it immediately after the error. Luckily, most mistakes are inadvertent deletions that you realize about one millisecond after touching *Backspace*.

The Cut and Copy Operations

In addition to deleting highlighted text, there are other operations that you can perform on selected text, the two most important being *Cut* and *Copy*. Cut is like Delete, except that the text deleted from the file isn't thrown away; it's moved to the Clipboard, a hidden and temporary repository for text.

Copy is similar, except that the highlighted text isn't deleted from the file; it is simply copied to the Clipboard.

The Paste Operation

The Clipboard wouldn't be useful without the *Paste* feature, which lets you move text out of it. The Paste operation inserts whatever text is in the Clipboard, from one character to thousands, at the insertion point. If you perform a Paste operation when text is highlighted, the pasted text replaces the highlighted text.

To sum up, Undo "erases" your more recent editing. Cut and Copy move text to the Clipboard; Paste takes text from the Clipboard. All these commands are in the Edit menu.

Scrolling

If you enter more text than can fit on the screen, either horizontally or vertically, the screen scrolls to show you that text.

Unlike most word-processing programs, the Turbo Pascal editor doesn't automatically wrap text when you get to the edge of the window. The window scrolls horizontally to accommodate any characters you continue to enter. To move down to the next line, you must press *Return*. This is because the Turbo Pascal editor is designed for creating Pascal source files, and Pascal source files are organized into sequences of lines (usually fairly short lines) with a Return control character at the end of each one.

Sizing and Moving Windows

The symbol in the extreme lower-right corner of an editing window is called a *size box*. By dragging the size box, you can make the editing window larger or smaller. This capability is particularly useful when more than one window is open on the screen.

You can move a window by dragging in the window's so-called title bar (the area with the horizontal lines and "Untitled").

Command-Key Equivalents

After working with Turbo Pascal for a while, you may find that it's a hassle to reach over, grab the mouse, and pull down a menu to perform every little Cut and Paste. For this reason, Turbo Pascal supports *Command-key equivalents* for its most common operations. (The Command key is another feature unique to the Macintosh. It's the one with the cloverleaf symbol [⌘] on it; on some keyboards, the cloverleaf symbol is joined by the Apple symbol.)

A Command-key equivalent is produced by holding down the *Command* key and typing a letter. If a menu option has a key equivalent, it will be listed to the right of the option. For example, the File menu defines a number of keyboard equivalents, including *Command-N* to open a new, empty file and *Command-O* to open an existing file.

A Quick Tour of the Menus

Like most Macintosh applications, Turbo Pascal is wholly controlled by the commands in its eight pull-down menus.

The Apple Menu

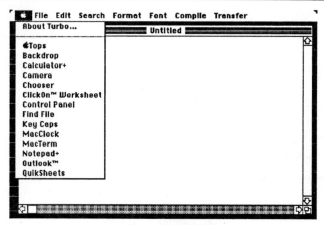

Figure 5.3: The Apple Menu

In the Apple menu, you'll find an About Turbo option that lists copyright and version information about the Turbo Pascal application itself. The various desk accessories you have installed in your system file are also listed.

The File Menu

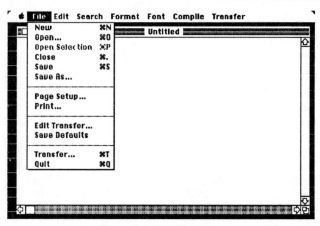

Figure 5.4: The File Menu

You'll use the File menu most often for opening, saving, and closing text files. In a moment, we're going to create a program, and we'll come to this menu to save it to disk.

The File menu also has commands for printing your source files on paper (Page Setup and Print).

The Edit Transfer option is more unusual. It allows you to create entries for the Transfer menu (the menu at the extreme right of the menu bar). The Transfer menu is a quick way to leave Turbo Pascal and run another application (typically, one related to the software development process) without the bother of quitting Turbo, returning to the Finder, and then launching that program.

Take a look at the Transfer menu. You will see the single dimmed message `No items installed`. Dimmed menu selections can't be chosen, usually because a particular option can't be chosen in the current context. For example, the Edit menu's Cut and Copy options are dimmed when no text is highlighted: There's no text to Cut or Copy.

As shipped from Borland, Turbo Pascal's Transfer menu is empty because we don't know what applications you'll want to Transfer to and what folders those applications will be in on your working floppy or hard disk. The Edit Transfer command is provided so that you can customize the Transfer menu to your own needs.

For example, one program that you will soon find convenient to transfer to is RMaker. You need this program, which is on the Utilities & Sample Programs Disk, to produce true Macintosh applications. To make transferring to RMaker an option under the Transfer menu, choose Edit Transfer from the File menu.

Turbo Pascal presents a dialog box in which to edit the name of the RMaker program (and as many as 30 others). Be sure to include the path and name of any directories that it may be concealed in. For example, if RMaker is in a folder called Utilities, you must include the name of this folder and the name of the disk that contains it, along with the name of the program, all separated by colons; for example, startup:utilities:RMaker.

After entering a path to a utility program, click OK. Now pull down the Transfer menu and see the change. Don't choose this option just yet, though. You've only performed a temporary patch of the Turbo Pascal program. Unless you make this patch permanent, it won't be available the next time you run the program.

To save this newly acquired entry to the Transfer menu, you must choose the next option in the File menu, Save Defaults. There will be a moment of disk activity as the default information is written to disk inside the Turbo program itself; the next time you start Turbo Pascal, the Transfer menu will be as you left it. This also means that the copy of Turbo Pascal on your working disk is no longer quite identical to the one on the original disk you have stored away.

The Transfer... option of the File menu (not to be confused with the Transfer menu itself, which you just edited) is a Finder-bypassing shortcut for running programs that aren't in the Transfer menu. It presents a standard Get-File box listing all the programs on the indicated disk.

The last option in the File menu is Quit (*Command-Q*); you'll use it to return to the Finder when you're finished with Turbo Pascal.

The Edit Menu

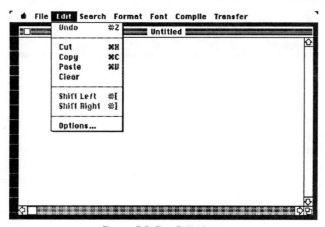

Figure 5.5: The Edit Menu

Most Macintosh applications have an Edit menu with the same first four options: Undo, Edit, Cut, Copy, and Paste. We discussed these commands earlier, under "Edit Menu Commands." Even if these operations don't mean anything to that application, many desk accessories (like the Notepad+) require that they be present.

Clear deletes selected text; this is the same operation performed by the Backspace key.

The Shift Left and Shift Right options are time savers when working with Pascal source programs. They shift all the characters in the highlighted block one column to the left or right. The Command-key equivalents

Command-[and *Command-]* are easier to use than choosing repeatedly from this menu.

The Search Menu

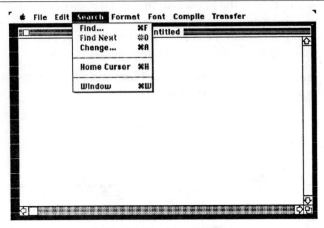

Figure 5.6: The Search Menu

The Search menu is primarily for Find and Find-and-Replace operations on text files. Use it to locate a particular spot in a large file—the Turbo Editor can work with files thousands of lines long, memory permitting—and to replace one word or phrase with another. For example, if you consistently misspelled the word "procedure" as "proccedure," you can use this menu's Change... option to make the correction throughout the file automatically.

The Format Menu

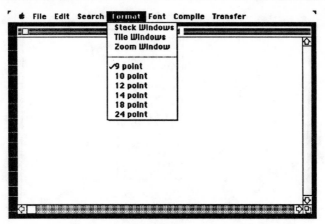

Figure 5.7: The Format Menu

The Format menu performs two functions: First, it has commands related to working with multiple windows. The Stack Windows option causes windows to overlap each other. The Tile Windows option organizes windows into a tile-like pattern so that no two windows overlap. Zoom Window expands the current window to the full width of the screen; if it's already full sized, then this command shrinks it to its regular size. You can also do this by double-clicking on a window's title bar.

Second, the Format menu lets you set the size of the text in the active (topmost) window. You can work with a different font and size in each window; however, since font information isn't stored on disk along with the text, you'll have to change it back from 9-point Monaco (the default) whenever you begin a session on a window.

The Font Menu

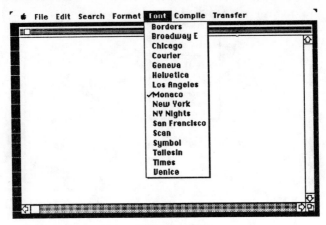

Figure 5.8: The Font Menu

The Font menu selects the font for the active window. Although you can create programs in any font that exists in your System file, most of the time you'll be working in the non-proportional Monaco font. The LaserWriter font Courier makes a decent programming font, although it isn't much use smaller than 12 point.

The Compile Menu

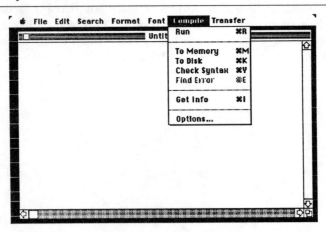

Figure 5.9: The Compile Menu

Here's the good stuff. Without the Compile menu, Turbo Pascal would be just an exceptionally fast eight-window text editor. The Run command executes programs from within Turbo Pascal. If the program represented by the active (topmost) window needs compiling, it'll be compiled first. When programs executed by the Run command terminate, Turbo Pascal regains control. With Run, it's easy to hop quickly back and forth between editing and executing programs.

The To Memory option compiles the contents of the active window to memory. It's the same operation performed by Run—except that the program isn't executed. The To Disk option causes the output of the compiler to be sent to disk rather than memory. The Check Syntax option performs a syntax analysis on the active window, but doesn't actually produce any code.

Entering a Program

Rather than go into each command in great detail (the *Turbo Pascal for the Macintosh* reference manual does that), we're going to show you how to use the most important commands by having you enter, compile, and run a program.

This manual, in keeping with Borland's style convention, prints certain key components of Pascal (reserved words) in boldface type (for example, **program, begin,** and **end**). This notation helps to clarify program structure. Turbo's editor doesn't support boldfacing (and if it did, the compiler wouldn't care anyway), so don't worry about duplicating this aspect of program FirstEffort.

Start with a clean window: Select every character in the window (named "Untitled") you've been practicing in and press *Backspace*. Now type in the following program exactly (except for the boldfacing, of course) as shown. Punctuation is important to the compiler, although spacing is not—you could insert twenty blank lines between the first and second lines and not affect the meaning of the program one bit. You can substitute your name, or some other proper noun, for Robin Jones. If you make a mistake, use *Backspace* or the mouse editing techniques to correct it.

```
program FirstEffort;
begin
  WriteLn('This program compliments of Robin Jones');
  ReadLn
end.
```

These five lines constitute a complete, if less than overwhelmingly useful, Turbo Pascal program. The first line starts with the word **program** and gives the program a name—in this case, FirstEffort. This line always ends with a semicolon; no Pascal compiler would tolerate this semicolon's absence. The next line contains only **begin**, which signals the beginning of the "action" part of the program.

The third line's *WriteLn* command displays on the screen the text enclosed in parentheses and single quote marks. Leave out a parenthesis or a quote mark, or use double quotes, and you've got a program that won't compile. There's a semicolon after this line as well.

The *ReadLn* command in the fourth line creates a pause in the program so that you can admire its output; without it, the program would execute so quickly you'd only get a glimpse of the line. The *ReadLn* statement pauses execution indefinitely until *Return* is pressed on the keyboard. Note that there *isn't* a semicolon after this line.

Finally, the word **end** followed by a period defines the stopping point of the program. These semicolons and periods almost call to mind an English sentence:

Here's the program's name; now do this; and this and you're done.

We'll delve deeply into Pascal punctuation in good time.

Compiling and Running FirstEffort

Check FirstEffort over one last time; a single misplaced character can reduce an otherwise perfect Pascal program to second-class status in the eyes of the compiler. Actually, it may be faster to let the compiler do the checking. Choose Check Syntax from the Compile menu (or use the Command-key equivalent, *Command-Y*). If the compiler finds something it doesn't like, it'll tell you so in an alert box.

In the following figure, *WriteLn* is misspelled, which makes the third line a mystery to the compiler. Turbo Pascal brings up an error box and highlights the questionable identifier on the screen.

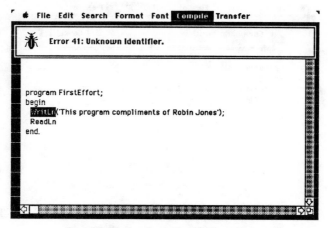

Figure 5.10: The Compiler Finds an Error

If Check Syntax finds something wrong with your program, don't take it personally. Simply click the mouse button (or press any key) to dismiss the error message, then edit your program to correct the error.

Once the Check Syntax option scans your version of FirstEffort without producing an error, it's ready to be run. Choose To Memory from the Compile menu; with Turbo Pascal, compiling to memory is over in seconds.

There are now two versions of FirstEffort in memory: a source form, created by you with the editor, and the resulting object program (68000-family machine language) created by the compiler. You can't see the object program, because there's no easy way to represent it for human consumption; it makes sense only to a CPU.

Now, let's execute the compiled object form of FirstEffort. Choose Run from the Compile menu (or use its keyboard equivalent, *Command-R*). The screen is quickly cleared and replaced by a lone window entitled FirstEffort.

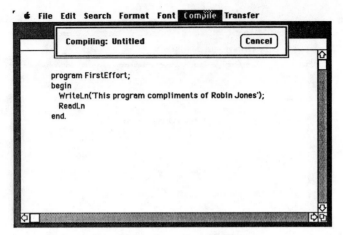

Figure 5.11: Compiling FirstEffort

This *terminal window* was created to give FirstEffort a well-defined place in which to write its output. The terminal window simulates a standard 80-column by 25-line character display (such as that on the IBM PC) and uses the same 9-point Monaco typeface as the editor.

These startup operations (clearing the screen and creating an 80-by-25 terminal window) are done automatically; FirstEffort didn't have to ask for it. FirstEffort's first action was to execute the *WriteLn* command and output the message `This program compliments of Robin Jones` to the screen. All this happened in a fraction of a second; meanwhile, the program has been executing the *ReadLn* command and waiting for you to press *Return*.

The flashing horizontal line on the display is the equivalent of the cursor used on traditional computers to indicate where future output will go. It started out on the first line of the terminal window, and the *WriteLn* command caused it to drop down to the second line.

There's no menu bar, for what would it contain? FirstEffort didn't define any menus. Unless you accidentally bump your mouse, there isn't any pointer either, because FirstEffort doesn't define any mouse interaction. You'll be well into your study of Pascal before you begin to add these user-interface niceties to your programs.

When the glow of pride at seeing your name in phosphor begins to fade, press *Return*. Since the *ReadLn* command is the last command in the program, FirstEffort is over when *ReadLn* finishes. (**end** isn't a command; it just indicates the end of a program.) This causes Turbo Pascal to regain control and display what was on the screen before the program was launched.

If all that happened too fast, do an instant replay: Simply choose Run from the Compile menu again.

Saving Your Source Program

The source form of FirstEffort (the text that you just entered) exists only in RAM at this point. If you (or a squirrel frolicking on a nearby transformer) were to suddenly deprive your Macintosh of power, your typing effort would be lost. To save this program to disk, choose Save from the File menu.

Turbo Pascal is reluctant to save a file named Untitled, so it asks you to give it a name and, optionally, to specify the folder in which it should be stored. This is done via the standard Save As dialog box. Enter

```
FirstEffort.Pas
```

as the title, and if you like, put it in a folder someplace. Actually, you can name the file anything. There doesn't have to be any similarity between the name of a text file that happens to be a Pascal program and the word that appears after the word **program** in that file. (**NOTE:** Don't use any colons in the file name unless you know what you're doing. Colons in file names are interpreted by the Macintosh's file-management routines to indicate volumes and folders, a subject we won't come to for many chapters.)

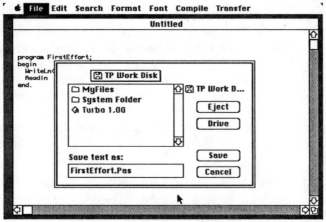

Figure 5.12: The Save As Dialog Box

After you name and save the file to disk, it remains in memory as well. The only visible change is that the window's title bar now reflects the file's name. As an exercise, let's close file FirstEffort. You can choose Close from the File menu (Command-key equivalent *Command-.*) or click the window's close box.

Now the editor has no open windows on the screen. Without a text window to refer to, many menu commands no longer make sense and so are dimmed (made unselectable), such as the File menu's Close and Save options.

Let's reload FirstEffort from disk. Choose Open from the File menu, and select FirstEffort.Pas. The beauty of Turbo Pascal is how easy it is to experiment with a program. Using the Lisa development system, it would take minutes to see the result of a one-character change to FirstEffort. Using Turbo Pascal, it takes about a second.

Change the message output by the *WriteLn* statement. Instead of the Compile-then-Run approach we used the first time, just choose Run. Turbo Pascal is smart enough to recognize that you've changed the program since the last compilation and automatically recompiles FirstEffort before running it.

Once a file has a name, it's almost painless to save it to disk. Press *Return* to return to the Turbo Pascal menu bar. Then simply choose Save from the File menu (or use its Command-key equivalent, *Command-S*).

Saving the Object Program

When you select the Run command, Turbo compiles the source program contained in the topmost window and runs it. The object form of the program is only in memory and will be lost when you turn off the power or exit Turbo Pascal back to the Finder. It's not that much of a problem since you've saved your source program and can recreate the object program in a matter of seconds. However, sometimes, that's not convenient. It would be better if you could save your executable program to disk, where it could be executed directly by the Finder without Turbo Pascal having to get involved.

You can do this by choosing the To Disk option of the Compile menu. This causes FirstEffort.Pas to be recompiled and the result of that compilation to be written to disk rather than memory. For a file name, Turbo uses the program name (FirstEffort), not the name of the source file. In fact, this is the only function served by the program's "internal" name.

After a few seconds of disk activity, Turbo Pascal will have created a file called FirstEffort.

Finishing Up

You've come a long way in this chapter. You started Turbo Pascal, typed in a program, and compiled it to memory. You ran the program in memory, saved the source code to disk, and finally, the object program as well. Now it's time to go to the Finder.

Choose Quit (*Command-Q*) from the File menu. If you've made changes to FirstEffort.Pas since your last Save, you'll get one last chance to save them.

When you're safely back at the Finder, look for the two files you created in this session: FirstEffort.Pas, a text file containing the source of the program, and FirstEffort, a brand-new application.

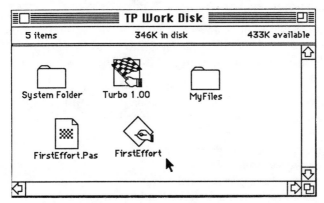

Figure 5.13: FirstEffort's Two Icons

FirstEffort.Pas is a text file, internally exactly like the text files created by MacWrite and a number of other applications, although the Finder knows to associate this file with Turbo Pascal. That's why the Finder gave it the checkered icon. If you were to double-click this file, the Finder would know to launch Turbo Pascal.

FirstEffort, on the other hand, is an application. It has the same status to the Finder as Turbo Pascal, MacPaint, or any other application. Since we didn't define a fancy icon, it gets the plain application icon. If you double-click it, you don't run Turbo Pascal; instead, you run this program.

Double-click FirstEffort. You'll see the same message in the same terminal window that you saw from within Turbo Pascal. When you press *Return* to end the program, however, you'll return to the Finder instead of Turbo Pascal.

Just for fun, perform the Finder's Get Info function on file FirstEffort (Get Info is an option under the File menu). You'll find that it's surprisingly big (about 5000 bytes). Does this mean that your compiled programs take up about 2500 bytes per executable statement? No, thank goodness. What you're seeing is about 100 bytes generated by the compilation and 4900 bytes worth of *library routines*.

Library routines are utility functions that are used as a resource by compiled programs; for example, the code that maintains the terminal window. These routines are within Turbo Pascal itself and are "glued" to programs that are compiled to disk as needed.

Review

There are obviously many more commands available in Turbo Pascal than what we've covered so far, but you can get by with what you've learned in this chapter for quite some time. You should now be able to do the following:

- Start Turbo Pascal from your bootable work disk or hard disk.
- Use the editor to create and edit source programs.
- Check the syntax of a source program.
- Compile your program into memory and run it.
- Save your source program on disk.
- Save your object program on disk.
- Exit from Turbo Pascal back to the Finder.
- Recognize the icons of Turbo Pascal text files and object programs.

You've cleared a substantial hurdle: You've used Turbo Pascal to write your first program. Now all you need to learn is how to create your own programs. And that's the subject of the rest of this book.

2

A PROGRAMMER'S GUIDE TO TURBO PASCAL

6

The Basics of Pascal

In the last chapter, you learned how to enter, compile, and run a simple Turbo Pascal program that displays some text on the screen. Before moving on, make sure you've acquired the skills necessary to

- Start up your Turbo Pascal work disk.
- Start up Turbo Pascal.
- Load or create a program source file.
- Enter and modify a source program.

If you're not comfortable performing these operations, review Chapter 5.

Some Pascal Terms

You're ready to learn some of the basic concepts of Pascal. Let's begin by defining some terms and the ideas behind them:

Data type	Variable	Comment
Identifier	Operator	Program heading
Reserved Word	Expression	Declaration part
Constant	Statement	Statement part

Data Types

Niklaus Wirth, the father of Pascal, once coined a marvelously succinct definition of computer programs:

Algorithms + Data Structures = Programs

An *algorithm* is a plan of action for accomplishing some goal. In Wirth's formula, algorithms refer to the action side of a program—the steps that a program takes to accomplish its goal; operations like adding two numbers, testing one number against another, and moving values in memory.

Data structures are the other primary components of programs—a component that most languages don't do justice to. Data structures are the objects in memory that algorithms act on. The better a program's data structures—the more closely they model the problem, the more options they offer the programmer—then the simpler (and usually faster and shorter) the algorithm necessary to work with them will be.

In other words, good data structures encourage good algorithms and therefore efficient programs. Pascal goes to great lengths to help you create effective data structures.

One of the underpinnings of Pascal is that all data structures (data objects) have a *type*; only certain operations are legal for data of a given type. Before Turbo Pascal can perform an operation on a piece of data, you must first specify what type of data it is. By specifying data types (which you'll learn how to do later), you define what operations can be performed on data of that type.

Suppose that your data consists of the numbers 3 and 4. Because 3 and 4 are numbers, it makes sense for Turbo Pascal to be able to add them and return the sum, 7.

Now suppose your data items consist of *Tuesday* and *March* (this may seem unlikely at this point, but Pascal can handle this sort of non-numeric data with ease). Clearly, it doesn't make much sense to add them together (that is, *Tuesday* + *March* is an illegal operation), and, in fact, Turbo Pascal won't let you. However, it may be possible to perform a different operation on these items, say, finding the first Tuesday in March. If you invent such an operation and explain to Turbo Pascal exactly how to go about doing it, Turbo Pascal will gladly perform the operation on data items of that type.

Predefined Data Types

Certain fundamental data types are used in almost every program. For this reason, Turbo Pascal provides you with a number of *predefined data types*:

Type	Examples		
Integer	3	0	–17382
LongInt	14	–150321	6681012
Real	3.14159	0.00	–6.67E-22
Char	'A'	'$'	'0'
Boolean	True	False	

We'll discuss the details of these types in later chapters. For the moment, here's a synopsis of their properties.

Integers are what mathematicians call "whole numbers," that is, numbers without a fractional component. Integers can be less than, equal to, or greater than zero. 5, –20, 0, and –32355 are all integers, but 3.5 is not, because it contains a decimal point and fractional part. Pascal *Integers* have a limited range of values: They can't be bigger than 32767 or smaller (more negative) than –32768. These size restrictions have an important basis in Macintosh hardware: Integers are formed from compact 2-byte chunks of memory that the Mac's processor can process with exceptional alacrity.

A *LongInt* (long integer) is a whole number with a much larger range than the standard *Integer* type, all the way from –2,147,483,648 to 2,147,483,647 (call it –2 billion to +2 billion) Long integers are handy in situations that require speed, but need more range than that afforded by integers. Long integers require 4 bytes of storage each and are processed efficiently by the processor (but not quite as quickly as integers).

A *Real* is a number that can (but doesn't have to) contain a fractional part, like 1.5, –0.33335, or 24E15. (The *E* means that the number is interpreted to be in scientific notation; that is, it is to be read as 24×10^{15}.) Data objects of type *Real* (which are sometimes called *floating-point* numbers) have a vast range—all the way from 1.4E-45 (a number microscopically close to zero: 0.000000000000000000000000000000000000000000014) to 3.4E38 (340,000,000,000,000,000,000,000,000,000,000,000,000). Values of type *Real* can be positive or negative and require 4 bytes of storage each.

If real numbers sound too good to be true (the vast range, including decimal points, in the same storage as a long integer), they are. Unlike integers and long integers, Turbo Pascal's internal representation of real numbers is not exact. Although you can represent very large and very small numbers, no single number has more than seven digits of accuracy. For example, 123,456,789 would be represented as a *Real* as 1.23456E8; the last three digits of precision are lost.

Furthermore, because of the internal structure used to represent reals, most decimal fractions, even those with seven or fewer digits, cannot be represented exactly. A figure like $1.10 can only be approximated by a *Real* value. That approximation may be very close ($1.0999999), but it still lacks the total accuracy provided by integers.

Turbo Pascal also offers three additional floating-point types—*Double*, *Extended*, and *Comp*—that offer more range and accuracy than type *Real*. For more information about floating-point types, see Chapter 26 of the *Turbo Pascal for the Macintosh* manual. Because the processor is significantly less efficient in performing calculations with real numbers, don't use type *Real* unless you need its range or fractional capability. A surprising variety of programs can be written without reals.

A *Char* is exactly what it sounds like: an ASCII character. It's useful for handling textual information, like a file from a word-processing program.

A *Boolean* is a data item that can have only two values, True and False, spelled out just like that. Boolean items are useful as *flags* when your program needs to remember whether something is true or not.

User-Defined Data Types

Besides having predefined data types, Turbo Pascal lets you define your own data types. For instance, in a scheduling program, it might be useful to define the days of the week as

```
type
  day = (Sunday, Monday, Tuesday, Wednesday, Thursday, Friday, Saturday);
```

Turbo Pascal would then recognize all of the words listed between the parentheses as being of the new type *Day*.

Turbo Pascal allows fantastic flexibility in creating and manipulating data types. In fact, data typing may be the single most notable aspect of Pascal relative to other languages. We'll cover the hows and whys of user-defined data types later in this tutorial.

Identifiers

Another term vital to your understanding of Pascal is *identifier*. An identifier is, very simply, a name for something—a piece of data, a part of your program, a place in your program, or a data type. When you write a program, you name its parts by declaring identifiers to represent them. In the last example, eight identifiers were used to name and declare the data type *Day*: *Day*, *Sunday*, *Monday*, *Tuesday*, *Wednesday*, *Thursday*, *Friday*, and *Saturday*.

Turbo Pascal automatically declares some identifiers for you. For instance, the names of the predefined data types (such as *Integer* and *LongInt*) are predeclared.

An identifier must begin with a letter; numbers and punctuation characters won't do. This first letter may be followed by any combination of letters and digits, *but may not contain spaces*! An identifier may be as short as a single character or as long as you like, although only the first 63 characters are significant.

Standard Pascal (that is, Pascal as described in the book *American National Standard Pascal Computer Programming Language*, published by the IEEE standards committee) allows only letters and digits in an identifier. Turbo Pascal, however, allows you to use one additional character, the underscore (_). Underscores are handy in place of spaces. So,

```
An Identifier
```

is illegal (it contains a space), but

```
An_Identifier
```

which reads almost the same, is acceptable.

The Turbo Pascal compiler ignores the case differences within an identifier; the following are all considered to be the same identifier:

```
STARTINGLOCATION
Startinglocation
startinglocation
StartingLocation
startingLocation
```

The last two forms are easier to read than the others, so identifiers are depicted these two ways in this manual and other Borland books. Note that adding an underscore is the same as adding another character—it completely changes the meaning of the identifier.

Here are some examples of legal identifiers:

```
TURBO
square
persons_counted
BirthDate
DayOfTheWeek
AVeryLongIdentifierIndeed
The_2nd_Extremely_Long_Yet_Quite_Acceptable_Identifier
```

And here are some illegal ones:

`3rd_Root`	Starts with a digit instead of a letter
`Two Words`	Contains a space
`Two&Two`	Contains an illegal character (&)

To illustrate how the pieces of Pascal go together, we'll use a visual aid known as a *syntax diagram*. Let's look at the syntax diagram for an identifier shown in Figure 6.1.

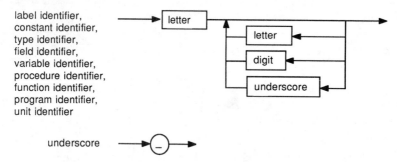

Figure 6.1: Syntax Diagram of an Identifier

Like all syntax diagrams, this one defines the language elements (parts of speech, if you will) named at the upper left-hand corner of the diagram. In this case, the diagram shows the syntax of all the different kinds of identifiers in the Pascal language.

How to Read a Syntax Diagram

Start at the arrow at the upper left-hand corner of the diagram; follow the arrows through any boxes, ovals, or circles until you reach the arrow that leaves the diagram at the right. As you pass through each box, oval, or circle, whatever is specified inside the figure must also appear (in that order) in the program element you are checking. If not, you must back up and try another path.

If you are able to make it through the syntax diagram without breaking any of these rules, then the syntax of the program element is correct.

The boxes, ovals, and circles in a syntax diagram have distinct meanings. A box contains a word that represents an object defined in another syntax diagram. An oval or a circle contains a symbol or a word that must be typed exactly as shown.

For example, the top left-hand corner of Figure 6.1 has a box with the word "letter" in it. This means, as mentioned earlier, that the first thing that must exist in an identifier is a letter. Following the arrow from the first box, you can either exit to the right (if your identifier consists of a single letter) or follow the path down to one of two boxes: one contains the word "letter," the other contains the word "digit." After leaving either of these boxes, you can follow the arrow up and exit, or you can go through the loop again, adding either another letter or another digit each time through.

Since each word in this diagram is enclosed in a box, each word is defined by another syntax diagram. Figure 6.2 shows the syntax diagram for letter.

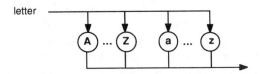

Figure 6.2: Syntax Diagram of Letter

Starting at the top left-hand corner of Figure 6.2, you are presented with a number of alternate paths, each to a single letter of the alphabet. Since each letter is in a circle, that letter must be entered exactly as shown. Finally, if you trace a path from any letter, you'll find that the only path is one that exits the diagram. This means that each time you see the word "letter" in any syntax diagram, only one letter may be used.

The syntax diagram for the word "digit" is shown in Figure 6.3.

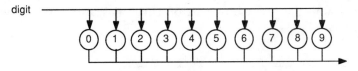

Figure 6.3: Syntax Diagram of Digit

You can read this diagram exactly as you did the letter diagram. Each pass through the diagram results in only one digit being selected.

Exercises

For practice, use the preceding syntax diagrams to check the syntax of the following "identifiers." Can you make it through the whole diagram with any of them? (The answers to all exercises are in Appendix B.)

Hen3ry
_Turbo_Pascal
5th_Amendment
Three+Four
Good Work

Syntax diagrams may be overkill for explaining identifiers, letters, and digits, but will prove valuable when we get to more complex constructs.

Reserved Words

When you begin writing programs, you'll see that identifiers are used virtually everywhere. You'll create identifiers for almost every data type, data object, and piece of code that you use. In addition to the syntax requirements just covered (for example, no spaces), there are a few combinations of letters that cannot be used as identifiers because Pascal uses them itself; these are called *reserved words*.

Reserved words (listed in Table 6.1) have special meaning to the Turbo Pascal compiler and cannot be used for any other purpose (except in comments—we'll talk more about that later on). For example, you can't declare a data type named **program** or name a program **begin**, because **program** and **begin** are reserved words. You can use reserved words only in the way Pascal decrees.

To help you distinguish reserved words in sample programs, they are shown in **boldface** type throughout this and other Borland manuals. (Remember that reserved words don't need to be bold when you type them into a program—the text editor part of Turbo Pascal doesn't know that they're special.)

Table 6.1: Pascal Reserved Words

and	external	mod	shl
array	file	nil	shr
begin	for	not	string
case	forward	of	type
const	function	or	unit

div	goto	then	until
do	if	to	uses
downto	otherwise	procedure	var
implementation	packed	program	while
in	inline	record	with
else	interface	repeat	xor
end	label	set	

Constants

A *constant* is a piece of information (a number, perhaps, or some text) that remains the same while you're running your program. Suppose you want to calculate a percentage based on a fraction, as follows:

```
100 * Numerator / Denominator
```

where * represents multiplication, / represents division, *Numerator* and *Denominator* are identifiers representing numbers, and "100" is a constant.

Constants are not limited to numbers, as shown in the sample program at the end of Part 1. When you write

```
WriteLn ('This program compliments of Robin Jones')
```

the sequence of characters "This program compliments of Robin Jones" is a constant; specifically, it is a *string constant*.

In addition to string constants, Standard Pascal allows you to use constants of types *Integer*, *LongInt*, *Real*, *Char*, and *Boolean*.

Constant Definitions

To show how a constant definition might be useful, consider the following example: A programmer at a bank has to write a program to compute compound interest on a bank account. An important *Real* value, known as *e* in math texts (the so-called base of natural logarithms, approximately 2.71828), is used in the compound-interest calculation.

Since the program needs this value in several different places, without constant definitions, the programmer would have to type it in at each place. This repetitiveness creates room for error—one that could cost the bank money. To avoid this problem, a constant is declared as an identifier to stand in for it:

```
const
   e = 2.71828;
```

This replaces the ponderous string of digits with a single character! After this definition, every use of the identifier *e* is equivalent to 2.71828. As you work through this book, you may think that we've gone overboard on constants—especially if you have a background in BASIC. But constants work to improve program readability, even if they're used only once.

Constants are defined in the *constant definition part* of a Pascal program. The syntax of this part of a program is shown in Figure 6.4.

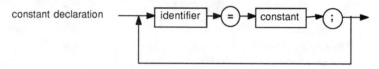

Figure 6.4: Syntax Diagram of a Constant Definition Part

To practice your use of syntax diagrams, you may want to again trace through the previous diagrams to verify that the declaration of *e* has the correct syntax.

Variables

Almost every program needs pieces of data whose values change during program execution. These data items are called *variables*. A variable is one or more bytes in memory where data is kept; the processor goes to this address to read or change the value of the variable.

All variables have names; this name is an identifier and must conform to the syntax for an identifier as shown previously. If you intend to use a variable in your program, you must give the compiler the variable's name and data type. This is called a *variable declaration*: It causes Turbo Pascal to set aside a place in memory for it and to remember its name.

Variable Declarations

Variables are declared in the *variable declaration part* of a program. Here are some examples:

```
var
   FirstInteger : Integer;
```

```
SecondInteger, ThirdInteger : Integer;
BigInteger: LongInt;
ASCII_Character : Char;
RealNumber : Real;
```

The preceding declarations define three variables of type *Integer*, plus one each of types *LongInt*, *Char*, and *Real*. Variables of the same type can be grouped into the same declaration, separated by commas. (*SecondInteger* and *ThirdInteger* are declared this way.)

The syntax of this part of a program is shown in Figure 6.5.

Figure 6.5: Syntax Diagram of a Variable Declaration Part

Operators

An *operator* is a punctuation symbol or reserved word that Turbo Pascal uses to indicate that some operation (such as addition) is to be performed on one or more pieces of data. Some operators, like +, are already familiar to you from arithmetic or algebra. Others, like / for division, represent familiar operations that have been adapted to the constraints of ASCII, which doesn't define the standard division symbol ÷. Still others, like **shl** and **or**, perform exotic *boolean* operations on data.

Here are Turbo Pascal's operators:

`-`	unary minus operator
`* / div mod + -`	math operators
`not and or xor`	boolean operators
`shl shr`	bit operators
`= < > <= >= <>`	relational (comparing) operators
`in`	set membership operator

The unary minus operator (-) works as you might expect: It changes a numeric value's sign. Thus, if variable *A* has the value *5*, writing *–A* yields the value *–5*.

The * and / operators indicate multiplication and division, respectively. The **div** operator represents *integer division*, in which the remainder is thrown away. **mod** (short for *modulo*), by contrast, divides two integers, throws away the quotient, and returns the remainder. + and – are the same folks you worked with in the first grade. They produce the sum and difference, respectively, of two numbers.

The **not** operator takes a boolean value (True or False) and inverts it. Thus, **not** True is the same as False, **not** False is the same as True, **not** (**not** True) is the same as True, and **not** (**not** (**not** True)) is False. (This is how George Boole got his kicks.)

The **and** and **or** operators work on pairs of boolean values. The value True is produced by **and** if both of its operands are True; it's produced by **or** if either of its operands are True. These two operators can also be used to do boolean math on integers; more on this in Chapter 25, "Computer Numbering Systems: Boolean Operations on Integers."

The **shl** and **shr** bit operators are special low-level operations that shift the bits of an integer or long integer. We describe how they work in later chapters.

The relational operators (=, <, >, <=, >=, and <>) compare numbers and return boolean values based on the results. They should all be familiar, except possibly <>, which means "not equal." The standard "not equal" symbol (≠) wasn't available on computer keyboards when Pascal was created (another ASCII omission).

Finally, the **in** operator determines whether or not an object is in a *set*. (We'll discuss sets shortly.)

Expressions

You've probably seen *expressions* before, perhaps in a science or math class as formulas. Formulas that calculate such things as the circumference of a circle or the velocity of a falling object with respect to time are pretty close to what Pascal means by an expression. In fact, FORTRAN (one of the earliest programming languages) stands for FORmula TRANslator.

Expressions are combinations of identifiers, constants, and operators that describe how to calculate a new piece of data from one or more existing ones. When an expression is evaluated, the operations within it are carried out. The result is a single value, which is often assigned to a variable.

Like all data used in a Turbo Pascal program, the result of an expression has a data type. This type is usually, but not necessarily, the same as that of the constants or variables within it. For instance, an expression such as

```
first_Integer + second_Integer + third_Integer
```

which adds the contents of three *Integer* variables, is said to be an *Integer* expression because evaluating it produces an *Integer* value. However, the expression

```
first_Integer < second_Integer
```

compares two integers and yields a boolean value (True or False), depending on whether or not *first_Integer* is less than *second_Integer*.

The Order of Operations in Expressions: Precedence

If you've taken a course in algebra, you may remember the *Order of Operations*—which means the order in which you perform operations in an expression. In this section, we demonstrate why this ordering (or *precedence*) is necessary and how Pascal handles expressions in which order makes a difference.

Suppose you ask Turbo Pascal to evaluate the expression *3 + 4 * 2* (remember that * denotes multiplication). The following shows two possible ways the computer could calculate the result:

```
      3                    4
    + 4                  * 2
   ─────                ─────
      7                    8
    * 2                  + 3
   ─────                ─────
     14                   11
```

The example on the left adds *3* to *4* totaling *7*, then multiplies the total by *2* to get *14*. The example on the right first multiplies *4* by *2* to get *8*, then adds *3* to get *11*. Which answer is correct? Well, a long time ago, mathematicians ran into this dilemma and set up a series of rules to determine how to evaluate expressions in an unambiguous way. Pascal follows these rules and adds a few of its own.

The first rule is that multiplication and division are performed before addition and subtraction, *unless* the addition or subtraction operation is enclosed in parentheses, thereby causing the multiplication or division operation to follow. By applying this rule, we can see that the expression in the previous example evaluates to 11, not 14. However, if we were to add parentheses to the previous expression to make *(3 + 4) * 2*, the addition is performed first and then the multiplication.

The second rule is that operations with the same precedence (multiplication and division, addition and subtraction) are performed from left to right. Thus, the expression *10 / 5 * 2* is evaluated as shown:

$$\begin{array}{c} 10 \\ /\ \ 5 \\ \hline 2 \\ *\ \ 2 \\ \hline 4 \end{array} \qquad \text{and } not \qquad \begin{array}{c} 5 \\ *\ \ 2 \\ \hline 10 \\ /\ \ 10 \\ \hline 1 \end{array}$$

To get the second answer, write the expression as *10 / (5 * 2)*. In this case, the parentheses indicate that the multiplication should occur first.

The third rule is that unary operations (that is, operations that operate on only one object) are performed before any of the others. For instance, in the expression *–5 + 10*, the unary minus before *5* applies only to the *5*, not to the whole expression *5 + 10*. The result of the expression therefore is *5*, not *–15*.

Parentheses can be used to override the order of operations for unary operators, as well. The expression *–(5 + 10)* evaluates to *–15*, as you might expect.

Pascal extends the rules just described to relational and set membership operations as well. Relational operations are performed after addition operations, and set membership operations follow. The complete table of operators given earlier was, in fact, intentionally laid out in order of precedence—that is, with the operations that are done first above those that are done afterward.

Exercises

Evaluate each of the following expressions according to the Order of Operations used in Pascal. (The answers are in Appendix B.)

1. 4 * 6 / 2 + 3

2. (4 * 6) / 2 + 3

3. 4 * (6 / 2 + 3)

4. (4 * (6 / 2) + 3)

5. 4 * ((6 / 2) + 3)

6. (4 * 6) / (2 + 3)

Now, insert the expressions into the following short program and run it to check your answers. The program as shown is ready to run the first example.

```
program calculate;
begin
  WriteLn( 4 * 6 / 2 + 3 );
  ReadLn;
end.
```

Statements

A *statement* is a part of a program that tells the computer to perform some action. In the sample program from Chapter 5, the statement

```
WriteLn('This program compliments of Robin Jones')
```

tells the computer to display a message on the screen. Usually, programs have many statements, and when statements occur in succession, they must be separated from one another by a semicolon (;). Here are more examples of statements:

```
Value1 := Value2 + Value3;
```

```
Radius := 40.25;
```

```
if Value1 > 100 then
   WriteLn('Value1 is greater than 100');
```

The first two examples are *assignment statements*. The first causes the computer to evaluate the expression *Value2 + Value3* and assign the result to variable *Value1*. (That is, it writes the result to the memory address reserved for *Value1*.) *Value1* retains this result until it is specifically changed by the program, for example, by another assignment statement. The second statement assigns the constant *40.25* to variable *Radius*.

The last example is an *if* statement. It instructs the computer to perform a certain action only if a particular condition is met; in this case, if *Value1* is greater than *100*. Note that this statement contains another statement (the *WriteLn* statement). This is a common occurrence in Pascal, and we'll say more about it later.

Comments

Lastly, there's the Pascal construct that causes the computer to do nothing at all: the *comment*. A comment is a string of characters starting with a left brace ({) and ending with a right brace (}). The space within the braces can contain any kind of text at all (except more braces, which would tend to confuse things). Everything within braces is ignored by the compiler. (Chapter 7 details another method of commenting.)

```
{ This is a comment. Turbo Pascal will ignore this text. }
```

If comments are ignored, why are they part of the language at all? Because comments assist the flesh-and-blood human being trying to understand a program. Even though Pascal is designed to make programs readable, it is still possible to come back to your own code a month after writing it and discover that even you no longer understand how it works.

A Programming Example

Let's write a Pascal program to accept two numbers typed at the keyboard, add them together, and display the result—in other words, a program that turns a state-of-the-art personal computer into a pale imitation of a $5 calculator. Before you read the discussion of it, look at the program carefully and try to understand how it works.

```
program Simple;                   { This is the Program Heading. }
{ A simple Pascal program to display the sum of two numbers.
 DATE:     March 19, 1987
AUTHOR:   put your name here }

{ This is the beginning of the Declaration Part of the program, where identifiers
are declared. }

const
  YourName = 'Friend'; { This is a string constant used in the greeting message.
                Change to contain your name if you'd like. }

var
  A,B,C : Integer;                          { Variables }

{ This is the beginning of the Statement Part of the program. It contains
statements--the parts of a Pascal program that tell the computer what to do. }

begin                        { Main body of program Simple }

{ Start by greeting the user. As in our very first program, we use a WriteLn
("Write Line") statement to write to the screen. }
```

```
WriteLn('Hello, ', YourName, '.');
```

{ The WriteLn statement can take a LIST of things to write on a line, as well as just one thing. We wrote three things: the constant string 'Hello, ', the value of the constant identifier YourName (another string), and a period (a character constant).}

{ Then write a string to the terminal asking the user for an Integer. A message like this, which requests a response of some kind, is often called a "prompt." }

```
WriteLn('Please type an Integer, followed by a Return.');
```

{ Wait for the user to type a number, then place that number in the variable A. ReadLn, which is read as "Read Line," tells the computer to wait for the Return key to be pressed before assuming that the number is complete. }

```
ReadLn(A);
```

{ Repeat the two steps for a second number. }

{ Prompt for another number }

```
WriteLn('Now please type another Integer, followed by a Return.');
ReadLn(B);          { Read the number and place it in  variable B. }
C := A + B;      { Add A and B and place the result in variable C. }
```

{ Write a line containing a message and the value of variable C. }

```
WriteLn('The sum of the two Integers is: ', C);
```

{ Putting an identifier (here, C) in the list of things that a WriteLn statement is to write causes its VALUE to be written, rather than its name. If we wanted to print the letter "C," we would enclose it in single quotes--as we did with the period in the first WriteLn statement. }

```
ReadLn
```

{ This ReadLn performs the same "delay" function that we saw in FirstEffort; without it, the screen would disappear before we had a chance to read the answer. }

end.   { of program Simple }

The first thing you should notice about this program (actually the second: the first is that we went overboard on comments) is that it is divided into three sections, each starting with a reserved word (**program**, **const**, and **begin**). Let's now discuss the functions of each part of the program.

The Program Heading

The first line (the one with the reserved word **program**) indicates that the lines of code are a program (later we'll learn about another structure Turbo Pascal can compile besides programs). It also gives the program's name,

"Simple." (The importance of program headings is discussed in detail in Chapter 7.)

```
program Simple;  { This is the Program Heading. }
```

The Declaration Part

Next is the *declaration part*, where identifiers are declared. As mentioned previously, an identifier is a name you give to something (a constant, a variable, a place in your code, or a piece of your code). The declaration part occurs after the program header and before the rest of the program. In this program, we declare the constant *YourName* and variables *A*, *B*, and *C*.

A constant declaration consists of two pieces of information that must be supplied to the compiler: the *name* of the constant and its *value*. These are separated by an equal sign (=), and the whole thing is followed by a semicolon. A group of one or more constant declarations is preceded by the reserved word **const**.

We declared the constant *YourName* as follows:

```
const
   YourName = 'Friend'; { This is a string constant used in
                          the greeting message. Change to
                          contain your name if you'd like. }
```

Remember that comments are ignored—even if they span more than one line in the program.

A variable declaration also provides the compiler with two facts: the *name* of the variable being declared and its *type*. These two pieces of information are separated by a colon, and each declaration statement must end with a semicolon. To let the compiler know that a group of one or more variable declarations is coming, we use the reserved word **var**:

```
var
  A,B,C : Integer;                    { Variables }
```

The variables in our program are *A*, *B*, and *C*, and they are all of the type *Integer*. Thus, the only type of data that variables *A*, *B*, and *C* can contain are integers (positive and negative numbers without fractional parts).

The Statement Part

The remainder of the program is enclosed by the reserved words **begin** and **end**. This part of the program consists of one or more statements and is therefore called the *statement part*. The computer starts with the first statement in the statement part and continues to execute the statements, in top to bottom order, until it reaches the final **end**:

```
begin        { Main body of program Simple }
   .
   .
   .
             ( Statements go here )
   .
   .
   .
end.         { of program Simple }
```

Adjoining statements are separated by semicolons. Since the last statement is not followed by another statement (**end** isn't a statement), no semicolon is needed—although having one doesn't hurt. (This is one of the few instances in which you'll get a break from Pascal syntax.) There is a period after the final **end** in the program. This lets the compiler know that the program is finished.

The first statement in the sample program is a *WriteLn* statement:

```
{ Start by greeting the user. As in our very first program, we use a WriteLn
("Write Line") statement to write a line to the screen. }

  WriteLn('Hello, ', YourName, '.');

{ The WriteLn statement can take a LIST of things to write on a line, as well as
just one thing. We wrote three things: the constant string 'Hello, ', the value of
the constant identifier YourName (another string), and a period (a character
constant). }
```

As mentioned in the comment, the *WriteLn* statement takes a list of variables, constants, or expressions and writes their value(s) to the screen. (It is also possible to have a *WriteLn* statement without a list of things to write, although we didn't show this in our program. The statement *WriteLn;* simply outputs a blank line to the screen.)

The program then *prompts* (that is, asks) for an *Integer* value to place in the variable *A*.

```
{ Then write a string to the terminal asking the user for an Integer. A message
like this, which requests a response of some kind, is often called a "prompt." }

  WriteLn('Please type an Integer, followed by a Return.');

{ Wait for the user to type a number, then place that number in the variable A.
ReadLn, which is read as "Read Line," tells the computer to wait for the Return key
to be pressed (starting a new line) before assuming that the number is complete. }

  ReadLn(A);
```

The *ReadLn* statement does the work of getting the *Integer* we asked for from the keyboard. Like *WriteLn*, *ReadLn* can take a list of values to get from the terminal or can be used with no list at all. The statement

```
ReadLn;
```

just waits for the user to press *Return*, as we saw in our first program.

Our program then does a second *WriteLn* and a second *ReadLn* to get another number and adds the first number to the second:

```
{ Repeat the two steps for a second number. }

{ Prompt for another number}

  WriteLn('Now please type another Integer, followed by a Return.');
  ReadLn(B);      { Read the number and place it in variable B. }
  C := A + B; { Add A and B and place the result in variable C. }
```

The last statement of the preceding group is an assignment. The expression *A + B* is evaluated by adding the values contained in variables *A* and *B* together. The result of this operation is then placed in variable *C*.

It helps to think of the assignment operator, :=, as an arrow pointing to the left, indicating the flow of information from the expression on the right-hand side to the variable on the left-hand side. When a program is read aloud, the assignment operator can be read as "gets," as in "C gets A plus B."

Now our sample program displays the value saved a moment ago in variable *C*:

```
{ Write a line containing a message and the value of the variable C. }

  WriteLn('The sum of the two Integers is: ', C)

{ Putting an identifier (here, C) in the list of things that a WriteLn statement is
to write causes its VALUE to be written, rather than its name. If we wanted to
print the letter "C," we would enclose it in single quotes--as we did with the
period in the first WriteLn statement. }
```

Finally, the program reaches the final **end** and stops.

Throughout the sample program, everything has been arranged in an orderly fashion. Since the compiler doesn't care about spacing between words (unless, of course, the spaces are within a quoted string of characters), we have spaced and aligned everything for clarity.

If you'd like to actually execute this program, type it in and run it under Turbo Pascal (feel free to expunge the comments). Alternatively, the source code of every example program in this book in contained in file Manual.Pas on the Turbo Tutor disk. Simply open this file under Turbo Pascal, locate the program Simple (do a Find operation on the string *Simple;*), and copy it into a new window.

We've covered a lot of ground in this chapter. So, before you move on, take the time to perform the following exercises. They are designed to reinforce what you have learned so far and prepare you for the material in chapters to come (answers in Appendix B).

Exercises

1. Review the previous sample program. How many identifiers can you find? (Hint: The names of data types, like *Integer*, are identifiers). How many constants? How many statements?

2. Use Turbo Pascal to load and run this program in its original form. Change the value of the constant *YourName* so that the computer writes your name when the program is run (don't cheat by typing in the name of one of the 25 bones in the human foot).

3. Modify the sample program so that it prints not only the sum of the two numbers ($A + B$), but the difference ($A - B$) as well. Add a new variable, D, to hold the difference.

4. Modify the program to return the following values:

   a. Twice the difference between A and B
   b. A minus twice B
   c. Five times A, minus the quantity three times B
   d. The product of A and B
   e. A *modulo* B (Watch out if you enter a value of 0 for B!)

   Check your work by accumulating results for several values of A and B.

5. Try typing a number with a decimal point when asked for one by the program. What happens? Can you explain why?

6. Now, change the variables in the program so that they are all of the type *Real*. Repeat Exercise 5 with this new program. Can you explain the results? (The compiler will complain if you try Exercise 4(e) with the variables A and B as *Real* numbers; the **mod** operator only works on integers.)

Review

Each of the topics presented in this chapter deserves (and gets) more explanation. Our objective here has been to define some of the basic concepts of Pascal, and you should have at least a basic understanding of the terms data type, identifier, reserved word, operator, constant, variable, expression, statement, and comment. If you feel comfortable using these terms, you're ready to go on to the next chapter.

7

Program Structure

In Chapter 6, we took a brief look at the most important Pascal terms and concepts and used them in a simple program. This chapter covers the rules governing the structure of a Pascal program.

Let's quickly review what we've learned about program structure. A Pascal program consists of three distinct parts: the program heading, the declaration part, and the statement part. Figure 7.1 shows the syntax of a program.

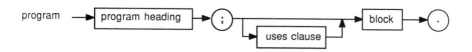

Figure 7.1: Syntax Diagram of a Program

The program heading's primary function is to name the program.

The declaration part consists of zero or more declarations that describe to Pascal the various pieces of data and code with which the program will work. It is possible to write simple programs without a declaration part (program FirstEffort from Chapter 5, for example).

Finally, the statement part (see Figure 7.3) is one or more program statements that describe the actual work to be performed, such as adding numbers, making assignments, and printing information to the screen. The statements are enclosed between the reserved words **begin** and **end**, followed by a period indicating the end of the program. This part of the program is also called the *main program*.

The Program Heading

In standard Pascal, the first non-comment line in a program must be a program declaration consisting of the following, in this order:

- the reserved word **program**
- the name you want to give to your program (which can be any legal identifier)
- a list of identifiers naming the files that the program will use (called "program parameters")
- a semicolon

The syntax diagram for the program heading is shown in Figure 7.2.

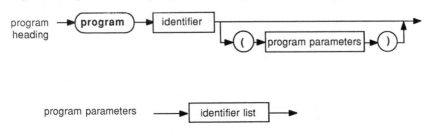

Figure 7.2: Syntax Diagram of a Program Heading

Here are some sample program headings:

```
program BudgetAnalysis;
program Digestion (input, output);
program With_A_Very_Long_Name_Indeed (file1, file2);
```

The optional program-parameters list gives some compilers information about the files the program will use. Many compilers require that programs that perform *ReadLn* and *WriteLn* operations declare the special files "input" and "output"; Turbo Pascal, however, does not—in fact, it totally ignores program parameters.

The Declaration Part

The declaration part of a program follows the program heading and consists of listing all labels, constants, types, variables, procedures, and functions that the program uses. (Procedures and functions are pieces of your program—something like BASIC's subroutines—that are invoked by name. More about them later.)

Each declaration lists one or more identifiers, then gives information about the meaning(s) of these identifiers. Label declarations are rare: They serve to tell the compiler that the associated identifier will be used as the target of a **goto** statement in the program, which are seldom used in Pascal.

The declaration part of a program may be divided into five subparts:

- Label declaration part
- Constant definition part
- Type definition part
- Variable declaration part
- Procedure and function declaration part

Standard Pascal requires that each of these subparts occur only once (if at all) and in the exact order listed. Turbo Pascal, however, doesn't care about the order in which things are declared, as long as they're declared *before they are used*. With Turbo Pascal, you can make any kind of declaration, any number of times, and in any order.

Since the compiler has no idea what an identifier means until you tell it, you must declare all of the identifiers you will use in your program (except, of course, the "standard" identifiers, like *ReadLn* and *WriteLn*, which are already part of Turbo Pascal). This includes all labels, constants, types, variables, and procedures and functions that you create as you build your program. If you use an identifier that has not been declared, Turbo (like all Pascal compilers) produces an error message and refuses to compile or run your program.

Pascal's rule of identifier declaration is so fundamental that we need to call special attention to it. Memorize this rule well: *All identifiers must be declared before they are used.*

Formatting Your Declarations

Pascal allows considerable freedom in how the declarations can be laid out in a source program. This section presents some sample variable declarations to illustrate this flexibility. The same principles apply to constant and type declarations.

A group of variable declarations (that is, a variable declaration part of a program) is preceded by the reserved word **var**. Each declaration consists of one or more names (identifiers) for variables, a colon, a type (another identifier) for the variable(s), and, finally, a semicolon. The result looks like this:

```
var
  A,B,C : Integer;
```

This example defines three variables of type *Integer*: *A*, *B*, and *C*.

The reserved word **var** can be followed by several variable declarations without being repeated. Thus, if you want to declare *A*, *B*, and *C* on separate lines in an effort to make your program more readable, you can write

```
var
  A: Integer;
  B: Integer;
  C: Integer;
```

without repeating the **var**.

Here are some sample variable declarations for each of the predefined types discussed in Chapter 6:

```
var
  Alive,Breathing   : Boolean;
  Age,Height,Weight : Integer;
  Income            : LongInt;
  Ratio,Percentage  : Real;
  First,Middle,Last : Char;
```

Pascal is a "free-format" language—it doesn't care how the text of your program is broken into lines (unlike BASIC and other languages that stick their noses into the text-editing business). As long as the syntax of the declarations agree with the syntax diagram, Pascal doesn't care how you arrange things. If, for some reason, you want to arrange your declarations in a long, narrow column, you could rewrite the previous example as

```
var
  Alive,
  Breathing
```

```
: Boolean;
Age,
Height,
Weight
: Integer;
Income
: LongInt;
Ratio,
Percentage
: Real;
First,
Middle,
Last
: Char;
```

Here's yet another variation:

```
var
  Alive : Boolean; Breathing : Boolean; Age : Integer;

  Height : Integer; Weight : Integer; Ratio : Real;
  Percentage :   Real; First: Char; Middle : Char; Last : Char;
```

In this book, we use a format that we think is easy to read and understand. Most Pascal programmers ultimately evolve a unique style—but our conventions make a good starting point.

The Statement Part

The statement part of a program consists of the reserved word **begin**, followed by any number of statements, then the reserved word **end** (see Figure 7.3). The statement part of a program is followed by a period (.) right after the closing **end** to indicate the program is finished. Execution starts with the first statement after **begin** and proceeds sequentially to the last statement before **end**, unless a statement directs the program flow elsewhere than to the next sequential statement. Other than a comment, the period after the last **end** must be the last thing in a Pascal program.

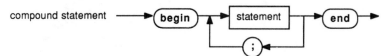

Figure 7.3: Syntax Diagram of a Statement Part

Formatting Your Statements

As mentioned earlier, spaces and line breaks don't affect the meaning of the program—unless, of course, they occur in the middle of a string. For this reason, we could have written our first program (FirstEffort) like this:

```
program MyName; begin WriteLn('This program compliments of...');ReadLn end.
```

Pascal also doesn't make a distinction between uppercase and lowercase letters. It doesn't care if you write *Program*, *PROGRAM*, or *program*, as long as you spell it right. This means more freedom in controlling the appearance of your program, which, initially, you should use with restraint. Again, the examples shown in this book are written in what we think is a readable, easy-to-use format that can be understood by anyone knowledgeable in Pascal.

Statement Types

A large portion of this tutorial is devoted to discussing the different kinds of statements available to you in Turbo Pascal. Let's look at the syntax diagram of a statement (shown in Figure 7.4) to get an overview of what's to come.

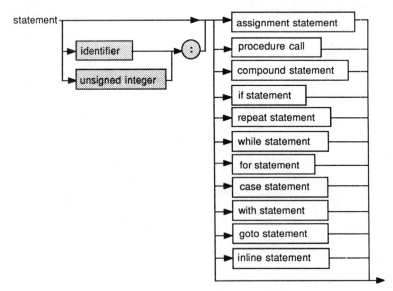

Figure 7.4: Syntax Diagram of a Statement

Turbo Pascal Tutor for the Macintosh

You have already been introduced to the first kind of statement shown in the diagram, the *assignment* statement. The assignment statement gives values to variables and, if necessary, evaluates expressions to produce this value.

A *procedure* statement causes the named procedure to be executed. The *ReadLn* and *WriteLn* statements used in the example programs thus far are actually procedure calls to procedures *ReadLn* and *WriteLn*, which are predefined by Turbo Pascal. We'll talk more about procedures, and how to define your own, in chapters to come.

A *compound* statement is zero or more statements grouped between the reserved words **begin** and **end**. If you think this sounds similar to the statement part of a program, you're absolutely right: The statement part is an example of a compound statement. Compound statements have other uses, which we'll discuss shortly. (If you've ever looked at a large Pascal program, with **begin**s and **end**s all over the place, then you know how common compound statements are.)

The **if** and **case** statements are used to make decisions about what the program should do next.

The **repeat**, **while**, and **for** statements are loop builders; all cause the computer to repeat actions until a particular condition is met. We say more about them in Chapter 10, "Control Structures."

The **with** statement helps the programmer by shortening certain variable names. We'll cover this in Chapter 14, "Records."

The **goto** statement tells the computer to jump to a particular place in the program (indicated by a label) and start executing statements there. Unlike less structured languages like Fortran and BASIC, Pascal never presents a situation where a **goto** is absolutely necessary, and you should avoid them. However, we've included a brief explanation of **goto** in Part 3.

If you have programmed in BASIC or Fortran, it is important to kick the **goto** habit, even though it may be difficult. Once you've mastered Pascal's structured techniques, then you can resort to **goto**s, if you must.

Finally, the **null** statement is represented by the arrow that completely bypasses all of the other statements in the previous syntax diagram (Figure 7.4). In some places where the Pascal language requires a statement, you can tell the computer to do nothing. The **null** statement provides you with a way to convey that message to the compiler.

The path shown in gray in Figure 7.4 shows the format of a label—the target of a **goto** statement. As previously mentioned, we strongly recommend against **goto** statements; this is shown simply for your information.

Comments: The Rest of the Story

An important part of any serious program is its documentation—text that explains what the program does and why. Comments are used to help the reader of the program understand how it works. Comments explain the uses of identifiers, the actions of the program, the situation that will occur when a certain condition is met, the date the program was written, the name of the author, and anything else the author thinks is relevant.

Commenting takes a little effort, but it is an invaluable aid in debugging, maintaining, and enhancing your programs. Someone other than yourself may have to modify the source code of your program someday: If your program didn't have comments, it would be like cooking a gourmet meal from a recipe that lists all the ingredients but gives no instructions on how to combine them.

As mentioned in Chapter 6, comments are ignored by the compiler, which means they have no effect whatsoever on an object program: They do not increase its size or affect its execution speed.

Comments begin with a left brace ({) and end with a right brace (}). These symbols are known as *comment delimiters*. A comment can start and end almost anywhere, and it can occupy as many lines as needed.

About the only potentially confusing aspect of comments is when you use *nested comments*—comments embedded within comments. Say you've written the following section of a program:

```
    .
    .
    .
WriteLn (date);                          { Write the date }
old_a := a;                        { Save the old value of a }
ReadLn (a);                         { Read a new value for a }
    .
    .
    .
```

Suppose you want to temporarily remove the last two statements shown. You don't want to delete them from the program forever, just keep them from being performed during this run. This can be done by "commenting out" a section of code. At first glance, it appears that you could simply put comment symbols before and after the statements you want to comment out, as follows:

```
       .
       .
       .
WriteLn (date);                          { Write the date }
{
old_a := a;                    { Save the old value of a }
ReadLn (a);                    { Read a new value for a }
}
       .
       .
       .
```

This approach doesn't work. The compiler recognizes the first comment (*{Write the date}*) and understands that the next left brace (at the beginning of the second line) is the beginning of another comment. However, when the compiler encounters the right brace at the end of the third line, it assumes the comment is over. Thus, the statement *ReadLn (a)* is compiled into the program, even though we didn't want that to happen.

In this particular case, the compiler then finds the extra right brace in the last line of the example and signals with an error message that something is wrong. Sometimes, however, this sort of error goes undetected, causing many debugging headaches.

One solution to this problem is to delete some of the comment symbols within the section that is commented out. But that would be more trouble (and probably cause more errors) than removing the entire section of code. Fortunately, there's a better way.

There's an alternate pair of comment symbols: a left parenthesis paired with an asterisk "(*" to begin a comment and an asterisk paired with a right parenthesis "*)" to end a comment.

Turbo Pascal allows you to place one kind of comment within the other, as a natural result of the way comments work. If you begin a comment with a left brace ({), everything after it is ignored, including the set of parentheses and asterisks ((* and *)), until the right brace (}) appears. The reverse is also true: When a comment begins with a left parenthesis and an asterisk ((*), everything up to the next asterisk and right parenthesis (*)) is ignored, including a set of braces ({ }).

So, the solution to the problem of nested comments is to always use one set of comment delimiters for descriptive comments, and the other set of comment delimiters for commenting out sections of code. In this manual, we use curly braces as comment delimiters for ordinary text comments. If the situation requires that sections of code be commented out, we use the parenthesis-asterisk comment delimiters. Now, let's rewrite our latest example using both sets of comment delimiters:

```
    .
    .
    .
WriteLn (date);                         { Write the date }
  (*
old_a := a;                   { Save the old value of a }
ReadLn (a);                   { Read a new value for a }
  *)
    .
    .
    .
```

The program runs just fine now, with the sections of code between (* and *) ignored by the compiler. You can use this technique to test various parts of programs, to isolate problems, or to prove that a section of your program does what you intend.

You can insert comments almost anywhere, except in the middle of an identifier or a reserved word, or inside a string. In the first case, the compiler thinks that the reserved word or identifier ends where the comment begins; in the second, it thinks that the comment is part of the string. The statement

```
WriteLn('Hello, world, my name is {not} Joe.');
```

produces the output

```
Hello, world, my name is {not} Joe.
```

Review

The structure of a Pascal program follows this form:

```
program Name ({optional file identifiers});

label     { label declarations here }
            .
            .
            .
const   { constant declarations here }
            .
            .
            .
type      { type declarations here }
            .
            .
            .
var         { variable declarations }
```

```
          .
          .
          .
{ subprograms (procedures and functions) declared here }
begin
{ main body of program }
end.
```

Pascal is a free-format language. It allows declarations and statements to be formatted in many ways, subject to certain simple constraints. Pascal provides a rich variety of statements from which to choose.

Turbo Pascal is more flexible than Standard Pascal in that **label**, **const**, **type**, **var**, and subprogram declarations can be placed in any order and can occur more than once.

Comments are used to document programs and to prevent certain sections of code from being run during tests. The two sets of comment delimiters—{ and } and (* and *)—allow the programmer to nest comments within one another. Comments can be used anywhere, except in the middle of a string, a reserved word, or an identifier.

Now you're ready to tackle predefined data types.

8

Predefined Data Types

In this chapter, we'll explore Turbo Pascal's predefined data types—the ones that you will use most often. They include *Integer*, *LongInt*, *Real*, *Boolean*, and *Char*. We'll explain and give examples of each. In addition, we'll cover *string types*, which allow you to manipulate textual data.

Every data object in a Pascal program has a *type*. You must therefore tell the compiler the type of every constant and every variable your program uses. For constants, the type is implicit in its declaration. For example,

```
const
  peopleCount = 13;
  e = 2.71818;
```

Given these declarations, the compiler figures out that *peopleCount* is an *Integer*, because it fits in the range of integers and has no decimal point. Similarly, *e*'s decimal point marks it as a *Real*.

In determining the type of variables, the compiler doesn't have to guess, because you are required to explicitly state the type in the declaration:

```
var
  HeadCount: Integer;
  Acreage: Real;
```

Pascal's data types can be classified as either *simple types*, which are used for information that is always manipulated as a whole, and *structured types*, which are used for information consisting of smaller pieces that can be manipulated individually or as a whole.

Turbo Pascal's predefined data types are the ones that you will use most often. All of Turbo's predefined types fall into the simple category; they include *Integer*, *LongInt*, *Real*, *Boolean*, and *Char*. *String types* allow you to manipulate textual data; while not part of Standard Pascal, strings are a common extension.

Integers

Integers are whole numbers, negative and positive, in the range –32768 to 32767. 12 is an integer, as are 456 and –12000. On the other hand, 1.234, 2.0, and –0.54234312 are not: They have decimal points. You use *Integer* data types when your data is strictly numeric, doesn't contain fractions, and fits in the prescribed range. Figure 8.1 shows the syntax diagram for an *unsigned integer* (an integer constant without a + or – sign).

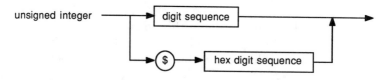

Figure 8.1: Syntax Diagram of an Unsigned Integer

In Turbo Pascal, you can specify an integer constant in *hexadecimal* (base 16, also known as *hex*) notation as well as ordinary decimal (base 10) notation. A hexadecimal constant consists of a series of hex digits (0 through 9 or *a* through *f*) preceded by a dollar sign ($). Declaring hex constants is an advanced technique we'll delve into in Chapter 25.

A Turbo Pascal integer occupies 2 bytes of memory. Because there are only so many unique values that can be expressed by 16 bits (65,536, to be exact), objects of type *Integer* are limited to the range –32768 through 32767. Each integer you declare will occupy 2 bytes regardless of its value; for example, the integers 0, 37, and 32,000 are all stored in 2 bytes. For your convenience, there's a predefined constant called *MaxInt* equal to 32767.

Integer Operators

In performing calculations with integers, you can use the operations that you expect to work on any kind of number: +, –, *, and /. (The / operator actually divides real numbers, but works on integers because its operands are converted to reals before the division. The result of the / operator is always of type *Real*.) If a value with a fractional part is assigned to an integer variable, the fraction is removed (truncated) and the integer assumes the value of the non-fractional part of the number.

The *relational operators* can also be used with integers. These include >, <, >=, <=, =, and <>. In addition, Turbo Pascal has two special operations that can be applied only to integers: **div** and **mod**.

The **div** operator performs *integer division*. Integer division works much like /-style division, except that the operands must both be integers and the result is always an integer (any fractional part is dropped during the division). Using **div** to process integers is preferable to using /, since integer division is processed by the Macintosh's processor approximately 10 times faster than real division.

The **mod** (*modulo*) operator divides its two operands, again using integer division, and returns the remainder. This operation is useful for "clock arithmetic." (As you know, the hours on a clock go up to 12, then start at 1 again, so the next hour is the current hour plus 1, **mod** 12.) The **mod** operator also helps determine if a number is a multiple of another (if A is a multiple of B, then A **mod** $B = 0$). For example, *48* **mod** *16 = 0*, because 16 goes into 48 three times, with a remainder of 0; therefore, 48 is a multiple of 16.

Integers and Arithmetic Overflow

We know that integers are limited to a specific range of values. What happens, you may ask, if the result of an integer operation falls outside this range—as in the following program:

```
program Test;
var
  A: integer;
begin
  A := 30000 + 30000
end.
```

The answer: A bad thing known as *arithmetic overflow*. If you calculate a value that is too positive or too negative to store in the –32768 to 32767 range of integers, overflow occurs. Overflow is especially pernicious when it occurs in the middle of a calculation.

For example, consider program MightOverflow:

```
program MightOverflow;
```

```
var
  A,B,C: Integer;
begin
  A := 1000;
  B := 100;
  C := A * B div 50;
  WriteLn(C);
  ReadLn
end.
```

This program doesn't assign to *C* the value you might expect (*2000*) because of overflow—even though *2000* is in the acceptable integer range. Instead, *C* gets the mysterious (and completely wrong) value, *–621*.

How did this happen—especially since arithmetic is the one thing computers do rapidly and dependably? Let's follow through the actions a Turbo Pascal program performs in executing this statement. First, Turbo Pascal multiplies *1000* by *100*. Since *A* and *B* are both *Integer* constants (the compiler can tell, just by looking), it uses integer multiplication.

This multiplication routine has only 16 bits in which to return an answer. Unfortunately, *100000* doesn't fit in 16 bits. So, the multiplication instead returns a value of *–31072*, which happens to be the value of the lower 16 bits of *100000*. The rest of the number is simply lost. *–31072* is then integer-divided by *50*, producing *–621*. The compiler and computer have both done their jobs correctly, yet still produce the wrong result.

Integers have two main benefits: They require only 2 bytes of storage, and operations on them execute fast (as much as 100 times faster than certain operations on reals). The price you pay for these benefits is the caution you must exercise when calculating. No run-time error is produced as a result of arithmetic overflow, so it's important to keep alert for this problem. In the previous example, writing the assignment as

```
C := A * (B div 50)
```

would have produced the correct result.

Exercises

Which of the following are valid constants of type *Integer*? Why aren't the others valid?

1. 40000
2. –10,000
3. $b

4. *MaxInt*

5. −32768

6. $A21H

7. 2.0

8. 0

Long Integers

There are times you'll need an *Integer* variable, but find the range constraints of integers too limiting. For such situations, Turbo Pascal provides the *LongInt* (long integer) type. Values of type *LongInt* must be whole numbers but can range all the way from −2,147,483,648 to 2,147,483,647 (call it ± 2 billion).

Converting Between Types LongInt and Integer

Turbo Pascal automatically performs the necessary conversion in assigning integer values to long integers and vice versa. For example,

```
program Test;
var
  A: Integer;
  B: LongInt;
begin
  A := 1234;
  B := A;
  B := 100000;
  A := B;
  WriteLn(A);
  ReadLn
end.
```

does not produce any compile-time or run-time errors. Turbo Pascal lets you freely mix operations involving integers and long integers. Going from integers to long integers never causes problems; however, overflow can result when you assign long integer values to integers, as in the example. This program writes *−31072* to the screen, which happens to be the lower 16 bits of *100,000*.

Real

A real constant, like all numeric constants, must begin with at least one digit. To be recognized as a real, it must then contain a decimal point followed by one or more digits, or an exponent. Thus, 100.0 and 1E2 are real constants, while 100 is an integer.

The Macintosh's processor isn't as comfortable working with real numbers as with integers. (You may have surmised this from our statement that real division and multiplication are slower than the corresponding integer operations.)

Real Operators

You can perform the four basic arithmetic operations (+, −, ×, and ÷) on values of type *Real*. It is important to note that if any of these operations is done on one value of type *Integer* and another of type *Real*, the result will be of type *Real*. In other words, in evaluating the expression *(50 × 50.0)* the *Integer* constant *50* is converted to a real before being multiplied with the *Real* constant *50.0*.

The relational operators may also be applied to values of type *Real*. Again, if operands of types *Integer* or *LongInt* are mixed with real numbers in an expression, they are converted to reals before the operation is performed.

Exponential Notation

What's an *exponent*? Since real numbers must encompass both very large and very small values, Pascal allows *exponential*, or scientific, notation to represent them. For instance, it is a well-known fact that Scotts Valley, California, is 5,890,000,000,000 inches from the sun. In college-level engineering texts, this important physical constant is represented as

5.89×10^{12}

To accommodate the lack of superscripts on most computer screens and keyboards, it is conventional in programming languages to replace the $\times 10$ part of the number with the letter E (for exponent). The Scotts Valley Solar Constant can be represented by a Turbo Pascal real as

`5.89E12`

Exponential notation is also used to represent very small numbers; that is, values that are close to zero. For example, Frank Borland's height, expressed in light years as 0.00000000000000019, is represented in scientific notation as

$$1.9 \times 10^{-16}$$

and as a Turbo Pascal real constant by

```
1.9E-16
```

The number to the left of the E is called the *mantissa*; the value to the right is the exponent. To convert a number from exponential notation to ordinary notation, move the decimal point in the mantissa the number of places to the right indicated by the exponent, and fill in any gap with zeros. (If the exponent is negative, you move the decimal point to the left.)

To convert a number to exponential notation, move the decimal point until it is just to the right of the leftmost non-zero digit in the number. The exponent then becomes the number of digits you move the decimal point. (If the number is negative, you move the decimal point to the right; if positive, you move it to the left.)

Values of type *Real* can store numbers in the range ±10E38. Of course, it takes more space to store this information than it does to store an integer, but there are times when no other type will do.

The following are examples of real numbers:

```
1E5
3.1415926
-3546.3
0.0034
32.E4
5.679E21
-1.324E-2
21343.0
0.0
0.1
```

The following are invalid real numbers:

```
-.123423    No digit to the left of the decimal
25.         No digit to the right of the decimal
E14         No mantissa
```

If you write a number that you intend to be a real constant without a decimal point or exponent, the compiler doesn't complain as long as the constant is within the range of integers (or long integers). Instead, the compiler interprets the number as an integer (or long integer). Since Turbo Pascal automatically converts integers to real numbers when necessary, this never causes your code to execute incorrectly; however, the conversion slows things down slightly.

Exercises

Convert each of the following numbers to a legal Pascal constant in scientific notation.

1. 20,000
2. −.000025
3. +42.77
4. −530000.5

Convert each of the following constants from scientific notation to standard notation.

1. 1.5E-10
2. −5.545454E12
3. 2E0

Boolean

Objects of the type *Boolean* are limited to only two values: True and False—spelled out, just like that. This type is named in honor of 19th-century English mathematician George Boole, who developed the rules (now called boolean algebra) that govern the operation of computers at the hardware level.

Pascal programs use boolean values to evaluate the truth of an assertion—especially when the computer must decide what to do next. You may recall that the results of all relational operators are of type *Boolean*; we show you how to use them to make decisions in Chapter 10, "Control Structures." Here's an example:

```
program BooleanDemo;
var
  A: Boolean;
begin
  A := True;
  if A then
    WriteLn('A is true')
  else
    WriteLn('A is false')
end.
```

Char

Data objects of type *Char* hold ASCII characters; that is, they hold a number from 0 to 127 that represents the corresponding printable or control character. Actually, a variable of type *Char* can have 256 values, including the 128 characters in the standard ASCII set and the Macintosh's extensions. (See Figure 2.2.)

As you may recall, the ASCII character set includes both printing and nonprinting characters. You represent printing characters by enclosing them in single quote marks, as follows:

'a'   '$'   ' '   'J'

Notice in the third example that a space is a printing character like any other and is represented as a space enclosed in single quotes.

Nonprinting characters can be represented by preceding a character's ASCII value with the pound-sign symbol (#). For example, #13 equals carriage return; #9 equals tab.

Strings

Briefly, a string is a sequence of characters with a specific length. A string can be treated as a single entity, and the characters that make it up can be accessed individually, hence its status as a structured type.

For example, *'Enter first value: '* is a string. The single quotes or apostrophes (') show where it starts and stops; the string contains the characters *E, n, t, e, r,* and so on. Its length—the number of characters between the single quotes—is 19, including the space before the close quote.

String Constants

A string constant consists of a group of characters, enclosed in single quotes. Figure 8.2 displays the syntax diagram for a string constant.

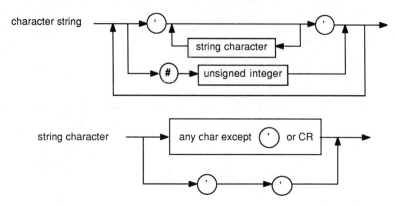

Figure 8.2: Syntax Diagram of a String Constant

The following are examples of legal string constants:

```
'a'    'Hello, how''s it going?'    'blipvert'    ''
```

The second of these examples demonstrates how to get a single quote into a string constant. Two consecutive single quotes represent a single quote. When this string is output to the screen, the result is

```
Hello, how's it going?
```

The fourth example, a string constant that consists of nothing but two single quotes, is called the null string. The null string has zero length and does not show anything when written.

Declaring String Variables

You declare a variable of a string type as you would declare any other variable: identifier, colon, and type. In this case, the type is a string type. Figure 8.3 shows how this works.

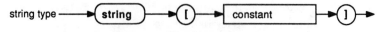

Figure 8.3: Syntax Diagram of a String Type

The unsigned integer in the string-type definition is a value from 1 to 255, which declares the maximum number of characters a string of that type can hold. A string can therefore be no longer than 255 characters. When you declare a variable of type **string**[*n*], where *n* is an integer, Turbo Pascal sets aside *n + 1* bytes of memory to hold that string's contents: *n* bytes to hold the characters themselves, and one byte to hold the current length of the string.

Here's an example of a string declaration:

```
var
  CompanyName : string[39];
```

This makes the compiler set aside 40 bytes for *CompanyName*. If you then execute the statement

```
CompanyName := 'Borland';
```

the current length of *CompanyName* is 7, even though the maximum length is still 39. We'll get into the storage format of strings in more detail later, but here's a sneak preview: Strings are stored as a series of characters in successive bytes of memory, with the very first byte of storage containing the current length. After string variable *CompanyName* is assigned the constant *'Borland'*, the first byte contains the value 7, the second byte the character *B*, the third byte the character *o*, and so on. The unused characters (positions 8 through 39) at the end of the string variable can contain anything at all; however, with the length information in the first byte, Turbo Pascal knows to not use them.

It's easy to confuse the maximum length of a string with its current length. It may be helpful to think of this distinction in terms of compile time versus run time. A string variable's maximum length is determined at compile time according to the type given the string in its declaration. This length serves as the upper limit on how much data can be placed in this string at run time. A variable of type **string**[*10*], for example, can never contain more than 10 characters.

The current length of a string variable, by contrast, varies during program execution according to the value most recently assigned to it. For example:

```
Program StringTest;
var
  s: string[10];
begin
  s := 'Hello';
  s := 'Hi';
end.
```

String *s* is allocated 11 bytes of storage by the compiler (10 plus 1 for the length byte). After executing the first assignment statement, its length becomes 5—but *s* still has 11 bytes of storage allocated for it. After the second assignment, its length byte has the value 2. Routines that access variable *s* (*WriteLn*, for instance) know to look at the length byte to see just how many of those bytes are in use.

Review

In this chapter, we introduced you to Turbo Pascal's predefined data types (*Integer*, *LongInt*, *Real*, *Boolean*, and *Char*) and to strings.

To summarize, an integer is a positive or negative whole number, including zero. Integers require 2 bytes of memory each, and can be in the range –32768 through 32767. Processing with integers is quicker than with any other numeric type.

A *LongInt* (long integer) is like an integer with a vastly expanded range, approximately ±2 billion. Long integers require 4 bytes of storage.

Real values consist of a mantissa and an optional positive or negative exponent. The mantissa may have up to seven significant digits. The range of reals is approximately ±1E38.

Logical values of True and False are handled by the data type *Boolean*. A *Boolean* value occupies one byte of memory.

The type *Char* is one of 256 ASCII characters, including both printing and nonprinting characters. *Char* data types occupy one byte of memory each.

Finally, the string data types can have a defined length of 1 to 255 characters and are declared with a maximum length. A string occupies 1 more byte in memory than its maximum length.

Now that you have a fundamental understanding of the predefined types, you are ready to tackle defined scalar types in the next chapter.

9

Defined Scalar Types

In the real world, there are many types of objects that have a limited range of values and a definite order. A day of the week, for example, ranges from Sunday to Saturday, and the days come one after the other in a fixed sequence. Pascal lets you define and manipulate this type of data as *scalar* types.

A scalar type is one in which all possible values can be said to be in order—from the first to the last—with no gaps. Some of the predefined types are scalar—namely, *Integer*, *LongInt*, *Boolean*, and *Char*.

Scalar types are representable internally by the same binary technique used for integers. *Real* is not a scalar type, because adding 1 to a real doesn't produce the next real number—in fact, there is no "next" real number after, say, 5.0. Between 5.0 and 6.0 come a host of values, including 5.01, 5.1, 5.11, 5.1109, 5.3, and so on. Similarly, string types are not scalar.

A *defined scalar type* has a user-defined range of values and a user-defined order. The range of values is defined by the number of elements you declare, and the order is defined by the order in which the elements are declared. Properly used, these types can result in a better representation of the real-world entity your program must process. Defined scalar types also improve readability, save memory space, and allow automatic checking to be performed on your program. We'll discuss two kinds of defined scalar types: *enumerated* and *subranges*.

Enumerated Scalar Types

Good programming style means being considerate of the human beings who have to read and understand your code (including yourself). For example, to hold a day of the week in a program, you could declare a variable *DayOfWeek* of type *Integer*, and then use numbers for the days. But it isn't clear which day you understand to be the first day of the week—Sunday or Monday? Nor is it obvious if your program represents the first day of the week by a 0 or a 1. Anyone who tries to modify your program has to determine what number stands for which day.

The way to address these potential problems is *not* to declare *DayOfWeek* to be of type *Integer*. Instead, you can declare a type specifically for the purpose of holding a day of the week and *enumerate*, or list, the values it can have:

```
program Day_Of_Week_Example;
type
  Days       = (Monday,Tuesday,Wednesday,Thursday,Friday,Saturday,Sunday);
var
  DayOfWeek  : Days;

begin
   DayOfWeek := Thursday;
   .
   if DayOfWeek = Saturday then
     WriteLn('It''s Saturday. Why are you at work?');
   .
   .
end.
```

Now there's no confusion over converting between numbers and days.

To declare a scalar type, you must first give an identifier for the type, then list in parentheses, in order, identifiers for all of the values the type can have. You can declare scalar types for just about any set of values, including those with no inherent order, for example,

```
type
  precipitation = (rain, snow, sleet);
  color = (black, white, blue, green, red, yellow);
```

If order is important, declare your list of values from the first to the last.

You define user-defined types in the *type definition part* of a program. The syntax of this part of the program is shown in Figure 9.1.

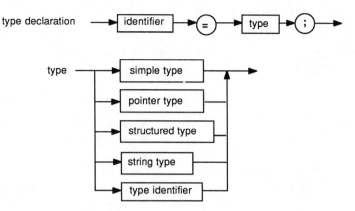

Figure 9.1: Syntax Diagram of a Type Definition Part

Each type definition names the type to be defined, then tells the compiler the details of the type. An enumerated scalar type is a simple type (see Figure 9.2).

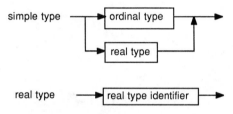

Figure 9.2: Syntax Diagram of a Simple Type

It is important to remember that when you list the values of an enumerated type, you are in fact declaring the names of those values as identifiers. It is therefore *not* legal to declare:

```
type
  Days    = (Monday,Tuesday,Wednesday,Thursday,Friday,Saturday,Sunday);
  DaysOff = (Saturday,Sunday);
```

because to do so would be to declare *Saturday* and *Sunday* twice. Each identifier must have one, and only one, type. (Later, we'll learn how to use *sets* to handle a situation like this gracefully.)

Ordinal Values

Enumerated scalar types (indeed, all scalar types) are inherently ordered. In other words, there is a lowest value, a highest value, and a number of distinct values in between. It is often convenient to turn a member of an enumerated type into the underlying integer value that represents it.

In type *Days* in the previous example, *Monday* is the lowest value and *Sunday* is the highest value. The lowest value is considered to have an ordinal value of 0, while the highest value has an ordinal value equal to the total number of values defined, minus 1 (because we started counting at 0; there are many cases in Pascal programming in which counting starts at 0, so be alert for this). For example, here are the ordinal values of the type *Days*:

```
Element         Ordinal Value
-------         -------------
Monday                0
Tuesday               1
Wednesday             2
Thursday              3
Friday                4
Saturday              5
Sunday                6
```

Standard Functions for Scalar Types

To simplify the use of enumerated types and scalar types in general, Pascal provides operations to manipulate objects of these types. In particular, these functions help you to find

- the value that comes before a value of the type (its predecessor)
- the value that comes after a value of the type (its successor)
- the position of a value in the list of values in the type definition

Here's a scenario that helps explain why this information can be useful. Imagine that in your program you have defined the type *Days* and two variables of that type, *DayOfWeek* and *NextDay*:

```
      .
      .
      .
type
   Days    = (Monday,Tuesday,Wednesday,Thursday,Friday,Saturday,Sunday);
var
   DayOfWeek, NextDay  : Days;
      .
      .
      .
```

Now suppose that somewhere in your program you want to set *NextDay* equal to the day following *DayOfWeek*. How do you do it?

Well, one thing you *cannot* do is add 1 to the value of *DayOfWeek*. The statement

```
NextDay := DayOfWeek + 1;
```

causes the compiler to give you a `Type Mismatch` error—and rightly so. The operation of addition is not defined for objects of the type *Days*. Yet you know intuitively that you want an operation that somehow adds 1 to a day of the week, finding its successor in the list of weekdays.

Pascal comes to the rescue by providing this exact operation in the form of the *Succ* (successor) function. Using it, you can write

```
NextDay := Succ(DayOfWeek);
```

and achieve the desired effect. If *DayOfWeek* has the value *Tuesday*, *NextDay* is assigned the value *Wednesday*. If it's *Wednesday* already, *NextDay* becomes *Thursday*, and so on.

A *function* is an operation that takes one or more values (called *parameters*, or sometimes *arguments*) and uses them to produce a new value. The sine function, for instance, takes an angle as a parameter and returns the sine of that angle. In the previous example, you made the function *Succ* work on the parameter *DayOfWeek* to produce (return) a new value, which was the next value in the type *Days*. The new value was then assigned to the variable *NextDay*.

The *Succ* function is one of three predefined "standard" functions that manipulate scalar types. The others are *Pred* and *Ord*.

As you might already have guessed, the *Pred* function is the reverse of the *Succ* function: It returns the predecessor of the value given to it as a parameter. The *Ord* function returns the ordinal value of its parameter.

Here are some examples of the results of using these functions. Given that *DayOfWeek* = *Wednesday*, then

```
Pred(DayOfWeek)          = Tuesday
Succ(DayOfWeek)          = Thursday
Pred(Pred(DayOfWeek))    = Monday
Succ(Succ(DayOfWeek))    = Friday
Pred(Succ(DayOfWeek))    = Wednesday
Succ(Pred(DayOfWeek))    = Wednesday
Ord(DayOfWeek)           = 2
Ord(Pred(DayOfWeek))     = 1
Ord(Succ(DayOfWeek))     = 3
```

Ord always returns a value greater than or equal to 0 for all scalar types except *Integer*. That is, except for integers, scalar types never have negative ordinal values; their first value always has an ordinal value of 0.

Given an integer or long integer parameter, *Ord* returns the actual integer value. There's no reason to use *Ord* with these types (although it's legal).

The examples also demonstrate that it is perfectly legal to *nest* functions—that is, to apply a function to the result of another. The expression *Pred(Pred(DayOfWeek))* is a convenient way to get the day two days before *DayOfWeek*.

Cyclical Enumerated Types and Range Errors

One thing to watch out for when using *Succ* and *Pred* is inadvertently calculating a nonexistent successor or predecessor. For instance, suppose variable *DayOfWeek* in the previous example had the value *Sunday*, and you tried to perform this assignment:

```
NextDay := Succ(DayOfWeek);
```

You might expect *NextDay* to roll over to the first day of the week, *Monday*. But Turbo Pascal has no way of knowing that the days of the week run in a cycle, so it tries to assign to *NextDay* a value with the ordinal value 7 (one more than the ordinal value of *Sunday*, which is 6).

The result of this assignment depends on the conditions present when you compiled your program. If you compiled your program with range-checking turned on (explained in the next section), it realizes that there is no successor for *Sunday*; the program stops and displays an error message. If range-checking wasn't turned on when the program was compiled (which is the default), the error isn't caught and your program will behave erratically, that is, who knows what value will be assigned to *NextDay*.

Neither of these reactions is especially desirable. To achieve the correct result, use an **if** statement to handle the special case:

```
if DayOfWeek = Sunday then
  NextDay := Monday
else
  NextDay := Succ(DayOfWeek);
```

While we haven't described the **if** statement in detail yet, the preceding example is a pretty clear English description of what needs to be done. If *DayOfWeek* has the value *Sunday*, then we want to explicitly set *NextDay* to the value *Monday*; otherwise, the *Succ* function will provide the correct value.

Exercises

Rewrite the previous code fragment to set the variable *Yesterday* to the day before *DayOfWeek*. How do you handle Sunday? (Solutions are in Appendix B.)

Of course, the same situation can arise even if the enumerated type in question is not cyclical—though it is less likely. If you define the type

```
Rank = (Programmer,Peon,Manager,SeniorMgr,VicePres,President,Chairman);
```

and try to find the next rank after Chairman, the same type of error occurs.

Compiler Directives: Range-Checking

Defined scalar types are designed to help you restrict the values of your variables to within certain predetermined limits. However, Turbo Pascal does not enforce those limits unless it is specifically told to do so. The previous example, in which we attempted to take the successor of the last value of an enumerated type, does not cause an error message in Turbo Pascal unless a feature called *range-checking* is enabled when the program is compiled.

Range-checking is turned on by a *compiler directive*. Pascal compilers traditionally use special "activated comments" as a way to control the compiler. A compiler directive (also called a *metastatement* or *metacommand*) consists of a comment in which the very first character is a dollar sign ($). For example,

```
{$U MyUnit}
{$I+}
```

demonstrate two of Turbo Pascal's directives. The $U directive tells the compiler to search disk file MyUnit for information that this program will use. The $I+ directive turns input/output (I/O) checking on; we'll learn more about it in Chapter 17. Units are explained in Chapter 18.

Compiler directives are unlike standard language elements like identifiers, key words, and statements in that they don't describe actions and data objects to be used at run time. Instead, they instruct and assist the compiler at compile time.

The compiler directive that turns range-checking on is {$R+}. {$R-} turns range-checking off; it's the default, so if you don't want range-checking you don't have to include it. We recommend that you put {$R+} before the program heading of every program you write; it will save you many hours of debugging. Once a program is known to be free of potential range errors, you can compile it a final time with range-checking turned off to generate a faster, more compact program.

A Useful Trick: Undefined Values in Enumerated Types

In working with defined scalar types, it can be useful to consider what will happen if no value is provided for a variable, or if your program must have a "none of the above" choice for a value. For example, there may be times when you need to begin a program with your variables set to a known value, but one that is not normally associated with your type. (Putting your variables into a known state before doing anything else is known as *initializing*.)

A good way to do this is to add an extra value to your type to reflect this "undefined" state. For instance, in the first example in this chapter, we could have written

```
program Day_Of_Week_Example;
type
  Days       = (Noday,Monday,Tuesday,Wednesday,Thursday,
               Friday,Saturday,Sunday);
var
  DayOfWeek  : Days;
begin
  DayOfWeek := Noday;
  .
  .
  .
end.
```

Now, when the program begins, *DayOfWeek* has a known value: *Noday*. If, later in the program, you want to test whether or not you have assigned a value to *DayOfWeek*, you can test to see whether *DayOfWeek* still equals *Noday*.

Subranges

Another important kind of scalar type is called a *subrange*. A subrange is a group of consecutive values that is part of another scalar type. It is useful when you want to limit the possible number of values a variable can have to a subset of the original type.

A subrange is specified by the minimum and maximum values to be allowed in the subrange, separated by two periods (..). This sounds more complicated than it really is. In the following example, we define an enumerated scalar type and two subranges of that type:

```
type
  Days    = (Noday,Monday,Tuesday,Wednesday,Thursday,
             Friday,Saturday,Sunday);
  Workdays = Monday..Friday;
  Weekend = Saturday..Sunday;
```

The type from which the subrange is derived is called the *base type* of the subrange. Therefore, *Workdays* is a subrange of *Days* and *Days* is the base type of *Workdays* and *Weekend*.

As you might expect in declaring subranges, the minimum value (the one specified first in the declaration) must not have a greater ordinal value than the maximum value (the one specified last in the declaration).

Here are more examples of subranges:

```
type
  CompassRange  = 0..360;  { Subrange of the base type Integer }
  ValidEntry    = 'A'..'F';   { Subrange of the base type Char }
  MonthlyIncome = 10000..30000;
  Hours         = 0..23;              { Subrange of integer }
  Minutes       = 0..59;            {   "       "    "    }

  { Here is a defined scalar type... }
  MusicType     = (Notype,Classical,Jazz,Folk,RhythmBlues,Rock,
                   HardRock,AcidRock,HeavyMetal);

  { ...and here is a subrange of that type. }
  MusicILike    = Classical..Rock; { Subrange of the base type MusicType }
```

Subranges can be used to design menus (or any other user-interface element of your program) in which the only valid entries are a subrange of an existing type.

Subranges are often used in defining other elements of Pascal, such as arrays and records; these uses are described in chapters 12 and 14.

Subranges as Anonymous Types

So far we've defined subranges in **type** declarations, implying that to use a subrange type you must first define it, then declare variables with it. You can also specify a subrange directly in the variable declaration.

For instance, after declaring

```
Days        = (Noday,Monday,Tuesday,Wednesday,Thursday,
                Friday,Saturday,Sunday);
```

you can write

```
var
  Workday     : Monday..Friday; { This subrange type has no name.}
```

rather than

```
type
  WorkingDay = Monday..Friday;
var
  Workday     : WorkingDay;
```

The ability to specify subranges in this way saves you from inventing a name for every subrange you want to use. Because the subrange type is never named, it is called an *anonymous type.*

Enumerated types can be defined anonymously as well, though this practice is not recommended. It is legal to declare

```
var
  Day1      : (Mon,Tue,Wed,Thu,Fri,Sat,Sun);
```

Note, however, that the identifiers *Mon* through *Sun* are now defined as part of the anonymous type and may not be used for anything else. For this reason, you may *not* declare

```
var
  Day1      : (Mon,Tue,Wed,Thu,Fri,Sat,Sun);
  Day2      : (Mon,Tue,Wed,Thu,Fri,Sat,Sun);
```

If you attempt to compile this, you will get an error when the compiler gets to the second declaration since the second anonymous, but distinct, type uses the same identifiers as the first. This declaration, however, would work:

```
var
  Day1,Day2 : (Mon,Tue,Wed,Thu,Fri,Sat,Sun);
```

Two other restrictions apply to anonymous enumerated types. First, you cannot coerce variables to an anonymous scalar type (that is, convert them from other types to an anonymous type), because the name of the type is required to perform the operation. Don't worry, this will make more sense when you learn about type coercion.

Second, you cannot pass such variables as typed parameters to a subroutine or procedure, since there is no data type to use in the declaration of the formal parameter. These restrictions will be more important to you later, when you begin writing code using these advanced features.

Input and Output

It would be convenient if you could read and write objects of enumerated scalar types directly, but Pascal doesn't allow it. For example, it would be handy to say the following to display the current value of *DayOfWeek*:

```
WriteLn('Today is ',DayOfWeek);
```

But this statement won't compile. The same is true for reading enumerated types from the keyboard:

```
ReadLn(DayOfWeek);
```

To overcome this limitation, you need to explicitly tell the compiler to write, or look for, specific strings. In chapters 10 and 12, respectively, we'll show you how to use the **case** statement and **arrays** to accomplish this.

Memory Usage

Another advantage of defined scalar types is that they use memory efficiently. A variable of a defined scalar type with up to 128 possible values uses only one byte of memory.

Furthermore, if you define a subrange of type *Integer* that has a minimum value greater than or equal to –128 and a maximum value less than or equal to 127, only one byte of storage is required for a variable of that type.

Review

Defined scalar types are data types that you define yourself. They include enumerated types and subranges of existing scalar types. Defined scalar types can be of great help in program development, documentation, and maintenance.

Take a moment to study the quiz on Scalars in the Turbo Tutor program on your distribution disk.

Now that you're clear on the use of types, you can move on to the use of control structures in Pascal.

10

Control Structures

In the sample programs we've seen thus far, statements are executed sequentially, top to bottom, from **begin**ning to **end**. While this sort of execution is straightforward and easy to understand, it doesn't lend itself to repetitive tasks or to making decisions and acting on them. If all Macintosh programs executed each statement once and once only, the machine would be about as useful as a dull Ginsu knife.

Fortunately, Pascal provides *control structures*—special statements that divert execution from the usual top to bottom sequence. These structures fall into four categories: *conditional* (the **if** statement), *iterative* (the **for**, **while**, and **repeat**...**until** statements), *case* (the **case** statement), and *goto* (the **goto** statement).

Conditional Execution: The If Statement

In earlier chapters, we touched briefly on the **if** statement, a Pascal device that tells the machine to do something only if a certain condition is true. Chapter 9 used this simple example:

```
if DayOfWeek = Saturday then
  WriteLn('It''s Saturday. Why are you at work?');
```

Here we tell the computer, "Compare the value of variable *DayOfWeek* to the constant *Saturday*. If they are equal, then perform this *WriteLn* statement; otherwise, do nothing."

This is the simplest form of the **if** statement:

- the reserved word **if**
- a boolean expression (that is, one that yields the value True or False)
- the reserved word **then**
- a statement

Note that the semicolon at the end of the example marks the end of the **if** statement, not of the enclosed *WriteLn* statement. If the **if** statement wasn't followed by another statement, the semicolon could be omitted. Semicolons are statement separators—not statement terminators.

An extension of the **if** statement allows the computer to choose one of two possible actions based on the truth of a boolean expression. In another example from the last chapter, we wrote

```
if DayOfWeek = Sunday then
  NextDay := Monday
else
  NextDay := Succ(DayOfWeek);
```

Here we've added the reserved word **else** and a statement to be executed if the expression *DayOfWeek = Sunday* isn't True. Since the **if** statement doesn't end after the enclosed statement *NextDay := Monday*, and there can be only one nested statement, there is no semicolon there. This is an important part of the format of the **if** statement. A semicolon before an **else** causes the compiler to generate an error message, because it tells the compiler that the **if** statement is over—and no Pascal statement type begins with the **else** keyword.

The syntax diagram for the **if** statement is shown in Figure 10.1.

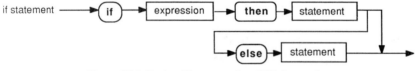

Figure 10.1: Syntax Diagram of an If Statement

The Compound Statement

As mentioned earlier (and as you can see from Figure 10.1), the **if** statement allows only one statement in the **if** clause and only one in the optional **else** clause. If this seems overly restrictive, we agree. In many cases, you need to have the computer do more than one thing if a certain condition is met.

A brute-force way to accomplish this would be to write a separate **if** statement for each and every statement you want to execute conditionally. However, this would tend to clutter a program with **if** statements and slow down execution, because the test must be performed repeatedly. Messy.

Not surprisingly, there's a better way. In Pascal, one can group a series of statements together so that the **if** statement controls the group as a whole. A group of statements that the compiler perceives as a single statement is called a *compound statement*. It's constructed by enclosing the statement group between the reserved words **begin** and **end**. This creates a sort of program within a program.

The syntax of a compound statement is, in fact, exactly the same as that of the statement part of a program, as shown in Figure 10.2. The ramifications of this are important: Any number of any type of statement can appear in a compound statement (including additional **if** statements), which themselves can contain still more compound statements. This is an example of Pascal's recursive, egg-within-an-egg character.

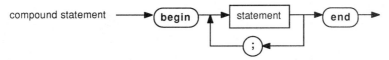

Figure 10.2: Syntax Diagram of a Compound Statement

Thus, if we want our first example to do more than one thing when it discovers that our user is working on Saturday, we could write

```
if DayOfWeek = Saturday then
begin
  WriteLn('It''s Saturday. Why are you at work?');
  WriteLn('Why not go home and watch TV instead?')
end;
```

Furthermore, if we want to put more than one statement into an **else** clause, we could do that as well:

```
if DayOfWeek = Saturday then
  WriteLn('It''s Saturday. Why are you at work?')
else
begin
  WriteLn('It isn''t Saturday.');
  WriteLn('Quit messing around and get to work!');
end;
```

You'll find compound statements (also known as **begin/end** blocks) useful when working with the **while** and **for** statements covered later in this chapter.

Boolean Expressions

The expression *DayOfWeek = Saturday* in the previous example is a boolean expression; when it's evaluated it yields a value of either True or False. (That is, the expression is either True or False.)

Boolean expressions are often formed by using the relational operators to compare two numbers. For example, suppose integer variables *Score* and *Maximum* are equal to 10 and 0, respectively. Here are some boolean expressions that apply relational operators to these variables and the results that they yield:

```
Score >  Maximum  --->  True     (is greater than)
Score =  Maximum  --->  False    (is equal to)
Score <  Maximum  --->  False    (is less than)
Score >= Maximum  --->  True     (is greater than or equal to)
Score <= Maximum  --->  False    (is less than or equal to)
Score <> Maximum  --->  True     (is not equal to)
```

The relational operators don't just apply to numbers, however. All of the relations shown can be applied to objects of any scalar type, even enumerated types (since enumerated types have a definite ordering). Thus, it is legal to write

```
if DayOfWeek > Friday then
  WriteLn('It''s the weekend!');
```

Relational operators aren't the only operators that yield boolean results. The **not** operator, for example, "inverts" its boolean operand: **not** False yields True, and **not** True yields False.

A boolean expression can, of course, also contain one or more variables of type *Boolean*, and a boolean variable can be assigned the result of a boolean expression. For instance, if we declare

```
var
  NewMaximum : Boolean;
```

then we can write the assignment statement

```
NewMaximum := Score > Maximum;
```

and use variable *NewMaximum* to remember the result of the comparison.

Combining this with our earlier example, we can create a series of statements that determines if the player of a game has set a new high score, then prints an appropriate message:

```
NewMaximum := Score > Maximum; { NewMaximum is True if new high score }
```

```
if NewMaximum then
begin
  Maximum := Score;
  WriteLn('Congratulations!');
  WriteLn('Your new high score is ', Maximum)
end
else
begin
  WriteLn('Your score was ', Score);
  WriteLn('Not bad for a carbon unit.')
end;
```

More Boolean Operators

You can create more complex expressions (for more elaborate tests) using the boolean operators **and**, **or**, and **xor**.

The **and** operator returns the value True if (and only if) both of its operands are True; thus,

```
False and False    ---> False
False and True     ---> False
True  and False    ---> False
True  and True     ---> True
```

It is convenient to show the effect of a boolean operator with a *truth table*. This table shows the result of the operation for all possible combinations of values of the operands, much like a multiplication table shows the results for various combinations of multiplication operands. The truth table for the **and** operation is

```
and| F | T |
---+---+---+
 F | F | F |
---+---+---+
 T | F | T |
---+---+---+
```

You read a truth table as you would a multiplication table: Find the values of the operands on the edges of the chart, then find where the row and column of the two operands intersect. The value in that box is the result of the operation.

For practice, try reading the results listed for the **and** operator in the previous truth table. Do they agree with the results shown earlier?

The **or** operator, as you might have already guessed, returns the value True if either or both of its operands are True. Its truth table looks like this:

```
or | F | T |
---+---+---+
 F | F | T |
---+---+---+
 T | T | T |
---+---+---+
```

Finally, the **xor**, or *exclusive or*, operator returns the value True if one, but not both, of its operands has the value True (in other words, if they have the opposite value). The truth table for the **xor** operation is

```
xor| F | T |
---+---+---+
 F | F | T |
---+---+---+
 T | T | F |
---+---+---+
```

Using these operators, you can create such expressions as

```
(Score > Maximum) or (Score > 30000)   (True if either Score is greater than
                                         Maximum, or Score is greater than 30000);
(Score > 10000) and (Score <= 20000)   (True if Score is both greater than 10000
                                         and less than or equal to 20000); or
not (NewMaximum or (Maximum = 0))      (True if neither NewMaximum nor the
                                         expression Maximum = 0 is True).
```

If we assume that *Score*, *Maximum*, and *NewMaximum* have the values *10*, *0*, and True, then the first expression yields the value True, while the other two yield False.

Note the copious use of parentheses in these examples. Since Turbo Pascal allows some of the boolean operators to apply to integer as well as boolean values (a feature we'll discuss in the advanced part of this tutorial), it is important to enclose your boolean expressions in parentheses to be sure they do what you intend them to.

Repetitive Tasks

Iteration

In Part 1, we said that computers are at their best performing tedious, repetitive tasks. Without the ability to execute instructions repetitively, a Macintosh would have the general-purpose utility of a shoehorn.

Pascal provides three ways of repeating one or more statements until some condition is met. Using the **while, repeat...until**, and **for** statements, you are able to say in effect, "Do this 10 times," or "Do this until the task is completed." This kind of repetitive processing is known as *iteration*, and the section of code that performs this activity is known collectively as a *loop*.

The While Statement

The first kind of iterative statement we'll discuss is the **while** statement. It tells the computer to repeat a nested statement (which may be a compound statement) as long as a certain condition remains true. Program WaitForKey illustrates:

```
program WaitForKey;
begin
  Write('Waiting for a keystroke');
  while not KeyPressed do  { Write dots continuously until a key is hit. }
    Write('.');                        { The KeyPressed function }
end.                     { returns True only after a key has been struck. }
```

Take a moment and type this program into Turbo Pascal, then compile and run it. The periods keep coming until you press a key.

The syntax of the **while** statement is shown in Figure 10.3.

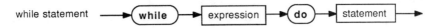

Figure 10.3: Syntax Diagram of a While Statement

The **while** statement consists of

- the reserved word **while**
- a boolean expression
- the reserved word **do**
- the statement to be repeated

When the **while** loop is encountered during execution of the program, the boolean expression is evaluated. If the expression is False, the nested statement inside the **while** statement is never executed at all. If the expression returns True, the nested statement is executed. The expression is then evaluated again, and the process of test-execute-test-execute continues until the expression returns False.

Repeat...Until

Like the **while** statement, the **repeat...until** statement causes a process to repeat until a condition is satisfied. The syntax of the **repeat...until** statement is shown in Figure 10.4.

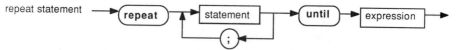

Figure 10.4: Syntax Diagram of a Repeat Statement

Unlike either the **if** or the **while** statement, the **repeat...until** statement can enclose as many statements as desired—separated by semicolons if there is more than one. Thus, there is no need to use a compound statement to make the **repeat...until** statement execute more than one statement on each iteration.

The **repeat...until** statement also differs from the **while** statement in that the statements within the loop are always executed at least once. The test for the loop terminating condition is performed *after* the enclosed statements are executed. If the expression yields the value False, the loop is repeated; otherwise, execution continues with the next sequential statement.

The following program illustrates the **repeat...until** statement. It asks the player to guess a number from 1 to 10. The player is always asked to guess at least once, but the game stops when the user gets the number right. It is therefore an apt situation for a **repeat...until** loop.

```
program GuessingGame;
{$R+ Turn range-checking on }
const
  Answer = 3;                 { Don't look at this line! }

var
  Guess : Integer;

begin
  WriteLn('In this program, you will guess an integer from 1 to 10.');
  repeat
    WriteLn('You have not guessed the number yet.');
    Write('Type an integer from 1 to 10 as your guess: ');
    ReadLn(Guess);
  until Guess = Answer;
end.
```

The For Statement

So far, we've discussed two kinds of iterative statements: One says "Do this *while* the following condition is True," and the other says "Repeat this *until* the following condition is True." We now come to the third type of looping statement in Pascal—one that says "Do this *n* times."

The **for** statement uses a scalar variable as a *counter* (or, in more formal terms, a *control variable*) to keep track of how many times a loop has been executed. You define the value at which the counter will be started and what the final value will be, and the compiler does the rest.

The syntax of the **for** statement is depicted in Figure 10.5.

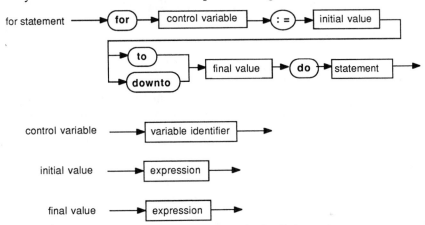

Figure 10.5: Syntax Diagram of a For Statement

In executing a **for** statement, the counter variable is assigned the value of the first expression. If the counter is less than or equal to the second expression, then the statement is executed. The counter is then incremented (if **to** is used) or decremented (if **downto** is used). This process continues until the value of the counter is greater than the second expression. (If the the first expression is greater than the second expression, then the statement isn't executed a single time.)

Here's an example. If the variable *Index* is declared to be of type *Integer*, then the loop

```
for Index := 1 to 10 do
  WriteLn('n = ',Index,' n*n = ', Index * Index);
```

writes out the integers from 1 to 10 in increasing order, each followed by its square. If you were to write the loop like this,

```
for Index := 10 downto 1 do
  WriteLn('n = ', Index, ' n*n = ', Index * Index);
```

then the same values would be printed but in decreasing order, from 10 down to 1.

Note that there is no rule that says you must use your control variable within the loop. In the statement

```
for Index := 1 to 10 do
  WriteLn('Hello!');
```

you merely tell the Mac to output the string *Hello!* 10 times.

One point about **for** loops catches many novice programmers unawares. The value of the counter variable is undefined after the **for** statement finishes; that is, it can have any value at all. For example, after completing this loop

```
for n := 1 to 10 do
  WriteLn('Hello');
```

you might expect *n* to have the value *11*. And, in fact, sometimes it will. But at other times, it won't—it may have the value *10* or even something else.

If you've used BASIC, you may be wondering how to specify a step value other than 1, that is, how to increment the control variable by 5 or 17 or 0.2 with each iteration. Well, in Pascal, you can't. You can cause the same effect with a **while** or **repeat** ...**until** loop, although you'll have to do most of the work yourself. For example, this BASIC For/Next loop

```
for n = 2 to 8 step 2
  print n
next n
print "Who do we appreciate?"
```

can be simulated in Pascal as

```
n := 2;
while n <= 8 do
begin
  WriteLn(n);
  n := n + 2;
end;
WriteLn('Who do we appreciate?');
```

Pascal doesn't permit such foolishness in a **for** loop, because it uses the counter variable to keep track of how many times the loop has been executed. From Pascal's point of view, it doesn't make sense to increment (or decrement) the counter by anything other than one each time.

However, Pascal *does* permit you to build loops that are impossible in BASIC: You can use any scalar type as the loop index, including *LongInt*, *Char*, *Boolean*, or any enumerated type you define. Given appropriate definitions and declarations, the following **for** loops are all valid:

```
for Ch := 'A' to 'Z' do
  WriteLn('Hello');

for Flag := True downto False do
  WriteLn('Hello');

for Day := Mon to Fri do
  WriteLn('Hello');
```

As with the **if** and **while** statements, a compound statement can be controlled by the **for** statement to make more than one thing happen each time through the loop:

```
for Index := 20 to 30 do
begin
                                     { First statement here }
   .
   .
   .
                                     { Last statement here }
end;
```

We claimed back in Chapter 2 that a Macintosh can count to a million in six seconds. Here's proof:

```
program FastCount;
var
  N : LongInt;
begin
  Write('Press Return to begin counting');
  ReadLn;
  for N := 0 to 1000000 do;    { don't do anything but count up }
   Write('Done!');
  ReadLn;
end.
```

Endless Loops

One of the mutations that you will doubtless create during your programming career is an *endless loop*—a loop that, for some reason, never finishes. Such a loop can occur due to bad data, or you may even have a reason for programming one intentionally. Most often, however, an endless loop is caused by programmer error.

The following program was intended by its author, a curious fellow, to list the integers between 1 and 20 that are evenly divisible by 3. He expected it to quickly display a few values and then stop. Instead, it never prints anything and runs forever. Can you find the bug?

```pascal
program Oops;
var
  N: Integer;
begin
  N := 1;
  repeat
    if (N mod 3) = 0 then { If true, then N is evenly divisible by 3 }
    begin
      WriteLn(N);
      N := Succ(N);                        { Increment N by 1 }
    end;
  until N = 20;
end.
```

The problem is that Oops only increments N if it is divisible by 3. Thus, the program considers the number 1 again and again and again at high speed, never moving on to test 2 or any other value.

This program can be repaired by moving N := Succ(N) to just before the **until**, so that N is incremented on every pass.

In Case of Infinite Loop, Break Glass

It's easy to recover from an infinite loop, thanks to some "programmer friendly" engineering built into the Mac—the so-called programmer's switch. It's a plastic widget that snaps into the slots on the bottom left side of the computer.

Once installed, the programmer's switch reaches through the ventilation slots to contact two pushbuttons on the logic board (you can see the pushbuttons if you look between the slots closely). The frontmost of the two buttons on the switch is labeled *Reset*; pressing it has precisely the same effect as turning the machine off and then on again—only without the hardware stress and strain associated with powering-on.

The second lever, labeled *Interrupt*, has a less drastic—and more useful—effect. When a program launched from Turbo Pascal is interrupted, you're (usually) able to get back to your source program and Turbo Pascal. Just how you accomplish this depends on whether or not you have a debugger (such as MacsBug) installed.

If MacsBug isn't installed, you'll end up in a mini-debugger built into ROM in the Mac Plus and SE (this doesn't work for Mac 512s). To return to Turbo

Turbo Pascal Tutor for the Macintosh

Pascal and your source program, enter the following strange, but effective, lines (be sure to press *Return* after each):

```
SM 0 A9F4
G 0
```

Assuming your program hasn't done anything too drastic, this restores control to Turbo with your source file uncorrupted.

If MacsBug *is* installed, pressing the interrupt switch puts you in MacsBug. Type ES ("Exit to Shell"), press *Return*, and you'll be back in Turbo; more on MacsBug in Chapter 41.

With the programmer's switch, recovering from an infinite loop such as that in program Oops is as simple as pressing a button. Without the switch, you have no choice but to cycle the power and reboot—a bitter pill if the latest version of your source program hasn't yet been saved to disk.

Even with the programmer's switch, it's good practice to save your source text before running experimental programs—especially those that work with pointers, which we introduce in Chapter 16. Pointers make it all too easy to write programs that can trash the system beyond hope of resumption. Nothing ruins a day quite like losing an hour of good work to a system crash. To Save, just press *Command-S* before every *Command-R*. To perform an automatic Save before every run, click on the Auto Save Text check box in the Options dialog box of the Compiler menu.

The Case Statement

In many of your programs, you will want the computer to perform one of a list of actions, depending on the current value of a variable. For example, you might want to display a menu, accept the user's choice, and then perform the action that was chosen. We already have the capability to do this with a series of **if** statements:

```
Write('Enter your choice:  U)p, D)own, L)eft, R)ight:');
ReadLn(Ch);        { Ch is of type Char }

if (Ch = 'U') then
  Y := Y + 1
else
  if (Ch = 'D') then
    Y := Y - 1
  else
    if (Ch = 'L') then
      X := X - 1
    else
```

```
if (Ch = 'R') then
   X := X + 1
else
   WriteLn('Invalid command!');
```

Note that we have nested a number of **if** statements; each time a condition is not satisfied, the program tries the next until it finds the appropriate action.

However, a long chain of **ifs** is messy and hard to follow. So, Pascal simplifies matters with its **case** statement.

In the **case** statement, you provide the compiler with an expression (which must be of a scalar type), followed by a list of values and actions (constants). When the program runs, the action associated with the current value of the variable is performed.

The following **case** statement expresses the intent of the previous example much more clearly:

```
Write('Enter your choice:  U)p, D)own, L)eft, R)ight:');
ReadLn(Ch);                              { Ch is of type Char }

case Ch of
   'U' : Y := Y + 1;
   'D' : Y := Y - 1;
   'L' : X := X - 1;
   'R' : X := X + 1;
otherwise
   WriteLn('Invalid command!'); { Do this if Ch is none of the above }
end;
```

The syntax of the **case** statement is shown in Figure 10.6.

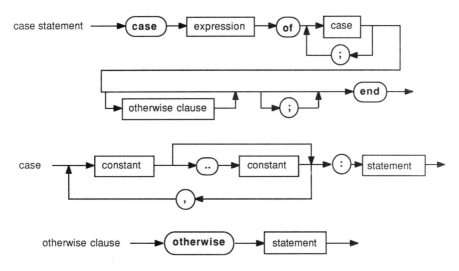

Figure 10.6: Syntax Diagram of a Case Statement

When the **case** statement is executed, the computer inspects the lists of constant values preceding each action. If the value of the expression is present in one of these lists, the specified action is taken. Each action must be expressed as a single statement; use a compound statement if more than one statement needs to be executed. The end of the **case** statement is marked by the reserved word **end**.

What if the expression has a value other than those listed in the **case** statement? Under the original definition of the Pascal language, the result is undefined. Turbo Pascal, however, extends this definition in a logical way.

With Turbo, you can specify the default action (the statement(s) to be executed if no match is found) in an **otherwise** clause. In an earlier example, we used the **otherwise** clause to make a noise and write an error message. There can be as many statements between the **otherwise** and the **case**'s final **end** statement as desired; a **begin/end** block isn't necessary.

If a **case** statement doesn't have an **otherwise** clause and none of the specified **case** conditions apply, execution continues with the statement following the **case**.

The Constant List

In the **case** statement, the list of constants for each possible action can be specified in a number of ways: as individual values, as a subrange, or as a combination of the two. A subrange is specified exactly as it is in the definition of a subrange type: the lower bound (boundary) followed by two periods and the upper bound.

Subranges can simplify **case** statements. The following two **case** statements are completely equivalent:

```
case Age of                    { Age is of type Integer }
   0, 1, 2, 3, 4, 5, 6, 7, 8, 9,
   10, 11, 12, 13, 14, 15, 16, 17:
   WriteLn('You are not old enough to vote yet.');
   otherwise
      WriteLn('You are old enough to vote. Who will you vote for?');
end; { case }

case Age of                    { Age is of type Integer }
   0..17: WriteLn('You are not old enough to vote yet.')
   otherwise
      WriteLn('You are old enough to vote. Who will you vote for?');
end; { case }
```

To mix subranges with individual items in the constant list, you need only separate them with commas. The following is perfectly legal:

```
case Age of
   0, 1, 2..5, 6, 7, 8, 9,
   10..17: WriteLn('You aren't old enough to vote yet.');
otherwise
   WriteLn('You are old enough to vote. Who will you vote for?');
end;
```

Review

In this chapter, we introduced Pascal's control structures—the statements that enable a program to make decisions and perform actions repetitively. We also discussed boolean expressions and operations in some detail and showed how the compound statement can be used to make one statement out of many.

You can test your understanding of the various control structures by studying the appropriate exercises in Turbo Tutor. These include ForDo, IfCase, RepeatUntil, and WhileDo.

Now that you know how to control the order in which your program's statements execute, you are ready to learn how to subdivide your code into logical groups called procedures and functions, making programs more readable and efficient.

11

Procedures and Functions

In previous chapters, procedures and functions (known collectively as subprograms) were used in some of the sample programs. This chapter describes the concepts behind subprograms and shows how and where to place them in a Pascal program. It also introduces the notion of *scope*, which determines what the identifiers used in a subprogram mean and where a subprogram can be called from. Finally, it discusses *parameters*, the data objects a subprogram works on.

Subprograms

You've learned that a Pascal program can be divided into the Big Three: a program heading, a declaration part, and a statement part (or main program). You've also learned that each statement in the main program is normally executed in order—from beginning to end—unless a conditional (**if** or **case**) or iterative (**for**, **repeat**...**until**, or **while**) statement alters that pattern.

Subprograms allow you to associate an identifier with a series of statements. Once defined, the actions represented by the subprogram can be invoked simply by naming the desired subprogram (calling it).

Here's an example of a situation in which a subprogram might come in handy. The following statement asks the user for a number, then checks the number to see if it is within range. If so, the value entered is assigned to the variable *NewNumber*.

```
WriteLn('Please enter an integer from ', Minimum, ' to ', Maximum, ': ');
ReadLn(Temporary);                      { Temporary is of type Integer }
while (Temporary < Minimum) or (Temporary > Maximum) do
begin
  WriteLn('The integer you have entered is out of range.');
  WriteLn('Please try again: ');
  ReadLn(Temporary);
end;

NewNumber := Temporary;                 { NewNumber is of type Integer }
```

Suppose there are several places in your program where you need to perform this function. A crude technique would be to copy all of these statements into each place. While a good text editor like Turbo Pascal's makes this approach feasible, it increases the size of both your source and executable programs and slows down compilations. Worse, if you had to make a change to this number-entry routine, you'd need to find and alter every occurrence.

Fortunately, Pascal (and virtually every other programming language) provides a solution to this problem. Instead of copying the group of statements, you can give it a name and cause the entire group to be executed by mentioning that name. In Pascal, such a group of statements is called either a *procedure* or a *function*; both correspond to what BASIC and FORTRAN call *subroutines*.

We'll look first at procedures; most of what we'll say about them applies to functions as well.

Procedures

To create a procedure, you declare its name as an identifier (as you declare all identifiers), and present the compiler with the code that is to go by that name. The syntax of a procedure declaration is shown in Figure 11.1.

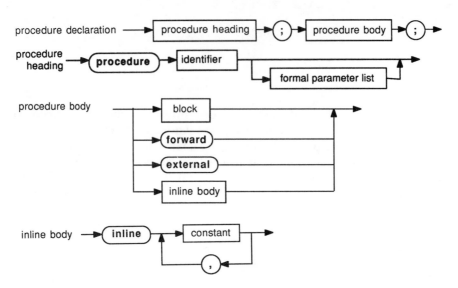

Figure 11.1: Syntax Diagram of a Procedure Declaration

A procedure declaration begins with the reserved word **procedure**, followed by the identifier to be associated with that procedure. Then there's an optional list of parameters (which we describe in the next paragraphs) and a semicolon. The body of the procedure follows, and a closing semicolon finishes things off.

A procedure body consists of the same sequence of declaration part/statement part that comes after the heading of a program. About the only difference is that the closing **end** is followed by a semicolon instead of a period.

A procedure is essentially a mini-program embedded within a larger program. A procedure can declare its own constants and variables, just like a main program. The acid test for "main program likeness" is, Can you declare a procedure from within a procedure? Yes! And you can declare procedures within *that* procedure, and so on ad infinitum. (Well, not quite. All compilers cop out this side of infinity; Turbo Pascal permits at least 16 levels—and programs rarely use more than three or four.)

Where do you put procedures in your program? In Standard Pascal, they come after all other declarations (label, constant, type, and variable) and before the opening **begin** of the main program. Turbo Pascal is more

Turbo Pascal Tutor for the Macintosh

flexible on this score and lets you place them anywhere in the declaration part.

Let's rewrite our earlier sequence of number-inputting statements as a procedure to show how we might build a small program around it.

```
program Sample;
const
  Ten = 10;
var
  NewNumber, Index : Integer;

procedure GetNumber;          { Get a number from the user and store }
const                         { it in the global variable NewNumber  }
  Minimum = 0;
  Maximum = 25;
type
  Response = Minimum..Maximum;        { A type for a legal response }
var
  Temporary : Response;   { A temporary place for the user's integer }
begin                         { Statement Part of procedure GetNumber }
  WriteLn('Please enter an integer from ', Minimum, ' to ', Maximum, ': ');
  ReadLn(Temporary);
  while (Temporary < Minimum) or (Temporary > Maximum) do
  begin
    WriteLn('The integer you have entered is not between 0 and 25,');
    WriteLn('inclusive. Please try again.');
    ReadLn(Temporary);
  end;
  NewNumber := Temporary;
end;                                          { procedure GetNumber }

begin                                { program Sample's main program }
  GetNumber;
  .
  .
  .
  for Index := 1 to 10 do
  begin
    GetNumber;
    .
  end
  .
  .
  GetNumber;
  case NewNumber of
    0: WriteLn('You have selected option 0');
    .
    .
    .
   25: WriteLn('This is option 25: ');
  end;
  .
  .
end.
```

Note that procedure *GetNumber*'s **const**, **type**, and **var** declarations are formatted exactly like those of a Pascal program.

Besides avoiding duplication, procedures make programs easier to write and understand. They allow you to break down big, complicated tasks into a series of smaller, easier tasks. This divide-and-conquer approach is *the* way to write programs, and if you only carry a single piece of mental baggage away from this book, this should be it.

As a rule of thumb, if a main program is too long to fit on a sheet of paper, it's too long—break it down into one or more procedures. And if one of those procedures ends up being longer than a page, break it down also. Ultimately you're left with a series of easy procedures that collectively perform a tough job.

In addition, procedures and functions can serve as reusable modules for pasting into new programs.

Changes to procedures instantly affect all parts of the program that call it—without any additional rewriting. Also, when a program involves more than one author, each programmer can write one or more procedures, then combine them into the finished product. This modular approach allows each author to perfect his or her part of the program without having to directly modify the work of others.

Scope

You know that you can't use the same identifier twice in the declaration part of a program. Since it is possible to declare types, constants, and variables in a procedure, you may well ask, What happens if the same identifier is declared in both the main program and a procedure? Or in two procedures?

Well, since each identifier can only refer to one thing, it seems as though the compiler would flag the second use of the identifier as an error.

Type in and check the syntax (*Command-Y*) of this program. (Don't bother to run it.)

```
program test1;
const
  J = 13;

procedure testProcedure;
var
  J: Integer;
```

```
begin
end;

begin
end.
```

If you performed this exercise, you know that no error resulted from redefining *J* in procedure *testProcedure*. But this next program *does* produce a Duplicate Identifier error:

```
program test2;
const
  J = 13;
var
  J: Integer;

begin
end.
```

What's the difference between these two programs? *Test2* declared two identifiers *at the same level*—in the declaration part of the main program. This is *verboten*. If it weren't, and you said *WriteLn(J)*, how would the compiler know if you were talking about variable *J* or constant *J*? *Test1*, however, declared an identifier named *J* at different levels; one at the highest level of the program and a second one at a lower level.

It would be easy to write a compiler that *wouldn't* accept *Test1*'s declaration of *J*. However, if Pascal worked that way, programming in modules would be difficult. You'd have to keep track of all the identifiers used in a program—and typing errors and other goofs would make it easy to alter variables unpredictably.

To avoid this problem, the concept of *scope* was developed. Pascal's scope rules specify, in a rigorous way, what object any identifier refers to at a given time. It is scoping rules that enable Turbo Pascal to cope with two identifiers with the same name in program *Test1*.

Scope Rule #1: Each identifier has meaning only within the block in which it is declared, and only after the point in that block at which it is declared.

Thus, in the previous example, variable *Temporary* only has meaning within the procedure *GetNumber*, and even then only after its declaration. By the same rule, the declarations

```
const
  Minimum = 0;
  Maximum = 25;
```

and

type
```
  Response = Minimum..Maximum;    { A type for a legal response }
```

can't occur in the reverse order. If they do, the constants *Minimum* and *Maximum* aren't defined when the type *Response* is defined using them, and the compiler indicates an error.

Another consequence of the first scope rule is that procedure *GetNumber* has access to variables that were declared before *GetNumber* in the declaration part of the program Sample. Thus, the statement

```
NewNumber := Temporary;
```

does what one would expect, assigning the value of *Temporary* to the variable *NewNumber*, which was declared in the main program. An identifier like *NewNumber*, which is declared at a higher level and is accessible within *GetNumber*, is said to be global to the procedure *GetNumber*.

The converse, however, is not true. In the main program, we cannot write the statement

```
Temporary := NewNumber;
```

because the variable *Temporary* is undefined outside of *GetNumber*. *Temporary* is said to be local to *GetNumber* and is not visible outside that block. By the time the compiler gets around to compiling the statements of the main program, it has forgotten everything it knew about variable *Temporary*.

Scope Rule #2: If a global identifier is redefined within a block, then the innermost (most deeply nested) definition takes precedence from the point of declaration until the end of the block.

What does this mean? The following program illustrates:

```
program A;
const                    { These are the "global" identifiers of program A. }
  J = 1;                      { They are visible everywhere within the program, }
  K = 2;             { unless hidden by local symbols with the same name. }
var
  R, S : Integer;

procedure B;
const
  L = K;                                  { L is defined to be 2 (NOT 3!) }
  K = 3; { K is now defined locally to be 3, "hiding" the K defined in A }
begin                                { Statement Part of procedure B }

  { Within the Statement Part of procedure B, the following
    identifiers are visible:
```

```
              identifier | defined in
              -----------+-----------
              B, J, R, S |    A
                   K, L  |    B
```

The local constant L derives its value from the GLOBAL constant
K, not the local one, since the global identifier was not yet
"hidden" when L was defined. Note that there is no identifier
A visible. Turbo Pascal, unlike most other compilers, ignores
the program heading entirely, including the program name. }
end;   { procedure B }

var
  T, U: Integer; { These identifiers are not visible within procedure B! }

procedure C;
var
  V : Integer;

procedure D;   { local to procedure C }
var
  R, T : Integer; { These declarations "hide" the R and T declared in A }
begin   { Statement Part of procedure D }

  { Within the Statement Part of procedure D, the following identifiers
    are visible:

```
              identifier   | defined in
              -------------+-----------
        B, C, J, K, S, U   |    A
                   D, V    |    C
                   R, T    |    D
```

    Note that the constant K is seen as having the value 2 here, since
    the local K (with a value of 3) defined in B is visible only there. }
end;

var
  B : integer;   { This declaration "hides" procedure B within
                        the Statement Part of procedure C. However,
                        procedure B is still callable from procedure D,
                        and this Integer is not visible to D. }
begin   { Statement Part of procedure C }

  { Within the Statement Part of procedure C, the following
    identifiers are visible:

```
              identifier     | defined in
              ---------------+-----------
        C, J, K, R, S, T, U  |    A
                   B, D, V   |    C
```

  }
end;   { procedure C }

begin   { program A }

  { Within the Statement Part of program A, the following identifiers

```
```

```
are visible:

            identifier        | defined in
    ------------------------+----------
        B, C, J, K, R, S, T, U |    A

    }
    end.                                            { program A }
```

In each procedure (and also within the statement part of the main program), we've listed which identifiers are visible and what they refer to.

To understand how this information is derived, it helps to pretend that you are the compiler, scanning the program from top to bottom. Each time you encounter a definition that overrides a previous one, you make a note of the new definition, and use it until the current block is exited. When you exit a block, all the identifiers declared locally within that block become undefined, and all the identifiers that were temporarily "hidden" by definitions in that block become visible once more.

Exercises

Consider the following program. At each of the points marked { 1 }, { 2 }, and { 3 }, list the identifiers that are accessible and the procedure (or program) where they were defined. For the constant identifiers, also list their values. For the variables and types, list their base types (that is, the predefined type from which their types are derived).

```
program ScopeTest;
type
  A = Integer;
  B = Real;
const
  J = 5;
  K = 14;
var
  Q : A;
  R : B;

procedure First;
type
  B = A;
var
  R : B;
const
  K = J;
  J = K;
begin                                   { procedure First }
  { 1 }
end;                                    { procedure First }
```

```
procedure Second;
var
  First : A;
const
  L = K;
  { 2 }
  K = 3;
type
  A = B;

procedure Third;
var
  First : A;
begin                                { procedure Third }
end;                                 { procedure Third }

begin                                { procedure Second }
end;                                 { procedure Second }

var
  S : A;

begin                                { program ScopeTest }
  { 3 }
end.                                 { program ScopeTest }
```

Now consider the following program. Will it compile without errors? What will it output to the screen when run? Why? Test your answer using Turbo Pascal.

```
program Scope2;
var
  A : Integer;

procedure SetA;
var
  A : Integer;
begin                    { Statement Part of procedure SetA }
  A := 4
end;                                 { procedure SetA }

begin                    { Statement Part of program Scope2 }
  A := 3;
  SetA;
  WriteLn(A)
end.                                 { program Scope2 }
```

The Lifetime of Local Variables

Unlike the global variables that are declared in the declaration part of the main program, a procedure's local variables are created (assigned places in memory) each time the procedure is called and destroyed (the memory they occupied is taken back) each time control returns to the calling program or procedure. Thus, the lifetime of a local variable—that is, the time during which it will be able to retain its assigned value—is limited to the current invocation of the procedure that contains it.

What does this mean? Well, suppose you have a procedure *A*, which declares the local *Integer* variable *X*. Now, call *A* and assign to *X* the value 3. When you call *A* again, can you assume that *X* will still be 3? No! The old *X* disappeared when procedure *A* returned the first time; with the next invocation of *A*, *X* can have any value whatsoever. *A procedure's local variables are undefined upon entrance to that procedure.*

Local variables are said to be *dynamically allocated*. Pascal compilers generate code that creates the storage for local variables on an internal structure called the *stack* just before a procedure is called, and that disposes of this storage as the procedure returns. Each time the procedure is called, the storage may have a different address; even if it has the same address, it will almost certainly have been overwritten with some other data since the last use. We return to the stack and dynamic allocation in later chapters.

Parameters

In our first example of a procedure (*GetNumber*), each call to the procedure causes a number the user types in to be assigned to global variable *NewNumber*—in fact, that assignment is *GetNumber*'s main job. Since the variable *NewNumber* is overwritten each time *GetNumber* is called, to keep track of the value the user entered it is necessary to save the value of *NewNumber* in some other variable immediately after the call, like this:

```
    .
    .
GetNumber;
Choice1 := NewNumber;

    .
    .
GetNumber;
Choice2 := NewNumber;
    .
    .
```

While this works, it has the potential for problems. First, you must always remember to perform the assignment. If you don't, the value the user entered is lost. Second, since *NewNumber* is the information-passing connection between *GetNumber* and the main program, it must be declared globally. If not, because of scope rules there would be no way to communicate between *GetNumber* and the main program. By making it global, we make it global for every procedure in the program. Even though only *GetNumber* has any business using it, we might forget and assign values to *NewNumber* from another place in the program—thus mucking up the communications channel.

There's a third problem: If *GetNumber* is called from a procedure that defines a local variable named *NewNumber*, then scoping rules cause that local identifier to mask the global identifier *NewNumber*, and it becomes impossible to communicate with *GetNumber*. All of these problems may seem somewhat far-fetched, and, in truth, many excellent programs have been produced with BASIC, a scopeless, parameterless language.

Still and all, any way you can reduce interference between subroutines and their callers is helpful: It's one less way a program can fail. One reason for using procedures is to avoid this sort of potential identifier conflict. Local variables solve this problem for data objects that are used entirely within a procedure, and a feature called *parameter passing* handles the problem of naming data that is passed to and from a procedure.

You already used parameters when you called the built-in procedures *ReadLn* and *WriteLn*. In the statement *ReadLn(A);* the variable *A* is passed as a parameter to the procedure *ReadLn*, which in turn gets data from the keyboard and places that data in the variable. In the statement

```
WriteLn('This program compliments of Robin Jones');
```

the string constant 'This program compliments of Robin Jones' is passed as a parameter to the *WriteLn* procedure.

Let's rewrite procedure *GetNumber* to return a number in a parameter, rather than in a global variable:

```
procedure GetNumber (var NewNumber : integer);
                        { Get a number from the user and return
                          it in the variable parameter NewNumber. }
const
  Minimum = 0;
  Maximum = 25;
type
  Response = Minimum..Maximum;        { A type for a legal response }
var
  Temporary : Response; { A temporary place for the user's integer }
begin                        { Statement Part of procedure GetNumber }
  WriteLn('Please enter an integer from ', Minimum, ' to ', Maximum, ': ');
  ReadLn(Temporary);
  while (Temporary < Minimum) or (Temporary > Maximum) do
  begin
    WriteLn('The integer you have entered is not between 0 and 25,');
    WriteLn('inclusive. Please try again.');
```

```
    ReadLn(Temporary);
  end;
  NewNumber := Temporary;
end;                                    { procedure GetNumber }
```

Note that the only change made to this procedure (not counting comments) was in the very first line, where we changed the procedure heading to read

procedure GetNumber (**var** NewNumber : integer);

What does this accomplish? First, it tells the compiler that when the procedure is called, it can expect to find the name of an integer variable in parentheses following the procedure name. Second, it says that, inside the procedure, that data object will be referred to by the name *NewNumber*, regardless of what it might have been named in the part of the program calling the procedure. Finally, the **var** preceding the name *NewNumber* indicates that a variable (rather than an expression or a constant) must be passed for that parameter, and that *GetNumber* has the ability to alter the value of that variable.

It is important to note that *NewNumber* is not a variable itself; rather, it is an identifier that "stands in" for another variable whose identity is decided at run time when the procedure is called. Such an object is called a *formal parameter* or *dummy parameter*. If we make a call to *GetNumber* as follows,

GetNumber(A);

then the procedure acts exactly as if variable *A* were present everywhere *NewNumber* is mentioned. In this situation, *A* is said to be the *actual parameter*. If we then made the call

GetNumber(B);

the actual parameter is *B*, and any assignments made inside *GetNumber* to its formal parameter *NewNumber* are actually made to variable *B*.

A procedure can also declare formal parameters without the reserved word **var**. This changes things at both the calling and receiving ends. First, *any* expression can be passed as the actual parameter, rather than only variables. Second, any changes (such as assignments) that are made to the formal parameter in the procedure don't affect the value of the actual parameter. Instead, they are made to a *copy* of the value of the expression, which is created when the procedure is entered.

Such parameters are called *value parameters*, and the one-way information flow they provide is useful for two reasons. First of all, they allow the values of constants and expressions, as well as variables, to serve as input to a procedure. Without them, statements such as

WriteLn('This program compliments of Robin Jones');

would be impossible, because 'This program. . .' isn't a variable.

The second benefit of value parameters is as a precautionary measure. Because a procedure works on a copy of a value parameter, rather than on the value parameter itself, it can't make unwanted, accidental modifications to that parameter.

A common mistake made by beginning programmers is to forget to declare a procedure parameter that needs to be alterable as a **var** parameter. If so, the compiler won't complain (it's legal to assign to non-**var** parameters in a procedure), but the variables you pass to this procedure never have their values altered.

Figure 11.2 shows the syntax of a formal parameter list—the part of a procedure declaration where you specify the names and types of the procedure's formal parameters.

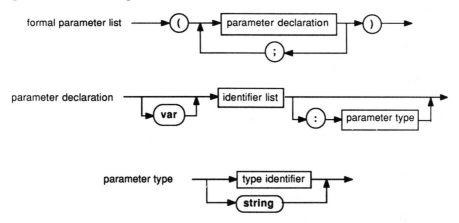

Figure 11.2: Syntax Diagram of a Formal Parameter List

A procedure can have any number of parameters of practically any type. In practice, though, most procedures declare only a few, and many none at all.

One more point: Because a procedure's formal parameters are considered to have the same scope as identifiers within the procedure, they can hide identifiers declared at a higher level of the program just as other local identifiers can. For this reason, a locally declared constant, type, or variable may not have the same identifier as a formal parameter.

Functions

As we've seen, a procedure can change the values of variable (**var**) parameters passed to it. Often you'll only want a single value back from the procedure, and it can be inconvenient to set aside a variable just to hold that value.

Suppose, for example, that you were to write a procedure to find the square root of an integer, approximated to the nearest integer:

```
procedure ISqrt(Val : Integer; var Root : Integer);
var
  OddSeq,Square    : Integer;
begin                                    { procedure ISqrt }
  OddSeq := -1;
  Square :=  0;
  repeat
    OddSeq := OddSeq + 2;
    Square := Square + OddSeq
  until Val < Square;
  Root := Succ(OddSeq div 2);
  if Val <= Square - Root
    then Root := Pred(Root)
end;                                     { procedure ISqrt }
```

Procedure *ISqrt* takes *Val*, determines its square root, and sets *Root* to that value. A calling program might use it as follows:

```
repeat
  Write('Enter value  (0 to quit):  '); ReadLn(Square);
  ISqrt(Square, Root);
  WriteLn('The square root is ', Root)
until Square = 0;
```

Variable *Root*'s only purpose is to carry the value of the square root from the call to *ISqrt* to the *WriteLn* statement. If there are many "transfer" variables like this in a program, it can become clumsy to keep track of them all—and since most of them will not be in use most of the time, memory is wasted.

Functions work to reduce the need for variables. You may remember from Chapter 9 that function identifiers appear in expressions. At run time, the function is called in the process of evaluating the expression. Structurally, a function is simply a procedure that returns a value.

Functions are declared just like procedures, with two exceptions. First, you must specify the type of the returned value in the header—so that Turbo Pascal knows how to fit the returned value into expressions properly.

Second, at some point in the body of the function, you must assign a value to the function's name; this determines the value the function returns.

The syntax of a function declaration is shown in Figure 11.3.

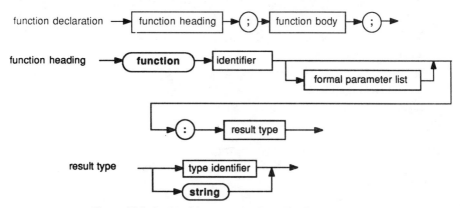

Figure 11.3: Syntax Diagram of a Function Declaration

Here's an example of a function equivalent to the square root procedure shown earlier. Note that there is no parameter to hold the root—the name of the function itself is used to represent the value.

```
function ISqrt(Val : Integer) : Integer;
var
  OddSeq,Square,Root    : Integer;
begin                          { Statement Part of function ISqrt }
  . . .                                   { same code as before }
  ISqrt := Root           { The value is returned by assigning to
                        the function name as if it were a variable }
end;                                          { function ISqrt }
```

The function can now be used in a program like this:

```
repeat
  Write('Enter value:  '); ReadLn(Square);
  WriteLn('The square root is ',ISqrt(Square))
until Square = 0;
```

With *ISqrt* written as a function, the main program doesn't need an additional variable to hold the square root. This means a simpler program, with less room for name conflicts and errors.

A function can be used anywhere that a constant or an expression of the same data type can be used. Suppose you want to find the fourth root of an *Integer*. You could say:

```
repeat
  Write('Enter value:  '); ReadLn(FourthPower);
```

```
    WriteLn('The fourth root is ',ISqrt(ISqrt(FourthPower)))
until FourthPower = 0;
```

When writing a function, take care to ensure that you have set the function identifier to some value before exiting. As shown previously, you do this by performing an assignment to the function name, as if it were a variable. Strictly speaking, the compiler doesn't require that you make any assignment at all.

While you can assign to the function identifier, you may *not* retrieve the value you assigned to that identifier by including it in an expression, even though it can be tempting to do so, as in,

```
ISqrt := ISqrt + 1;
```

Why? Because the compiler interprets that use of the function name as another call to *ISqrt*. This is why we made *Root* a local variable, rather than eliminating it entirely from our function in the previous example. Had we tried to use the identifier *ISqrt* to hold the intermediate values of the root as it was being computed, we would have had no way of getting them back.

Since an attempt to get the value of the function identifier within a function is construed by the compiler as another call to the same function, it follows that functions (and procedures as well) *can call themselves*. This is impossible in many languages. But in Pascal, the ability of a subroutine to call itself produces the opportunity for spectacular algorithms (and equally spectacular confusion). Procedures or functions that call themselves are said to be *recursive*.

Recursive Procedures

Sometimes, the easiest way to describe a task or object is in terms of itself. For example, there's an operation in mathematics called the factorial function. Used extensively in statistics (and in Pascal tutorials for describing recursion), a factorial of an integer is the product of all the positive integers up to, and including, that integer. For instance, 5 factorial (written as 5!) is $5 \times 4 \times 3 \times 2 \times 1$ (120), and 8 factorial is $8 \times 7 \times 6 \times 5 \times 4 \times 3 \times 2 \times 1$ (40,320). Factorials are usually defined in math books this way:

For a positive integer n, if n is greater than 1, then n! = n * (n-1)!; if n equals 1, then n! = 1

This definition is recursive. It says that the factorial of a number is equal to the number times the factorial of the number minus 1. It is possible to

Turbo Pascal Tutor for the Macintosh

translate this definition almost verbatim into a working Pascal program to calculate factorials.

Here's a recursive implementation of the factorial operation:

```
function Factorial(N : Integer) : Real;
begin
  if N > 1 then
    Factorial := N * Factorial(N - 1) { the statement that causes recursion }
  else
    Factorial := 1
end;
```

We defined *Factorial* to accept an *Integer* parameter—and produce a *Real* result, because factorials have a way of getting big in a hurry ($30! = 2.65 \times 10^{32}$).

When this function is called, it looks to see if the value of the parameter *N* is equal to *1*. If it is, there is no multiplying to be done, since *1!* is *1* by definition (and, incidentally, *0!* is considered to be *1* as well). Otherwise, we set the function identifier *Factorial* equal to *N* times the *Factorial* of *N* − *1*.

Note the very different meanings when a function identifier appears on the left- and right-hand sides of the assignment operator. On the left, the identifier is used without a list of parameters and represents the return value of the function. On the right, the same identifier is used with a list of parameters to represent the result of a call to that function. The calls "nest" more and more deeply until *Factorial* is finally called with the value 1; at that point, the calls unwind, doing the necessary multiplication at each step.

Factorials don't have to be calculated recursively. A simple loop suffices and, in fact, executes more quickly than the recursive routine:

```
function Factorial(N : Integer) : Real;
var
  Total: Real;
  M: Integer;
begin
  Total := 1;
  for M := 1 to N do
    Total := Total * M;
  Factorial := Total;
end;                               { function Factorial }
```

Procedures can be recursive as well. It is also possible to build complex recursive structures where one procedure or function calls a second, which calls the first, which calls the second, and so on. This is called *indirect recursion*.

Recursive procedures can simplify certain programming problems. But beware, because like loops (another repetitive process), it is possible for recursion to get out of control. The calls nest until the machine no longer has enough memory to keep track of them. (Remember, space for local variables is allocated each time a procedure is called. Thus, each call uses up a block of memory, and the available space can be exhausted very quickly.)

So use recursion with care. Make sure that there's at least one path through the routine that doesn't cause more recursion (like the previous statement *Factorial: = 1*) in every recursive procedure.

Forward Declarations

Occasionally, Pascal's rule that all identifiers must be declared before they are used can cause problems in defining recursive programs. For instance, as mentioned earlier, you may want to write a procedure that calls another, which in turn calls the first, and so on. The problem is, Which appears first in your program? No matter which one you choose, the other procedure will not have been defined yet, and therefore you will not be able to call it. This program illustrates the problem:

```
program Example;
var
  Alpha : integer;
procedure Test1(var A : integer);
begin                                { procedure Test1 }
  A := A - 1;
  if A > 0 then
    Test2(A);
  WriteLn(A);
end;                                 { procedure Test1 }

procedure Test2(var A : integer);
begin                                { procedure Test2 }
  A := A div 2;
  if A > 0 then
    Test1(A);
  WriteLn(A);
end;                                 { procedure Test2 }

begin                    { Statement Part of program Example }
  Alpha := 15;
  Test1(Alpha)
end.                                 { program Example }
```

Test1 calls *Test2*, and *Test2* calls *Test1*. As it stands, this program won't compile: You'll get an `Unknown identifier` error when it finds the reference to *Test2* within *Test1*. If you swapped *Test1* and *Test2*, you'd get a similar error within *Test2*.

The solution to this problem is to tell the compiler, *before* it gets to the procedure *Test1*, that the procedure *Test2* will be declared later. This is done with a **forward** declaration, as shown in the following example:

```
program Example;
var
  Alpha              : Integer;

procedure Test2(var A : Integer); forward;

procedure Test1(var A : Integer);
begin                              { procedure Test1 }
  ...
end;                               { procedure Test1 }

procedure Test2 {(var A : Integer)};  { We've commented out the }
begin                                 { procedure Test2 }
                                      { parameter list; it was }
  ...                                 { supplied earlier. }
end;                                  { procedure Test2 }

begin                              { Statement Part of program Example }
  Alpha := 15;
  Test1(Alpha)
end.                               { program Example }
```

The **forward** declaration of *Test2* contains only its heading and the reserved word **forward**—the information necessary for the compiler to check any calls to it for a correct name and parameter list. The actual body of *Test2* occurs after *Test1*. Now *Test1* can call *Test2* (because of the **forward** declaration) and *Test2* can call *Test1* (since the latter precedes the former).

Note that when *Test2* is finally declared, its parameter list is omitted (though we recommend showing it in a comment as a reminder of what the parameters and their types are). The parameter list may not be repeated; Turbo Pascal already knows what the parameters are and doesn't need the redundant (and possibly inconsistent) information.

Scope and Recursion

The subject of recursion brings us to Pascal's third and final scope rule. As you may remember, Scope Rule 2 states that if an identifier is declared in an outer block and then again in an inner block, the inner declaration takes precedence until the end of the inner block. This is true regardless of which procedures call which others; it is the position of the variables in the text of the program at compile time that decides which symbol refers to which object.

The problem of scope becomes more complex when recursion is involved. For instance, suppose we wrote the following set of nested procedures, and then called function A with the parameter 5. What would be written? And what would A return?

```
function A(G : Integer): Integer;
var
  X : Integer;

procedure B;
begin
  WriteLn(X);
end;

begin
  if G > 1 then
    X := A(G - 1)
  else
    X := 0;
  B;
  A := G;
end;
```

To understand the result of this program, we need **Scope Rule 3**: When procedures are invoked recursively, a reference to a global variable always refers to the instance of the variable in the most recent invocation of the procedure in which that variable is defined.

This rule applies to the previous procedure B, when it references variable X defined in function A. So when B is invoked and executes the statement *WriteLn(X)*, the X that is written is the one that exists in the storage area allocated by the most recent call of the procedure A. The correct answer to our question then is that $A(5)$ would return the value 5, and would write the numbers 0, 1, 2, 3, and 4.

The Exit Procedure

Sometimes in writing a procedure or function, you reach a point in the middle of the body of the procedure at which it would be handy to return *immediately*—without executing the rest of the procedure—to the calling program. Standard Pascal offers no way to do this; you must structure the procedure (using **if** statements, perhaps) so that all statements from then on to the end of the procedure can be skipped.

Here's a sample program that shows how involved things can get in Standard Pascal. Function *RunningTotal* accepts numbers from the keyboard, one at a time, then returns the total:

```pascal
function RunningTotal : Real;
var
  Subtotal, NewNumber : Real;
begin
  Subtotal := 0.0;
  repeat
    Write ('Enter a number (-1 to quit): ');
    ReadLn (NewNumber);
    if NewNumber <> -1.0 then    { Only add if number is not -1 }
      Subtotal := Subtotal + NewNumber;
  until NewNumber = -1.0;        { Exit the loop if number is -1 }
  RunningTotal := Subtotal;
end;
```

Note that *RunningTotal* returns when the user enters a special value: *–1*. Such a value, used as a signal to the program to do something, is known as a *sentinel*. Here, the sentinel value *–1* indicates that there are no more numbers to be entered. While *RunningTotal* works, it is both confusing and inefficient. In particular, we test twice to see if variable *NewNumber* has the value *–1*: once to determine whether to add it to the running total and a second time to see if we should leave the procedure.

The second test wouldn't be necessary if we could put a statement in the **repeat**...**until** loop that says, "If *NewNumber* is *–1*, return the total immediately without doing anything else." Turbo Pascal allows a return from any point in a procedure or function with the predefined procedure *Exit*. Using *Exit* both simplifies and speeds up *RunningTotal*:

```pascal
function RunningTotal : Real;
var
  Subtotal, NewNumber : Real;
begin
  Subtotal := 0.0;
  repeat
    Write ('Enter a number (-1 to quit): ');
    ReadLn (NewNumber);
    if NewNumber = -1.0 then
    begin
      RunningTotal := Subtotal; { Set the function result and exit }
      Exit
    end
    else
      Subtotal := Subtotal + NewNumber

  until False;            { Since we exit the loop from the middle,
                            we never want the until to be satisfied }
end;
```

This technique becomes even more important when the point from which you want to exit is deeply nested in structured statements, such as **if**s and **while**s. It can also make your program more readable, since the reader will be able to recognize immediately where the exit occurs and what value is returned.

As you might guess, calling *Exit* from within the main program causes the program to terminate—it's like hitting the final **end**.

Review

In this chapter, we introduced the two types of program subdividers in Pascal: procedures and functions. We described the format of procedure and function declarations, and we explained Pascal's rules about the scope and lifetime of identifiers declared within procedures and functions.

We touched on the topic of recursion. We discussed how to declare **forward** procedures and functions and how to determine the scope of identifiers during recursion. Finally, we presented the predefined procedure *Exit*, which causes an immediate exit from a subprogram or main program.

In the next chapter, we cover arrays: what they are and how to use them.

C　　H　　A　　P　　T　　E　　R

12

Arrays

We've discussed the five predefined data types—*Integer, LongInt, Real, Boolean,* and *Char*—as well as declared scalar types. A variable of one of these types can hold only one value at a time. For example, if you define

```
var
  Index      : Integer;
```

Index has a single value at any moment. There are situations in which it's convenient for a single identifier to represent a series of values, such as a list of numbers or characters. That's where *arrays* come in.

Suppose, for example, you want to write a program to balance your checkbook. One thing your program will need is a list of all your checks and the amounts they were written for. To reserve space for this information, you could declare a variable for each check:

```
var
  Check1 : Real; { Amount of check 1 }
  Check2 : Real; { Amount of check 2 }
  Check3 : Real; { Amount of check 3 }
  .
  .
  .
  Check50 : Real; { Amount of check 50 }
```

This approach quickly becomes tedious if you write a lot of checks. Also, it is impossible to write a loop to go through all the checks and do something with each—say, add them to a running total. You can't write the following:

```
for Check := Check1 to Check50 do
  Total := Total + Check;
```

How, then, do we accomplish the task we've described? The answer is to store the check amounts in an array.

An array is a list of variables of identical type, each of which can be referred to by specifying the name of the list and the variable's position in the list. Suppose that you declare

```
var
  Check : array[1..10] of Real;
```

This declaration tells the compiler that identifier *Check* refers to a list of ten variables of type *Real*, each with a number (called its *index*) from 1 to 10.

Each item of an array is referred to by the name of the array, followed by its index enclosed in square brackets ([]). Thus, array *Check* contains the 10 variables *Check[1], Check[2], Check[3], Check[4], Check[5], Check[6], Check[7], Check[8], Check[9],* and *Check[10]*. You can use any of these variables wherever you would use a regular *Real* variable. Furthermore—and this is what makes arrays useful—the index value doesn't have to be a constant. It can be any expression that yields an integer in the range 1..10. For example, if the variable Index is of the type *Integer*, the statement

```
for Index := 1 to 10 do
  Check[Index] := 0.0;
```

zeros each variable.

How do arrays solve the problem of adding up check amounts? You can now refer to each check by its index and write

```
Total := 0.0;                    { initialize the "accumulator" variable }
for Index := 1 to 10 do
  Total := Total + Check[Index];
```

Figure 12.1 shows the syntax of an array type.

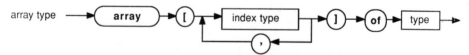

Figure 12.1: Syntax Diagram of an Array Type

To specify an array type, you must give the compiler two pieces of information: the array's *index type* and the type of each of the items of the array, the *base type*.

Turbo Pascal Tutor for the Macintosh

The index type, which appears between the square brackets, must be scalar, usually an integer subrange, for example, *1..10*. Occasionally another type is appropriate. For example, for a program to encrypt a secret message using a cipher, you might want an array that holds the code for each possible object of the type *Char*. In that case, you could declare the array

```
var
  Cipher : array [char] of char;
```

filling each location of the array with the replacement character for the corresponding index character. Then, to encode a character, you could write

```
MsgChar := Cipher[MsgChar];
```

and each character in the secret message would be replaced by the code for that character.

There are other limits to the index type of an array, one being that the type cannot have so many possible values that the total size of the array is greater than 32,767 bytes (32K). The declaration

```
type
  BigArrayType  = array[1..20000] of Integer;
```

causes a `Structure Too Large` error during compilation, because a list of 20,000 integers, at 2 bytes each, requires 40,000 bytes.

The reason for this constraint stems from the Macintosh's processor. While the processor can work with objects larger than 32K, its most efficient (fastest) addressing mode is restricted to objects less than 32K bytes long. We'll come up against the 32K limitation again in other contexts as well.

There are various ways around the 32K array size limitation, allowing the creation of objects as large as you have memory for. We'll deal with this topic in detail in Chapters 16 and 23.

It can be handy to use an enumerated type in declaring an array:

```
type
  Days         = (Mon,Tues,Wed,Thur,Fri,Sat,Sun);

var
  Regular      : array[Mon..Fri] of Integer;
  Overtime     : array[Days] of Integer;
  Present      : array[Days] of Boolean;
```

Array *Regular* has a subrange of type *Days* as its index type, while the arrays *Overtime* and *Present* have the entire type *Days* as their index type. Array *Regular* consists of five integers. If an *Integer* variable occupies 2 bytes and a *Boolean* 1 byte, can you tell the total amount of memory (in bytes) taken up by each array? (Note that the compiler always pads data structures out to an even length, for example, 5-byte data structures are padded to 6 bytes.) The answers are 10, 14, and 8.

The base type of an array can be almost any data type at all—just as long as the total size of the array does not exceed 32,767 bytes. In fact, you can declare arrays that contain other structured types, including other arrays—there's that recursive quality of Pascal again. Arrays of arrays (called *multidimensional arrays*) are useful for describing objects in a table or grid, such as a cell in a spreadsheet (which is located by its row and column) or a point on a piece of graph paper (located by its horizontal and vertical coordinates).

Consider a program that plays checkers. An important data structure for this program would be the array that tracks the state of the board. One way to represent the board might be like this:

```
type
  Square = (RedSquare, EmptyBlackSquare, RedPiece, BlackPiece,
           RedKing, BlackKing);     {possible contents of a square}

var
  CheckerBoard : array [1..8] {outer array} of
                  array [1..8] {inner array} of Square;
```

How would you access a particular square of the board given this declaration of array *CheckerBoard*? In Pascal, you specify the subscript of the *outer array*, followed by the subscript of the *inner array*. Thus, if you let each of the inner arrays be a column (horizontal file) of the board, you could specify the square in the third column from one player's left and the fourth row (vertical rank) from the same side of the board (see Figure 12.2).

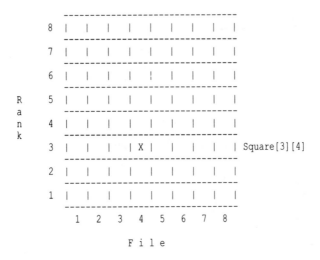

Figure 12.2: Accessing the Game Board

Because it is inconvenient to type multiple sets of brackets, Pascal allows a shorthand notation for multidimensional arrays. Instead of *Square[3][4]*, you can substitute *Square[3,4]*. Similarly, when specifying array *CheckerBoard*'s type, you can write

var
```
  CheckerBoard : array [1..8, 1..8] of Square;
```

which is equivalent to what's shown in Figure 12.1.

You can create arrays with three or more dimensions. For example, here's the board for five-dimensional (neo-Vulcan) chess:

var
```
  Chess5D : array [1..8, 1..8, 1..3, 1..3, 1..9] of Chess5DSquareType;
```

Turbo Pascal allows an array to have as many dimensions as you want, as long as you observe the 32K total limit.

Array Assignments

Standard Pascal permits assignments on the individual objects within an array, but not on an array as a whole. Thus, if you declare

```
var
  A, B: array [1..10,1..20] of Integer;
```

and you want to transfer all the elements of *A* into *B*, you'd have to write the double loop

```
for I := 1 to 10 do
  for J := 1 to 20 do
    B[I,J] := A[I,J];
```

This loop transfers each element of *A* into *B*, one at a time. Can you see how it works?

While this approach gets the job done, what we really want is code that automatically takes everything in *A* and moves it to *B*. Turbo Pascal permits this, as long as both arrays have the same type. Thus, the single assignment

```
B := A;
```

does the job in one fell swoop. Turbo Pascal also lets you work with arrays that are nested within other arrays. Thus, if you want to transfer just one row of array *A* to a row of array *B*, you could write

```
A[8] := B[3];
```

Remember that the declaration

```
var
  A, B: array [1..10,1..20] of Integer;
```

is shorthand for

```
var
  A, B: array [1..10] of array [1..20] of Integer;
```

so that *B[3]* means "the third 20-element array of *B*." These special features of Turbo Pascal make working with arrays easier.

Range-Checking and Arrays

A common run-time error involving arrays is trying to access elements that don't exist. For instance, if you declare

```
var
  Check : array[1..10] of Real;
```

and then process it with this loop,

```
```

```
for i := 1 to 11 do
  WriteLn(Check[i]);
```

you're asking for trouble. The first 10 values in array *Check* would be written to the screen. But what happens on the last pass when the program tries to find *Check[11]*?

The answer depends on whether or not range-checking was enabled (using the $R directive) when the program was compiled. If range-checking is off (which is the default), the program looks where it thinks *Check[11]* ought to be in memory, namely, immediately after *Check[10]*. It then interprets whatever is there to be a real number and writes that number to the screen. This place in memory could be another variable, a combination of two smaller variables, or even part of a program; the number displayed is meaningless.

With range-checking turned on, run time error 5, `Range Check Error`, occurs when the program attempts to access array *Check*'s eleventh element.

Reading an out-of-range array element is bad enough; writing to one is even worse:

```
for N := 1 to 11 do
  Check[N] := 0;
```

With range-checking turned off, this loop fills 4 bytes of memory just past the end of array *Check* with zeros, overwriting whatever was there before.

We can't overemphasize the importance of making sure that array subscripts (as well as variables of subrange and enumerated types) do not go out of range. Until you are sure a program is free from errors of this sort, compile with range-checking on. Get into the habit of making {$R+} the first line of every program you write.

Initializing Arrays

Like any variable, before you use an array you must initialize it, that is, set its elements equal to some starting set of values. (Before a variable is assigned a value, it can have any value at all.) If all values are to be the same, the process is simple. For example, suppose you want to set all elements in the array *A* (defined earlier) to 0. One way to do this is to use a pair of **for** loops:

```
for X := 1 to 10 do
```

```
for Y := 1 to 20 do
   A[X,Y] := 0;
```

This method works, although it could be faster and it uses up a bit of space for code and variables. Turbo Pascal, however, provides you with a faster way: the predefined procedure *FillChar*. A call to *FillChar* looks like this:

```
FillChar(Dest,Length,Data);
```

where *Dest* is the variable (of any type) to be filled, *Length* is the number of bytes to initialize, and *Data* is an integer value between 0 and 255 to be written to each byte. You want to fill *B* with the integer 0, which is represented as 2 bytes of 0s. So, use *B* for *Dest*, and *0* for the data byte.

Now you just need the length in bytes. You can calculate this value given your knowledge of arrays and the storage requirements of various types. For example, array *A*, of type array *[1..10, 1..20]* of *Integer*, contains *10 * 20* integers at 2 bytes each, and therefore occupies 800 bytes.

A better way is to use the built-in function *SizeOf* and let the compiler do the work for you. *SizeOf* takes as its only parameter either a variable or a data type and returns the size of that variable (or that type) in bytes. So to initialize *A*, you could write either

```
FillChar(A,800,0)
```

or

```
FillChar(A,SizeOf(A),0);
```

This statement sets each byte in the memory-address range occupied by array *A* to 0. The combination of *FillChar* and *SizeOf* is the fastest way to initialize an array variable in Turbo Pascal (although the nested **for** loop method isn't all that slow).

Be warned, however, that the *FillChar* technique may not work as intended when you wish to initialize all the elements of an array to a value other than *0*. If you try to set all of the elements of *B* to *1* by using the statement

```
FillChar(B,SizeOf(B),1);
```

you would discover that, after this "initialization," each element of *B* has the value *257*, not *1*. This is because *B* is an array of type *Integer*, and an integer with both of its bytes set to 1 equals 257. So be careful when using *FillChar* to initialize arrays whose components are larger than a single byte.

Turbo Pascal Tutor for the Macintosh

Representing an Array in Memory

The elements of an array are stored in memory in a specific order. If the array is one-dimensional—that is, if it has only one index—then the elements are stored in ascending order. For example, array *Check* (defined as **array**[1..10] **of** Real) stores *Check[1]* at the lowest address, *Check[2]* at an address 4 bytes higher than *Check[1]*, and so on, as you might expect. But what about multidimensional arrays, like *CheckerBoard*:

```
var
    CheckerBoard : array [1..8, 1..8] of Square;
```

Are the elements in *CheckerBoard* stored as *CheckerBoard[1,1]*, *CheckerBoard[2,1]*, *CheckerBoard[3,1]*, and so on? Or are they stored as *CheckerBoard[1,1]*, *CheckerBoard[1,2]*, *CheckerBoard[1,3]*, and so on?

Pascal hints at the answer to this question. Remember that the previous definition is just shorthand for

var CheckerBoard : **array** [1..8] **of array** [1..8] **of** Square;

Thus, the first index of *CheckerBoard[3,4]* (which can also be written as *CheckerBoard[3][4]*) selects a column of the board, which is an **array**[1..8] **of** Square. The second index selects a square within that array, and those elements are stored sequentially, just as in *Check*. *CheckerBoard[1,1]* says to pick the first element of the first array; *CheckerBoard[1,2]*, the second element of the first array; and so on. The squares are stored in the order

```
CheckerBoard[1, 1]
CheckerBoard[1, 2]
CheckerBoard[1, 3]
   . . .
CheckerBoard[2, 1]
CheckerBoard[2, 2]
   . . .
CheckerBoard[8, 7]
CheckerBoard[8, 8]
```

Remember that the index furthest to the right—the last index—changes the fastest, regardless of the number of dimensions in the array. The array

var BigOne : **array**[0..3,0..4,0..5,0..2] **of** byte;

is stored as

```
BigOne[0,0,0,0]
BigOne[0,0,0,1]
BigOne[0,0,0,2]
BigOne[0,0,1,0]
BigOne[0,0,1,1]
```

```
. . .
BigOne[3,4,5,1]
BigOne[3,4,5,2]
```

Packed Arrays

To save space, arrays can be *packed*. Packed arrays, indicated with the **packed** keyword, make more efficient use of storage for byte-sized array elements such as characters and small integer subranges (with 256 or fewer values). For example, consider the following two types:

```
type
  T1 = array [1..10] of char;
  T2 = packed array [1..10] of char;
```

Variables of type T1 are 20 bytes long and those of type T2 are 10 bytes long.

Review

In this chapter, you learned how to declare and access arrays, which is a structured type that consists of a list of variables of any type. You further saw how to work with multidimensional arrays and how to initialize arrays. Also described was how arrays are stored in memory.

Take a moment to study the two array exercises in Turbo Tutor.

You'll see arrays used throughout the rest of this book. Chapter 13 introduces string types, a special application for arrays.

13

Strings

Niklaus Wirth had mainframes, not Macintoshes, in mind when he designed Pascal. This orientation is evident when we study strings and how this concept has been expanded in Turbo Pascal.

The mainframes of the late 1960s accepted programs and information in the form of punched cards and magnetic tapes. Programs were submitted as "batch jobs"; the program and data (usually numbers) went in, the computer worked on them, and the results came out. No one communicated with the program while it was running.

In time, this situation changed. "Timesharing" computers capable of serving many users at once became common. CRT terminals became available to more users. Minicomputers became popular, and users began to insist on *interactive programs*—programs that communicated with the user while being run. Many of these programs performed functions, such as word processing, that would have been impossible as batch programs.

Because it originated in the world of batch-oriented, number-crunching mainframes, Standard Pascal was not given facilities for working with strings (groups of ASCII characters). In Standard Pascal, strings can only be stored as arrays of characters, and no special operations for reading, writing, or processing them are provided. This makes writing programs to handle text difficult.

Turbo Pascal, like many modern versions of Pascal, has extensions for handling strings simply and quickly.

String Types

A **string** is a one-dimensional array of ASCII characters, that is, an array of type *Char*. Turbo Pascal keeps track of both a string's contents and its length. Using various operators and built-in procedures and functions, you can manipulate a string: Add characters to it, delete characters from it, combine it with other strings, and more.

You create a string variable by declaring it to be of a **string** type. To specify a string type, you tell the compiler the maximum number of characters that a string of that type can contain (so it can reserve enough memory). The syntax of a string type is shown in Figure 13.1.

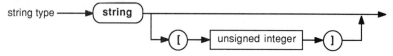

Figure 13.1: Syntax Diagram of a String Type

The constant in the specification of the string type must be in the range 1..255. Here is a sample declaration of string types:

```
const
  MaxstringSize = 255;
type
  Bigstring    : string[MaxstringSize];
  Littlestring : string[15];
```

Here are some string variable declarations:

```
var
  MyName      : string[80];
  Token       : Littlestring;
  MyBigString : Bigstring;
```

The constant used in the specification of a string type sets the maximum number of characters each string can hold. The variable *MyName* holds up to 80 characters; *Token* holds only 15. The following assignment

```
Token := 'this is too long a string for Token';
```

would store only the first 15 characters ("this is too lon") into *Token*. *MyBigString* has the maximum length possible for a string in Turbo Pascal: 255 characters. This string length has particular relevance in Macintosh programming, as we shall see in Part 5 of this book.

String Operators, Functions, and Procedures

Turbo provides a rich assortment of operators, procedures, and functions to manipulate variables of string types, as shown in Table 13.1.

Table 13.1: String Procedures and Functions

Procedure/Function	Definition
Concat(St1, St2 {, St3,...,Stn})	Returns string composed of St1 through Stn concatenated together; the plus sign (+) can also be used.
Copy(St, Position, Len)	Returns string composed of St[Position] ... St[Position+Len-1].
Delete(St, Position, Num)	Deletes Num characters from St starting at St[Position].
Insert(Source, Destination, Position)	Inserts Source into Destination starting at Destination[Position].
Length(St)	Returns current length of St.
Pos(Pattern,Target)	Returns position (index) of Pattern within Target.

String Assignments

Assignments to string variables work pretty much as they do with other variable types, with one difference: If the destination string is too small to hold all the characters assigned to it, those characters are dropped. (In other words, the string is *truncated*.) For instance, if string variable *Fruit* is of type **string***[5]*, then the assignment

```
Fruit := 'Watermelon';
```

gives *Fruit* the value *'Water'*.

The Length Function

One of the most frequently used string functions is *Length*, which returns the current length of a string. (Don't confuse this with the maximum possible length of the string that is declared as part of its type.) If *St* is a string variable, then the expression

```
Length(St)
```

returns the number of characters currently in *St*. The following example demonstrates the *Length* function.

```
program LengthTest;
type
  SmallStr    = string[15];
var
  Test        : SmallStr;

procedure ShowLength(St : SmallStr);
{ Write out a string and its length }
begin
  WriteLn('The length of "',St,'" is ',Length(St))
end;

begin
  Test := 'hello, there';
  ShowLength(Test);
  Test := 'hi';
  ShowLength(Test);
  Test := '';                    { the null string }
  ShowLength(Test);
  ReadLn
end.
```

Procedure *ShowLength* accepts a string as its parameter, and then writes out the string, followed by its length. When this program is run, it produces the output

```
The length of "hello, there" is 12
The length of "hi" is 2
The length of "" is 0
```

The Concat Function and the + Operator

Another useful function is *Concat*, which concatenates (combines) two or more strings to make one large string. If *St1* is a string variable with the value *'Robin Jones'*, then the expression

```
Concat('This program compliments of ', St1, '.')
```

yields

```
 This program compliments of Robin Jones.
```

The general syntax of the *Concat* function is

```
Concat(St1, St2 {, St3,...,Stn})
```

where *St1*, *St2*, and so on are string variables or constants.

Like *WriteLn*, *Concat* can accept a variable number of parameters; unlike *WriteLn*, it must have at least two. Beyond this, its only restriction is that the total length of all the concatenated strings must be less than or equal to 255. Characters past position 255 are lost.

In lieu of calling the *Concat* function, Turbo Pascal lets you concatenate strings using the plus sign as an operator. The expression

```
'This program compliments of ' + St1 + '.'
```

performs exactly the same operation as the earlier *Concat* example.

The Copy Function

The next string function that you may find useful is *Copy*, which allows you to make a copy of any part of a string (that is, a substring). It takes as parameters the string, two integers indicating the position of the first character at which to begin copying, and the number of characters to copy. The expression

```
Copy('This string has no character', 20, 9);
```

returns the value *'character'*. The syntax of the *Copy* function is

```
Copy(Source, Position, Len)
```

where *Source* is a string and *Position* and *Len* are integers.

There are a few restrictions on the parameters passed to *Copy*. The second parameter, which indicates the position at which to start copying from the string, must be in the range 1 through 255. Secondly, if you try to use *Copy* to copy beyond the end of a string, only the characters within the string will be returned. If the starting position is already beyond the end of the string, then *Copy* will return a *null string*, that is, a string with a length of 0 containing no characters at all.

The Pos Function

Another handy string function is *Pos*. It looks for the first occurrence of a substring inside another string; if it finds the substring, it tells you where. *Pos*'s syntax is as follows:

```
Function Pos(Substring, S);
```

where *Substring* and *S* are both **string** expressions. *Pos* takes the string to search *for* as its first parameter, and the string to search *in* as its second parameter. If it finds *Substring* lurking in *S*, *Pos* returns an integer giving the location in *S* where *Substring* begins; otherwise, *Pos* returns 0.

Suppose you want to see if the word "to" occurs in string variable *S*:

```
S:= 'To be or not to be';

Location := Pos('to', S);
```

Variable *Location* (assumed to be of type *Integer*) would get the value *14*. (NOTE: Case *is* significant, so the *To* at the beginning of *S* isn't matched.) If the target string is not found, *Pos* returns the value 0.

The Delete and Insert Procedures

Two operations you'll undoubtedly perform on strings are to delete characters from and insert characters into them. The *Delete* procedure lets you remove a section of a string; like *Copy*, it requires the string, the starting position, and the number of characters to delete.

Suppose you've found the word "to" in a soliloquy somewhere and want to remove it and the following blank space from the string. You can do this by calling the following *Delete* procedure:

```
Delete (S, Location, 3);
```

It removes three characters from *S*, starting at the character indicated by *Location*. Alternatively, you could perform the entire operation in one masterstroke by writing

```
Delete (S, Pos('to', S), 3);
```

which omits the need for variable *Location* entirely. In either case, *S* becomes *'To be or not be.'*

The syntax of the *Delete* procedure is

```
Delete(S, Position, Num)
```

where *S* is a string and *Position* and *Num* are integers.

If *Position* is beyond the last character of the string, no characters are removed. If it is not a value from *1* to *255*, a run-time error occurs. Even if you attempt to delete past the end of the string, only characters in the string are removed.

Combined with *Pos* and *Copy*, you can use *Delete* to separate a string of text into individual words. The following procedure gets the first word from a line of text (where "word" is defined to be a sequence of characters starting with a non-space character and followed by a space).

```
procedure GetWord(var Line, Word : BigStr);
                              { Get the next word from the string line }
const
  Space       = ' ';
var
  Len      : Integer;
begin
  while Pos(Space,Line) = 1 do                    { remove leading blanks }
    Delete(Line,1,1);
  Len := Pos(Space,Line) - 1;                        { look for blank }
  if Len = 0 then                                   { no blanks left }
  begin
    Word := Line;              { get word--might be null string if none left }
    Line := ''                             { now make line the null string }
  end
  else
  begin                                  { get word and delete from line }
    Word := Copy(Line,1,Len);                    { get all but blank }
    Delete(Line,1,Len + 1)                   { delete word plus blank }
  end
end;                                                 { procedure GetWord }
```

The *Insert* procedure is the reverse of the *Copy/Delete* operation: It takes one string and stuffs it inside another. The first parameter of *Insert* is the string to insert, the second is the string into which it's to be inserted, and the last is the location where the insertion should occur.

For example, if you want to put "to " back into *S*, you can write:

```
Insert(S, Location, 'to ');
```

The syntax of the *Insert* procedure is

```
Insert(Source, Destination, Position)
```

where *Source* and *Destination* are strings and *Position* is an integer.

Position must be in the range *1..255*. If the result is longer than the maximum length of *Destination*, the extra characters at the end are truncated. Furthermore, if an attempt is made to insert a string at a position after the end of *Destination* (that is, *Position* is greater than *Length(Destination)*), then *Source* is concatenated onto the end of *Destination*.

Insert and *Delete* can be used together to substitute one substring for another. Suppose you are writing a program that takes a form letter and inserts the appropriate names, dates, and so on. Within the form letter, these name and date strings can be represented by tokens (groups of symbols that show you where to put the information). For example, the salutation might look like this:

```
Dear <title> <last name>:
```

where the information to be filled in is represented using variable-like tokens such as "<title>". The following procedure, then, can be used for replacement purposes:

```
procedure Replace(var Line : BigStr; Token,Sub : TokStr);
                          { Look for Token in Line and replace with Sub }
var
  Index,Len        : Integer;
begin
  repeat
    Index := Pos(Token,Line);
    if Index > 0 then
    begin
      Delete(Line,Index,Length(Token));
      Insert(Sub,Line,Index)
    end
  until Index = 0
end;                                        { procedure Replace }
```

The statements

```
Line := 'And so, <title> <last>, the entire <last> family';
Replace(Line,'<title>','Dr.');
Replace(Line,'<last>','Lewis');
WriteLn(Line);
```

produce

```
And so, Dr. Lewis, the entire Lewis family
```

This is how personalized junk mail is generated, as you might have guessed.

The Chr Function

The *Chr* function takes a value of any scalar type with an ordinal value of *0* to *255* and returns the corresponding character (a data object of type *Char*) with that ASCII code. This sounds like double talk, since we know that a character is nothing but an ASCII value anyway. All *Chr* does is change the compiler's perspective on the underlying ordinal value—it doesn't perform any action at run time; no memory is changed or moved. For instance, the following program prints all of the characters in the font (Monaco) used in the terminal window:

```
program PrintASCII;
{Print the characters corresponding to codes 0 to 255.}
var i :Integer;
begin
  for i := 0 to 255 do
    WriteLn(i, ' --> ', Chr(i));
  ReadLn;
end.
```

Any parameter passed to *Chr* should be between *0* and *255*. If it isn't, no run-time error occurs, but the parameter *modulo 256* (that is, the lower byte of the parameter) is used.

Representing Strings in Memory: Strings as Arrays

You can work with strings as complete entities, and the characters that make up a string can be accessed individually. A variable of type **string**[n] can be treated as though it were an **array**[0..n] **of** *Char*.

That the array starts with *0* and not *1* is significant. You can reference individual characters in a string variable using standard array notation—for instance, the first character of *Token* (of type **string**[80]) is *Token[1]*, the second is *Token[2]*, and so on. The first element of the array—the one with an index of 0—contains the current length of the string. If you execute the assignment

```
Token := 'this string';
```

then *Token[0]* is a character with ASCII value 11, since there are 11 characters in *'this string'*. This implies that *Token[0]* performs the same function as *Length(Token)*. It does, but beware: You've got to play by Pascal's typing rules if you want to look in position 0 to get a string's length, as this program shows:

```
program Mismatch;
var
  Token          : string[15];
  Len            : Integer;
begin
  Token := 'this string';
  Len := Token[0];               { The compiler won't like this line }
  WriteLn('The length of Token is ',Len)
end.
```

Type in and compile this program. What's wrong with the seventh line?

Since *Token[0]* is of type *Char*, the compiler won't let you assign it to an *Integer* variable, any more than it would let you perform the assignment

```
Len := 'c';
```

Your intentions are honorable, but Pascal is picky about mixing and matching types in assignment statements. You can reassure the compiler by substituting the statement

```
Len := Ord(Token[0]);
```

which returns the ordinal (numeric) value of *Token[0]*, which happens to be 11. Of course, the *Length* function does this for you, so there is usually no need for this technique.

Using array notation, you can access any individual character of a string. As mentioned previously, each element of a string is a variable of type *Char*, and you can treat it as such. For example, here's a procedure to convert all letters in a string to uppercase ('A'..'Z'):

```
type
  MaxString = string[255];

procedure UpperCase (var S: MaxString);
var
  Index      : Integer;
begin
  for Index := 1 to Length(S) do
    if (S[Index] >= 'a') and (S[Index] <= 'z') then
      S[Index] := Chr(Ord(S[Index] - 32));
end;
```

At times, even Pascal lovers get put out by the grief Pascal puts you through when performing numeric operations on character data. Let's work through the next to the last line of procedure *UpperCase*:

```
S[Index] := Chr(Ord(S[Index] - 32));
```

At this point, we know that *S[Index]* is a lowercase letter. ASCII is designed so that each lowercase letter has a code value 32 greater than the corresponding uppercase character. It would therefore be nice to say

```
S[Index] := S[Index] - 32;
```

In weakly typed languages like C, this is exactly what you'd do. But Pascal won't let you subtract apples from oranges, months from days, or integers from characters. Even though you and I know there's a numeric value hiding in the byte of memory represented by *S[Index]*, Pascal requires that we first change *S[Index]* into an integer value (*Ord(S[Index])*), perform the subtraction, and then convert the whole thing back into a character for assignment to the string.

The *Chr* and *Ord* functions are unlike most of Pascal's built-in functions in that they don't cause any run-time processing. They simply perform type coercion; that is, they cause the compiler to permit operations that typing considerations would otherwise prevent. The code generated by this line would therefore be simple and quick. Wirth made Pascal picky to make sure you know what you're doing when you put together such a statement.

Now that you know how strings work internally, be careful. Avoid messing with any elements beyond the current length of the string. Turbo Pascal won't give you any sort of error, but you need to be aware that you've just changed a portion of the string and it won't print unless you change the length as well. For example, the sequence

```
Token := 'Hello';
Token[6] := '!';
WriteLn(Token);
```

outputs *Hello* rather than *Hello!*. This is because *Token[0]* still contains a value of *5*, and that's what the *WriteLn* procedure looks at when it gets ready to display the contents of *Token*. If you add the statement *Token[0] := Chr(6)* just before the *WriteLn* command, you'll write out the complete string. Usually, this sort of "string surgery" isn't necessary, because of the many string functions available. The correct way to add emphasis to *Token* is

```
Token := Concat(Token,'!');
```

or, perhaps more intuitively,

```
Token := Token + '!';
```

String Comparisons

Strings can be compared to each other with the same operators that you use for numbers: =, <, >, <=, >=, and <>. But the meanings of these operations aren't as obvious as for numbers. For example, what does it mean to use the less-than symbol to compare two strings?

```
if 'cat' < 'dog' then ...
```

Strings are compared using two criteria: their underlying ASCII values and their length, in that order. For example, *cat* is less than *dog* because the ASCII value of *c* is less than the ASCII value of *d*. Two strings are equal only if they contain exactly the same characters. If two strings have different lengths, but are identical up to the length of the shorter string, then the shorter string is considered to be less than the longer string. This means that *cat* is less than *cats*.

Case is significant in string comparisons. *Cat* is less than *cat* because uppercase letters have lower ASCII values than their lowercase equivalent. For this reason, you will probably want to call a case-conversion routine before comparing two strings, unless you know ahead of time that case distinctions won't cloud the issue. It is worth noting that all characters (spaces, symbols, and control characters as well) are included in the comparison according to their ASCII value; for example, *cat#* is less than *cat/* because # has a lower value than /.

Passing Strings to Procedures and Functions

You may have noticed in these examples that whenever we've passed a string to a procedure or function, we've always given that parameter a named type, like *BigStr* or *TokStr*, rather than an anonymous string type like **string**[80]. For example, we used

```
procedure GetWord(var Line, Word : BigStr);
```

instead of

```
procedure GetWord(var Line, Word : string[255]);
```

not to be tidy or pedantic, but because Turbo Pascal requires it. Think of it from the compiler's point of view. Because of Pascal's strong typing, the compiler won't allow you to pass a parameter to a procedure unless both the parameter to be passed and the formal parameter used to define the procedure are the same type of object. And if they don't have the same type, the compiler considers them to be different.

When passing strings as parameters to procedures, it is often a good idea to pass them as **var** parameters, rather than value parameters (that is, not preceded by **var** in the parameter list). Parameters passed by value are copied when the subprogram is called—requiring more time and stack space than **var** parameters, which require only that a 4-byte address be passed. Passing a string of type **string**[255] by value requires 256 bytes of stack space, as well as the time to make the copy. Doing the same transfer by reference takes 4 bytes (and concomitantly less time).

However, when a string is passed as a **var** parameter, the compiler imposes an important restriction: Namely, that the formal and actual parameters have the same maximum length. This program won't compile:

```
program StringTest;
type
  String10 = string[10];
  String20 = string[20];
var
  Str: String20;

procedure P(var s: String10);
begin
end;

begin
  P(Str)
end.
```

because the compiler won't generate code that sends a 21-byte object (variable *Str*) to be processed by a procedure defined to process an 11-byte object (a *String10*). You'll get a `Type Mismatch` error at the point where the main program calls procedure *P*.

If you think about it, you'll see why. Except under rare circumstances, Pascal doesn't permit a variable of one type to be assigned a value of another type. Passing a variable to a procedure as a **var** parameter is treated just like an assignment, because the called procedure is free to change the value of that variable. Therefore, it doesn't let you pass *Real* variables to procedures that accept *Integer* parameters, nor a value of type **string**[20] to a procedure defined to accept parameters of type **string**[10] (or vice versa).

The IBM version of Turbo Pascal has a compiler directive that causes the compiler to permit passing strings of differing lengths as **var** parameters; Turbo Pascal for the Macintosh does not. One way around the problem is to make all strings the same type, say, **string**[80] or **string**[255]. You can minimize the potential for wasting space (four strings of type **string**[255] require 1K of RAM) by declaring strings as local variables, so that they are allocated on the stack.

Review

In this chapter, we learned about Turbo Pascal's string types, and how to use them to create arrays of characters. We looked at the syntax of a **string** type declaration and discussed such operations as string comparison, string assignment, and Turbo Pascal's built-in string procedures and functions. We ended with a discussion of some of the finer points of using string parameters.

There are two exercises on strings in Turbo Tutor. Take a moment to study them now.

In the next chapter, we discuss records, a structured type for combining data of different types into one neat packet.

14

Records

So far, you've learned about two structured types, arrays and strings. Both are collections of objects of the same type. Pascal also allows you to create structures called *records*, which are named groupings of different types.

This chapter explains records, the **with** statement, variant records, and free unions, followed by exercises that incorporate these features.

Let's return to the checkbook example at the start of Chapter 12. Originally, we declared an array of real numbers to hold the check amounts:

```
var
  Check : array[1..10] of  Real;
```

Suppose that, in addition to the amount of each check, you want to store information such as the date it was written on and who it was made out to.

You could declare many arrays, each using the check number as an index, to hold each piece of information about a check. The arrays might look something like this:

```
type
  CheckNumType = 1..1000;
  MonthType    = (January, February, March, April, May, June,
                  July, August, September, October, November, December);
  DayType      = 1..31;
  YearType     = 1980..2000;
  PayeeType    = string[40];
var
  CheckAmt    : array[CheckNumType] of  Real;
  CheckMonth  : array[CheckNumType] of  MonthType;
  CheckDay    : array[CheckNumType] of  DayType;
  CheckYear   : array[CheckNumType] of  YearType;
```

```
CheckPayee   : array[CheckNumType] of PayeeType;
```

This technique is used in some languages (BASIC, for instance), because they have no alternative. Intuitively, however, it doesn't seem logical to break a single entity (in this case, a check) into five separate pieces. Furthermore, the code resulting from this approach is messy. You'd need five assignments to make a working copy of the information for check *N*, for instance:

```
CheckCopyAmt    := CheckAmt[N];
CheckCopyMonth  := CheckMonth[N];
CheckCopyDay    := CheckDay[N];
CheckCopyYear   := CheckYear[N];
CheckCopyPayee  := CheckPayee[N];
```

Instead, you should be able to write something like

```
CheckCopy     := Check[N];
```

and transfer all of the information with a single statement.

Pascal's records solve this problem by allowing you to create a data object that consists of smaller objects of different types bundled together. These smaller objects, called *fields*, can be accessed individually, or you can refer to the record as a whole by name. This structuring lets you model many real-world situations and, as you gain familiarity with the technique, will become one of your most important problem-solving tools.

To create a record type for the checkbook example, you want each variable of this type to contain all information related to a single check: amount, date, and to whom it was written. Here's how the record type might be declared:

```
type
  Check = record          { "record" identifies a record type }
  Amt   : Real; {each field of the record has a name and a type }
  Month : MonthType;
  Day   : DayType;
  Year  : YearType;
  Payee : PayeeType;
end;                       { "end" marks the end of the record }
```

What does this definition mean? It defines a record type called *Check*. Each object of type *Check* consists of a group of five fields, each with a name and a type. Field *Amt*, which holds the check amount, is of type *Real*; the next field, *Month*, contains an object of type *MonthType*, which holds the month the check was written; and so on.

Now, suppose you have a variable called *MyCheck*, which you have declared to be of type *Check*. You access the individual objects within *MyCheck* by writing the name of the record variable (*MyCheck*) followed by a period, followed by the name of the field. Thus, you can refer to the amount of *MyCheck* by writing

```
MyCheck.Amt
```

MyCheck.Amt can be used wherever you would use a conventional *Real* variable. Here is a program fragment that declares the variable *MyCheck* and fill its fields with values.

```
var
  MyCheck  :  Check;

begin
  MyCheck.Amt   := 100.00;
  MyCheck.Month := February;
  MyCheck.Day   := 10;
  MyCheck.Year  := 1987;
  MyCheck.Payee := 'Philippe Kahn';
end.
```

As suggested previously, one of the benefits of records is that they can be copied all at once by a single assignment statement. If *MyCheck* and *YourCheck* are both variables of type *Check*, then the statement

```
YourCheck := MyCheck;
```

copies all of the fields from *MyCheck* into *YourCheck*.

What kinds of data objects can you use as the fields of a record? As you have probably come to expect of Pascal, practically anything—arrays, strings, scalars, and *even other records*—can be the fields of a record.

Suppose you declared a record type like this:

```
type
  Transaction = record
    Purpose : string[80];
    Payment : Check;
  end;
```

The record type *Transaction* contains two fields: *Purpose*, a string of 80 characters, and *Payment*, a record of type *Check*. If *Sale* were a variable of type *Transaction*, then you could refer to the *Payment* field of *Sale* as *Sale.Payment*, and to the *Amt* field of *Sale.Payment* as *Sale.Payment.Amt*. And so on and so on. (Yes, Pascal *is* a remarkable language.)

You can also use records in conjunction with other structured types. One especially handy construction is an array of records. For example, we can rewrite the data structures for this checkbook-balancing program as

```
type
   MonthType    = (January, February, March, April, May, June,
                     July, August, September, October, November, December);
   DayType      = 1..31;
   YearType     = 1980..2000;
   PayeeType    = string[40];

   Check = record
      Amt   : Real;
      Month : MonthType;
      Day   : DayType;
      Year  : YearType;
      Payee : PayeeType;
      end;

var
   CheckBook  : array[1..500] of  Check;
```

which is exactly what we wanted in the first place. We chose the size of the array carefully. Each check uses 50 bytes of storage, so 500 checks represent a 25,000-byte array, which begins to push the 32K limit. 500 checks is too severe a limit, so, in Chapter 23, we'll disclose a technique to smash the 500-check barrier.

To work with an individual field of a check within the array *CheckBook*, we could write statements of the form

```
for N := 1 to NumChecks do           { Total the amounts of the checks }
   Total := Total + CheckBook[N].Amt;
```

Figures 14.1 and 14.2 depict the formal syntax diagrams for a **record** type declaration. For the moment, disregard the box labeled "variant part."

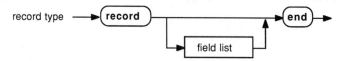

Figure 14.1: Syntax Diagram of a Record Type

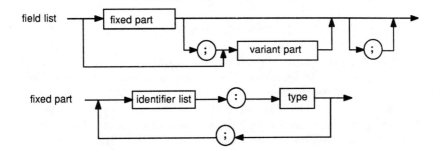

Figure 14.2: Syntax Diagram of a Field List

The With Statement

Previously, we showed you how to access each field of a record individually in order to assign values to those fields. You typed in the name of the record variable, a period, and the name of the field for every assignment:

```
MyCheck.Amt   := 100.00;
MyCheck.Month := February;
MyCheck.Day   := 10;
   ...
```

This can get tedious, especially if many fields are to be assigned—and records are common in Pascal programming. Some Macintosh data structures covered in Part 5 are records with dozens of fields. For this reason, Pascal provides you with a typing shortcut: the **with** statement.

Using the **with** statement, you can tell the compiler the name of the record variable you are using and then refer to its fields using the field names only. The following code sample uses **with** to perform the same assignments as the previous example:

```
with MyCheck do
  begin
    Amt   := 100.00;            { Assigns to MyCheck.Amt }
    Month := February;         { Assigns to MyCheck.Month }
    Day   := 10;               { Assigns to MyCheck.Day }
  end;
```

The syntax diagram of the **with** statement is shown in Figure 14.3.

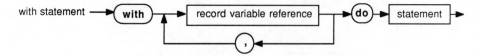

*Figure 14.3: Syntax Diagram of a **with** Statement*

While it isn't good practice, Pascal allows you to have field identifiers that are the same as the names of variables, types, constants, procedures, and so on. Thus, when using the **with** statement, you are creating a special scope in which the field names take precedence over—and perhaps hide—other identifiers. Had there been a global variable called *Month* in the previous example, it would not have been accessible within the **with** statement.

with statements can be nested:

```
var
  Sale : Transaction;       { As defined in the earlier example }
  ...
begin
  ...
  with Sale do
    with Payment do
    begin
      Amt    := 100.00;          { Assigns to Sale.Payment.Amt }
      Month := February;         { Assigns to Sale.Payment.Month }
      Day    := 10;              { Assigns to Sale.Payment.Day }
      ...
    end;
end.
```

Of course, the variables specified in the nested **with** statements need not have any relationship to each other at all. For example, we can write

```
var
  FirstRecord : record            { An "anonymous" record type }
    Field1, Field2 : Integer; { If fields are of the same type,
                                { we can declare them together }
    Field3        : Real;
  end;

  SecondRecord : record         { Another "anonymous" record type }
    Field4     : Real;
    Field5     : Integer;
  end;

begin
    ...
  with FirstRecord do
    with SecondRecord do
    begin
        ...     { Within this begin/end block, the fields of both
                records (Field1...Field5) can be accessed by their field names }
```

```
    end;
end.
```

However, if **with** statements are nested and two of the **with** variables have fields of the same name, the most deeply nested **with** takes precedence. If we modify the previous example so that some of the field names are the same, we can see what happens:

```
var
  FirstRecord : record
    Field1, Field2  : Integer;
    Field3          : Real;
  end;

  SecondRecord : record
    Field1      : Real;
    Field2      : Integer;
  end;

begin
    . . .
  with FirstRecord do
    with SecondRecord do
    begin
    . . .
{ Within this compound statement, the identifiers Field1 and
  Field2 refer to SecondRecord.Field1 and SecondRecord.Field2,
  respectively. Field3 still refers to FirstRecord.Field3, since
  there is no overlap. The "hidden" fields of FirstRecord can
  still be accessed by their full names: FirstRecord.Field1 and
  FirstRecord.Field2.}
    end;
```

Instead of nesting **with** statements, you may specify a list of record variables in a single **with** statement to accomplish the same thing. The statement

```
with FirstRecord, SecondRecord do
    . . .
```

is precisely equivalent to

```
with FirstRecord do
  with SecondRecord do
    . . .
```

There's one more point to remember when using the **with** statement: When the **with** variable is an element of an array, do not change the value of the index inside the **with** statement. This code demonstrates what *not* to do:

```
program UnsafeWith;
var
```

```
c : array[1..2] of record
                    a, b: Integer;
               end;
N : Integer;
begin
  c[1].a := 1; c[1].b := 2;
  c[2].a := 3; c[2].b := 4;
  N := 1;
  with c[N] do
  begin
    WriteLn(a,' ',b);
    N := 2;
    WriteLn(a,' ',b);
    ReadLn;
  end;
end.
```

This program outputs *1 2* both times, because the compiler doesn't consider the possibility that you might change the index of *C* within the **with** block. Therefore, even after the assignment to *N*, the **with** statement continues to refer to *C[1]*.

with statements can get you into trouble in a couple of other ways. While we haven't discussed *pointer variables* yet, the same restriction applies when the **with** variable is pointed to by a pointer: The pointer may not be changed. In general, the rule is *Don't do anything that might change the identity of the **with** variable*. This is an important consideration in Part 5 of this book.

These warnings notwithstanding, the **with** statement results in concise source code and, as a bonus, faster execution.

Variant Records

Occasionally, you'll need a record to store one set of fields under certain circumstances and a second set under others. For instance, imagine a **record** type to keep track of sales transactions in a store. You'll want to track some information under all conditions—for example, the amount of the purchase and the date of the transaction.

Other facts related to the transaction could vary according to the type of transaction. For example, if the person pays with a credit card, you'll want to record the kind of credit card, the credit card number, and the expiration date. And if the person pays with a check, you'll want the check number, the amount of the check (in case the customer got cash back from the transaction), and the customer's driver's license number.

One way to handle this is to allocate a separate field for every possible piece of information and, at run time, simply not fill in fields that don't apply. The **record** type definition might look something like this:

```
type
  MonthType    = (January, February, March, April, May, June,
                  July August, September, October, November, December);
  DayType      = 1..31;
  YearType     = 1980..2000;
  PaymentType  = (Cash, Check, CreditCard);
  CardType     = (Amex, Visa, MC);

  Purchase = record
    Amount : Real;
    Month  : MonthType;
    Day    : DayType;
    Year   : YearType;
    Hour   : 0..23;
    Minute : 0..59;
    MethodOfPayment: PaymentType;
    CheckNumber: Integer;  { These fields used for check purchases only }
    CheckAmt: Real;
    LicenseNumber: string[20];
    Card : CardType;         { These fields used for card purchases only }
    ExpMonth: MonthType;
    ExpYear: YearType;
  end;                                           { record Purchase }
```

While this approach works, it wastes storage. No matter what kind of purchase is made, some of the fields are guaranteed to be left empty.

To alleviate this situation, Pascal provides a feature called a *variant record*, which allows mutually exclusive fields (fields that will never be used at the same time) to share the same storage space within the record. This can result in a dramatic reduction in memory consumption.

Here's how to define a variant part for the previous record, allowing the mutually exclusive fields for check and credit card information to overlap. Note that the variant part of a record must come after all normally existing fields (the *fixed part*).

```
Purchase = record
  Amount : Real;
     ...
  Minute : 0..59;
  case MethodOfPayment : PaymentType of    { Beginning of variant part }
    Check    : ( CheckNumber : Integer;            { First variant: }
                 CheckAmt: Real;           { MethodOfPayment = Check }
                 LicenseNumber: string[20] );
    CreditCard : ( Card : CardType;                { Second variant: }
                   ExpMonth: MonthType;  { MethodOfPayment = CreditCard }
                   ExpYear: YearType );
  end;                                           { record Purchase }
```

The variant part of a record begins with the reserved word **case** (unrelated to its use in the **case** statement), followed by the name and type of a special field of the record, called the *tag field*. Here the tag field is *MethodOfPayment*. This field, besides carrying information about the purchase, serves another purpose: By looking at *MethodOfPayment*, your program can decide what information it expects to find in the rest of the record.

The reserved word **of** follows the definition of the tag field, then one or more lists of field definitions. Each list, called a *variant*, describes how the remaining space in the record is used for a different value of the tag field.

If the value of *MethodOfPayment* is *Check*, then the rest of the space in the record holds the fields *CheckNumber* (the number of the check), *CheckAmount* (the amount of the check), and *LicenseNumber* (the driver's license number of the issuer of the check).

On the other hand, if *MethodOfPayment* has the value *CreditCard*, then the same space holds the fields *Card* (the kind of credit card used), *ExpMonth* (the expiration month of the card), and *ExpYear* (the expiration year of the card). If *MethodOfPayment* has the value *Cash*, there are no additional fields in the record and the remaining space contains no useful information.

The syntax of this optional part of a record definition, the variant part, is shown in Figure 14.4.

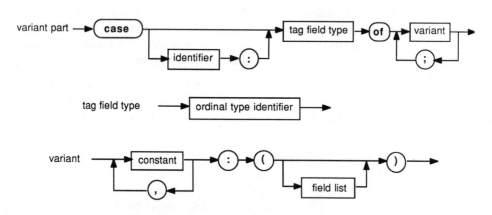

Figure 14.4: Syntax Diagram of a Variant Part

As you can see in the diagram, the same variant might be used for more than one value of the tag field. To illustrate this, suppose we add the value *TCheck* (for traveler's check) to the type *PaymentType*, and we want the same information for this form of payment as we do for a check. We could redefine the program as follows:

```
type
  PaymentType  = (Cash, Check, CreditCard);
      ...
  Purchase = record
    Amount : Real;
        ...
    Minute : 0..59;
    case  MethodOfPayment : PaymentType of
      Check, TCheck : ( CheckNumber: Integer; { Variant now serves for 2 values }
                        CheckAmt: Real;
                        LicenseNumber: string[20] );
      CreditCard    : ( Card    : CardType;
                        ExpMonth: MonthType;
                        ExpYear: YearType );
    end;                                        { record Purchase }
```

When using variant records, it is important to keep track of which variant you are using at any given moment. Despite the fact that Pascal lets you define different field names and types for different values of the tag field, it does *not* check to make sure you are using the right ones. Careless use of variant records can lead to scrambled data and disaster.

A **case** statement is ideal for handling the variants of a record:

```
case ThisPurchase.MethodOfPayment of
  Cash:  begin
            ...
         end;

  Check, TCheck:
         begin
            ...
            CheckAmt := ...etc.
            ...
         end;
  CreditCard:
         begin
            ...
            Card := ...etc.
            ...
         end;
end.
```

Free Unions: Omitting the Tag Field

The computer-science term for a variant record that includes a tag field is a *discriminated union*, which is a combination, or union, of field definitions that are discriminated from one another by the value of the tag field. Pascal also allows you to use another kind of variant record, or union, called a *free union*.

In the syntax diagram for a variant part (Figure 14.4), you may have noticed a path not mention earlier: There is an arrow that goes around the identifier (and the subsequent colon) for the tag field. This means that it is possible to define a variant part with *no* tag field, though a type must still be given.

A free union is a variant record with no tag field. Usually, it is used in one of two cases: when the correct set of fields to be used can be determined some other way than from a tag field, or when the programmer intentionally wants to look at a location in memory that is of two different types simultaneously—depending on which field name is being used. Here's an example of a free union:

```
program  FreeUnionDemo;
type
  FreeUnionRec = Record
    case  Boolean of
      False: (i: LongInt);
      True: (r: Real);
    end;
var
   num: FreeUnionRec;
begin
  num.i := 12345678;
  WriteLn(num.i,num.r);
  num.r := 3.14159;
  WriteLn(num.i,num.r);
  ReadLn
end.
```

Note that the declaration of type *FreeUnionRec* contains no constant part—only a variant part. Type *Boolean* is used in the declaration to tell the compiler that two variations are forthcoming.

In this example, variable *num* occupies 4 bytes in memory. If we choose to interpret those 4 bytes as a long integer, we select the first variant (*num.i*); to treat them as a real, use the second (*num.r*). The underlying 4 bytes don't change; only the way the program interprets them does. We'll show you how this can be useful in Part 3 of this tutorial.

Turbo Pascal Tutor for the Macintosh

Review

In this chapter, we introduced an important structured type, called records, that hold collections of variables of other types. Records consist of fields that hold these variables, with each field having a distinct name and type. Records are a natural device for making a program's data structures more like the real-world objects they represent—and more natural data structures always result in simpler, more efficient programs.

The **with** statement can be used to make referring to the fields of records easier. Variant records can save storage space by using the space in a record variable to hold more than one data object, depending on the value of a tag field.

Free unions (or variant records without tag fields) can be used when there is no need for a tag field, or for when there is a need for some advanced programming techniques.

In the next chapter, we'll discuss one more kind of structured type—the **set** type.

15

Sets

You may remember sets from an early math class. Well, Pascal sets are similar. This chapter explains how to build a set and define a set type, as well as the different set operations.

In Pascal, a set is a collection of zero or more objects of the same scalar type (called the base type). Sets have certain properties that make them especially efficient for representing certain types of information.

You may occasionally want to check whether a value of a scalar type (for example, *Integer*, *Char*, or *Boolean*) belongs to a set of values of that type. For example, suppose a spelling-checking program needs to test whether *Ch*, a variable of type *Char*, contains a vowel. With what you've learned so far about Pascal, you'd accomplish that by a long, drawn-out **if** statement:

```
if (Ch = 'A') or (Ch = 'E') or (Ch = 'I') or
   (Ch = 'O') or (Ch = 'U') then
   ...
```

Intuitively, it seems that Pascal should offer a better way than this messy approach—and it does.

To rewrite the previous test using sets, we could create a set that contains all the vowels by listing them between square brackets. Then, we could use the special set operator **in** to see if *Ch* is a "member" of that set. Using sets, the test becomes

```
if Ch in ['A','E','I','O','U'] then ...
```

which is easier to read and understand.

['A','E','I','O','U'] happens to be a set of characters, but a set can hold objects of any scalar data type. There is one restriction: The base type of the set (the type of objects contained within it) must not have more than 256 possible values. Thus, you can define a set of objects of the type *Char*, which has exactly the maximum number of possible values, or a set of objects of the subrange type 75..98. But you can *not* define a set of objects of the type *Integer*, because it would have 65,536 possible values.

Pascal sets are what mathematicians call *proper sets*. This means that no object can be contained in a set more than once, that is, ['a','b','a'] is illegal. Thus, a Pascal set can have at most 256 members. To remember whether or not an object is in a set, Pascal sets or clears a single bit in memory. A set of 256 members is only 32 (256/8) bytes long—an efficient use of storage.

Building a Set: The Set Constructor

A *set constructor* is a list of expressions of the same scalar type, separated by commas and enclosed by square brackets ([and]). If there are elements with consecutive ordinal values, you can use subrange notation, that is, two expressions separated by two periods ('..'). Here are some examples of set constructors:

```
[]                       { empty set--contains nothing }
[1,3,5,7,9]                { set of integer subrange }
['A'..'Z']                        { set of Char }
[Mon,Wed..Fri]                    { set of Days }
[Jan..Aug,Oct..Dec]             { set of Months }
```

The objects within a set constructor need not be constants. They can be any kind of expression whose result is of the base type of the set. This feature makes the use of sets even more convenient. For instance, suppose *A* is a variable of type *Char*. To construct a set that consists of all the characters from the character stored in *A* to the letter *'w'*, you could write the set constructor

```
[A..'w']
```

Of course, if there are no characters between *A* and *'w'* (that is, *A* is past *'w'* in the ASCII character set), the result is an empty set.

Defining a Set Type

To define an object of a set type, use the reserved words **set of**, followed by the name of the base type. Or, you can supply an anonymous type—usually a subrange—as the base type. Here are some examples of set types:

```
type
  CharSet = set of char;        { Set of objects of the type Char }
  MonthDays = set of 1..31;            { Set of objects of the
                                 (anonymous) subrange type "1..31" }
  DayType = (Sun, Mon, Tue, Wed, Thur, Fri, Sat);
  Days = set of DayType;            { Set of objects of DayType }
  WorkWeek = set of Mon..Fri;         { Set of objects of the
                                 (anonymous) subrange type "Mon..Fri". }
  Colors = set of (Red, Green, Blue);   { Set of objects of the
                         anonymous enumerated type (Red, Green, Blue) }
```

The syntax diagram in Figure 15.1 shows how to specify a set type.

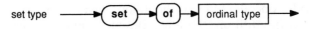

Figure 15.1: Syntax Diagram of a Set Type

Here's an example that shows a good use for sets: It makes sure that a character input from the user is a legal command for a program.

```
program CharTest;
type
  CharSet      = set of Char;
  Prompt       = string[80];
var
  Cmd          : Char;

procedure GetChar(var Ch : Char; Msg : Prompt; OKSet : CharSet);

{ Write a message, then get a character from the user. Ignore any
  character not in the set OKSet. }

begin
  Write(Msg);
  repeat
    Ch := ReadChar                { Get a character without echo }
  until Ch in OKSet;
  WriteLn(Ch)
end;

  begin
    repeat
      Getchar(Cmd,'CharTest> S)peak, C)ount, Q)uit: ',
              ['S','C','Q']);
      case Cmd of
        'S'    : WriteLn('Woof! Woof!');
```

```
      'C'   : WriteLn('1, 2, 3, 4, 5, 6, 7, 8, 9, 10')
    end
  until Cmd = 'Q'
end.
```

GetChar prompts the user with a message, then lets him or her type in a single character. It then checks to see if the letter typed is a valid command (that is, *S, C,* or *Q*). If not (note that this program is case sensitive), it waits until a valid character is entered. The **in** operator checks that the character is in the set of legal characters.

The **in** operator is only one of a large selection of operations available for use on sets, as you will see in the next section.

Set Operations

Pascal provides operators to find the union, intersection, and difference of any two sets. In addition, there are the membership operator (**in**), the subset operators (<= and >=), and the equality operators (= and <>).

Set Membership: The In Operator

In the sample program, we used the operator **in** to determine whether a character was part of a set of characters. The expression

```
Object in SetOfObjects
```

returns True if and only if *Object* is of the base type of *SetOfObjects*, and *Object* is a member of *SetOfObjects*. Note that *Object* can also be represented by an expression as long as it is of the proper type.

Set Equality and Inequality

The equality and inequality operators, = and <>, do precisely what you might expect. Two sets are equal if and only if they have exactly the same members. In setting up tests for equality and inequality, it isn't required that the sets have exactly the same base type, as long as the base types are compatible. Try to predict the output of the following program fragment:

```
program EqualityTest;
```

```
var
  Set1 : set of Char;
  Set2 : set of 'a'..'x';
begin
  Set2 := ['a', 'b', 'g'..'w'];
  Set1 := ['g'..'w', 'a', 'b'];
  WriteLn(Set1 = Set2);
  ReadLn
end.
```

If you guessed True, you are correct. Since *Set1* and *Set2* contain the same characters, they are considered to be equal. (Order doesn't matter.)

Set Union, Intersection, and Difference

The set union operator (+) returns a set that contains all members of either of its operands. The set intersection operator (*) returns the elements that are common to both of its operands. The set difference operator (-) returns the elements that are in its first operand, but not in its second.

Here are some examples that illustrate the use of these operators. Given the sets *A*, *B*, and *C*, all of the type **set of** *Char*, suppose

```
A  := ['A'..'Z']
B  := ['A', 'C', 'E', 'G']
C  := ['A'..'D', 'Z'].
```

then

```
A * B = ['A','C','E','G']        A + B = ['A'..'Z']
A * C = ['A'..'D','Z']           A + C = ['A'..'Z']
B * C = ['A','C']                B + C = ['A'..'D','E','G','Z']

A - B = ['B','D','F','H'..'Z']   B - A = []
A - C = ['E'..'Y']               C - A = []
B - C = ['E','G']                C - B = ['B','D','Z']
```

Set Inclusion Operators

The operators <= and >= have special meanings when used with sets. The >= operator returns True when its second operand is a proper subset of the first; that is, when all the elements of the second operand are included in the first. Similarly, the <= operator returns True if and only if the first operand is a proper subset of the second. Thus, given *A*, *B*, and *C* from the previous example,

```
A <= B , B => A  -->  False    B <= A , A => B -->  True
A <= C , C => A  -->  False    C <= A , A => B -->  True
B <= C , C => B  -->  False    C <= B , B => C -->  False
```

Set Disjunction

Finally, the condition of *set disjunction*, in which two sets have no members in common, can be tested by evaluating the expression

```
A * B = []
```

That is, if the set of elements in common between the two sets is the empty set, then they are disjoint.

Review

In this chapter, we explained Pascal sets: how they're constructed, how set types are defined, and the operations that can be performed on sets.

This would be a good time to study the two exercises on sets in Turbo Tutor. In the next chapter, we'll begin our discussion of pointers—the facility that allows Pascal programs to create and dispose of data objects while running.

16

Pointers and Dynamic Allocation

This chapter introduces the concept of pointers and the various pointer types. The address operator @ and the *New* procedure are also explained. Finally, it shows you how to create a linked list and to use *Dispose* to get back dynamically allocated memory.

Up to this point, whenever we've created a data structure, we've had to allocate storage for the structure in advance. In the checkbook example from Chapter 15, we reserved space for an array variable of 500 records, each holding information about a single check:

```
type
  CheckNumType =  1..500;
  MonthType    = (January, February, March, April, May, June,
                    July, August, September, October, November, December);
  DayType      = 1..31;
  PayeeType    = string[40];

  Check = record
    Amt   : Real;
    Month : MonthType;
    Day   : DayType;
    Year  : YearType;
    Payee : PayeeType;
  end;

var
  CheckBook  : array [CheckNumType] of Check;
```

Variable *CheckBook* contains space for 500 checks; its size (25,000 bytes) is an inseparable part of its type.

This approach is inflexible, and it wastes memory. If the program were called upon to balance a large checkbook, 500 records might not be enough. Conversely, if only a few checks were involved, memory would be wasted (50 bytes per unused record).

How, then, do we allocate just enough memory for our data? How can we change our minds about how much memory we need while the program is running? With Pascal's *pointer* and *dynamic memory allocation* features. Pointers are a key concept in true Macintosh programming, as explained further in Part 5 of this book, so pay close attention.

Pointers

In a single sentence, *a pointer is a variable that holds the address of a variable.* Instead of data, a pointer contains the address of data. A pointer is said to "point to" a variable. Pointers are used to access dynamically created data objects; that is, those created at run time, rather than compile time.

A few examples make this concept clearer.

Suppose, for instance, a program needs to be able to create new data objects of the record type *Check* as it runs. To do this, you'd need at least one pointer variable to keep track of check data. So, you might declare a pointer variable as follows:

```
var
   ChkPointer :^Check;
```

The notation ^*Check* is called a *pointer type* and is read as "pointer to Check." When we declare variable *ChkPointer* to be of type ^*Check*, we are saying that *ChkPointer* is a pointer, and that, moreover, it points to objects of the type *Check*. *ChkPointer* itself isn't a *Check* record, so you can't go around assigning *Check* information to it. For example, this assignment won't compile:

```
ChkPointer.amount := 99.95;
```

You can create pointer types that point to any type of data object, and you can define as many pointer variables of that type as you like. For instance, here's how to define a pointer type to point to a record of type *Check* and create a few pointers of that type:

```
type
   CheckPointerType = ^Check;     { A type of pointer which is to be
                                    used to point to objects of the type Check }
```

```
var
  CheckPointer1 : CheckPointerType; { Three pointer variables, each of which }
  CheckPointer2 : CheckPointerType; { can point to an object of type Check }
  CheckPointer3 : CheckPointerType;
```

The syntax used to specify a pointer type is shown in Figure 16.1.

Assigning to Pointer Types

As we said, you can't go around assigning *Check* fields to check pointer variables; they point to checks but aren't themselves checks. Pointers contain memory addresses—and though memory addresses at a low level happen to be binary numbers indistinguishable from long integers, it can be dangerous to blithely assign numeric values to them. So the compiler throws roadblocks in your path.

What you *can* assign to pointer types is addresses. One way to get an address is to use the address operator—the at sign (@)—on a variable. If *X* is an *Integer* variable, then @*X* represents the address in memory at which *X* is stored, and this value can be assigned to a pointer variable.

For example,

```
type
  ptr = ^Integer;
var
  N: Integer;
  P1, P2: ptr;
begin
  N := 6;          { A normal assignment to an Integer variable }
  P1 := N;    { Illegal and won't compile; the types don't match }
  P1 := @N;             { P1 now holds the address of variable N }
  P2 := P1;             { P1 and P2 "point to" the Integer value 6 }
end.
```

Dereferencing Pointers

Now it gets interesting. Pointer variables can be treated as though they were variables of the type that they point to, by simply putting a caret (^) after their identifier. This is called dereferencing the pointer. For example, continuing the pointer games from the last paragraphs:

```
type
  ptr = ^Integer;
var
```

```
     N,M: Integer;
     P1, P2: ptr;
begin
     N := 6;          { A normal assignment to an Integer variable }
     P1 := @N;                              { P1 --> N }
     WriteLn(P1^);                          { Prints 6 }
     P2 := P1;                              { P2 --> N }
     M := P2^;                     { Like saying M := N; }
     WriteLn(M);                            { Prints 6 }
     WriteLn(P2);          { Illegal--can't print addresses }
end.
```

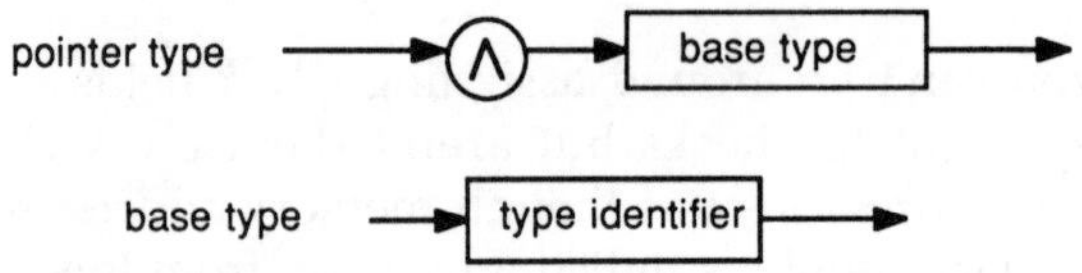

Figure 16.1: Syntax Diagram of a Pointer Type

Dynamic Allocation: The New Procedure

Let's now look at how pointers allow us to create and manipulate data objects at run time. To create a new data object, Pascal provides a routine that does the bulk of the work: the *New* procedure.

In the first example, we'll use the pointer variable *ChkPointer* (defined earlier) to create storage for a variable of type *Check*. This takes only a call to *New*:

```
New(ChkPointer);
```

This call creates a new variable of type *Check* in an unused portion of memory. Actually, "creates" may be too strong a word: We've simply caused a 50-byte area of memory to be reserved. It doesn't yet have any particular check character; it's just a range of bytes (with undefined values) that we can now treat like a *Check* record. Pointer variable *ChkPointer* is changed to point to the new variable.

So, *New* performs two operations. In addition to finding a place in memory to put a *Check* record (it knows to reserve 50 bytes, because it's smart enough to know that record type is 50 bytes long), it also assigns the address of that spot to *ChkPointer*.

What happens if we make the call *New(ChkPointer)* a second time? Well, Pascal obliges us by reserving space for yet another variable of type *Check* and changes *ChkPointer* to point to that object.

What happens to the 50-byte area previously allocated? Does it go away? No, its place in memory is reserved just as before. However, the second call to *New* overwrote the old value of *ChkPointer*, which was the only record of that variable's location. The variable is still there (that is, the 50 bytes are still allocated), but we have both literally and figuratively lost its address.

A dereferenced pointer can be used anywhere it would be legal to use an object of the type that it points to. If a pointer points to an array, then element selection braces follow immediately after the caret. For instance,

```
type
  BigArray = array [0..9999] of Integer;
var
  BigArrayPtr: ^BigArray;
  i: Integer;
begin
  New(BigArrayPtr);                { reserve 20,000 bytes }
  for i := 0 to 9999 do
    BigArrayPtr^[i] := 0;          { initialize it }
```

Similarly, if we want to write out the fifth letter in the name of the payee of a check pointed to by *ChkPointer*, we can write

```
Write(ChkPointer^.Payee[5]);
```

In fact, the convoluted notation *ChkPointer^.Payee[5]* can be used anywhere a value of type *Char* is permitted. If you can look at *ChkPointer^.Payee[5]* and see a variable of type *Char*, you're starting to think in Pascal.

Work through it:

- *ChkPointer* is a pointer.
- *ChkPointer^* is a check.
- *ChkPointer^.payee* is a **string***[40]*.
- *ChkPointer^.payee[5]* is a character.

Assigning to Pointers

Pointers, like all variables, can be assigned the value of variables of the same type, that is, of *pointers that point to the same type they do*. The assignment

```
CheckPointer2 := CheckPointer1;
```

does what you'd expect: It assigns the value of *CheckPointer1* to *CheckPointer2*, so that both point to the same data object, that is, to the same memory address. This means that if you change the information in *CheckPointer1^*, you'll simultaneously change *CheckPointer2^*.

Conversely, it's illegal to assign a pointer that points to type *X* to a pointer that points to type *Y*. The statement

```
IntPointer := CheckPointer1;
```

won't compile, even though *IntPointer* and *CheckPointer1* are both pointers. Later, we'll learn ways to relax the compiler's stance on assignments of this sort.

We've covered some rugged country so far in this chapter, so let's do a quick review.

Pointer variables are variables that hold the address of objects of some type. They are declared by putting a caret before a data type, in effect telling the compiler that they point to an object of that type. Pointer variables hold machine addresses, which under normal circumstances aren't printed out or examined directly. Pointer variables can be assigned values in one of three ways: by assigning the result of applying the address operator (@) to a variable, by the *New* procedure, or by assigning a pointer variable of the same type to them:

```
{ Three ways to assign a value to a pointer variable }
var
  P,Q,R: ^Integer;
  N: Integer;
begin
  P := @N;                          { Address operator }
  New(Q);                             { New Procedure }
  R := Q;        { Assignment from a pointer of the same type }
end ;
```

The *New* procedure allocates blocks of memory at run time. *New* is passed a pointer variable, and it finds an unused block of memory just large enough for the type of object that the pointer points to. It then assigns the address of that block to the pointer variable passed to it. A dereferenced pointer (a pointer variable followed by a caret) can be used in any statement where you'd use a variable of the type that the pointer points to.

The Special Pointer Value Nil

Pointers can produce subtle and elegant solutions to storage problems. They can also get you into trouble in a hurry:

```
program Kerpow;
var
  P: ^Integer;
begin
  P^ := 1234
end .
```

This seemingly innocent six-liner contains the seeds of utter destruction, although it will compile without error. What's wrong with it?

The compiler will generate code to write the value 1234 to memory, at the address stored in pointer variable *P*. But since we never assigned to *P* with the @ operator or by calling *New*, its value at the moment of the assignment is undefined. Like all variables in Pascal, a pointer variable can initially have any value at all. So the address to which the 1234 is written might be one of the thousands of important addresses that system routines use to keep track of the time or to read the keyboard or disk drive.

Few programs appreciate having a number dropped, bomb-like, into their midst. You may get lucky and hit an unused area of memory—or you may get unlucky and clobber an important system routine, but not see its effect until you're ready to save a text file you've been working on for an hour.

When you dereference a pointer, make sure that the pointer contains a reasonable address. This is one error that can't be checked at run time. Changing the memory location pointed to by such a pointer can alter any part of memory at all, including the operating system, your program, or its data.

To help avoid this calamity, Pascal provides a special value to which you can set a pointer as a signal that it doesn't point to anything and shouldn't be dereferenced. This value is represented by the reserved word **nil**.

Pascal's handling of pointers illuminates an important difference between Pascal and its macho cousin, C. Both languages provide pointer manipulations. In Pascal, pointer variables are considered to contain semi-imaginary values that, theoretically, can't be printed out, added, subtracted, or otherwise manipulated. In C, none of these restrictions exist. Since addresses are 4-byte binary numbers exactly like long integers, C says "Be my guest" when you assign to them directly.

Whenever you use pointers, it's good practice to set them to **nil** when you know they don't currently point to valid data, and then test pointers against **nil** before using them.

The special value **nil** can be assigned to any variable of a pointer type—regardless of the type the pointer is bound to. You can test to see whether a pointer is equal to **nil** or not by using a comparison of the form

```
if IntPointer = nil
```

or

```
if IntPointer <> nil
```

Equality and inequality are the only relational operators that can be used on pointers. Therefore, even though there are numbers lurking behind pointer variables, you can't say

```
var
  P1,P2: ^Integer;
begin
  if P1 < P2 then ...      { illegal! }
```

Pointers and Checkbook Data

Armed with what we've learned about pointers, we're ready to find better solutions to the problem of maintaining checkbook data.

One approach is to store check data with an array of pointers, one for each check. Then, as needed, create new variables to hold the check information itself. For example, consider these declarations:

```
type
  CheckNumType =  1..500;
  MonthType    = (January, February, March, April, May, June,
                  July, August, September, October, November, December);
  DayType      = 1..31;
  YearType     = 1980..2000;
  PayeeType    = string[40];

  Check = record
    Amt   : Real;
    Month : MonthType;
    Day   : DayType;
    Year  : YearType;
    Payee : PayeeType;
  end;

  CheckPointer = ^Check;

var
  CheckBook : array [CheckNumType] of CheckPointer; { Now an array of pointers }
```

In Chapter 15, array *CheckBook* was a 500-element array of records of type *Check*. Now it's a 500-element array of pointers, variables of type *CheckPointer*. How does this save space?

Remember that a record of type *Check* consumes 50 bytes of memory. A pointer, however, takes only 4 bytes. Thus, we have initially allocated only 2,000 bytes (500 * 4), instead of 25,000 bytes (500 * 50). We'll allocate space for the checks themselves only as needed. This also makes it possible to store over 8,000 checks before we come up against the 32K array limitation. (32K/4 bytes per pointer).

Before using this data structure, we should first initialize all of the elements of the *CheckBook* array to **nil**.

```
for N := 1 to 500 do
  CheckBook[N] := nil;
```

As checks are written, we call the *New* procedure on progressively higher elements of array *CheckBook*. For example, assuming *Integer* variable *CheckCount* tracks the number of checks that have been written so far, here's how to allocate a new check:

```
procedure NewCheck;
begin
  CheckCount := CheckCount + 1;
  New(Checkbook[CheckCount]);
end.
```

To access information stored on check number *N*, we dereference pointer number *N* in array *CheckBook*:

```
if CheckBook[N] = nil then
  WriteLn('No information on this check!')
else
  WriteLn('The amount of check #',N,' is ', CheckBook[N]^.Amt);
```

Again, before using it, we check that the pointer about to be dereferenced is something other than **nil**.

While this array-of-pointers-to-checks method is much more efficient than the array-of-checks approach, it still wastes space if a substantial percentage of the pointers in array *CheckBook* aren't used. Also, if the number of checks turns out to be larger than the number of pointers in *CheckBook*, we'd once again face the problem of running out of room in the array. It comes close but doesn't quite live up to the promise of a storage scheme that doesn't waste a single byte of memory, regardless of the number of checks involved.

A Second Approach: The Linked List

With some unobvious programming, it's possible to dynamically allocate not only the records, *but the pointers to them as well*. The key is a data structure built from dynamically allocated record variables held together with pointers: the *linked list*.

Using a linked list, we can string check records together like beads on a string, because each block of check information contains a pointer to the next record in the list. Thus, each time we allocate a new record, we allocate a new pointer as well, so that there is always a pointer available to point to the next object added.

Like many sophisticated operations in Pascal, linked lists are a consequence of a sophisticated data structure. Let's look at a new declaration for type *Check*, one which includes a pointer to the next check in the list.

```
type
  CheckPointer = ^Check;
  Check = record
    CheckNumber : CheckNumType;
    Amt         : Real;
    Month       : MonthType;
    Day         : DayType;
    Year        : YearType;
    Payee       : PayeeType;
    NextCheck   : CheckPointer;
  end;
```

You win a gold star if you noticed a Pascal axiom being tarnished in this example. These declarations demonstrate an exception to the rule that identifiers must be declared before they are used. We declare the pointer type *CheckPointer* before we declare the type it points to (namely *Check*), so that we can use it as the type of a field in *Check* itself.

Having defined the type *CheckPointer*, we can include a field of this type in the record type *Check* (called *NextCheck*). Each *NextCheck* field provides the link with which the checks will be strung together.

Before we can create that first check, there needs to be an anchor to which to connect the start of the linked list. Let's define a single variable of type *CheckPointer* for this purpose. We'll want to set it to **nil** to begin with, so that the program can tell that there are no items in the list.

```
var
  FirstCheck : CheckPointer;
begin
  .
  .
```

```
.
FirstCheck := nil;
.
.
.
```

Until we store the first check, pointer variable *FirstCheck* (at 4 bytes) is all the storage needed; compare this value to the 25,000 bytes and 2,000 bytes of overhead, respectively, for the previous two solutions to the check storage problem.

Adding Checks to the List

When it comes time to create a record for the first check, we use the statement

```
New(FirstCheck);
```

We've taken the first step to create our linked list. To understand the situation that exists in memory after this call, let's have another drill:

- *FirstCheck* is a pointer.
- *FirstCheck^* is a check record.
- *FirstCheck^.amount* is a real.
- *FirstCheck^.payee[5]* is a character.
- *FirstCheck^.nextCheck* is a pointer.
- *FirstCheck^.nextCheck^* is another check record, or at least, it has the potential to be. Right now, since *FirstCheck^.nextCheck* has never been assigned a value, it doesn't point to anything and can't be safely dereferenced.

We'll want to set the *NextCheck* field of the new record to **nil**, to indicate that there is no next check in the list. That's done like this:

```
FirstCheck^.NextCheck := nil;
```

As additional checks are written, we reserve storage for each new check by calling *New* with the *NextCheck* field of the record currently at the end of the chain. We make the *NextCheck* pointer of the previous check on the list point to the new check, and we set the *NextCheck* pointer of the *new* last check to **nil**. After three checks, the list looks like this:

```
              --------------
CheckBook-> (Check Info)|   --------------
            | NextCheck--|-> (Check Info)|   --------------
            --------------  | NextCheck--|-> (Check Info)|
                            --------------  | NextCheck--|-> nil
                                            --------------
```

This figure goes left to right for convenience only; there's no guarantee or requirement that all subsequent records get spots in memory higher than the previous record. In practice, they go wherever the allocation routines can find 50 free bytes.

To find a check with a particular number, we scan the list from beginning to end until we find the one we're looking for. The following shows a function that takes a check number and a pointer to a list of checks and returns a pointer to the check with that number:

```
function  FindCheck (Num: CheckNumType;
          FirstCheck : CheckPointer) : CheckPointer;

{ Given Num, the number of a check, and FirstCheck, a pointer to
  the first of a linked list of checks, return a pointer to the
  first check found on that list with the given number. If no
  check with that number is found, return nil. }

begin                                         { FindCheck }
  FindCheck := nil ;                { Start by assuming failure }
  while  FirstCheck <> nil do            { Stop if end of list }
    if  FirstCheck^.CheckNum = Num then        { Check found? }
    begin
      FindCheck := FirstCheck;{If so, set the function result and }
      Exit                     { Exit from the routine right away }
    end
    else
      FirstCheck := FirstCheck^.NextCheck;{ Number doesn't match; }
                               { point to next check, if any }
                               { Note that since FirstCheck }
                               { is not a var parameter, we }
                               { only change our local copy }
end;
```

This program uses some tricks to save memory and make the code as efficient as possible. First, since *FirstCheck* is not passed as a **var** parameter, we use it as the "moving" pointer to scan the list. (If *FirstCheck* were a **var** parameter, we couldn't change it without losing the main program's only pointer to the list.) We also use the special built-in procedure, *Exit*, to exit from the middle of the function. If we didn't have this out, we'd have to either traverse the rest of the list unnecessarily or force the loop to terminate by setting *FirstCheck* to **nil**. The use of *Exit* here is simpler and more efficient than the previously described techniques.

This process of reading through a linked list is called *traversing* the list, and it can be done with surprising quickness. Using pointer variables and linked lists results in fast programs, because they rely on a characteristic of computers that often isn't fully exploited, namely, that central processing units, like the Macintosh's processor, are inherently random-access devices. In addition to their talent for performing arithmetic, processors are absolute magicians when it comes to reading and writing memory. The processor can read from addresses millions of locations apart almost as easily as it can access adjacent addresses.

The Heap

We've learned that the *New* procedure finds a place in memory for dynamically allocated variables. For instance, if we use *New* on pointer variable *CheckPointer1* (as defined earlier), we would allocate 50 bytes for the new variable and return the address of that variable in *CheckPointer1*.

These 50 bytes come from "free space," that is, memory that isn't currently being used for anything else. When a Turbo Pascal program runs, a large chunk of memory known as the *heap* is reserved for the program's use. Depending on the amount of memory in your Macintosh and other factors (such as whether or not Switcher is around), the heap can range from a few thousand bytes to several megabytes.

Unlike the operation of the heap in most versions of Pascal, including Turbo Pascal for the IBM PC, Macintosh Turbo Pascal's heap is shared by other routines. For example, the 9-point Monaco font used by the terminal window routines resides in the heap right along with objects you create with the *New* procedure. In Part 5 of this book, we discuss more about the heap and memory management in general.

The MaxAvail Function

How can you make sure that there's enough room on the heap to allocate a variable? The predefined function *MaxAvail* gives you the size of the largest free block of space currently available on the heap. For example, suppose you'd like to create a large array:

```
type
  bigArray = array [1..16000] of Integer;
var
```

```
theArray: ^bigArray;
```

Creating an object of type *bigArray* requires that the heap have a contiguous chunk of 32,000 bytes available. *MaxAvail* tells you whether or not it does:

```
if  MaxAvail >= sizeof(bigArray) then
begin
  New(theArray)
  for  N := 1 to  16000 do                    { initialize it }
    theArray^[N] := 0
end
else
  WriteLn('Not enough memory');
```

If you don't use *MaxAvail* before attempting to declare a heap object, you run the risk that the *New* procedure will be unable to accommodate your request. If it can't find the needed memory, *New* assigns **nil** to the pointer passed to it, and testing for that value upon return is a valid detection method for successful allocation. For example, if there were only 20,000 bytes available, after

```
New(theArray);
```

theArray would have the value **nil**.

Deallocation of Dynamic Variables: Memory Management

Once *New* creates a variable, the storage allocated for it remains reserved until the program terminates, or until the space is explicitly freed with the *Dispose* procedure.

Dispose

When a dynamically allocated variable is no longer needed, call the *Dispose* procedure and pass to it a pointer to the memory block no longer needed. The memory formerly allocated to this variable is then released; the next call to *New* is free to use the deallocated block as it sees fit. For instance, to release the 50 bytes of memory allocated for a check record pointed to by variable *CheckPointer*, you would write

```
Dispose(CheckPointer);
```

Dispose complements *New*: *New* allocates space from the heap, *Dispose* gives it back. Calls to *New* are therefore usually matched by calls to *Dispose*, unless memory is to remain allocated until the program terminates (when all heap objects are destroyed automatically).

Dangling Pointers

In the process of deallocating heap space, you'd expect the *Dispose* procedure to set the pointer variable passed to it to **nil**—as it no longer points to anything reasonable—but it doesn't. For example, the value of *CheckPointer* doesn't change after a call to *Dispose*. The check record that *CheckPointer* formerly pointed to will be overwritten if the heap allocation routines see fit to put some other object there. This may or may not happen in the course of the program, depending on memory usage factors, so such problems can be hard to detect. Until it is assigned another legitimate value (or the value **nil**), *CheckPointer* points to an address in the heap that is no longer reserved.

Such a pointer is called a *dangling pointer*. Dangling pointers are every bit as dangerous as uninitialized pointers—they can destroy data, Turbo Pascal's internal data structures, or both. And if you attempt to *Dispose* an uninitialized or dangling pointer, you will almost certainly cause a crash: Memory management routines wreak havoc when told to deallocate memory that was never allocated in the first place.

Multiple Pointers to the Same Object

After using pointers for a while, you start to get brave with them. It becomes easy to think of a dereferenced pointer being exactly like a variable of that type, which it isn't.

For example, consider this code fragment:

```
var
  A,B: ^lnteger;
begin
  New(A);
  A^ := 15;        { A --> 15 }
  B := A;          { B --> 15 }
  .
  .  { In this range, we can safely assume that B^ = 15 }
  .
  WriteLn(B^);
```

```
   Dispose(A);
   .
   .  { Down here, assuming that B^ = 15 is unsafe }
   .
   WriteLn(B^);
end .
```

Depending on the amount of heap activity that has transpired since *A* was disposed, *B* may or may not point to the value *15* any more, so any integer value may be printed.

Review

In this chapter, we introduced pointers—variables that hold the addresses of other variables. We explained the notion of a pointer type, a type that is bound to the type of object it points to. We touched on the address operator, which returns the address of a variable for assignment to a pointer variable. We also explained the use of the *New* procedure to allocate anonymous variables that are referenced using pointers. We then showed how to create a linked list and how to use *Dispose* to reclaim dynamically allocated memory.

Part 5 of this book examines Macintosh heap management, including "pointers to pointers" (called *handles*) that offer even more flexible and powerful solutions to dynamic storage.

Study the exercise Pointers in Turbo Tutor at this time.

In the next chapter, we'll discuss file handling. You'll learn how to read and write disk files, and how to treat the keyboard and terminal window as special files.

17

Files

You've worked your way through dozens of programs that create and manipulate various data structures and have stored check information alone three different ways. But all of these programs have been memory based: When Chapter 16's linked-list checkbook program ends, through either normal mechanisms or a sudden power failure, the linked list and the data it holds disappear. If you had just entered 114 checks, you wouldn't appreciate having to retype the information.

How, then, can data survive the death of a program? By being stored in a *file*. A file is a named sequence of bytes that can be written from memory to a peripheral device (usually a disk drive) or vice versa.

Turbo Pascal's I/O Procedures

We've used *Read*, *Write*, *ReadLn*, and *WriteLn* to send information to the screen and read it from the keyboard. These same four procedures are employed to exchange information with a disk drive.

We've been able to use them so far without knowing anything about files, because when you don't explicitly tell these procedures what file to read or write, they automatically refer to two standard "device" files: Input (also known as the keyboard) for *Read* and *ReadLn* and Output (the screen) for *Write* and *WriteLn*. First, let's discuss in more detail the properties of these basic procedures.

Read and ReadLn

The *Read* and *ReadLn* procedures read one or more data objects from a file. Their syntax is as follows:

```
Read({FileVariable,} {Var1, Var2...VarN});
ReadLn({FileVariable,} {Var1, Var2...VarN});
```

The optional *FileVariable* parameter specifies the file that the procedure is to work with. If no file is specified, which is the way we've always used them, the keyboard becomes the source of input.

Read reads data and returns it immediately, while *ReadLn* waits for the end of a line. When reading data from the keyboard, however, both procedures wait for the end of the line, that is, for the Return key to be pressed. (If *Read* didn't wait for a return, it would have no way of knowing when you were finished.) When reading from other places, like a disk drive, *Read* doesn't wait for a return character.

Both *Read* and *ReadLn* can be called without any parameters at all, in which case the parentheses must be omitted. This causes Turbo to simply wait for Return to be pressed. If *Read* is called with a file variable but no other parameters, it skips over the next object in that file on that line. If *ReadLn* is called in the same way, it skips to the next line in the file.

Write and WriteLn

The *Write* and *WriteLn* procedures write one or more data objects to a file. Their syntax is as follows:

```
Write({FileVariable,} {, Var1, Var2...VarN});
WriteLn({FileVariable,} {, Var1, Var2...VarN});
```

The *Write* procedure writes the objects listed to the indicated file. *WriteLn* does the same and follows the information with a carriage return. The optional parameter *FileVariable* again specifies the file the procedure is to work with. If no file is specified, the output is sent to the screen.

When *Write* is called with no parameters, or with only a file variable as a parameter, nothing happens. However, when *WriteLn* is called with no parameters, a new line is started on the screen. When *WriteLn* is called with only a file variable as a parameter, a new line is started in that file (that is, a carriage return is output to that file).

As with *Read* and *ReadLn*, when *Write* or *WriteLn* is called without parameters, the parentheses must be omitted.

Controlling Numeric Formatting: Write Parameters

A *write parameter* is an argument to the *Write* and *WriteLn* procedures that contains formatting information piggybacked onto the expression to be output. This formatting information takes the form of integers separated by colons. For example,

```
WriteLn(N:8);
```

outputs the string equivalent of integer variable N at the current cursor position, with leading spaces added as necessary to pad the output to eight characters. For example, if $N = 1$, then seven spaces are added; if $N = 1000$, four spaces are added; for $N = -1$, six spaces are appended. If the width data provided after the colon is 0, or less than the minimum required to display the value, then it displays in exactly as many columns as necessary. For example, *Write(N:1)*, where *N=5000*, displays 5000 with no appended spaces. Write parameters make it easy to produce neatly aligned tables.

```
for N := 0 to 10
  WriteLn{N:8,N*25:8)
```

produces

```
        0         0
        1        25
        2        50
        3        75
        4       100
        .
        .
        .
```

For controlling the presentation of values of type *Real*, two integers of formatting information may be specified. The first, as for integers, indicates the total width of the field; the optional second, the number of places to the right of the decimal point to be displayed. For example, if real variable *Pi* = 3.14159, then:

```
WriteLn(Pi:10:2);
```

produces

```
3.14
```

and

```
WriteLn(Pi:10:4);
```

results in

```
3.1416
```

As with integer expressions, the first value indicates field width. If the second (decimal point position) value is omitted, then the real is output in standard floating-point notation. For example,

```
WriteLn(Pi:10);
```

produces

```
3.1e+0
```

For more information about write parameters, see the description of the `Write` procedure in the Input/Output chapter of the Turbo Pascal reference manual.

File Types

Files, like all Pascal data objects, have types. Like array types, file types consist of a series of elements. Unlike arrays, however, only one element is available at a time, and the length of the series isn't part of the type. Instead, file size is limited only by external factors (such as the capacity of a disk).

The formal syntax of a file type is similar to that of arrays and sets (see Figure 17.1). For example, to access a file consisting of a series of integers, declare it as follows:

```
var
  MyDiskFile : file of Integer;
```

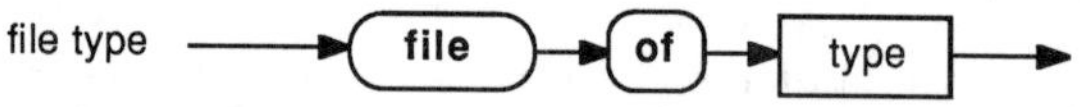

Figure 17.1: Syntax Diagram of File Type

Files can have as their *component* type any Pascal type, with the exception of another file type. In other words, Turbo Pascal permits files of arrays, arrays of arrays, arrays of files, arrays of records, records of arrays, files of records, and many, many other permutations—but *not* files of files. Here are some sample file-type definitions:

```
type
  CheckFile = file of Check;      { File of objects of type Check }
  SetFile = file of set of Char;      { File of objects of the
                                 anonymous type "set of Char" }
  ScreenFile = file of array[1..25] of string[80];
```

```
{ File in which each record consists of 25 strings
  of max length 80 (possibly used to hold copies of
  a terminal window) }
```

Because so-called text files (files consisting of printable ASCII characters segmented into lines by carriage return characters) are especially common, Turbo provides a predefined identifier named *Text* to represent this variety of file. File type *Text* is compatible with many Mac applications, including the Turbo Pascal editor, MacWrite, Microsoft Word, and the Sidekick Notepad+. (Note that by default Word and MacWrite don't produce text files; you have to ask for one specifically, using the Text Only option of the Save as... dialog box.)

The idea of text files didn't begin with Macintosh; a communications program lets you exchange text files with practically any computer that has a phone number. In fact, the text that makes up this book originated on an IBM Personal Computer, was edited extensively on a Macintosh Plus, and returned to an IBM Personal Computer for final typesetting.

Reading and Writing Text Files

A text file usually holds readable information; that is, information that makes sense to a human being once it has gone through a printer or text-editing program. The characters within a text file are divided into *lines*, which are sequences of ASCII characters; the end of each line is marked by the control-character carriage return (ASCII code 13). Indeed, it's the return characters that make the lines lines.

Text files imported from non-Macintosh computers tend to throw in a linefeed character (ASCII code 10) with every carriage return. Turbo Pascal's editor shows linefeeds as box characters; typically, at the start of each line in the file except the first.

To delete these linefeeds, select the first box character, then choose Change... from the Search menu. This option automatically uses whatever's highlighted as the suggested Find string, which is especially handy in this instance because there's no way to generate a linefeed character from the keyboard. Once the first linefeed (box character) is located, click the All button and in a second or two your file will be purged of this anachronistic control character.

A program reads and writes text files using the same four procedures for screen and keyboard I/O: *Read*, *Write*, *ReadLn*, and *WriteLn*. Turbo Pascal also has a number of auxiliary functions to expedite text file processing.

Read and ReadLn with Text Files

It is convenient to think of files as having an associated *file pointer* that indicates the next object in the file. When a file is being written, that pointer always points just past the end of the last data to be written to the file. When the file is being read, it points to the next object to be read (if any).

When *Read* is called with a text file and a variable as its arguments, it reads the next object (if any) on the current line of the file into the variable, and advances the file pointer past that object. However, when the data on that line is exhausted, *Read* won't advance the file pointer to the next line, that is, to the first item after the terminating carriage return character. Attempting to use *Read* at the end of a line in a text file has no effect at all; you must call the procedure *ReadLn* to advance to the next line (if it exists).

ReadLn moves the file pointer to the next line immediately after it reads the information it requires from the current line. Any other information on the line is ignored.

Eof, Eoln, SeekEof, and SeekEoln

The *Eof* and *Eoln* (end of file and end of line, respectively) functions are used to discover whether the program has read up to the end of a file, or up to the end of a line. Both return boolean values and allow the creation of **while** loops that systematically process text files line by line.

```
Eof(FileVariable);
Eoln(TextFileVariable);
SeekEof(TextFileVariable);
SeekEoln(TextFileVariable);
```

Eof returns True when the file pointer is at the end of the file. *Eoln* indicates whether the file pointer is at the end of a line in a text file and, consequently, has no meaning for non-text files. When *Eof* is True for a given text file, *Eoln* is also True.

SeekEof and *SeekEoln* have the same syntax as *Eof* and *Eoln* and only have meaning for text files. They skip over spaces and tabs before they test for the end of the file or line. These functions are useful when you don't know the number of objects on a line or in a file. With them, you can avoid getting the *Read* procedure stuck at the end of a line or a file, and find out whether there is another object available or not. You can then call *ReadLn* to finish processing the file, if necessary.

The Macintosh File System

In order to carry out file operations, Macintosh Turbo Pascal programs get help from a number of built-in ROM routines known collectively as the *File Manager* (or simply *file system*). In Part 5 of this book, we'll learn how to use the built-in file routines directly; for now, we'll describe basic file-system conventions.

As citizens of a Mac file-system world, the files you process with Turbo Pascal programs must abide by Mac file-system rules. Two entities are involved: Turbo Pascal's file-related commands, and the ways and means of the file system. To use files, you must know something about each. First, some terminology.

Volumes

A *volume* is a named medium for storing files. For example, a floppy disk represents a single volume (that is, there is a one-to-one correspondence between volumes and floppy disks). Some hard disks are formatted as single volumes; others are organized as multiple volumes; see your owner's manual for information about your particular drive.

The beauty of the volume scheme is that an application program doesn't have to know anything about the physical characteristics of the storage device to use the files it contains. Whether a volume is a single- or double-sided floppy, a 20-megabyte hard disk interfaced through the external floppy port, a 2-megabyte partition of a hard disk attached to the scuzzy (SCSI) port, or a RAM disk, it behaves like a volume.

Files

Files are named groupings of bytes, stored in volumes.

The Macintosh file system is generous almost to a fault in file naming. Where many computers restrict file names to six to eight characters followed by a period and optional three-character extension, the Mac permits file names up to thirty-one characters long, including any printable character you can generate from the keyboard, including spaces but *excepting colons (:).* The file system retains the case of the file name, but case distinctions aren't otherwise significant. For example, file Screen Data will be stored as Screen Data, but attempts to open it under the names SCREEN DATA and screen data will succeed. But Screen Data (two spaces between the *n* and the *D*) won't!

Colons and File Names: Path Names

Colons (:) have special significance to the file system. If a file name provided in a *Reset* or *Rewrite* statement contains no colons, then the file is assumed to be in the default volume, that is, the volume from which the application was launched. If one or more colons are included, then the file name specifies the directory path, starting with a volume name, that leads to the file. (As we will learn shortly, these procedures form a bridge between the Mac file system and Pascal.)

The Mac uses *path names* to describe a specific file on a specific volume. A path name consists of a file name optionally preceded by a volume name and a colon. For example,

```
Turbo Work Disk:My File
Startup:MyFile
```

On all but the oldest Macintoshes, the File Manager supports a hierarchical file system (HFS). This scheme organizes files in a given volume into an arrangement resembling the root system of a tree, in which at any level files can be either normal files or subdirectories (containing other files and potentially other subdirectories). The Finder represents subdirectories with the folder metaphor. Figure 17.2 shows a schematic of the hierarchical scheme.

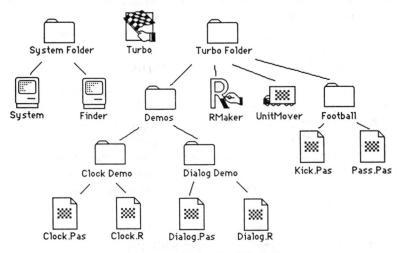

Figure 17.2: The Hierarchical File System

To locate a file on an HFS volume, you list each of the folders (directories) that leads to the file, separated by colons, starting with name of the volume and ending with the name of the file. For example, the specification

```
Hard Disk:Turbo Pascal:Data Files:MyFile
```

refers to file *MyFile*, which is in folder *Data Files* of folder *Turbo Pascal* on volume *Hard Disk*. To describe a file within a subfolder of the current folder—without specifying just what the current folder is—specify the partial path name with a leading colon. For example, if the current folder is *Hard Disk:Turbo Pascal*, then the partial path name

```
:Examples:CheckBook.Pas
```

refers to file *CheckBook.Pas* in folder *Hard Disk:Turbo Pascal:Examples*.

Types and Creators

In addition to their name and contents, Macintosh files have two attributes that control how they are treated by the file system in general and by the Finder in particular: a *type* (not to be confused with a type in the Pascal sense) and a *creator*.

A file's type is a four-character string describing, in a general way, the type of data it contains. For example, the files created by MacPaint are type *'PNTG'* (painting) and those created by Microsoft Word default to type *'WDBN'* (Word binary format). It's the file type that causes only files of type *'TEXT'* to show up when you choose Open... from Turbo Pascal's File menu.

Since the editor can only work with files of type *TEXT*, it tells the Toolbox's *GetFile* routine to filter out files with any other type. Similarly, in MacPaint, when you choose Open, you only see files that MacPaint can work with.

An application (that is, executable programs), be it Turbo Pascal or the result of compiling a program to disk with Turbo Pascal, always has the type *APPL* (application). It is this signature that tells the Finder that programs are programs—that it should load and give them control when they are double-clicked.

You're free to create your own unique types. For example, a data file for an accounting application could have type *ACCT*.

Creator

Files also have a four-character signature called a creator. This information is used by the Finder to determine what icon it should draw to represent the file, as well as what application to start should that file be opened. For example, the files created by the Turbo Pascal editor have type *TEXT* and creator *TPAS*. So, Turbo Pascal is started automatically when you double-click one of its source files from the Finder—even though, internally, the editor's files have the same structure as a MacWrite file of type *TEXT*.

Applications can use anything for a creator; often, it's the initials of the programmer (to avoid potential conflicts, commercial applications should have their creator strings approved by Apple). We'll learn more about types and creators in Part 5.

Data Forks and Resource Forks

You may have heard rumors about how Mac files are divided into two parts, a resource fork and a data fork. In Part 5, we describe this peculiar dichotomy in more detail. For now, note that the files you create and access with Turbo Pascal store and read data from the data fork only; their resource forks are always empty.

Creating a Text File with Turbo Pascal

Here's a simple program that creates and writes a few lines to a file. It demonstrates the Big Three of text file processing:

1. How to open a file (prepare it for writing)
2. How to write text to it
3. How to close it (tell the file system you're finished with it)

```
program CreateTest;
var
  TheFile : Text;            { Text is a predeclared file type }
  Line    : string[255];
  N : Integer;

begin
  Rewrite(TheFile,'MyFile.Text');
  WriteLn(TheFile, 'Hello, World!');
  WriteLn(TheFile, 'This is my first file.');
  for N := 1 to 10 do
    WriteLn(TheFile, N:2);
  WriteLn(TheFile, '------End of file------');
  Close(TheFile)
end.
```

Type in and execute *CreateTest*. When it executes, you won't see anything on the screen; its *WriteLn* statements are directed at text file *MyFile.Text* (which is known to the program as *TheFile*). Instead, there will be a brief flurry of disk activity. When the program finishes, use Turbo Pascal's Open command to peek inside the file you just created. The editor won't know the difference between *MyFile.Text* and files created by hand; they both have the same *'TEXT'* type signature—and, at Finder level, the same icon. Here's what you'll see in *MyFile.Text*:

```
Hello, World!
This is my first file.
 1
 2
 3
 4
 5
 6
 7
 8
 9
10
------End of file------
```

As we've mentioned, one of the better things about text files is that they make sense to human beings. This file contains exactly what the terminal window would have contained had this program's *WriteLn* statements been sent to the screen rather than a file.

Let's work our way through this program statement by statement.

Rewrite

The first step in file operations is opening the file. In this case, opening also means creating the file. This is accomplished by the two-parameter *Rewrite* procedure, specifying the file variable and the name of the file to create.

```
Rewrite(TheFile,'MyFile.Text');
```

Rewrite creates an empty file with the file system name you specify in the second argument. Had we used a name like *'startup:examples:MyFile.Text'*, we could have simultaneously specified the folder in which MyFile.Text would be created. As it is, without path name information, the file is created in the current (default) folder.

Note well the distinction between a Pascal file variable (TheFile) and a Macintosh file system name (MyFile.Text). They aren't the same. The file system name is only used once; in subsequent operations involving this file, we refer to it with the Pascal variable (TheFile) that represents it.

Note that some other Pascals, including the IBM version of Turbo Pascal, perform the *Rewrite* operation in two steps, first using the *Assign* procedure to connect a file system name with a file variable, and then *Rewrite*. Since these statements must always be used in pairs, Macintosh Turbo Pascal simplifies things (slightly) by performing both operations in a single step.

Rewrite creates files. In a moment, we'll learn about the *Reset* procedure, which opens existing files. If a file with the name specified in a call to *Rewrite* exists already, it is deleted. So, use this command with care, or you're liable to *Rewrite* a file containing something you don't want to lose.

After the *Rewrite*, an empty file named *MyFile.Text* is created in the default folder—the volume and folder from which you launched Turbo Pascal (or to which you have recently saved or opened a file).

Sending Text to TheFile

After the *Rewrite*, any call to *Write* or *WriteLn* that specifies file variable *TheFile* sends text to file *MyFile.Text*, exactly as though it were the terminal window.

```
WriteLn(TheFile, 'Hello, World!');
WriteLn(TheFile, 'This is my first file.');
```

Since we used *WriteLn* and not *Write*, a carriage return control character is sent after the last character of each line. This same carriage return character is sent to the terminal window by "normal" *WriteLn*s (that is, those that don't specify a file variable); the terminal emulation routines built into Turbo Pascal know to interpret this particular character as a signal that the cursor should be moved to the left edge of the window and down a notch (start a new line), rather than representing a character for display.

The loop

```
for N := 1 to 10 do
    WriteLn(MyFile, N:2);
```

writes out ten lines of text, each line containing the ASCII equivalent of the integers 1 through 10 and ending with a return. Note the use of a *Write* parameter (*N:2*) to cause single-digit values of *N* to be padded with a space; this keeps the column of numbers even.

Close

The *Close* procedure performs the third and final step in file processing, terminating the relationship between variable *MyFile* and the disk file *MyFirst.Text*.

```
Close(TheFile)
```

Closing a file also helps to ensure that information it contains is properly updated by file system routines. If we tried to perform another *WriteLn* to *MyFile* after closing, an I/O error would result (more on I/O errors in a bit).

Now exit to the Finder and locate *MyFirst.Text*. What sort of icon does it have? Use the Get Info function to learn more about it. Do its length and creation times seem reasonable? How does the Finder know that *MyFirst.Text* is a Turbo document? If you double-click its icon, what happens?

Reading a Text File

Now let's look at a program for getting text back out of *MyFirst.Text*.

```
program ReadTest;
var
  aFile : Text;
  Line  : string[255];
  LineCounter : Integer;

begin
  Reset(aFile,'MyFile.Text');
  LineCounter := 0;
  while not Eof(aFile) do
  begin
    LineCounter := LineCounter + 1;
    ReadLn(aFile, Line);
    WriteLn('Contents of line ', LineCounter:2, ' --> ', Line);
  end;
  Close(aFile);
  ReadLn
end.
```

ReadTest uses the *Reset* procedure, not *Rewrite*, to open *MyFile.Text*. Using *Rewrite* would be disastrous, because when it discovers that a file with that name already exists, the file would be erased and a new, empty file created. Remember: Use *Rewrite* to create and write to a new, empty text file; use *Reset* to read an existing file.

The program then enters a loop. With each pass, *ReadLn* loads one line of the file into string variable *Line*. The line count and contents are then written to the terminal window.

The loop controlled by **while not** *EoF(aFile)* **do** is an especially convenient structure for processing text files. This loop statement can be imaginatively read as "While not at the end of MyFile do..." It automatically sees to it that we process exactly as many lines as there are in the file, whether there are none or thousands. *EOF(MyFile)* returns True only when Myfile has been totally exhausted of lines. Therefore **not** *EOF(MyFile)* is true as long as it does contain one or more lines.

As before, *Close* tells the file system that we won't be working with this file any more.

Random-Access Files

Text files are suitable for applications in which it is natural to process data one line after another, from the first to the last. For example, if you were writing a Pascal compiler, text files would be ideal for inputting source programs and perhaps outputting a listing.

For applications that must read and write data from the same file, however, the one-way trait of text files renders them less than ideal. For example, to store checkbook data, you'd have to read in all the existing data at once at the start of the program, work with it in memory (preferably in a linked list) as the program runs, and, just before the user quits, write it all back out. This approach works and, depending on the amount of data to be stored and the availability of heap space, may even work well.

Text files have additional disadvantages. Numbers that are normally stored in memory in binary form are represented on disk in decimal form, that is, as sequences of ASCII digits, plus and minus signs, decimal points, and Es. Before numbers can be written to or read from a text file, they must be converted from their internal binary form to ASCII and vice versa. This translation process takes time. If the resulting file isn't going to be read by a human being, the time has been wasted.

Because the lines of a text file can be of varying lengths, the only way to find the next line is to read the previous one to its end. Thus, text files are inherently sequential. The objects in the file must be read and written in order: To read line 9741, one must work through the first 9740.

Turbo Pascal lets you create files without this restriction. So-called typed files consist of a sequence of objects of a fixed length, like check records. Objects in typed files don't have to be read in sequence, because the position of any object in the file can be calculated by multiplying the size of an object by the number of objects that come before it. In other words, if we want to look at check 472, we know that it begins at byte position 472 * 50 in the file. This knowledge permits us to go directly to that point to get information, without reading any of the others. Because records within them can be accessed in any order, typed files are also called *random-access* files.

In typed files, numeric data is stored exactly as it appears in memory; no translation is necessary. This saves processing time both when the file is written and when it is read. It also (usually) saves space. However, a human being won't have much luck interpreting the contents of a random file, should it somehow be printed out. Such is life.

Properties of Random-Access Files

Many of the operations that apply to text files also apply to random-access files. For instance, the procedures *Reset*, *Rewrite*, and *Close* work exactly the same on random-access files as does the function *Eof*. Others work essentially the same, but with restrictions. For example, *Read* and *Write* work on random files, but can't be used without a second parameter as they can be with text files. For example, *Read(filevar)*, where *filevar* is a text file, causes the file pointer to skip to the next object on the line. The same operation for a random file doesn't make sense, because there are no lines. Similarly, *ReadLn* and *WriteLn* have no meaning for random files.

When a random-access file is opened, the file pointer is positioned at the beginning of the file, just as it is in a text file. If successive reads or writes are performed on the file, the file is accessed sequentially (the file pointer advances to the next record after each operation). Unlike text files, however, random-access files allow either read or write operations to be performed at any time. Furthermore, by using the *Seek* procedure, it is possible to read or write the components of the file in any order.

The Seek Procedure

The *Seek* procedure is the key to taking advantage of the random-access quality of typed files. *Seek* allows you to position the file pointer at the beginning of any component of a file, so that the next read or write operation is performed on that component (or, as they are more commonly known, *record*). The syntax of the *Seek* procedure is as follows:

```
Seek(FileVariable, RecordNumber);
```

where *FileVariable* is a random file and *RecordNumber* is a long integer expression. The first record of a file is considered to be record 0, and the last is the size of the file (in records, minus 1). If we use procedure *MakeCheckFile* to create a file of checks, we could get the information on check *CheckNumber* by writing

```
Seek(CheckFile, CheckNumber - 1);
Read(CheckFile, ThisCheck);
```

(Assuming there's exactly one record for every check number, the variables are all defined and the file is open.)

A random-access file can be expanded simply by writing new records at the end of the file, that is, with the file pointer pointing just past the end of the last component. To position the file pointer at this location, you can read through the file until the *Eof* function returns True. Better yet, you can use Turbo's predeclared function *FileSize* along with the *Seek* procedure to move the file pointer directly to the end. *FileSize* returns a long integer representing the number of components in a file; therefore, to append new records to the end of the file, you can perform the call

```
Seek(FileVariable, FileSize(FileVariable));
```

and then write the new information.

The FilePos Function

The *FilePos* function, which works only on random-access files, returns the number of the component at which the file pointer is currently positioned as a long integer. The first component, or record, of a file is considered to have the number 0. The file must be open at the time of the call.

```
FilePos(FileVariable);
```

Creating a Random File

Suppose, just for the sake of argument, that you're writing a program to maintain your checkbook. To store the data, you could use a random-access file in which each record contains the data for a check, so that the number of checks you could record would be limited only by the size of your disk. To do this, you'd first define the record type for a check, then create a file with that type as its component type:

```
program CheckFile;

type
  CheckNumType =  1..10000;
  MonthType    = (January, February, March, April, May, June,
                  July, August, September, October, November,
                  December);
  DayType      = 1..31;
  YearType     = 1980..2000;
  PayeeType    = string[40];

  Check = record
    CheckNum : CheckNumType;
```

```
   Amt    : Real;
   Month  : MonthType;
   Day    : DayType;
   Year   : YearType;
   Payee  : PayeeType;
 end;

var
  CheckFile : file of Check;
  ThisCheck : Check;
```

Given these definitions and declarations, here's a routine to get checkbook information from the user and write it into a file:

```
procedure MakeCheckFile;
var
  MonthNumber : 1..12;

begin
  Rewrite(CheckFile,'Checkbook.Data');
  with ThisCheck do repeat
    Write('Enter check number (0 to exit): ');
    ReadLn(CheckNum);
    if CheckNum = 0 then
    begin
      Close(CheckFile);
      Exit;
    end;
    Write('Month (1-12): ');
    ReadLn(MonthNumber);
    Month := MonthType(MonthNumber - 1);
    Write('Day (1-31): ');
    ReadLn(Day);
    Write('Year (1980 - 2000): ');
    ReadLn(Year);
    Write('Payee (40 characters max): ');
    ReadLn(Payee);
    Write(CheckFile, ThisCheck);
  until False;
end;
```

MakeCheckFile is built around an endless loop (everything between the **repeat** and **until** False statements), with an *Exit* statement in the middle to get out. This prevents us from having to use a more awkward structure (such as an **if** statement, plus another test in the **until** at the bottom of the loop).

The technique used for reading in the month demonstrates *type coercion*, which is an extension to Standard Pascal that circumvents Pascal's rigid typing rules (avoiding nasty Type Mismatch errors) when inputting defined scalar types. In the statements

```
ReadLn(MonthNumber);
Month := MonthType(MonthNumber - 1);
```

we read in the month as an *Integer* subrange and convert it to the enumerated type *Month* (January..December) for storage in the record. Alternatively, we could have used a long **case** statement:

```
case MonthNumber of
  1: Month := January;
  2: Month := February;
  .
  .
  .
  12: Month := December;
end;
```

But type coercion is simpler and more efficient. Since all scalar variables are represented the same way internally (as an integer from 0 to *n*), Turbo Pascal lets you convert from one scalar type to another by temporarily suspending type checking. We indicate the type that we want the value to have by using the name of that type as if it were a function; in this case, *MonthType(MonthNumber –1)*. This converts the number *MonthType-1* to the object of the type *MonthType* with the same ordinal value, giving us the result we need.

At run time, there's no conversion involved. Type coercion just reassures the compiler that we know what we're doing in making an apparently nonsensical assignment of an integer to a month.

Miscellaneous File Routines

You can delete files from the disk by calling

```
Erase(filename);
```

where *filename* is a string expression representing a file system name, optionally including a folder path name. This is equivalent to dragging a file to the trash can icon from the Finder and choosing Empty Trash from the Special menu.

To rename a file, call

```
Rename(oldName, newName);
```

where *oldName* and *newName* are both string expressions.

Talking to Your Computer's Peripherals: Device I/O

In this section, we'll explore how you can use file operations to communicate with the keyboard, screen, and printer.

Logical Devices

Turbo Pascal supports *logical devices*, that is, special file names that are used to treat the keyboard, screen, and printer as though they were files of type *Text*. These files are predeclared and, as befits their special status, don't need to be opened with *Reset*, *Rewrite*, or *Closed*.

Turbo Pascal recognizes the logical devices *Console* and *Printer*. For example, this program sends text to a printer:

```
program PrinterOutput;
uses PasPrinter;
begin
  WriteLn(Printer,'this is a test');
end.
```

We'll learn more about the **uses** statement in Chapter 30; for now, all you need to know is that a **uses** clause adds capability to Turbo Pascal that isn't there otherwise. In the case of program *PrinterOutput*, it brings the ability to work with the predefined device file named Printer.

Advanced Keyboard Handling: KeyPressed and ReadChar

In certain applications, you want a program to continue to run while it is waiting for user input. For instance, in an arcade-style game, you want the invaders to continue to advance while the program tests to see if a key has been pressed.

So far, the input methods we've described are of the "blocking" type; the program is prevented from doing any other tasks while it is waiting for input. When you execute the statement

```
Read(C);
```

(where *C* is type *Char*), execution stops until the user types a character and a return. The *ReadChar* function performs the same action without requiring a return, or putting anything on the screen

```
C := ReadChar;
```

although *ReadChar*, too, stops the action until a key is pressed. How can you avoid this? By not making the call to *ReadChar* until you know that there is a character waiting to be read. For this reason, Turbo Pascal provides the boolean function *KeyPressed*.

KeyPressed returns True only if a character is ready to be read from the keyboard. The following routine, *CheckCommand*, is an example of how to use it. *CheckCommand* might be called periodically from a game program to see if a key has been pressed, and if so, act on it.

```
procedure CheckCommand;
var
  Cmd           : Char;
  begin
    if KeyPressed then
    begin
      Cmd := ReadChar;             { read key w/out echo }
    case Cmd of
        .
        .                              { Handle commands }
        .
      otherwise Write(^G);        { beep at illegal cmd }
    end
  end
end;
```

I/O Error Handling

Even perfectly written programs must deal with the unpleasant prospect of run-time errors due to I/O problems. You can test your code until Zaire freezes over, but if a user accidentally deletes or moves a file the program expects to open and use, something's got to give.

What happens when a program tries to *Reset* a nonexistent file? To find out, key in and execute this program:

```
program CantFind;
var
  aFile: Text;
begin
```

```
    Reset(aFile,'A Non-Existent File');
    Close(aFile);
end.
```

Running this program produces a run-time error alert. The bomb results from the inability of Turbo's file-handling library routines to find a file named *A Non-Existent File* in the default folder. When you resume your way back to Turbo Pascal, it declares that an `Input/Output Check fail error` has occurred and points to the *Reset* statement as the culprit. Had this program been launched from the Finder, you'd have no choice but to return to the Finder.

Once interrupted by an I/O error, any work in progress by a program can't be completed. This sort of behavior is okay for short, experimental programs, but for real software with real users it can cause data stored in memory (and time and effort) to be lost. This can make users angry.

To provide control over this situation, Turbo Pascal lets you disable these error messages and handle the error condition yourself. For example, if a program discovered that it hadn't found a file, it could prompt the user to insert a disk containing the file or at least give him or her some options about how to proceed.

To turn off I/O error checking (which is on by default), use the $I compiler directive. {$I-}, along with function *IOResult*, lets you build "bulletproof" programs, that is, programs that always do the smart thing, even when given improper user input and uncooperative hardware.

For example, suppose your program asks the user for the name of a file to read. There's always a chance that the user could mistype the file name, or that the disk with that file might not be in the drive. To keep the program from stopping immediately as a result of such an error, you could write

```
var
    inFile: Text;
    inFileName: string[80];
{$I-}
Write('Enter input file:  ');
ReadLn(InFileName);
Reset(InFile,InFileName);
{$I+}
```

Simply turning off the standard response to I/O errors doesn't solve the problem—in fact, it's made things worse. Now you've got a program that thinks it's opened a file but hasn't. Somehow the program needs to find out that something has gone wrong so that it can take appropriate action.

Turbo Pascal Tutor for the Macintosh

To detect errors, Turbo Pascal provides the built-in integer function *IOResult*. *IOResult* returns a numeric code that indicates the success or failure of the last I/O operation. If successful, *IOResult* returns a value of 0; otherwise, the code indicates what the problem was. If you were to rewrite the previous example using *IOResult*, you might come up with something like this:

```
program OpenTest;
var
  infilename: string[50];
  InFile: Text;
begin
  {$I-}
  repeat
     Write('Enter input file:  ');
     ReadLn(InFileName);
     Reset(InFile,InFileName)
  until IOResult = 0;
  {$I+}
end.
```

Note that *IOResult* only returns a nonzero code once for a given error. Successive calls to *IOResult* will return 0 until another error occurs. Also, if an error does occur, your program must call *IOResult* before attempting additional I/O. If you continue to do I/O on a file when *IOResult* has returned a nonzero result for that file, unpredictable (that is, bad) results may occur.

If all this error handling seems like a lot of trouble, you're right. It's not unusual for programs to devote more code to error handling than to the file operations themselves.

The following program demonstrates I/O error-handling techniques. You may want to adapt it for use in your own programs.

```
program MyProgram;
var
  IOErr : Boolean;
type
  Prompt       = string[80];

procedure Error(Msg : Prompt);
{ Write error Msg out on line 24 and wait for a key }
var
  Ch     : Char;
begin
  GoToXY(1,24); ClearEol;
  Write(^G, Msg, '--Press any key to continue...');
repeat until KeyPressed
end;

procedure IOCheck;
```

```
{ Check for I/O error; print message if needed }
var
  IOCode  : integer;
begin
  IOCode := IOResult;
  IOErr := (IOCode <> 0);
  if IOErr then begin
    case IOCode of
      -33   : Error('Volume directory full');
      -34   : Error('Volume is full');
      -35   : Error('Volume doesn''t exist');
      -36   : Error('Disk I/O Error');
      -37   : Error('Bad file or volume name');
      -38   : Error('File not open');
      -43   : Error('File not found');
      -44   : Error('Volume is hardware write protected');
      otherwise
        Error('Unknown I/O error');
    end { case }
  end {if IOErr}
end;

var
  aFile: Text;
begin
{$I-}
  Reset(aFile, 'NonExistent.Text'); IOCheck;
  if IOErr then {...}
end.
```

Procedure *IOCheck* is designed to be called after every I/O operation and does a number of good things. First, it calls *IOResult* and recognizes any error. Second, it sets the global flag *IOErr*, so that other parts of the program can quickly tell whether or not there has been an error and can act accordingly. Third, it prints out an error message at the bottom of the terminal window, pausing until the user hits any key. Finally, it uses the **otherwise** clause of the **case** statement to handle any undefined I/O errors.

Review

In this chapter we introduced files, a mechanism through which a Pascal program can communicate with the outside world. We discussed procedures, functions, and techniques for handling two basic categories of files: text files and random access (typed) files. Finally, we discussed I/O error checking, and how to handle I/O errors within a program.

There are two file exercises in Turbo Tutor: ReadText and WriteText.

18

Units

Pascal was designed as a teaching language, and early versions ran only on large mainframe computers. While most of Professor Wirth's efforts apply beautifully to the Macintosh (a machine barely dreamed of in 1970), he left out some facilities needed in personal-computer software development, such as decent string and file-handling tools. Standard Pascal also has characteristics that make it less than ideal for tackling large programming projects.

This chapter first shows you how to use the $Include compiler directive when writing large programs. It then introduces and explains units, an important extension of Turbo Pascal.

Pascal and Big Programs

As originally defined, a Pascal source program consists of a single file: a continuous stream of text, from the opening **program** to the closing **end**. This scheme works well for short programs but less well for large ones.

It's not unusual for Pascal source programs to be thousands of lines long. A 10,000-line, 400K source file (180 pages printed out) poses a number of pragmatic problems. For one thing, a 400K disk file is unwieldy. It doesn't fit on a single-sided disk, and it takes an editor a long time to load and save—if it even consents to work with a file this large. Within the editor, Find operations are sluggish, and microscopic movements of the scroll box move you hundreds of lines. A programmer can get lost in a big file ("Where'd that procedure go?").

In large programs, the list of global variables, types, and constants gets so long you forget what some are for, even with comments. Hundreds of procedures and functions accumulate. Furthermore, a long program threatens to exceed one or more of the compiler's internal limits, such as symbol table size. (A symbol table stores the name and other information about identifiers encountered during compilation.) 10,000 lines of code represent a lot of identifiers.

These problems notwithstanding, the worst thing about working with big source programs is that *they take a long time to compile*. MPW Pascal takes every bit of five minutes to compile 10,000 lines. Even Turbo Pascal takes almost a minute.

No matter how trivial a change you make to a 10,000-line program, even if it's just adding a pesky semicolon to the 9,741st line, you have to recompile the whole thing to see the effect of that change. If you didn't add the semicolon correctly, you won't find out until the compiler has worked its way to the 9,741st line. There are phases in every program's development when compiling is almost continuous—and if each takes seven minutes, that's a lot of waiting.

The $I(nclude) Directive

There's a partial solution to the large-program problem, involving the $I(nclude) compiler directive (not to be confused with the $I+- directive for trapping I/O errors). The $I(nclude) directive requires a file name and instructs the compiler to temporarily stop reading from the current file and to load and start compiling the named file. When this file is exhausted, compilation resumes where it left off in the original file.

For example, consider files Constdef.Pas and Includetest.Pas:

```
{ File Constdef.Pas }

const
  Pi := 3.14159;
  C = 2.99E8;

{ File IncludeTest.Pas }

program IncludeTest;
{$I Constdef.Pas}
var
```

```
  r: Real;
begin
  Write('Input radius: ');
  ReadLn(r);
  WriteLn('Area of circle = ', (Pi * r * r):0:2)
end.
```

When Turbo Pascal encounters the $I(nclude) directive in the second line
when compiling Includetest.Pas, it opens and begins to read file
Constdef.Pas. When this file is exhausted, compilation continues with the
third line of Includetest.Pas. As far as the compiler is concerned, it's as
though the lines that make up Constdef.Pas were physically inside
Includetest.Pas. So the definition of constants *Pi* and *C*, which are in
Constdef.Pas, are known to that program.

If an included file isn't in the current directory, you must specify its entire
path name. For example, if file Constdef.Pas were in folder Turbo of
volume Startup, the $I directive would be

```
{$I startup:turbo:ConstDef.pas}
```

If a file to be included is in a particular subfolder in the current folder, then
you can specify a partial path name. For example,

```
{$I :includes:constDef.pas }
```

refers to a file in subfolder Includes of the current directory, regardless of
the name of the current directory. Note the colon before the partial path
name; this must be present or the file system will think you're referring to a
volume named Includes.

Because long path names can be awkward, Turbo provides a short cut. The
Compile menu has a selection called Options....

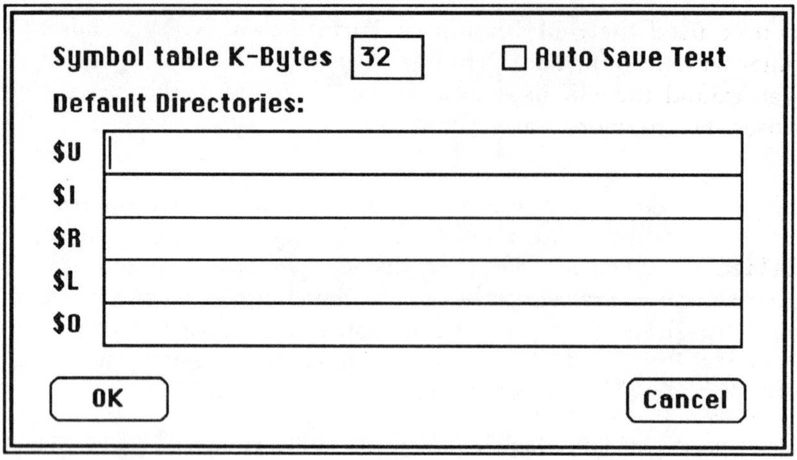

```
┌─────────────────────────────────────────────────┐
│ ┌─────────────────────────────────────────────┐ │
│ │                                             │ │
│ │  Symbol table K-Bytes  ┌──┐   ☐ Auto Save Text │ │
│ │                        │32│                  │ │
│ │                        └──┘                  │ │
│ │  Default Directories:                        │ │
│ │                                             │ │
│ │  $U ┌───────────────────────────────────┐   │ │
│ │     │                                   │   │ │
│ │  $I │───────────────────────────────────│   │ │
│ │     │                                   │   │ │
│ │  $R │───────────────────────────────────│   │ │
│ │     │                                   │   │ │
│ │  $L │───────────────────────────────────│   │ │
│ │     │                                   │   │ │
│ │  $O └───────────────────────────────────┘   │ │
│ │                                             │ │
│ │  ╭──────────╮              ╭──────────╮     │ │
│ │  │    OK    │              │  Cancel  │     │ │
│ │  ╰──────────╯              ╰──────────╯     │ │
│ └─────────────────────────────────────────────┘ │
└─────────────────────────────────────────────────┘
```

Figure 18.1: The Compile/Options Dialog Box

If you tend to include files from the same folder, you can simplify your $I(nclude) directives by specifying the path name of that folder in the $I box. This text is then concatenated with text specified in an $I(nclude) directive. For example, if your Include files are usually in folder Startup:Turbo:Includes, then put exactly that text in this box. Like the application names you provide for the Transfer menu, you must choose the Save Defaults option of the File menu to save this information when you exit Turbo Pascal (so that you won't have to specify it again when you restart Turbo Pascal).

The $I(nclude) directive allows a program to be broken into pieces, thereby simplifying editing and storage. For example, the main file of a 10,000-line application could be 12 lines long:

```
program BigProg;
{$I Const.Pas}
{$I Types.Pas}
{$I Var.Pas}
{$I InputRoutine.Pas}
{$I SortRoutine.Pas}
{$I PrintRoutine.Pas}
begin
  InputData;
  SortData;
  PrintResults
end.
```

At compile time, *BigProg* is effectively reassembled into one big piece. Note that Turbo Pascal doesn't permit $I(nclude) directives to be nested; that is, only the main file can contain $I directives. If file Types.Pas in the previous example contained any $I directives, they would be flagged as errors.

If you've used the IBM version of Turbo Pascal, you're undoubtedly familiar with the $I(nclude) technique. This is because it's a good technique to get around the 64K limit on text files that IBM Turbo Pascal's editor imposes. Furthermore, early versions of IBM Turbo Pascal didn't allow units.

Units

While the $I(nclude) methodology solves certain aspects of the big source-file problem, it doesn't help compilation speed. In fact, compilation actually slows down, as multiple files must be opened and closed. Even if it weren't for the speed problem, there's something *messy* about having to recompile 9,999 good lines of Pascal just to add one semicolon. And Turbo Pascal isn't messy.

Macintosh Turbo Pascal allows you to break large programs down into pieces called *units* that are edited *and compiled* separately. When a 10,000-line program is written as ten 1000-line units (with a short main program to hold it all together), you can add a semicolon to the last line of any individual unit and recompile in five seconds. Better?

Moreover, units offer you another level of detail hiding or masking, another way to make available to the main program or calling routine only those elements of a process that they need to know about. Like parameter passing and local variables, the thoughtful application of units reduces unexpected and undesirable interactions between different parts of a program.

How Units Work

Units are best explained by example. Consider the following program:

```
program CalcVolume;

function SphereVol(Radius: Real): Real;
const
  Pi = 3.14159;
begin
  SphereVol := (4.0 / 3.0) * Pi * Radius * Radius * Radius;
end;

function CylVol(Radius, Length: Real): Real;
const
  Pi = 3.14159;
begin
```

```
    CylVol := Pi * Radius * Radius * Length;
end;

var
  L, R: Real;
  C: Char;

begin
  while True do
  begin
    Write('Sphere or cylinder (S/C/Quit): ');
    ReadLn(C);
    case C of
      'S','s': begin
                 Write('Enter radius: ');
                 ReadLn(R);
                 WriteLn('Volume = ',SphereVol(R):0:4)
               end;
      'C','c': begin
                 Write('Enter radius: ');
                 ReadLn(R);
                 Write('Enter length: ');
                 ReadLn(L);
                 WriteLn('Volume = ',CylVol(R,L):0:4);
               end;
      'Q','q': Exit;
    end                                    { case }
  end                                      { while }
end.
```

For the sake of argument, imagine this program stretched to thousand-line extremes. What we have here are some utility routines (*SphereVol*, *CylVol*) and a main program that uses them. The main program is really what *CalcVolume* is all about. Function *SphereVol* is a black box; its internals, once known to be working, are of no further interest. The author of *CalcVolume* may even have written *SphereVol* months ago for a different program and simply borrowed it for this one.

In fairness, we must admit that Standard Pascal handles reusable routines fairly well. With some cutting and pasting, *CylVol* and *SphereVol* are easily inserted into new programs and, thanks to their use of the local constant *Pi* and parameter passing, are free of potential identifier conflicts.

The $I(nclude) directive makes things even better. With $I(nclude), we can insert *CylVol* and *SphereVol* (stored in a file with a clever name like, say, Geometryaids.Inc) into a new program without the muss and fuss of physically pasting them in:

```
program CalcVolumes;
{$I GeometryAids.Inc}                   { Inc = 'include'}
var
  L, R: Real;
  C: Char;
```

```
begin
   .
   .
   .
end.
```

Using $I(nclude) directives helps; this version of *CalcVolumes* visually indicates the support role of file Geometryaids.Inc. But it's possible to go a step further. Since the content of the geometry toolkit doesn't change, no matter how many programs use it, each time the compiler compiles it is redundant: The exact same code is generated. Redundancy wastes time—how much time depends on the size of Geometryaids.Inc.

Ideally, we'd compile the file of auxiliary routines once, and then use the various formulas it contains over and over, without the bother of repeating their definitions and recompiling every time in each program. That is, we'd treat *SphereVol* as if it were a built-in talent of Turbo Pascal.

This is precisely the concept behind units.

If you're impressed at the implications of this idea, you should be. Units are more than a way to speed up compilations. They let you customize the language: to add functions and procedures that have essentially the same status as built-in routines like *Insert* and *Cos*; to boldly extend Turbo Pascal where no compiler has gone before. You can set up a unit for calculating the volumes of geometric solids, a unit for financial analysis, a unit for sort routines, or a unit for drawing graphic objects and text on a bit-mapped CRT (coming soon, called QuickDraw).

Unit Syntax: Interface and Implementation

With the unit approach to program partitioning, the *CalcVolume* application becomes two files: a main program source file (Calcvolume.Pas) and a unit source file (Geometryaids.Pas). This sounds superficially like the separation provided by the $I(nclude) methodology but has an important difference. Once debugged, unit Geometryaids.Pas need only be compiled once, no matter how many programs use it.

A unit source file looks much like a program source file; both contain constants, types, variables, procedures, and functions. Both can be compiled by Turbo Pascal, and both end with **end.**

A unit consists of two parts: an *interface* and an *implementation*. The interface is the unit's "public" part. It describes the goodies that are available for use within it. The implementation is the "private" part of the unit and contains the nuts and bolts of each of the procedures and functions declared in the interface. Unit syntax is shown in the following syntax diagram.

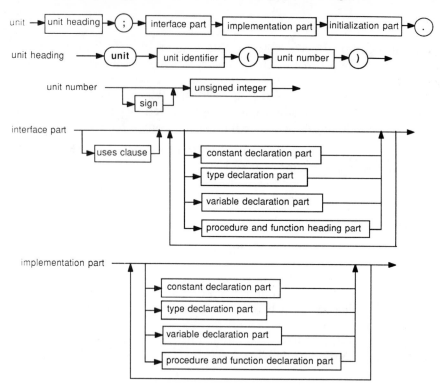

Figure 18.2: Syntax Diagram of a Unit

Different Pascal compilers implement units differently (everyone wants to try his or her hand at being Niklaus Wirth). Turbo Pascal's unit mechanism is one of the best you'll come across—uncomplicated and efficient. Here's unit *GeometryAids*:

```
unit GeometryAids(1);
interface

function SphereVol(Radius: Real): Real;
function CylVol(Radius, Length: Real): Real;

implementation

const
  Pi = 3.14159;

function Cube(X: Real): Real;
```

```
begin
  Cube := X * X * X;
end;

function CircleArea(Radius: Real): Real;
begin
  CircleArea := Pi * Radius * Radius;
end;

function SphereVol{(Radius: Real): Real};
begin
  SphereVol := (4.0 * Pi * Cube(Radius)) / 3.0
end;

function CylVol{(Radius, Length: Real): Real};
begin
  CylVol := CircleArea(Radius) * Length
end;

end.
```

The first non-comment line in a unit must be the unit header:

```
unit GeometryAids(1);
```

This line identifies the file to the compiler as a unit, rather than a program, and gives it a name. The number in parentheses after the unit identifier is the *unit number*; it can be any positive integer as long as each unit used by a given program has a unique value.

Everything between the keywords **interface** and **implementation** is the interface. In this case, the headers of functions *SphereVol* and *CylVol* make up the interface. It determines what is visible to programs that use a given unit. Note that only the headings of these functions are present; the bodies are elsewhere. Syntax diagrams of units are shown in Chapter 23 of the Turbo Pascal reference manual.

From keyword **implementation** on down is unit *GeometryAids*'s implementation. Among other things, this part of the unit contains the bodies of procedures and functions defined in the interface. Note that the parameter lists of *CylVol* and *SphereVol* aren't repeated in the implementation. The compiler has this information already and having it in two places would force Turbo to check that they're identical, wasting time. (This is also how we handled procedures and functions declared as **forward** in Chapter 11. Rather than deleting them entirely, we commented out the parameter lists, to serve as a reminder of what they are.)

Note functions *CalcArea* and *Cube*. They appear only in the implementation and not in the interface. They simplify the calculation performed by *SphereVol*, but, since they don't appear in the interface, can't be called by programs that use unit *GeometryAids*. *CalcArea*, *Cube*, and the constant *pi* aren't visible outside the implementation of *GeometryAids*. At times, a unit will declare a single procedure in its interface, yet use dozens of supporting types, variables, and procedures in its implementation. That's detail hiding, and the more of it a program has, the better.

Incidentally, file Geometryaids.Pas can have $I(nclude) directives—and, for that matter, practically any compiler directive.

Take a couple of minutes to type in and compile Geometryaids.Pas to memory. The compiler knows that it's dealing with a unit and not a program when it encounters the keyword **unit** rather than **program** in the first line.

Unlike programs, units can't be executed. (What would you run first? *SphereVol*? What would happen to the value it returns?) Therefore, Turbo's Run command does nothing if the editor's topmost window happens to be a unit. Furthermore, if you compile to disk, the resulting object file won't be perceived by the Finder as an application (that is, it won't have file type *APPL*).

So just what *does* go to disk when you compile a unit? The icon for a unit is a suitcase (similar to that used by the Font Mover), to symbolize a packet of pre-compiled utility routines that can be carried over and used by various programs.

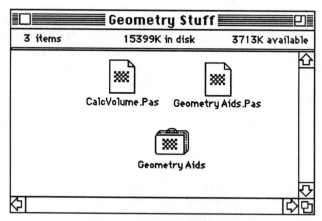

Figure 18.3: A Compiled Unit

Turbo Pascal Tutor for the Macintosh

Using a Unit

Now that we know how to build and compile a unit, how about the syntax for using one in a main program? Consider the new, improved *CalcVolume*:

```
program CalcVolume;
{$U startup:pascal:GeometryAids}
uses GeometryAids;
var
  L, R: Real;
  C: Char;

begin
  while True do
  begin
    Write('Sphere or Cylinder (S/C/Quit): ');
    ReadLn(C);
    case C of
      'S','s': begin
                 Write('Enter radius: ');
                 ReadLn(R);
                 WriteLn('Volume = ',SphereVol(R):0:4)
               end;
      'C','c': begin
                 Write('Enter radius: ');
                 ReadLn(R);
                 Write('Enter length: ');
                 ReadLn(L);
                 WriteLn('Volume = ',CylVol(R,L):0:4);
               end;
      'Q','q': Exit;
    end                                        { case }
  end                                          { while }
end.
```

The third line, **uses** GeometryAids, says it all. From this point on down, *CalcVolume* has access to the identifiers declared in the interface of unit *GeometryAids*. Without this **uses** statement, you'd get **Unknown Identifier** errors wherever *SphereVol* and *CylVol* appear. The compiler needs to know that *SphereVol* represents a function and, moreover, that it returns a value of type *Real* and expects to have one real parameter passed by value to it. Without this information, the compiler can't generate code to access the function.

Since the compiler can't read your mind, you need to tell it where on disk the unit resides so that it can check *GeometryAids*'s interface and learn what sort of objects it defines. This is done with the $U(nit) compiler directive.

Like $I, $U expects a file name, with or without a path name before it. You provide the name of the unit's object file (*GeometryAids*), not the source file (Geometryaids.Pas), in the $U directive. Unlike some Pascal compilers,

Turbo Pascal interfaces are stored in a binary form along with the compilation of the implementation. If a unit has been compiled to memory and its source window is still open, you don't have to do this; Turbo Pascal will find what it needs in memory automatically.

Now enter and compile *CalcVolume* to memory—but don't execute it just yet.

Linking

In traditional software-development environments, a process known as *linking* is a distinct (and usually slow) final step that must occur before a program can be executed. Linking merges the output of two or more separate compilations into a single file. Turbo Pascal also performs linking, but since most of the code is in memory, linking happens almost instantly when you compile. It's a step that you don't have to think about.

If you choose to compile *CalcVolume* to disk, Turbo's linking routines will output an application file that contains the result of both *GeometryAids* and *CalcVolume*'s compilation.

Initializing a Unit

Even though units aren't programs and can't be executed directly, it's still possible to give one a "main program." If a unit's implementation ends with a **begin/end** pair rather than just an **end**, then the compiler expects to find statements between them. These statements constitute the unit's initialization code; they are executed automatically when a program that uses this unit begins to run (before control is given to the application's main program).

As an example of how initialization code can be useful, unit *GeometryAids* might want to initialize a variable equal to (4/3 * *Pi*). This makes *SphereVol* quicker (it saves one multiplication and one division per call). Here's how:

```
unit GeometryAids(1);
interface

function SphereVol(Radius: Real): Real;
function CylVol(Radius, Length: Real): Real;

implementation
```

```
var
  pi,
  FourThirdsPi: Real;

function Cube(X: Real): Real;
begin
  Cube := X * X * X
end;

function CircleArea(Radius: Real): Real;
begin
  CircleArea := pi * Radius * Radius
end;

function SphereVol{(radius: Real): Real};
begin
  SphereVol := FourThirdsPi * Cube(Radius)
end;

function CylVol{(Radius, Length: Real): Real};
begin
  CylVol := CircleArea(Radius) * Length
end;

begin
  Pi := 4.0 * ArcTan(1.0);          { this equals pi, strangely enough }
  FourThirdsPi := (4.0 / 3.0) * Pi
end.
```

If a unit doesn't require initialization, then its implementation simply concludes with **end**, as in the original version of *GeometryAids*.

Moving Units into Turbo Pascal

When compiling a program that uses a unit, Turbo Pascal looks for it on disk under the name you specify in a $U directive. This read-from-disk process takes a bit of time. It also requires that you keep track of the volume-and-folder whereabouts of each compiled unit you'll be using.

This is a small enough price to pay for the benefits of units, but Turbo goes a step farther by allowing you to place thoroughly debugged, frequently needed units inside the Turbo Pascal application itself. Turbo automatically knows about all the units contained within itself, so $U directives are unnecessary—although you still need a **uses** clause.

For example, if you write applications daily that require functions *CylVol* and *SphereVol*, it would be worth a few seconds to move the compiled *GeometryAids* unit directly into Turbo Pascal. Once inside Turbo Pascal, you can omit the {$U GeometryAids} directive when compiling programs that use it; compilation speed will also be enhanced.

Moving a unit into Turbo Pascal is accomplished by a stand-alone application named UnitMover. It's on your Turbo Pascal Utilities & Sample Programs Disk. Instructions on its use can be found in Chapter 8 of the *Turbo Pascal User's Guide and Reference Manual* (although anyone who's ever put Font/DAMover through its paces shouldn't have much trouble figuring it out).

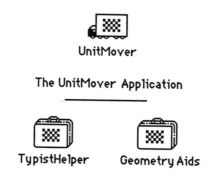

UnitMover

The UnitMover Application

TypistHelper   Geometry Aids

UnitMover Documents (compiled units)

Figure 18.4: UnitMover

Since units can be placed inside Turbo Pascal, you may wonder whether there are some there already. As shipped from Borland, about 70 percent of the size of Turbo Pascal is the result of some 15 units stored inside it. These units—some large, some small—provide run-time support for terminal window-oriented programs and allow contact with the thousands of constants, types, variables, procedures, and functions built into the Macintosh.

We'll learn more about taking advantage of these Macintosh units in Parts 4 and 5 of this book. For now, take a couple of minutes and browse through Appendix D of the Turbo Pascal manual. It contains a listing of the various interfaces and describes the constants, data types, variables, procedures, and functions available in each.

Review

Large source programs can be broken into separate files by using the $I(nclude) compiler directive and by using units. Units are a tool for extending and customizing Turbo Pascal, as well as for partitioning large programming tasks into manageable, quick-to-compile pieces. Units can be compiled just like programs, although they cannot be executed.

Units consist of a public part, the interface, and a private part, the implementation. The implementation defines how the public portion works. Once perfected, units can be merged into Turbo Pascal itself with the UnitMover application for fast, easy access.

19

A Sample Program

We've spent the last 200 pages discussing the fundamentals of Pascal. In this final chapter of Part 2, all of the previously discussed concepts have been put to work in a sample program.

Turbo Typist

Turbo Typist is a typing game. It reads a word or phrase from a text file, displays the word, and then waits for the user to type it correctly before retrieving the next word from the file. To make the game more fun, we've added scoring, and—the most difficult aspect—some animation. The program has three major components:

- file I/O to get words from a disk file
- animation: driving a "car" across the screen
- real-time keyboard handling to get characters from the keyboard while simultaneously updating the screen

If your computer is at hand, try compiling and running the program Typist.Pas. (You'll need to have unit file *TypistHelper* present in the same directory.) If you're far from a Macintosh, here's what the main screen looks like:

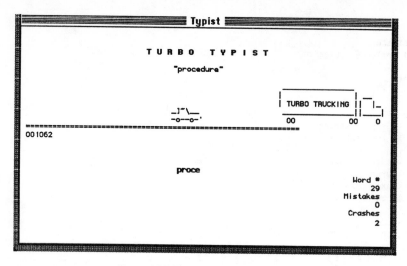

Figure 19.1: The Turbo Typist Screen

The goal of the player at this moment is to type the word **procedure**. The car (currently in the middle of the screen) drives forward until it rear-ends the truck or until the target word is typed correctly. The car has logged 21 miles this round, and the user has already typed the characters *proce*. When the user thinks **procedure** has been typed correctly, s/he presses *Return* and the score is updated accordingly: Either a new word is displayed or the mistake count is incremented.

To manage these tasks, Typist uses a host of data structures, statement types, and other features of Turbo Pascal:

Data Structures/Types	Pascal Features
Sets (of characters) Strings	Procedures/functions **case (if then else)**
Arrays (of strings)	Loops (**for, while, repeat**)
Records Booleans (both functions and variables) Enumerated scalars Files (for reading text)	File I/O Keyboard and video I/O Units

This program's source code is on your Tutor disk in folder Turbo Typist. Typist.Pas is the main program; TypistHelper.Pas is a unit used by the main program. Rather than reprint its entire source code, let's cover the overall structure of the program and then focus on some specific areas.

For starters, here's unit *TypistHelper*'s interface:

```
interface
uses MemTypes, QuickDraw, OSIntf;

const
  BS = #8;

type
  MaxString = string[50];
  CharSet = set of Char;
  String80 = string[80];

procedure BoldPrint;
procedure NormalPrint;
procedure Pause(var Tenths : Integer);
function  UpCase(c:Char):Char;
procedure AbortCheck(Ch : Char);
function  CenterStr(S : String80) : Byte;
function  GetWord(var F : text; var Word : MaxString) : Boolean;
function  GetString(X, Y: Byte;                  { starting row,col }
                    var St : MaxString;           { string to edit }
                    MaxLen : Byte;                { max length of st }
                    KeyQuota : Byte;          { used to limit # chars }
                    DelayTime : Integer;     { limits time spent editing }
                    TermSet : CharSet    { exit if one of these is typed }
                    ) : Char;                    { returns terminating Char }
```

Typist (and any program you write) is free to use the various data structures and routines defined in this interface. One of the benefits of units is that the client program doesn't have to know a thing about how a procedure in a unit works. It only needs to know how to call it.

About TypistHelper's Uses Clause

Like programs, units can use other units, and *TypistHelper* won't compile without the **uses** clause in the second line. The three units required by *TypistHelper* are built into Turbo Pascal, so no $U directives are necessary. Unit *MemTypes* defines some useful data types, including *Byte*, which is used by the *CenterString* and *GetString* functions. *QuickDraw* is a large, important unit we'll learn much more about in Part 5 of this book; it's used here to support the *BoldPrint* and *NormalPrint* functions. *OSIntf* (operating system interface) is needed to carry out the *Pause* function.

NOTE: Remember, the interfaces to all the built-in units are listed in Appendix D of the Turbo Pascal manual. Over time, this is sure to become a much used section of your manual.

Many of the routines in *TypistHelper* are general purpose. For example, *Pause* causes the system to delay for the specified number of tenths of a second. Function *UpCase* turns a character into its uppercase equivalent. If you'd like to use unit *TypistHelper* in one of your own programs, it's as simple as adding a **uses** clause:

```
program MyProgram;
{$U TypistHelper}
uses MemTypes, QuickDraw, OSIntf, TypistHelper;
begin
   WriteLn(UpCase('$'), UpCase('c'), UpCase('C'));
end.
```

Because of the way the compiler works, your **uses** clause must include all the units used by any units you might use—even if they aren't used by the program itself. So even though MyProgram doesn't use anything in *MemTypes*, *QuickDraw*, and *OSIntf*, it has to declare them, because it does use *TypistHelper*.

Getting back to Typist.Pas, keep in mind that it has access to everything declared in the interface of *TypistHelper*.

Step 1: The Main Program

In trying to understand a Pascal program, the place to start is at the end. Here's Typist's main program:

```
begin
  Initialize;
  repeat
    OpenFile;
    if GetWord(WordFile, TargetWord) then
      PlayOneRound(TargetWord)
    else
    begin
      GotoXY(1, Pred(MaxRows));
      WriteLn('That file is empty.');
    end;
    GotoXY(1, MaxRows);
    BoldPrint; Write('Try again?  '); NormalPrint;
  until UpCase(ReadChar) <> 'Y';
end.
```

Thanks to clear programming, the high-level flow of this program is easy to grasp. After some one-time initialization, we enter a **repeat/until** loop. Each pass through the loop represents one full game of Turbo Typist.

When you play a game, you call the *OpenFile* routine, which displays the startup screen and opens file TYPIST.DATA (where the words to be typed are listed). The program checks to see that there's at least one line (word) in file Typist.Data. If there isn't anything, the program complains. If there is at least one word in the file, then procedure *PlayOneRound* is called; this is where everything happens. The program ends when the user types something other than *Y* in response to the 'Try again?' *query*.

Step 2: File I/O

The disk file handling in Typist is straightforward. The task is to open a text file and read a line at a time until the word list (file) has been exhausted.

Procedure *InitProgram* paints the welcoming screen and opens Typist.Data. Once this file is successfully opened, control returns to the main program. The *Boolean* function *GetWord* retrieves the next word from the file; it returns True if a word is successfully retrieved; if the file is exhausted, it returns False.

Step 3: The Main Control Loop

Procedure *PlayOneRound* is the heart of Turbo Typist and has a number of procedures nested within it. Here's its operation, expressed in a sort of pidgin Pascal known as *pseudocode*:

1. Get a word from the file and display it.
2. Erase the car, increment its *X* coordinate, and increment and display the odometer.
3. If the car collides with the truck, then simulate a collision and back the car up to the start. Otherwise, display the car and read characters from the keyboard.
4. If the user presses *Command-C*, exit the program.
5. If the user presses *Return*, process the word.

   a. If the word typed matches the target word and more words remain in the file, then get the next word, display it, update the scoring information, and back up the car.

   b. Otherwise, if the word typed does not match the target word, update and display the score.
6. Repeat steps 2 through 5 until all the words have been retrieved, displayed, and typed.

Animation

Real-time animation refers to the ability to simulate movement on a computer screen while simultaneously collecting information controlling the simulation from the user. Turbo Typist demonstrates this capability by reading and displaying words from a file, updating the score, and so on, while simultaneously reading characters typed at the keyboard and acting upon them. Even though the program manages several processes concurrently, the car moves realistically (well, realistically enough for a car built out of dashes and quote marks, with lowercase Os for wheels).

At several places in the main loop (in *PlayOneRound*), a *GoToXY* statement is used to place an underscore character near the characters the user has already typed. This draws attention to the user's goal—that of typing more characters.

The animation itself is minimal—fourteen characters, two rows of seven columns each, are alternately drawn, erased, then redrawn a little to the left or right. Running this simple program will help you to understand the discussion that follows:

```
program SimpleCartoon;
{ Simple animation--run it a few times and try to understand it.
  Then try making the object string longer.  Try incrementing the
  row as well as the column.  Vary the delay interval. Can you
  modify this program to simulate a bouncing ball? }
var
  column : Integer;                        { loop variable }
  Object : string[10];          { object being animated }
  N: Integer;
begin
  ClearScreen;
  Object := 'o';      { start simple--try this string next: o-o }
  for column := 1 to 80 do
  begin
    GoToXY(column, 1);              { current column, first row }
    Write(Object);                       { display the object }
    for N := 1 to 10000 do;{ kill time for a fraction of a sec. }
    GoToXY(column, 1);     { place cursor back on top of object }
    Write(' ':Length(Object));         { erase previous object }
  end;
end.
```

Procedure *GetString* (located in unit *TypistHelper*) is unusual.

Most string-editing utility routines exit when the user types a terminating character (for example, Return). Typist's *GetString* function, however, exits for two other reasons as well:

1. The user has used up the alloted quota of keystrokes.
2. The allotted time for editing between "cartoon cycles" has expired.

The following pseudocode demonstrates a major dilemma in real-time programming:

```
1:   procedure GetString;
        { This routine is called to edit a string.  The routine
          terminates when the user types a carriage return. }
     begin
2:   repeat
3:     Read a character;
4:     Process the character; { legal char? backspace? etc. }
5:   until character=carriage return;
     end;  { GetString }
6:   repeat
7:     Move the car one "mile" forward;
8:     GetString;                              { the string }
9:     Process the string;   { legal word? update score, etc. }
10:  until no_more_words;
```

At first glance, the **repeat** loop beginning on line 6 looks reasonable: The car will advance one "mile" each time the loop is executed. However, several problems aren't addressed.

What if the user holds down one key and never presses *Return* (the beast!). Line 7 moves the car, and then the editing routine is called. While *GetString* is waiting for the player to press *Return*, the car is ticketed for parking in the red zone! Instead of driving smoothly across the screen, the car stays in the same place. And if the user holds down *Return*, the car zips across the screen in one meaningless motion.

The solution here is to pass a parameter to *GetString*, instructing it to return after a certain number of keystrokes have been typed—even if the user doesn't press *Return*. Of course, pressing *Return* will still cause *GetString* to return to the main loop.

```
*1:   procedure GetString(KeyQuota : Integer);
         { This routine is called to edit a string. The routine terminates
           when the user types a carriage return or when KeyQuota keystrokes
           have been typed. }
      begin
2:    repeat
3:      Read a character;
*3a:    Decrement KeyQuota; { subtract one from number remaining }
4:      Process the character;     { legal char? backspace? etc. }
5:    until (character = carriage return) or
*5a:         (KeyQuota <= 0);
      end;  { GetString }

6:    repeat
7:      Move the car one "mile" forward;
```

```
*8:     GetString(5 keystrokes);              { edit the string }
                                              { allow 5 keystrokes }
 9:     if user typed carriage return then
 9a:       process the string;    { legal word? update score, etc. }
10:     until no_more_words;
```

We have modified five lines (those marked by an asterisk) and completely overhauled the program's animation. Now *GetString* returns to the main loop every five characters or when *Return* is pressed, whichever comes first. Of course, we only want to check the string for validity if *Return* has been pressed. Either way, we can update our cartoon often enough to please the eye.

Now we're getting somewhere—except that the car will still go nowhere if our obstinate operator refuses to press a single key! Think about it. We display the car, then call *GetString*. *GetString* waits for a carriage return or five characters from the keyboard. If they never come, *GetString* never returns to the loop from whence it came.

The solution? Look at lines 6 to 10 of the original **repeat** loop. What we want is quite reasonable: We want *GetString* to always take approximately the same amount of time, whether *Return* is pressed, no characters are typed, or a key is held down the entire time. If "processing the string" also requires a fixed amount of time each time it is called, then the car will run smoothly from one side of the screen to the other.

```
!1:     procedure GetString(KeyQuota, TimeQuota : Integer);
        { This routine is called to edit a string. The routine terminates
          when the user types a carriage return, when KeyQuota keystrokes
          have been typed, or when TimeQuota milliseconds (or some other
          unit) have elapsed. }
        begin
 2:       repeat
 3:         if a character is in the buffer:
!3a:          read a character;
!3b:          Decrement KeyQuota;{ subtract one from number remaining }
!3c:          Decrement TimeQuota; { subtract one from number remaining }
 4:           Process the character;     { legal char? backspace? etc. }
 5:         until (character = carriage return) or
*5a:              (KeyQuota = 0);
!5b:              (TimeQuota = 0);
        end; { GetString }

 6:     repeat
 7:       Move the car one "mile" forward;
!8:       GetString(5 keystrokes, 100 milliseconds); {edit the string }
 9:       if user typed carriage return then
 9a:        process the string;        {legal word? update score, etc. }
10:     until no_more_words;
```

The modified lines are marked with an exclamation point. They do a decent job of accomplishing our goal. If we add any other routines anywhere in the main loop, we must carefully test and readjust our keystroke and time quotas.

Work your way through procedure *PlayOneRound* line by line, ignoring fine details like scoring and cursor placement. Once you understand the major steps in the loop, fine tune your focus a little and make another pass; repeat this process until you're satisfied with your understanding of the program.

Dare to Experiment

If you followed the preceding discussion, you can understand the program's source code. Be daring: Make a copy of the program and modify it. You can certainly find ways to improve it.

If you had difficulty understanding this material, try playing "human computer" and follow on paper exactly what the program does when it executes. Then, modify the simple animation example (program *SimpleCartoon*). Change it so it lets you type characters while it is moving its object across the screen. Try to keep the animation constant no matter how many or how few keys the user types. Keep making the program more and more sophisticated.

By enhancing this simple example, you will eventually run into and, hopefully, solve the same problems addressed by Typist.Pas.

Review

Turbo Typist demonstrates many Pascal structures and statements. Our discussion began with a description of the overall program structure, including the fact that a unit (*TypistHelper*) is used to reduce the workload of the program itself. Next, we did a best-case/worst-case analysis: The slowest typist refused to touch a single key; the fastest held down one key continuously. We then focused on solutions to some programming issues that were raised.

Turbo Pascal Tutor for the Macintosh

ADVANCED TOPICS IN TURBO PASCAL

20

Stacks, Queues, Deques, and Lists

Chapter 16 introduced the concepts of pointers and the dynamic allocation of variables, and hinted at their potential. Pointers and heap-resident variables allow you to create structures out of thin air and link them to other such variables—creating intricate webs of data. This chapter tells you how to use linked lists to combine these data structures in a linear or a circular manner.

Linked Lists

A linked list can store a variable number of data items without the waste of fixed-size arrays. To understand linked lists, we first must talk about *nodes*, the data structures (usually records) that contain both the raw information to be stored in a given location in the linked list and the pointers necessary to link to other nodes in the list. For the sake of simplicity, let's say that the information to be stored in this sample list are integers—that is, this will be a linked list of integers. (In practice, it would probably be something more complex, like a check record.) The simplest node definition you could construct would be like this one from Chapter 16:

```
type
  NodePtr = ^Node;
  Node =
    record
        Data  : Integer;
        Next  : NodePtr
    end;
```

This node declaration again shows the one exception to Pascal's otherwise unbreakable rule that identifiers must be defined before they can be used. Here you can use the data type *Node* before it has been defined, so that you can define *NodePtr* and use it within the definition of *Node*.

Single versus Double Links

Note that the preceding node definition has only one pointer in it (*Next*), which points to the next node in the list:

```
...-->Node-->Node-->Node-->...
```

It is possible to use two pointers instead of one, with the extra pointer linking back to the previous node in the list:

```
...<-->Node<-->Node<-->Node<-->...
```

The Pascal definition would then change to something like this:

```
type
  NodePtr      = ^Node;
  Node =
    record
      Data      : Integer;
      Last,Next : NodePtr
    end;
```

A list built of nodes like this is known as a *doubly linked list*. A doubly linked list is usually easier to work with because it allows you to move back and forth; a *singly linked list* only allows forward movement.

There is, of course, a price for this capability: Each node takes up 4 more bytes of memory. The additional size is most significant if the data section is small relative to the size requirements of the pointers. For example, the previous node definition would increase in size from 6 bytes to 10. However, if the data section is fairly large, then the additional pointer represents a minor size increase and a major increase in power and flexibility.

Starting a Linked List

Since all nodes in a linked list are created as needed, you have to decide how to get the whole thing started, that is, how do you create that first node? There are a number of approaches, but the easiest is to use a *Header node*. A Header node is created at the start of a program; its pointer(s) is either set to the special pointer value **nil** (which means it isn't pointing to anything) or to itself (if you're using a *circular linked list*). The data field(s) often isn't used, at least not in the way it's used in other nodes in the list.

You usually declare the Header node as a pointer variable. At the start of the program, you create the node and set the fields accordingly:

```
program LinkedLists;
  type
    NodePtr       = ^Node;
    Node =
      record
        Data      : Integer;
        Next      : NodePtr
      end;
  var
    Header        : NodePtr;
  ...
  begin
    New(Header);
    with Header^ do
    begin
      Data := 0;
      Next := nil
    end;
    ...
  end.
```

This code assumes you have a singly linked list (*linear* or *noncircular list*). For circular lists, things change a little.

Circular Linked Lists

A linear list has the Header node pointing to the first node, while the last node points to nothing (it is assigned the value **nil**). Such a list looks like this:

```
Header-->Node-->Node--> . . . -->Node-->Node-->[nil]
```

This type of list can make search loops messy. For instance, suppose you have an unsorted list of nodes like the ones already defined, and you want to see if there's a node with a given value in it. Your first impulse might be to write a loop like this (assuming the value you're looking for is in *Val*):

```
TPtr := Header^.Next;
while (TPtr <> nil) and (TPtr^.Data <> Val) do
  TPtr := TPtr^.Next;
```

The problem, of course, is that if you hit the end of the list (TPtr = **nil**), you'll get a run-time error when the program tries to evaluate the expression *TPtr^.Data <> Val*. This problem can sneak up on you again and again (such as when doing insertion and deletion with a doubly linked list).

One solution is to use a circular linked list. Instead of having the last node point to **nil**, you can point it to the Header node instead:

```
Header-->Node-->Node-->...-->Node-->Node-->Header
```

When you create your Header node, you point it to itself:

```
New(Header);
with Header^ do
begin
  Data := 0;
  Next := Header
end;
```

Thus, your search loop will run without any difficulty:

```
TPtr := Header^.Next;
while (TPtr <> Header) and (TPtr^.Data <> Val) do
  TPtr := TPtr^.Next;
```

For a doubly linked list, start the Header with both its pointers pointing to itself (add the statement *Last := Header* to the previous code). As you add nodes, Header will point to both the first and last nodes in the list.

Insertion

After setting up the Header, the first function you need to perform is adding nodes to the list. This is called *insertion*—you add the node between two other nodes, or between a node and the end of the list.

Before inserting, you must do two things. First, create the node to be inserted (using the *New* command) and set all the data fields to their appropriate values. We'll call the pointer to this node *NPtr*. For the sample node already given, the program might look like this:

```
New(NPtr);
NPtr^.Data := NewValue; { whatever it happens to be }
NPtr^.Next := nil;
```

Note that setting *NPtr^.Next* equal to **nil** usually isn't necessary, but it's not a bad idea to initialize all fields of a node.

Second, find, in the list, the node after which you wish to insert the new node. If the new node belongs at the start of the list (or if it's the first node in the list), then it will be inserted after the Header node. Typically, you start at the Header and continue until you've found the node you're looking for. We'll call this node *TPtr*.

The process of insertion itself is simple. Given *NPtr* and *TPtr* (as defined earlier), and assuming this is a singly linked list, do the following:

1. Set *NPtr^.Next* equal to *TPtr^.Next*. This ensures that *NPtr* and *TPtr* are both pointing to the same node.

2. Set *TPtr^.Next* equal to *NPtr*. This makes *TPtr* point to *NPtr*.

The final result is that *TPtr* points to *NPtr*, and *NPtr* points to the node that *TPtr* used to point to. The Pascal code for this is simple:

```
NPtr^.Next := TPtr^.Next;
TPtr^.Next := NPtr;
```

For a doubly linked list, you must do a little more work since you have twice as many pointers to change. Here's the code for a linear list:

```
NPtr^.Next := TPtr^.Next;
NPtr^.Last := TPtr;
TPtr^.Next := NPtr;
if NPtr^.Next <> nil then
  NPtr^.Next^.Last := NPtr;
```

First, note that both of *NPtr*'s pointers have changed, pointing to the nodes that precede and follow it. *TPtr* is then changed to point to *NPtr*. Finally, the node following *NPtr* (which you can reference as *NPtr^.Next^*) is changed to point back to *NPtr*. If the list is circular, you can drop the test for **nil** and always make the assignment to *NPtr^.Next^.Last*.

Deletion

The process of deletion is similar to insertion: First, find the node you want to delete, then make the *preceding* node point to the *following* node. If you have a singly linked list, then you must keep track of the node preceding the one to be deleted (otherwise, you'll have no way to get back to it). If *NPtr* points to the node to be deleted and *TPtr* points to the preceding node, then the statement

```
TPtr^.Next := NPtr^.Next;
```

removes *NPtr* from the list.

With a doubly linked list, you only need to know the node to be deleted:

```
NPtr^.Last^.Next := NPtr^.Next;
if NPtr^.Next <> nil
  then NPtr^.Next^.Last := Nptr^.Last;
```

The first statement points the preceding node to the following one; the second points the following node to the preceding one. As with insertion, if you're using a circular list, you don't need to check for *NPtr^.Next <> nil*.

Having changed the pointers, the statement

```
Dispose(NPtr);
```

reclaims the memory used by *NPtr^*.

Stacks

A *stack* is a storage device for data objects with certain rules about how you add to or remove from it: You cannot simply insert or delete nodes anywhere in the list. Instead, all nodes added to the list must be added at the very front (beginning); likewise, all nodes taken from it must be taken from the very front. If you think about this for a minute, you'll realize that any node you remove will always be the one (of all those left in the list) most recently added. Because of this, a stack is sometimes known as a *last in, first out* (or LIFO) list. When you add to a stack, you're usually said to be "pushing" a node onto it; when you remove from it, you're "popping" a node.

Stacks can be handy in any situation where you need to remember what you're doing (and what you've done) before you can perform some other action (often the same action on a different set of data), then pick up where you left off. Usually, you can just call procedures and functions (sometimes recursively), and Pascal takes care of all that for you. However, situations may arise where you need (or want) to handle that explicitly, either to avoid recursion or direct control over the stack.

The following code implements a stack as a linear, singly linked list:

```
type
  NodePtr    = ^Node;
  Node =
    record
      Data    : Integer;
      Next    : NodePtr
```

```pascal
      end;

var
  StackPtr    : NodePtr;  { Header for stack }
  StackEmpty  : Boolean;  { flag for empty stack }

procedure CreateStack;
begin
  New(StackPtr);
  with StackPtr^ do
  begin
    Next := nil;
    Data := 0;
  end;
  StackEmpty := True;
end;  { CreateStack }

procedure Pop(var Val : Integer);
var
  NPtr : NodePtr;
begin
  if not StackEmpty then
  begin
    NPtr := StackPtr^.Next;
    StackPtr^.Next := NPtr^.Next;
    Val := NPtr^.Data
    Dispose(NPtr);
    StackEmpty := (StackPtr^.Next = nil);
  end;
end;  { Pop }

procedure Push(Val : Integer);
var
  NPtr      : NodePtr;
begin
  StackEmpty := False;
  New(NPtr);
  NPtr^.Data := Val;
  NPtr^.Next := StackPtr^.Next;
  StackPtr^.Next := NPtr;
end;  { Push }

procedure DeleteStack;
var
  Temp        : Integer;
begin
  while not StackEmpty do
    Pop(Temp);
  Dispose(StackPtr);
end;  { DeleteStack }
```

CreateStack must be called before any other stack routine. It creates the Header node (called *StackPtr*) and sets the *StackEmpty* flag to True. *Push* adds a value to the stack. Note that it just passes a value; you don't have to worry about what the node data structure looks like. Likewise, *Pop* just returns a value, hiding the node removal and deletion from you. Finally, the routine *DeleteStack* disposes of all the nodes in the stack, and then gets rid of *StackPtr* itself. You then must call *CreateStack* again before using the stack.

Queues

As we've just shown, a stack follows the LIFO principle. Sometimes though, you'll want to treat nodes on a first come, first served basis. In programming, a *queue* is a list of nodes treated just this way, technically called *first in, first out* (FIFO). You always add a node to the end of the list, and you always remove a node from the front of the list.

Like stacks, queues are simple to implement. However, since you have to deal with both ends of the list, you'll probably find it easier to use a circular, doubly linked list rather than a linear, singly linked one. You should probably use a queue whenever things keep cropping up faster than you can handle them, and you want to look at them in the exact order they appear. Here's an implementation:

```
type
  NodePtr     = ^Node;
  Node =
    record
      Data      : Integer;
      Last,Next: NodePtr
    end;

var
  Header       : NodePtr;      { Header for stack  }
  QueueEmpty   : Boolean;   { flag for empty stack }

procedure CreateQueue;
begin
  New(Header);
  with Header^ do
  begin
    Next := Header;
    Last := Header;
    Data := 0;
  end;
  QueueEmpty := True;
end;  { CreateQueue }

procedure GetValue(var Val : Integer);
var
  NPtr         : NodePtr;
begin
  if not QueueEmpty then
```

```
  begin
    NPtr := Header^.Next;
    Header^.Next := NPtr^.Next;
    Header^.Next^.Last := Header;
    Val := NPtr^.Data;
    Dispose(NPtr);
    QueueEmpty := (Header^.Next = Header);
  end
end;

procedure PutVal(Val : Integer);
var
  NPtr          : NodePtr;
begin
  QueueEmpty := False;
  New(NPtr);
  with NPtr^ do
  begin
    Data := Val;
    Next := Header;
    Last := Header^.Last;
  end;
  Header^.Next := NPtr;
  NPtr^.Last^.Next := NPtr;
end;   { PutVal }

procedure DeleteQueue;
var
  TVal          : Integer;
begin
  while not QueueEmpty do
    GetVal(TVal);
  Dispose(Header);
end;   { DeleteQueue }
```

CreateQueue must be called before any of the other queue procedures. *PutVal* creates a new node and inserts it between the Header and the end of the queue. *GetVal* gets the value from the node at the start of the queue, removes that node, and then disposes of it. And, of course, *DeleteQueue* cleans up the whole thing.

Deques

In his classic work *Fundamental Algorithms*, Donald Knuth describes yet another list type: a *deque* (pronounced *deck*) or double-ended queue. While a queue adds nodes on only one end and removes them only from the other, a deque lets you add and remove nodes from either end.

Implementing a deque isn't much harder than implementing a queue. The only real difference is that the *GetVal* and *PutVal* routines now have to know whether to use the front (*Header^.Next*) or the rear (*Header^.Last*) of the list. Also, you'll almost certainly want to use a circular, doubly linked list for a deque.

Here's an implementation:

```
const
  Front      = True;
  Rear       = False;

type
  NodePtr      = ^Node;
  Node =
    record
      Data      : Integer;
      Last,Next: NodePtr
    end;

var
  Header       : NodePtr;      { Header for stack }
  DequeEmpty   : Boolean;   { flag for empty stack }

procedure CreateDeque;
begin
  New(Header);
  with Header^ do
  begin
    Next := Header;
    Last := Header;
    Data := 0
  end;
  DequeEmpty := True;
end;   { CreateDeque }

procedure InsertNode(var NPtr,TPtr : NodePtr);
begin
  NPtr^.Next := TPtr^.Next;
  NPtr^.Last := TPtr;
  TPtr^.Next := NPtr;
  NPtr^.Next^.Last := NPtr;
end; { InsertNode }

procedure RemoveNode(var NPtr,TPtr : NodePtr);
begin
  NPtr := TPtr;
  NPtr^.Next^.Last := NPtr^.Last;
  NPtr^.Last^.Next := NPtr^.Next;
end;   { RemoveNode }

procedure GetValue(var Val : Integer; theFront : Boolean); var
  NPtr         : NodePtr;
begin
  if not DequeEmpty then
  begin
    if theFront then
      RemoveNode(NPtr,Header^.Next)
```

```
  else
    RemoveNode(NPtr,Header^.Last);
  Val := NPtr^.Data;
  Dispose(NPtr);
  DequeEmpty := (Header^.Next = Header);
  end;
end;   { Pop }

procedure PutVal(Val : Integer; theFront : Boolean); var
  NPtr          : NodePtr;
begin
  DequeEmpty := False;
  New(NPtr);
  NPtr^.Data := Val;
  if theFront then
    InsertNode(NPtr,Header)
  else
    InsertNode(NPtr,Header^.Last);
end;   { PutVal }

procedure DeleteDeque;
var
  TVal          : Integer;
begin
  while not DequeEmpty do
    GetVal(TVal,Front);
  Dispose(Header);
end;   { DeleteDeque }
```

As you can see, we've gone on to general routines for *InsertNode* and *RemoveNode*. These routines are then called by *GetVal* and *PutVal*, with the boolean parameter *theFront* indicating whether to access the front or end of the deque.

Lists

In the linked list data structures we've looked at, we've given *GetVal* and *PutVal* greater access to the list. In every case, however, that access has been at one end or the other. What if you want to insert or delete nodes in the middle of the list?

You can do just that, and you can do it easily. With the creation of the *InsertNode* and *RemoveNode* procedures, you can now get to any node by stepping through the list. Given a circular list, the code to do that is as follows:

```
TPtr := Header^.Next;
while (TPtr <> Header) and ({ whatever condition }) do
  TPtr := TPtr^.Next;
if TPtr = Header
```

```
then    { node not found }
else       { node found }
```

The test *(TPtr <> Header)* keeps you looking until you've gone through the loop; the test *({ whatever condition })* determines what you're looking for. For example, if you were looking for a node with a particular value *(theVal)*, then the **while** statement might look like this:

```
while (TPtr <> Header) and (TPtr^.Data <> theVal) do
  TPtr := TPtr^.Next;
```

General lists have all kinds of uses. As shown in Chapter 17, they can hold a list of data structures (such as records) in a more flexible form than an array (although you can index into an array faster than you can search through a list). They also don't come up against the 32K size limitation of arrays. Another good use for linked lists is to create and maintain a sorted list of items, especially if you don't know ahead of time how many items you'll need to sort. With a linked list, you just insert the item in its proper place as you read it in.

Review

In this chapter, we've discussed linked lists in detail, elaborating on how they can be used to build different data structures (both linear and circular). Chapter 21 describes how to use linked lists to build nonlinear structures.

If you're interested in learning more on data structures, here are two books to guide you:

- Horowitz, E., and Sahni, S. *Fundamentals of Data Structures in Pascal*. Rockville: Computer Science Press, Inc., 1984.

- Knuth, D. E. *Fundamental Algorithms*. Vol. 1 of *The Art of Computer Programming*. 2d ed. Reading: Addison-Wesley, 1973.

21

Trees, Graphs, and Other Nonlinear Structures

In Chapter 20, you learned more about linked lists and how to use them to build various data structures, including stacks, queues, and deques. All of these structures have one thing in common: The nodes in them are strung together, like beads on a string. Sometimes, though, you need a different kind of structure, one that isn't so linear. This chapter describes such structures.

The most common nonlinear structure is the *tree*, which allows a node to point to several other nodes. There's also the *graph*, which allows *rings* and other intricate paths to form. *Sparse arrays* let you implement large, multidimensional arrays without wasting space. Let's look at each of these nonlinear structures.

An Introduction to Trees

A tree is like a linked list with branches. In a linked list, each node points ahead to, at most, one more node (though it may point back to the previous node as well). In a tree, each node can point ahead (or "down") to more than one node.

The *root* of a tree is the first (or topmost) node. (Note that this kind of tree has the root at the top and the leaves at the bottom—computer scientists are notoriously poor botanists.) A *subtree* consists of a non-root node and all the nodes (if any) below it. A *terminal node* (or *leaf*) is a node with no other nodes below it. Any given node has a *parent* (the node directly above it), unless it's the root. A node may have *siblings* (other nodes pointed to by its parent) and *children* (nodes directly below it that it points to). A *tree* can now be defined as a root with zero or more subtrees; a *forest* is a set of zero or more unconnected trees.

Trees are useful when relating data in a hierarchical fashion, that is, in order of grade or class. Each leaf in a tree then represents a small component of the whole.

Another common use for trees is in the area of artificial intelligence (AI), where a complex goal or task can be broken down into small, performable subgoals or subtasks. Game-playing programs often use game trees to "look ahead" for good (or bad) moves. The root represents the current board position. Possible moves by one side generate new board states or children to the root. Moves by the other side produce the next generation of children (grandchildren to the root), and so on.

These applications are beyond the scope of this book, but the following sections describe some simpler uses of trees.

Binary Trees

The most commonly used tree is known as a binary tree: Each node has no more than two subtrees attached to it. Usually, these subtrees are labeled as left and right. You could use the following node definition for a binary tree:

```
type
  NodePtr          = ^Node;
  Node =
    record
      Data          : Integer;
      Left,Right    : NodePtr
    end;
```

A minimum of pointers is used. Each node points only to its children (the nodes directly below it), with a value of **nil** indicating an unused link. A leaf, then, is a node whose left and right pointers are both **nil**.

For this example, we'll assume the tree is *sorted*; that is, values are added according to certain rules. In this case, we'll assume that lower values are stored to the left and higher values to the right.

The program Animals.Pas on your Turbo Tutor distribution disk uses a binary tree to organize data about the animal kingdom. It prompts you to think of an animal and tries to "guess" it using its binary tree of animal facts. If it doesn't recognize your animal, it gives up and lets you "teach" it a new one.

Searching Binary Trees

To add or remove any value from the tree, we must first see if the value is in the tree. The following boolean function (based on the algorithm described in *How to Solve It by Computer*; see the end of this chapter) looks for a given value in the tree. If found, the function returns True and passes back both the node containing the value as well as its parent; otherwise, it returns False.

```
function FoundInTree(var TPtr,Parent : NodePtr; Val : Integer): Boolean;
var
  Found : Boolean;
begin
  TPtr := Root;
  Parent := nil;
  Found := False;
  while (TPtr <> nil) and not Found do
  with TPtr^ do
  begin
    if Data = Val
      then Found := True
    else
    begin
      Parent := TPtr;
      if Data > Val
        then TPtr := Left
        else TPtr := Right;
    end;
  end;
    FoundInTree := Found;
end;  { FoundInTree }
```

This function works its way down the tree until it either finds the given value or runs into a **nil** pointer. There are two reasons why both the node itself and its parent are passed back. First, if you want to add a node, then you'll automatically have the parent node to add it to. Second, if you want to delete a node, then you also have the parent node to patch things back up to.

Inserting into Binary Trees

To have a tree to search, you must first build it, add values to it, and place them in the proper locations. For starters, you need a pointer, *Root* of type *NodePtr*, that is initialized to **nil**. When you add your first value, that case is checked for (see the following routine) and *Root* is given that value. From then on, each value goes either to the left or right, depending upon whether it's less than or greater than *Root*'s data.

To add a new value, first check to see if it's already in the tree (using the function *FoundInTree*). If it's present, you needn't do anything; otherwise, you have the parent node to add it to, and you need only decide whether it goes to the left or the right. This routine does it all:

```
procedure AddToTree(Val : Integer);
var
  TPtr,Parent,NPtr   : NodePtr;
  Done               : Boolean;
begin
  if not FoundInTree(TPtr,Parent,Val) then
  begin
    if GetNode(NPtr) then
    begin
      NPtr^.Data := Val;
      if Root = nil then
        Root := NPtr
      else
        with Parent^ do
          if Data > Val then Left := NPtr
          else Right := NPtr;
    end;
  end;
end;   { AddToTree }
```

Note: The boolean function *GetNode* creates the node, checking for sufficient memory and initializing the different record fields. If there isn't enough memory, it returns False, preventing the node from being created and added.

Traversing Binary Trees

There's only one way to move through a linked list: straight ahead. There are at least three ways to traverse a binary tree: *preorder*, *inorder*, and *postorder*.

Preorder prints out the data of the current node *before* printing out that of either subtree. Inorder prints the current node *between* the left and right subtrees. Postorder writes out the current node *after* both subtrees. All are recursive, described in terms of *visiting* a root and its subtrees. Visiting a node means handling it in some way (for example, printing a value or comparing it to another value), since you will often pass and ignore nodes on your way to visit other ones.

The following set of routines traverses the binary tree you've created, writing out the values in the appropriate order. As you can see, it's easiest to define the traversal recursively. (The only difference between the three traversal methods is the point at which the data of the current node is written out.) Given the previous insertion routine, the procedure *InOrder* prints out the values in the tree in numerical order:

```
procedure WriteData(Data : Integer; var Row,Col : Byte);
begin
  GoToXY(Col,Row);
  Write(Data:9);
  Row := Row + 1;
end; { proc WriteData }

procedure PreOrder(Node : NodePtr; var Row,Col : Byte);
begin
  if Node <> nil then
  with Node^ do
  begin
    WriteData(Data,Row,Col);
    PreOrder(Left,Row,Col);
    PreOrder(Right,Row,Col);
  end;
end; { PreOrder }

procedure InOrder(Node : NodePtr; var Row,Col : Byte);
begin
  if Node <> nil then with Node^ do
  begin
    InOrder(Left,Row,Col);
    WriteData(Data,Row,Col);
    InOrder(Right,Row,Col);
  end
end; { InOrder }

procedure PostOrder(Node : NodePtr; var Row,Col : Byte);
begin
  if Node <> nil then with Node^ do
  begin
    PostOrder(Left,Row,Col);
    PostOrder(Right,Row,Col);
    WriteData(Data,Row,Col);
  end;
end; { PostOrder }
```

Deleting Nodes and Subtrees

The easiest deletion to do on a binary tree is to remove an entire subtree. You can disconnect it by setting the appropriate *Left* or *Right* pointer on its parent to **nil**. However, you must also track down and dispose of all nodes in the subtree to recover the memory used by them. This procedure does just that:

```
procedure PruneTree(var TPtr : NodePtr);
begin
```

```
   if TPtr <> nil then with TPtr^ do
   begin
     PruneTree(Left);
     PruneTree(Right);
     if (Left = nil) and (Right = nil) then
     begin
       Dispose(TPtr);
       TPtr := nil;
     end;
   end;
end;  { PruneTree }
```

If you wanted to remove, say, the entire left subtree of *Root*, you could simply call *PruneTree(Root^.Left)*, which would dispose of all the nodes and set *Root^.Left* equal to **nil**. And if you wanted to remove the entire tree, you'd just call *PruneTree(Root)*.

A far trickier matter is to remove a single node, especially if that node has subtrees below it. Think for a moment: You've removed a single node that frees up exactly one pointer (either *Left* or *Right*) on its parent, but you might have two subtrees to graft back in somewhere. Where do you put them? If there's only one subtree, then no problem arises; two subtrees can be messy.

There is a well-defined, if complex, solution. The basic rule is this: If the node deleted is to the left of its parent, then its left subtree gets grafted in its place; likewise, if the node is deleted to the right, its right subtree is grafted in. The root of the ungrafted subtree is then added to the grafted subtree, with the root's subtree still hanging below.

Non-Binary Trees

Not all trees are binary: Nowhere is it written that a given node can have only two children. There are applications with nodes of three or more, allowing finer distinctions between subtrees. We won't describe these applications here, but we will show you how you might implement non-binary trees.

Your first problem is the node data structure. If you allow exactly three (or four or five) subtrees, you can simply declare that many pointers. But what if you want a more general tree structure? What if you don't know ahead of time the maximum number of children a given node will have?

Believe it or not, you can implement a general tree using a binary tree node. Let's redefine our earlier data structure:

```
type
  NodePtr              = ^Node;
  Node  =
    record
      Data             : Integer;
      Child,Sibling    : NodePtr;
    end;
```

As you can see, the node is identical in size and content; we've just renamed *Left* and *Right* to be *Child* and *Sibling*. For a given node, *Child* points to the first (leftmost) child of that node, while *Sibling* points to the first sibling to the right.

Since we no longer have a binary tree, our concept of order has disappeared to a certain extent. A given node can have several subtrees below it. How then do their relative positions correspond to the values they contain? A number of approaches can be taken. Each child can have some sort of cut-off value or range of values. The child itself can hold that value (or values) so the tree becomes self-regulating.

Manipulation of non-binary trees tends to be specific to a given implementation, so we won't discuss the topic in any more detail. However, the books listed at the end of this chapter and of Chapter 20 deal with non-binary trees in more depth.

Graphs

You may remember that our definition of a tree includes the provision that all subtrees of a given node are disjoint; that is, the nodes in one subtree are not found in any other subtree. This guarantees exactly one path from the root to any given node. Cases can exist where two different nodes contain the same information, but they are still distinct nodes with different parents and in different subtrees.

What if we let a given node have parents? This seems like a small change, but it can have dramatic effects. Imagine multiple paths from one node to another, with one path better than another. Or imagine a node as a parent to one of its own ancestors, forming a ring of nodes that can be looped through indefinitely.

Such a data structure is generally called a *graph*. You can think of a graph as a tree with fewer restrictions—or, better yet, think of a tree as a special, restricted graph. (Often, the distinction between the two is blurred, and what one person might call a graph is accepted by someone else as a tree.)

In any case, a graph is a set of nodes that point to one another; different limitations may exist on how the nodes point. If a pointer goes only one way—like a tree, where the parent points to the child but not vice versa—then you have a *directed graph*. However, if a given pointer links two nodes equally (that is, you can't tell which is pointing to which), then you have an *undirected graph*. The link between two nodes in a graph is called an *edge*. In some graphs, the edge may have a value (or *weight*) assigned to it, in which case you have a *weighted graph*.

Graphs are used much like trees and are common in artificial intelligence work, where their greater flexibility is advantageous. Directed, weighted graphs are particularly useful in goal decomposition (breaking up a large, difficult goal into many small, easy goals). Researchers in the physical sciences, such as biology and chemistry, often use graphs to represent systems or molecules.

Again, it is beyond the scope of this book to treat graphs in any depth. If you're interested, look at *Fundamentals of Data Structures in Pascal* (referred to at the end of Chapter 20), which devotes an entire chapter to the subject.

Sparse Arrays

From time to time, you may need to work with large arrays; possibly multidimensional large arrays. If you're not careful, you can quickly exceed Turbo's 32K structure limit. To illustrate,

```
var
  PicData     : array[1..500,1..500] of Integer;
```

At first glance *PicData* may not seem like an especially large variable. A little math, however, shows that it requires 500,000 bytes of RAM (500 * 500 * 2 bytes per integer). If you try to compile a program with this declaration, you'll get a "Structure Too Large" error.

If you've got the heap space for it (that is, if *MaxAvail* > 500000), a pointer approach overcomes the problem:

```
type
  yCoordinates = array [1..500] of integer;  {a 1000 byte structure}
var
  PicData: array [1..500] of ^yCoordinates;  {a 2000 byte structure}
  N, X, Y: integer;
begin
  for N := 1 to 500 do
    New(PicData[N]); { each call allocates 1000 bytes of heap space}
    for X := 1 to 500 do                     { initialize each element }
```

```
  for Y := 1 to 500 do
    PicData[X]^[Y] := 0;
.
.   { use the array }
.
end.
```

Here we've simulated a large two-dimensional array with an array of pointers, each element pointing to a unique 500-element integer array on the heap.

Any single element can be addressed using an X-coordinate value to index the array of pointers (and thereby select one particular 500-element array), and a Y coordinate to index into that array. For example, element (476,2) is referenced as :=PicData[476]^[2].

Pretty sneaky, although it still takes memory to work. What if you don't have the memory? Suppose that you need this array, but you don't need it to hold very many values. (We'll talk later about how many values are "too many.") Maybe you had a thousand or so non-zero values to place in the array; the remaining 249,000 elements would all be zero. Such a structure is called a *sparse array*, since the number of significant values is small compared to the total number of storage locations. Is there some way to store only the non-zero values?

There is indeed a way—by using a linked data structure. Suppose you defined the following node:

```
type
  NodePtr         = ^Node;
  Node =
    record
      Val           : Integer;
      X,Y           : Integer;
      Next,Last     : NodePtr;
    end;
```

Now, for each non-zero entry in the array, we use the Node data structure. The non-zero integer value is held in *Val*, the coordinates are kept in *X* and *Y*, and *Next* and *Last* point to the adjacent nodes along the X-axis. In the following example, each node has the value *(X,Y=Val)*:

```
-->(99,110=205)<--->(99,375=-10321)<--->(99,422=32032)<--
```

The general idea is that nodes with the same *X* value form a doubly linked list using the pointers *Next* and *Last*. Furthermore, the list is sorted by the Y coordinate along the X-axis. In other words, given nodes *A* and *B*, if $A^\wedge.Next = B$, then $A^\wedge.Y <= B^\wedge.Y$. This makes searches faster, since you may not need to search all nodes in a given list to find the one you're looking for.

You could implement this using a singly linked list, but it makes insertions and deletions more difficult. If you're tight on space, or if you're going to build the array and not change it, a single link reduces space.

So now you have several doubly linked lists, where each list represents all values having the same X coordinate. How do you find a given list, and how do you find a node within that list? One solution is to define a Header node for each list, and then link all the Header nodes together. To do that, you'll need a few extra pointers (for the Header nodes only—the Header nodes don't need the Y and *Val* values, only the X). Note that everything must link together. Let's modify the definition of node as follows:

```
Node =
  record
    Next,Last      : NodePtr;
      case Header : Boolean of
      False : (   Val          : Integer;
                  X,Y          : ARange);
      True  : (   XVal         : Integer;
                  Up,Down      : NodePtr)
  end;
```

We've created a variant record. The field Header decides what type of node this is. If Header equals True, then the node has the fields *XVal* (X coordinate for the axis) and *Up* and *Down* (pointers to other Header nodes). Using *Up* and *Down*, you can implement a doubly linked circular list of Header nodes. Each Header then uses Next and Last to form a doubly linked circular list of data nodes (Header equals False).

Here is boolean function *NodeFound*, which takes (X,Y) coordinates and returns a pointer to the corresponding node (if it exists):

```
function NodeFound(TX,TY : Integer; var TPtr : NodePtr) :Boolean;
var
  Found            : Boolean;
begin
  TPtr := theHead^.Up;
  Found := False;
  while (TPtr^.XVal < TX) and (TPtr <> theHead) do TPtr := TPtr^.Up;
  if TPtr^.XVal = TX then
  begin
    TPtr := TPtr^.Next;
    while (TPtr^.Y < TY) and not TPtr^.Header do
      TPtr := TPtr^.Next;
    Found := (TPtr^.Y = TY);
  end;
  NodeFound := Found;
end;  { NodeFound }
```

Global variable *theHead* is of type *NodePtr* and is the master Header node for the entire structure. This function first seeks to find a Header node for the X coordinate desired. If a Header node is found, *theHead* searches the list of data nodes until the Y coordinate desired is found. In either case, the search ends (fails) if a coordinate greater than the one sought is found, or if the list circles back to the initial Header.

Even when *NodeFound* returns False, it produces valuable information. In such cases, *TPtr* points to the closest node. For example, suppose you're looking for (259,321). It doesn't exist, but the nodes (259,17) and (259,421) do. *TPtr* returns from *NodeFound* pointing to (259,421), which means that if you want to add (259,321), you're at the correct point for insertion. Even if there are no nodes with X coordinate 259, *TPtr* still helps: It points to the Header node of the list just above 259. So, once again, you are pointing to the appropriate spot to insert a new Header node.

Mixed Sparse Arrays

There are many variations on sparse arrays, depending on how much space you have and how fast the program must be. Suppose you need the program to run faster and have memory to spare. You might keep your original definition of Node and declare the following array:

```
var
  Header                 : array[1..500] of NodePtr;
```

Instead of a linked list of Headers, you have a fixed array of all 500 Headers, one for each possible X coordinate. Initialize all elements in this array to be **nil**, then create linked lists as needed. The function *NodeFound* then looks like this:

```
function NodeFound(TX,TY : Integer; var TPtr : NodePtr) : Boolean;
var
  Done                 : Boolean;
begin
  TPtr := Header[TX];
  NodeFound := False;
  if TPtr <> nil then
  begin
    Done := False;
    repeat
      if (TPtr^.Y >= TY)
        then Done := True
        else TPtr := TPtr^.Next
    until Done or (TPtr = nil);
    if Done
      then NodeFound := (TPtr^.Y = TY);
  end;
end;   { NodeFound }
```

The inner search loop has been changed. Our linked lists are no longer circular, since the nodes can't point to the elements in the array Header. This forces us to make the test $TPtr^\wedge.Y >= TY$ inside the loop, since at the **until** statement there's a chance that $TPtr = $ **nil** (which makes the other comparison illegal). To use this routine, you would have to do some benchmarks to see if the increase in speed is worth the additional memory required.

When to Use Sparse Arrays

The toughest question about sparse arrays is when to use them. How can you tell if a linked list implementation will be smaller? The easiest way is to define a normal array and find its size using the *SizeOf* function. Then define a node for your linked list structure, and find out its size as well. Divide the array's size by the node's size. This tells you the point (in terms of number of nodes) at which your linked list version is eating up more memory than the normal array.

In much the same manner, you can divide the dynamic memory size (given at the end of a compilation) by the size of a node and find the maximum number of nodes allowable.

You should realize that pointers, at 4 bytes each, can eat up space. There's also between 8 and 20 bytes of overhead for every object you allocate in the heap, so if your actual data is small compared to the rest of the node, you may be better off with a regular array. On the other hand, if the data is rather large, such as a complete record, then the linked list approach looks better and better: The additional overhead for pointers becomes less significant, and the wasted space in a regular array becomes very significant.

Review

As a balance to Chapter 20, we examined nodes linked into nonlinear structures such as graphs, trees, and arrays. Here are two books (in addition to those mentioned in Chapter 20) that will provide you with more detail about trees, graphs, and other linked structures.

- Dromey, R. G. *How to Solve it by Computer*. Englewood Cliffs: Prentice-Hall International, 1982.

■ Knuth, D. E. *Searching and Sorting*, Vol. 3 of *The Art of Computer Programming*. Reading: Addison-Wesley, 1973.

22

Sorting and Searching

Searching and sorting are tasks common to virtually all applications for computers, from games to word processing to database management. Yet poorly written search and sort routines can result in unacceptably slow programs. So, more research has been done and more papers submitted on these topics than all others in computer science put together, with the possible exception of programming languages. As there are many books on these topics, we'll review only the basic examples of sorting and searching in this chapter.

Sorting

Sorting can be done on various levels. For instance, you can sort by grouping similar items together (all two-story homes, for example, could make up a group). You can also sort and order a group of similar items by predetermined ascending or descending values (all two-story houses valued from $125,000 to $195,000, listed in ascending order). Let's look at a few sorting methods, using a list of integers as the data to be sorted. They range from the simple and slow to the sneaky and fast.

Insertion Sort

In Part 1 of this book, we presented a sample program to sort a list of integers using *insertion sort* method:

```
procedure InsertSort(ListMax : Integer);
var
  Indx,Jndx,Val    : Integer;
begin
  for Indx := 2 to ListMax do
  begin
    Val := List[Indx];
    Jndx := Indx;
    while List[Jndx-1] > Val do
    begin
      List[Jndx] := List[Jndx-1];
      Jndx := Jndx - 1
    end;
    List[Jndx] := Val
  end
end;
```

This procedure assumes that *List* is declared as an **array[1..ListMax] of** *integer*. An insertion sort takes each number in the list and moves it toward the top of the list (leftmost element), shuffling the other numbers as it goes, until all the numbers preceding it are of a lower value. Starting at the top of the list, the sort works its way down the list, so that the upper portion of the list is always sorted. Suppose that, partway through the sort, the list looked like this:

-10 -2 15 19 55 69 0 -20 42 100

The next low-value number we come across is *0*, and that number keeps moving left until it finds a number less than itself (-2). The list would then look like this:

-10 -2 0 15 19 55 69 -20 42 100

The next number to be moved, *–20*, illustrates a special case in insertion sorts. The number *–20* is of the lowest value in the list of numbers; you must know how to stop when you hit the top of the list since you'll never encounter a lower value in the list itself.

Three possible solutions present themselves. First, if you're working with a list of *N* elements, then declare the array to have *N + 1* elements (*0..N*) and store the lowest possible value in location *0*. For example, you might do the following:

const

```
  ListMax        = 10;
var
  List : array[0..ListMax] of integer;
begin
  List[0] := -MaxInt - 1;
  ...
end.
```

The values you want sorted are stored in locations 1 through *ListMax*. The location *List[0]* acts as a stopper or *sentinel*; since it's the lowest possible integer value, nothing can move beyond it.

In some cases, you won't be able to use this extra location. For example, when sorting part of a list, there may not be a "free" location there. You can then use the second approach: Before starting the sort, find the lowest value in the list and move it to *List[1]* as the sentinel, substituting it for the present sentinel value. For example, if our original list to be sorted looked like this,

```
-10 19 15 -2 69 55 0 -20 42 100
```

after the search and swap, the list would look like this:

```
-20 19 15 -2 69 55 0 -10 42 100
```

As you can see, the values *–20* and *–10* traded places. Now, all other values in the list are greater than *–20*, thus all values will stop moving when they reach *–20* (if not before).

The third solution is to put a **goto** statement in the inner loop, jumping out of the loop if *Jndx* gets down to *1*.

Shellsort

The insertion sort, while effective, suffers from the large number of comparisons and exchanges needed to move a number from its starting position to its final one. A computer scientist named Donald Shell suggested that, since most numbers sorted are going to move a fair amount anyway, it might be more efficient to compare and swap numbers of greatest distance from each other first, shrinking the distance between numbers until you return to the ones in closest proximity to each other. This method is known as *shellsort* or sorting by diminishing increment.

Two issues immediately arise in considering shellsort. First is the sort method to use, since shellsort only states to sort those numbers some distance from each other, not how to sort them.

The second issue is deciding what incremental value to use. *Shellsort* is difficult to analyze; most studies of its effectiveness are based on trial-and-error testing. The literature suggests at least three approaches. Assuming a list of *N* integers, you might use one of the following sets of diminishing increments:

- Start with *Inc* = *N* **div** 2; divide *Inc* by 2 each time.
- Start with *Inc* = (2^P)-1, where *P* = *Trunc(N log 2)*; decrement *P* by 1 each time.
- Set *Inc* = 1, then continue to set *Inc* := 3*Inc + 1 until *Inc* > *N*; divide *Inc* by 3 at the start of each loop.

The following example of *Shellsort* (adapted from *Algorithms*; see the end of this chapter) uses the third method:

```
procedure ShellSort();
          { purpose: sort list using shell algorithm }
label
  ExitLoop;
var
  Indx,Jndx,Val,Inc : integer;
begin
  Inc := 1;
  repeat
    Inc := 3*Inc + 1
  until Inc > ListMax;
  repeat
    Inc := Inc div 3;
    for Indx := Inc+1 to ListMax do
    begin
      Val := List[Indx];
      Jndx := Indx;
      while List[Jndx-Inc] > Val do
      begin
        List[Jndx] := List[Jndx-Inc];
        Jndx := Jndx - Inc;
        if Jndx <= Inc
          then goto ExitLoop
      end;
ExitLoop:
      List[Jndx] := Val
    end
  until Inc = 1
end; { ShellSort }
```

At the center of the program is the insertion sort routine (using the **goto** solution) with one major change: The number 1 has been replaced by the variable *Inc*. Because of the way *Inc* is initialized, it will equal 1 the last time through the loop and will do a regular insertion sort. By that time, the list will be mostly sorted. The remaining few that have to be moved don't have far to go.

Quicksort

Shellsort is a simple, efficient sorting method. However, you may find yourself in a situation where you need the list sorted as quickly as possible. In such cases, your best bet is probably *Quicksort*, an algorithm developed by C.A.R. Hoare.

The basic idea of *Quicksort* is as follows: Using the list of integers *List[1..ListMax]*, perform the following steps:

- Pick some number in *List*, which we'll call *Val*.

- Move all the numbers in *List* so that *Val* is in its correct location, *List[Indx]*. This means that all the numbers in *List[1..Indxl-1]* are less than *Val* (although not necessarily sorted), and that all the numbers in *List[Indx+1..ListMax]* are greater than *Val* (also not necessarily sorted).

- Now perform the same operation for each sublist, *List[1..Indx-1]* and *List[Indx+1..ListMax]*. This continues until each sublist is too small to sort.

The simplest implementation of quicksort is a recursive one. Adapting again from Sedgewick, you have the following implementation:

```
function Partition(Left,Right : integer) : integer; { partition list into two
sublists }
var
  Val,Indx,Jndx,Temp : integer;
begin
  Val  := List[Right];
  Indx := Left - 1; Jndx := Right;
  repeat
    repeat Indx := Indx + 1 until List[Indx] >= Val;
      repeat Jndx := Jndx - 1 until List[Jndx] <= Val;
      Temp := List[Indx];
      List[Indx] := List[Jndx];
      List[Jndx] := Temp
  until Jndx <= Indx;
  List[Jndx] := List[Indx];
  List[Indx] := List[Right];
  List[Right] := Temp;
  Partition := Indx
end; { Partition }

procedure QuickSort(Left,Right : integer);
        { recursive implementation of Quicksort }
var
  Indx : integer;
begin  { main body of proc QuickSort }
  if Left <= Right then begin
    Indx := Partition(Left,Right);
    QuickSort(Left,Indx-1);
    QuickSort(Indx+1,Right)
```

```
  end
end;   { QuickSort }
```

The procedure *Partition* uses the last value (*List[Right]*) in the current sublist as *Val*, the one to be moved to its correct location. It then starts at both ends of the list and moves toward the center, swapping numbers on the left greater than *Val* with those on the right less than *Val*. Once it hits the center, it picks the last number greater than *Val* (*List[Indx]*) and swaps it with *Val* (which is still sitting at *List[Right]*). *Val* is now in its final location, and *Indx* becomes the new dividing point. The procedure *QuickSort* calls *Partition* for the current list, then calls itself for the left and right sublists that *Indx* divides.

You may not want to use a recursive approach in some situations. If the list is large, the stack might overflow. This happens when the stack runs into the heap—which is bad news for data stored in the upper regions of the heap. You can avoid recursion by implementing your own stack, either with an array or with a linked list (as shown in Chapter 20).

Here's a non-recursive version of *QuickSort*, assuming you have a set of stack routines (*ClearStack, Push, Pop, StackEmpty*):

```
procedure QuickSort;
         { non-recursive implementation of Quicksort }
var
  Left,Right,Indx       : Integer;
  Done                  : Boolean;
begin
  Left := 1; Right := ListMax;
  ClearStack;  Done := False;
  repeat
    if Left <= Right then
    begin
      Indx := Partition(Left,Right);
      if (Indx-Left) > (Right-Indx) then
      begin
        Push(Left); Push(Indx-1);
        Left := Indx + 1
      end
      else
      begin
        Push(Indx+1); Push(Right);
        Right := Indx -1
      end;
    end
    else if not StackEmpty then
    begin
      Pop(Right); Pop(Left)
    end
    else Done := True
  until Done
end;   { QuickSort }
```

This version always pushes the larger sublist on the stack, looping back to partition the smaller one first. This helps reduce the number of values pushed onto the stack; the upper limit is about *lg ListMax* (*lg* means log base 2). If *ListMax = 10*, then the stack need only hold four sets of values. Your best bet is probably to use an array-based stack, since the overhead for a linked list stack isn't worth it.

Searching

As mentioned at the start of this chapter, searching techniques help you determine the location (if any) of specific data, in order to retrieve, modify, or verify its existence or place more data nearby (as in sorting). Usually, you're searching for a *key*, some part of the information that identifies the rest of it. In the simplest case, such as a list of integers, the key is the information itself. In more complex settings, such as a list of records, the key might be an ID number, a name, or something even more complex. In every case, you know the key, and you want to find its location. Let's look at a few methods of searching.

Sequential Search

Given a list of values (such as integers), the most straightforward way to find a given value (or key) is to start at the top of the list and search it sequentially until you come to the end. With certain data structures, such as linear linked lists, this is your only option, since you usually have no way of jumping into the middle of the list. (Arrays provide more options, which we'll examine momentarily.) Right now, let's assume we're looking for a given integer value in the integer array *List[1..ListMax]*. Our routine might look like this:

```
function Found(Val : Integer; var Indx : Integer) : Boolean;
var
  Flag : Boolean;
begin
  Flag := False;
  Indx := 1;
  while not Flag and (Indx <= ListMax) do
    if List[Indx] = Val then
      Flag := True
    else
      Indx := Indx + 1;
  Found := Flag
end;   { Found }
```

This function returns True if *Val* is found in *List* and sets *Indx* to the appropriate location; otherwise, it returns False and *Indx* equals *ListMax+1*. If *List* has been sorted, then it can be made a bit more efficient:

```
function Found(Val : Integer; var Indx : Integer) : Boolean;
var
  Done : Boolean;
begin
  Found := False;
  Done  := False;
  Indx := 1;
  while not Done and (Indx <= ListMax) do
    if List[Indx] = Val then
    begin
      Done := True;
      Found := True
    end
    else
      if List[Indx] > Val then
        Done := True
      else
        Indx := Indx + 1
end;   { Found }
```

Now the search function knows to quit as soon as it encounters a number greater than *Val*, since the rest of the list will also be greater than *Val*. Unless *List* is short, however, you're better off using a binary search.

Binary Search

Think for a moment about looking for a given value in a sorted list of numbers. Instead of starting to the left and going through the list, suppose you start in the middle. If you happen to hit the exact value you want, you're done. If the value is too large, then you know to search the left half; otherwise, search the right half. Repeat this process on the appropriate half until you find the value or run out of lists.

You've just performed a *binary search*—a zeroing-in process that isn't too different from the way you look up words in a dictionary. Here's an implementation:

```
function BFound(Val : integer; var Indx : integer) : boolean;
var
  Left,Right   : integer;
begin
  Left  := 1; Right := ListMax;
  repeat
    Indx := (Left+Right) shr 1; { = div 2 }
    if Value < List[Indx]
```

```
      then Right := Indx - 1
      else Left  := Indx + 1
  until (Value = List[Indx]) or (Left > Right);
  BFound := (Left <= Right)
end;  { BFound }
```

The advantage of a binary search is that the most comparisons you'll have to do is *lg* of *ListMax*. With a sequential search, you'll average *ListMax*/2 comparisons, and your worst case is *ListMax*.

If *ListMax* = *MaxInt* (32767), here are the best, worse, and average performances of sequential and binary searches:

	Best	**Worst**	**Average**
Sequential	1	32767	16383
Binary	1	16	8

As you can see, there's quite a difference between the two methods. However, if you will be changing the list a lot, keeping it sorted could be unacceptably slow, unless you're using a linked list. If you're using a linked list, however, you can't use the binary search method. Fortunately, there is yet another technique that combines the two approaches: *hashing*.

Hashing

You can easily maintain (add to and remove from) a sorted linked list, but you must search it sequentially. Sorted arrays are easily searched, but you have to do a lot of work to keep them sorted. Hashing takes the best of both approaches. For example, suppose you have the following definitions:

```
const
  HMax              = 63;
type
  NodePtr           = ^Node;
  Node =
    record
      Next          : NodePtr;
      Data          : integer
    end;
var
  HList             : array[0..HMax] of NodePtr;
```

HList is an array of Header nodes, each one possibly pointing to a linked list. To add a value to the list, you must first use a hashing function to choose among the header nodes. This function takes the data subfield (on which we're sorting) and returns some result in the range *0..HMax*. It always returns the same result for the same data value (or you couldn't find the stored data). Also, it tries to spread the hash values evenly over the range *0..HMax*, so that most of your values don't end up in only a few locations.

Once you have the hash value, you can use it as an index into *HList*. You now have a linked list to which you can add your value. This list can be sorted or not, as you prefer. Finding a number involves the same process: You must use the hash function to find the Header node in *HList*, then search the linked list until you find the value or reach the end.

Do you see how this is a compromise between pure arrays and pure linked lists? If *HMax = 0*, then you've got a simple linked list; if *HMax = the number of values to be stored* (and you drop the hash function), then you've got a regular array. The value of *HMax* determines just how much you're leaning toward one or the other. A large *HMax* reduces collisions (when two or more values map to the same index) and speeds up the search, while a small *HMax* reduces the amount of memory initially allocated.

External Search

Sometimes the data you're after is in a file. The file may be too large to have in memory, so you pull in selected records as you need them. Each time you read a record from the file, it costs you a certain amount of time. Your goal, then, is to read as few records as possible when searching for the one desired.

The worst case is to start at the beginning of the file and read each record until you find the one you want. This method would be necessary if you could only read files sequentially. Luckily, Turbo Pascal allows random access of files (via the *Seek* procedure). So, if a file is sorted, you can use a variation of the binary search to look for a given record.

However, sorting a file is even messier than sorting an array, and you still might have to read several records before finding the record (or verifying that it isn't there). More efficient techniques are needed.

One approach is to maintain a separate list, called an *index table*, consisting of keys and record numbers for all the records in the file. Suppose an accounting application needs to retrieve a particular customer's record from a sales file, based on the customer's name. You might make the following definition:

```
type
  CustIndex =
    record
      Name            : NameStr;
```

```
    Index           : integer
  end;
```

You now have a data type for each entry in the index table, associating a name with a record number in the file. The question is, what data structure do you use for the table itself? The answer depends on how big the table will be and if it will tend to change in size a lot. Essentially, you have the choices we've already presented: array, linked list, or hash table. You can even add some twists, such as faking a dynamically sized array. And you'll probably want to write the index table itself out to disk, to avoid having to recreate it each time by reading through the entire file of customer records.

Given the choice of an index table, you can then use the searching and sorting options to find the name, get the index, and read in the appropriate record.

```
var
  ITable        : array[1..TabMax] of CustIndex;
  ICount        : 0..TabMax;
  CFile         : file of CustRec;
  .
  .
  .
function RecFound(FName : NameStr; var Cust : CustRec) : Boolean;
var
  Tndx : Integer;
begin
  Tndx := 1; RecFound := False;
  while (Tndx <= ICount) do with ITable[Tndx] do
    if FName = Name then
    begin
      RecFound := True;
      Seek(CFile,Index);
      Read(CFile,Cust);
      Tndx := ICount + 1
    end
    else Tndx := Tndx + 1
end;  { RecFound }
```

This routine does not assume that the index table (*ITable*) is sorted. It does a sequential search for the name. If the name is found, the routine reads in the appropriate record and returns True; otherwise, it returns False.

Review

In this chapter, we uncovered the rudiments of sorting and searching. After our discussion of the insertion sort method, *Shellsort*, *Quicksort*, hashing, and sequential, binary, and external searching, you may want to investigate further. There are many books on the topic, including the following and the ones mentioned in previous chapters, which provide more detailed information.

- Sedgewick, R. *Algorithms*. Reading: Addison-Wesley, 1984.
- Knuth, D. E. "Searching and Sorting," *The Art of Computer Programming*, Vol. 3. Reading: Addison-Wesley, 1983.

23

Writing Large Programs

The programs presented thus far in this book haven't stretched the capacity of either Turbo Pascal or the Macintosh—not by a long shot. Many programmers will never have occasion to produce programs any larger than Turbo Typist. If you're in that group, count yourself lucky: You'll never experience the heartaches that result from stretching a given computer/compiler combination to the limit.

This chapter is dedicated to those of you that will someday produce a large Macintosh application—a program with thousands of lines of source code or huge memory requirements, or both.

As drawn up by Professor Wirth in his cozy study at the University of Zurich, Pascal has no limitations. It runs on an imaginary computer with infinite RAM, capable of accommodating an arbitrary number of arbitrarily large arrays, with an infinite amount of memory left over for huge code blocks and bottomless stacks for infinitely deep recursion. However, in real life, Turbo Pascal has boundaries—and, depending in what direction you stretch things and how far, you will eventually bump into one.

These boundaries result from judgment calls by the author of the compiler. The author of Turbo Pascal, for example, decreed that sets shall have no more than 256 elements. It was decided that this number was large enough for most uses and that larger sets would eat up too much memory and be too slow to work with.

Faking Large Arrays

A restriction we're familiar with by now is the 32K limit of any single data structure. Turbo Pascal permits no type definitions where a variable of that type would occupy more than 32K. This problem, which is especially galling in light of the Macintosh's potential to address 4 million bytes of RAM, also stems from a design decision. Because of a quirk in the instruction set of the processor, structures any larger are significantly slower to access.

Arrays are most likely to come up against this constraint, so let's investigate a couple of strategies for faking big arrays.

In Chapter 21, we learned a trick for simulating large two-dimensional arrays. In a nutshell, instead of declaring variable *PicData* to be

```
var PicData : array[1..500,1..500] of Integer;
begin
  PicData[14,312] := 1234;
  . . .
```

we defined it as

```
var PicData : array[1..500] of ^array[1..500] of Integer;
begin
  PicData[14]^[312] := 1234;
  . . .
```

A more general solution is to abandon array notation entirely. Suppose an application requires a one-dimensional array of 30,000 reals. Since

```
var
  theArray : array [1..30000] of Real;
```

won't compile (this structure is 120,000 bytes long), let dedicated procedures and functions simulate the array structure for you, as shown here:

```
program FakeBigArray;
type
  arrayHelper = array[1..7500] of Real; { a 30,000-byte structure}
var
  Part1, Part2, Part3, Part4: ^arrayHelper; {16 bytes of global data}

function GetReal(Index: integer): Real;
var
  N: integer;
begin
  N := Index mod 7500;
  case Index of
```

```
      00001..07500: GetReal := Part1^[N];
      07501..15000: GetReal := Part2^[N];
      15001..22500: GetReal := Part3^[N];
      22501..30000: GetReal := Part4^[N];
    end;
  end;

  procedure PutReal(Index: integer; R: real);
  var
    N: Integer;
  begin
    N := Index mod 7500;
    case Index of
      00001..07500: Part1^[N] := R;
      07501..15000: Part2^[N] := R;
      15001..22500: Part3^[N] := R;
      22501..30000: Part4^[N] := R;
    end;
  end;
  var
    N: integer;
  begin
    New(part1); New(part2); New(part3); New(part4); { allocate space }
    for N := 1 to 30000 do
      PutReal(N,0.0);   { initialize }
    .
    .  { Use GetReal to read the array;  write to it with PutReal }
    .
  end.
```

This program uses four arrays on the heap to simulate one large one. The simulation is based on using *GetReal* and *PutReal* instead of array notation in accessing the simulated array. Wherever you'd normally say

```
theArray[X] := 3.14159
```

instead use

```
PutReal(X, 3.14159).
```

And instead of

```
WriteLn(theArray[X]);
```

use

```
WriteLn(GetReal[X]);
```

In Part 5 of this book, we'll learn more elegant and general solutions to large structures involving the Toolbox calls *NewPtr* and *NewHandle*. These routines can create effective arrays as large as available heap space, from 20 to 2,000,000 bytes. The "handle" approach is particularly interesting, because it allows a heap object to grow (and shrink) as conditions dictate, much like a file.

32K of Global Variables

The same processor quirk behind the 32K structure maximum also prevents a program from declaring more than 32K of global variables. Similarly, no single procedure or function can declare more than 32K of local variables. For example, this program refuses to compile:

```
program TooMuchGlobal;
type
  array10K = array [1..5000] of integer;
var
  A,B,C,D: array10K;   { 10K each; 40K total }
begin
end.
```

Try it and you'll get the compile-time message `Too many global variables`. A more accurate description would be, "More than 32K of global variables." *TooMuchGlobal* won't compile even in a 4-megabyte Macintosh, although this program will:

```
program CompilesFine;
type
  array10K = array [1..5000] of integer;
var
  A,B,C,D: ^array10K;
begin
  New(A); New(B); New(C); New(D);
end.
```

CompilesFine has 16 bytes of global storage. Of course, whether or not it succeeds in allocating 40,000 bytes of heap storage at run time is another story.

Stack Data

At run time, Turbo Pascal programs automatically create, use, and finally destroy the local variables of procedures and functions using a last-in, first-out methodology known as the stack. Depending on the amount of memory in your machine and other factors, there can be anywhere from hundreds of thousands of bytes to only about 8K available for the stack.

When the stack fills up and attempts to store data outside the area reserved for it, a Stack Overflow run-time error occurs.

The stack is used for

- the return address of each routine that has called a currently active procedure or function
- parameters passed to procedures and functions
- the local variables of all active procedures and functions

Programs are most likely to cause a stack overflow if they perform the following operations, especially in combination:

- declare large local variables
- pass large variables by value
- use recursive algorithms

Large Local Variables

The following program demonstrates how the stack is used for storing local variables. *Proc1* and *Proc2* each declare 30K of local variables, variables that exist only when their enclosing procedure is active.

```
program LocalVars;
type
  array10K = array [1..5000] of integer;

procedure Proc1;
var
  A,B,C: array10K;
begin
  WriteLn('60K of local variables on stack');
  ReadLn;
end;

procedure Proc2;
var
  A,B,C: array10K;
begin
  WriteLn('30K of local variables on stack');
  ReadLn;
  Proc1;
  WriteLn('30K of local variables on stack');
  ReadLn;
end;
begin
  WriteLn('No local variables on stack');
  ReadLn;
  Proc2;
```

```
    WriteLn('No local variables on stack');
    ReadLn;
end.
```

If your machine is tight on memory, you'll get a `Stack Overflow` when either *Proc1* or *Proc2* attempts to allocate space for its arrays.

Passing Large Structures by Value

When passing a structure by value to a procedure, a copy is made of the structure and placed on the stack. For example,

```
program StackPassing;
type
  array10K = array [1..5000] of integer;
var
  X: Array10K;

procedure Proc1(anArray: array10K);
begin
end;

begin
  Proc1(X);
end.
```

In the process of calling *Proc1* from the main program at run time, a copy of array *X* is placed on the stack. This consumes 10K of stack space and takes time. This space remains occupied until *Proc1* returns. Had *Proc1* declared its parameter with the **var** attribute instead,

```
procedure Proc1(var anArray: array10K);
```

all that would have gone on the stack would be the address of array *X*—4 bytes instead of 10,000.

This is not to say that all parameters should be passed by reference; passing by value allows better separation between caller and client and therefore fewer chances of unexpected interactions. But when working with arrays (even large strings), keep in mind the overhead cost of pass-by-value.

Recursion

The third primary cause of stack overflow is recursion. Since a recursive routine may call itself hundreds or thousands of times, there's an excellent chance of stack overflow unless its local variable and parameter storage requirements are small. For example, this program recurses endlessly, using up 10K of stack with each call, until the error handler finally takes over:

```
program EndlessRecursion;
type
  array10K = array [1..5000] of integer;
var
  RecursionCount: integer;

procedure Proc1;
var
  A: array10K;
begin
  RecursionCount := RecursionCount + 1;
  WriteLn('Number of KBytes now on stack: ',RecursionCount * 10);
  Proc1;                                    { recursive call }
end;

begin
  RecursionCount := 0;
  Proc1;
end.
```

Again, don't take this to mean that you shouldn't write recursive algorithms. Such programs are often the most efficient and elegant solution to a given problem. Just be aware of the program's stack requirements: How many bytes of local variables and parameters does the routine use? What's the worst-case depth to which the routine might nest?

The stack starts in high memory and grows down; the heap starts low and grows up. A stack overflow occurs when the two meet. The heap grows slowly, about 6K at a time, in accordance with allocation requests via *New*. Note, however, that the *MaxAvail* function expands the heap to its maximum, resulting in approximately 8K of stack space. If this isn't enough stack for your application, be careful not to call *MaxAvail*. We return to the subject of stack allocation in more detail in Chapter 30, where we describe techniques to allocate heap and stack space more equitably.

Segmentation: The $S Directive

Turbo Pascal follows standard Macintosh practice by dividing the programs that it creates into chunks known as *segments*. (This term is unrelated to the concept of segments used in 8086 family processors, such as used in the IBM PC.) Macintosh architecture breaks large programs into segments so that code modules can be independently loaded into memory and later expunged.

This allows routines that aren't needed in a given situation to stay on disk until required. For example, a lengthy initialization routine need only be in memory at the start of a program's execution. Once its task is complete, the memory it occupies can be given back.

When the compilation of a particular program or unit hits the 32K barrier, you are forced to segment your code whether you want the benefits of automatic segment loading or not. To segment a program or unit, turn on segmentation at the start of the program with {$S+}. Then, before each procedure and function, use a $S directive to specify the segment that procedure or function should belong to. For example,

```
program SegDemo;
{$S+}                          { Turn segmentation on; it's off by default }

procedure Proc0;        { By default, code goes to the "blank" segment }
begin
end;
{$S seg1}               { Until next $S directive, put all code generated }
procedure Proc1; { into a code segment named 'seg1'--case is significant }
begin
end;
procedure Proc2;                         { Also in segment 'seg1' }
begin
end;
{$S }
procedure Proc3;        { Like Proc0, a member of the "blank" segment }
begin
end;
begin                                 { Ditto for the main program }
  ReadLn;
  Proc1;
  ReadLn;
end.
```

Enter and compile program *SegDemo* to disk. Then exit Turbo and execute this program (use the Transfer option of the File menu). When this program first gets control, only the procedures in the blank segment are initially in memory. The call to *Proc1* automatically brings in segment *seg1*, so listen for disk activity just after pressing *Return* to satisfy the *ReadLn*. For more information on segmentation, see Chapter 9 of the *Turbo Pascal User's Guide and Reference Manual*.

Compile-Time Memory

It's possible to run out of memory when compiling a program with a large number of identifiers. Turbo Pascal allocates a certain amount of space for storing symbol table information. If this space fills up, you've got to go back and find some space.

There is a good and a bad way to reduce the number of identifiers in a program. The bad way is to "de-Pascalize" your program, to strip it of high-level niceties such as enumerated data types and plentiful constants.

The good way is to convert your program into one or more units. Then the compiler only has to tackle the identifiers in a given unit or main program. You'll make things even easier on the compiler if you keep the number of identifiers in each unit's interface to a minimum. This approach produces a good result all around: no identifier crisis, fast compilations, and detail hiding.

Now that you know some techniques for overcoming size limitations in Turbo Pascal, let's move on to the **goto** statement.

24

The Goto Statement

In this chapter, we'll study the black sheep of the Pascal family: the **goto** statement. A **goto** causes an unconditional transfer of control to another point in the program, a point marked by a special construct called a *label*.

Syntax of the Goto Statement

A **goto** statement consists of the reserved word **goto**, followed by a number or identifier that has been declared as a label in the declaration part of the currently executing procedure (or function or main program). You cannot use **goto** to jump into or out of a procedure (or function or main program) but only to another statement within that procedure (or function or main program). Its syntax diagram is shown in Figure 24.1.

Figure 24.1: Syntax Diagram of Goto Statement

The label marking the destination of a **goto** statement must be declared in the declaration part of a program, procedure, or function. Figure 24.2 shows the syntax of a label declaration part in Turbo Pascal.

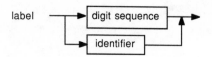

In Standard Pascal, labels cannot be identifiers; they can only be unsigned integers (for example, '1', '100'). Turbo allows labels to be normal identifiers, to better describe the place in the program to which they refer.

How to Use the Goto Statement—And Why Not to

Early programming languages had fewer flow control and decision-making statements than are available in Pascal. For instance, the original FORTRAN had no **else** clause in its version of the **if** statement. Here are two versions of a program fragment, one written in Pascal, the other in FORTRAN.

```
Pascal                      FORTRAN

if A < 27 then                IF A .LT. 27 THEN GOTO 1
  A := A + 2                  A = A + 1
else                         GOTO 2
  A := A + 1;               1 A = A + 2
                            2 CONTINUE
```

The FORTRAN version is almost laughably complicated. If the value of variable *A* is less than *27*, execution continues on the line with the number *1* (a label) before it. (.LT. is FORTRAN's way of saying "less than" because keyboards didn't always have < and > back when FORTRAN was defined.) Otherwise, the statement *A = A + 1* is executed. (FORTRAN uses = for assignment; Pascal uses :=.) Then the computer executes the statement *GOTO 2*, which jumps to the statement with the word *CONTINUE* in it. (The *CONTINUE* statement does nothing; it is merely a place holder for a label.)

How much clearer the Pascal version is! Instead of thinking in terms of machine language-like jumps, you can express an algorithm in near-English. Because of the descriptive power of Pascal's structured statements, there's little need for **goto**s and labels.

However, a **goto** can be helpful once in a while. One instance is when you must exit from the middle of a loop, such as a **for** or a **while** loop. Consider this loop:

```
for I := 1 to 10 do                        { Get 10 numbers }
begin
  Write('Enter a number ( < 0 to stop ): ');
  ReadLn(Number[I]);
if Number < 0 then
  goto NoMore;
end;
NoMore:
  .
  .
  .
```

This loop normally gets 10 numbers from the user, but it terminates at once if the user enters a negative number.

Even in this case, it would be better programming style to make the loop a separate procedure, and use *Exit* to leave the procedure (and therefore the loop) when you get a negative number.

Here's another example of how confusing **goto**s can be. Can you predict what this program writes to the screen?

```
program Spaghetti;
label
  One, Two, Three, Four;
var
  A : integer;
begin
  A := 0;
  One:    if A > 3 then goto Three;
  Two:    A := A + 5; goto Four;
  Three:  A := A + 3; goto Two;
  Four:   if A mod 3 <> 0 then goto One;

  WriteLn(A);
  ReadLn;
end.
```

The answer is 21.

Review

As Niklaus Wirth and Kathleen Jensen say in *The Pascal User Manual and Report*: "The presence of **goto**s in a Pascal program is often an indication that the programmer has not yet learned 'to think' in Pascal (as this is a necessary construct in other programming languages)."

We agree, and we encourage you to build programs without them.

25

Computer Numbering Systems: Boolean Operations on Integers

In our discussion of operators in Chapter 9, we mention that it is possible to use the operators normally reserved for boolean values with integers and long integers. In this chapter, we explore the meaning and application of such apparently nonsensical expressions as *3* **and** *25* and *2541* **or** *12*.

Numbers as Bits and Bytes: Representing Integers in Memory

To understand how boolean operators work on integers, you must first understand how integers are stored in memory. As you may recall from earlier discussions, all data is represented internally as 1s and 0s, that is, as bits. How does a group of bits "get together" to describe the value of an integer? The "code" is similar to what we normally use to represent numbers. We will examine the base 10, or decimal, system we use daily and see how we can make it work when there are only two possible values for a digit: 0 and 1.

Place Value

When we count to 10, we begin with single digits, like so:

0	9 digits left
1	8 " "
2	7 " "
3	6 " "
4	5 " "
5	4 " "
6	3 " "
7	2 " "
8	1 " "
9	no digits left

After counting to 9, we move on to 10 without thinking—a 1 followed by a 0.

What are we really doing here? We're reusing symbols to avoid inventing new ones. The 1 in the number 10 is the symbol for 1, but because of its place in the number it represents a value of ten: The 0, a place holder, represents a value of *nothing*. Similarly, the 2 in the number 20 represents a value of *twenty* and the 3 in 35 represents a value of *thirty* (with the 5 still representing a value of *five*). The idea of having a digit represent a different value depending on its location in the number is called *positional notation*, and it is the central idea behind all modern numbering systems (including binary and hexadecimal).

The second digit from the right in a decimal number is said to be in the "tens" place; similarly, the 5 in the number 543 is said to be in the "hundreds" place. Each place to the left has a value of 10 times its predecessor, ad infinitum. It's no accident that the multiplying factor between places is 10 and not 14, 4, or 7: It's the number of fingers owned by Cro-Magnon mathematicians.

If the digits 8 and 9 suddenly disappear, we would have no way of representing them with a single digit. However, we could make the symbol 10 stand for the value eight, 11 for nine, and so on. In this case, we'd be counting in *octal* (base 8).

If we continue our exercise by eliminating all the digits down to 7, 6, or 5, then the single-digit numbers decrease correspondingly—and the multiplying factor for the numbers in successively higher places decrease as well. Base 2 uses two digits and a multiplying factor of two between places. Here's a table that shows what happens:

Base	Available Digits	Place Values	Value of Symbol '10'
Base 10	0,1,2,3,4,5,6,7,8,9	1,10,100,1000,...	Ten
Base 8	0,1,2,3,4,5,6,7	1,8,64,256,...	Eight
Base 7	0,1,2,3,4,5,6	1,7,49,343,...	Seven
Base 3	0,1,2	1,3,9,27,81,...	Three
Base 2	0,1	1,2,4,8,16,32,64...	Two

Using these place values, we can understand how to read a number in any base. For instance, in the number 143_7 (where the subscript indicates that the number is expressed in base 7), we can look at the places as follows:

$$
\begin{aligned}
1 \times 7^2 &= 49 \\
4 \times 7^1 &= 28 \\
3 \times 7^0 &= + \ 3 \\
\hline
& 72
\end{aligned}
$$

1   4   3

How about the number 00111001_2? It would read

$$
\begin{aligned}
1 \times 2^5 &= 32 \\
1 \times 2^4 &= 16 \\
1 \times 2^3 &= 8 \\
1 \times 2^0 &= + \ 1 \\
\hline
& 57
\end{aligned}
$$

0 0 1 1 1 0 0 1

It is possible to have a numbering system with *more* than 10 digits. Hexadecimal (hex for short) has 16 digits—0 through 9 plus *A* through *F*. The digit *A* has the value *ten*, *B* is *eleven*, and so on up to *F*, which is *fifteen*. Here's an example of how to read hex:

$$
\begin{aligned}
3 \times 16^2 &= 768 \\
15 \times 16^1 &= 240 \\
14 \times 16^0 &= + \ 14 \\
\hline
& 1022
\end{aligned}
$$

$3 F E

Hexadecimal numbers are usually indicated by a preceding dollar sign or, in some systems, with a letter *H* at the end. Turbo Pascal uses the dollar-sign convention. So, 100 represents a decimal value, and $100 is a hexadecimal value equal to 256 decimal.

The values of the places in hex go up by a factor of 16 each time you move to the left. Thus, it is possible to write large numbers in only a few hex digits. ($10000 equals 64K; $100000 equals 1 megabyte—1048576 decimal.) A numbering system with more single digits (that is, with a higher base) always expresses a number more compactly than one with fewer possible digits (a lower base).

Exercises

Translate these numbers to base 10. (The answers are in Appendix B.)

1. 1212_3
2. 8435_9
3. 111111_2
4. 3051_7
5. $3FF

Reversing Base Values

It is also useful to understand how to reverse the process, to convert numbers from decimal to an arbitrary base. To do this, consider the values of the places in the base you are converting *to*, and find the largest number that is less than the one you are converting *from*. Then, divide the number you are converting by the value of that place, and place the quotient in that place. Next, take the remainder from the division and repeat the process, filling in unused places with 0s.

To show this technique in action, let's convert the decimal number 37 to binary. As shown in Table 25.1, the places in binary have the values 1, 2, 4, 8, 16, 32, 64, and so on, which are the powers of 2 from 0 on up. Since 37 is less than 64, the left-most digit (also called the *most significant digit*) of the binary representation of 37 must be in the 32s place:

	32s	16s	8s	4s	2s	1s
37/32 = 1, remainder = 5	1	?	?	?	?	?

Now, resume with the remainder 5. Since 5 is smaller than 16 or 8, those places are filled in with 0s; however, since 5 is greater than 4, we do another division operation:

5/4 = 1, remainder = 1   1   0   0   1   ?   ?

Finally, only a 1 remains. We therefore put a 0 in the 2s place, and the 1 fits into the 1s place with a remainder of 0:

1/1 = 1, remainder = 0   1   0   0   1   0   1

Thus, the binary representation of 37_{10} is 100101_2.

Before we give you some examples to try, let's run through another example, converting the number 50085_{10} to hex.

	4096s	256s	16s	1s
50085/4096 = 12 = $C, remainder = 933	C	?	?	?
933/256 = 3, remainder = 165	C	3	?	?
165/16 = 10 = $A, remainder = 5	C	3	A	5

In this example, we converted all quotients produced by division to single digits of the base we were converting to. Thus, the quotient of 12 decimal from the first division was converted to the single digit C. Two divisions later, we converted 10 decimal to the value A. In *all* cases, you must be able to convert the result to a single digit, or you've made a mistake.

Exercises

Convert the following numbers to the bases indicated (see Appendix B for solutions):

1. 6673_{10} to base 5
2. 65533_{10} to hex
3. 45_{10} to binary
4. 3262_{10} to base 7

The Special Relationship between Binary and Hex

Since 16 is a power of two, you might expect to find a relationship between binary and hexadecimal. In fact, this turns out to be the case, and the resulting relationship makes it easy to represent binary numbers using hex. It is for this reason and no other that hex is used by programmers.

Let's look at the number 151 expressed in both binary and hex. The binary form of 151 is

1 0 0 1 0 1 1 1

In hex, the same value is

9   7

If you group the digits in the binary number into clusters of four (sometimes called a *nibble*) and convert those groups to hex digits, then you get the equivalent number in hex. Similarly, you can convert hex to binary. The hex number $AF can be converted to binary by remembering that $A = $10_{10} = 1010_2$, and $F = $15_{10} = 1111_2$. Thus,

A   F

equals

1 0 1 0 1 1 1 1

To mentally convert between binary and hex, memorize the binary equivalent of each of hex's 16 digits:

Binary	Hex	Binary	Hex
0000	0	1000	8
0001	1	1001	9
0010	2	1010	A
0011	3	1011	B
0100	4	1100	C
0101	5	1101	D
0110	6	1110	E
0111	7	1111	F

Hex is easier to use than binary: Even though a value like $C30 isn't as natural to use as a decimal number, it's a lot easier to deal with than

110000110000. With a little practice, conversion between hex and binary becomes second nature.

Representing Numbers in Memory

With what you've learned about the binary system, how do you suppose integers are represented using the bits and bytes that constitute the memory circuits of a Macintosh? Integers occupy two bytes of memory. Two bytes of memory represent a sequence of 16 ones and zeros:

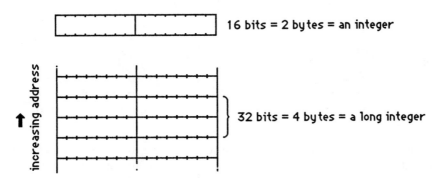

Figure 25.1: Memory Corresponding to a 16-bit Binary Number

Long integers (and pointers) are represented by four consecutive bytes (32 bits). Unlike some processors (like the 8086 family used on IBM personal computers), long integers are stored with the most significant 16 bits stored first, that is, at the lowest address. This makes it much easier to understand what you're looking at when using a debugging program.

Two's Complement Notation: Representing Negative Integers

We haven't yet talked about representing negative numbers. In Turbo, an integer can range from –32768 to 32767. How does Turbo know whether a number is positive or negative?

Turbo Pascal, like virtually all CPUs and the languages that run on them, uses *two's complement* notation to represent integers. An integer is stored in 16 bits (2 bytes) of memory. If we only wanted to represent positive numbers with the *Integer* data type, the largest value we could represent would be 1111111111111111_2 (64K-1) and the smallest would be 0—a total of 64K combinations. In order to also represent negative numbers with type *Integer*, two's complement notation divides the combinations of 16-bit numbers into two equal groups: 32768 positive numbers (0 to 32767) and 32768 negative ones (-1 to –32768).

To signify whether a number is positive or negative, the left-most bit of the binary number is used as the *sign bit*. If the left-most bit is a 0, the number is positive; if it is a 1, the number is negative.

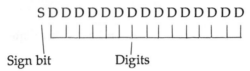

Sign bit   Digits

If the number is positive, the digits are encoded the same as any binary number. If the number is negative, however, they are encoded so that it's easy to do arithmetic with them—as the two's complement of the corresponding positive number.

The two's complement of a binary number is the result of changing all 1s to 0s and all 0s to 1s, plus 1. (For 16-bit numbers, you can also subtract the number from 65536—the value of the next place after the left-most place of the number—and get the two's complement and the sign bit.)

Why are negative numbers represented this way, rather than as ordinary positive numbers with a sign? One reason is to avoid having two representations for 0 (+0 and –0). Since storage space in a computer is a valuable commodity, it is wasteful to use two combinations of bits to represent the same number. It also makes the circuitry of the computer more complex, as it has to recognize both "kinds" of 0. The second reason is that logic circuits that work with two's complement numbers are easy to design and build and are included in virtually every microprocessor on the market today. Turbo Pascal uses these circuits to do integer math as quickly and efficiently as possible.

The way the "complement plus 1" plan works out, 0 is encoded as 0, –1 as 1111111111111111, –2 as 1111111111111110, –3 as 11111111111101, and so on all the way to –32768, 1000000000000000.

Boolean Operations on Integers

Now that we understand how integers are represented in memory, we are ready to learn what it means to use the boolean operators on them.

Given boolean operands, the **and** operator produces a value of True if and only if both of its operands are True. Since it doesn't make sense to talk about an integer as being "true" or "false" (Is 0 true? How about 14? Which is the truest?), what does it mean to use **and** on them?

The answer lies in the way integers are stored as bits in memory. Each bit of each integer can be thought of as a boolean value—where 1 represents True and 0 False. When we do an **and** of two integers, we are actually telling the computer to perform 16 simultaneous **and**s between the corresponding bits of the two integers. For example,

5 **and** 97 =

$$\begin{array}{ll} & 0000000000000101 \ (= \ 5 \ \text{decimal}) \\ \textbf{and} & 0000000001100001 \ (= 97 \ \text{decimal}) \\ \hline & 0000000000000001 \ (= 1, \text{so}, 5 \ \textbf{and} \ 97 = 1) \end{array}$$

The same is true for the **or** and **xor** operations. Here are some examples of how these operations work on integers:

$$\begin{array}{ll} & 1111111111111111 \ (= -1_{10}) \\ \textbf{xor} & 000000000001101 \ (= 14_{10}) \\ \hline & 1111111111110010 \ (= -14_{10}) \end{array} \qquad \begin{array}{ll} & 0000000001100011 \ (= 99_{10}) \\ \textbf{or} & 0000001111111111 \ (=1023_{10}) \\ \hline & 0000001111111111 \ (=1023_{10}) \end{array}$$

The **not** operator also works on integers, changing all 1s to 0s and all 0s to 1s. Thus,

$$\textbf{not} \ \ 1010111001010001 \ \ = \ \ 0101000110101110$$

Some operations are especially efficient using boolean operators—irresistably so. One application of the **and** operator is to clear (force to 0) a particular bit position of an integer. This process is called *masking*.

Fixing Bit 7 of W.S. Files

Masking with the **and** operator is useful when working with text files produced by a well-known word processing program (which shall remain nameless but which runs on the IBM PC and has the initials "W.S.").

W.S. sometimes sets the high-order bit of the bytes that represent the characters of your text. Since ASCII is a seven-bit code, W.S. can change the high-order bit without affecting the meaning of the encoded character. While this format works well for W.S., it makes its files something of a mystery to programs that care about the value of the high-order bit, such as MacWrite. A W.S.-to-MacWrite translation program must "mask off" the high bit of every byte in a W.S. file to make it palatable to MacWrite.

The **and** operator is just the ticket:

```
      11000001   ($C1 = ASCII "A" ($41) with high bit set)
and   01111111   ($7F = a mask for clearing bit 7)
      --------
      01000001   ($41 = normal ASCII "A")
```

In Turbo Pascal, the conversion looks like this:

```
N := Ord(C)
N := N and $7F;
C := Chr(N);
```

where *C* is a character and *N* is an integer.

By performing an **and** on every byte of the file, you go a long way toward rendering it readable by MacWrite. Then you have only the problem of squeezing a 5 1/4-inch floppy into a Macintosh's 3 1/2-inch slot—but that's another story.

Using And for Fast Modulo Arithmetic

Another application of the **and** operator is fast modulo arithmetic, when working with a divisor that is a power of 2 (2, 4, 8, 16, and so on). Explaining why it works is beyond the scope of this book, but to evaluate the expression

```
T := 14371 mod 16
```

that is, the integer remainder after dividing 14371 by 16, one could equivalently use

```
T := 14371 and $F
```

$F, decimal 15, has an underlying binary value of 00000000 00001111. Using **and** with this number has the effect of masking off all the bits in the first operand except the least significant four, which retain whatever value they had previously. Magically, these four bits represent the remainder. If you use the **mod** operator to perform these actions, you'll get the same answer, but more slowly, because the compiler generates a 68000 divide instruction, which executes much more slowly than an **and**.

This doesn't mean you should go around trying to turn every **mod** into an **and**. If you don't need the speed, **mod** is preferable because its meaning is clearer. This is simply another trick to salt away in your programmer's toolkit.

The Shift Operators: Shl and Shr

Turbo's **shl** (shift left) and **shr** (shift right) operators provide you with direct access to processor instructions that slide all the bits within an integer or long integer to the left or the right. They have no counterparts in Standard Pascal.

Given integer variable N equal to $7F, here are the results of applying the **shl** and **shr** operations to N and an integer from 1 to 16:

N shr	1	= 0000000001111111	N shl	1	= 0000000111111110
N shr	2	= 0000000000111111	N shl	2	= 0000001111111100
N shr	3	= 0000000000011111	N shl	3	= 0000011111111000
N shr	4	= 0000000000001111	N shl	4	= 0000111111110000
N shr	5	= 0000000000000111	N shl	5	= 0001111111100000
N shr	6	= 0000000000000011	N shl	6	= 0011111111000000
N shr	7	= 0000000000000001	N shl	7	= 0111111110000000
N shr	8	= 0000000000000000	N shl	8	= 1111111100000000
N shr	9	= 0000000000000000	N shl	9	= 1111111000000000
N shr	10	= 0000000000000000	N shl	10	= 1111110000000000
N shr	11	= 0000000000000000	N shl	11	= 1111100000000000
N shr	12	= 0000000000000000	N shl	12	= 1111000000000000
N shr	13	= 0000000000000000	N shl	13	= 1110000000000000
N shr	14	= 0000000000000000	N shl	14	= 1100000000000000
N shr	15	= 0000000000000000	N shl	15	= 1000000000000000
N shr	16	= 0000000000000000	N shl	16	= 0000000000000000

As you can see, the **shr** operator works by shifting all of the bits of the first operand to the right by the number of places indicated in the second operand and then adds 0s to the left. Similarly, the **shl** operator shifts its operand to the left and adds 0s to the right.

What are these operators good for? From our previous discussion of place value, you may recall that the values of the places in a binary number increase by a factor of 2 as you move to the left. Thus, N **shl** 1 is equivalent to $N * 2$, N **shl** 2 is the same as $N * 4$, N **shl** 3 is the same as $N * 8$, and so on. Note that this only works when the multiplier is a power of two—and you must be careful not to change the sign bit. For example,

01000000 00000000 = 16,384

Shifting left one position changes the sign bit, producing

10000000 00000000 = −32,768

which is definitely *not* the product of 16384 * 2. As with other operations involving integers, Turbo will not provide a warning if overflow occurs, so use these operations with care.

Similarly, N **shr** 1 is equivalent to N **div** 2, N **shr** 2 is the same as N **div** 4, and so on, for all positive integers and long integers. Because the Macintosh's processor takes significantly longer to perform multiplication and (especially) division than a shift, you can make your programs faster by using shift operations in well-chosen places.

Review

In this chapter, we looked at positional numbering systems, including decimal, binary, and hexadecimal. We also learned how integers and long integers are represented in memory, and how the boolean and shift operators can be used on them to perform machine-level operations in programs, enhancing both flexibility and speed.

4

USING THE POWER OF THE MACINTOSH

If you've made it this far in Turbo Tutor, give yourself a pat on the back: You've learned Pascal. Of course, you'll get better with every program you write, but parts 2 and 3 of this book pretty well exposed Pascal's entire bag of tricks.

You've also practiced with a particular Macintosh implementation of the language and know how to load, save, edit, compile, and test programs. You've come a long way—in fact, were this book about programming a more conventional personal computer, all that would remain would be appendices and a stirring rendition of "Pomp and Circumstance."

On the Macintosh, however, you've only just begun. You've learned Pascal as a general-purpose tool but have yet to use that tool to create software that behaves in a "Macintosh-like" fashion.

The sample programs discussed thus far have been devoid of Macintosh flair. You've balanced checkbooks four different ways, none of which had niceties like pull-down menus and dialog boxes. When you sent characters to the screen with *WriteLn*, they always came out in 9-point Monaco. The mouse collected dust as you executed *ReadLn*s and *ReadChar*s to get commands and data from the keyboard.

The demo programs were written this way for a good reason: to set aside Macintosh user-interface considerations while we addressed the primary task, namely, teaching Pascal. As we shall see, it is considerably easier to collect a command from the user with `ReadLn(Command);` than with a dialog box.

The time has come to take what you've learned about Pascal in previous sections and discover how true Macintosh applications are put together.

Beyond ReadLn and WriteLn

Part 4 of this book describes the design philosophy of the Macintosh and includes an overview of the machine's hardware and built-in software. We'll touch on its primary hardware elements, including the mouse, graphics display, and microprocessor. We'll also introduce the 600-odd utility routines provided by Apple to help programs be "Macintosh-like"—the so-called Toolbox.

Part 5 then delves into the nuts and bolts of writing Macintosh programs. You'll learn how to create programs that use graphics and pull-down menus and dialog boxes and multiple windows and fancy typefaces and all the other things that put the Macintosh a step and a half ahead of conventional personal computers.

26

The Visual User Interface

Why is the Macintosh so revolutionary? After all, despite its unconventional looks, it's built around standard personal-computer ingredients like disk drives, microprocessors, and a video display. Why do well-written Macintosh programs make equally well-written MS-DOS programs look bland by comparison? Why are Macintosh programs singularly easy to learn and use? Several reasons:

- a consistent, intuitive, visual user interface
- the mouse—a natural way to interact with objects on the screen
- the Toolbox, some 600 routines built into every Macintosh to implement the user interface and many auxiliary functions
- a high-resolution, bit-mapped display able to show and animate detailed graphic objects

In this and the next two chapters, we'll take a closer look at these elements.

The User Interface: Human Meets Machine

At the core of the Macintosh's design is a simple idea: *A computer should be easy to use*. In this context, ease of use refers both to the level of difficulty of learning a new program, as well as to the effort an experienced user must expend to do useful work.

Despite ad copy to the contrary, most programs for traditional personal computers—especially powerful ones—aren't especially easy to use. They require time and effort to learn initially, and frequent sojourns to the manuals thereafter. This is because, in large measure, they embody an awkward and inconsistent *user interface*.

User interface is a term thrown about rather loosely these days. Just what is a user interface, and what makes one good or bad?

In science, an interface refers to the boundary between two dissimilar materials; for example, between water and air. What materials could be more dissimilar than a plastic, glass, metal, and silicon personal computer and a human being? Their nontrivial physical differences aside, people and computers have profoundly different methods of thinking.

Internally, the Macintosh is a numerical beast. Its CPU is adept at manipulating binary numbers at high speed and precious little else. In fact, "thinking" is too good a word to apply to this number shuffling. Human beings, in contrast, are intuitive, visual thinkers. They do arithmetic only when they have to, and then not especially well.

A user interface can be defined as the set of methods by which a human being communicates with a particular program running on a particular computer: how he or she provides the program with commands and data, and how the program informs him or her of results and options. A good user interface recognizes the visual, common-sense quality of human thought.

The Macintosh user interface is based on several key concepts:

- simulating the real world
- standardized conventions such as overlapping windows, pull-down menus, dialog boxes, and text-editing techniques
- using the mouse rather than the keyboard as the primary command giver

Simulating the Real World

Thanks to its crisp display, on-board graphics software, and mouse, the Macintosh supports the design of software that simulates events and objects of the real world. You don't have to read even a short manual to operate the Calculator desk accessory, because that program successfully mimics real, three-dimensional calculators.

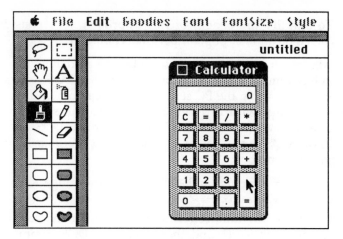

Figure 26.1: The Calculator Desk Accessory

Similarly, MacPaint represents drawing tools with symbols (icons) that imply their functions. Macintosh word-processing programs such as MacWrite emulate the real world with an electronic sheet-of-paper metaphor. Like real paper documents, MacWrite uses black "ink" on white "paper." Such simulation is a powerful concept in creating easy to use software, because users intuitively know how to use such software without having to relearn everything.

Standardization

Still, there is more to the Macintosh user interface than emulating the real world. Emulating a sheet of paper with a word-processing program is a good start, but a computer program must move into areas without real-world analogs. You can't exactly move paragraphs around on a sheet of paper, and spreadsheet programs can do much more than any calculator can.

The next best thing is to make sure what's learned in one program transfers easily to another program.

Here the Macintosh again scores, by stressing consistent behavior. Macintosh programs all behave like Macintosh programs. That is, Macintosh applications use dialog boxes and menu bars and windows, and these devices behave in a consistent way. Pulling down a menu or editing text in one program is like pulling down a menu or editing text in another program. To amplify the benefit of this approach, let's consider how software evolved on another popular personal computer.

Before the Macintosh, there were no user-interface guidelines for personal computers. Over time, a Tower of Babel arose in MS-DOS software land. Software developers using the PC series—and programmers are notorious mavericks—came up with different ways to do the same thing. For example, consider what an owner of four major MS-DOS applications (Lotus 1-2-3, MS-DOS Turbo Pascal, dBASE II, and WordStar) must do to print a document from each:

- To print in 1-2-3, type */PR* and then specify the range to print, type *Return*, and, finally, press *G*.
- To print a source program from MS-DOS Turbo Pascal, you first leave the program (*Control-KDQ*) and then execute a DOS command: COPY MYFIRST.PAS LPT1:.
- With dBASE II, you type SET PRINT ON, then LIST ALL.
- To print a WordStar file, return to No File Menu (type *Control-KD* or *Control-KQ*), type *P*, specify the file name, and, finally, answer six Yes/No questions.

There's little cumulative knowledge gained in using these four programs: A year of printing 1-2-3 files daily doesn't help you understand the meaning of WordStar's fourth print-time query, USE FORM FEEDS (Y/N):___.

The designers of these programs weren't sadistic; their programs wouldn't have made it to the top of the software sales charts if they embodied quirky, erratic programming. Rather, each individual designer faced the problem of getting something sent to the printer and solved it in a way that was best for his or her particular application. This multiplicity of rules, of four ways to do the same thing, confuses beginners and sends even savvy veterans to their manuals.

Thanks to user-interface consistency, Macintosh programs with a Print option—be they word processors, integrated Pascal editor/compilers, spreadsheets, or database managers—invariably have a Print... option under a pull-down menu named File. Choosing this option brings up a standard dialog box:

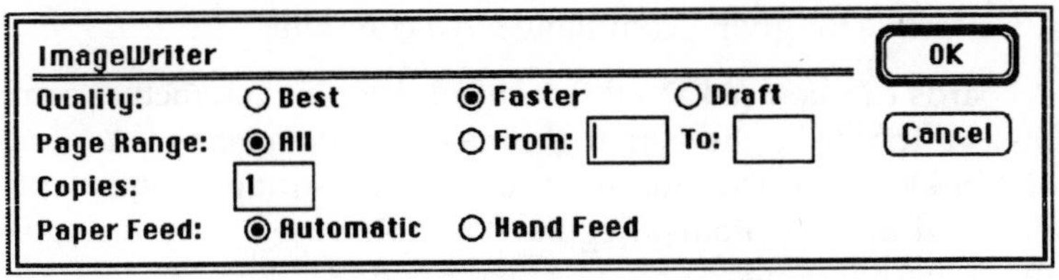

```
┌─────────────────────────────────────────────────────────┐
│  ImageWriter ─────────────────────────────    ╭────────╮ │
│                                                │   OK   │ │
│  Quality:      ○ Best      ⦿ Faster   ○ Draft  ╰────────╯ │
│  Page Range:   ⦿ All       ○ From: │  │ To: │  │ ╭──────╮ │
│  Copies:       │ 1 │                            │Cancel│ │
│  Paper Feed:   ⦿ Automatic ○ Hand Feed          ╰──────╯ │
└─────────────────────────────────────────────────────────┘
```

Figure 26.2: Turbo Pascal's Print Dialog Box

It didn't work out this way by accident. When Apple rolled out the Macintosh in January 1984, they not only gave the programming community tools for programming (Lisa and Lisa Pascal), they simultaneously published a document describing how programs should act. Like an Emily Post etiquette guide for well-bred Macintosh software, the "User Interface Guidelines" chapter in *Inside Macintosh* describes in no uncertain terms how windows should look and behave; about menus and keyboard equivalents; radio buttons, regular buttons, check boxes, and dialog boxes; and text editing and the Undo, Copy, Cut, and Paste features.

In addition, Apple's first generation of Macintosh software—the Finder, MacWrite, MacPaint, MacDraw, MacTerminal, and MacProject—all did things the same way. So, although printing a MacPaint file is internally very different from printing a six-page MacWrite document, externally the user sees the same Print... option under the same File menu.

The Mouse

When you engage a non-Macintosh computer enthusiast in a conversation, the first image that pops into his or her mind is *Macintosh, The Computer That Uses A Mouse*. The Macintosh was the first machine to bring the clickable rodent from the ivory towers of corporate think-tanks and research universities to the masses.

The mouse allows you to use an on-screen cursor as an extension of your own arm and hand—to interact with software as naturally as you reach for a stapler. The Macintosh user interface wholeheartedly embraces the mouse. You can run many applications productively without plugging the keyboard in, but you can't get to first base without the mouse.

Typewriter keyboards were invented in the late nineteenth century for creating text. When computers appeared, typewriter-like units were adapted to communicate with them. Today, the keyboard and computer seem inseparable, yet there is growing evidence that keyboards aren't especially effective for giving commands to a computer.

That keyboards can be used at all to control complex interactive computer programs is a tribute to the verbal abilities of human beings. Experienced users of MS-DOS applications have dozens of strange control phrases rattling around in their brains. Regular WordStar users may recognize the following: `Control Cue Are; Control Cue Ef En Em 300 Escape.` (Translation: Move to line 300.)

With the mouse as primary command device, the keyboard is reserved for what it does best: entering text.

Review

There are a number of important concepts at work in the Macintosh that make the machine easy to use. Macintosh software emulates the real world and uses standardized user-interface techniques, to reduce the amount of learning required when moving from application to application. The Macintosh user interface relies primarily on the mouse to communicate commands.

In the next chapter, we'll learn more about the hardware necessary to implement this user interface.

27

Macintosh Hardware

Programmers and programming books have a tendency to shortchange hardware. After all, didn't we say early on that, without software, a Macintosh just sits there getting warm? That's certainly true, but the reverse is equally true. Without hardware on which to execute, software is but a peculiarly tortuous mental exercise.

Much as human beings are constrained by the laws of physics as manifested on planet Earth, so programs are constrained by the qualities of the computer on which they execute. It's to our advantage to spend some time getting acquainted with the capabilities of the 20-pound beige box known as a Macintosh. Let's address each major element of Macintosh hardware individually.

The Processor

Following a tradition begun in the Apple II, the Macintosh was designed to be "chip efficient." At the January 1984 Macintosh introduction, then-chairman Steven Jobs pointed out that there were fewer integrated circuits in the entire Macintosh than on the video adapter board of an IBM PC. All things being equal, a computer with fewer chips costs less to build, consumes less power, can be made physically smaller, and breaks down less often than a computer with more chips.

Chip efficiency is accomplished by using complex or custom parts that do the work of many simpler chips, and by using software to perform functions that would otherwise be provided by hardware.

The most important and largest chip on the Macintosh logic board is a Motorola 68000 microprocessor (CPU), a third-generation microprocessor. The Macintosh would not have been possible without this chip's speed. Table 27.0 compares the processor to the Apple II's 6502 processor and to the 8088 chip that drives most IBM PCs and compatibles.

	6502	8088	68000
Internal data path	8 bits	16 bits	32 bits
External data path	8 bits	8 bits	16 bits
General registers	3 8-bit	8 16-bit	16 32-bit
Addressable memory	64K	1 Mb	16 Mb

Generally speaking, the processor is ten times faster than the 6502 and four times faster than the 8088 at the operations typically performed by personal computer CPUs. The processor was something of a daring choice when Apple selected it for the Macintosh in 1980; in retrospect, the two have been very good for each other.

Since Turbo Pascal performs the translation from Pascal source into processor machine language automatically, you don't really need to know how to read and write processor machine language. It *can* be handy, especially in tracking down bugs, to know more about the processor, so Chapter 41 discusses this in more detail.

The Display

The Mac's cathode ray tube (CRT) is only the most visible of a number of components responsible for creating displays. Screen images consist of tens of thousands of tiny picture elements (pixels), which are either black ("on") or white ("off"). (Mac II users have color pixels and a larger display, but we won't go into that here.) The pixels are arranged into a grid measuring 512 pixels horizontally by 342 pixels vertically. Images are created by making some pixels black and others white.

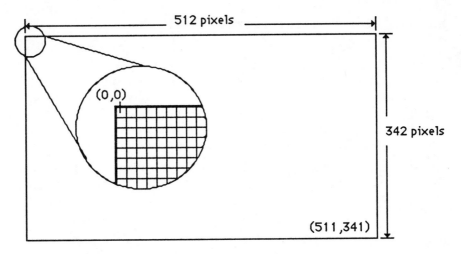

Figure 27.1: The Mac's 512 by 342 Grid

The Macintosh uses "memory mapped" video, a flexible and chip-efficient means of generating a CRT image: flexible because the display is totally controlled by software, and chip efficient because it takes advantage of components such as the processor and memory that are already there.

Memory mapping in the Macintosh centers around 21,888 bytes of memory called the *screen buffer*. The screen buffer appears to the CPU as ordinary RAM; under program control, the CPU can store and retrieve binary numbers in this range. It is simultaneously available to the Macintosh's video circuits, the part of the machine that controls whether each of the 175,000 pixels on the CRT are black or white. These circuits (which operate pretty much independently of the processor) scan the buffer and redraw ("refresh") the screen, according to what they find, 60 times a second. Without this constant refreshing, the CRT image would fade away in a split second.

The bottom line is this: When you change bits in the screen buffer, you change pixels on the screen. Most popular personal computers have multiple video display modes: typically, a *text* mode for displaying text and a *bit-mapped graphics* mode for games, pie charts, and whenever you want to create graphic images that cannot be resolved into individual characters.

The Macintosh, in contrast, has one and only one display mode—512 by 342 bit-mapped graphics. Every letter, digit, punctuation symbol, and line is drawn to the screen pixel by pixel.

Accessing the Screen Buffer Directly

You can think of the CRT as a window on the screen buffer. 0 bits display as white; 1 bits display as black. For example, writing the integer value 255 (binary equivalent 11111111) into the screen buffer creates an eight-pixel long horizontal black line; just where the line appears on the screen depends on the particular memory address written to. Writing the integer value 3855 (00001111 00001111 binary) produces a short dotted line.

Just for fun, key in and contemplate this program. What do you think it does?

```
program ScreenBufferTest;
var
  P: ^LongInt;
begin
  P  := Pointer(501504);          { for a 1 Mb machine, change to 1025792 }
  P^ := 252645135;         { $0F0F0F0F, 00001111 00001111 00001111 00001111 }
  Readln
end.
```

ScreenBufferTest's only variable is *P*, a pointer to a long integer. This means that the notation *P^* refers to a long integer—just *where* in memory this long integer resides at any given moment depends on the value assigned to *P*. Rather than taking the address of something (which is normally how one assigns a value to a pointer variable), this program stuffs a number into *P* directly. The *Pointer* type coercion function is necessary to keep the compiler happy.

501,504 happens to be the address of the first byte of the 512K Mac's screen buffer; the buffer is clearly near the top of RAM. Address 501,504 represents the top-left corner of the screen; that is, the first 32 pixels on the top line of the screen are represented in the display buffer by the long integer that begins at 501,504, the next 32 are stored in the long integer at address 501,508, and so on.

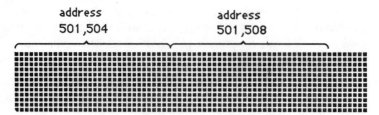

Figure 27.2: Display Buffer Addressing

After the assignment, *P* points to the first byte in the screen buffer; *P^* therefore represents the first four bytes of the buffer. The effect of assigning an integer constant to *P^* writes that value into four bytes of display memory—and unlike most memory writes, is instantly reflected on the screen.

252645135 has an underlying binary representation of 00001111 00001111 00001111 00001111, so a short, dotted-line pattern appears in the upper left-hand corner of the display. Turbo Pascal's terminal window routines don't know that you've tampered with the screen, and so make no attempt to repair the "damage." If you were to change the assignment to *P^ := –1*, you'd make the same 32 pixels all black, because the long integer constant –1 is represented in binary as 11111111 11111111 11111111 11111111. *P^ = 0* makes them all white.

As we mentioned, the screen measures 512 pixels horizontally by 342 pixels vertically; 512 pixels at 8 pixels per byte equals 64 bytes per row of pixels. That means that the second line of the display starts at 501,568, the third at 501,632, and so on. The screen buffer therefore requires 342 lines * 64 bytes per line or 21,888 bytes.

This next program fills the entire buffer with binary 1s, thereby blacking it out:

```
program BlackScreen;
var
  P: ^LongInt;
  N: Integer;
begin
  P := Pointer(501504);        { for a 1-Mb machine, change to 1025792 }
  for N := 1 to 5472 do
  begin
    P^ := -1;                  { 11111111 11111111 11111111 11111111 }
    P := Pointer(Ord4(P) + 4);          { advance to next LongInt }
  end;
  Readln
end.
```

BlackScreen's **for** loop executes once for every long integer in the screen buffer (5472 = 21888/4). Running this program clears the screen, except for a small patch under the cursor (which was actually cleared and then quickly redrawn).

It's one thing to poke a 32-pixel horizontal line into screen memory; it's quite another to create intricate blends of text and graphics. If every Macintosh programmer had to create unique screen-writing routines, we'd be lucky to have half a dozen Macintosh applications. Fortunately, there are powerful, efficient routines in ROM for this purpose, known collectively as QuickDraw. Turbo Pascal's terminal window emulation routines call

QuickDraw routines to draw 9-point Monaco characters. We'll discuss QuickDraw thoroughly in Part 5; for now, know that QuickDraw is so fast—and so complete—that writing to screen memory directly is never necessary.

The Mouse

From a hardware standpoint, the mouse is two independent subsystems: one for tracking movement and another for button activity. Every time you move the mouse, an interrupt is generated. (An interrupt is a hardware signal that causes the processor to temporarily stop working on the current program and jump to a program for handling the device that caused the interrupt.) The software that services this interrupt uses the motion information generated by the mouse to position the cursor.

Programs collect mouse information by calling Toolbox routines. One routine returns the location on the screen where the pointer is at a given instant, another tells whether or not the mouse button is currently down, and so on.

For example, this program outputs periods to the terminal window until the mouse button is pressed (using the *ToolIntf* unit's *Button* routine):

```
program WaitForMouse;
uses MemTypes, QuickDraw, OSIntf, ToolIntf;
begin
  repeat
    Write('.')
  until Button; { returns True if button down; otherwise False }
end.
```

The Keyboard

The Macintosh Plus's standard detachable keyboard resembles that of a typewriter, with certain additions and omissions. All the ASCII printable characters are supported: This explains why oddballs like ', ~, |, and \ are included, and why some typewriter standbys like ¢ are missing.

Some keys traditionally present on personal computers are conspicuously absent on the Macintosh Plus, including *Control, Escape, Delete,* and sundry function keys. They *do* exist on the keyboards for the II and SE, and on extended keyboards. These keys have no meaning in the Macintosh user interface. They are useful only when you're using a communications program to talk with another computer that assumes you have these keys at your disposal; such programs use various techniques to fake these keys.

Special Keys

The Option key allows you to go beyond the limitations of ASCII and generate dozens of additional characters. Use the Key Caps desk accessory to determine the characters that are available in a particular font as well as what keys to press to produce them.

The Command key ( ) is defined by the user-interface guidelines as a pull-down menu substitute. Most applications (Turbo Pascal included) define Command-key equivalents for certain common menu actions, such as *Command-X* for the Cut command. Some applications use exotic combinations of *Command, Shift,* and *Option* to increase the number of keyboard equivalents.

Keyboard Hardware

The cable provides power and a two-way communications link to the logic board. When a key is pressed, the keyboard's electronics send a unique key number down the cable, where the processor translates the key value into ASCII form and places it into a queue. The current application can then retrieve it with the Toolbox routine *GetNextEvent*; we'll dissect this in Chapter 32.

The Control Panel desk accessory can modify the keyboard's auto-repeat characteristics, including the speed with which keys repeat, as well as the delay before the appearance of the first repeated character.

Internal Drive

The Macintosh was one of the first personal computers to use Sony's 3 1/2-inch floppy disk drives. Some high points of an internal drive include:

- This book's terminology notwithstanding, externally, Macintosh disks aren't a bit floppy. The delicate magnetic media is protected by a rigid plastic shell. A spring-loaded shutter keeps dust and fingerprints out.

- Because of the protection afforded by the shell, recording densities are stepped up (800K on a surface area about one third of that used by standard 5 1/4-inch disks).

- Software-controlled disk ejection keeps the user from removing disks until the file system (or application) is ready for that to happen. This improves file integrity.

- A disk insertion sensor allows a program to discover when a disk has been inserted and to respond appropriately.

- Best of all, the disks fit in a shirt pocket.

Speaker

The Macintosh can create elaborate musical and sound effects. On the Plus and SE, sound is controlled by half a dozen routines known collectively as the *Sound Driver*, which work with a 740-byte range of memory called the sound buffer. The sound buffer is to the built-in speaker what the screen buffer is to the display: When you change a value stored in the buffer, you change the sound generated by the speaker.

In fact, the sound buffer is addressed just above the screen buffer and, like it, typically isn't accessed directly but instead with the Sound Driver's routines. You can create tones that operate in the background (that is, while the program is doing something else, such as manipulating the display) and control both the volume and tonal characteristics of that sound.

The Macintosh II can emulate most of the preceding and more: It can produce stereo sound.

Expansion Connectors: Closed versus Open Architecture

The original Macintosh was designed with an impressive complement of expansion connectors (sometimes called *ports*) on the back of the machine. Apple's aim, not fully realized, was to build a computer so complete that the user would never need to open the case and make changes. The Macintosh was therefore designed as a "closed" system—meaning it was difficult (and therefore expensive) to expand. The market has since spoken on the issue; it said, rather loudly: We Want To Open The Case And Fiddle

Around. Apple has since released the Macintosh SE and Macintosh II, which have slots for expansion boards.

There's a positive side to closed architecture. A Macintosh Plus may be hard to upgrade, but, as a programmer, you're assured that one is like any other: the same screen, the same keyboard, the same mouse, the same serial ports, the same sound capabilities, the same everything. Macintosh software is therefore more likely to exercise every single muscle in the machine, from the basic mouse/windows/pull-down menus environment to exotic features like synthetic speech, than a corresponding IBM PC program.

On open systems like the IBM PC and Apple II, it is all too easy to write programs that run on one system perfectly and on another not at all or, worse, erratically. The "slotted" Macs will undoubtedly usher in an era of similar trade-offs for Macintosh programmers.

The Ports

The standard Macintosh is well-equipped for various forms of input/output (I/O). From left to right on the back of the machine are the mouse port, a connector for an external floppy or hard disk drive, two high-speed serial ports, and a mini phone jack for sending sound to an audio amplifier in lieu of the built-in speaker. A Macintosh Plus includes a Small Computer Standard Interface (SCSI, pronounced "scuzzy") port as well. SCSI is an increasingly popular standard for fast data transmission over short distances (under 20 feet), ideal for connecting hard disks and tape backup units.

Battery-Protected Clock and Option Settings

You may have noticed that you can unplug a Macintosh from the wall and still have the correct time on the Alarm Clock desk accessory the next time you use the machine, an hour or a month later. This is possible because a battery (located just above the power switch on the Plus and on the motherboard on the II and SE) keeps certain components running even when the machine is unplugged. Among other benefits, this means that the Finder and other programs that work with files can assume that the time stamps applied to files are correct.

In addition to the time and date, all of the settings you can make with the Control Panel desk accessory, such as the desktop pattern and key-repeat rate, are retained.

Review

Here's a nuts and bolts summary of the Macintosh's hardware features.

Macintosh Plus

- 128K ROM, 512K or 1 Mb RAM, 7.8 MHz 68000 CPU
- 800K 3 1/2-inch disk drive
- 9-inch monitor with 512 by 342 bit graphics (no text mode)
- Two 230K baud serial ports
- SCSI port
- Sound synthesizer with built-in speaker
- Detached keyboard (*Option* key for generating more characters; *Command* key for menu substitutes) with software-definable touch and repeat rates

Macintosh SE

- 256K ROM, 1-Mb RAM, 7.8 MHz 68000 CPU
- Two 800K 3 1/2-inch drives or one 800K 3 1/2-inch drive and a 20-Mb hard disk
- Same monitor as the Plus
- Same serial ports as the Plus
- SCSI port
- Sound synthesizer with built-in speakers
- Detached keyboard (with Option and Command keys) with software-definable touch and repeat rates
- One expansion slot

28

ROM Software: The Toolbox

This chapter explains the utility routines available in the Mac's read-only memory (ROM) and shows you how to use them.

The Hardware/Software Pyramid

It's useful to think of the Macintosh and the software that executes on it as a multilevel pyramid. At the top of the pyramid are the applications—programs like MacPaint, Turbo Typist, and Turbo Pascal itself. From this lofty perch, applications are insulated from hardware concerns.

When you write a program that uses disk files, for example, you work with abstract terms like "volumes," "path name," and "files." Low-level routines flesh out these abstractions into specific hardware activities, such as moving read/write heads about and accessing specific regions of a particular floppy disk. Programs that rely on Turbo's terminal window, like Typist, are even farther removed from reality: They think they're running on an 80-column by 25-line CRT terminal.

Hardware devices like disk drives and mice can, in fact, be directly accessed by application programs. Generally speaking, however, you'd never get much done if it were your job to run the disk drive and handle keyboard interrupts.

Two layers of ROM code support application programs: A high-level *User Interface Toolbox* and a low-level *operating system*. This distinction of Toolbox versus operating system isn't hard and fast; generally speaking, the services performed by the Toolbox are more complex and removed from hardware than operating system routines.

A third class of ROM routines is *QuickDraw*, the graphics software you use to put text and graphics on the screen. *QuickDraw* is called both by Toolbox routines and directly by application programs.

At the bottom of the Macintosh pyramid is the hardware itself: the keyswitches, cables, and integrated circuits you can see and touch. Beneath the pyramid, gazing in wonder at the screen, is the user, the point of the whole exercise.

These software layers simplify the task faced by an application. Much as well-written Pascal programs use the divide-and-conquer approach to turn lengthy main programs into a series of short procedures, the Macintosh itself provides a layering of utility programs. Your program is therefore able to remain blissfully ignorant of the complexities of hardware—and to call on powerful, debugged software building blocks.

The Routines in ROM

Despite its long list of hardware features, two drab integrated circuits on the logic board ultimately give the Macintosh most of its character. These ROM chips hold up to 256K of machine-language code and represent many years of work by talented programmers.

Permanently encoded in these chips are hundreds of subroutines that can be called by your programs. As mentioned, they can be organized into three large groups: QuickDraw, the User Interface Toolbox, and the operating system. These routines, which we'll refer to collectively as the Toolbox, are the true masters of Macintosh hardware. You don't check hardware status ports to see if the mouse button is depressed; instead, you call a ROM routine that does it for you. You don't set bits in screen memory to cause lines to be drawn; you call a QuickDraw routine and tell it where the line should go, and it is drawn for you. You don't tell the disk drive to seek to track 13 and read sector 8; you call a File Manager routine and tell it to read *x* bytes from file *y*.

The benefits of using the Toolbox are many: Your programs are smaller and easier to write, because you don't have to duplicate code that already exists. Your programs are more dependable, because the Toolbox routines are tested and known to work. Your programs are fast, because Apple's programmers made the ROM routines fast. Your programs are transportable to future generations of Macs that may have more memory, larger displays, and different keyboards, because the ROMs in those as yet unbuilt machines will present the same interface to your program.

Pascal and Macintosh: A Perfect Marriage

The ROM has hundreds of utility subroutines. We're using Turbo Pascal, which creates object programs in RAM. What's the connection between the code generated by our compilations and the Toolbox? How are they held together?

Lucky for us, the ROM was created with Pascal in mind. Although written largely in assembly language, the routines are designed to be called from Pascal programs; that is, they follow Pascal parameter-passing conventions.

Units and the Toolbox

In Chapter 18, we discussed units as a way to extend and customize Turbo Pascal. To review, units consist of two parts, an interface and an implementation. The interface provides the compiler with information about the public components of a unit, when compiling a program that uses that unit. After the interface comes the implementation, containing the nuts and bolts of the various procedures and functions described in the interface.

Once compiled, units can either be used from disk or, for thoroughly debugged and often used units, stored inside the Turbo Pascal application itself. As shipped from Borland, Turbo Pascal has 15 units. Some of these units provide support for terminal window operations. Most, however, are for tapping the power of the Toolbox.

Tapping the Toolbox

The Toolbox interface is implemented as 12 units that are treated exactly like *TypistHelper* (from Chapter 19) or, for that matter, like the units you build yourself. Since the Toolbox units are already inside Turbo Pascal, you can use them without $U directives. The bottom line is this: With the addition of a single **uses** clause at the start of a program, you can use Turbo Pascal as though it had 650 built-in functions and procedures instead of 50.

The interface of each Toolbox unit is listed in Appendix D of the Turbo Pascal reference manual, a section that should soon become dog-eared with use. Let's quickly list the most important ones.

Unit Memtypes

MemTypes defines about a dozen general-purpose data types, and nothing else. It's short enough to print in its entirety here:

```
unit MemTypes(-6);

interface

type
  SignedByte = -128..127;
  Byte = 0..255;

  Ptr = ^SignedByte;
  Handle = ^Ptr;                   { a pointer to a pointer! }
  ProcPtr = Ptr;
  Fixed = LongInt;

  Str255 = string[255];
  StringPtr = ^Str255;
  StringHandle = ^StringPtr;
```

Here's a tip you'll want to remember: When writing an application to be spread over several units, it helps to create a small unit consisting of nothing but type definitions needed by all modules.

The most important types defined in *MemTypes* are *Ptr* and *Handle*. In an upcoming chapter on memory management, we explain how these types are used to manage the storage of blocks of memory from a dozen to thousands of bytes long.

Unit QuickDraw

QuickDraw uses unit *MemTypes* and contains a vast assortment of drawing tools. Anything on a Macintosh application screen, be it text or graphics, was probably put there by a *QuickDraw* routine. *QuickDraw* is often called by a Toolbox routine rather than by the application directly; for example, the menu bar is created and manipulated using Menu Manager routines, which in turn use *QuickDraw* tools. A couple of chapters down the road, we'll learn the *QuickDraw* way of looking at memory as drawing paper.

Unit OSIntf

The operating system is conceptually the lowest level of Macintosh ROM software. It performs operations directly related to hardware. Operating system tasks range from the important, including disk I/O and memory management, to the obscure: serial drivers and the AppleTalk and Vertical Retrace managers. It uses *MemTypes* and *QuickDraw*.

Unit ToolIntf

ToolIntf uses *MemTypes*, *QuickDraw*, and *OSIntf* and provides user-interface building blocks. The Toolbox unit defines hundreds of data types, constants, and routines involved in implementing the user interface. It's represented by the following chapters in *Inside Macintosh*: "Resource Manager," "Control Manager," "Event Manager," "Font Manager," "TextEdit," "Dialog Manager," "Window Manager," and "Menu Manager."

Unit PackIntf

PackIntf uses *MemTypes*, *QuickDraw*, *OSIntf*, and *ToolIntf* and controls the use of packages. Packages are collections of utility routines that because of either their occasional-use status or large size were denied valuable space in ROM. Packages span a wide range of applications, from handling disk initialization to various string utilities. Many of the original packages in the Macintosh 128 and 512 were put into ROM with the 128K (Macintosh Plus) release of the ROMs, although the software interface to them is the same.

The Trap Mechanism

Let's quickly describe the process of how program flow passes from your program into a ROM or RAM routine and back again. This material is helpful for program writing but not strictly necessary. So, if machine language isn't your cup of tea, bail out and meet us at the start of the next chapter.

The Inline Directives

Normally, procedure and function headings are followed by a block of statements, which the compiler examines to determine the processor machine code (a sequence of 16-bit numbers) that will represent that function or procedure. The following figure shows this process.

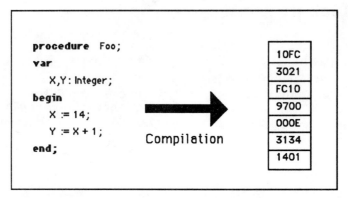

Figure 28.1: Text to Hex

The optional **inline** directive after a procedure or function heading overrides the standard pattern, telling the compiler not to expect a block of statements but instead to accept a series of integer constants, verbatim, as the code to represent this procedure or function. Put another way, **inline** says "take our word for it" as to what the machine-language expression of this procedure should be.

Type in and study this program:

```
program HideCursorTest;

procedure HideCursor; inline $A852;

begin
  HideCursor;
  WriteLn('Look, ma, no cursor!');
  ReadLn;
end.
```

Ordinarily, when you execute a program in the terminal window, the cursor (which is what *Inside Macintosh* calls the mouse pointer) disappears temporarily; the first movement of the mouse makes it visible again. Just to get it out of the way, compile and run this program. As advertised, the cursor disappears and no amount of mouse movement can bring it back. It won't reappear until you return to Turbo Pascal.

In order to understand what went on in the first few microseconds of *HideCursorTest*'s execution when the cursor vanished, think for a moment about how the compiler processes this program. The compiler's job is to translate the text of this source program into a sequence of processor instructions (that is, an object program).

When the compiler sees the **inline** keyword after *HideCursor*'s header, it knows it won't find a standard declaration part/statement part for this procedure. Instead, it expects a list of one or more integer constants, separated by commas and terminated with a semicolon. In this case, there's exactly one, $A852 (which could alternatively have been written as its decimal equivalent, –22446). The compiler knows to associate the machine code represented numerically as $A852 with the procedure identifier *HideCursor*. It doesn't do anything yet; it simply makes note of the association:

identifier 'HideCursor' = a procedure with no parameters = $A852

The *HideCursor* routine, which causes the cursor to disappear temporarily, was built into your computer at the factory. We haven't recreated it with this short **inline** declaration, we've simply created a way for our program to access that ROM code.

On with the compilation. Soon the compiler finds the identifier *HideCursor* as the first statement in the main program. We told it that the code for *HideCursor* is $A852, so in the corresponding position of the object code, it places the value $A852. Next, the compiler encounters the more conventional *WriteLn* and *ReadLn* statements. The compiler uses its knowledge of Pascal and the processor to generate code to perform these operations, accumulating more 16-bit chunks of object code (each requires several integers).

After the compilation, the resulting object program looks something like this:

```
$A852
$486D
$FFC2
$487A
$0024
$4267
$4EBA
$F9FC
$4EBA
$F9A2
```

Programs are executed by causing the processor to fetch and execute instructions from a particular region of memory. In the case of *HideCursorTest*, let's say the compiler stored the program at address 100,000.

The first instruction at address 100,000 is $A852. Somehow, this 16-bit number causes the built-in routine to hide the cursor to be executed. This happens through a complex sequence of actions known as a *trap*.

A-Line Traps

Instructions that begin with the hex character 'A' (binary 1010) have a singular effect on the processor. They cause it to automatically execute a program known as the *trap dispatcher*. The trap dispatcher (which was written by Apple and is placed into memory when the system is booted up) looks at the lower 12 bits of the trap instruction. This particular trap,

$852 = 1000\ 0101\ 0010$

tells the dispatcher to execute the routine defined in *Inside Macintosh* as *HideCursor*. We don't know exactly where it is in ROM, how long it is, or how it works. We know only that it makes the cursor disappear.

After the cursor has been banished, the rest of the instructions in the program are executed, causing a message to be sent to the terminal window. After you satisfy the *ReadLn* routine by pressing *Return*, the program ends. A program ends by sending the processor off to execute instructions in some other program, in this case, Turbo Pascal. This quickly restores the screen (and the cursor), and it's business as usual.

The trap mechanism is the key to hooking into the Toolbox. With this mechanism, it's almost as though the instruction set of the processor included a routine named *HideCursor*.

Units and Inline Directives

Normally, when you use Toolbox routines, you don't define them as **inline** but rather use the units that contain them. For example, *HideCursorTest* could have been written more conventionally as

```
program HideCursorTest;
uses MemTypes, QuickDraw;
begin
```

```
HideCursor;
WriteLn('Look, ma, no cursor!');
ReadLn;
end.
```

Turn to the interface listing of unit *QuickDraw* in Appendix D of the Turbo Pascal reference manual. Can you find the declaration of *HideCursor*? (Look under the comment "Cursor routines.") What do you suppose the routine listed right beneath it (*ShowCursor*) does? Test your theory with a short program.

Note that virtually all of the Toolbox routines defined in the 12 units use **inline** declarations. Incidentally, when **inline** functions and procedures are declared in a unit, the **inline** attribute appears in the interface, and the procedure doesn't appear in the implementation at all.

Review

In this chapter, we discussed the utility routines in ROM: what they are and how they are accessed in a program via the unit mechanism. We learned, in some detail, the sequence of actions that occurs when invoking a routine defined with an **inline** directive as a trap instruction.

PROGRAMMING THE MACINTOSH

Part 5 of this book is a journey to the lush valley of True Macintosh Programming—a place where programs like Reflex, Turbo Pascal, Excel, and SideKick grow in profusion; where checkbook-balancing programs are commanded with points and clicks, not *ReadLns*. Standing in your way is the forbidding, snow-covered hulk of Toolbox Mountain.

In the years since its introduction, Macintosh programming has earned a reputation for being hard to learn. There are reasons for this reputation.

First, without a working knowledge of Pascal, the learning curve is impossibly steep. Many have tried to learn Pascal and the Toolbox simultaneously; for most, this approach is destined to fail. You can't struggle with **while** loops and enumerated types and expect to pick up on the Toolbox at the same time. That's why we took 28 chapters to drill Pascal into your head before starting the climb.

More than a few seasoned Pascal programmers have failed to conquer Toolbox Mountain. Some freeze in blizzards of documentation overload: They attempt to read and understand every word of *Inside Macintosh* before tackling even a simple program. Others wander in endless loops, able to mimic sample programs but unable to conceptually complete the circle on their own.

It isn't so much that any single aspect of the Mac program development process is difficult. Taken individually, the Memory Manager, QuickDraw, and the rest are easily learned. The problem is quantitative rather than qualitative: The Toolbox encompasses some 600 procedures and functions and countless constant, type, and variable declarations. Many of the types are records with dozens of fields.

So, how do we propose to take *you* on this precipitous journey?

In a word, carefully. We've provided a good guide, and we've chosen a logical route. Perhaps most importantly, we're using the best equipment—Turbo Pascal.

29

Memory Management: Theory

Stack and Heap: The Memory Map

Let's spend some time learning more about how programs execute in memory. This chapter explains the theory behind managing your computer's memory, while the next chapter shows you how to practice good memory management.

When you compile and run a Pascal program, it undergoes a complex transformation from a static list of ASCII characters (a source program) into a dynamic software machine (an executing object program). Some of the questions you may have had about this run-time machine include: Where in memory do the compiled routines go? Where are my global variables? Where's the local data? Where's the stack? Where's the heap? Where do Toolbox routines place their data?

A tool for understanding the run-time model is the *memory map*, a diagram that shows where code and various classes of data reside in memory.

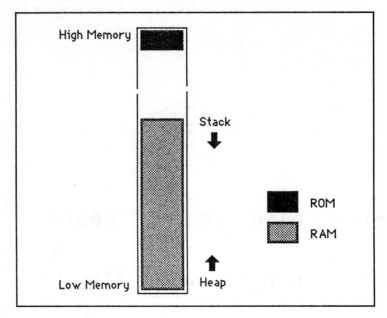

Figure 29.1: A Simple Memory Map

About the Stack

Because of its importance in the run-time model, let's focus first on the stack. A stack is a memory-allocation scheme, that is, a technique for storing information that is used constantly by all Pascal programs, whether you're aware of it or not.

Stacks store data like programmers store computer magazines near a favorite reading chair: At the top of the magazine pile are glossy new *MacWorld*s; at the bottom, musty issues of *Interface Age* circa 1978. Storage activity ("popping" a magazine off the pile and "pushing" a magazine onto the pile) occurs at the top of the stack. This causes stacks to be known as *LIFO* (last in, first out) data structures.

The stack used by a Turbo Pascal program is managed directly by the CPU. The processor's stack consists of two components, working in concert: a range of memory (potentially, any vacant place in RAM) and a register inside the processor known as the *stack pointer*. (A register is simply a storage location for binary numbers located inside the processor.) By definition, the value in the stack pointer defines the top of the stack; that is, it "points" to the top of the stack. "Pushing" a value onto the stack means writing the value to the address the stack pointer points to and then reducing the stack pointer register. As items are popped off the stack, the stack pointer register is increased. The stack pointer is like a pointer variable; dereferencing the stack pointer indicates the data at the top of the stack.

By convention, the stack starts in high memory and works down. In the following figure, the stack pointer shows that 1074 is the value at the top of the stack. If you were to remove 1074—that is, to "pop" it off the stack—the value at the next higher address (900140) becomes the top of the stack.

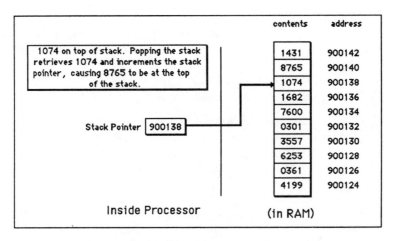

Figure 29.2: Processor Stack

Every Turbo Pascal program uses the stack to store

- return addresses when calling procedures and functions
- parameters passed to procedures and functions
- the local variables of procedures and functions
- the values returned by functions

Although program *StackDemo* creates no output, we can learn a lot about stack usage by closely studying its execution.

```
program StackDemo;
var
  X, Y: Integer;

procedure Proc2;
var
  A,B,C: Integer;
```

```
begin
  A := 1234;
  X := 5678;
end;

procedure Proc1(param: Integer);
var
  I,J: Integer;
begin
  I := param;
  Proc2;
end;

begin
  Proc1(1234);
end.
```

It's the compiler's job to generate stack-handling code, so let's think about compiling this program for a moment. Part of the compilation process involves replacing variable names (in the source code) with addresses (in the object code). A variable identifier is translated into the address of a section of RAM just large enough to hold it.

StackDemo declares two global integer variables: *X* and *Y*. They are called global because their declarations appear at the highest level of the program. This global quality is manifested at run time: Storage for *X* and *Y* is reserved before *StackDemo* even begins to run; let's say address 900,002 for *X* and 900,000 for *Y*. For the duration of the program, these addresses do not change. For example, the assignment to *X* in *Proc2* is translated to machine language that reads something like this:

```
move 5678 --> address 900,002
```

The same cannot be said for the variables declared within procedures *Proc1* and *Proc2*. In fact, when *StackDemo* first begins to execute, *A, B, C, I,* and *J* don't exist; that is, no memory has been reserved to hold them. Although space doesn't exist for them at first, code to manipulate them *does*.

This seems impossible—how can code exist to manipulate a variable that hasn't yet been assigned an address? Thanks to a capability of the processor known as *register relative addressing*, local variables are known by their position relative to the stack pointer register, that is, to the top of the stack. If you were to peer inside the compiled form of *StackDemo* at the code representing the assignment to local variable *A* in *Proc2*, you'd see the machine code equivalent of

```
move 1234 --> address 2 bytes from top of the stack
```

Note that this code doesn't say what the top of the stack is. When *Proc1* is called, as you'll see in a minute, the stack pointer register will have a real value, (say, 850,000), and at that time "2 bytes from the top of the stack" will refer unambiguously to address 850,002.

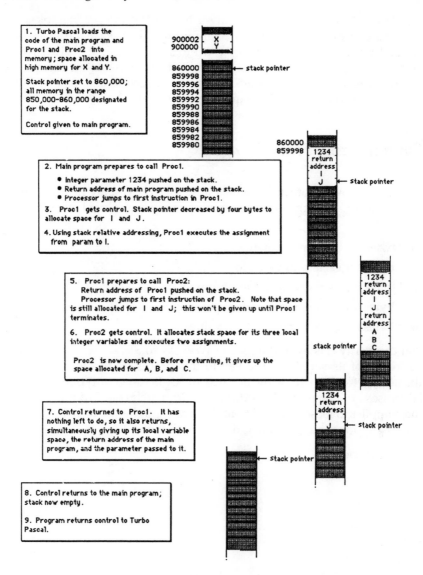

Figure 29.3: Executing StackDemo

Size Limits of Stack Variables

StackDemo's procedures declare only a handful of integer variables, but a procedure or function is free to declare up to 32K of local variables of any type. Surprisingly, it doesn't take any longer to allocate 256 bytes—**string**[255]—on the stack than it does to create an integer. Both involve a reduction in the stack pointer; subtracting 256, or even 32,000, from the stack pointer is just as quick as subtracting 2.

Summarizing Stack Usage

The stack grows according to which nested levels you are in when you call a procedure, and the size of those procedure's local variables and parameters:

- 8 bytes for each level down
- *n* bytes for each local variable
- 4 bytes for each **var** (reference) parameter
- *n* bytes for each non-**var** (value) parameter
- *n* bytes for each function return value

You can verify this by adding some *WriteLn*s to *StackDemo* to print out the addresses of its variables. The key to this process is the address operator, the at sign (@; @X equals the address of X). Because of typing constraints, addresses can't be printed out directly. Fortunately, the *Ord* function causes the compiler to loosen up and treat them as though they were long integers. (Internally, long integers and addresses are identical.)

```
program StackDemo2;
var
  X, Y: Integer;

procedure Proc2;
var
  A,B,C: Integer;
begin
  A := 1234;
  X := 5678;
  WriteLn('Address of A, B, C = ', Ord(@A):10, Ord(@B):10, Ord(@C):10);
 end;

procedure Proc1(param: Integer);
var
  I,J: Integer;
begin
```

```
    I := param;
    Proc2;
    WriteLn('Address of I, J = ', Ord(@I):10, Ord(@J):10);
end;

begin
    Proc1(1234);
    WriteLn('Address of X, Y = ', Ord(@X):10, Ord(@Y):10); ReadLn;
end.
```

Let's examine the output of this program to see how reasonable it is, given our understanding of stack usage.

A 1-Mb Mac Plus created the following:

```
Address of A, B, C =  972588    972586    972584
Address of I, J =     972600    972598
Address of X, Y =     972646    972644
```

Note that the global variables are stored in a higher address than the first set of local variables. In fact, those addresses are what determined the initial top of stack value; it's initially set to just below the last global variable. *Proc1*'s variables have higher addresses than *Proc2*'s , because they are created earlier (remember, the stack grows down).

The addresses of this program's local variables change according to the value of the stack pointer when they are called. For example, if you change the main program to call *Proc2* directly instead of *Proc1*, A, B, and C will have slightly higher addresses. The addresses of X and Y won't change.

```
begin
    Proc2;
    WriteLn('Address of X, Y = ', Ord(@X):10, Ord(@Y):10); ReadLn;
end.
```

results in

```
Address of A, B, C =  972602    972600    972598
Address of X, Y =     972646    972644
```

Do some experimenting on your own. Declare a large global array variable. Does the storage allocated for local variables move down a corresponding amount?

Suppose we were devious and printed out the addresses of *Proc1*'s local variables from within the main program. This catches Pascal with its pants down, because, at this point, *I* and *J* don't yet exist. So just what value will *Ord(@J)* return when used in the main program? The address it will have when *Proc1* is called? Zero? A random value? Add this line to the start of the main program and find out:

```
WriteLn('Address of I, J = ', Ord(@I):10, Ord(@J):10);
```

Surprise! Professor Wirth is way ahead of us. Pascal's scope rules prevent us from even performing the experiment. Since *I* and *J* aren't visible to the main program, you can't use their identifiers here. *I* and *J* can only be used within *Proc1*—which, not coincidentally, is the only time they've been assigned an address in memory.

Stack Overflow

The compiler handles the stack for you, creating code that automatically pushes data on the stack and pops it off as a program executes. This is one more good reason for using Pascal instead of assembly language. Assembly-language programmers must manage the stack themselves, and one little mistake causes a machine to hang.

When using Pascal, problems arise only when a program uses so much stack that it overwrites part of the heap. This is called *stack overflow* and always results in a system error. Programs are most likely to cause a stack overflow if they perform the following operations, especially in combination:

- declare large local variables
- pass large variables by value
- use recursive algorithms

Under the Stack: The Heap

Let's review what we learned about the heap back in Chapter 16. The heap is an initially unused area of memory located beneath the stack. The *New* procedure allocates memory from this region, which is then accessed via a pointer, and *Dispose* gives it back. This program demonstrates:

```
program AllocateTest;
type
  BigArray = array [1..1000] of integer;
  BigArrayPtr = ^BigArray;
var
  theArray : BigArrayPtr;
begin
  New(theArray);  { heap now has 2,000 fewer free bytes }
  .. { use the array by dereferencing the pointer, e.g., theArray^[56] := 123 }
  Dispose(theArray);
```

end.

When *AllocateTest* calls *New*, two things happen. First, an unused block of memory large enough to hold 1000 integers (2000 bytes) is located in the heap. Nothing is moved or altered, but simply flagged as "in use." How *New* can look in the heap and tell what's in use and what's not isn't our concern. It's possible that there isn't a 2000-byte contiguous chunk available. In this case, *New* sets *theArray* to **nil** and returns.

If the *New* procedure *does* find 2000 free bytes, after flagging the block as in use, it sets *theArray* to the address of the first byte of the block and returns control to the calling routine. Since the allocated block isn't initialized to any special value, one operation we might perform on the array is to initialize every element to zero:

```
for N := 1 to 1000 do
  theArray^[N] := 0;
```

Now *theArray^* is ready to store check numbers, test scores, or whatever.

If the program finishes with *theArray^* before the program ends, it should give back the memory it occupies. Otherwise, these 2000 bytes won't be available for reuse. Do this too many times and you'll run out of heap space. For this reason, *AllocateTest* balances the call to *New* with a call to *Dispose*:

```
Dispose(theArray);
```

In this particular case, there's really no need for it, since the program ends immediately thereafter and when a program ends, all heap structures are released.

A Pascal program's stack grows down toward its heap, which in turn grows up toward the stack. You run out of room when the two meet. The heap never expands into the stack—but the stack will overwrite the heap. When a Mac program first starts to run, the heap is simply an unused area of RAM of approximately 6K, in as low a memory location (that is, as far from the stack) as possible.

If a program allocates more than 6K of heap space, then the heap automatically grows to accommodate each request. It can ultimately expand to a limit that by default is 8K less than the original top of the stack. This means that if your program's stack requirement is less than 8K (which isn't hard to achieve unless you have large local variables or pass large variables by value), the stack won't overflow no matter how large the heap should grow. In an upcoming section, we'll describe the routines that set the stack/heap boundary point, so that you can achieve the optimal balance for your particular application.

Rather than letting it grow in bits and pieces, it's possible to expand the heap to its full extent all at once. One way to do this is to call Turbo's *MaxAvail* function, which expands the heap to its limit and returns the length of the largest single contiguous block it contains. Typically, *MaxAvail* is used just before a call to *New* to see if there's room for the object you're about to create.

Sharing the Heap

When you use Pascal on traditional personal computers, the heap is only for the benefit of your program. If you never make a call to *New* on such a machine, heap memory never changes. In the Mac, however, programs share the heap with Toolbox routines, and the programmers behind these routines had a passion for heap allocation. Toolbox routines put objects in the heap like crazy.

Consider fonts, for instance. We take for granted the ability of Turbo Pascal's editor to display text in various fonts and sizes. This ability is supported by QuickDraw (which actually draws the text on the screen) and by the Font Manager, which provides QuickDraw with character data.

Each font is represented by a data structure thousands of bytes long that must be entirely in memory before a single character can be drawn in that font and size. If you had to write the Toolbox code that Turbo calls when ordered to display a program in 24-point New York, where would you store this 7K chunk of data—a place where you could easily get rid of it later on when it wasn't needed any more? In the heap, of course.

Figure 29.4: Check Records and Fonts on Heap

In a Mac program, your heap data objects are liable to have anything for a neighbor—linked lists of check records intertwined with font data. This also means that even if *MaxAvail* says the heap has 300,000 bytes available, you can't count on that number being right ten minutes later. Even if your program didn't change the heap during that interval, a Toolbox routine you used, either directly or indirectly, may have allocated (or deallocated) space.

Review

Macintosh programs make extensive use of both the stack and heap to store variables. Because the compiler generates stack-handling code for you, you can't get into much trouble with it. Stack overflow is unlikely if you pay attention to the size of parameters you pass to procedures and functions and the size of local variables.

The heap is another matter. It's a busy area shared by your programs and by the Toolbox routines. Moreover, the compiler doesn't give you any help in using it. It's up to you—using pointers along with the routines of the Memory Manager—to stay on top of the heap.

30

Memory Management: Practice

When writing programs for a heap overachiever like the Macintosh, you need more powerful tools than *New* and *Dispose*. ROM contains dozens of routines that perform heap-management tasks, known collectively as the *Memory Manager*.

Incidentally, Apple's technical writers adopted the "manager" notation to divide the Toolbox into functional groups for documentation purposes. Don't be misled into thinking about the Memory Manager as a single process or program that manages all aspects of the heap in a godlike fashion. It's simply a collection of constants, types, variables, procedures, and functions that perform memory-related activities. From a Pascal standpoint, the Memory Manager is defined in unit *OSIntf*.

Heap Zones

The Memory Manager can work with multiple heaps (officially called *heap zones*). At any given time in a booted-up Macintosh, exactly two are in use: the *system heap* and the *application heap*.

The system heap is in low memory. This area is created when the system first boots up and is rarely accessed directly by applications. An important characteristic of the system heap is that it retains its contents between a transfer from one application to another. It is used, among other things, to keep track of volumes and files.

Just above the system heap is the application heap. It's intended for the current application's use and is what we've simply been calling "the heap." The application heap is destroyed and a new one created whenever a new application starts up (that is, every time you enter or exit the Finder). By default, most Memory Manager calls apply to the application heap—as does the information in this chapter.

NewPtr = New

When writing True Macintosh Programs, you usually forgo *New* in favor of *NewPtr*, the Toolbox equivalent. *NewPtr* is both better and worse than *New* for creating heap objects: It's more powerful, but it's also more trouble, mainly because *NewPtr* involves hand-to-hand combat with the compiler over typing considerations.

The nice thing about *New* is that it's a built-in part of the language and, as such, has certain privileges not accorded ordinary procedures and functions. Much as *WriteLn* can accept from zero to dozens of parameters, *New* has no problem accommodating variables of differing types:

```
type
  BigArray = array [1..1000] of Integer;
  BigArrayPtr = ^BigArray;
  Check = record
            Amt    : Real;
            Month  :(Jan,Feb,Mar,Apr,May,Jun,Jul,Aug,Sep,Oct,Nov,Dec);
            Day    : 1..31;
            Year   : 1980..2000;
            Payee  : string[40];
          end;
  CheckPtr = ^Check;
var
  A: BigArrayPtr;
  C: CheckPtr;
begin
  New(A);  { allocate 2000 bytes }
  New(C);    { allocate 50 bytes }
end.
```

New accepts a pointer to a check record as readily as it does a pointer to an array of integers. In fact, any pointer type is acceptable. The compiler isn't as generous with your own routines. For example, if you write a procedure to accept a parameter of type *CheckPtr*

```
procedure NewCheck(theCheck: CheckPtr);
```

the compiler, with your best interests at heart, won't let you send anything but variables of type *CheckPtr* to *NewCheck*. If *P* isn't a *CheckPtr*, then

```
NewCheck(P)
```

produces a `Type Mismatch` error. That is, unless you apply a little compiler voodoo known as *type coercion* (or, alternatively, *typecasting*). You can send other pointer types to *NewCheck* only if you reassure the compiler that you know what you're doing by wrapping the parameter with the name of the correct type. For example, as long as variable *P* is some pointer type (*bigArrayPtr, ^LongInt*, for example), then

```
NewCheck(CheckPtr(P));
```

causes the compiler to accept it as a parameter to *NewCheck*. It looks as though we're calling a function named *CheckPtr* here, but we're not. Surrounding *P* with *CheckPtr()* tells the compiler to treat *P* as though it really were a value of type *CheckPtr*, thus satisfying *NewCheck*'s requirement that it be passed items of this type.

Typing restrictions also apply to Toolbox routines accessed through Turbo's unit mechanism. Armed with the tool of type coercion, let's take a look at the formal declaration of the Toolbox's *NewPtr* routine. You'll find it in unit *OSIntf* (described in Appendix D of the Turbo Pascal manual and Volume II of *Inside Macintosh*).

```
function NewPtr(byteCount: Size): Ptr;
```

The *Size* data type is defined in unit *OSIntf* as a synonym for *LongInt*, so you can pass any integer or long integer value to *NewPtr*. *NewPtr* returns a value of type *Ptr*, which is defined in unit *MemTypes* as

```
type
  Ptr = ^SignedByte;
```

where *SignedByte* is itself declared as the integer subrange –128..127 (the largest subrange that can be stored in 1 byte of memory). *Ptr* is declared to point to *SignedByte* not because individual bytes are such useful objects, but rather as a sort of heap "standard currency." You'll create pointers to the types of objects your program needs to use and then use type coercion to make them compatible with type *Ptr*—which is the type expected by Memory Manager routines.

Because of typing constraints, the only sort of objects you can assign to with *NewPtr* is a variable of type *Ptr*. Therefore, allocating heap space with *NewPtr* for a check record or a *BigArray* requires type coercion.

Here's how to use *NewPtr* to allocate space for an integer array:

```
program NewPtrTest;
```

```
uses
  MemTypes, QuickDraw, OSIntf;
type
  BigArray = array [1..1000] of Integer;
  BigArrayPtr = ^BigArray;
var
  theArray: BigArrayPtr;
begin
  theArray:=BigArrayPtr(NewPtr(2000));  { instead of: New(theArray) }
end.
```

Note the differences between *New* and *NewPtr*. First, *NewPtr* is a function—it returns the address of the allocated block, rather than being called as a procedure. Second, type coercion is required to get the compiler to agree to the assignment of a *Ptr* to a *BigArrayPtr*. Third, *NewPtr* requires a numeric parameter describing the number of bytes to allocate. In contrast, as a built-in routine, *New* gains this value automatically because of the compiler's knowledge of the pointer type passed to it.

The *SizeOf* function is a better way to provide *NewPtr* with size information. It returns a number equal to the size in bytes of a variable of a given type or, alternatively, the type itself. So, this statement is equivalent:

```
theArray := BigArrayPtr(NewPtr(SizeOf(BigArray)));
```

You're probably thinking, *NewPtr* is so *messy* compared to *New*:

```
New(theArray);
```

And, visually, it is. Surprisingly, though, using *NewPtr* to allocate *theArray* involves no more run-time processing than *New*. Here's why. First, type coercion doesn't affect run-time code; it simply causes the compiler to agree to an otherwise illegal type conflict. Similarly, *SizeOf* doesn't cause any run-time processing. By the time this program gets around to running, the expression *SizeOf(BigArray)* will have already been turned into the value 2000. From a run-time standpoint, the statement

```
theArray := BigArrayPtr(NewPtr(SizeOf(BigArray)));
```

generates exactly the same code as

```
P := NewPtr(2000);  { where P is of type Ptr }
```

Finally, because Turbo Pascal's built-in routines use the Memory Manager to implement heap management, a call to *New* ultimately results in a call to *NewPtr* anyway. By calling it directly, we skip the middleman.

This theme repeats again and again in using the Toolbox: statements that are visually complicated, with long identifiers and a forest of nested parentheses, but which result in fast, compact run-time code.

If you're still not convinced *NewPtr* is worth the clutter, here's something it can do that *New* can't: Declare an object greater than 32K. *NewPtr* accepts a size parameter of up to 2 billion.

```
program BigBlock;
uses
  MemTypes, QuickDraw, OSIntf;
var
  P: Ptr;
begin
  P := NewPtr(100000);
end.
```

This program claims 100,000 contiguous bytes of heap space, the first byte of which is at the address stored in *P*. Like *New*, *NewPtr* returns **nil** if it can't fulfill the allocation request. *NewPtr*'s ability to create big blocks goes a long way toward alleviating the pain of the 32K structure limitation. You can't use array notation to access any bytes past the 32K point, but a little "pointer arithmetic" allows you to treat a large block in any way you like (we describe this process later).

After using *NewPtr* to allocate heap space, don't use *Dispose* to give it back. Instead, call the complementary Memory Manager routine *DisposPtr*.

```
procedure DisposPtr(p: Ptr);
```

Since it only accepts parameters of type *Ptr*, a variable of any other type must be coerced to type *Ptr*—for example, to dispose of *theArray* from the earlier example:

```
DisposPtr(Ptr(theArray));
```

The Fragmented Heap

NewPtr (and by extension *New*, since it ultimately results in a call to *NewPtr*) creates fixed (*nonrelocatable*) blocks on the heap. Unlike stack space, heap space can be allocated and deallocated in any order. That's simultaneously its greatest attribute and its worst problem. After a heap-using program has run for a while, the heap becomes a Swiss cheese of vacant holes and allocated space.

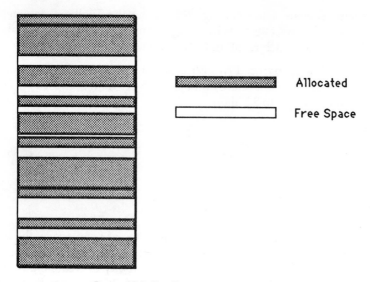

Allocated

Free Space

Figure 30.1: The Fragmented Heap

This is called *fragmentation*, and it's the nemesis of heap management. It is possible to have tens of thousands of bytes of free space, but no single contiguous block larger than a few hundred bytes. So, even though the heap theoretically has room, any attempt to allocate even a thousand bytes fails.

This program demonstrates the tragedy of fragmentation.

```
program FragmentationDemo;
uses
  MemTypes, QuickDraw, OSIntf;
var
  ArrayOfPtr: array[1..400] of Ptr;
  N: Integer;
  Temp: LongInt;
begin
  MaxApplZone; { Expand the heap to its maximum (8K below top of stack) }
  N := 0;
  repeat
    N := N + 1;
    WriteLn('Now allocating array ',N);
    ArrayOfPtr[N] := NewPtr(10000);
  until ArrayOfPtr[N] = nil;
  ReadLn;

  N := N - 1;
  repeat
    WriteLn('Now disposing array ',N);
    DisposPtr(ArrayOfPtr[N]);
    N := N - 2;
```

Turbo Pascal Tutor for the Macintosh

```
until N <= 0;
WriteLn(FreeMem,MaxMem(Temp):10);
ReadLn;
end.
```

This program first calls the Memory Manager's *MaxApplZone* procedure to expand the heap to its limit (that is, to within 8K of the top of the stack). Then, depending how much memory your machine contains, *FragmentationDemo* creates several—possibly dozens of—nonrelocatable 10,000 byte objects. It keeps track of each with an entry in *ArrayOfPtr*. In a 1-Mb machine, *FragmentationDemo* allocates roughly 75 such blocks (750K).

It stops creating them when *NewPtr* finally returns **nil**, indicating that the heap is too full to accept any more 10K blocks. The text in the terminal window may get a little distorted at this point, due to a phenomenon known as *purging* (described later). Then *FragmentationDemo* methodically deallocates every other block. By the time this program works its way to the final *WriteLn* statement, the heap is striped like a zebra with alternating free space and allocated blocks.

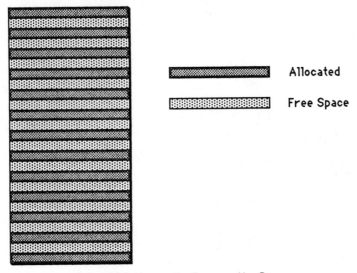

Figure 30.2: Heap after Program Has Run

This program forgoes Turbo's built-in heap status routines *MemAvail* and *MaxAvail* in favor of Toolbox functions that do the same thing. The Memory Manager function *FreeMem* returns the total amount of free memory in the heap. *MaxMem* returns the size of the largest single contiguous block. (It returns in *Temp* the size by which the heap can still grow; since we used *MaxApplZone* already, *Temp* returns as zero.)

On a 1-Mb machine, *FragmentationDemo*'s final *WriteLn* produces numbers somewhere in this vicinity:

360000   18066

This is the tragedy of fragmentation: 360,000 bytes of free memory, yet we can't create a 20K block.

Compacting the Heap

Apple's programmers created the fragmentation problem with their abundant use of the heap to store various and sundry Toolbox data objects. So they devised a scheme that periodically packs all the allocated blocks snugly at the bottom of the heap, resulting in a consolidation of free space at the top. This is called *compacting* the heap.

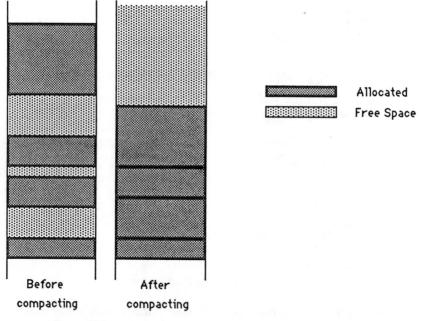

Before compacting   After compacting

Figure 30.3

Let's think about the ramifications of compacting the heap. Imagine that a program has been running for a while and has allocated a number of blocks. One object in particular is accessed through pointer variable *theArray* (of type *BigArrayPtr*), which currently holds the value 201,220 (that is, 201,220 is the address of *theArray^[1]*).

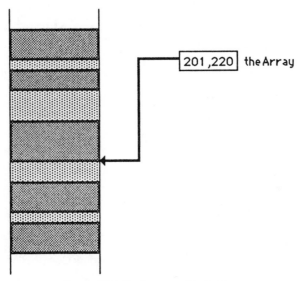

201,220 theArray

Figure 30.4: theArray on the Heap

Up to this point, there's been enough room to create every block that the program (or a Toolbox routine) asked for without any compaction necessary. But now, a desk accessory requiring 7K is activated. The Toolbox's *OpenDeskAcc* function asks for a 7000-byte block on the heap. The Memory Manager discovers that 7000 contiguous bytes don't exist. So it compacts the heap, packing the allocated blocks into a solid chunk at the bottom, and frees up 20,000 bytes at the top.

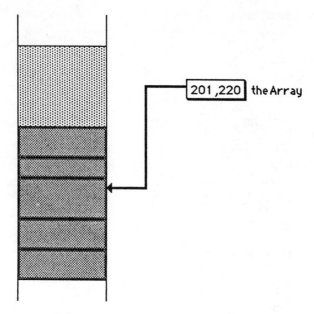

Figure 30.5: New Address of theArray after Compaction

The desk accessory does its thing and our program gets control back. All is well—or is it? Before too long, the desk accessory tries to access the array formerly at address 201,220 (pointer variable *theArray* still holds this value). But the array isn't there any more—it's been moved to address 102,188. Since the program has no way of knowing this, it goes through the motions of treating the 2000 bytes at address 201,220 as though they still represented the array. Every read of *theArray* gets erroneous values; every write clobbers 2 bytes of some other routine's data.

The same situation exists for other routines that had declared heap objects before the compaction—all start working with data that isn't right any more, and things run amuck. Bomb alerts appear. Users tear out their hair.

It seems that heap-management routines shouldn't go around moving memory blocks, because the pointers used to keep track of them aren't updated to reflect the movement. But there's an improvement to blocks and pointers that permits compaction.

Turbo Pascal Tutor for the Macintosh

Relocatable Blocks and Handles

The Memory Manager offers two sets of tools for working with heap memory. The first are the ones we've been working with thus far: pointers to nonrelocatable blocks in the heap. They're created with *NewPtr* (or *New*, for that matter); accessed by dereferencing pointer variables; and disposed of with *DisposPtr* (or *Dispose*). Using nonrelocatable blocks invites fragmentation.

The second approach uses *pointers to pointers to relocatable blocks*. Relocatable blocks are created with the Memory Manager's *NewHandle* routine and disposed of with the complementary *DisposHandle*. Relocatable blocks permit heap compaction and therefore eliminate (or at least reduce) the fragmentation problem.

Relocatable blocks are made possible by an ingenious scheme involving a middleman called a *master pointer*. Relocatable blocks are accessed with pointer variables that point to master pointers, which in turn contain the addresses of the objects themselves. The pointer to the master pointer is called a *handle*.

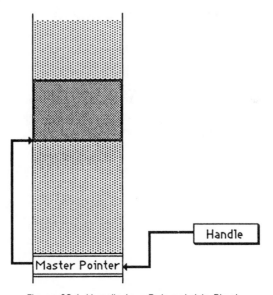

Figure 30.6: Handle to a Relocatable Block

When, during compaction, a heap-management routine sees fit to move the object that a master pointer points to, it knows to change the value in the master pointer so that the master pointer continues to point to the object in its new location. (There's a backward link between each relocatable block and its associated master pointer.) Since the master pointer itself didn't move, the pointer to it (the handle) maintains access to the block.

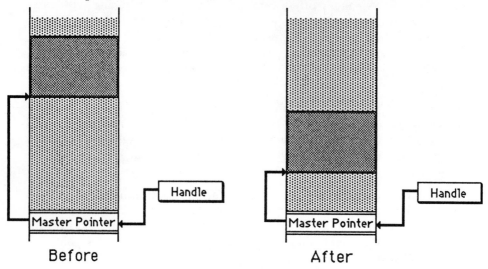

Figure 30.7: Handle to a Moved Relocatable Block

Here's the official declaration of *NewHandle* in unit *OSIntf*:

```
function NewHandle(byteCount: Size): Handle;
```

NewHandle is analogous to *NewPtr*. You tell it how many bytes long the relocatable block should be, and it returns a 4-byte object of type *Handle*, where *Handle* is defined in unit *MemTypes* as

```
type
  Handle = ^Ptr;
```

This means that given

```
var
  H: Handle;
```

then

- *H* is a *Handle*
- *H^* is a *Ptr*
- *H^^* is a *SignedByte*

Turbo Pascal Tutor for the Macintosh

Handle variables require two dereferences and, therefore, two carets alongside the handle identifier to get to the object indicated by the handle. For example,

```
type
  CheckPtr = ^Check;
  CheckHdl = ^CheckPtr;
var
  aCheck: CheckHdl;
```

After allocating the block with NewHandle,

```
aCheck := CheckHdl(NewHandle(Sizeof(Check));
```

- *aCheck^* is a *CheckPtr*
- *aCheck^^* is a check record
- *aCheck^^.amt* is a real
- *aCheck^^.payee* is a string
- *aCheck^^.payee[5]* is a character

Just as you can't dereference pointer variables unless they really point to something, you can't dereference a handle unless you've previously used *NewHandle* to allocate a master pointer and relocatable block. (You can try, but the results are usually catastrophic.) For example, when executing the statement

```
aCheck^^.payee := 'Alice Carlson'
```

the Macintosh uses the address in *aCheck* to locate the address of the check record itself, so that it can assign to its payee field. If *aCheck* doesn't point to a master pointer or if that master pointer doesn't point to an appropriate heap block, then executing this statement is liable to assign string data to any address in memory.

Let's review: When a program wants to allocate some heap memory (and reduce the likelihood that the heap will become unusably fragmented), it calls function *NewHandle*. *NewHandle* returns the address of a master pointer. In turn, this master pointer contains the address of the relocatable block of data of the prescribed length that's been allocated in the heap. When you're compacting the heap and a block requires moving, the memory-management routines need only update this master pointer with the new address of the block. The Pascal routine that allocated the block still has the address of the master pointer, which itself doesn't move.

This next program show how handles and relocatable blocks result in a more usable heap.

```
program NoFragmentationDemo;
uses MemTypes, QuickDraw, OSIntf;
var
  ArrayOfHdl: array [1..400] of Handle;
  N: Integer;
  Temp: Longint;
begin
  MaxApplZone; N := 0;
  repeat
    N := N + 1;
    WriteLn('Now allocating array ',N);
    ArrayOfHdl[N] := NewHandle(10000);
  until ArrayOfHdl[N] = nil;
  ReadLn;
  N := N - 1;
  repeat
    WriteLn('Now disposing array ',N);
    DisposHandle(ArrayOfHdl[N]);
    N := N - 2;
  until N <= 0;
  WriteLn(FreeMem,MaxMem(Temp):10);
  ReadLn;
end.
```

This program creates relocatable blocks instead of fixed blocks, and therefore allows heap compaction to work. At the instant of the final *WriteLn*, the heap is striped much like before.

The payoff comes when *MaxMem* invokes heap compaction. The compaction is so successful that *MaxMem* and *FreeMem* return almost the same value, meaning that you can create a block almost as large as the heap's free space.

It's Up to You

In practice, Macintosh programs create both types of blocks, and the Memory Manager takes both in stride. Nonrelocatable blocks are always placed in as low a memory location as possible, moving relocatable blocks up as necessary, to reduce the potential for permanent fragmentation. This process works best when the heap is largely empty, so try to allocate nonrelocatable space early on in a program's execution.

Where you have a choice, use relocatable blocks.

Applications for Relocatable Blocks

A handy characteristic of relocatable blocks is that they can be easily lengthened and shortened—treated almost like disk files. The keys to this are the Memory Manager's *SetHandleSize* and *GetHandleSize* routines.

Procedure *SetHandleSize* allows you to enlarge or reduce a relocatable block.

```
procedure SetHandleSize(h: Handle; newSize: Size);
```

To find out how long a relocatable block is at any given time, call function *GetHandleSize*:

```
function GetHandleSize(h: Handle): Size;
```

Checkbook Program #49

Using a relocatable block to store check data uses less memory than even a linked list. We won't show an entire program here—just enough to demonstrate how a 0-byte relocatable block is allocated initially, then expanded by one check's worth with each call to procedure *AddCheck*.

```
type
  CheckArray = array [1..640] of check;
  CheckArrayPtr = ^CheckArray;
  CheckArrayHdl = ^CheckArrayPtr;
var
  checkbook: CheckArrayHdl;

procedure AddCheck(theCheck: Check);
{ add a check record to the end of the block }
var
  N: LongInt;
  checkCount: Integer;
begin
  N := GetHandleSize(Handle(checkbook));               { how large is it now? }
  SetHandleSize(Handle(Checkbook),N + Sizeof(Check)); { now one check bigger }
  checkCount := sizeNow div Sizeof(Check);   { calculate index for new entry }
  checkbook^^[checkCount] := theCheck;     { store check data at end of block }
end;

begin
  checkbook := CheckArrayHdl(NewHandle(0));          { allocate a 0-byte block }
  .
  . { accept and store check data }
  .
end.
```

Since this program uses array notation to access the relocatable block, it is still subject to the 32K structure limitation. That's why type *CheckArray* is defined the way it is—640 check records are as many as can be shoehorned into 32K.

There are similar calls for retrieving and setting the size of nonrelocatable blocks—*GetPtrSize* and *SetPtrSize*. They're rarely used, however, mainly because *SetPtrSize* will usually fail a request to increase the size of a nonrelocatable block. If there's a nonrelocatable block above a nonrelocatable block (and there usually is, since the Memory Manager puts all nonrelocatable blocks together at the bottom of the heap), then any effort to expand that block will fail.

Error Detection

After performing any Memory Manager function, you can determine the success or failure of the operation by calling the *MemError* routine. For example, when attempting to expand a relocatable block with *SetHandleSize*, check the value returned by *MemError* immediately thereafter to see if it worked:

```
SetHandleSize(Handle(CheckArray));
if MemError <> noErr then          { noErr is an integer constant }
  OutOfMemory;                            { defined in OSIntf }
```

Unit *OSIntf* defines a number of integer constants useful in interpreting the value returned by *MemError*. See *OSIntf*'s interface in Appendix D of this and the Turbo Pascal manual for more information.

Master Pointer Blocks

The Memory Manager allocates 64 master pointers when it first sets up the application heap zone. These master pointers reside in a 512-byte nonrelocatable block at the very bottom of the heap. Additional nonrelocatable blocks of 64 master pointers each are created as needed. If you watch the execution of *NoFragmentationDemo* carefully, you may notice a brief pause as the 40th or 50th block is allocated. This delay is caused by the allocation of a fresh block of master pointers at the bottom of the heap. It requires several hundred thousand bytes worth of relocatable blocks to be moved up 512 bytes, creating a slight pause.

Should a program need more than 64 master pointers (and they have a way of getting used up), it's safest to allocate them early on yourself, to reduce the risk of fragmentation. The parameterless *MoreMasters* procedure creates 64 master pointers with each call. To create more than 64 master pointers, call *MoreMasters* more than once. Some applications call it a dozen times or more as part of their initialization code.

Purging and Heap Compaction

Heap management, Macintosh-style, gets even more interesting. In accommodating a request for a block larger than what's currently available, the allocation routines will do more than simply compact the heap. If, after moving all the relocatable blocks together, there still isn't enough memory available, the Memory Manager checks if any blocks are flagged as *purgeable*.

A purgeable block is a relocatable block whose user (either you or a Toolbox routine) has told the Memory Manager, in effect, "If you ever need to use the memory occupied by this relocatable block for something else, feel free. Just let me know that you've taken it." This is known as making a block *purgeable* and is performed by calling the *HPurge* routine:

```
procedure HPurge(h: Handle);
```

It may be hard to imagine allowing a block to be purged—after all, if you're going to let it be overwritten, why bother to allocate it in the first place? You certainly don't want to lose carefully acquired checkbook data this way. But there are cases where purging is tolerable.

Consider the Toolbox's font-handling routines. A given font must be in memory before QuickDraw can use it to draw text. But there's an exact duplicate of that font data out on disk (in the System file, where it came from in the first place). So, if a program allows a 7K block of font data that hasn't been used in the last 30 minutes to be purged so that more checks can be entered, there's no great loss. The font is simply loaded from disk again the next time it's needed—at which time the memory situation may have changed.

It's a classic programming trade-off: speed versus memory. We sacrifice the time spent going to the disk to reread the purged font for the benefit of using its memory for something more important. For bulky, read-only, occasional-use data that can be easily recreated or reloaded from disk, purgeable blocks free up memory for routines that really need it. Incidentally, font data usually *is* purgeable; that's why this chapter's heap-filling demos may result in strange-looking text on your machine.

Blocks aren't purged except as a last resort. Here are the steps the Memory Manager follows when trying to allocate an *n*-byte block:

- Check the current heap zone for an *n*-byte free space.
- Compact the heap and check again.
- Increase the heap zone (if it isn't already at the limit).

■ Purge purgeable blocks.

This program demonstrates purging:

```
program PurgeDemo;
uses MemTypes, QuickDraw, OSIntf;
var
  ArrayOfHdl: array [1..400] of Handle;
  N: Integer;
  Temp: LongInt;
begin
  MaxApplZone;
  N := 0;
  repeat
    N := N + 1;
    WriteLn('Now allocating array ',N);
    ArrayOfHdl[N] := NewHandle(10000);
  until ArrayOfHdl[N] = nil;
  WriteLn(MaxMem(Temp):10);
  ReadLn;
  N := N - 1;
  repeat
    WriteLn('Now flagging array ', N:0, ' as purgeable');
    HPurge(ArrayOfHdl[N]);
    N := N - 2;
  until N <= 0;
  WriteLn(MaxMem(Temp):10);
  ReadLn;
end.
```

This program stuffs the heap with relocatable blocks until it can't accept another one. By default, blocks created with *NewHandle* are not purgeable, so calling *MaxMem* the first time displays a value of less than 10K. Then *PurgeDemo* proceeds to flag every other block as purgeable. When the heap compaction/purging process is triggered again by the *MaxMem* statement in the final *WriteLn*, half the original size of the heap is regained.

How an Application Can Tell if a Block Has Been Purged

If you've made a block purgeable, you must be able to find out whether it's been purged since you last used it. You can tell whether the block still exists by looking at its master pointer (not the handle itself, but the pointer it points to; this takes one dereferencing caret). The Memory Manger sets the master pointer of a freshly purged block to **nil**. For example, if the Font Manager didn't take care of this already, you could test whether a font has been purged thusly:

```
var
  NewYork24Pt : Handle;  { to 7000 bytes worth of purgeable font data }
  .
  .
  .
  if NewYork24Pt^ = nil then
  begin                              { using the same master pointer, }
    ReallocHandle(NewYork24Pt, 7000); { create a 7K relocatable block }
    LoadFont;                                       { load it back }
    HPurge(NewYork24Pt);             { and make it purgeable again }
  end;
  .
  . { use the font }
  .
```

ReallocHandle is designed to be used after you've discovered that a block has been purged. Alternatively, you could call *NewHandle* again, but you'd waste a master pointer.

Locking a Relocatable Block

Occasionally, you'll want to tell the Memory Manager not to relocate a relocatable block until further notice; that is, to temporarily treat it as though it had been declared with *NewPtr*. One instance would be when using File Manager routines to read a file.

The Toolbox's file routines (which are described in Chapter 39) work by being told what file to work with and where in memory to write to. This memory location is communicated with a pointer to the heap block that should be written to. The problem is that the File Manager itself must occasionally allocate heap space to accomplish the read, and it's just possible that this allocation will trigger heap compaction. As a result, the block no longer resides where you specified, and the File Manager cheerfully clobbers some other routine's data.

The solution is to temporarily *lock* the block just before the read, then to unlock it afterwards. Block locking and unlocking is performed by the *HLock* and *HUnlock* procedures:

```
procedure HLock(h: Handle);
procedure HUnlock(h: Handle);
```

A locked relocatable block is the worst sort of heap citizen, so be sure to unlock it as soon as possible. Relocatable blocks can be anywhere and locking even a small one that happens to be in the middle of the heap severely limits the ability of the Memory Manager to collect free space. This is known as creating an "island" in the heap. A single 50-byte locked block in the middle of an otherwise empty heap reduces the size of the largest block that can be allocated by half.

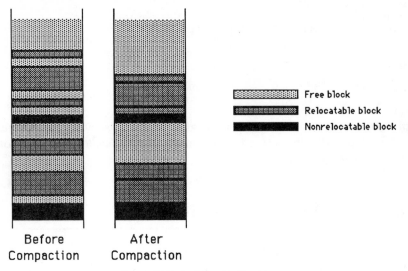

| Before | After |
| Compaction | Compaction |

⬛⬛⬛⬛⬛ Free block
⬛⬛⬛⬛⬛ Relocatable block
⬛⬛⬛⬛⬛ Nonrelocatable block

Figure 30.8: An Island in the Heap

Setting the Boundary between Stack and Heap

By default, the application heap is allowed to grow to within 8K of the stack's initial value. In a program that uses recursion or declares large stack variables, you'll want to adjust this dividing line to give the stack more elbow room. Use the following calls early on in the program's initialization:

```
function GetApplLimit : Ptr;
procedure SetApplLimit (zoneLimit: Ptr);
```

The following statement sets the heap limit to 100K less than the start of the stack:

```
SetApplLimit(Ptr(Ord(GetApplLimit) - 92000)); { Stack is 8K by default }
```

In a 1-Mb machine, the heap still has hundreds of thousands of bytes of elbow room.

Simulating Big Arrays

Both relocatable and nonrelocatable blocks can be used to simulate arrays larger than 32K. For example, this program simulates a 100,000-element array of real numbers.

```
program BigArraySimulation;
uses
    MemTypes, QuickDraw, OSIntf;
var
  theArray: Handle;

procedure PutReal(index: LongInt; value: Real);
var
  aReal : ^Real;
begin
  aReal := Pointer(Ord(theArray^) + index * 4);
  aReal^ := value;
end;

function GetReal(index: LongInt): Real;
var
  aReal : ^Real;
begin
  aReal := Pointer(Ord(theArray^) + index * 4);
  GetReal := aReal^;
end;

var
  N: LongInt;
begin
  theArray := NewHandle(400000);   { = array [0..99999] of real }
  if theArray = nil then Exit;              { insufficient memory }
    for N := 0 to 99999 do
      PutReal(N,0.0);                                     { heat }

                                             { and serve... }
  .
  .
  .
end.
```

The *PutReal* and *GetReal* routines use pointer arithmetic to calculate where a given element of this pseudo array resides in memory:

```
aReal := Pointer(Ord(theArray^) + index * 4);
```

This statement says to take the value currently in *theArray's* master pointer (*theArray^*) and add to it the result of multiplying the *index* parameter by 4. Values of type *Real* are 4 bytes long, so the second element in the array starts 4 bytes beyond the start of the block, the third at position 8, and so on.

Typing considerations force us to first turn *theArray^* (a pointer type) into a number with the *Ord* function, so that we can perform arithmetic with it. Finally, the *Pointer* function coerces the result back into a pointer type so that it can be assigned to *aReal*. After this assignment, *aReal* holds the address of the proper spot in the block, so we can assign the indicated value to *aReal^*. At the risk of making this statement even more complex, we could replace the multiplication with a left shift to speed things up:

```
aReal := Pointer(Ord(theArray^) + (index shl 2));
```

Review

Macintosh programs make extensive use of both stack and heap for data storage. Stack management is handled by the compiler and occurs automatically as procedures and functions are called and returned from. Heap objects can be either nonrelocatable (created by *NewPtr* and accessed through simple pointers) or relocatable (created by *NewHandle* and accessed through handles and master pointers). Relocatable blocks can be temporarily locked (prevented from moving). In addition, relocatable blocks can be flagged as purgeable; that is, the Memory Manager has permission to take back their memory if it needs to.

There can be several heaps in memory at once, and there are always at least two: the system heap (which keeps track of such things as volumes and files), and the application heap, which stores data for the lifetime of the current application. The application heap disappears when a program terminates; the system heap doesn't.

31

Resources and Resource Files

One aspect of Macintosh programming has no counterpart in traditional programming environments: the notion of *resources*. Originally intended simply to separate an application's country-specific information from its code—for example, the text of a pull-down menu from the code that puts the menu on the screen—resources grew in importance as the Macintosh Toolbox evolved.

Resources are packets of data residing on disk, which are loaded into memory as required by an application or Toolbox routine. Just where on the disk? In what file(s)? The answer indicates the significance of resources in Macintosh programming: potentially, in every single file on the disk.

The Need for Resources

Like your own programs, Toolbox routines need data on which to operate: QuickDraw requires font information; the Window Manager needs window description data; the Menu Manager requires the text for each pull-down menu. These data objects, of various Pascal types, typically reside on the heap as relocatable blocks and are accessed through handles. Consider type *MenuHandle*, the Menu Manager's primary data type:

```
MenuHandle = ^MenuPtr;
MenuPtr = ^MenuInfo;
MenuInfo = record
              menuID: Integer;
              menuWidth: Integer;
```

```
    menuHeight: Integer;
    menuProc: Handle;
    enableFlags: Longint;
    menuData: Str255;
  end;
```

Without worrying at this point what the fields in a *MenuInfo* record are for, note that whenever an application executes, there's exactly one of these records out in the heap for each menu. To define its complement of pull-down menus, for example, Turbo Pascal has eight menu handles to eight relocatable blocks.

Before they can be used by the Menu Manager, *MenuInfo* records are loaded from disk (usually from the application file) and placed as relocatable objects in the heap. Other Toolbox routines follow this "load from disk to heap" pattern; the Font Manager goes through similar gyrations collecting font data.

Over time, the Resource Manager evolved into a general-purpose tool for moving chiefly read-only data from disk to heap—a tool much easier to use than the traditional Open/Seek/Read/Close way of working with files.

Data and Resource Forks

As mentioned in Chapter 17, every Macintosh file is actually two files going under the same name: One part is called the *data fork*; the other, the *resource fork*. The Finder represents both forks by a single icon and works hard to maintain this illusion. When it copies, deletes, or renames a file, it automatically processes both forks.

One fork is often empty. In most application files (programs), the data fork is the empty one. Conversely, data files (such as a MacPaint document or Turbo Pascal text file) generally have empty resource forks. For the purposes of this chapter, we're going to call every file with a non-empty resource fork a *resource file*.

Standard Pascal's file-handling tools all operate implicitly on data forks. Similarly, by default, the File Manager's routines (which we'll work with in Chapter 36) also manipulate the data fork.

It isn't necessary to understand the internal structure of a resource file, because of the wealth of access tools provided by the Resource Manager. Every resource is known by a unique four-character type and integer ID code (and optionally, by a name).

```
type
    ResType: packed array [1..4] of Char;
```

Resources can be arbitrarily divided into two categories: *system resources* and *application resources*. System resources are those that tend to be used by all programs and by Toolbox routines. Application resources are those used exclusively by a particular program.

Examples of resources include

- **Fonts**—A collection of symbol images and width data needed by QuickDraw to draw characters in a given typeface and size (ResType = 'FONT').

- **Menus**—Each pull-down menu of an application is a resource, consisting of its title and each entry (ResType = 'MENU').

- **Icons**—The 32-by-32 pixel symbols used by the Finder to represent files and disks (ResType = 'ICON').

- **Strings**—Sequences of ASCII characters with a length byte at the beginning (ResType = 'STR ').

The System File

System resources are held in one large resource file named *System*. A file with this name must be present whenever a Macintosh boots up. The System file can be thought of as the Toolbox's toolbox: a repository of information considered too changeable and/or bulky to be placed in valuable ROM.

To keep users safe from themselves, the active System file can't be renamed or deleted. Along with hundreds of other resources, desk accessories and fonts are stored in the System file. Depending on the number of DAs and fonts it contains, a System file can range from about 50K in size to 600K and beyond.

Application Resources

Application resources are held within the resource fork of the application file itself. These resources are less general than the resources of the system file, although the methods for accessing them are identical.

To get a resource, you need only specify the type and the ID number. The Resource Manager does the rest, locating the specified data in an open resource file, allocating a suitably sized relocatable block on the heap, reading the resource to the block, and, finally, returning a handle to it. Typically, you won't even specify the file to read from. The Resource Manager looks first for a resource in the current application's resource file. If it can't find it there, it looks in the System file.

Resource Manager Routines

If a program intends to use resources in a resource file other than its own resource fork or the System file, it calls *OpenResFile*:

```
function OpenResFile(fileName: Str255): Integer;
```

OpenResFile opens the indicated file on the default volume. If the file can't be opened successfully, *OpenResFile* returns –1; otherwise, it returns the file's *reference number*, the value by which you'll refer to this file in future calls. For example, the reference number is required to close a resource file:

```
procedure CloseResFile(refNum: Integer);
```

To determine how many resources of a particular type exist in all open resource files, call *CountResources*:

```
function CountResources(theType: ResType): Integer;
```

For example,

```
WriteLn(CountResources('FONT'))
```

displays the number of font resources available. Since usually only the System file contains font data, this returns the same number of fonts you'd see if you ran the Font/DA Mover application on that system file. (A font is a given typeface in a given size; 12-point Los Angeles and 24-point Los Angeles are two fonts.)

To read each resource of a given type, call the *GetIndResource* function repeatedly:

```
function GetIndResource(theType: ResType; index: Integer): Handle;
```
For example, if we knew as a result of a call to *CountResources* that there are 14 font resources available, we could load and get a handle to each by calling *GetIndResource* repeatedly with an index ranging from 1 to 14:

```
for N := 1 to 14 do
  fontArray[N] := GetIndResource('FONT',N); {fontArray is an array of handles }
```

The most important Resource Manager call is *GetResource*:

```
function GetResource (theType: ResType; theID: Integer): Handle;
```
Called indirectly by many Toolbox routines and directly by your programs, *GetResource* returns a handle to the requested resource given the type and ID number. Note that resources of different types can have the same ID number.

Releasing Resources

As with any heap-allocated object, when you're through working with a resource, you must make sure that the space it occupies is released. This is done by the *ReleaseResource* call:

```
procedure ReleaseResource(theResource: Handle);
```

A Sample Program

This program demonstrates the *CountResources* and *GetResource* calls.

```
program GetFonts;
uses
  MemTypes,QuickDraw,OSIntf,ToolIntf,PackIntf;
var
  H : Handle;
  N : Integer;
begin
  WriteLn('This system file has ',CountResources('FONT'),' font resources.');
  for N := 9 to 24 do                          { check each potential size }
  begin
    H := GetResource('FONT',128 * newYork + N);      { font resource IDs are }
    if H <> nil then                           { based on a formula using }
    begin                                      { the font number and size }
      Write('New York is available in point size ',N,'; Size = ');
      WriteLn(GetHandleSize(H));
      ReleaseResource(H);                           { deallocate the storage }
    end;
  end;
  ReadLn;
end.
```

Creating a Resource File: RMaker

We mentioned earlier that the data fork of most applications is empty. In other words, most applications consist of nothing but resources. The code itself is divided into one or more resources of type *CODE*.

If application files are nothing but a collection of resources, how do the resources associated with a program get there? The program most responsible for this is called RMaker, which is on your Turbo Pascal Utilities & Sample Programs Disk. Apple calls RMaker a "resource compiler." It isn't a compiler in the sense that Turbo Pascal is: It has no knowledge of the 68000 family and produces no machine code. Instead, it translates textual descriptions of resources written in "RMaker language" into binary form and writes them to a newly created resource file.

You can use RMaker to produce any sort of resource as long as you know the structure of the resource and the RMaker statements necessary to define it.

Following is an example of an RMaker source program. Fortunately, RMaker language isn't nearly as tricky as Pascal. RMaker input files consist of a series of short (three- to six-line) entries, each describing a single resource. The format varies according to the type of resource being defined.

```
MyResourceFile.Rsrc

Type STR    ;; double semicolons delimit comments
  ,128      ;; ID = 128; the comma separates optional name
This string came from a resource file . . .

Type STR    ;; be sure to include a trailing space after "STR "
  ,129
And so did this one.
```

The first line of an RMaker file is the name you've chosen for the resulting resource file. In this case, after RMaker has finished processing MyResourceFile.R, the string resources generated are placed in a new resource file called MyResourceFile.Rsrc. (This file will have an empty data fork.) Note that the extensions *.R* and *.Rsrc* to represent RMaker input and output files, respectively, are standard in Macintosh development. This particular file describes two resources of type *STR* by simply listing the ID number and then the string itself.

Running RMaker

Use Turbo's editor to enter MyResourceFile.R. Now try to compile it. It didn't work, did it? Of course not, it isn't a Pascal program. The only compiler in the world able to make sense of this text is RMaker.

Transfer to the RMaker application (it's an excellent candidate for membership in the Transfer menu). RMaker has few options; it asks you to select a file for processing (by default, only text files ending in .R show up in the Open box) and then quickly creates the resource file

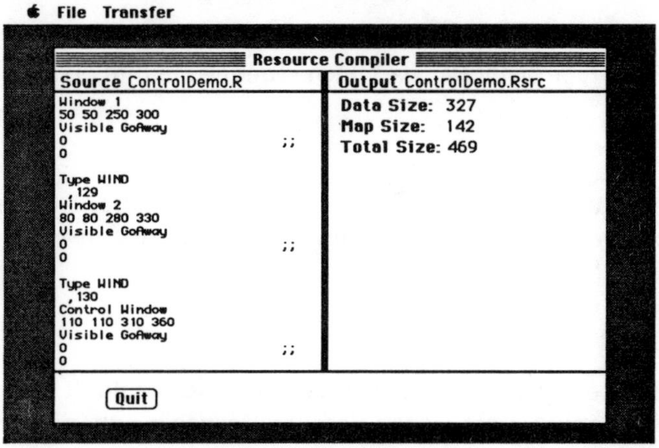

Figure 31.1: RMaker Working

For instructions on using RMaker, see Chapter 12 of the Turbo Pascal manual.

Assuming you didn't make any errors in entering MyResourceFile.R—you *did* include a space after 'STR ' and a final carriage return to terminate the last string, right—RMaker now produces a new resource file named MyResourceFile.Rsrc. It contains only two string resources.

Quit RMaker to the Finder. Can you locate this newly created file? It'll have the generic document icon.

Now, let's write a Turbo Pascal program that uses these string resources:

```
program ResourceGetter;
uses
  Memtypes,QuickDraw,OSIntf,ToolIntf;
var
  S: StringHandle;
  refNum: Integer;
begin
```

```
  refNum := OpenResFile('MyResourceFile.Rsrc');
  if refNum = -1 then
  begin
    WriteLn('Couldn''t open the resource file...');
    Exit;
  end;
  S := StringHandle(GetResource('STR ',128));
  WriteLn(S^^);  ReleaseResource(Handle(S));
  S := StringHandle(GetResource('STR ',129));
  WriteLn(S^^);  ReleaseResource(Handle(S));
  S := StringHandle(GetResource('STR ',0));
  WriteLn(S^^);  ReleaseResource(Handle(S));
  CloseResFile(refNum);
  ReadLn;
end.
```

Variable *S* has type *StringHandle*, which is defined in unit *OSIntf* as

```
StringPtr = ^Str255;
StringHandle = ^StringPtr;
```

By defining this string variable as a handle, we reduced this program's global memory requirement to 6 bytes. Had we declared instead

```
var
  S: Str255;
  refNum: Integer;
```

there would be 258 bytes of global data. We also couldn't have used the resource mechanism, because the Resource Manager only works with data that can be accessed through handles.

This program's first move is to the resource file containing the strings:

```
refNum := OpenResFile('MyResourceFile.Rsrc');
```

It adds MyResourceFile.Rsrc to the resource search chain when hunting for resources, by implementing its "resource map," which describes the type, ID number, and location in the file of all resources the file contains. The chain already contains the System file. If *OpenResFile* returns –1, then the file couldn't be opened, because either it isn't in the current directory or its name was misspelled.

Once the file is open, we can take advantage of the resource mechanism. We can read string data from the file without concern for the internal structure of MyResourceFile.Rsrc (in fact, without even caring if it's in MyResourceFile.Rsrc or the System file).

```
S := StringHandle(GetResource('STR ',128));
```

A simple call to *GetResource*, telling it the type of resource we want and a unique ID number, is all it takes. Type coercion is necessary because *GetResource* returns the type *Handle*. After this call,

- *S* is a *StringHandle*
- *S^* is a *StringPtr*
- *S^^* is a *Str255*

Each call to *GetResource* is matched by a *ReleaseResource* call. Otherwise, we'd tie up the heap with data we no longer care about.

The third *GetResource* call (using ID = 0) retrieves a string hidden away in the System file that describes the version number and release date of the system file. (By definition, all ID numbers less than 128 refer to system resources. Values 128 through 32767 are reserved for your own use.) Note that, except for the ID number, the process is exactly the same.

Review

The Resource Manager is a convenient mechanism by which Pascal programs and Toolbox routines are able to load data from files into the heap. The Resource Manager works with resource files, that is, with the resource fork of files. All resources have a unique four-character type and integer ID number.

System resources are stored in the System file and are used by both applications and Toolbox routines. Application resources are used only by applications and are usually stored in the resource fork of the application file itself.

The RMaker application produces resource files by compiling textual descriptions of resources and generating the appropriate resources in a file.

32

QuickDraw: Theory

Most personal computers work almost exclusively in text mode. If they have a graphics capability at all, it is used mostly for games or for pie charts and graphs. The Macintosh was the first widely distributed personal computer without a so-called text mode: Every letter, number, and punctuation symbol—*and* drawing—is drawn to the Macintosh screen pixel by pixel.

Where other personal computers have text-mode hardware, the Macintosh has QuickDraw. Don't be misled by QuickDraw's relatively insignificant status in *Inside Macintosh*. QuickDraw takes up only 78 pages out of that book's 1,200, yet is the most significant aspect of the Toolbox. If you understand it, the rest will come easy. Skimp on understanding QuickDraw, and you can memorize every word of the Vertical Retrace Manager and still not get programs to work.

Because of the volume of structures and routines it contains, QuickDraw is one of the tougher stretches of the Mount Toolbox climb; so stay with the group (and don't look down).

Some of the things QuickDraw helps you draw, quickly, include

- text in various fonts, sizes, and styles
- straight lines of variable thickness and pattern
- rectangles, rounded-corner rectangles, ovals, and polygons

QuickDraw allows multiple independent drawing regions to exist simultaneously, each with a unique set of drawing criteria, such as text size and style. QuickDraw's "picture" facility allows you to accumulate dozens of drawing calls into a single entity that can be stored as a resource to disk or played back with a single call.

In addition, QuickDraw has a well-developed ability to "clip" drawings—to control what areas on the screen get drawn to and what don't.

Points, Rectangles, and the Coordinate Plane

QuickDraw operations are based on an imaginary two-dimensional grid (or plane). Each horizontal and vertical line (not the gaps between the lines) on the grid is numbered, from –32767 on the top and left corners to 32767 on the bottom and right corners (see Figure 32.1).

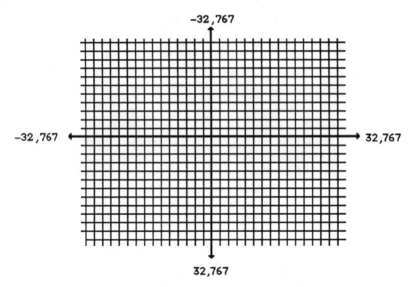

Figure 32.1: The QuickDraw Coordinate Plane

These values weren't chosen for their decimal beauty, but rather for their binary convenience. They're the largest numbers you can express with a value of type *Integer*, integers being an efficient object for the Macintosh's 68000 processor family.

The grid lines of the QuickDraw plane are infinitely thin. At each intersection of a horizontal and vertical grid line lies a QuickDraw *point*. Points are infinitely small; they have a position, but no length or width.

Turbo Pascal Tutor for the Macintosh

The only attribute of a point is its location, specified by the horizontal and vertical grid lines that pass through it. We use the notation (*x,y*) to describe points. For example, (20,10) is the point defined by the intersection of vertical grid line 20 and horizontal grid line 10.

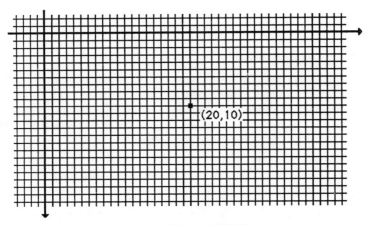

Figure 32.2: Point (20,10)

This point is slightly to the right and down from the center (origin) of the QuickDraw grid, point (0,0). The point (-32767,-32767) is the extreme upper left; (32767,32767) is the extreme lower right. With 64K lines along both the horizontal and vertical axes, there are some 4 billion points on the QuickDraw plane (64K * 64K). That's more than enough to define fancy displays.

The QuickDraw plane and the Cartesian plane of coordinate geometry that you probably learned in school are similar, except that

■ The QuickDraw plane isn't infinitely large.

■ It's impossible to specify a point between grid lines, such as (0.5,15) or (12.1,67). For speed, QuickDraw works strictly with integers.

■ Y-axis values get larger as you move *down* the QuickDraw plane rather than up.

Pascal and Points

QuickDraw defines the objects it works on with good, clean Pascal; it is accessed through unit QuickDraw. Here's how QuickDraw defines a point:

```
type
  VHSelect = (v,h);
  Point = record case Integer of
          0: (v,h: Integer);
          1: (vh: array [VHSelect] of Integer)
        end;
```

This definition is surprisingly complicated. Unfortunately, the programmer behind QuickDraw didn't choose the data structures for the benefit of an introductory tutorial. Let's work through the definition and, in the process, review what we learned about variant records in Chapter 14.

This definition offers two different ways to think about a point. Ignoring enumerated type *VHSelect* for a moment, **case** `Integer` **of** in the Point record is a signal to the compiler that two or more variations of the record are forthcoming, each enclosed in parentheses. Since it's **case** *Integer*, there could be as many as 32,767 variants (lucky for it—and us—there are only two). This particular variant record is a *free union*; it doesn't contain a "tag field" that defines when a particular variant should be used, so both are equally legal.

The first variant allows us to treat a point as a record consisting of two integer fields, named *v* and *h*. This code fragment defines a QuickDraw point at (37,19), slightly down and to the right of the origin:

```
var
  aPoint: Point;
begin
  aPoint.v := 19;
  aPoint.h := 37;
end.
```

Note that assigning information to a variable of type *Point* doesn't cause the screen to change. This illustrates an important QuickDraw concept: the distinction between mathematical entities such as points and rectangles and the commands that actually draw them on the screen.

The second variant of the record allows us to describe a point as a two-element array of integers. *VHSelect* (for "vertical/horizontal select") is an enumerated type. (Remember type *Days* from Chapter 9 with elements *Sunday, Monday,* and so on?) *VHSelect* consists of two elements, *v* and *h*. For example, we could declare a variable of type *VHSelect* and then assign either *v* or *h* to it.

This scrap of code uses the array variant to describe the same point as the previous example:

```
var
  aPoint: Point;
begin
```

```
    aPoint.vh[v]  := 19;
    aPoint.vh[h]  := 37;
end.
```

You'll use the first (record) variant more often. Note that no matter which notation you use, a variable of type *Point* has the same 4-byte structure: The first 2 bytes hold the vertical information, the second 2 bytes, the horizontal.

Rectangles

Rectangles are the next QuickDraw object of interest. A rectangle is defined by two points: those at the upper left and lower right corners. The edges of a rectangle (QuickDraw gridlines) are infinitely thin. As with points, we can describe rectangles in two ways through a variant record type definition:

```
type
  Rect = record case Integer of
           0: (top,left,bottom,right: Integer);
           1: (topLeft,botRight: Point);
         end;
```

The first option uses four integers; the second, two points. The following code fragment uses both ways to specify the same 20-by-100 rectangle 40 points down and 40 points to the right of the center of the QuickDraw grid are

```
var
  r1,r2: Rect;
  p1,p2: Point;
begin
  r1.top := 40; r1.left := 40;
  r1.bottom := 140; r1.right := 60;

  p1.v := 40; p1.h := 40;
  p2.v := 140; p2.h := 60;
  r2.topLeft := p1; r2.botRight := p2;
end.
```

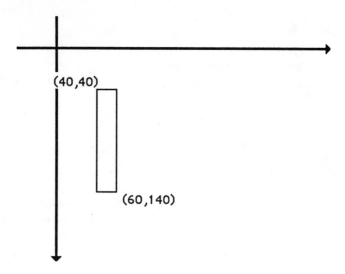

Figure 32.3: The Rectangle

After executing this code, rectangles *r1* and *r2* are identical—that is, the memory allocated for each contains the same pattern of bits. Since rectangle assignments are so common, there's a QuickDraw call that performs it and is visually neat:

```
procedure SetRect(var r: Rect; left, top, right, bottom: Integer);
```

For example,

```
SetRect(myRect,40,40,60,140)
```

sets rectangle *myRect* to the same coordinates as the previous example. (Incidentally, *SetRect* may be visually clean relative to assigning to the fields directly, but it takes longer—not long, mind you, but longer—to execute because of the overhead of parameter passing and the trap mechanism.)

Imaginary grids, infinitesimal points, and rectangles with infinitely thin sides—how does QuickDraw get around to drawing on the screen?

Drawing into Bits

Viewed from one perspective, QuickDraw is an engine for setting and clearing bits in memory. If those bits happen to be in the screen buffer, then pixels on the screen change.

Human beings usually draw on white paper with black ink; QuickDraw draws in RAM with 1s and 0s. 1 bits mean black; 0 bits mean white. Any memory suffices as long as you define the address of that memory and how QuickDraw should think of it as being organized.

Bit Images

To an imaginative programmer, computer memory is the ultimate clay: It lends itself to any number of visual representations. A common model sees Macintosh RAM as a continuous highway of 16-bit integers (or *words*, in the parlance of the processor), starting at address 0 and working up to 512K or 1 Mb or however much memory is installed.

But the highway model doesn't account for the fact that widely "separated" addresses can be accessed almost simultaneously; that address 500,000 is no "farther" in terms of accessibility from address 0 than is address 6.

QuickDraw takes advantage of the random-access characteristic of the 68000 family of processors to model memory into rectangular matrices called *bit images*. You decide exactly how wide and how deep the matrix is.

Lowest Address

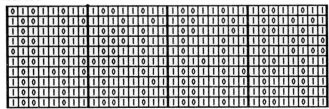

Highest address

Figure 32.4: A 32-by-10 Bit Grid

Inside Macintosh describes a bit image this way:

> Take a collection of words in memory and lay them end to end so that bit 15 of the lowest-numbered word is on the left and bit 0 of the highest-numbered word is on the far right. Then take this array of bits and divide it, on word boundaries, into a number of equal-size rows. Stack these rows vertically so that the first row is on the top and the last row is on the bottom. The result is a matrix. . .with each row containing the same number of words. The number of bytes in each row of the bit image is called the row width of that image. A bit image can be any length that's a multiple of the row width. (Volume I, 143)

For example, suppose we tell QuickDraw to work with a 50-by-50 bit image, in an area of RAM far from the screen buffer.

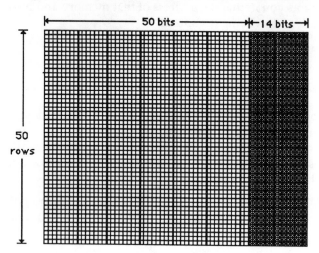

A 50 by 50 bit image; 14 bits of waste in each row of eight bytes each.

Figure 32.5: 50-by-50 Bit Grid

How much memory should we allocate for this bit image?

50 * 50 = 2500 bits = (2500/8) bytes = 312 1/2 bytes

This is close to, but not quite, the right answer. So that the processor can deal with memory most efficiently, QuickDraw requires bit images to be aligned on word (16 bit) boundaries. So unless the width of a bit image happens to be an exact multiple of 16, there's some waste at the end of each row:

50 bits divided by 16 bits per word equals 4 words equals 8 bytes, with 14 unused bits at the end of every row. So exactly 8 times 50 or 400 bytes are required for a 50-by-50 bit image. A good place to grab a 400-byte space is in the heap:

```
var
  bitImagePtr: Ptr;
begin
  bitImagePtr = NewPtr(400);
```

It doesn't matter where the bit image is allocated, only that it won't be bothered until we're through with it. We used heap-strangling *NewPtr* rather than *NewHandle* because that's the way QuickDraw's author decided it should be.

O.K., now variable *bitImagePtr* points to a 400-byte block of memory. We've determined that's just enough for a 50-by-50 sheet of QuickDraw paper.

Before QuickDraw can start drawing lines or text into this memory range, we must describe the bit image to QuickDraw. After all, it has no way of knowing that this particular 400-byte block off in an obscure corner of the heap is intended for drawing purposes. So we provide QuickDraw with a data structure known as a *BitMap*, a Pascal record type that defines a bit image.

```
type BitMap = record
            baseAddr:Ptr;
            rowBytes: Integer;
            bounds: Rect;
        end;
```

A variable of type *BitMap* communicates both the location (*baseAddr*) and structure (*rowBytes*, *bounds*) of a bit image. *BaseAddr* points to the first (lowest) address of the block reserved for drawing. Like any pointer, it should point to the correct place, or QuickDraw is liable to spray bits anywhere.

The *rowBytes* field tells QuickDraw the width (in bytes) of each line in the bit image. For our 50-pixel-wide drawing paper, *rowBytes* is 8. We don't need to tell QuickDraw how many rows the bit image contains, because that is evident from the third field, the *bounds* rectangle. As a rectangle, it contains either four integers (top, left, bottom, right) or two points (*topLeft*, *botRight*), whichever is more convenient. *Bounds* is the bit map's *boundary rectangle*: It encloses and thereby brings a numbering system to the bit image. Its grid lines fit with conceptual snugness between bits.

For our 50-by-50 drawing space, we'd probably choose to make *bounds.topLeft* the point (0,0) and *bounds.botRight* (50,50)—although we could describe it as (10,20)(60,70), (-50,0)(0,50), or any 50-by-50 rectangle. But we better not describe a boundary rectangle larger than the reserved bit image, or we're liable to clobber some memory.

It's impossible to make QuickDraw set pixels outside of the boundary rectangle of its current *BitMap*. For example, attempts to set pixel (57,0) or (999,1012) or (-2,25) have no effect; no errors are generated and no memory changed. This is the first of several levels of clipping provided by QuickDraw.

By default, QuickDraw works with a bit map that describes the address and organization of the screen buffer, that two-way area in high memory linked to the display. We'll learn more about this particular bit map, called *screenBits*, later.

Of Points and Pixels

A point is a location on the QuickDraw grid, described by the intersection of a horizontal and vertical gridline. Points have zero width and length.

Pixels are visual building blocks that make up computer displays. Unlike points, pixels have a height and width. For example, on a well-adjusted Macintosh screen, they are 1/72-inch square. When a bit image doesn't happen to be in screen memory, you can imagine a pixel (that is, a bit) to be any size you like.

By superimposing a boundary rectangle over a bit image, the *BitMap* data structure allows us to use point notation to describe pixels. By convention, pixel (*x*,*y*) is the pixel just below and to the right of point (*x*,*y*).

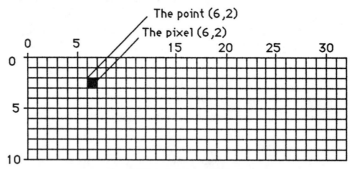

Figure 32.6: Points and Pixels

Note that for a 50-by-50 bit image with *bounds.topLeft* equal to (0,0), the pixel identified by point (50,50) falls *outside* the bit image. The lower rightmost pixel is associated with point (49,49). When working with the screen, the same sort of thing applies. There are 512 pixels horizontally, numbered 0 through 511, and 342 pixels vertically, numbered 0 through 341.

More QuickDraw Data Types

QuickDraw uses *patterns*, repeating 8-by-8 bit images to fill areas on the screen or to draw lines, almost as if they were colors. Their Pascal definition is

```
type
  Pattern = packed array [0..7] of 0..255;
```

A *cursor* (the data structure behind the Macintosh's familiar arrow and I-beam) is defined as two 16-by-16 bit images (data and *mask*), with a "hot spot" that indicates exactly which pixel is being pointed at.

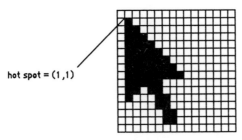

Figure 32.7: A Cursor

```
type
  Bits16 = array [0..15] of Integer;
  Cursor = record
             data: Bits16;
             mask: Bits16;
             hotSpot: Point;
           end;
```

GrafPorts

QuickDraw is flexible: It accepts bit maps other than *screenBits*. It draws lines of varying thicknesses and patterns. It displays text in different fonts, sizes, and styles.

To provide defaults and yet still allow for customization, QuickDraw features a record construct known as the *GrafPort*. Don't take this term too literally. It sounds as though it's a porthole through which QuickDraw stretches a digital hand for sketching, and *Inside Macintosh* promotes this image with statements like, "All drawing takes place inside the current GrafPort." While this has a certain ring, it is more accurate to say, "All drawing is done according to the fields of the current *GrafPort* record."

A *GrafPort* is simply a Pascal record type with fields that control QuickDraw's behavior. *GrafPort*s allow an application with multiple windows to invoke drawing operations that are appropriate for each window, simply by telling QuickDraw to use a different *GrafPort* record. If there are four windows on the screen, there are usually at least five variables of type *GrafPort* in memory (one for each window and one to manage the entire screen). The *GrafPort* record is a bear; even though we've left out half its fields, what's left is going to take some serious explaining.

```
type
  GrafPort = record
               portBits: BitMap;
               portRect: Rect;
               visRgn, clipRgn: RgnHandle;
               pnLoc, pnSize: Point;
               pnPat: Pattern;
               txFont: Integer;
               txFace: Style;
               txSize: Integer;
               .
               . (plus a host of others...)
               .
             end;
```

*GrafPort*s are often accessed through pointers, so an important data type for their use is

```
type
  GrafPtr: ^GrafPort;
```

The first significant structure in a *GrafPort* is its *portBits* field. *portBits* has type *BitMap*. It tells QuickDraw where in memory it should set and clear bits when carrying out drawing commands when using a given *GrafPort*.

Given variable *myPortPtr* of type GrafPtr, then

- *myPortPtr* is a pointer.
- *myPortPtr^* is a *GrafPort* record.
- *myPortPtr^.portBits* is a *BitMap* record.
- *myPortPtr^.portBits.baseAddr* is a pointer (of type *Ptr*).
- *myPortPtr^.portBits.rowBytes* is an integer.
- *myPortPtr^.portBits.bounds* is a rectangle record.
- *myPortPtr^.portBits.bounds.top* is an integer.
- *myPortPtr^.portBits.bounds.topLeft* is a point.
- *myPortPtr^.portBits.bounds.topLeft.v* is an integer.
- *myPortPtr^.portBits.bounds.topLeft.vh[v]* is the same integer.

(Now you know why we asked you to pay attention back in Chapter 14, when we first discussed records.)

QuickDraw's Global Variables

Variables declared in the interface of units have the same status as global variables in your program: All must fit into the same 32K maximum space, and all are available at every level of a program. Unit QuickDraw defines nine global variables:

```
var
  thePort:    GrafPtr;
  white:      Pattern;
  black:      Pattern;
  gray:       Pattern;
  ltGray:     Pattern;
  dkGray:     Pattern;
  arrow:      Cursor;
  screenBits: BitMap;
  randSeed:   LongInt;
```

Whenever QuickDraw gets a drawing command, it dereferences *thePort* to find the *GrafPort* record it should use to carry out that command. Changing to a different *GrafPort* simply involves causing *thePort* to point to a different one. This can be done by assigning to *thePort* directly or by using the *GetPort* and *SavePort* calls.

```
procedure GetPort (var port: GrafPtr);
procedure SetPort (port: GrafPtr);
```

Note that these routines expect a pointer to a *GrafPort* (type *GrafPtr*), not a *GrafPort* itself. The following code fragment demonstrates a common ritual in Macintosh programming: changing from one *GrafPort* to another—drawing something—and then changing back to the original port.

```
var
  port1Ptr, port2Ptr, port3Ptr: GrafPtr;  { three pointers to three GrafPorts }

procedure DrawInPort1;
var
  savePort: GrafPtr;
begin
  GetPort(savePort);       { assign the current value of thePort to savePort }
  SetPort(port1Ptr);       { make thePort = port1Ptr; i.e., both point to the }
  .                        { same GrafPort }

  .
  .   { draw in GrafPort port1Ptr^ }
  .
  SetPort(savePort);
end;
```

The Pen

Drawing always takes place using the parameters in the *GrafPort* record variable currently pointed to by *thePort*. Drawing usually occurs at the location of the QuickDraw pen, which has a variable size tip and "ink color" (pattern).

Since most drawing is performed by the pen, you'd expect a variety of Toolbox functions for moving it around and controlling its characteristics. The pen's current location is defined by a point and is returned by the *GetPen* call:

```
procedure GetPen(var pt: Point);
```

The Move and MoveTo commands move the pen:

```
procedure MoveTo(h,v: integer);
procedure Move(dh,dv: integer);
```

MoveTo (an absolute move) sets the pen at the indicated point. *Move* adjusts the pen relative to where it is now.

To set the pen's thickness (size), which by default is one pixel square, use *PenSize*. To set its drawing "mode" (which we're about to describe), use *PenMode*. *PenPattern* sets the pattern it writes with; by default, it's solid black.

```
procedure PenSize(width,height: integer);
procedure PenMode(mode: integer);
procedure PenPat(pat: pattern);
```

Pen Transfer Modes

When drawing a line from Point A to Point B, you can control the low-level boolean algebra that transfers the pen's pattern to what's in the bit image already. There are four basic choices: Copy, Or, Xor, and Bic (bit clear).

The default is mode *srcCopy*, where what used to be in the destination bit image is simply overlaid with the pen's pattern. The other three options leave the pixels under the white part of the pattern alone. They differ only in how they affect pixels under the black part of the pattern:

- **Or** replaces those pixels with black pixels.
- **Xor** inverts the pixels under the black part.
- **Bic** sets them to white.

Finally, for each mode, there's a variation in which every pixel in the pattern is inverted before performing the operation.

The eight drawing modes are supported by integer constant definitions in QuickDraw.

```
const
  patCopy    = 8;    { the default penMode }
  patOr      = 9;
  patXor     = 10;
  patBic     = 11;
  notPatCopy = 12;
  notPatOr   = 13;
  notPatXor  = 14;
  notPatBic  = 15;
```

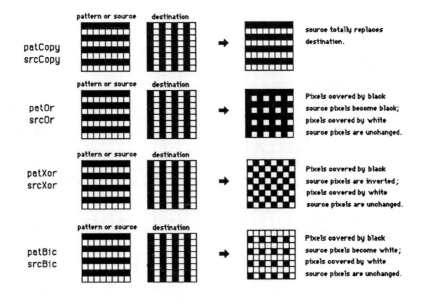

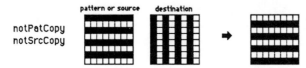

Figure 32.8: Transfer Modes

Clipping and Regions

Earlier, we mentioned that QuickDraw never harms a single byte outside of its current bit map. Stated more rigorously, QuickDraw never sets or clears bits outside of *thePort^.portBits.bounds*. This protective behavior, termed clipping, keeps memory outside of the designated bit image safe.

Clipping is such a good thing that QuickDraw offers multiple levels of it. These additional levels of clipping are for protecting areas within *portBits.bounds* and are based on QuickDraw entities known as *regions*.

Like rectangles and lines, regions are theoretical constructions: They enclose arbitrary collections of points. Regions divide the plane into two sets of points: those inside the region and those outside. Regions can have any shape. They don't have to be contiguous and can even have holes on the inside.

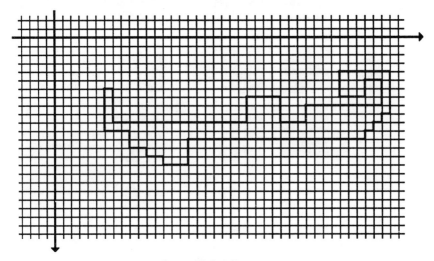

Figure 32.9: A Region

In Pascal, they look like this:

```
type
  RgnHandle = ^RgnPtr;
  RgnPtr = ^Region
  Region = record
             rgnSize: Integer;
             rgnBBox: Rect;
             { additional data if nonrectangular }
           end;
```

This structure of regions points up a weakness of Pascal that is addressed by the Memory Manager's handle/relocatable block scheme. Pascal types have a fixed length; integers are 2 bytes, points are 8 bytes, and **string**[49]s are 50 bytes. Regions don't have a particular length; they're never less than 10 bytes and often longer than 100.

Regions get longer as the areas they define get more complex, as more twists and turns are taken by the defining commands. Storing region data in a relocatable block makes it possible for regions to expand and contract as necessary.

From Pascal, you can look at the region's first two fields: *rgnSize* (its total length, in bytes, including the size field), and *rgnBBox*, its bounding box—the smallest rectangle that contains every point in the region. The simplest and shortest regions are rectangular and are exactly 10 bytes long (2 for the size and 8 for the rectangle). Since QuickDraw's region-manipulation routines all expect handles to regions rather than regions themselves, it is easy for QuickDraw to expand and shrink the region's variable size area as necessary. You don't need to know what QuickDraw puts out past the *rgnBBox* to use regions.

Regions can be drawn, moved, expanded, and reduced on the screen. Various mathematic operations can be performed on two regions. For example, you can tell the program to add Region A to Region B and call the result Region C.

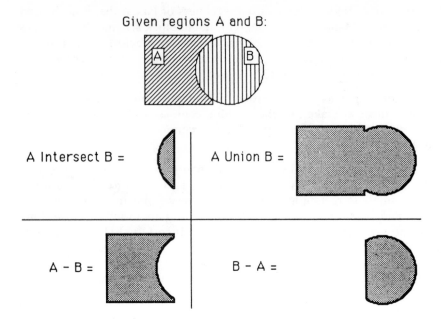

Given regions A and B:

A Intersect B =   A Union B =

A - B =   B - A =

Figure 32.10: Region Math

Now, let's move on to some QuickDraw sample programs.

33

QuickDraw: Sample Programs

Despite any misgivings you may have, QuickDraw is the fun part of the Toolbox. Before you start working with the following example programs, write the word *Experiment!* on a piece of paper and stick it right below the screen.

You should be able to devise modifications to each program and successfully predict the result of those modifications—or at least understand the results. It takes all of a second to recompile a short program. (And if you encounter an occasional system error, take comfort in the knowledge that there are only two kinds of Macintosh programs: those that crash in development and those that haven't been written yet.)

Doing without the Terminal Window

We're about to shake an addiction, and the following program is the first step. It's the model upon which we will base this chapter's experiments. You'll find it in the QuickDraw Examples folder of the Turbo Tutor disk.

```
program InitQuickDraw;
{$U-}
uses MemTypes, QuickDraw, OSIntf, ToolIntf;
var myPort: GrafPort;
begin
  InitGraf(@thePort);
  OpenPort(@myPort);
  FillRect(myPort.portBits.Bounds,white);
```

```
  repeat
  until Button;
end.
```

The {$U-} directive tells the compiler that this program won't be using the built-in units *PasInOut* and *PasConsole* (which are automatically **use**d by default). *PasInOut* implements Standard Pascal's I/O routines, including *ReadLn, WriteLn, Reset,* and *Rewrite.* The *PasConsole* unit is responsible for routines related to the terminal window, among them *GotoXY* and *ReadChar.*

After a {$U-} directive, as far as the compiler is concerned, these routines don't exist. If a program wants to send something to the screen, read the keyboard, or write to a disk, it must now do it the Toolbox's way.

All programs that intend to use QuickDraw must initialize QuickDraw and create at least one *GrafPort* record. These functions—which were previously performed automatically by a routine in *PasConsole*—are accomplished by this program's first two lines. Let's take them one at a time.

```
InitGraf(@thePort);
```

thePort is a global variable defined by unit QuickDraw (look for it in Appendix D of the Turbo Pascal manual). `InitGraf(@thePort)` tells QuickDraw to initialize its global variables (for example, so that the white pattern is really white and not simply the result of whatever happened to be there previously). The `@thePort` parameter tells QuickDraw where in memory this initialization should take place—namely, at the address reserved by the compiler for *thePort* and the rest of QuickDraw's variables.

Making this call doesn't have any effect on the screen; it simply paves the way for future drawing. Next, we create a *GrafPort*:

```
OpenPort(@myPort);
```

As we learned in the last section, QuickDraw draws according to the fields in a record variable of type *GrafPort*. It so happens that this program's only variable, *myPort*, is a *GrafPort*. Oddly, *OpenPort* doesn't want to be passed a *GrafPort* variable directly, but rather a pointer to a *GrafPort*. Two objects meet this description: a variable of type *GrafPtr* and the result of applying the address operator to a *GrafPort* variable. We're telling the *OpenPort* routine, "Initialize a *GrafPort* at this address and make it the current *GrafPort*."

The *OpenPort* routine carefully massages the bytes in record variable *myPort* into a default *GrafPort*.

Initialization complete, our first drawing act is to make the entire screen solid white:

```
FillRect(myPort.portBits.Bounds,white);
```
The *FillRect* call takes two parameters, a rectangle and a pattern. It so happens that the rectangle we supply, `myPort.portBits.Bounds`
, surrounds every pixel in screen memory.

- *myPort* is a *GrafPort*.
- *myPort.portBits* is a *BitMap*.
- *myPort.portBits.baseAddr* is a pointer to the start of screen memory.
- *myPort.portBits.bounds* is the rectangle (0,0)(512,342).

White is one of QuickDraw's globals stored in high memory just under *thePort*, a variable of type *Pattern*. After the *FillRect* call, the screen is totally filled with white.

If you haven't already, execute this program. You should now be looking at an all-white screen (with the exception of the cursor, which will still be the checkered flag left by the compiler).

Note the square corners. The screen buffer is perfectly rectangular. We're used to nicely rounded corners because most applications lead off with a call to the Window Manager's *InitWindows* call, which creates a round-cornered rectangle (filled with the pattern you've selected with the Control Panel), with an empty menu bar at the top.

The last line of this program simply creates a delay that lasts until you press the mouse button. It serves the same function as **repeat until** `KeyPressed` in terminal window programs. (*KeyPressed* resides in unit *PasConsole*; it doesn't exist in the {$U-} world.)

Drawing Lines

The following program draws a thin horizontal line on the screen connecting points (50,20) and (300,20). Enter and execute program *DrawLine* (it adds only two lines to *InitQuickDraw*):

```
program DrawLine;
{$U-}
uses MemTypes, QuickDraw, OSIntf, ToolIntf;
var
  myPort: GrafPort;
begin
  InitGraf(@thePort); OpenPort(@myPort);
```

```
FillRect(myPort.portBits.Bounds,white);     { the "terrible three" }

MoveTo(50,20);
Line(300,0);

    repeat until Button;
end.
```

When a *GrafPort* is freshly opened, its pen is given location (0,0). To create a line from point (50,20) to point (350,20), we must first move the pen to the starting point of that line:

`MoveTo(50,20)`

This code does just that; it doesn't create any drawing. We've simply picked up the pen and moved it. The next statement does the drawing:

`Line(300,0);`

This says to start at the current pen location and draw a line extending 300 pixels to the right and 0 pixels down. Note that this is a relative move—that is, relative to the current position of the pen. There's also an absolute line-drawing call. Had we used

`LineTo(300,0)`

we'd have created a diagonal line between point (50,20) and point (300,0). After drawing a line, the pen is left at the last point to be drawn. Therefore, these three calls

```
MoveTo(50,20);
Line(300,0);
Line(0,200);
```

create a right-angle shape, as the second *Line* call connects points (350,20) and (350,220).

Experiment by adding *Move* and *Line* calls of your own to this program. Draw the first letter of your name; create a simple geometric shape. What happens if you enter a horizontal or vertical coordinate value greater than the dimensions of the screen—as in `LineTo(600,942)`: Does the line wrap around on the opposite side of the screen? Do you suppose memory outside the bit image defined by `myPort.portBits` is affected? (Answers: No and no; clipping prevents both.)

As a final enhancement to program *DrawLine*, change the cursor from Turbo's checkered flag to the standard arrow by including a call to the parameterless procedure *InitCursor*.

Drawing Lines with the Mouse

Next, let's consider a more sophisticated program that draws lines based on the position of the mouse.

```
program Sketch;
{$U-}
uses MemTypes, QuickDraw, OSIntf, ToolIntf;
var
  myPort: GrafPort;
  theLoc: Point;
begin
  InitGraf(@thePort); OpenPort(@myPort);
  FillRect(myPort.portBits.Bounds,white);
  InitCursor;

  repeat
    GetMouse(theLoc);
    LineTo(theLoc.h,theLoc.v);
  until Button;
end.
```

This program uses the Toolbox's *GetMouse* routine to fetch the current position of the cursor's hot spot.

```
procedure GetMouse(var mouseLoc: Point);
```
Within a loop, *Sketch* breaks down the point returned by *GetMouse* into its horizontal and vertical components, then passes them to the *LineTo* procedure. The result is a continuous line following the cursor, until you press the mouse button to terminate the program.

Why does the line start at the upper left-hand corner? (Because *OpenPort* initializes *myPort*'s *penPos* field to (0,0).)

As an experiment, insert the following line just above the loop:

```
PenSize(4,4);
```

This causes the pen associated with *myPort* to be four pixels by four pixels, rather than the default one-pixel size. It's like changing to a thicker brush in a paint program.

You can also change the "ink" (pattern) with which the pen draws, by calling *PenPat* (pen pattern). Use any of the predefined patterns—ltGray, Gray, dkGray, and black—except white. Finally, experiment with different drawing modes. We've been using the default, *patCopy*. Try

```
PenMode(patOr)
```

Automatic Art: The Random Function

Next we're going to turn QuickDraw loose to create semi-artistic patterns without human intervention. The key to this process is the QuickDraw function *Random*. Unlike random-number generators you may have used in other languages, QuickDraw's *Random* returns integers between –32768 and 32767, for speed's sake.

```
function Random: Integer;
```

Let's temporarily resurrect the terminal window to demonstrate *Random*.

```
program RandomTest;
uses MemTypes, QuickDraw;
begin
  repeat
    WriteLn(Random:7)
  until Keypressed
end.
```

For our purposes, *Random* would be more useful if it returned numbers in a definable range. The following routine fills the bill: It accepts a positive integer *N* and returns a value between 0 and *N-1*, inclusive.

```
function Rnd(limit: Integer): Integer;
begin
  Rnd := Abs(Random mod limit)
end;
```

Now, back to the {$U-} world and computer art.

```
program RandomLines;
{$U-}
uses MemTypes, QuickDraw, OSIntf, ToolIntf;
var
  myPort: GrafPort;

function Rnd(limit: Integer): Integer;
begin
  Rnd := Abs(Random mod limit)
end;

begin
  InitGraf(@thePort); OpenPort(@myPort);
  FillRect(myPort.portBits.Bounds,white); InitCursor;

  repeat
    LineTo(Rnd(512),Rnd(342));
  until Button;
end.
```

Execute *RandomLines* and stand back.

This program produces a wildly growing thin black line. You can vary the thickness of the line by adding this statement to the loop:

```
PenSize(Rnd(8)+1, Rnd(8)+1);
```

With this modification, the screen quickly fills up too quickly with black. What we need are random changes of the pen's pattern as well. Add this **case** statement to the loop:

```
case Rnd(5) of
  0: PenPat(Black);
  1: PenPat(dkGray);
  2: PenPat(Gray);
  3: PenPat(ltGray);
  4: PenPat(white);
end;
```

Now you've got a legitimate masterpiece creator.

Drawing Rectangles

Let's move on to a slightly more complex QuickDraw object, the rectangle. Consider this program:

```
program Rectangle1;
{$U-}
uses MemTypes, QuickDraw, OSIntf, ToolIntf;
var
  myPort: GrafPort;
  myRect: Rect;

begin
  InitGraf(@thePort); OpenPort(@myPort);
  FillRect(myPort.portBits.Bounds,white); InitCursor;

  myRect.Top := 50; myRect.Bottom := 300;
  myRect.Left := 20; myRect.Right := 400;

  repeat
  until Button;
end.
```

Type in and execute this program. What appears on the screen? Not a darn thing. Even though this program assigns coordinate values to rectangle *myRect*, it doesn't cause the rectangle to be drawn. We've merely defined a rectangle; we haven't changed any pixels in screen memory. This illustrates the distinction between QuickDraw geometric entities and the pixels they enclose.

Getting this program to draw a rectangle on the screen requires the following call after defining it.

```
FrameRect(myRect);
```

The *FrameRect* routine causes pixels just inside the defined rectangle to be filled in using the pen's current size and pattern. Since the pen defaults to a one-pixel size, you'll see the rectangle framed by a one-pixel thick line. Use *PenSize* to increase the size of the pen and verify that the thickness of the frame applied by *FrameRect* changes accordingly.

Besides *FrameRect*, there are a number of other options for drawing *myRect* once it's defined.

```
procedure PaintRect(r: Rect);
procedure EraseRect(r: Rect);
procedure InvertRect(r: Rect);
procedure FillRect(r: Rect; pat: Pattern);
```

FillRect is the routine we've been using to clear the screen at the start of each program. If you add

```
FillRect(myRect, gray)
```

to *Rectangle1*, you'll cause the rectangle to be filled with the familiar gray pattern.

The *InvertRect* call complements all the pixels in a rectangle (black pixels become white and vice versa). It's handy for nondestructively highlighting areas of the screen, because a second *InvertRect* call on the same rectangle restores an area to the condition it was in previously. For example, Turbo Pascal uses *InvertRect* to highlight text, and the Menu Manager uses it to call attention to a menu's title and the current selection.

Calling *InvertRect* repeatedly on the same rectangle causes the enclosed pixels to alternate quickly between black and white. Add this code fragment to *Rectangle1* and run it. As you stare at the screen, repeat softly to yourself, "I must buy all Borland software."

```
myRect.Top := 50; myRect.Bottom := 290;
myRect.Left := 130; myRect.Right := 370;
repeat
  InvertRect(myRect);
until Button;
```

Drawing Ovals

In addition to straight lines and right angles, QuickDraw can also draw ovals—one variety of which is a circle. A reasonable person might expect that QuickDraw would define a circle something like this:

```
type
  Circle = record
           center: Point;
           radius: Integer;
         end;
```

Not so. Surprisingly, circles are defined as rectangles. To draw a circle, define a square (that is, a rectangle of equal height and width) that just encloses the desired circle, and then call one of the oval drawing routines. These calls parallel those for drawing rectangles. There's *FrameOval*, *FillOval*, *InvertOval*, *PaintOval*, and *EraseOval*.

If you replace the *FrameRect* call of program *Rectangle1* with

```
FrameOval(myRect);
```

you'll create an oval rather than a rectangle. This is one reason why QuickDraw makes a distinction between simply defining a rectangle and actually drawing one. Rectangles can be used to draw, fill, and invert rectangles and to draw, fill, and invert ovals.

Round-Cornered Rectangles

Round-cornered rectangles (RCRs) are a pleasing variation on the rectangle theme. The outline of the Calculator desk accessory is a good example of a QuickDraw RCR.

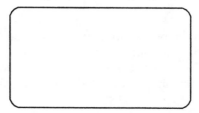

Figure 33.1: A Round-Cornered Rectangle

Since RCRs are a combination of ovals and rectangles, their drawing routines require both oval and rectangle parameters:

```pascal
procedure FrameRoundRect(r: Rect; ovalWidth, ovalHeight: Integer);
```

ovalWidth and *ovalHeight* control the degree of curvature of the corners. Larger values produce more rounded corners.

The drawing routines for RCRs follow the pattern established by oval and rectangle drawing:

```pascal
procedure PaintRoundRect(r: Rect; ovalWidth, ovalHeight: Integer);
procedure EraseRoundRect(r: Rect; ovalWidth, ovalHeight: Integer);
procedure InvertRoundRect(r: Rect; ovalWidth, ovalHeight: Integer);
procedure FillRoundRect(r: Rect; ovalWidth, ovalHeight: Integer);
```

This program uses RCRs to create something approximating the standard desktop:

```pascal
program GreyRCR;
{$U-}
uses MemTypes, QuickDraw, OSIntf, ToolIntf;
var
  myPort: GrafPort;
begin
  InitGraf(@thePort); OpenPort(@myPort);
  FillRect(myPort.portBits.Bounds,black);  { first erase it to black }
  FillRoundRect(myPort.portBits.Bounds,20,20,gray);
  repeat
  until Button;
end.
```

Drawing Text

In the {$U-} environment, our faithful I/O companions *Write* and *WriteLn* aren't available. This is both good and bad news. It's bad in that without them we must work harder to send text to the screen. It's good in that we have much more control over the appearance of text. Another classic programming trade-off: flexibility (and attendant complexity) versus simplicity.

Text drawing occurs at the pen location and causes the pen to be moved to the right an appropriate amount after drawing each character. Text is always drawn using the current *GrafPort*'s *txFont*, *txFace*, and *txSize* fields, which can be set by assigning to the *GrafPort* record directly or with the following three calls:

```pascal
procedure TextFont(font: Integer);
procedure TextFace(face: Style);
procedure TextSize(size: Integer);
```

Fonts are described to *TextFont* by integers but, thanks to constant definitions in unit *ToolIntf*, it's possible to refer to them by name:

```
const
  systemFont = 0;   { a.k.a. chicago }
  applFont   = 1;   { a.k.a. geneva }
  newYork    = 2;
  geneva     = 3;
  monaco     = 4;
  venice     = 5;
  london     = 6;
  athens     = 7;
  sanFran    = 8;
  toronto    = 9;
  cairo      = 11;
  losAngeles = 12;
  times      = 20;
  helvetica  = 21;
  courier    = 22;
  symbol     = 23;
  taliesin   = 24;
```

The Text-Drawing Routines

QuickDraw has three calls that actually put text on the screen.

```
procedure DrawChar(c: Char);
procedure DrawString(s: Str255);
procedure DrawText(textBuf: Ptr; firstByte, byteCount: Integer);
```

DrawChar is passed a single character; that character is drawn at the pen position and the pen position adjusted an appropriate distance to the right.

DrawString draws each character of its *Str255* parameter. For *DrawText*, you pass a pointer to character data and include numeric parameters that describe where to start relative to the pointer and how many characters to draw.

Neither *DrawString* nor *DrawText* performs any sort of formatting. Carriage returns, line feeds, and tabs are ignored.

Consider program *BigTalk*:

```
program BigTalk;
{$U-}
uses MemTypes, QuickDraw, OSIntf, ToolIntf;
var
  myPort: GrafPort;
begin
  InitGraf(@thePort); OpenPort(@myPort);
  FillRect(myPort.portBits.Bounds,white);
  InitCursor;
```

```
    MoveTo(20,50);
    TextFont(newYork);
    TextFace([shadow]);
    TextSize(18);
    DrawString('This program compliments of ');
    TextFace([]);
    DrawString('Robin Jones');
    repeat
    until Button;
end.
```

This program writes in 18-point, shadowed New York type. The statement

```
TextFont(newYork);
```

demonstrates the value of constants. Would the intent of

```
TextFont(2)
```

have been as clear? Hardly.

If you've worked with a Macintosh much, you're undoubtedly familiar with the various text permutations it can produce—for example, bold, underline, and italic. Since these attributes can be applied singly (bold only) and in combination (bold plus italic plus shadow), the set data structure is ideal for representing this quality. The following definitions

```
type
    StyleItem = (bold,italic,underline,outline,shadow,condense,extend);
    Style = set of StyleItem;

procedure TextFace(face: Style);
```

work together to specify the style of text printed by the current *GrafPort*. Program *BigTalk*'s call to *TextFace*

```
TextFace([shadow]);
```

passes the routine a set constant. Until told otherwise, this *GrafPort*'s text-drawing statements will produce shadowed text. Normal text (text with no style attributes) is produced by passing the empty set:

```
TextFace([]);
```

Fancier Text

Program *GrowingTalk* outputs each character of a string in an ever-increasing point size.

```
program GrowingTalk;
{$U-}
```

```
uses MemTypes, QuickDraw, OSIntf, ToolIntf;
var
  myPort: GrafPort;
  N: integer;
  S: Str255;
begin
  InitGraf(@thePort); OpenPort(@myPort);
  FillRect(myPort.portBits.Bounds,white);
  InitCursor;

  S := 'Turbo Pascal by Borland International';
  MoveTo(20,180);
  TextFont(newYork);
  for N := 1 to Length(S) do
  begin
    TextSize(N+4);
    DrawChar(S[N])
  end;
  repeat
  until Button;
end.
```

Running this program results in a lot of disk activity. This is because font data must be fetched from disk periodically by the Resource Manager. You may notice that some of the characters look better than others.

Explaining this phenomenon requires a digression on the relationship between QuickDraw and its lackey, the Font Manager. Before drawing a character in font X and size Y, QuickDraw asks the Font Manager for character data on that font and size. If the Resource Manager (every manager's lackey) indicates that font X exists in the System file in size Y, the Font Manager returns the character data to its boss, which can then draw good quality characters. If it doesn't exist, then the Font Manager tries to come up with the next best thing:

- First it looks for font X in size $2 * Y$. If found, it scales this font down and uses that. This scaling looks very good.

- Next, it looks for font X in size $Y/2$. If found, it scales this font up. This scaling looks blocky but symmetrical.

- Failing that, if looks for font X in the smallest size $> Y$. If it finds one, it scales down. This results in good detail, but with asymmetrical irregularities.

- If not, it looks for font X in the largest size $< Y$. If it finds one, it scales up. Usually, this scaling doesn't look very good.

- If the Font Manager gets to this point, then font X doesn't exist at all in the System file. In its stead, the application font (Geneva) is used, scaling as necessary, according to the same decision process.

■ If the application font doesn't exist in any size, the Font Manager substitutes the system font (Chicago), scaling as necessary, according to the same decision process.

Converting Numbers to Text

In programming, as in life, we often don't fully appreciate something until it's gone. *Write* and *WriteLn*, Standard Pascal's main weapons against blank screens, are a case in point. Not only can they output a dozen strings in a single call, they can also handle numbers—something that *DrawString* will have no part of.

Try as you might, you'll never get

```
DrawString(n * 3.14159)
```

to compile. *Write* and *Writeln* are able to output numeric expressions because they implicitly perform number to string conversions.

Think about it for a minute. Executing the statement

```
Write(n * 3.14159)
```

requires some work at run time. First, the expression (*n * 3.14159*) must be evaluated. This produces a single value of type *Real*. Real numbers are 4-byte entities in a complex internal format, so before the result can be put on the screen, these 4 bytes must be translated into a form that human beings can understand—as a sequence of ASCII characters (mainly digits, with perhaps a decimal point, *E*, and plus sign thrown in). Finally, once converted into an appropriate string of characters, *DrawString* is called.

Without the assistance of *Write* and *WriteLn*, you must explicitly call number to string conversion routines to send numbers to the screen. Unit *PackIntf* contains a routine called *NumToString*; it handles integers and long integers:

```
procedure NumToString(theNum: Longint; var theString: Str255);
```

To convert reals, you'll need to use the Standard Apple Numeric Environment (SANE) unit. It has dozens of assorted floating-point routines, including the following conversion types and procedures:

```
type
  DecForm = record
            Style : (floatDecimal, fixedDecimal);
            Digits: Integer;
          end;
```

```
procedure Num2Str(format: DecForm; theNum: Extended; theString: Str255);
```

Type *Extended* is an extended precision real; values of type real and double are automatically converted to type extended when passed to this routine.

This program demonstrates how to output numbers without *WriteLn*'s help.

```
program FancyNumbers;
{$U-}
uses MemTypes, QuickDraw, OSIntf, ToolIntf, PackIntf, SANE;
     { Calculate and display factorials of 1 - 15 }
var
  myPort: GrafPort;
  N : Integer;
  R : Real;
  NS : Str255;
  RS : Str255;
  format: DecForm;                    { defined in SANE for controlling }
                                      { real-to-string conversions }
begin
  InitGraf(@thePort);
  OpenPort(@myPort);
  FillRect(myPort.portBits.Bounds,white);
  InitCursor;

  TextFont(newYork);
  TextFace([italic,bold]);            { use default size (12 point) }
  format.style := FixedDecimal; { don't use floating-point notation }
  format.digits := 0;                          { no decimal point }
  R := 1.0;
  for N := 1 to 15 do
  begin
    R := R * N;                               { accumulate factorial }
    NumToString(N,NS);                   { convert integer to string NS }
    Num2Str(format,R,RS);        { convert real number R to string RS }
    MoveTo(20,N * 20);
    DrawString(NS + '! = ' + RS);
  end;
  repeat
  until Button;
end.
```

Manipulating Rectangles

Besides simply assigning to them, there are other operations you can perform on rectangles that don't cause anything to appear on the screen. *InsetRect* shrinks or enlarges a rectangle. *OffsetRect* moves a rectangle on the QuickDraw plane.

```
procedure InsetRect(var r: Rect; dh,dv: Integer);
```

```
procedure OffsetRect(var r: Rect; dh,dv: Integer);
```

A call to *InsetRect* pulls in the sides of a rectangle according to parameters *dh* and *dv*. Negative parameters to *InsetRect* cause the rectangle to grow.

Now let's do some rectangle drawing, using *OffsetRect* and *InsetRect* to manipulate the rectangle between drawing calls.

```
program ManipulateRects;
{$U-}
uses MemTypes, QuickDraw, OSIntf, ToolIntf;
var
  myPort: GrafPort;
  myRect: Rect;
  N: Integer;
begin
  InitGraf(@thePort); OpenPort(@myPort);
  FillRect(myPort.portBits.Bounds,white);
  InitCursor;

  myRect := myPort.portBits.Bounds;
  for N := 1 to 50 do
  begin
    InsetRect(myRect,4,4);
    FrameRect(myRect);
  end;
  while not Button do
end.
```

This program creates an illusion of motion, by framing a series of progressively smaller rectangles. Change the *InsetRect* call to *OffsetRect* and you'll see a different effect. This time, the rectangles don't change in size. Instead, they are moved down and to the right.

When working with complex images, it is often useful to know whether a point is within a given rectangle. The boolean function *PtInRect* takes as parameters a point and a rectangle and returns True if the point is enclosed by the rectangle. The following program uses sound to return information; a one-second tone means that *PtInRect* has returned True. (**NOTE:** I f you've turned your sound all the way down with the Control Panel, *SysBeep* makes the menu bar blink.)

```
program NoDrawing;
{$U-}
uses MemTypes, QuickDraw, OSIntf, ToolIntf;
var
  myRect: Rect;
  myPoint: Point;
begin
  SetRect(myRect,20,50,400,300);
  myPoint.h := 100; myPoint.v := 100;
  if PtInRect(myPoint,myRect) then
    SysBeep(60);                    { 60 sixtieths of a second = 1 second }
```

Turbo Pascal Tutor for the Macintosh

```
    while not Button do
end.
```

Regions and Clipping

In addition to working with regularly shaped geometric objects such as rectangles, QuickDraw also supports arbitrarily shaped objects known as regions.

Regions are formed by making a sequence of calls to drawing routines, such as *FrameRect* and *LineTo*, that collectively form some shape. The basic process goes like this:

1. Tell QuickDraw you're forming a new region.
2. Make as many drawing calls as necessary to define the outline of the region.
3. Tell QuickDraw that you're finished and to give you the region.

Once defined, regions can be filled, framed, and, most importantly, used as a clipping boundary. This program defines and then frames a circular region as large as the screen:

```
program BuildRegion;
{$U-}
uses MemTypes, QuickDraw, OSIntf, ToolIntf;
var
  myPort: GrafPort;
  myRect: Rect;
  myRgn: RgnHandle;
begin
  InitGraf(@thePort); OpenPort(@myPort);
  FillRect(myPort.portBits.Bounds,white); InitCursor;

  myRgn := NewRgn;
  OpenRgn;
    SetRect(myRect,85,0,512-85,342);
    FrameOval(myRect);
  CloseRgn(myRgn);
  FrameRgn(myRgn);                        { show the region }
  repeat
  until Button;
end.
```

Usually, regions aren't used to create screen images directly but indirectly, by defining clipping boundaries—that is, controlling what part of the current *GrafPort*'s bit image may be written to. Every *GrafPort* has an associated clipping region called *clipRgn*. QuickDraw will never set any bits not enclosed by this region. When first initialized (with the *OpenPort* call), a *GrafPort*'s *clipRgn* is set to a rectangular region covering the entire QuickDraw grid, extending from a top left point of (-32768,-32768) to a bottom right of (32767,32767). This has the effect of causing no clipping at all. (Every QuickDraw point is in this rectangle.)

Clipping regions are a powerful drawing aid. Suppose you want to create some random art inside a circular "porthole." Without clipping regions, this would be next to impossible. With them, it's simple:

1. Define a circular region.
2. Make that region the current *GrafPort*'s *clipRgn*.
3. Draw the random art.

```pascal
program ClippedRandomLines;
{$U-}
uses MemTypes, QuickDraw, OSIntf, ToolIntf;
var
  myPort: GrafPort;
  myRect: Rect;
  myRgn: RgnHandle;

function Rnd(limit: Integer): integer;
begin
  Rnd := Abs(Random mod limit)
end;

begin
  InitGraf(@thePort); OpenPort(@myPort);
  FillRect(myPort.portBits.Bounds,black); HideCursor;

  myRgn := NewRgn;
  OpenRgn;
    SetRect(myRect,85,0,512-85,342);
    FrameOval(myRect);
  CloseRgn(myRgn);
  SetClip(myRgn);

  repeat
    PenSize(Rnd(8), Rnd(8));
    case Rnd(5) of
      0: PenPat(Black);
      1: PenPat(dkGray);
      2: PenPat(Gray);
      3: PenPat(ltGray);
      4: PenPat(white);
    end;
    LineTo(Rnd(512),Rnd(342));
  until Button;
end.
```

Even though this program never actually draws the circle-shaped region, a circle quickly appears. No matter how long this program runs, *LineTo* will never alter a single pixel outside *myPort.clipRgn*.

The more complex the clipping region (the greater its *rgnSize* field), the longer it takes QuickDraw to perform clipping calculations. Not surprisingly, the most efficient clipping regions are simple rectangles. Change the region in *ClippedRandomRects* to a rectangular shape and run the program again. Does it run faster?

ScreenBits and Other BitMaps

The most important field in the *GrafPort* record is *portBits*. It defines the binary drawing paper that QuickDraw will use. *PortBits* is of type *BitMap*, which is defined as

```
BitMap = record
         baseAddr: Ptr;
         rowBytes: Integer;
         bounds: Rect
       end;
```

When we made the call

```
Line(0,300)
```

in the very first program of this section, why were only bits in screen memory changed and not elsewhere? Because, at the moment of that call, *myPort.portBits* was set to indicate the screen buffer. QuickDraw defines a global variable of type *bitMap* called *screenBits*, which defines the screen buffer of the Macintosh in use. Initializing a *GrafPort* sets its *portBits* field equal to *screenBits*. This program displays its contents:

```
program ScreenBitsTest;
{$U-}
uses MemTypes, QuickDraw, OSIntf, ToolIntf, PackIntf;
var
  myPort: GrafPort;

procedure OutNum(h,v: Integer; theNum:LongInt);
var
  theString : Str255;
begin
    NumToString(theNum,theString);
    MoveTo(h,v);
    DrawString(theString);
end;

begin
```

```
InitGraf(@thePort); OpenPort(@myPort);
FillRect(myPort.portBits.Bounds,white);
InitCursor;

with screenBits do
begin
   OutNum(30,30,ord4(baseAddr));
   OutNum(30,60,rowBytes);
   OutNum(30,90,bounds.top); OutNum(60,90,bounds.left);
   OutNum(90,90,bounds.bottom); OutNum(120,90,bounds.right);
end;
repeat until Button;
end.
```

Enter and execute this program.

A 1-Mb Macintosh Plus produced this output:

```
1025792
64
0    0    342    512
```

Let's decipher these results. 1025792 is the address of the first byte of screen memory in a Macintosh Plus. 64 is the *rowBytes* parameter (64 * 8 = 512, the number of pixels horizontally on the standard Macintosh Plus display); since 512 is evenly divisible by 16, there's no waste. Finally, points (0,0) and (512,342) define the boundary rectangle for *screenBits*.

Just because *OpenPort* makes a *GrafPort*'s *portBits* field equal to *screenBits* doesn't mean you have to leave it this way. You can set a port's *portBits* to indicate any bit image and thereby cause drawing in any area of memory. This allows you to create an image offscreen and later "stamp" this image onto the screen, that is, to *screenBits*.

Moving data from an offscreen bit map to *screenBits* is performed by QuickDraw's *CopyBits* routine.

```
procedure CopyBits (srcBits, dstBits: BitMap; srcRect, dstRect: Rect;
                    mode: Integer; maskRgn: RgnHandle);
```

CopyBits moves bits between two bit images. All the bits in the image defined by *srcBits* and bounded by rectangle *srcRect* are copied into the image defined by *dstBits* and bounded by rectangle *dstRect*. If *dstRect* and *srcRect* aren't the same size, then *CopyBits* automatically performs scaling so that all of *dstRect* is filled with the pattern in *srcRect*.

Mode defines the transfer's boolean algebra; generally, you use *srcCopy* mode, which causes the destination bits to be totally overlaid with the source bits. *MaskRgn* defines a clipping area in the destination bit map you may choose to use. If you don't require clipping or the current *GrafPort*'s *clipRgn* is sufficient, pass **nil** for this value.

The following program demonstrates offscreen drawing into an alternate bit map, then using *CopyBits* to move the drawing to screen memory.

```
program OffScreenDrawing;
{$U-}
uses MemTypes, QuickDraw, OSIntf, ToolIntf;
var
  myPort: GrafPort;
  aRect, bRect: Rect;
  offscreenBitMap: BitMap;

begin
  InitGraf(@thePort); OpenPort(@myPort);
  FillRect(myPort.portBits.Bounds,white); InitCursor;

  with offscreenBitMap do
  begin
    baseAddr := NewPtr(8 * 60);  { allocate a bit image on the heap }
    rowBytes := 8;       { 8 bytes per row; 4 bits of waste per row }
    SetRect(bounds,0,0,60,60);
  end;
  SetPortBits(offscreenBitMap);

  SetRect(aRect,5,5,55,55);
  FillRect(aRect,gray);

  CopyBits(offscreenBitMap,screenBits,aRect,aRect,srcCopy,nil);
  repeat until Button;

  CopyBits(offscreenBitMap,screenBits,aRect,screenBits.bounds,srcCopy,nil);
  repeat until Button;

end.
```

Let's work through this program. It draws a pattern in an offscreen 60-by-60 bit image. The three assignments controlled by the **with** OffScreenBitMap statement define this alternate bit image:

```
with offscreenBitMap do
begin
  baseAddr := NewPtr(8 * 60);
  rowBytes := 8;
  SetRect(bounds,0,0,60,60);
end;
```

The most important thing is to provide a safe area of memory in which to draw—we don't want QuickDraw to start decorating bits within our program or on top of the disk driver. The statement

```
BaseAddr := NewPtr(8 * 60)
```

allocates 480 bytes of heap and assigns the address of those 480 bytes to pointer variable *BaseAddr*. Why 480 bytes? The image we're going to create in this offscreen buffer requires that the buffer be organized as 60 by 60 pixels. Each pixel takes one bit of memory. 60 pixels divided by 8 pixels per byte equals 7 1/2 bytes, but since QuickDraw requires word boundaries, we round this value to 8 bytes. So each line of the bit map is 8 bytes long, and there are 60 such lines; 60 times 8 equals 480.

For QuickDraw to correctly interpret the dimensions of this bit map, we must tell it how long a row is, by setting *rowBytes* to 8. Finally, we define the boundary rectangle:

```
SetRect(bounds,0,0,60,60);
```

A *BitMap*'s boundary rectangle performs two functions: It encloses the active area of the bit image (for example, bits 60-63 on each row aren't part of the bit map, even though they're present in the bit image). The boundary rectangle also provides a coordinate system for the bit map. For example, after `SetRect(bounds,0,0,60,60)`, the pixel in the upper left-hand corner of the bit map is known as (0,0); the lower right corner is (59,59). Had we defined the boundary rectangle as

```
SetRect(bounds,50,50,110,110);
```

then this first pixel would have gone under the name (50,50); either way, it's the same bit in the same memory location.

Now that we've defined the bit map, we are ready to begin drawing into it. First, set *MyPort*'s *portBits* field to *offscreenBitMap*:

```
SetPortBits(OffscreenBitMap);
```

From this point on, all drawing commands take effect in this offscreen *BitMap* rather than in *screenBits*; nothing will be seen on the screen. This bit map is significantly smaller than *screenBits*; any attempt to plot a pixel less than 0 or greater than 59 will fail.

The *FillRect* call

```
FillRect(aRect,gray);
```

fills a 50-pixel square in the offscreen bit image with gray.

Drawing offscreen isn't good for much unless you ultimately cause what has been drawn to become visible. So, this program next calls *CopyBits*, a routine for moving rectangular chunks of bits from one bit image into another. This call moves the gray rectangle just drawn into screen memory, where we can look at it:

```
CopyBits(offscreenBitMap,screenBits,aRect,aRect,srcCopy,nil);
```

The second *CopyBits* call demonstrates its scaling capability. Instead of *aRect* as the destination rectangle, we specify *screenBits.bounds*—a rectangle as large as the screen. This copy operation expands the gray pattern into something resembling a checkerboard. The horizontal axis is scaled more than the vertical; that's because there are more pixels along that axis.

We'll return to *CopyBits* in a later chapter, as an important ingredient in the animation process.

Drawing Pictures

QuickDraw has the ability to accumulate many drawing operations into a single data structure, which can then be output with a single call. For example, a program may define a complex image consisting of dozens of filled rectangles and ovals, text in various fonts and styles, and even use a clipping region to control drawing. Rather than repeat each drawing statement individually whenever the image needs redrawing, the *picture* mechanism allows you to define an image once—during a program's initialization—and then reproduce the image with a single call to the *DrawPicture* routine. Resources of type PICT can be accessed by the Resource Manager as well, for example,

```
program Pictures;
{$U-}
uses MemTypes, QuickDraw, OSIntf, ToolIntf;
var
  myPort: GrafPort;
  aRect, bRect: Rect;
  myPic: PicHandle;
  N: Integer;

begin
  InitGraf(@thePort); OpenPort(@myPort);
  FillRect(myPort.portBits.Bounds,white);
  InitCursor;

  RectRgn(myPort.clipRgn,screenBits.bounds); { required for correct playback }
  SetRect(aRect,5,5,55,55);
  myPic := OpenPicture(aRect);
    MoveTo(10,10);
    LineTo(40,50);
    LineTo(50,40);
    LineTo(30,50);
    LineTo(10,10);
    MoveTo(15,15);
    TextFace([italic]);
    TextSize(8);
    DrawString('Pascal');
  ClosePicture;

  SetRect(aRect,100,100,200,200);
  for N := 1 to 4 do
```

```
  begin
    DrawPicture(myPic, aRect);
    InsetRect(aRect,-(N * 20), -(N * 20));
  end;
  repeat until Button;
end.
```

Program *DrawPicture* doesn't create an especially complex image, but you get the general idea. Like regions, QuickDraw pictures are stored as relocatable blocks.

Variable *myPic* is a *PicHandle*, a pointer to a pointer to a Picture record. The Picture collection routines allow you to specify a so-called picture frame, a rectangle that encloses the picture to be drawn. This rectangle allows you to scale the picture later on when it is drawn to the screen. For example, if you choose to use the picture mechanism to draw the contents of a resizeable window, then this scaling feature causes QuickDraw to always scale the picture to the exact size of the box.

The statement

```
RectRgn(myPort.clipRgn,screenBits.bounds);
```

is required to reduce `myPort.clipRgn`
 from its original whole-plane size to something less. Without this reduction, *DrawPicture* doesn't work.

For creating *myPic*, we choose a 50-by-50 picture frame. *OpenPicture* is passed a picture frame and returns a handle to a newly created picture. From this point until a call to *ClosePicture*, drawing calls don't appear on the screen but instead only serve to define *myPic*. *myPic* gets longer and more complex with each call.

Once constructed, this program proceeds to call *DrawPicture* multiple times, each time with a different destination rectangle. Note the automatic scaling.

Stuff a Wild Cursor

QuickDraw defines a number of utility routines. A particularly interesting one is *StuffHex*:

procedure StuffHex (thingPtr: Ptr; s: Str255);

StuffHex is a quick-and-dirty way of initializing data structures. *StuffHex* takes a string of hexadecimal characters and writes its binary equivalent to memory, starting at the address passed in *thingPtr* and working up. For example, the following statement initializes rectangle *r* to (12,10)(240,256):

```
StuffHex(r,'000A000C010000F0')
```

Remember that a rectangle contains four integers, in this order: top, left, bottom, right. The 16-character string represents these values in hex, complete with leading zeros: $000A = 10; $000C = 12; $0100 = 256; $00F0 = 240.

StuffHex is handy in short, experimental programs (that is, the types of programs you're likely to be writing at this stage of the game). *StuffHex* isn't easy to use unless you're reasonably comfortable with the decimal-to-hex-and-back-again process. If hexadecimal isn't your thing just yet, try not to worry about it; *StuffHex* isn't a make-or-break routine. The next program demonstrates its use to define a new cursor.

```
program MysteryCursor;
{$U-}
uses MemTypes,QuickDraw,OSIntf,ToolIntf;
var
  myPort: GrafPort;
  myCursor: Cursor;
begin
  InitGraf(@thePort); OpenPort(@myPort);
  FillRect(myPort.portBits.Bounds,white);

  with myCursor do
  begin
    hotspot.h := 8; hotspot.v := 8;
    StuffHex(@Data, '3FC01830181818181818181818301FE0' +
                    '18301818181C181C181C181818383FF0');
   mask := data; { when mask = data, white pixels of cursor are transparent }
  end;
  SetCursor(myCursor);
  repeat
  until Button;
end.
```

Review

QuickDraw is a set of ROM-based routines for drawing text, lines, and various shapes, including rectangles, round rectangles, ovals, and polygons. QuickDraw applies an integer numbering scheme to rectangular matrices of memory called bit images. Bit images are defined by record types called *BitMaps*, which define the address and structure of memory to be used for drawing purposes. QuickDraw operations are controlled by the fields of a record type called *GrafPort*, and there can be many *GrafPort*s in memory at once, although only one is the current *GrafPort*.

Drawing always takes place at the position of the current *GrafPort*'s pen, whose size, pattern, and transfer characteristics are adjustable. Regions are variable-length structures accessed through handles that serve to define clipping boundaries. Pictures are stored collections of drawing commands that can be sent to the screen with a single call.

Both regions and pictures are defined by opening an initially empty structure and then accumulating various drawing calls into this structure. The *CopyBits* routine allows you to move rectangular groups of bits from one bit image to another. *StuffHex* provides a quick means of loading an arbitrary sequence of bytes to any address in memory.

Compiling a program with the {$U-} compiler directive forces a program to rely on its own resources and the Toolbox for initializing QuickDraw and creating output. QuickDraw can create text in different sizes, styles, and fonts, although it doesn't perform automatic number-to-string conversions.

34

Events

By definition, interactive computer programs must periodically get input from the user and act upon that input. On conventional personal computers, "getting input from the user" means reacting to keys pressed on the keyboard. Software for these machines therefore requires only two low-level user input routines:

```
function KeyPressed: Boolean;
```

to see if a key is ready to be read, and

```
function ReadChar: Char;
```

to read a key when one is known to be available.

On the Macintosh, there are other means by which a user can affect a program, the most important being manipulations of the mouse. The Event Manager describes constants, data types, and a key function that make it possible for an application to respond to any user-caused "event" with a single function call and **case** statement.

The GetNextEvent Routine

Most Macintosh programs get all their user input from a single routine:

```
function GetNextEvent(eventMask:Integer;var theEvent:EventRecord): Boolean;
```

Macintosh programs call *GetNextEvent* early and often throughout their entire lifetime. *GetNextEvent* returns True if there's an event, that is, some sort of user activity to report; otherwise it returns False. This single routine covers all the various forms of information the user can supply, thanks to the structure of **var** parameter *theEvent*, a record of type *EventRecord*.

```
type
  EventRecord =
record
  what     : Integer;
  message  : LongInt;
  when     : LongInt;
  where    : Point;
  modifiers: Integer;
end;
```

This 16-byte structure communicates information about both keyboard and mouse activity, and more esoteric "events" as well.

The *eventMask* parameter controls the types of events that are returned by a call to *GetNextEvent*. This lets a program give priority to certain events (say, keyboard events at the expense of mouse events). Passing the integer value –1 (11111111 11111111 binary) causes all events to be returned. Typically, information on all events is requested, and a program simply ignores events that mean nothing to it, much the way terminal window programs ignore mouse activity.

(Incidentally, if you're following along in *Inside Macintosh*, Apple's documentation people divided the Event Manager into two parts: A Toolbox (high level) Event Manager, described in Volume 1, and an Operating System (low level) Event Manager in Volume II.)

Using GetNextEvent

After *GetNextEvent* is called and returns True, a program tests the five fields of the *EventRecord* variable to discover

- the type of event (*what*)
- the time the event occurred (*when*)
- the position of the cursor at the moment of the event (*where*)
- the state of the mouse button and the keyboard's *Shift, Option, Caps Lock,* and *Command* keys at the moment of the event (*modifiers*)
- event-specific information (*message*)

The *what* field is an integer. It returns a value between 0 and 15, and a slew of descriptive constants are defined in unit *OSIntf* to represent its possible values. A list of these constants is effectively a list of the various event types a Macintosh program potentially has to deal with.

```
const
    nullEvent   =        0;
    mouseDown =          1;
    mouseUp     =        2;
    keyDown     =        3;
    keyUp       =        4;
    autoKey     =        5;
    updateEvt =          6;
    diskEvt     =        7;
    activateEvt =        8;
    networkEvt =         10;
    driverEvt   =        11;
    app1Evt =            12;
    app2Evt =            13;
    app3Evt =            14;
    app4Evt =            15;
```

This list is probably longer than you expected—but don't let it scare you. You may never have to worry about half of these event types. *GetNextEvent*'s role grew as the Toolbox evolved, from simply a place where a program could learn what the user was doing to a function that helps manage overlapping windows and pass information from one part of a program to another.

Buffering

The Event Manager stores events into a queue, so that a program doesn't have to deal with an event at the instant it occurs. The event is stored in the queue and handled in the order received, something like phone calls to an airline during the Christmas season. If the buffer fills up because events come in faster than the application can process them, then the oldest events are lost.

This queuing process is called *buffering*.

Null Events

The null event type (*nullEvent*) is returned in the event record's *what* field whenever *GetNextEvent* returns False. A null event means that there's nothing for the program to act on right now. Programs often take this opportunity to address fine points such as whether the cursor has the right shape according to its position on the screen. For example, Turbo Pascal changes the cursor from an arrow to an I-beam when it enters a text window.

Common Keyboard Events

A user can create three event types at the keyboard: *keyDown*, *keyUp*, and *autoKey*. A key-down event is produced by pressing any key other than the modifier keys. These are *Shift*, *Caps Lock*, *Command*, and *Option*; they serve only to affect the code produced by other keys.

Whenever a program detects an event record's what field equal to *keyDown*, it knows that within the event record is a *ReadChar* yearning to breathe free. The meat of a key-down event is hidden in the least significant byte of the message field; it contains the ASCII value of the key pressed.

This value can be plucked from the message by performing modulo 256 division or, more to the point, by masking off the three most significant bytes with the **and** operator:

```
theChar := Chr(message and $000000FF);
```

This statement sets character variable *theChar* equal to the lower 8 bits of the message field. The *Chr* function provides the type coercion necessary to get the compiler's blessing on assigning a *LongInt* to a *Char*. For example, after a *keyDown*, if the message field is $10003141,

```
    $10003141
and $000000FF
    $00000041 = 65 decimal = "A"
```

As for all events, the time of a key-down event can be gleaned from the when field (in sixtieth of a second "clock ticks" from when the system most recently booted up) and the position of the cursor from the where field.

A key-up event is produced by releasing any key other than the modifier keys. In practice, applications are so rarely interested in *keyUps* that they are automatically blocked by the Event Manager. Even if you tell *GetNextEvent* to return key-up events with an *eventMask* parameter of −1, it still won't. You won't miss them.

An auto-key event is like a key-down event, except that it results not from a fresh keystroke but from holding a key down and letting it repeat. Typically, you'll treat auto-key events like key-down events, except where a user would be unlikely to deliberately repeat a keystroke, for example, in handling *Command*-key menu equivalents.

Mouse Events

There are two event types that the user can create with the mouse: *mouseDown* (produced by pressing the button), and *mouseUp* (produced by releasing the button). In the eyes of the Event Manager, simply moving the mouse around doesn't constitute an event. If you want to know what the mouse is up to at times other than the instant of a *mouseDown* or *mouseUp*, use the Event Manager's *GetMouse* call, which we used in Chapter 31's sketching program.

The *message* field is undefined for mouse-down events; *when* tells when the button was pressed, and *where* indicates the hot spot of the cursor at the instant the button went down. The *modifiers* field can be used to discover if one of the modifier keys (*Option, Caps Lock, Shift, Command*) was also down at that moment.

A mouse-down requires more processing than any other event type, because its meaning varies according to the position of the cursor. Taking Turbo Pascal itself as an example, here's what it must do to decode a mouse-down.

If the mouse-down occurs in

Menu bar   Call a Menu Manager routine to pull down and make a selection from a menu.

Inactive window   Make it the active window.

Active text window:

    Text area   Prepare to select text or set insertion point.
    Close box   Prepare to close window.
    Size box   Prepare to resize window.
    Title bar   Prepare to drag or grow window.

Scroll bar:

    Scroll box   Scroll text the indicated amount.
    Arrow   Scroll text one line up or down.
    Between arrow/scroll box Scroll text one screenful up or down.

Active DA window   Call a Desk Manager routine to give the desk accessory the information,

otherwise   (if in no window at all) do nothing.

We'll learn more about the strange science of interpreting *mouseDowns* in the next chapter.

A mouse-up event is generated whenever you release the mouse button. Surprisingly, applications are seldom interested in mouse-ups. A program typically detects a mouse-down in some area of the screen, and then relies on a Toolbox routine to monitor its state until a mouse-up occurs. When there's a mouse-down in the menu bar, for example, an application calls the *MenuSelect* routine, which doesn't return until the button has been released. The mouse-up never makes it to the event queue.

GetNextEvent and the Structure of Macintosh Programs

After initialization, most Macintosh programs settle into a loop that goes something like this:

```
repeat
  Get an event;

  case event of
    typeA: Handle typeA Events;
    typeB: Handle typeB Events;
    typeC: Handle typeC Events;
  end;

until program done
```

This structure is called a program's *main event loop*. Macintosh applications cycle endlessly through their main event loop: Get an event, process it; get an event, process it; get an event, process it. . . .

The EventWorkbench Sample Program

Program *EventWorkbench* (in the Miscellaneous folder) demonstrates event processing, in particular, mouse-down, mouse-up, key-down, and auto-key events. Like last chapter's QuickDraw experiments, it runs in the terminal-windowless ($U-) environment. To display numbers, it borrows the standard QuickDraw initialization sequence and the *OutNum* procedure from the last chapter.

The event workbench displays information on the top three "lines" of the screen about mouse-down, mouse-up, and key-down events, respectively. For all three, the time of the event is displayed, representing how many clock ticks have transpired since the system was booted. The position of the mouse at the time of the event is displayed as the horizontal and vertical coordinates of the cursor's hot spot at the moment of the event.

For keyboard events, the event workbench displays the ASCII value of the key pressed, as well as the character equivalent of that key.

Should an event of any other type occur, it is simply noted at the bottom of the screen.

Type in this program (or load it from folder Miscellaneous on your Tutor disk).

```
program EventWorkbench;
{$U-}
uses
  MemTypes, QuickDraw, OSIntf, ToolIntf, Packintf;

var
  myPort   : GrafPort;
  theEvent : EventRecord;
  theChar  : Char;
  done     : Boolean;

procedure OutNum(h,v: Integer; theNum:LongInt);

var
  theString : Str255;
begin
  NumToString(theNum,theString);
  while Length(theString) < 8 do        { pad the string w/ leading spaces }
    Insert(' ',theString,1);
  MoveTo(h,v);
  DrawString(theString);
end;

procedure Initialize;
begin
  InitGraf(@thePort);
  OpenPort(@myPort);
  InitCursor;
  FillRect(myPort.portBits.Bounds,white);
  TextFont(monaco);
  TextMode(SrcCopy);
  done := False;
  MoveTo(30,30);
  DrawString('  Time          -X---Location---Y-        Code  Character');
end;

procedure MiscEvent(s: Str255);
begin
```

```
     MoveTo(30,300);
     DrawString(s);
  end;

begin
  Initialize;
  repeat
    if GetNextEvent(everyEvent,theEvent) then { everyEvent = a const = -1 }
      with theEvent do                  { this with makes the fields }
        case what of                    { of theEvent known everywhere }
          mouseDown : begin             { in this large case statement }
                        OutNum(30,60,when);
                        OutNum(130,60,where.h);
                        OutNum(230,60,where.v)
                      end;
          mouseUp :   begin
                        OutNum(30,90,when);
                        OutNum(130,90,where.h);
                        OutNum(230,90,where.v)
                      end;
          keyDown,
          autoKey :   begin
                        OutNum(30,120,when);
                        OutNum(130,120,where.h);
                        OutNum(230,120,where.v);
                        if what = autoKey then
                          SysBeep(1);
                        theChar := Chr(message and $000000FF);
                        OutNum(330,120,Ord(theChar));
                        MoveTo(430,120); DrawChar(theChar);
                        if (theChar = 'c') and
                          ((modifiers and $100) <> 0) then
                          done := True;
                        if theChar = '~' then
                        if PostEvent(app3Evt,0) > 0 then
                          SysBeep(1);
                      end;
          keyUp:      MiscEvent('keyUp');
          updateEvt:  MiscEvent('updateEvt');
          diskEvt:    MiscEvent('diskEvt');
          activateEvt:MiscEvent('activateEvt');
          networkEvt: MiscEvent('networkEvt');
          driverEvt : MiscEvent('driverEvt ');
          app1Evt:    MiscEvent('app1Evt');
          app2Evt:    MiscEvent('app2Evt');
          app3Evt:    MiscEvent('app3Evt');
          app4Evt:    MiscEvent('app4Evt');
        end;                                              { case }
  until done;
end.
```

Running EventWorkbench

Now run the program. Let's experiment first with key-down events. Type a capital A. Even though this involves pressing two keys (*Shift* and *A*), only a single key-down event is generated. The shift keys are modifiers; pressing either or both doesn't generate a key-down event, but instead serves to modify the event should another key be pressed.

Suppose the following values appear:

```
1163764    258    218    65    A
```

Let's interpret this output.

1163764 ticks equals 1163764/3600 minutes equals 323 minutes since the system booted. (In processing *keyDowns*, we're usually not interested in the position of the cursor—but the information is here, just in case.) At the instant *A* was pressed, the cursor's hot spot was (*258,218*). Finally, *65* is the ASCII code for *A*.

Press Tab. Tab doesn't have a printable equivalent, so the *DrawChar* routine outputs nothing, given a parameter of *Chr(9)*. Now experiment: What's the ASCII code produced by the Return key? The Enter key? A Macintosh Plus's arrow keys?

When you're done, press *Command-c* to leave the program.

Testing the Modifiers Field

The test involving the *modifiers* field in the key-down block checks for a particular key-down event: a lowercase *c* pressed along with *Command*. This is determined by checking a particular bit in the modifiers field.

```
if (theChar = 'c') and ((modifiers and $100) <> 0) then
   done := True;
```

Here we've used the **and** operator two ways: to test two boolean operands and to perform a logical **and** on two integers. This statement reads, "If the character typed is a lowercase *c* and if *Command* was down when this key was typed, then set the done flag." Thus, this program reprises an old standby of Standard Pascal: *Control-c* to terminate a program.

The modifiers field contains six flags:

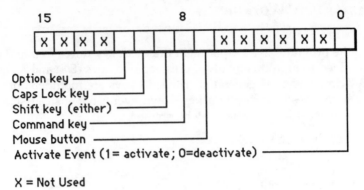

Option key
Caps Lock key
Shift key (either)
Command key
Mouse button
Activate Event (1= activate; 0=deactivate)

X = Not Used

Figure 34.1: Modifiers Word

Since the Command-key status is stored in bit 8 of this word, **and**ing the modifiers value with $100 (00000001 00000000) produces a nonzero value if and only if the Command-key bit was set—regardless of the values of the other bits in this word. The following constant definitions in the *ToolIntf* unit simplify this test:

```
const
  activeFlag = 1;      {$0001}
  btnState   = 128;    {$0080}
  cmdKey     = 256;    {$0100}
  shiftKey   = 512;    {$0200}
  alphaLock  = 1024;   {$0400}
  optionKey  = 2048;   {$0800}
```

Generate an auto-key event by holding a key down. Since this program processes auto-key events with the same code block as key-down events, the only difference is the call to *SysBeep*.

Studying Mouse Events

Move the cursor to a pleasing place on the screen, and click the mouse button (press and release). This generates a mouse-down event and, immediately thereafter, a mouse-up. Suppose the following values appear:

```
1164202  101   214 1164206   101    214
```

These six numbers succinctly define the click. The button went down at 1164202 ticks and back up at 1164206 ticks, a fifteenth of a second later. The cursor was in the same position at both times: point (101,214).

Disk Insertion Events

Press *Command-Shift-1* to eject the disk in the internal drive. Now, reinsert this disk. (**Hard disk users**: Insert any formatted disk.) A second or so after the insertion, a *diskInsertEvt* occurs. Applications normally don't have to worry about disk insertions.

Application-Defined Events

Since the execution of a Macintosh program never strays far from its main event loop, it can be convenient to use *GetNextEvent* as a means of communication between the various parts of a program. The *EventWorkbench* demonstrates this technique. Whenever you type a tilde (~), the key-down handler "posts" an application-3 event:

```
if theChar = '~' then
  if PostEvent(app3Evt,0) > 0 then
    SysBeep(1);
```

This statement places *app3Evt* into the event queue, right along with the *keyDown*s and *mouseDown*s that you create with your fingers. The main event loop, in turn, fetches this event as it would any event and then acts on it however it sees fit. *PostEvent* is an integer function; if it returns a non-zero value, then the posting failed for some reason (and the *EventWorkbench* beeps).

function PostEvent (eventCode: Integer; eventMsg: LongInt): OSErr;

The *eventMsg* parameter (0, in our example) shows up in the message field of the newly created event record.

Extra Credit

Why does *OutNum* pad numbers with leading spaces? Take out the code that does this and see what happens. What function is served by the *TextMode(srcCopy)* call in procedure *Initialize*? Delete it and see. (Hint: The default text-drawing mode is *srcOr*, which doesn't erase pixels in the bit image that are already black.)

While we're on the subject of text, why does this program use the Monaco font? Change the font to something other than Monaco. What goes wrong, and why? (Hint: In every font except Monaco, spaces are half as wide as numbers.)

Review

The Event Manager gives Macintosh applications a consistent way of dealing with all forms of user input. The primary types of "events" that a user creates are mouse-down, mouse-up, and key-down.

The *GetNextEvent* call fetches events from a queue. It returns in its *EventRecord* parameter detailed information about the event, including the type of event, when it occurred, where the cursor was on the screen when it occurred, and other supplemental information.

Macintosh programs typically are structured around a single main event loop, that repeatedly calls *GetNextEvent* and then processes each event type appropriately.

35

Windows

Overlapping, resizable, movable windows—a fundamental precept of the Macintosh user interface—are made possible by a series of procedures and functions known collectively as the Window Manager. Once woven into the fabric of an application just so and called at the right time in the right way, these routines create the illusion of a desktop containing multiple "documents" and tools.

Apple's User Interface Guidelines don't permit much flexibility in window behavior, and neither does the Window Manager. It allows an application to achieve the behavior described in the guidelines—nothing more and nothing less. In this sense, the Window Manager is very different from more general-purpose tools such as the Memory Manager and QuickDraw. The Window Manager is for programming artisans, not artists; save your creativity for the content of your windows.

What's a Window?

Figure 35.1 is a typical Macintosh window (in this case, one of Turbo Pascal's).

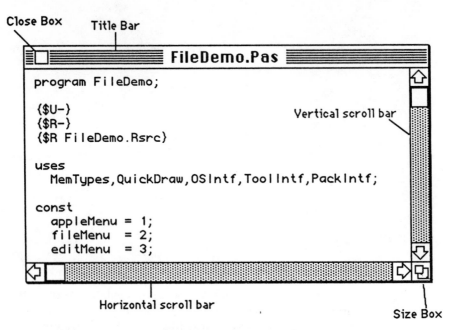

Figure 35.1: A Typical Window

This is what the Window Manager calls a *document* window. Document windows have a title bar, containing a centered string (the window's name) displayed in 12-point Chicago. Document windows can also have a close box, a size box, and horizontal and vertical scroll bars (which aren't really handled by the Window Manager but by one of its assistants, the Control Manager).

There are five other standard window types, as shown in Figure 35.2. Type *rDocProc* is often used for desk accessories and types *dBoxProc* and *plainDBox* for dialogs and alerts. You can even create your own types, provided you're willing to devote your life to contemplative study of *Inside Macintosh*.

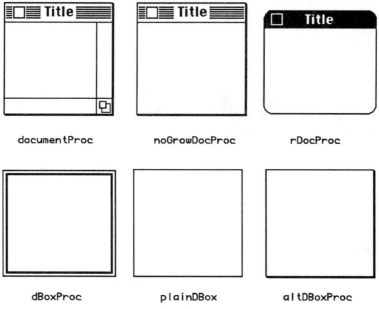

documentProc   noGrowDocProc   rDocProc

dBoxProc   plainDBox   altDBoxProc

Figure 35.2: Standard Window Types

Regardless of type, once drawn, windows are treated pretty much the same by the Window Manager. (Incidentally, windows created by desk accessories are called *system windows*; those created by applications are *application windows*.) While many windows can be on the screen at once, only one is the *active* window. All the rest are *inactive*. The active window is visually and logically on top of the others, and it is the window to which all user actions apply, including keystrokes and menu selections.

The active window is visually distinct from inactive windows. For example, the Window Manager indicates that a standard document window is active by adding horizontal lines to its title bar.

The content of a window also may change when it becomes inactive. For example, for text-editing windows, any highlighting disappears, as does the insertion point. At least that's what the guidelines recommend; it's up to each application to implement this behavior. (Quiz: What does Turbo Pascal do?)

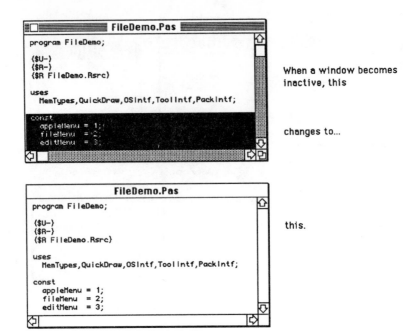

Figure 35.3: Inactive versus Active Windows

Only an active window can have a close box or grow box. Clicking once in any exposed part of an inactive window brings it to the top of the stack and makes it the active window. The former active window becomes the second in the stack. This click serves the activation function and no other.

What the Window Manager Does for You

The Window Manager offers a workable, if somewhat convoluted, solution to the enormous technical problems presented by overlapping windows. By automatically making appropriate QuickDraw calls to manipulate clipping regions, the Window Manager allows an application to draw into a window without concern for its size, location on the screen, or position relative to other windows. If the part of the window that's being drawn to is visible, then the drawing shows; if it isn't, clipping protects the other windows.

Windows Equal GrafPorts

Stated bluntly, *a window is a GrafPort*. Each window has a unique bit image, port rectangle, pen pattern and location, and all the other fields of the *GrafPort* record.

A window record is a *GrafPort*, but not vice versa; window records contain additional information. Let's take a look at the Pascal expression of a window record:

```
type
  WindowRecord = record
    port:          GrafPort;   { i.e., portBits, portRect, visRgn, etc. }
    windowKind:    Integer;
    visible:       Boolean;
    hilited:       Boolean;
    goAwayFlag:    Boolean;
    spareFlag:     Boolean;
    strucRgn:      RgnHandle;
    contRgn:       RgnHandle;
    updateRgn:     RgnHandle;
    windowDefProc:Handle;
    dataHandle:    Handle;
    titleHandle:   StringHandle;
    titleWidth:    Integer;
    controlList:   ControlHandle;
    nextWindow:    WindowPeek;
    windowPic:     PicHandle;
    refCon:        LongInt;
  end;
```

Since the very first thing in a *WindowRecord* is a *GrafPort*, given variable *W* of type *WindowRecord*, you have access to an entire *GrafPort* of fields:

- *W.port.penPattern* is a Pattern.
- *W.port.portBits.bounds* is a Rectangle.
- *W.port.visRgn* is a RgnHandle, and so on.

The Fields beyond the GrafPort

WindowKind is an integer defining the "class" of a window and, for windows created by an application to 8 defaults. You can check this field to learn whether a given window belongs to a desk accessory (*windowKind* < 0), or if it was put on the screen by the Dialog Manager as a dialog box or alert (*windowKind* = 2). Values greater than 8 can be used for an application's own purposes in discriminating windows.

The *visible* flag tells if it's currently invisible or visible. (Windows can be logically on the screen but invisible; note that this condition is distinct from a window simply covered by other windows.) The *hilited* flag tells whether a window is currently highlighted, that is, active. The *goAwayFlag* indicates whether or not a window has a close box.

Structure and Content Regions

The *strucRgn, contRgn,* and *upDateRgn* fields are handles to regions that are automatically manipulated by the Window Manager in drawing window frames and contents.

Every window has a *content region* and a *structure region*. The content region is the area of the window into which an application draws. The structure region is a combination of the content region plus the window frame itself.

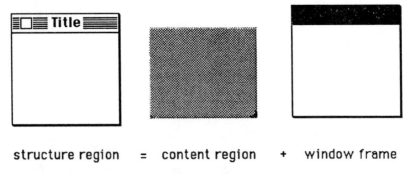

structure region   =   content region   +   window frame

Figure 35.4: Content and Structure Regions

The window's title is accessed through a *StringHandle* (defined in unit *MemTypes* as a pointer to a pointer to a Str255). A window may have one or more *controls* associated with it: Controls are mouse-driven user interface niceties such as radio buttons and scroll bars. If so, *controlList* is the anchor of a linked list of the controls attached to this window.

The last field of a window record, *refCon*, is for applications to use any way they see fit. It's often used to point to additional data belonging to a window. For example, a word-processing program may use the *refCon* of a text-editing window as a handle to a block of ASCII characters.

Pointers, GrafPorts, WindowRecords, and Type Coercion

Like *GrafPorts*, window records are usually allocated on the heap as nonrelocatable blocks and accessed through pointers. Also like *GrafPorts*, pointers are used to access window records far more often than variables of type *WindowRecord*.

Note well the following Window Manager type definition:

```
type
   WindowPtr = GrafPtr;
```

This says that a *WindowPtr* is the same thing as a *GrafPtr*, namely, a pointer to a *GrafPort*—not a pointer to a *WindowRecord*. This allows you to send window records off to QuickDraw routines that expect *GrafPtr* parameters (such as *InitPort* and *GetPort*). This chicanery works because a *GrafPort* happens to be the very first field in a window record.

As a result, dereferencing a variable of type *WindowPtr* doesn't result in a *WindowRecord* but rather a *GrafPort*. If *W* is a variable of type *WindowPtr*, then *W^.penLoc* is a Point and *W^.goAwayFlag* doesn't exist, because *GrafPorts* don't have a *goAwayFlag* field.

This is fine if you only care about the *GrafPort* component of a window record, and, 51 percent of the time, this is the case. To get Turbo Pascal to process the additional fields in a window record, you must use a different pointer type declared by the Window Manager:

```
type
   WindowPeek = ^WindowRecord;
```

In other words, given a single *WindowRecord* in the heap, you can access its *GrafPort* fields with a variable of type *WindowPtr* or all its fields, including the *GrafPort*, with a variable of type *WindowPeek*. In either case, the value of the pointer is the same: the address of the first byte of the *WindowRecord*.

To illustrate, consider the following segment of code.

```
var
  W: WindowPtr;
  W2: WindowPeek;
begin
  W := NewWindow (a,b,c,d,e,f,g,h,i)     { allocate a window record }
  W2 := WindowPeek(W);            { type coercion; W2,W --> window rec }
  InitPort(W);                           { this works, because WindowPtr }
                                    { and GrafPtr are one and the same }
  InitPort(W2);               { illegal--can't send apples to oranges }
```

```
   W^.penPattern := gray;
   W2^.port.penPattern := gray;     { this assigns to the same field,
                                      i.e., the same address in memory }
   W2^.visible := True;
   W^.visible := True;              { illegal; no such field in a GrafPort }
   WindowPeek(W)^.visible := True; { legal, thanks to type coercion }
end;
```

Drawing a Window

Windows are drawn in a two-step process. First, the Window Manager draws an empty window frame. Second, the application is signaled to draw its contents. This signaling is provided by *GetNextEvent*, which, in addition to looking for mouse and keyboard activity, checks to see if there are windows that require redrawing (for example, because an overlaying window has been moved). If it finds such a window, *GetNextEvent* returns an "update event" with the message field a pointer to the window in question. Upon fetching and decoding an update event, the application then draws that window's contents.

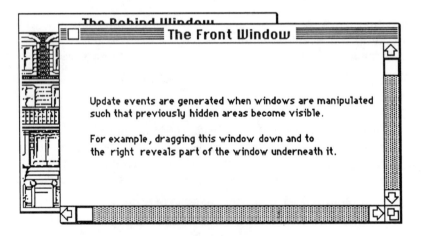

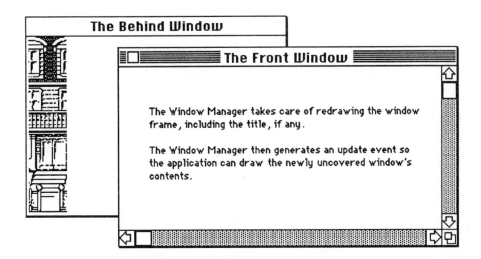

The Behind Window

The Front Window

The Window Manager takes care of redrawing the window frame, including the title, if any.

The Window Manager then generates an update event so the application can draw the newly uncovered window's contents.

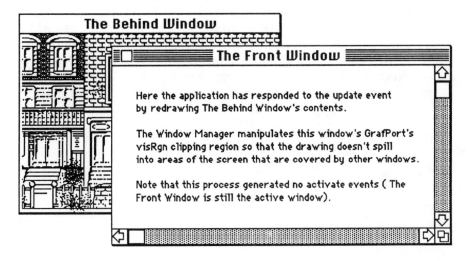

The Behind Window

The Front Window

Here the application has responded to the update event by redrawing The Behind Window's contents.

The Window Manager manipulates this window's GrafPort's visRgn clipping region so that the drawing doesn't spill into areas of the screen that are covered by other windows.

Note that this process generated no activate events (The Front Window is still the active window).

Figure 35.5: Update Events

Key Window Manager Routines

The parameterless *InitWindows* routine initializes the Window Manager; as a bonus, it allocates a *GrafPort* in the heap (called the "Window Manager port") and uses this port to draw the desktop and menu bar. Call *InitWindows* after *InitGraf* and *InitFonts* and before making any other Window Manager call. A pointer to the Window Manager port can be had by calling procedure *GetWMgrPort*:

procedure GetWMgrPort (**var** wPort: GrafPtr);

There are two calls for creating a window: *NewWindow*, a function requiring umpteen parameters to define the new window (type, size, and so on), and *GetNewWindow*, which gets most of the defining parameters from a 'WIND' template in a resource file. Both calls draw the window on the screen and return a pointer to the newly allocated window record. We'll show how to use *GetNewWindow* in an upcoming demo program.

To erase a window from the desktop and its various data structures from memory, call *DisposeWindow*, passing it a pointer to the underlying WindowRecord.

The Window Manager maintains a linked list of all the windows on the desktop. It is the position of each *WindowRecord* in this list that controls the "plane" in which the window is drawn (that is, who covers who). A pointer to the topmost window is available at any given time with the *FrontWindow* function:

function FrontWindow: WindowPtr;

The list is maintained using the *nextWindow* field of each window record. The bottom window has a *nextWindow* value of **nil**. If there are no windows on the screen at all, *FrontWindow* returns **nil**. The following procedure demonstrates how to traverse this list. It beeps as it encounters negative *windowKind* fields (that is, desk accessory windows).

```
procedure BeepForDAs;
var
  myPtr: WindowPeek;
begin
  myPtr := WindowPeek(FrontWindow);
  while myPtr <> nil do
  begin
    if myPtr^.windowKind < 0 then
      SysBeep(10);
    myPtr := myPtr^.nextWindow;
  end;
end;
```

This is the same sort of linked list traversing we did back in Chapter 16. If you need to, review the relevant sections.

The *SelectWindow* routine takes a *WindowPtr* parameter and makes the window record it points to the active window. If it was the active window already, then nothing happens and no harm is done.

procedure SelectWindow(theWindow: WindowPtr);

A program calls *SelectWindow* when there's been a mouse-down event in any inactive window. *SelectWindow* automatically generates appropriate update events so that the application is able to redraw the windows in their new order.

For an application with multiple windows, the key to handling mouse-downs is the Window Manager's *FindWindow* function.

function FindWindow(thePt: Point; **var** whichWindow: WindowPtr): Integer;

You pass this routine one fact (a point), and get back two: An integer code that can be tested to learn more about the *mouseDown* and, returned in *whichWindow*, a *WindowPtr* indicating the window (active or inactive) in which the *mouseDown* occurred. If the *mouseDown* wasn't in a window, then *whichWindow* returns **nil**.

The following constants are defined in unit *ToolIntf* for your convenience in testing the value returned by *FindWindow*, much the way one tests the what field of an event record:

```
const
  inDesk      = 0;                    { i.e., you missed everything }
  inMenuBar   = 1;  { somewhere in the white at the top of the screen }
  inSysWindow = 2;       { i.e., anywhere in a desk accessory window }
  inContent   = 3;  { in the content region of an application window }
  inDrag      = 4;       { in the title bar of an application window }
  inGrow      = 5;        { in the grow box of an application window }
  inGoAway    = 6;     { in the goAwaybox of an application window }
```

The Toolbox has routines to call in response to various codes returned by *FindWindow*. For example, handling everything involved in dragging a window to a new location requires a single call to the *DragWindow* function.

Using the Window Manager

FindWindow, *SelectWindow*, and the rest don't make all that much sense taken out of context. The best way to learn is to watch them in action and then implement a similar pattern in your own programs. Remember, when it comes to window management, strive for craftsmanship, not artistry.

The following demonstration program is possibly the most difficult presented so far in this book. It's also the first one that behaves like a real Macintosh program. Take your time. Be consoled by the knowledge that when you can say, "I understand how this program works," the worst of the Toolbox climb will be behind you.

```pascal
program WindowDemo;
{$U-}
uses
  MemTypes,QuickDraw,OSIntf,ToolIntf;

var
  done:     Boolean;
  theEvent: EventRecord;
  dragRect: Rect;

procedure DoUpdate;
var
  theWindow: WindowPtr;
  myRect:    Rect;
  n:         Integer;
begin
  theWindow := WindowPtr(theEvent.message);
  SetPort(theWindow);
  BeginUpdate(theWindow);

  if WindowPeek(theWindow)^.refCon = 0 then
  begin
    myRect := theWindow^.portRect;
    for N := 1 to 12 do
    begin
      InsetRect(myRect,8,8);
      FrameRect(myRect);
    end;
  end
  else
  begin
    MoveTo(10,100);
    DrawString(StringHandle(windowPeek(theWindow)^.refCon)^^);
  end;

  EndUpdate(theWindow);
end;

procedure doMouseDown;
var
  theWindow: WindowPtr;
  code:      Integer;
begin
  code := FindWindow(theEvent.where,theWindow);
  case code of
    inMenuBar: SysBeep(1);
```

```
      inContent: if theWindow = FrontWindow then SysBeep(10)
                 else SelectWindow(theWindow);
      inDrag:    DragWindow(theWindow,theEvent.where,DragRect);
      inGoAway:  if TrackGoAway(theWindow,theEvent.where) then done := True;
    end;
end;

procedure Initialize;
var
  r: Rect;
  aWindow: WindowPtr;
begin
  MoreMasters;
  InitGraf(@thePort);
  InitFonts;
  InitWindows;
  InitCursor;
  done := False;

  SetRect(r,50,50,300,250);
  aWindow:=NewWindow(nil,r,'Window 1',True,documentProc,Pointer(-1),True,0);
  aWindow^.txFace := [bold]; aWindow^.txFont := SystemFont;
  windowPeek(aWindow)^.refCon := Longint(NewString('Contents of window 1'));

  OffsetRect(r,30,30);
  aWindow:=NewWindow(nil,r,'Window 2',True,documentProc,Pointer(-1),True,0);
  aWindow^.txFace := [italic]; aWindow^.txFont := SystemFont;
  windowPeek(aWindow)^.refCon := Longint(NewString('Contents of window 2'));

  OffsetRect(r,30,30);
  aWindow:=NewWindow(nil,r,'Window 3',True,documentProc,Pointer(-1),True,0);

  dragRect := screenbits.bounds; InsetRect(dragRect,25,25);
end;

begin
  Initialize;
  repeat
    if GetNextEvent(everyEvent,theEvent) then
      case theEvent.what of
        mouseDown:  DoMouseDown;
        keyDown:    SysBeep(10);
        updateEvt:  DoUpdate;
        activateEvt: ;
      end;
  until done;
end.
```

Unless you need the typing practice, don't enter this program by hand. It's on your Turbo Tutor disk in folder Miscellaneous. Now compile and run this program.

WindowDemo doesn't really do anything, but it has the Macintosh feel. Move windows around. Click on an inactive window to make it the active window. Note that when you drag a window from in front of another, the formerly hidden contents appear. Click in various areas on the screen, such as the menu bar, inside the current window, and in the desktop. What happens? To exit, click the active window's close box.

About WindowDemo.Pas

The main program has a structure reminiscent of EventDemo's. After performing some one-time initialization, it enters a "main event loop" that repeatedly calls *GetNextEvent* and acts on the value returned in *theEvent.what*.

Initializing

Procedure *Initialize* first calls the Memory Manager's *MoreMasters* procedure. This gives the program 64 additional master pointers to work with, down at the bottom of the heap where they belong. With as many as 11 master pointers required per window, the default block of 64 can get used up in a hurry.

Next we initialize QuickDraw, the Font Manager, and the Window Manager, in that order. At no time do we explicitly initialize a *GrafPort*. There's no *OpenPort* call, nor does this program declare any *GrafPort* variables. A *GrafPort* (the Window Manager port) is created on the heap automatically by *InitWindows*, which is then used to draw the familiar gray desktop and an empty menu bar.

Creating a Window

Next, the program creates three windows, with three calls to *NewWindow*.

```
procedure NewWindow(wStorage: Ptr; boundsRect: Rect; title: Str255;
                    visible: Boolean; procID: Integer; behind: WindowPtr;
                    goAwayFlag: Boolean; refCon: LongInt);
```

As windows are complex objects with many options, *NewWindow* takes many parameters. This routine both allocates and initializes a window record, and draws its on-screen manifestation, a window. Let's examine the first call to this function in detail:

```
aWindow:=NewWindow(nil,r,'Window1',True,documentProc,Pointer(-1),True,0);
```

Each parameter helps to define the window to be created. The *wStorage* argument is a pointer to the storage that's been allocated for the about-to-be-created window record. In this case, we haven't allocated any storage; instead, we want the *NewWindow* routine to do the allocation for us. This desire is communicated to *NewWindow* by passing **nil** as the *wStorage argument*.

The *boundsRect* parameter defines the size and location of the content region of the new window. This rectangle is specified in "global coordinates," that is, point (0,0) represents the pixel in the extreme upper-left-hand corner of the screen. Keep in mind that the frame of a document window extends 20 pixels above the top of the content region; therefore, a top-left point of (0,0) creates a window with a title bar hidden under the menu bar.

The string you provide as the *title* parameter shows up in the title bar when the window is drawn (assuming it's a window type with a title bar, like a document window). It'll also be stored in handle form in the *WindowRecord*'s *titleHandle* field.

visible controls whether or not the window will initially be visible. Sometimes it is useful to bring a window onto the screen "invisibly," adjust it in some way, and then make it visible. In this case, we want to see the new window immediately.

procID defines the type of window you want. Unit *ToolIntf* defines integer constants representing the six standard window types, *documentProc* being the identifier representing document windows.

behind controls the plane in which the window will appear when drawn. Use **nil** to place a new window underneath all existing windows, and *Pointer(-1)* to draw it on top.

If your application dictates that the new window should have a close box, then pass True for the *goAwayFlag* parameter.

Finally, the *refCon* parameter sets the window's initial value for the all-purpose "reference constant." We're going to use this field in just a minute, but for now, we'll just let it be zero.

The Window Appears

The call to *NewWindow* does a number of things: First, space for a new *WindowRecord* is allocated in the heap; its fields initialized to default values (except for those explicitly provided, such as *goAwayFlag*); and the address of this block is assigned to *aWindow*. Finally, a document window entitled "Window 1" appears on the screen.

Since a window record contains an embedded *GrafPort*, you may wonder if this *GrafPort* is initialized as well. It is; *NewWindow* makes a call to *OpenPort* (although when *NewWindow* returns the current port is the Window Manager port).

This new *GrafPort* has a local coordinate system such that the first pixel enclosed by its *portRect*—the first pixel in its content region—is addressed as (0,0). This is the same pixel that we called (50,50) in our earlier QuickDraw experiments. In effect, the *GrafPort* represented by *Window^* is a miniature screen onto itself, in which we can make QuickDraw calls—drawing lines, round-corner rectangles, text.

WindowDemo assigns the address of the new window record to pointer variable *aWindow*. This means that by dereferencing *aWindow*, we gain access to the window record—as shown in the next two statements:

```
aWindow^.txFace := [bold]; aWindow^.txFont := SystemFont;
```

To reiterate the typing problems of window records: Since *aWindow* is a *WindowPtr* (a pointer to a *GrafPort*), getting to the fields beyond the *GrafPort* requires type coercion. It is type coercion that makes the next statement so strange:

```
windowPeek(aWindow)^.refCon := LongInt(NewString('Contents of
window 1'));
```

Were it not for type coercion, this statement would be

```
aWindow^.refCon := NewString('Contents of window 1');
```

The intent here is to use the *refCon* field to associate a string (the window's "contents") with this window. It uses *NewString*, a utility routine that allocates a relocatable block of string data and returns a typed handle to it:

```
function NewString(theString: Str255) : StringHandle;
```

NewString is one of two dozen routines lumped under the title "Toolbox Utilities" and documented in Chapter 16 (Volume I) of *Inside Macintosh*. Toolbox Utilities "perform generally useful operations such as fixed-point arithmetic, string manipulation, and logical operations on bits," says the reference work.

Once string data has been "handle-ized" by *NewString*, you can refer it by double-dereferencing the handle. To illustrate,

```
var
  sHandle: StringHandle;
begin
  sHandle := NewString('I know not what course others may take,')
  WriteLn(sHandle^^ + ' but, as for me, I''m going to Quebec.');
end.
```

Back to WindowDemo. What we're doing in the assignment to *refCon* is tying the "contents" of the window to its record. A real application would probably declare a handle to a record type able to store various facts about the window's contents.

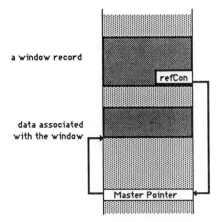

Figure 35.6: Storing Window Data

To get at the window record's *refCon* field, *aWindow* must first be coerced into a pointer of type *WindowPeek*. The expression

```
WindowPeek(aWindow)
```

has the same underlying value as *aWindow*. We've simply coerced the compiler into treating it as though it were type *WindowPeek*. Therefore,

- *windowPeek(aWindow)* is a pointer to a *WindowRecord*.
- *windowPeek(aWindow)^* is a *WindowRecord*.
- *windowPeek(aWindow)^.refCon* is a *LongInt*.

Finally, the *StringHandle* returned by *NewString* must be coerced to a long integer before the compiler will permit its assignment to a window record's *refCon* field.

Let's recap. At this point, we've created a new window record and drawn an empty document window titled "Window 1" on the screen. We've set its *GrafPort* to draw in the System font and size (12-point Chicago—by default, *GrafPorts* within window records created by *NewWindow* use Geneva). Finally, we attached a string to its *refCon* field.

Once More, with Feeling

Next, we go through the same process to create two more windows, each offset slightly down and to the right of the previous one.

In calling *NewWindow* to create Window #2, we're again assigning to *aWindow*—which happens to be our program's only record of the address of Window #1. Similarly, creating #3 overwrites the address of #2's window record. To make matters worse, since *aWindow* is local to procedure *Initialize*, we'll lose track of #3 the moment this routine finishes.

With the addresses of their window records lost, how will we be able to work with our windows? For now, we won't. But the Window Manager can find all three, thanks to the linked list it maintains. In another part of the program, one of its routines will give us the address of a window record on a silver platter when we need it.

Window #3 doesn't get a content string. It contains rectangles (or will, shortly).

The last operation performed by procedure *Initialize* is to set global variable *dragRect* to enclose an area somewhat smaller than the screen:

```
dragRect := screenbits.bounds; InsetRect(dragRect,25,25);
```

We'll use this rectangle later to limit how far a window can be dragged.

Update Event Processing

At the instant procedure *Initialize* ends, the screen looks like this:

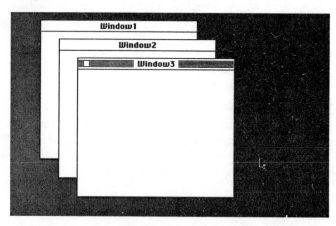

Figure 35.7: The Three Windows

We haven't yet drawn any window contents. Simply assigning a handle to a Str255 to the *refCon* field isn't enough: The Window Manager can't guess that you intend this data to be drawn inside the window. How are their contents finally drawn? Through the good auspices of *GetNextEvent* and the main event loop.

Creating a window automatically generates an update event for that window. So, after procedure *Initialize* finishes, three *updateEvts* lie waiting in the event queue, waiting to be fetched by *GetNextEvent*, right along with *mouseDowns* and *autoKeys*.

Procedure DoUpdate

The main event loop responds to update events by calling this program's *DoUpdate* routine. *DoUpdate*'s job is to draw the contents of the window represented by a given update event.

Even when only a part of a window needs updating, *DoUpdate* (and most Macintosh applications) draws the whole thing. The Window Manager's manipulation of each window's *visRgn* keeps areas that don't need to be redrawn from being repeated. (The program goes through the motions of redrawing everything, but clipping protects bits in screen memory that don't require updating.)

DoUpdate first decodes the information in global variable *theEvent* (of type *EventRecord*) to discover which window needs updating. It so happens that for update events *theEvent.message* is nothing less than this pointer masquerading as a long integer.

For convenience in working with it, *DoUpdate* assigns this value to a local variable of type *WindowPtr*. The assignment requires our old friend, type coercion:

```
theWindow := WindowPtr(theEvent.message);
```

Now *theWindow* points to the window that needs updating. The actual updating proceeds according to this pseudocode:

```
Make theWindow^ the current GrafPort;
  if theWindow^.refCon = 0 then
    this must be Window #3, so draw the nested rectangles
  else
    draw the string pointed to by the refCon field at (10,100).
```

Here's where the Window Manager pays off. We don't care where on the screen this window is or whether other windows are wholly or partially blocking it. Thanks to the Window Manager's manipulation of this

GrafPort's *visRgn* field, we can make QuickDraw calls indefinitely without fear of drawing outside of the window. If we need the assistance of a clipping region to draw in this port, we are free to use *clipRgn*.

The Window Manager expects to be told when you start updating a window and when you've finished. This is accomplished by bracketing the routines that draw in the window with calls to the procedures *BeginUpdate* and *EndUpdate*.

For Window #3, drawing is a matter of 12 calls to *FrameRect*, each smaller than the one before (a la the QuickDraw demonstration program *ManipulateRects*). This *GrafPort's* port rectangle is always (0,0),(250,200), no matter where its window is on the screen.

For Windows 1 and 2, drawing entails sending the string pointed to by *refCon* off to QuickDraw's *DrawString* routine. This would be duck soup were it not for type coercion. We could say

```
DrawString(theWindow^.refCon^^);
```

but since *theWindow* isn't type *WindowPeek* and since *refCon* isn't a *StringHandle*, we must muck things up with type names and parentheses:

```
DrawString(StringHandle(windowPeek(theWindow)^.refCon)^^);
```

(If you ever find yourself getting irritated with Pascal's strong typing, repeat ten times "Type coercion is for my own good.")

We created three windows, so when program flow returns from *DoUpdate* to the main loop, there are two more update events waiting in the queue. *GetNextEvent* returns update events according to their position on the screen (front windows first), not the order in which they were generated. So Window #3 is updated first, and Window #1 (the first to be drawn) is updated last.

All this main event loop activity happens without the user lifting a finger. After all three windows have been updated, the program continues calling *GetNextEvent*, hundreds of times a second, while waiting for you to do something.

Besides update events, this program responds to *mouseDowns* and (halfheartedly) to *keyDowns*. This program's mouse-down processing is a model for all Macintosh programs:

```
procedure doMouseDown;
var
  theWindow: WindowPtr;
  code:      Integer;
begin
  code := FindWindow(theEvent.where,theWindow);
```

```
  case code of
    inMenuBar: SysBeep(1);
    inContent: if theWindow = FrontWindow then SysBeep(10)
               else SelectWindow(theWindow);
    inDrag:    DragWindow(theWindow,theEvent.where,DragRect);
    inGoAway:  if TrackGoAway(theWindow,theEvent.where) then done := True;
  end;
end;
```

Let's review what an *EventRecord* variable contains after a mouse-down event: The tick count, in the *when* field; the state of various shift keys in the *modifiers* field; nothing in the *message* field; and, most importantly, in the *where* field, the location of the cursor's hot spot when the button went down.

The key to mouse-down processing is the Window Manager's *FindWindow* routine:

```
code := FindWindow(theEvent.where,theWindow);
```

FindWindow returns a numeric value and sets *theWindow* equal to a pointer to the window in which the mouse-down occurred, if any. Using a **case** statement, this program tests the return code against predefined integer constants that cover every possibility:

```
  case code of
    inMenuBar: SysBeep(1);
    inContent: if theWindow = FrontWindow then SysBeep(10)
               else SelectWindow(theWindow);
    inDrag:    DragWindow(theWindow,theEvent.where,DragRect);
    inGoAway:  if TrackGoAway(theWindow,theEvent.where) then
                  done := True;          { i.e., in close box }
  end;
```

For mouse-down in the (empty) menu bar, we beep. (When we start adding menus to our programs, at this point, we'll call a Menu Manager routine that does all the processing necessary to pull down the appropriate menu, highlight selections, and so on.)

The next possibility is more interesting. If *FindWindow* returns a value equal to *inContent*, then we know that the content region of one of our three windows was clicked (the content region being everything except the frame). For lack of anything better to do, a mouse-down in the active window results in a one-sixth second beep. Windows that contain controls (for example, scroll bars, radio buttons) require more work to handle a mouse-down in the active window's content.

As required by the User Interface Guidelines, a mouse-down in an inactive window makes that window active. *DoMouseDown* can tell if the window receiving the mouse-down is the active window by comparing *theWindow* to the *WindowPtr* returned by the *FrontWindow* routine:

```
inContent: if theWindow = FrontWindow then SysBeep(10)
           else SelectWindow(theWindow);
```

Making an inactive window the active window is accomplished by calling *SelectWindow*. It takes care of drawing the appropriate window frames and generates the necessary update events so that the main event loop again calls *DoUpdate* to redraw the contents.

The remaining two possibilities, *inDrag* and *inGoAway*, are also handled by calls to the appropriate Menu Manager routine.

```
procedure DragWindow(theWindow; startPt: Point; boundsRect: Rect);
```

DragWindow doesn't return until the mouse button is finally released, and no *mouseUp* event ever makes it to the event queue. It pulls the familiar gray outline around the screen until the button is released, at which time the window is moved to its new location (and appropriate update events generated should part of an underlying window become exposed). The *boundsRect* parameter limits how far the window can be moved, largely to keep the user from moving it off the screen altogether. If the button is released with the cursor's hot spot outside this rectangle, then the window stays where it was initially.

If the window you've dragged isn't the active window already, then it becomes the active window thereafter (as though you had called *SelectWindow* yourself). This effect can be overridden by holding Command down as you click in the drag area; this is yet another user-interface standard built into the Window Manager.

TrackGoAway

Call *TrackGoAway* if *FindWindow* indicates that the mouse-down occurred in the active window's close box. (Since inactive windows never have close boxes, it's guaranteed to be the active window.)

```
function TrackGoAway(theWindow: WindowPtr; thePt: Point): Boolean;
```

It's *TrackGoAway* that draws the "bubble bursting" asterisk in the close box and erases it if the cursor moves out of the box. Like *DragWindow*, *TrackGoAway* doesn't return until the mouse button has been released. If it returns True, then the user was still in the close box as he or she released the button; if not, then he or she moved the cursor out of the box before releasing.

The program's response to a click in the close box may be to close that window or, as in the case of WindowDemo, to end the program altogether. Setting global boolean variable *done* to True ends the program in microseconds, as control returns to the main event loop and falls through the **until**-done test.

Activate Events

WindowDemo chooses not to respond to activate events, the event type that results when a window makes the transition from active to inactive and vice versa (its windows don't have contents worth deactivating).

Just for fun, insert a *SysBeep(1)* where the main event loop's **case** statement decodes activate events. This creates a beep whenever an activate or deactivate event occurs. Since they always occur in pairs in this program, you'll hear two beeps whenever you click an inactive window—one beep as the current active window becomes inactive, a second as the window you clicked in becomes active. Since activate events have a higher priority than update events, you'll hear two quick beeps before any content drawing is performed.

So that you'll be able to tell when update events occur, place a signaling beep at the start of *DoUpdate*. Make it longer so you can tell the two types apart, say, *SysBeep(30)*.

Update events often accompany activate events and vice versa, but not necessarily. For example, if two windows don't overlap, then making one of them active generates two activate events—but no update events, because no contents need redrawing. On the other hand, if you drag the active window in such a way as to uncover part of one or more windows, you'll produce an update without an activate. Experiment until you're comfortable with the distinction between update and activate events.

Experiment

You're using the fastest Pascal compiler in captivity. Take advantage of its one-second turnaround to tweak the parameters to *NewWindow*. Change the name of Window 3 to "Graphics Window." Make Window 2 a 100-pixel-square window in the lower left-hand part of the screen. What happens if the window is too small to contain its title? Pass a *boundsRect* parameter such that the window is partially under the menu bar. Pass **nil** as the *behind* parameter to make a window go underneath existing windows.

Change *procID* to created a different window type. Create a window without a close box.

With astute cutting and pasting, you could make this program open dozens of windows. Maybe you could call *NewWindow* repetitively inside a **for** loop. Is there a limit on how many windows can be on the desktop at once? (No.)

Review

This program is the most complex we've worked with yet in this book, so it's understandable if you don't immediately understand parts of it. By the time you've written your hundredth Macintosh program, it will make perfect sense.

The Window Manager provides data types and routines for implementing windows according to the User Interface Guidelines. Windows are represented internally by a record type that begins with an embedded *GrafPort*. Consequently, pointers to windows (of type *WindowPtr*) may be passed to QuickDraw routines that expect pointers to *GrafPort*s. Accessing the additional fields of a *GrafPort* requires coercion to a pointer of type *WindowPeek*.

The *NewWindow* and *GetNewWindow* routines allocate window records and draw the new window on the screen; the latter gets most of the window's definition information from a resource file. When an application has finished with a window, it calls *DisposeWindow*.

Window frames are drawn automatically by the Window Manager. Window contents are drawn by the application in response to update events. The *FindWindow* routine is called after mouse-down events to learn in what window or region of the screen the mouse-down occurred. The *SelectWindow* routine is called when a mouse-down occurs in an inactive window. The *DragWindow* routine handles moving a window from one point to another. The *TrackGoAway* function tests the user's actions after a mouse-down in a close box.

36

Controls

The Macintosh notion of *controls* is another component of the user interface. Controls are graphic objects that can be manipulated with the mouse (with graphic feedback) to cause an immediate action or to affect a future action.

The Control Manager is a repository of types and routines for handling controls. There are routines to create and dispose of controls, to draw controls, to call when the user clicks in a control, and to read and write a control's value. Although *Inside Macintosh* explains at length how to create custom controls, most programs—certainly those that you'll be writing at first—can make do with the four standard ones: *buttons, radio buttons, check boxes,* and *scroll bars.*

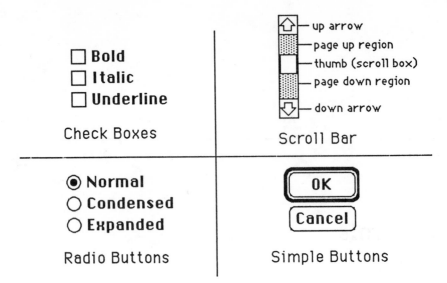

Figure 36.1: The Four Types of Controls

Buttons are small, round-cornered rectangles with text centered inside. Unlike other control types, buttons don't retain a value, but instead immediately result in some action.

Radio buttons are for presenting options that fit into a "one of several" category. Pressing one button "pushes out" the others, so that exactly one is on at all times.

Check boxes are like boolean variables on the screen: They're either on (checked) or off (unchecked). Conceptually, check boxes are for options that can be applied singly or in combination. For example, a word-processing program could offer the user seven check boxes to control the text style. Internally, individual radio buttons and check boxes have a value of either 0 or 1.

Scroll bars are the only predefined member of a class of control called *dials*. Dials permit the user to select from a continuous range of values, like the volume knob on a radio. Scroll bars are used in document windows when the document is larger than the window.

It's worth noting that even though scroll bars appear to have the same status as the frame of a document window, all controls, including scroll bars, are in fact part of a window's content region. As such, they must be drawn by the application.

Controls: Active and Inactive

Controls are always associated with a window. Since the User Interface Guidelines state that user actions apply only to the active window, there would be confusion if an inactive (but visible) window contained normal-looking controls.

To avoid this situation, controls, like the windows that contain them, can be made inactive. An inactive control is distinctively "dimmed" to indicate that clicking in it will have no effect.

Part Codes

To support complex controls like scroll bars containing multiple components, the Control Manager relies on the notion of *part codes*. Various routines that process controls accept and return part-code data. Simple controls like buttons, radio buttons, and check boxes have a single part code; scroll bars have five.

The Control Record

A control is represented in memory by a variable of type *ControlRecord*:

```
type
  ControlPtr    = ^ControlRecord;
  ControlHdl    = ^ControlPtr;
  ControlRecord = packed record
                    nextControl:    ControlHandle;
                    contrlOwner:    WindowPtr;
                    contrlRect:     Rect;
                    contrlVis:      Byte;
                    contrlHilite:   Byte;
                    contrlValue:    Integer;
                    contrlMin:      Integer;
                    contrlMax:      Integer
                    contrlDefProc:  Handle;
                    contrlData:     Handle;
                    contrlAction:   ProcPtr;
                    contrlRfCon:    LongInt;
                    contrlTitle:    Str255;
                  end;
```

Let's work through these fields. *NextControl* is a link to the next control in the linked list (the first is stored in the window record of the window containing these controls). If a control happens to be the last in the list, then *nextControl* equals **nil**.

The "owning" window of a control is pointed to by its *contrlOwner* field. *ContrlRect* is this control's boundary rectangle. It encloses the control, including any associated text. This rectangle controls whether or not a *mouseDown* is considered to affect a control. Therefore, clicking on the text of a radio button or check box has the same effect as clicking inside the circle or square itself.

ContrlVis determines whether or not the control will be visible. A value of *255* makes it visible; *0* is invisible.

ContrlHilite determines whether or not a control is currently active. A value of *255* means it's active; a value of *0* indicates inactive. An inactive control is dimmed and can't be manipulated with the mouse.

ContrlValue is the value currently stored by the control. For radio buttons and check boxes, this field is either *1* (filled in) or *0* (empty). For plain buttons, this field is always *0*, because buttons don't store information. For dials (scroll bars), this field can be any value between *contrlMin* and *contrlMax*.

You never have to worry with the *contrlDefProc*, *contrlData*, and *contrlAction* fields when using the standard control types—so we won't go into them.

ContrlRfCon, like the *refCon* of a window record, is for anything you want to use it for. Finally, *contrlTitle* is the text to be associated with the control (inside a simple button, or alongside a radio button or check box).

Key Control Manager Routines

As with windows, you have two options in creating controls: Create a control on the spot with *NewControl*, passing numerous parameters defining the fields in the *ControlRecord*; or fetch a control template from a resource file with *GetNewControl*. In practice, controls are usually stored in and read from resource files, and this is the method we use in this section's demonstration program:

```
function GetNewControl(controlID:Integer;theWindow:WindowPtr):ControlHandle;
```

To erase a control from its window and free up the memory it occupies, call *DisposeControl*:

```
procedure DisposeControl(theControl: ControlHandle);
```

Since the Window Manager's *DisposeWindow* call automatically disposes of all the controls associated with a particular window, you may never need to dispose of a control individually.

To draw all the controls in a window's control list, call *DrawControls*:

```
procedure DrawControls (theWindow: WindowPtr);
```

Calling this procedure draws all of the visible controls (either active or inactive, depending on their *contrlHilite* field) associated with *theWindow*. As always, the drawing won't have any effect if that part of the window is covered by other windows. Typically, you'll call *DrawControls* in response to an update event.

To change the status of a control from active to inactive or vice versa, and to redraw the control to indicate the transition, call

```
procedure HiliteControl(theControl: ControlHandle; hiliteState: Integer);
```

Passing *hiliteState = 0* makes the control active. A value between *1* and *253* means that particular part code should be highlighted (this applies to scroll bars only). A value of *255* makes the control inactive.

When a mouse-down occurs in the content of an active window containing controls, a program checks to see if the mouse-down occurred in one of them. The *FindControl* function makes this determination:

```
function FindControl(thePoint: Point; theWindow: WindowPtr;
                     var whichControl: ControlHandle): Integer;
```

If you notice a parallel between this call and *FindWindow*, you're starting to think the way the architects of the Toolbox intended. *FindControl* is passed both the point at which the *mouseDown* occurred and a pointer to the window in which it occurred. If the mouseDown didn't hit an active control, then *FindControl* sets *whichControl* to **nil** and returns the value *0*.

If the *mouseDown* happens in an active control, this function returns the part code of the control. The following integer constants are defined in unit *ToolIntf* for ease in testing the value returned by *FindControl*:

```
const
  inButton     = 10;                       { simple button }
  inCheckBox   = 11;        { a radio button or check box }
  inUpButton   = 20;              { scroll bar's Up arrow }
  inDownButton = 21;            { scroll bar's Down arrow }
  inPageUp     = 22;        { scroll bar's "page up" area }
  inPageDown   = 23;      { scroll bar's "page down" area }
  inThumb      = 129;                      { scroll box }
```

Controls

Note that *inCheckBox* (part code 11) applies equally to radio buttons. From the user's point of view, check boxes and radio buttons are very different; from a programming standpoint, they're identical.

There's one complicating factor to decoding *mouseDown* in controls, having to do with global and local coordinates. The Window Manager's *FindWindow* call (which must be able to return information about any window on the screen) works with global coordinates; that is, (0,0) is at the upper left-hand corner of the screen. By contrast, *FindControl* already knows the window in which the *mouseButton* occurs and, since controls live in the *GrafPort* of that window, expects points to be expressed in that *GrafPort*'s local coordinate system. So, (0,0) is the upper left-hand corner of the window's content region.

As a practical matter, all this means is that you must make QuickDraw's *GlobalToLocal* call on the point of the *mouseDown* before calling *FindControl*. We'll show how in just a minute.

If *FindControl* determines that a *mouseDown* did in fact occur in an active control, the next step is to call *TrackControl*:

```
function TrackControl(theControl:ControlHandle;startPt:Point;
                      actionProc:ProcPtr:Integer;
```

This routine doesn't return until the user releases the button, at which time you study the value returned to figure out what to do next. If it returns as *0*, then the user moved out of the control before releasing the button, in which case you do nothing. If it returns with the same part code that *FindControl* returned originally, then the user really intends to manipulate that control and you need to take action. For example, a radio button needs its value set to *1*; a check box must be set to the opposite of its current value.

Reading and Writing a Control's Value

Call *SetCtlValue* to set a control's value and *GetCtlValue* to read it. *GetCtlValue* redraws the control to indicate its new value.

```
procedure SetCtlValue(theControl: ControlHandle; theValue: Integer);
function GetCtlValue(theControl: ControlHandle): Integer;
```

ControlDemo.Pas

The following program, which is in folder Control Demo, builds on the foundation established by WindowDemo.Pas. One major difference is that

ControlDemo.Pas gets its window and control resources from a resource file. Therefore, instead of using *NewWindow* and *NewControl* (and passing 819 parameters to each), it uses *GetNewWindow* and *GetNewControl* (and passes only a couple of parameters).

This means that before you'll be able to execute this program, a resource file containing these resources must be available. To create the file, use RMaker on ControlDemo.R; it creates ControlDemo.Rsrc which has the necessary resources.

ControlDemo.R

This file contains "RMaker language" descriptions for three windows and five controls. Let's look at the definitions for one of each.

```
* resource file for Control demo program
* defines five controls and three windows

ControlDemo.Rsrc  ;; the output filename

Type CNTL
 ,128                ;; the resource ID
Soft                 ;; the button's text
144 15 160 75        ;; boundary rectangle (local coordinates)
Visible              ;; initially visible
2                    ;; i.e., radio button
1                    ;; refCon field initialized to 1
0 1 1                ;; minimum, maximum, startup value

Type WIND
 ,128                ;; the resource ID
Window 1             ;; the window's title
50 50 250 300        ;; boundary of window's content region (global)
Visible GoAway       ;; initially visible, has a close box
0                    ;; i.e., standard document window
0                    ;; refCon field initialized to 0
```

The first non-comment in an RMaker source file is the name to be given to the resultant resource file. This must match the name specified in the $R (use Resource file) compiler directive at the start of ControlDemo.Pas. This directive at the start of ControlDemo.Pas

```
{$R ControlDemo.Rsrc}
```

causes the resource file to be opened just before giving control to *ControlDemo*, so that its resources are available without the program having to make an explicit *OpenResFile* call.

Defining CNTL Resources

Control templates are defined by listing the following on consecutive lines:

- the resource ID
- the text of the control
- the boundary rectangle of the control (in local coordinates, top-left-bottom-right)
- the initial visibility status of the control
- the control type (unfortunately, constants aren't available here; 2 means a radio button)
- the control's reference constant
- the control's minimum, maximum, and startup values

For check boxes and radio buttons, use minimum = *0* and maximum = *1*. This particular radio button is initially on.

Defining WIND Resources

Window definitions contain the window's resource ID, title, and placement rectangle (in global coordinates, top-left-bottom-right). Next comes its initial visibility status and whether or not it contains a close box. Following is the window's type (*0* = standard document window) and, finally, its default reference constant value.

For more information about RMaker syntax, see Chapter 12 of the Turbo Pascal reference manual.

Running ControlDemo

Now compile and run ControlDemo.Pas. Play around with it for a while. The radio-button cluster controls the volume of the tone produced by the two simple buttons at the top. One thing to look for is this program's response to activate events. WindowDemo.Pas didn't worry about activate events because its windows had no controls to activate and deactivate. ControlDemo.Pas must ensure that any time the "control window" *isn't* the active window, its controls are dimmed. Similarly, when it becomes active, its controls must be undimmed.

To see this effect in action, drag the control window off the right so that no part of it overlaps the other windows (partially offscreen, if necessary). Click on one of the inactive windows. The screen now looks like this:

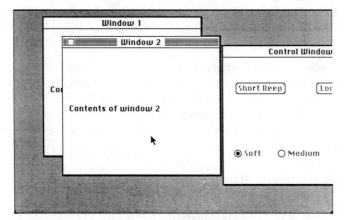

Figure 36.2: Inactive Controls

The controls are now inactive, to visually indicate that clicking inside them at this time would have no effect. Now click once anywhere in the control window. The program responds to the activate event by redrawing the controls in an undimmed state. No update events were generated, because no window contents were changed by this action.

Initializing ControlDemo

The Sound Manager

This program manipulates the volume of *SysBeep*s by calling the Sound Manager's *SetSoundVol* and *GetSoundVol* routines.

procedure GetSoundVol(level: Integer);

procedure SetSoundVol(level: Integer);

Level ranges from *0* (total silence) to *7* (case shaking). Since sound volume is a parameter users like to think they control with the Control Panel, this program saves this default setting at the start of the program and restores it at the very end.

Much of the burden of initialization has been shifted to RMaker and the resource mechanism. The line

```
aWindow:=GetNewWindow(128,nil,Pointer(-1));
```

causes a window template with resource ID 128 to be loaded from ControlDemo.Rsrc (a window record created in memory) and a document window to be drawn on the screen. The **nil** and Pointer(-1) parameters perform the same function as in the *NewWindow* call (**nil** = allocate storage for us; Pointer(-1) = open as topmost window).

In general, use resources where you can. Not only does this relieve your program's run-time workload, it allows the object form of a program to be adjusted by various resource-editing tools such as *ResEdit*. With a resource editor, we could adjust the positions of the controls and the default placement and size of all three windows without recompiling the application.

Loading Control Resources

Five controls (two buttons and three radio buttons) are attached to the third window with this loop:

```
for n := 128 to 132 do
   aControl := GetNewControl(n,aWindow);
```

Each call to *GetNewControl* reads the indicated control template from ControlDemo.Rsrc, allocates a *ControlRecord* and draws an active control with the appropriate default value at the appropriate place in the control window.

As we saw in WindowDemo when creating windows, each call to *GetNewControl* overwrites the address that was in *aControl* previously—effectively erasing a link to the control record. Much as the Window Manager tracks windows with a linked list, the controls associated with a given window are also in a list (incidentally, in the reverse order of creation—the "Long Beep" button is the first entry in the list).

The anchor of this list is the *controlList* field of the window record pointed to by *aWindow*. We'll lose this anchor when procedure *Initialize* ends and its local variables (*aWindow*, among them) disappear. But, as in WindowDemo, we'll get this pointer back when we need it.

Two observations about the window records now in memory: The first two have empty control lists (*controlList* = **nil**) and nonzero *refCon* fields (because of the assignment from *NewString*). The situation is reversed for the control window. It has a non-**nil** *controlList* and a zero *refCon*. These facts will come in handy later figuring out which window is which.

Update Events and Controls

Controls must be drawn in response to an update event just like everything else in a window's content region. The following statement determines whether the window involved in this particular event is the Control Window (in which case it draws the controls) or one of the other two (in which case it draws the string pointed to by *refCon*). It makes this determination by checking for a zero *refCon* field.

```
if windowPeek(theWindow)^.refCon = 0 then
  DrawControls(theWindow)
else
  {draw string}
```

Processing Activate Events

Clicking in an inactive window generates two activate events: A deactivate event for the window that used to be the active window, and an activate event for the new active window. Both are handled by this program's *DoActivate* procedure.

```
procedure DoActivate;
var
  theWindow: WindowPtr;
  theControl: ControlHandle;
begin
  theWindow := WindowPtr(theEvent.message);
  SetPort(theWindow);

  theControl := windowPeek(theWindow)^.controlList;
  while theControl <> nil do
  begin
    if Odd(theEvent.modifiers) then
      HiliteControl(theControl,0)
    else
      HiliteControl(theControl,255);
    theControl := theControl^^.nextControl;
  end;
end;
```

Whether an *activateEvt* represents a deactivate or an activate event is stored away in bit *0* of the *EventRecord*'s *modifiers* field. A *1* in this position indicates an activate event; *0* means a deactivate event. This routine works its way through the linked list of controls associated with this window (for Windows 1 and 2, it's a very short list).

Each control along the way is made either active (0 parameter for *HiliteControl*) or inactive (255). The binary numbering system is such that odd integers have a *1* in the least significant bit, so the expression

Odd(modifiers) is true only for activate events. You could alternatively make this determination with an **and** operation:

```
if (modifiers and 1) <> 0 then ...
```

Mouse-Downs

Because of the testing that must be performed after a mouse-down in the control window, this program's mouse-down processing is more involved than WindowDemo's. The nested *TestControls* procedure is called after the program has figured out that the mouse-down occurred in an active control window. Here's the code that makes that determination:

```
inContent: if theWindow <> FrontWindow then
               SelectWindow(theWindow)
           else
               if windowPeek(theWindow)^.refCon <> 0 then
                 SysBeep(10)
               else
                 TestControls;
```

Windows 1 and 2 have non-zero *refCon* fields, and the program's only response to a click in their content is to beep the speaker.

```
procedure TestControls;
var
   theControl: ControlHandle;
   tempControl: ControlHandle;

begin
   SetPort(theWindow);
   GlobalToLocal(theEvent.where);
   if FindControl(theEvent.where,theWindow,theControl) > 0 then
     case TrackControl(theControl,theEvent.where,nil) of
        inButton:   SysBeep(theControl^^.contrlRfCon);
        inCheckBox: begin
                      SetCtlValue(theControl,1);
                      case theControl^^.contrlRfCon of
                        1: SetSoundVol(1);
                        2: SetSoundVol(4);
                        3: SetSoundVol(7);
                      end;
                      tempControl := windowPeek(theWindow)^.controlList;
                      while tempControl <> nil do
                      begin
                        if (tempControl^^.contrlRfCon <= 3) and
                           (tempControl <> theControl) then
                           SetCtlValue(tempControl,0);
                        tempControl := tempControl^^.nextControl;
                      end;                            { while }
                    end;                         { inCheckBox }
       end;                             { case TrackControl }
   end;                                 { procedure TestControls }
```

First *TestControls* translates the position of the mouse-down from global (screen) coordinates into local (window) coordinates. So, after making *theWindow^* the current *GrafPort*, it calls *GlobalToLocal* to translate *theEvent.where* to the control window's local coordinate system.

The *FindControl* routine determines if any controls happened to be at this point. If so, it returns a positive value and *theControl* is set to point to the control that was clicked on. By examining the control record's reference constant (*theControl^^.contrlRfCon*), we can determine which control was pressed. (In ControlDemo.R, each control had a unique reference constant.)

Now that we know one of the five controls was hit, we call *TrackControl*. This routine provides visual feedback to the user by highlighting the control (and turning off the highlighting, if the user drags the mouse out of the control's active area). *TrackControl* returns when the mouse button is finally released.

At this point, the program has three possibilities to consider.

1. The button was released out of the control's active area, in which case it does nothing (the user changed his or her mind).
2. It was released in the active area of one of this window's two simple buttons.
3. It was released in one of this window's three radio buttons.

Assuming the second case (*inButton*), the program simply calls *SysBeep*, passing it a ticks parameter equal to the button's *contrlRfCon* field, which we set in the resource file to *10* for the "short" button and *60* for the "long" one.

Handling the Radio Buttons

Radio buttons connote a "one and only one" option—only one can be toggled *on* at any one time. Surprisingly, this characteristic isn't supported by the Control Manager; it's up to *ControlDemo* to make sure that when one of its radio buttons is clicked, that button gets turned on and the others turned off. If the mouse-down occurred in one of the radio buttons, we first turn on that button (whether it is already on or not):

```
SetCtlValue(theControl,1);
```

Next, based on its *contrlRfCon* field (1, 2, or 3), we use *SetSoundVol* to set the volume. The next click of the "short" or "long" button will now output a tone of the appropriate volume. Finally, we turn off the other two radio buttons—without regard for their current state. This is accomplished by traversing the linked list of controls associated with this window. We set to zero all controls that aren't simple buttons (we can tell the difference because they've got larger reference constants) **and** aren't *theControl*, which is the one that's supposed to be set (and already is).

Other than the new *DoActivate* routine and more complicated mouse-down processing, ControlDemo isn't that different from WindowDemo.

Review

Controls are graphic objects that can be manipulated with the mouse to cause an immediate action or control a future action. There are four predefined control types: simple buttons, radio buttons, check boxes, and scroll bars. Controls are always associated with a window and appear in the content region of that window. Control locations are specified in the local coordinate system of their owning window.

Control information is heap based and usually loaded from a resource file. Windows containing controls must draw their controls in response to update events, and controls in an inactive window must be inactivated (dimmed). After mouse-down events in an active window containing controls, a program checks to see which control (if any) the mouse-down occurred in. If a control was pressed, then the program tracks the mouse and sets the value of the control (and possibly related controls) appropriately.

37

Menus and Desk Accessories

Last chapter's control demonstration program came close to being a true (if skimpy) Macintosh application. In this chapter, we add a handful of statements and take it to full-fledged Macintosh status.

Menu Data Structures

Menus are accessed almost exclusively through handles. You will probably never have occasion to dereference a menu handle to look at any of the fields in a menu record, but, for the record, here they are:

```
type
  MenuHandle = ^MenuPtr;
  MenuPtr    = ^MenuInfo;
  MenuInfo = record
               menuID:      Integer;
               menuWidth:   Integer;
               menuHeight:  Integer;
               menuProc:    Integer;
               enableFlags: Integer;
               menuData:    Str255;
               {plus additional data}
             end;
```

Menus are almost always fetched from resource files. The term "menu" refers to a single pull-down menu, not the full collection of menus an application puts in its menu bar. In an RMaker source file, menus are described by listing a resource ID, a title (the text that goes on the menu bar), and, beneath it, the text of each option of that menu. Here's an example:

```
type MENU
  ,3 (4)           ;; ID = 3; attribute = 4 = pre-loaded
Edit               ;; title of menu
  Undo/Z           ;; first option = Undo; command-key equivalent
  (-               ;; a dimmed line separating Undo and Cut
  Cut/X
  Copy/C
  Paste/V
```

All resources have an associated *flag byte*. The placement of these so-called resource attributes within the flag byte is shown in the following figure.

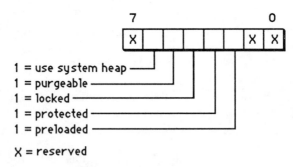

Figure 37.1: The Attribute Byte

For example, if the flag byte is 36 (hexadecimal 24, binary 0010 0100), then the associated resource is both purgeable and preloaded—that is, loaded into memory when the resource file is first opened.

When resources are defined in an RMaker source file, a value for the attribute byte can be specified along with the resource definition data; if no value is specified, then it is assumed to be zero. The flag byte is specified on the same line as the resource ID and enclosed in parentheses. For example, the MENU resource resulting from this RMaker definition

```
type MENU
,3 (4)           ;;4 = 0000 0100 = preload
Edit
  Undo/Z
  (-
  Cut/X
  Copy/C
  Paste/V
```

will be loaded into the application heap, unlocked and unpurgeable. It will be read into the heap when its resource file is first opened. To work correctly, menu resources must always be preloaded and unpurgeable.

Special Characters in the Menu Item String

The string defining a menu item can contain certain characters for creating special effects. For example, a slash followed by a capital letter (Copy/C) causes that item to be given a *Command*-key equivalent:

Figure 37.2: Command-Key Equivalents

Starting an entry with a left parenthesis produces a menu item that is initially disabled (dimmmed; unselectable). The string (- from the previous example produces a line separating options. This technique is useful to separate logically distinct choices in the same menu.

An RMaker syntax convention is that a backslash (\) followed by two hexadecimal digits indicates the character with that ASCII value. This is the sort of exotic detail we minimized in this book, but it so happens that this technique is required to produce the Apple symbol used to represent the desk accessory menu. The Apple character appears only in the Chicago font, so you typically indicate this character in an RMaker source file by its code value, which happens to be 14 hex. Wherever you see "\14," think Apple symbol.

Menu Manager Routines

Before using any Menu Manager routine, call *InitMenus*:

procedure InitMenus;

An application begins the process of setting up its menu bar by calling *GetMenu* as necessary, to fetch each menu template from a resource file.

function GetMenu(resourceID: Integer): MenuHandle;

The address of each menu record returned by *Getmenu* is assigned to a variable of type *MenuHandle*. A program usually has as many global variables of type *MenuHandle* as it has menus.

Unlike *GetNewControl* and *GetNewWindow*, *GetMenu* doesn't put the menu on the screen, only into memory. Once an application has fetched all its menus, they're inserted into the menu bar with *InsertMenu* and drawn by the *DrawMenuBar* procedure.

```
procedure InsertMenu (theMenu: MenuHandle; beforeID: Integer);
procedure DrawMenuBar;
```

There's a minor complication to this process. Part of a well-bred application's job is to support desk accessories (DAs). Your users expect the first menu to be named "\14" and, in it, they expect to find the unique assortment of DAs installed in their System file. This makes the Apple menu unlike the others, in that its contents can't be fully defined in the RMaker file. The Toolbox handles this situation with the *AddResMenu* call, which in one fell swoop adds the names of all desk accessories to a variable of type *MenuHandle*.

```
procedure AddResMenu (theMenu: MenuHandle; theType: ResType);
```

The *ResType* of desk accessories isn't anything reasonable like 'DACC' or 'DSKA' but 'DRVR' (for driver).

Interpreting MouseDowns in the Menu Bar

Having drawn some menu titles, an application needs to respond to them. If you recall, there's a predefined constant named *inMenuBar* used to decode the return value of the *FindWindow* call. The lion's share of the response is calling the Menu Manager's *MenuSelect* routine once you know that a *mouseDown* has occurred in the menu bar:

```
function MenuSelect(startPt: Point): LongInt;
```

This routine handles everything until the mouse button goes up—pulling down the appropriate menu, highlighting selections as you drag down, pulling down another menu should you drag into another menu's area, the works. The long integer it returns contains the number of the menu selected (1 = leftmost menu) in its most significant word and the number of the option selected (1 = topmost item) in its least significant word. Typically, an application branches to a procedure based on the menu selected and then handles each selection appropriately.

Fine Points

That's about it for the Menu Manager. Of course, there are all sorts of options: Individual menu items and entire menus can (and should) be dimmed (that is, made unselectable) whenever choosing them would be inappropriate. For example, Turbo Pascal dims several menu items when there's no text window open and therefore nothing for the commands to act on.

It's possible to add entire menus to the menu bar after it has already been displayed and to add items to individual menus. You can alter the content of existing menus. You can cause items to be marked with a check mark or other character, displayed in a particular text style (such as boldface), or have an associated icon. You can even set how many times a selection flashes when chosen.

To perform these feats, read *Inside Macintosh's* Menu Manager chapter.

Supporting Desk Accessories

An application that has an Apple menu containing DA names had better be ready to perform should a user choose a DA. Supporting DAs isn't especially difficult, just strange. Some things the DA does for itself; others you have to do for it.

If the user chooses a DA from the Apple menu, the application's response is to call *OpenDeskAcc*:

function OpenDeskAcc(theAcc: Str255): Integer;

Parameter *theAcc*—the name of the DA—is obtained by the Menu Manager's *GetItem* routine:

procedure GetItem(theMenu:MenuHandle;theItem:Integer; **var** itemString:Str255);

GetItem returns in *itemString* the text of a menu's *theItem*th selection. Remember that an application doesn't have this information until run time; *AddResMenu* fetches the names and puts them in the Apple menu without telling us what they were.

DAs—their code, resources, and other data—all go in the application heap, so after opening one you have less memory in the heap than previously. DAs generally open windows that go into the Window Manager's linked list right along with yours. Guess whose job it is to see to it that this window is handled correctly?

Mouse-Downs and DA Windows

If *FindWindow* returns the value equal to the predefined constant *inSysWindow*, then you know that the click happened inside a DA. Without determining which one, simply call

procedure SystemClick(theEvent: EventRecord; theWindow: WindowPtr);

The Toolbox passes the event information to the appropriate DA.

DA Menus

Many DAs perform standard editing operations (Undo, Cut, Copy, Paste, and Clear). The User Interface Guidelines require that, if an application supports DAs, it have an Edit menu. Moreover, that menu's first six lines should contain Undo, a blank line, Cut, Copy, Paste, and Clear, in that order.

That's why applications for which "cutting" and "copying" don't make sense have an Edit menu with these options. (Admittedly, it's not one of the most intuitive aspects of the user interface.) It's your job to make sure that a DA that uses Cut, Copy, et al., gets wind of these selections when they're made. This operation is performed by the Desk Manager's *SystemEdit* routine:

function SystemEdit(editCmd: Integer): Boolean;

Call *SystemEdit* when the user chooses one of the Edit menu's first five commands. If you've arranged this menu in the standard way and determined that a selection from the Edit menu has occurred, the expression

SystemEdit(menuItem-1);

is required, where *menuItem* is the low-order word returned by *MenuSelect*. *SystemEdit* returns False if the active window *isn't* a DA—meaning that if your application works with this menu, it should do so now. If it returns True, then that selection did in fact apply to a DA and you don't have to worry about it.

DAs require even more favors from their hosts. Some DAs need processor attention every so often if their window is active or not. For example, the Alarm Clock DA continues to count off the seconds as you edit text within Turbo Pascal.

An application sees to it that DAs needing attention get it by periodically calling the *SystemTask* routine, preferably from within the main event loop:

```
procedure SystemTask;
```

If no DAs have been opened or if they don't require periodic updates, then *SystemTask* quickly returns.

Summarizing DA Support Requirements

To support DAs, an application must

- have an Apple menu
- load this menu with the names of all DAs in the System file
- launch the DA when one is chosen
- pass control of mouse-down events when one occurs in a DA's window
- make selections of the five standard Edit menu items available to DAs
- call *SystemTask* in the main event loop

MenuDemo.Pas

The next evolution of our demonstration program is called MenuDemo.Pas; it, too, can be found on your Turbo Tutor disk. A true Macintosh application, MenuDemo supports DAs and has overlapping windows, controls, and pull-down menus.

Play around with this program for a while. Open a DA, perhaps the Alarm Clock. Note how the formerly topmost window becomes inactive. Now click in one of the application's windows. The clock is deactivated but keeps right on ticking, thanks to the attention it gets from *SystemTask*. Open half a dozen desk accessories; notice the juggling performed by the Window Manager (called by our program). Our program doesn't have to get any more complicated to deal with sixteen windows rather than four.

Only a handful of changes were necessary to turn ControlDemo.Pas into MenuDemo.Pas. Each change is flagged by the notation "(* addition *)." Let's work through them.

New Data Structures

This program's four menu records are tracked by a new global variable:

```
theMenus: array [1..4] of MenuHandle;
```

Each element of this array represents a menu. The first element will represent the Apple menu, the second the File menu, and so on.

Procedure Initialize

In addition to what it did before, *Initialize* now sets up four menus. We inserted a call to *InitMenus* after calls to initialize QuickDraw and the Font and Window managers.

The menus are loaded from the resource file in this **for** loop:

```
for n := 1 to 4 do
   theMenus[n] := GetMenu(n);
```

At this point, the raw menu information structure has been allocated in memory, but not in a form that can be put in the menu bar. Moreover, the Apple menu is initially devoid of the names of the DAs in the current System file. The next statement takes care of that problem:

```
AddResMenu(theMenus[1],'DRVR');
```

Designed for just this purpose, procedure *AddResMenu* adds the name of every resource of type 'DRVR' to the *menuRecord* associated with *theMenus[1]*. Next, all four menus are placed in the menu bar with *InsertMenu*:

```
InsertMenu(theMenus[n],0);
```

The zero parameter in this call means to add this menu to the end of the current menu bar, that is, to the right of the rightmost menu. Note that "adding to the menu bar" doesn't put anything on the screen. That's accomplished by the final statement of procedure *Initialize*:

```
DrawMenuBar;
```

At this point, we've draw four menu titles in the menu bar. A program with menus had better be prepared should the user choose one of these menus. Let's follow through the processing this program performs in dealing with a mouse-down on top of the Beep menu. We'll start at the main event loop—assume that the update events drawing the contents of the three windows have already been completed.

```
repeat
  SystemTask;
  if GetNextEvent(everyEvent,theEvent) then
    case theEvent.what of
      mouseDown:   DoMouseDown;
      keyDown:     DoKeyDown;
```

```
        autoKey:     SysBeep(1);
        updateEvt:   DoUpdate;
        activateEvt: DoActivate;
      end;
until done;
```

The call to *SystemTask* returns almost instantly because, at this moment, there aren't any DAs open that need processing. Next we call *GetNextEvent*, and it returns *theEvent.what* value representing a mouse-down. So we call the routine that decodes mouse-down events:

```
procedure DoMouseDown;
  .
  .
  .
  case code of
    inMenuBar:    DoCommand(MenuSelect(theEvent.where));
  .
  .
  .
end;
```

Before we simply beeped at menu bar mouse-downs; now we've got four menus to handle. Virtually all of the work involved in decoding a mouse-down in the menu bar is handled by the call to the Toolbox's *MenuSelect* function, which we call in passing on our way to this program's *DoCommand* procedure.

Calling *MenuSelect* this way has the effect of passing a long integer parameter to *DoCommand*; this long integer represents the number of the menu chosen (if any) and the individual item of that menu chosen (if any). Here's *DoCommand*:

```
procedure DoCommand(menuResult:LongInt);
begin
  theMenu := HiWord(menuResult);
  theItem := LoWord(menuResult);
  case theMenu of
    1: DoAppleMenu;
    2: done := True;
    3: if SystemEdit(theItem-1) then;
    4: if theItem = 1 then SysBeep(60) else SysBeep(10);
  end;
  HiliteMenu(0);
end;
```

DoCommand's first move is to decode this long integer with Turbo's built-in long integer separators, *HiWord* and *LoWord*. *HiWord* returns the most significant word of a long integer; *LoWord* the least significant word.

Most of this program's menu processing occurs within a single **case** statement based on the menu chosen. For example, for a choice within menu #2 (the File menu), we set done to True; since Quit is the only option of this menu, we don't bother to check *theItem*. For the Beep menu (#4), we call *SysBeep* with an appropriate ticks parameter.

While the operation required by a menu selection is being performed, the name of the menu is highlighted in the menu bar (*MenuSelect* leaves it this way). *DoCommand*'s final act is to turn off this highlighting:

```
HiliteMenu(0);
```

DAs and Menus

The other two choices (Apple menu and Edit menu) relate to DAs. As we mentioned, DAs frequently perform editing operations. We must therefore pass control to the *SystemEdit* routine when such a menu selection occurs. *SystemEdit* returns True if the menu selection was in fact intended for a DA and False if it wasn't. Since our program doesn't do cutting and pasting, we don't care what it returns. Calling it in a dummy **if** statement saves us the aggravation of declaring a local boolean variable to hold this value.

A selection from the Apple menu means that the user has picked a DA. It's our job to start that DA running. This is accomplished by the two-statement *DoAppleMenu* procedure:

```
procedure DoAppleMenu;
var
  name: Str255;
begin
  GetItem(theMenus[1],theItem,name);
  if OpenDeskAcc(name) > 0 then ;
end;
```

Since the *OpenDeskAcc* routine requires the name of the DA to be opened, we first fetch that string with a call to the Menu Manager's *GetItem* procedure. We pass it a handle to the Apple menu and the number of the item that was chosen on it.

With or without an open DA, program flow continues back at the main event loop.

Key-Down Processing for Command-Key Equivalents

Unlike its predecessor, this program responds intelligently to key-down events. This is not because we're going to do word processing in one of its windows, but to permit menu selection with Command-key equivalents.

Key-down events (but not auto-key events) are sent off to be processed by this program's *DoKeyDown* procedure:

```
procedure DoKeydown;
var
  c: Char;
begin
  c := Chr(theEvent.message and charCodeMask);
  if (theEvent.modifiers and cmdKey) <> 0 then
    DoCommand(MenuKey(c))
  else
    SysBeep(1);
end;
```

This program only cares about key-downs if an examination of the EventRecord's modifier field reveals that the Command key was down when this key-down was generated. If it wasn't, then the program simply beeps.

If Command was down, regardless of what character was typed, we call the Menu Manager's *MenuKey* function. *MenuKey* does for *Command*-key equivalents what *MenuSelect* does for mouse-downs in the menu bar. If the character passed to *MenuKey* happens to be defined by any item in any menu, then it highlights the indicated menu and returns a long integer value equal to what *MenuSelect* would have returned for a selection of that item. Consequently, we're able to call the same *DoCommand* routine that's called after mouse-downs in the menu bar. If the character typed doesn't happen to be a Command-key equivalent, then *MenuKey* returns zero in its most significant word, a value ignored by *DoCommand*.

Extra Credit

Give this program an option to beep once for every open DA window. This requires adding the *BeepForDAs* routine we presented in Chapter 35. Call this routine after a selection of a new, third item in the Beep menu (Beep for DAs); you'll have to add this item to the Beep menu in MenuDemo.R and recompile the resource file.

Review

MenuDemo.Pas *is* a true Macintosh program: It supports DAs, pull-down menus, and controls; and it has multiple overlapping windows. Much of its length is devoted to decoding mouse-downs and other standard functions. MenuDemo.Pas can serve as a template for your own applications.

Like controls, menus are usually read from resource files and accessed through handles. RMaker allows you to define as many menus as you need. Menus are loaded from resource files and placed in the menu bar at program initialization time. An application responds to a mouse-down in the menu bar by calling the *MenuSelect* routine, which returns the menu number and item chosen. For keyboard equivalents, call *MenuKey*.

To support DAs, an application must have an Apple menu containing the names of the DAs in the current System file. When a selection is made from this menu, launch the DA with *OpenDeskAcc*. Call *SystemEdit* when the user chooses a standard Edit menu item. To give open DAs processing time, call *SystemTask* in the main event loop.

38

Dialogs

As ControlDemo shows, it's awkward to decode mouse-downs when the active window contains controls. If an application requires a dozen or more such windows, it can become hellishly awkward. To simplify the process of working with controls, the architects of the Toolbox created the notion of a *dialog box*—basically, a window containing controls. A dialog box communicates with background text and the placement and value of its controls; the user talks back with the mouse and keyboard. Thus, a "dialog" takes place.

In addition to background text and controls, dialog boxes can contain pictures (in the QuickDraw sense), icons, and "editText" items in which the user can enter and edit text.

Strictly speaking, the Dialog Manager and the dialog boxes it creates aren't really necessary, since the same thing can be done with appropriate calls to other routines, as in ControlDemo.Pas. The Dialog Manager simply makes it easier.

Classes of Dialogs

There are three basic kinds of dialog boxes. *Modal* dialog boxes are the most common. They're called modal because, when one appears, the mode of the program changes. When a modal dialog box is on the screen, you can't do some things that the user interface normally permits, like pull down menus and activate other windows. In other words, you're in a mode.

Modal dialogs aren't processed in the main event loop; that's one reason they're easier to work with than standard windows containing controls. Instead, dialogs are brought onto the screen as a result of a menu selection or some other action, and program flow doesn't return to the main event loop until the dialog has gone away. For example, choosing Print... from Turbo Pascal's File menu invokes the following modal dialog box:

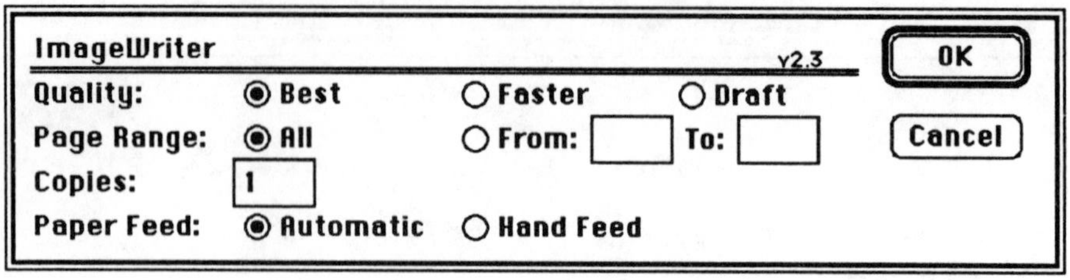

Figure 38.1: A Modal Dialog Box

A *modeless* dialog, on the other hand, is a lot like the control window of ControlDemo.Pas. Modeless dialogs behave like just another window on the desktop. Whether active or inactive, you continue to have access to other windows and to the menu bar. Some word processors use modeless dialogs to implement Find and Replace functions (Turbo Pascal uses modal boxes).

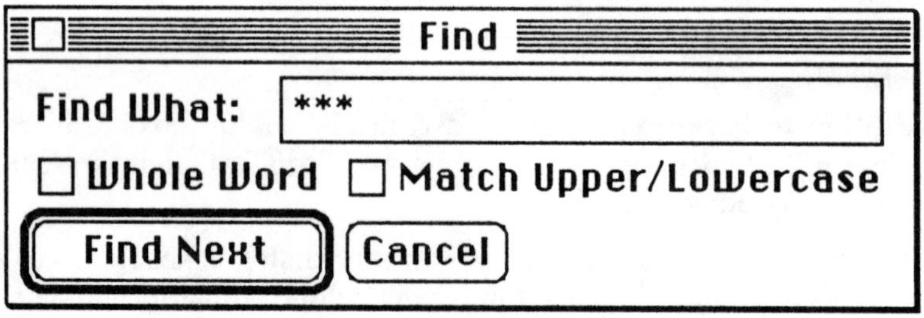

Figure 38.2: A Modeless Dialog Box

An *alert* is a simple form of modal dialog used for warnings and reporting errors. It contains at most two controls, typically, "OK" and "Cancel." The user doesn't "dialog" with an alert box; he or she simply reads and then dismisses it.

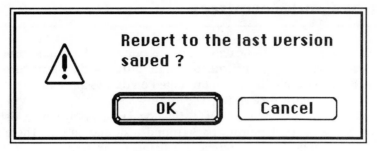

Figure 38.3: An Alert

Dialog Data Structures

The primary data structure of the Dialog Manager is the Dialog record.

```
type DialogRecord = record
                window:    WindowRecord;
                items:     handle;
                textH:     TEHandle;
                editField: Integer;
                editOpen:  Integer;
                aDefItem:  Integer;
            end
```

The *items* field points to the dialog's *item list*—the series of controls, icons, background text—that are the contents of this dialog. The majority of the fields in this record have to do with *editText* items, a topic we'll discuss shortly. The first field in a *DialogRecord* is a *WindowRecord*. The Dialog Manager is therefore able to get away with the following definition:

```
type DialogPtr = WindowPtr;
```

Since a *WindowPtr* is the same thing as a *GrafPtr*, a *DialogPtr* is a *GrafPtr* too. Consequently, you can pass variables of type *DialogPtr* to QuickDraw routines that expect *GrafPtr* parameters (for example, *GetPort*). And, as a *DialogPtr* points to a window, you can make Window Manager calls with them. To get at the fields past the embedded *WindowRecord*, you require a pointer of type *DialogPeek*:

```
type DialogPeek = ^DialogRecord;
```

In practice, you'll almost never need variables of type *DialogPeek*. There are routines built into the Dialog Manager you'll use in lieu of accessing the fields of a dialog record directly.

Dialogs and Resources

The Dialog Manager leans heavily on the resource mechanism to provide it with data structures; it's difficult to create a dialog data structure from scratch. Basically, each dialog is represented on disk as a resource of *resType* DLOG—a template describing the dialog's size, window type, and title—and a resource of type DITL (Dialog ITem List), which lists the content of the dialog (controls, background text, and so on). There's one entry in the item list for each item in the dialog. For example, a radio button counts as one entry, as does a string of background text.

Dialogs and RMaker

The following RMaker fragment defines a fairly complex (10-item) modal dialog box, consisting of DLOG resource 256 and DITL resource 256.

```
type DLOG
    ,256 (36)          ;; 36 = 32 (purgeable) + 4 (preloaded)
sample dialog          ;; title (won't show in this type of window)
30 100 230 412         ;; bounding box
Visible NoGoAway
1                      ;; dBoxProc type window--standard modal dialog wind
0                      ;; refCon
256                    ;; resource ID of its associated item list

Type DITL              ;; DLOG #256's item list
    ,256 (36)          ;; this number must match last number of DLOG def
10                     ;; number of items following

BtnItem Enabled        ;; item #1; a simple button
180 240 200 300
Cancel

BtnItem Enabled        ;; item #2; ditto
70 70 90 130
Long

BtnItem Enabled        ;; item #3; ditto
70 170 90 230
Short

RadioItem Enabled      ;; item #4; a radio button
120 15 140 75
Soft

RadioItem Enabled      ;; item #5; ditto
120 90 140 160
Medium
```

```
RadioItem Enabled          ;; item #6; ditto
120 195 140 250
Loud

CheckItem Enabled          ;; item #7, a check box
145 15 165 200
Double duration

EditTextItem Enabled       ;; item #8, an EditText item
180 180 200 210
60

StatText Disabled          ;; item #9, background (static) text
180 15 200 170
Duration of long beep

StatText Disabled          ;; item #10, ditto
10 100 30 350
Beep Dialog Box
```

The description of a DLOG template is similar to that of a window, except that it contains a "hook" to an item list. The particular dialog box described here will be stored as DLOG resource 256 and its item list as DITL resource 256 (they don't have to be the same, but usually are). At run time, you specify the resource ID of the DLOG template; its associated item list is fetched automatically.

Describing Items in the Item List

The description of controls in an item list is considerably terser than that ordinarily required for controls. It takes eight lines to describe a radio button as a CNTL resource,

```
type CNTL
 ,128
Soft
144 15 160 75
Visible
2                          ;; i.e., radio button
1                          ;; rfCon field
0 1 1                      ;; minimum, maximum, startup value
```

and only three in an item list,

```
RadioButton
144 15 160 75
Soft
```

Unfortunately, you can't set the startup value or reference constant of a control in an item list—but there are ways around this limitation.

RMaker knows how to make several types of dialog items: Static (background) text, editable text, simple buttons, radio buttons, check boxes, icons, and, for more elaborate graphics, QuickDraw pictures. The general syntax for defining an item is

```
ItemType
boundingBox (top-left-bottom-right)
associatedText (or resourceID)
```

RMaker doesn't have an incredibly sophisticated parser; only the first letter of an item type is significant. Consequently,

```
RadioButtons
RaptureOfTheDeep
```

both define a radio button item.

Each entry in a dialog's item list can be either *enabled* or *disabled*; by default, all items are enabled. An item is disabled by adding any word that starts with "D" after the item name. The user can't interact with a dialog's disabled items. Clicking in them has no effect. Typically, only *StatText* items are disabled.

For more information on RMaker's item list syntax, see Chapter 12 of the Turbo Pascal reference manual.

EditText Items

EditText items are miniature word-processing windows embedded within dialog boxes.

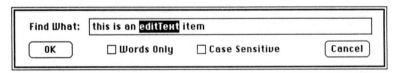

Figure 38.4: An EditText Item

The Dialog Manager implements these items by making appropriate calls to *TextEdit* (a manager that *Inside Macintosh* doesn't call a manager, for some reason). *TextEdit* provides sufficient editing muscle to build an entire editor around. (In fact, creating editors is the traditional subject matter of Macintosh programming tutorials.)

In practice, most programs let the Dialog Manager make the *TextExit* calls to manipulate the values of these items. The Dialog Manager has routines to read and write the string contents of *editText* items.

Dialog Manager Routines

A program that intends to use dialogs sees to it that appropriate resources of type DLOG are available at run time. Then, as circumstances warrant, the program loads them into memory and draws them on the screen with *GetNewDialog*:

```
function GetNewDialog(dialogID: Integer; dStorage: Ptr; behind: WindowPtr)
                    : DialogPtr;
```

This call is reminiscent of *GetNewWindow*—especially as *DialogPtr* equals *WindowPtr*. As with *GetNewWindow*, pass **nil** as the *dStorage* parameter and *GetNewDialog* creates storage on the heap for the dialog record. Pass *Pointer(-1)* as the *behind* parameter to open the dialog on top of existing windows.

When you're through with a dialog, call *DisposDialog* to erase it from the screen and free up the memory it occupies:

```
procedure DisposDialog(theDialog: DialogPtr);
```

ProcPtrs: Customizing ModalDialog

After *GetNewDialog* has read a dialog template and its item list into memory and drawn it on the screen, a program enters a loop in which it repeatedly calls the lynchpin of dialog processing, *ModalDialog*, and acts on the integer value it returns.

```
procedure ModalDialog(filterProc: ProcPtr; var itemHit: Integer);
```

With practically no controlling parameters, *ModalDialog* isn't the ultimate in flexibility. So, like many Toolbox routines, *ModalDialog* allows you to customize its operation with a routine of your own. You inform *ModalDialog* of this by passing a non-**nil** *filterProc* parameter that points to the routine, which then gets control every time an event is generated when the dialog is on the screen. It's up to the filter routine to decide what to do about it.

Unit *MemTypes* defines a *ProcPtr* as the same thing as a *Ptr*. In practice, you create one by applying the @ operator to the name of a procedure:

```
ModalDialog(@MyCustomRoutine,itemHit);
```

If you're happy with the default operation of *ModalDialog*—as we are in this chapter's demo program—then pass **nil** as the *filterProc* parameter. If you need more control, pass the address of a suitable filter procedure (and read the Dialog Manager chapter of *Inside Macintosh*).

Processing ItemHit

ModalDialog doesn't return until the user has clicked in the rectangle of an enabled item. During this interval, the user won't be able to work with other windows or menus; a click outside the dialog produces a warning beep. *ModalDialog* does, however, see to the needs of DAs that may be open, by calling *SystemTask* periodically.

When it finally returns, *ModalDialog* will have set its *itemHit* parameter to the item number of the radio button or *editText* item or whatever was clicked on. The first item listed in the RMaker source file is item number 1.

What happens next depends on what sort of item *itemHit* is. If it represents a simple button named OK or Cancel, you'll probably dispose the dialog and proceed accordingly. If it was an *editText* item, you'll want to read the string contents of that field. If *itemHit* is a radio button, you'll want to set its value to 1 (and turn off the other radio buttons in that group). Unfortunately, the Dialog Manager doesn't automatically set control values for us.

Getting Information on the Items in the Item List

To set the value of a control, you need to call *SetCtlValue*. Since *SetCtlValue* expects a handle to the control record (which *GetNewDialog* put out in the heap, somewhere), you'll have to get a handle to the control that needs setting. This is a task for the Dialog Manager's *GetDItem* routine:

```
procedure GetDItem(theDialog: DialogPtr; itemNo: Integer;
                var itemType: Integer;
                var item: Handle;
                var box: Rect);
```

GetDItem takes in two bits of information and returns three. Given the indicated dialog and item number, it returns the information about that particular item: its type (such as *radioButton* or *staticText*, encoded as an integer); a handle to its underlying data structure (for controls, this is a *ControlHandle*); and, finally, its bounding box.

For example, if *ModalDialog* returns an *itemHit* value of 3 and the program knows that the third item in the list is a radio button, it could make the following calls to get the handle to the button's control record and then set its value to 1:

```
GetDItem(theDialog,3,temp,Handle(myControlHandle),r);
SetCtlVal(myControlHandle,1);
```

temp is an integer variable (we already know that item three is a radio button, so we don't care what it returns) and *r* is a rectangle. After setting this button to 1 (and other radio buttons in its cluster to 0), we call *ModalDialog* again to handle the next thing the user does. (He or she may click another radio button in the same group.)

A Dialog Manager convention is that pressing Return is a substitute for clicking the first item in the item list. Therefore, many dialog boxes make a simple button entitled "OK" the first item in the item list. If *ModalDialog* returns *itemHit* equal to 1, then you don't know—and don't care—if the user pressed Return or clicked the OK button.

Changing this standard behavior is a classic application for a filter procedure.

Getting Information About EditText Items

The key to working with *editText* items is to use the *GetIText* and *SetIText* procedures:

```
procedure GetIText(item: Handle; var text: Str255);
procedure SetIText(item: Handle; text: Str255);
```

An *editText* item begins life with the string content assigned by its definition in an RMaker file. After the user has played with it (as determined by a suitable *itemHit* value returned by *ModalDialog*), use *GetIText* to see what the value is now. To change the text (perhaps to suggest a different response), use *SetIText*. Both routines expect a handle to the structure used to store this text; you get this from *GetDItem*.

Program DialogDemo.Pas

Your Turbo Tutor disk contains a text file named DialogDemo.Pas, with a matching RMaker source file, DialogDemo.R. If the resource file isn't already created (DialogDemo.Rsrc), then you need to bring RMaker's talents to bear on DialogDemo.R. Bring each file up in a separate text window and then compile and run the program.

The Beep menu from MenuDemo.Pas is gone. This function is supplanted by an elaborate dialog box, invoked by choosing Beep... from the File menu. The ellipsis after "Beep" isn't accidental: The User Interface Guidelines require that menu selections that invoke dialog boxes include ellipses to indicate that there's more to come.

DialogDemo.R defines two dialogs, each with a matching item list. The first is described earlier in this chapter. The second is simpler and contains mostly static text; it comes up in response to the About DialogDemo... selection of the   menu. Let's zero in on this dialog's item list:

```
type DITL
  ,257 (36)
4                             ;; four items

BtnItem Enabled
170 240 190 300
OK

StatText Disabled
65 55 85 300
Dialog Demo of Turbo Tutor

StatText Disabled
100 55 120 300
(C) 1987 Borland International

StatText Disabled
175 10 195 200
Memory: ^0  ^1
```

Its fourth item is peculiar—a static text item containing the string *Memory: ^0 ^1*. If you've run the program, you know that these digits and carets don't appear in the About DialogDemo... box. *^0* and *^1* stand in for text provided at run time—RMaker language string variables, if you will. Before this box is put on the screen, a Dialog Manager routine called *ParamText* provides the string data to be plugged into these stand-ins:

procedure ParamText(s1,s2,s3,s4: Str255);

s1 replaces *^0*, *s2* replaces *^1*, and so on. If a dialog box doesn't require four stand-ins, then simply pass the null string ('') for the extras.

DialogDemo uses this feature to display the size of largest contiguous block in the heap (returned by the Memory Manager's *MaxMem* call), as well as the total number of bytes in the heap (returned by *FreeMem*). If your heap is relatively unfragmented, these values will be close.

Experiment with this simple heap diagnostic by repeatedly opening desk accessories and choosing About DialogDemo. How much memory does each DA steal from the heap? When the DA terminates, is all the memory given back? It's not unknown for DAs to leave permanent islands in the heap even after they've said good night. (When creating your own DAs, remember that a good DA behaves like a visitor to a national park, leaving nothing but footprints.)

Working with the Beep Dialog

The Dialog Manager simplifies things, but not as much as you may hope. This program's *DoBeepDialog* routine, called in response to choosing the first item under the File menu, demonstrates the nontrivial process of interacting with the user as he or she manipulates the controls of a dialog.

```
procedure DoBeepDialog;
const
  cancelBtn    = 1;
  longBtn      = 2;
  shortBtn     = 3;
  softBtn      = 4;
  mediumBtn    = 5;
  loudBtn      = 6;
  doubleCkBox  = 7;
  durationText = 8;

var
  saveSoundVol: Integer;
  theDialog : DialogPtr;
  itemHit: Integer;
  theType: Integer;
  r: Rect;
  radButton: array [softBtn..loudBtn] of ControlHandle;
  checkBox: ControlHandle;
  done: Boolean;
  n: Integer;

  h: Handle;
  s: Str255;
  duration: LongInt;
```

```pascal
begin
  GetSoundVol(saveSoundVol);
  SetSoundVol(1);
  duration := 60;

  theDialog := GetNewDialog(256, nil, Pointer(-1));
  for n := softBtn to loudBtn do
    GetDItem(theDialog,n,theType,Handle(radButton[n]),r);
    SetCtlValue (radButton[softBtn],1);

    GetDItem(theDialog,doubleCkBox,theType,Handle(checkBox),r);
    GetDItem(theDialog,durationText,theType,h,r);

  done := False;
  repeat
    ModalDialog(nil,itemHit);
    case itemHit of
      cancelBtn    : done := True;
      longBtn      : SysBeep(duration + duration * GetCtlValue(checkBox));
      shortBtn     : SysBeep(10 + 10 * GetCtlValue(checkBox));
      softBtn      : begin
                        SetSoundVol(1);
                        for n := softBtn to loudBtn do
                          SetCtlValue(radButton[n],Ord(n = itemHit));
                     end;
      mediumBtn    : begin
                        SetSoundVol(4);
                        for n := softBtn to loudBtn do
                          SetCtlValue(radButton[n],Ord(n = itemHit));
                     end;
      loudBtn      : begin
                        SetSoundVol(7);
                        for n := softBtn to loudBtn do
                          SetCtlValue(radButton[n],Ord(n = itemHit));
                     end;
      doubleCkBox  : begin
                        n := GetCtlValue(checkBox);
                        n := n xor 1;
                        SetCtlValue(checkBox,n);
                     end;
      durationText : begin
                        GetIText(h,s);
                        StringToNum(s,duration);
                     end;
    end;
  until done;
  DisposDialog(theDialog);
  SetSoundVol(saveSoundVol);
end;
```

Copious Constants

It's good practice to create an integer constant corresponding to the item number of each selectable item in a dialog's item list. This takes extra work on the front end, but the readability it brings to a routine compensates in reduced debugging time.

The beauty of modal dialog processing is that it's far from the confusion of the main event loop. The call to *GetNewDialog* at the start reads the dialog (and its item list) from disk and puts it on the screen. *GetNewDialog* also takes care of deactivating the window it covers. The beep dialog stays on the screen until it is disposed at the end of the procedure.

The most complex processing of *DoBeepDialog* involves radio buttons. For efficiency in turning on the selected button of a group (and turning off the unselected ones), this program calls *GetDItem* to fetch the control handle for each of the three radio buttons. These handles are stored in array *radButton* for later retrieval.

We use the handle to the Soft button immediately to turn it on with *SetCtlValue*. (By default, radio buttons and check boxes read from an item list initially have a value of 0.) The poor user should never be subjected to a group of radio buttons without any being pushed in.

This setting up is performed every time procedure *DoBeepDialog* is entered. So, no matter where you leave the volume set, it'll be back at Soft the next time you bring up this box. This isn't desirable in all cases. If you want the value to hang around between invocations, you'll need global variables to track the state of the dialog's controls between invocations.

Next, *DoBeepDialog* enters a sort of mini event loop, in which *ModalDialog* assumes the task of reading the keyboard and watching for *mouseDowns*. *ModalDialog* doesn't return until the user performs a *mouseDown* in one of the enabled items, then it assigns the number of this item to local variable *itemHit*. Actually, since this routine has an *editText* item, *keyDown* events result in an *itemHit* for the *editText* item.

Most of *DoBeepDialog*'s work is performed by a **case** statement that tests *itemHit* against constants that relate to each item.

For the cancel button, we set *done* to True and thereby terminate the loop.

For the long button, we perform a beep of either *duration* ticks or, if the "double duration" checkbox is on, 2 × *duration* ticks. *duration*'s length depends on the value in the *editText* item; it is *60* by default.

For the three radio buttons, processing is tricky. First, the volume is set to a suitable level. Next, we execute a loop that executes the following statement for each radio button:

```
SetCtlValue(radButton[n],Ord(n = itemHit));
```

As the second parameter to *SetCtlValue*, this statement passes the ordinal value of the boolean expression *n = itemHit*. The ordinal value of True is *1*; False = *0*. The effect is to send a *1* to the button that needs turning on and *0* to those that need turning off.

Code of this sort almost constitutes showing off. This idea could been more clearly expressed as

```
if n = itemHit then
  SetCtlValue(radButton[n],1)
else
  SetCtlValue(radButton[n],0)
```

We reduced four clear lines of code into one dense line. You decide if it's worth trading clarity for efficiency.

Processing Check Boxes

Check-box processing can be summarized this way: If a check box is currently checked, then uncheck it; if it's currently unchecked, then check it. In other words, if its underlying control value is *1*, then make it *0*, and vice versa. The task of complementing integers like this belongs to the **xor** operator.

Using **not** would work if *SetCtlValue* expected a boolean parameter, but it doesn't: It expects an integer. Using **not** on an integer flips the value of all 16 bits; **not** 0 = 11111111 11111111 = -1 is an undefined value for a check box.

The next three statements fetch the current value of *checkBox^^.contrlValue*, complement its least significant bit, and use this value as the parameter to *SetCtlValue*.

```
n := GetCtlValue(checkBox);
n := n xor 1;
SetCtlValue(checkBox,n);
```

We don't have to concern ourselves with other controls—each check box is an independent entity. We could squeeze these three lines into one and do away with variable *n* like this:

```
SetCtlValue(GetCtlValue(checkBox) xor 1));
```

Handling the EditText Field

If the user has clicked in an *EditText* item (*keyDown*s result in an *itemHit* for this field as well), then call *GetIText* for the current state of that item's text. The string value it returns is turned into a number by *StringToNum*, the complementary procedure of our old friend *NumToString*:

```
procedure StringToNum(theString: Str255; var theNum: LongInt);
```

No error checking whatsoever is performed by *StringToNum*. If the string you pass to this routine doesn't represent a reasonable long integer, *StringToNum* won't complain and *theNum* is liable to be set any (potentially huge) value. For example,

```
StringToNum('Borland', n);
```

sets *n* to 3,532,244 without the hint of an error. To be safe, a program must take a hard look at the text in *theString* before putting any trust in the value returned by *StringToNum*. (Each character should be in the set ['0'..'9','+','-'].) Otherwise, you're liable to have 16-hour long beeps.

The dialog processing loop ends when the user clicks the Cancel button, causing boolean variable *done* to be set to true. Note that this *done* is local to *DoBeepDialog* and, therefore, unrelated to the global variable *done* that controls termination of the program as a whole. There's a pleasing symmetry in using the same variable name to control this minor event loop as in the main event loop.

It may help to understand the flow of control in *DoBeepDialog* to insert a diagnostic *SysBeep(1)* just after the call to *ModalDialog*. This generates a beep each time *ModalDialog* returns.

The *DoAppleMenu* procedure is responsible for opening DAs and putting up the About DialogDemo message. In performing the latter, it first converts the values returned by *MaxMem* and *FreeMem* to strings and then calls *ParamText*:

```
ParamText(s1,s2,'','');
```

At the instant of this call, the About DialogDemo... box isn't even on the screen yet. *GetNewDialog* automatically substitutes the strings provided in the most recent invocation of *ParamText* into any text items containing the magic placeholders ^0, ^1, ^2, and ^3. With that accomplished, the actual dialog processing is easy. With only one enabled item (the Cancel button), we know that, as soon as *ModalDialog* returns, we're finished.

Experiment

If you think the appearance of the Beep dialog can be improved, be our guest. There are two basic approaches to editing a dialog box. First, there's the "Edit the Rmaker Source" method. Go into DialogDemo.R and tweak the boundary rectangles for each item in its item list to your heart's content. Then recompile, test, and repeat. Second, there's the "Edit the Resource File" method, using a tool such as *ResEdit, REdit,* or *Servant* to directly manipulate the DLOG and DITL resources in DialogDemo.Rsrc.

The advantage of the first approach is that, should you later decide to add some stuff to DialogDemo.R, your changes won't be lost as soon as you recompile. On the other hand, direct resource-file editing is your only alternative when working with resource files for which you don't have an RMaker source file. *ResEdit* can work with Turbo Pascal's "Find What" box as easily as those in DialogDemo.Rsrc.

MemoryDemo.Pas

Turn DialogDemo.Pas into a heap demonstrator by making calls to *NewHandle* and *NewPtr* to periodically allocate blocks of, say, 500 bytes. Perhaps you can call *NewHandle(500)* in response to a click on the Long button—in lieu of making a tone—and *NewPtr(500)* for a Short button click. If you want to get fancy, you can even change the names of the buttons.

Now click these buttons a few times and see if the memory status information returned in the About... dialog is reasonable.

Review

The Dialog Manager provides routines and data types that simplify the process of using windows and controls to communicate with the user. Dialog boxes are windows containing text, controls, and other objects. There are three basic classes of dialogs: modal dialogs (the type we discussed in this chapter), modeless dialogs (which behave more like application-created windows), and alerts, a simple form of modal dialog used to communicate error information and warnings.

Dialogs are almost always created by fetching a resource of type DLOG from a resource file. Associated with this resource is the ID of a resource of type DITL (dialog item list), which contains a description of each "item" (control, background text, and so on) associated with a dialog. RMaker allows you to create lists containing eight distinct types of dialog items. Items can either be enabled (selectable by the user) or disabled.

Dialog resources are fetched from disk and put on the screen by the *GetNewDialog* routine. Most interaction between the user and the dialog is handled by the *ModalDialog* routine, which doesn't return until the user has clicked an enabled item. At this point, the program performs actions appropriate to the item that was manipulated: toggling check-box items, setting and clearing various members of a radio-button cluster, and reading the content of *EditText* items.

39

Reading and Writing Files

Macintosh programs process files with the Toolbox's File Manager and the supplemental Standard File Package. Together, they constitute powerful, easy to use tools for reading and writing files.

The File Manager takes a somewhat different approach to file processing than Turbo Pascal's *Reset/Rewrite/Read/Write* methods, covered in Chapter 17. These built-in routines are able to process two basic file types: text files (lines of ASCII characters) and random-access (typed) files, which consist of a series of values of the same type. However, there are times when neither approach is suitable.

Often, the structure of a file is immaterial. For example, if an application must duplicate a file, it doesn't care if the file is text, check records, or mean temperature data from Barrow, Alaska: It simply has to recreate *n* bytes of data. At other times, files require a structure too complex for either of the built-in approaches. A data file may need a fixed length "header" record at the start and, following that, a sequence of records of a different type.

The File Manager takes a simple, cohesive view of all files: It treats them as numbered collections of bytes and makes no effort to associate Pascal concepts such as types or text to these bytes. This approach is both flexible and efficient.

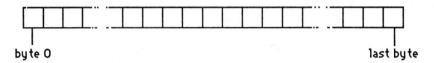

byte 0   last byte

Figure 39.1: Numbered Bytes of Files

Terminology: Volumes and Files

To restate some definitions from Chapter 17, a *volume* is a named medium for storing files. There's a one-to-one correspondence between volumes and floppy disks. Most hard disks are formatted as single volumes; some contain multiple volumes.

On all but the oldest Macs, the File Manager supports a "hierarchical" file system (HFS). This scheme organizes a given volume into an arrangement resembling the root system of a tree, in which files at any level can be either normal files or subdirectories (containing more files and more subdirectories). The Finder indicates subdirectories with its folder metaphor.

Files are named sequences of bytes stored in volumes. Macintosh files consist of two *forks*, *data* and *resource*. Resource forks are usually accessed through the routines of the Resource Manager; the data fork is the province of the File Manager. For this chapter's purposes, a "file" means "the data fork of a file."

File names can be up to 31 characters long and can contain any printable character except the colon (:).

Path Names

The File Manager uses *path names* to describe a specific file on a specific volume. A path name consists of a file name optionally preceded by a volume name and a colon, for example, *Turbo Work Disk:Turbo* (file Turbo on volume Turbo Work Disk).

Types and Creators

In addition to their name and contents, Macintosh files have two attributes that determine certain aspects of their treatment by the file system and Finder: a *type* (not to be confused with a type in the Pascal or Resource Manager senses) and a *creator*.

A file's type is a four-character string describing, tersely, the sort of data it contains. For example, the files created by MacPaint are type PNTG (painting) and those created by Turbo Pascal's editor are type TEXT.

By convention, programs have type APPL (application). That's how the Finder knows that programs are programs, so that it can load them into memory and give them control when they are double-clicked.

The Finder relies on the four-character creator string to determine the icon with which to represent the file, as well as what application should be started up when the file is opened. For example, files created by the Turbo Pascal editor have creator TPAS; that's why they have the checkered icon and why Turbo Pascal is started when you double-click one from the Finder.

The $T   (type) compiler directive controls the type and creator of Turbo programs compiled to disk. By default, the type is APPL and the creator is ????. For example, {$T APPLJOHN} sets a program's type to APPL and its creator to JOHN.

The File Manager's View of Files

Since a file is a string of bytes, each byte in a file is known uniquely by its distance from the start of the file. By convention, the first byte is byte #0; the second is byte #1; and the last byte in a file of length n is byte #$n-1$.

For every open file, the File Manager associates a position indicator called the *mark* to determine where the next read or write will take place.

When a file is first opened, its mark is set to byte 0. There's a routine to adjust the mark to any position in the file and a complementary routine to retrieve its position. The mark moves n bytes toward the end of the file after reading or writing n bytes.

The File Manager also keeps track of each file's length. The end of a file is known numerically as a long integer with a value one greater than the last byte in the file. That is, a file of length *n*'s last byte is #*n* − 1, and its "end of file" (EOF) is at position *n*, as shown in Figure 39.2.

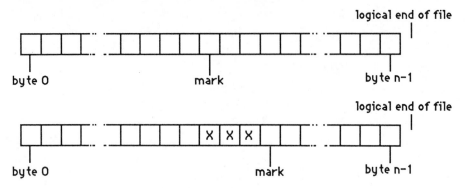

after reading three bytes (marked by X)

Figure 39.2: Reading Files

This is the so-called "logical" EOF. There's also a physical EOF, which programs usually don't care about. The physical end of file is usually a little farther out from the logical EOF because, for efficiency, files are allocated in discrete chunks called *allocation blocks*—and rarely is a file exactly as long as its last allocation block.

It's an error to try to read bytes or set the mark past a file's logical EOF (you can't read what doesn't exist). Writing is different: Writing to a file past the current EOF extends the EOF.

Working with Files: The Routines

Inside Macintosh divides the File Manager into high-level routines and low-level, "parameter-block" routines. We'll describe only the former. Powerful and complete, they're all most programs will ever need.

Before you can read or write a file, it must first be opened with *FSOpen*:

```
function FSOpen(fileName:Str255;vRefNum:Integer; var refNum:Integer): OSErr;
```

FSOpen prepares a file for reading or writing and sets its mark to position 0, the first byte in the file.

Type OSErr and I/O Error Handling

Each File Manager call is structured as a function returning error information (type OSErr is simply a synonym for *Integer*). Unit *OSIntf* defines a flock of constants so that your programs can take appropriate action if things don't go well. Here's a partial list of the error codes associated with *FSOpen*:

```
const
   noErr    = 0;      { file opened without incident }
   fnfErr   = -43;    { no such file in this volume }
   ioErr    = -36;             { I/O error }
   nsvErr   = -35;           { no such volume }
   tmfoErr  = -42;    { too many files open already }
```

As with Standard Pascal file processing, file input/output (I/O) is easy if you make simple-minded assumptions about errors (such as, there will never be any) and not so easy if you think out and prepare for worst-case scenarios. The former approach is suitable for demonstration programs, but real users won't be satisfied with a program that locks up when they try to save a data file they've been working on for hours to a write-protected floppy disk.

Back to FSOpen

FSOpen takes in two facts, a file name and a volume reference number (more about volume reference numbers in a minute). It also returns two facts: an error code (the function's return value) and the file's all-important *reference number*. Once a file has been successfully opened, you'll use this value rather than the file's name when reading and writing it.

To read a file once it's been *FSOpen*-ed, call *FSRead*:

```
function FSRead(refNum: Integer; var count: LongInt; buffPtr: Ptr): OSErr;
```

FSRead pulls *count* bytes from file *refNum*, starting at the position of its mark, and places these bytes in memory starting at address *buffPtr* and working up. After the read, the mark will have been moved *count* bytes deeper into the file.

If you've got the heap space, *FSRead* can read a file as large as a double-sided disk in a single call. For the fastest possible response, read files in chunks as large as memory permits. ("As large as memory permits" can be determined by calling the Memory Manager's *MaxMem* function.)

Surprisingly, *count* is a **var** parameter. Not only does it tell *FSRead* how many bytes to read, but, in case of an error of some sort, it returns equal to the number of bytes actually read. If all goes well, *count* returns with the same value it had initially.

Setting the Mark

To control the position of the read, set the file's mark beforehand with *SetFPos*:

```
function SetFPos(refNum: Integer; posMode: Integer; posOff: LongInt): OSErr;
```

You'll always pass a value between 0 and 3 for *posMode*, using one of the following predefined constants:

```
const
  fsAtMark    = 0;
  fsFromStart = 1;
  fsFromLEOF  = 2;
  fsFromMark  = 3;
```

Typically, you'll use *fsFromStart* as the *posMode* parameter. For example,

```
errCode := SetFPos(refNo,fsFromStart,512);
count   := 64;
errCode := FSRead(refNo,count,@myArray);
```

These statements set the mark of the file opened as reference number *refNo* to byte #512, and then read bytes 512 through 575 into memory starting at the address of variable *myArray*. After this operation, the file's mark will be at byte 576.

When you're through with a file, call *FSClose*:

```
function FSClose(refNum: Integer): OSErr;
```

FSClose terminates the relationship between a file and its reference number. Before you can work again with this file, you'll have to reopen it and get another reference number (probably not the same value) before working with it again.

Getting Volume Reference Numbers

The *FSOpen* call requires two facts to uniquely identify a file: a file name and a volume reference number. On HFS volumes (which constitute 99.9 percent of the volumes your programs are likely to encounter), the volume reference number is really a "working directory" reference number, identifying both a volume and a particular directory (folder) on that volume.

If you use 0 as the working directory reference number in a call to *FSOpen*, the File Manager knows to look for the file in the directory from which the application was launched. This is the so-called default directory. To get the working directory reference number for the default directory, call *GetVol*:

```
function GetVol (volName: StringPtr; var vRefNum: Integer): OSErr;
```

GetVol returns the default directory's reference number in its *vRefNum* parameter, and the volume's name is written to the address indicated by the *volName* parameter. If you're not interested in the name (and usually you won't be), pass **nil** for the *volName* parameter. *GetVol* doesn't return a path name for this directory, even if the default directory is many levels down in the file system; it gives you the name of the volume only. This call's lack of symmetry results from the way Apple implemented compatibility between the old "flat" file system and HFS.

It's hard (and almost never necessary) for a program to know the names of all the files and subdirectories it finds at run time. It's easy, however, to access the directory that it was launched from; simply pass 0 wherever a File Manager routine expects a volume reference number (for example, *FSOpen*). This allows your programs to locate key data files without asking the user where he or she's put them.

In addition, the *SFGetFile* and *SFPutFile* calls let the user specify exactly where in his or her unique file system a file is stored or should be created. We'll describe them in just a bit.

Reading Files: Putting It All Together

For the sake of argument, suppose we wanted to read the data on the *n*th check in a file of check records, located in the application's default directory. Procedure *ReadCheck* reads the information on the check designated by its *checkNo* parameter into **var** parameter *theCheck*.

```
procedure ReadCheck(checkNo; var theCheck: CheckRecord);
var
  refNum, errCode: Integer;
  byteCount: LongInt;
begin
  errCode   := FSOpen('Check.Data',0,refNum);              { open the file }
  errCode   := SetFPos(refNum,fsFromStart,(checkNo-1)*Sizeof(CheckRecord));
  byteCount := SizeOf(CheckRecord);
  errCode   := FSRead(refNum,byteCount,@theCheck);         { do the read }
  errCode   := FSClose(refNum);
end;
```

ReadCheck fails if there isn't a file named Check.Data in the default
directory, or if it doesn't contain at least *checkNo* checks. Actually, there's
one other place where this file could be and still be found. The File
Manager searches the directory containing the current System file when a
file specified in an *FSOpen* call can't be found in the default directory. Many
applications (especially DAs, since they don't have a default directory) use
this technique to access data files. If *FSOpen* doesn't return an error, your
application doesn't know—or care—if the file is in the default or the
System directory.

The read itself is performed by this statement:

```
errCode := FSRead(refNum,byteCount,@theCheck);
```

This says to read *byteCount* bytes from the file opened as file *refNum* and to
place them at the address in memory occupied by **var** parameter *theCheck*.
The actual parameter passed at run time to *ReadCheck* may be on the stack,
in global memory, or in the heap; it doesn't matter. *FSRead* will write to any
address you specify, so if you accidentally read too much or to the wrong
spot, it's possible to overwrite code or system data structures and cause a
crash.

Writing a File

Writing to a file is similar to reading. Again, you're limited only by
memory and disk space. Here's *FSWrite*:

```
function FSWrite(refNum: Integer; var count: LongInt; buffPtr: Ptr): OSErr;
```

*Write*s occur at the mark of an open file and advance the mark an amount
equal to the number of bytes written. If the file doesn't exist already, you'll/
need to *Create* it beforehand:

```
function Create(fileName:Str255;vRefNum:Integer;creator,fType:OSType): OSErr;
```

Because caching may be in use on the device that physically implements a given volume, it's good practice to call the File Manager's *FlushVol* routine immediately after closing a file that you've written to. Then you can be sure that the directory information on that file is properly updated.

```
function FlushVol(volName: StringPtr; vRefNum: Integer): OSErr;
```

There's no need to call *FlushVol* if you've only been reading from a file.

An Example of Writing to a File

A block of check records in the heap practically begs to be written to disk. Procedure *WriteCheckData* creates and opens file Check.Data in the working directory, and it then fills the file with the contents of the relocatable block indicated by its handle parameter.

```
procedure WriteCheckData(h: Handle);
var
  refNum,errCode: Integer;
  byteCount: LongInt;
begin
  errCode := Create('Check.Data',0,'CHEK','CBAP'); { "checkbook appl." }
  errCode := FSOpen('Check.Data',0,refNum);               { open it up }
  byteCount := GetHandleSize(h);           { we'll write this many bytes }
  HLock(h);
  errCode := FSWrite(refNum,byteCount,h^);                { send it out }
  HUnlock(h);
  errCode := FSClose(refNum);
  errCode := FlushVol(nil,0);   { flush the volume as a safety measure }
end;
```

We lock the relocatable block indicated by *h* before the write. If we didn't, the call to *FSWrite* could trigger heap movement before the write occurs and cause our check data to no longer be where we said it was.

A single call to *FSWrite* can write one or a thousand check records to disk, disk and heap space permitting.

Miscellaneous File Manager Routines

Functions *FSDelete* and *Rename* delete files from the file system and change their names, respectively.

```
function FSDelete(fileName: Str255; vRefNum: Integer): OSErr;
function Rename(oldName: Str255; vRefNum: Integer,newName: Str255): OSErr;
```

An open file can't be deleted. Either an open or closed file may be renamed.

Fetching Finder Information

The File Manager maintains certain facts about each file on a volume for the Finder's benefit. This information is held in a record of type FInfo (Finder info).

```
type FInfo = record
               fdType    : OSType;  { the type }
               fdCreator : OSType;  { the creator }
               fdFlags   : Integer; { miscellaneous flags }
               fdLocation: Point;   { position of file's icon in its window }
               fdFldr    : Integer; { the folder containing this icon }
             end;
```

The File Manager has routines to both read and write this packet of information on a particular file, which may be open or closed.

```
function GetFInfo(fileName: Str255; vRefNum: Integer;
                  var theInfo: FInfo):OSErr;
function SetFInfo(fileName: Str255; vRefNum: Integer; theInfo: FInfo):OSErr;
```

To determine the length of an open file (of its data fork), use *GetEOF*:

```
function GetEOF(refNum: Integer; var fileLength: LongInt): OSErr;
```

To read the current position of an open file's mark, use *GetFPos*:

```
function GetFPos(refNum: Integer; var filePos: LongInt): OSErr;
```

The Standard File Package

Applications get a big boost in file processing from two sophisticated procedures known as *SFPutFile* and *SFGetFile*. These routines are described in Volume I of *Inside Macintosh* under the heading "Standard File Package"—far from the rest of the information about files. From a unit standpoint, they're declared in unit *PackIntf*.

This segregation from the File Manager results from their implementation as a "package." The Standard File Package isn't in ROM, but instead is read from the System file into RAM when you call one of its routines. All this happens transparently to your program (assuming there's 10K or so of heap space available).

SFPutFile

```
procedure SFPutFile(where: Point; prompt,origName: Str255; dlgHook:
                    ProcPtr; var reply: SFReply);
```

Call *SFPutFile* ("Standard File PutFile") when your program needs to save a data file with the name, volume, and directory selected by the user. *SFPutFile* puts up the familiar dialog that Turbo Pascal (and practically every other Macintosh application) uses when saving files to disk. It takes care of moving between volumes, of ejecting disks, and accepting new ones. If the user inserts a blank disk, *SFPutFile* checks that it is properly formatted and named. If the user specifies a directory and volume that already contains a file with this name, *SFPutFile* asks if you want to replace it:

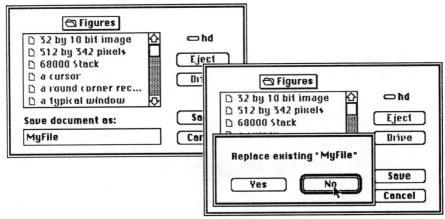

Figure 39.3: PutFile in Action

If the user accidentally inserts a write-protected disk, *SFPutFile* says so. All this in a one-line procedure call—talk about powerful, high-level routines.

SFPutFile doesn't actually create files or write data. It simply returns the name the user wants the file to have and where (volume and directory) he or she wants it stored. It's up to you to create the file and write to it based on what's returned in the *reply* parameter.

The *SFReply* record type returned by both *SFPutFile* and *SFGetFile* is the key to decoding the user's response:

```
type SFReply = record
               good:   Boolean;
               copy:   Boolean;
               fType:  OSType;
```

```
        vRefNum: Integer;
        version: Integer;
        fName:   String[63];
end;
```

Let's consider a sample call to *SFPutFile*:

```
SFPutFile(p,'Save check data as','Check.Data',nil,theReply);
```
Point parameter *p* specifies the position of the top-left corner of the standard *PutFile* dialog box. This location information, along with the *prompt* and *origName* strings, gives us the opportunity to customize the *PutFile* dialog just a bit. The box resulting from this call looks like this:

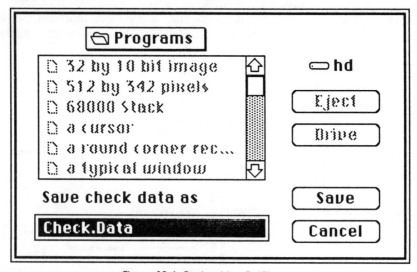

Figure 39.4: Customizing PutFile

The user is free to change the file name to something other than your suggestion (*origName*). The **nil** *dlgHook* parameter tells *SFPutFile* to behave in its default way, that is, we won't customize its operation. As we saw with *ModalDialog*, there's a *ProcPtr* parameter that offers flexibility in exchange for some *Inside Macintosh* migraines.

When *SFPutfile* returns, we must study the fields in *theReply* to find out where the user wants the file to go, and what he or she has decided to call it. The *good* field tells whether or not the user clicked the dialog's Cancel button. If *good* returns False, then Cancel was clicked, so we can't trust the data in *reply*'s other fields. If it's True, the name selected is stored in *fName*, and the desired working directory reference number for the directory for the file chosen returns in *vRefNum*.

The *copy*, *fType*, and *version* fields of *theReply* can be ignored.

SFGetFile

SFGetFile is complementary to *SFPutFile*. Call it to let the user choose a particular existing file in a particular directory of a particular volume for opening.

```
procedure SFGetFile (where: Point; prompt:Str255; fileFilter: ProcPtr;
                     numTypes: Integer; typeList: SFTypeList, dlgHook:
                     ProcPtr; var reply: SFReply);
```

where *SFTypeList* is defined as

```
type
  SFTypeList = array [0..3] of OSType; { OSType = packed array [1..4] of char }
```

SFGetFile uses its *typeList* parameter to filter out inappropriate file types. For example, when Turbo Pascal calls it in response to your choosing Open from its File menu, *SFGetFile* shows only files of type TEXT. Similarly, the Transfer option of the File menu shows only files of type APPL. You request this filtering process by preparing a variable of type *SFTypeList* containing up to four types and by passing *numTypes* equal to the number of types used. Passing –1 for *numTypes* causes all types to appear, regardless of the content of *typeList*.

For more sophisticated filtering, *Inside Macintosh* describes how to create a filter routine and pass its address as the *fileFilter* parameter. This allows your application ultimate flexibility; for example, it can display only files that end in *.R* or cause files that have already been opened to be omitted.

As with *SFPutFile*, the user's response to *SFGetFile* can be learned by examining the *reply* record. If *reply.good* is True, then the user wants to open the file indicated by *replay.fName* in directory *reply.vRefNum*. This chapter's demonstration program, FileDemo.Pas, includes a call to *SFGetFile*.

Macintosh File I/O: The Short Form

Here's what an application must do to open and read a file specified by the user:

1. Call *SFGetFile* to get the working directory reference number and name of the file.

2. Call *FSOpen*, passing the directory reference number and file name returned by *SFGetFile*.

3. Call *SetFPos* to set the file's mark.

4. Call *FSRead* to read *n* bytes from the file into a buffer in memory. (Steps 3 and 4 can be repeated as necessary.)

5. Call *FSClose* to terminate I/O to this file.

Here's how to create and write a file specified by the user:

1. Call *SFPutFile* to get the working directory reference number of the volume/directory combination where the user wants to put the file and the name he or she wants the file to have.

2. Call *Create*, passing the working directory reference number and file name returned by *SFPutFile*.

3. Call *FSOpen* to open the file and get a reference number for it.

4. Call *SetFPos* to set the file's mark.

5. Call *FSWrite* to write to the file from a buffer in memory. (Steps 4 and 5 can be repeated as necessary.)

6. Call *FSClose* to terminate I/O to this file.

7. Call *FlushVol* to ensure that buffers are flushed and the volume properly updated.

FileDemo.Pas

FileDemo.Pas demonstrates key File Manager routines. It can also be useful. Compile and run this program now.

When you choose Open from its File menu, after letting you select from the *GetFile* dialog box, it displays the file's length, type, and creator, as well as its first 50 bytes.

To illustrate, choose file FileDemo.R. The program responds by displaying the following information:

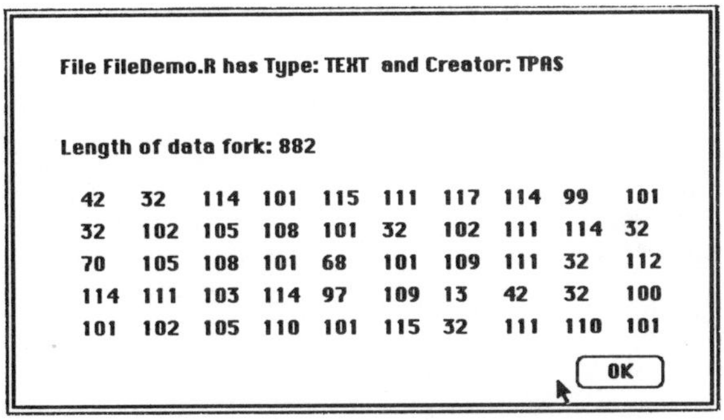

```
┌─────────────────────────────────────────────┐
│ ┌─────────────────────────────────────────┐ │
│ │                                         │ │
│ │  File FileDemo.R has Type: TEXT  and Creator: TPAS │ │
│ │                                         │ │
│ │                                         │ │
│ │  Length of data fork: 882               │ │
│ │                                         │ │
│ │    42    32   114  101  115  111  117  114   99  101 │ │
│ │    32   102  105  108  101   32  102  111  114   32 │ │
│ │    70   105  108  101   68  101  109  111   32  112 │ │
│ │   114  111  103  114   97  109   13   42   32  100 │ │
│ │   101  102  105  110  101  115   32  111  110  101 │ │
│ │                                   ┌──────┐  │ │
│ │                                   │  OK  │  │ │
│ │                               ▲   └──────┘  │ │
│ └─────────────────────────────────────────┘ │
└─────────────────────────────────────────────┘
```

Figure 39.5: FileDemo.R's Output

According to this figure, FileDemo.R has type TEXT and a creator of TPAS (Turbo Pascal). It's 882 bytes long. Are the values that supposedly represent its first 50 bytes reasonable? Theoretically, TEXT files contain nothing but printable ASCII characters, with an occasional Carriage Return (code 13) thrown in. Using the ASCII chart in Appendix E, take a few minutes to translate these values into text form. Do they match what Turbo's editor says FileDemo.R contains?

It isn't very smart about short data forks; it goes through the motions of reading and displaying the first 50 bytes even if the file isn't 50 bytes long. In this case, the "content" part of this display isn't meaningful, and you may have noticed a beep as *FSRead* indicated a failure to perform the requested operation.

Use FileDemo to probe your file system. What type and creator does Turbo Pascal itself have? The Finder? The System file? Are these files mainly resource fork or data fork files?

Inside FileDemo.Pas

From a window-handling standpoint, FileDemo is simpler than previous example programs: With the exception of its two dialog boxes, there aren't any windows to be concerned with. No windows means we can dispense with processing activate and update events from the main loop.

The meat of this program is procedure *DoOpen*, called as a result of choosing the File menu's first option.

```pascal
procedure DoOpen;
var
  reply       : SFReply;
  typeList    : SFTypeList;
  findrInfo   : FInfo;

  refNum      : Integer;
  buffer,aByte: Ptr;
  row,column  : Integer;
  fileLength, readCount: LongInt;

  theDialog   : DialogPtr;
  p           : Point;
  s           : Str255;

begin
  p.h := 100; p.v := 60;
  SFGetFile(p,'',nil,-1,typeList,nil,reply);

  if not reply.good then Exit;

  if GetFInfo(reply.fname,reply.vRefNum,findrInfo) <> 0 then SysBeep(1);
  if FSOpen(reply.fname,reply.vRefNum,refNum) <> 0 then SysBeep(1);
  if GetEOF(refNum,fileLength) <> 0 then SysBeep(1);
  NumToString(fileLength,s);

  ParamText(reply.fname,findrInfo.fdType,findrInfo.fdCreator,s);
  theDialog := GetNewDialog(256,nil,Pointer(-1));
  SetPort(theDialog);

  readCount := 50;
  buffer := NewPtr(readCount);
  if FSRead(refNum,readCount,buffer) <> 0 then SysBeep(1);
  if FSClose(refNum) <> 0 then SysBeep(1);

  aByte := buffer;
    for row := 1 to 5 do
      for column := 1 to 10 do
      begin
        NumToString(aByte^,s);
        MoveTo(38 * column, 100 + row*20);
        DrawString(s);
        aByte := Pointer(Ord(aByte)+1);
      end;

  ModalDialog(nil,row);
  DisposDialog(theDialog);
end;
```

DoOpen's Local Variables

Reply and *typeList* are needed by *SFGetFile*; a record of type FInfo is required by *GetFInfo*. Integer variable *refNum* is used in the *FSOpen* call. The two pointers (*buffer*, *abyte*) are for reading and displaying the first 50 bytes of the chosen file.

DoOpen has some long integer variables for matters relating to file length. (These must be long integers because you can read more than 32K in a single call.) Finally, there's a *DialogPtr* for accessing the box that displays all this information.

Calling SFGetFile

An amazing amount of work is done by *DoOpen*'s second line.

```
SFGetFile(p,'',nil,-1,typeList,nil,reply);
```

Since *SFGetFile* ignores its *prompt* parameter anyway, we simply pass the null string. Passing –1 as the *numTypes* parameter causes all types to be shown, regardless of the contents of *typeList* (which we didn't bother to initialize).

To cause this program to open only files of types TEXT and PNTG (MacPaint files), appropriate assignments to *typeList* before the call to *SFGetFile* are required:

```
typeList[0] := 'TEXT';
typeList[1] := 'PNTG';
SFGetFile(p,'',nil,2,typeList,nil,reply);
```

When *SFGetFile* returns, the information supplied by the user comes back in record variable *reply*. If its *good* field isn't True, then the user clicked the Cancel button, so the contents of *reply*'s other fields are meaningless. Our response to this condition is simply to leave *DoOpen*.

If *reply.good* is True, the program proceeds to probe for information about the file chosen by the user, which is represented by the *reply* record's *fname* and *vRefNum* fields. First, it calls *GetFInfo* to collect the file's type and creator. Files don't have to be opened before you can fetch their Finder information.

```
if GetFInfo(reply.fname,reply.vRefNum,findrInfo) <> 0 then SysBeep(1);
```

FileDemo's "error handling" isn't the greatest. It tells you that something is amiss (with a beep), but doesn't tell you what went wrong nor does it do anything about it. After the call to *GetFInfo*, we let the information cool its heels in *findrInfo* until we're ready for it.

Opening the File

Next, we open the file by passing *FSOpen* the same file name and working directory reference number used in the *GetFInfo* call. If the file can be opened, *refNum* is set to the all-important reference number, which we'll use in subsequent calls to refer to this file.

```
if FSOpen(reply.fname,reply.vRefNum,refNum) <> 0 then SysBeep(1);
```

This operation is almost guaranteed to work, because *SFGetFile* can't return file names and working directory reference numbers that don't exist.

The call to *GetEOF* places the length of the chosen file in long integer variable *fileLength*, which is then converted to string form.

Next comes a call to *ParamText*, setting the ^0 through ^3 placeholders of the next dialog box to be fetched by *GetNewDialog* to the file's name, type, creator, and length, respectively. This information makes its appearance on the screen with the call to *GetNewDialog*:

```
theDialog := GetNewDialog(256,nil,Pointer(-1));
```

Reading File RefNum

At this point, the dialog is displayed (including the type and length information, but not the content bytes). We set the current *GrafPort* to the new dialog box, because we're about to do some *DrawString*-ing into the lower part of the box. Since *DialogPtr*s are really *GrafPtr*s, they can be passed without coercion hassles to QuickDraw routines that expect pointers to *GrafPort*s.

Reading the file represented by integer variable *refNum* is accomplished by the following statements:

```
readCount := 50;
buffer    := NewPtr(readCount);
if FSRead(refNum,readCount,buffer) <> 0 then SysBeep(1);
```

The first line allocates a 50-byte space in the heap for the data about to be read; the second performs the read itself. If this particular file has less than 50 bytes in its data fork, the program will beep at this point.

Sending Content Bytes to the Screen

Having read 50 bytes into the buffer, we output them to the screen. Since they're displayed as 5 rows of 10 bytes each, a pair of nested **for** loops are a natural structure for this process.

You may recall that a *Ptr* is defined in unit *MemTypes* as a ^*SignedByte* (where *SignedByte* = –128..127). Therefore, dereferencing a variable of type *Ptr* results in an integer between –128 and 127, representing the 256 possible combinations of eight bits. After converting this value to string form and *DrawString*-ing it to an appropriate spot in the window, we increment pointer variable *aByte* to point to the buffer's next byte:

```
aByte := Pointer(Ord(aByte)+1);
```

As we've come to expect when working directly with the contents of pointers, this statement is more fat (type coercion) than meat (incrementing *aByte* by 1).

After all 50 bytes are on the screen, we call *ModalDialog* to take care of event processing until the user clicks the dialog's one and only enabled item, the OK button. When it returns, we dispose the dialog—erasing it from the screen and its various data structures from memory. We're now done, at least until the next Open command.

Find the Bug

We've deliberately left a bug in FileDemo to give you some practice in finding and fixing problems.

This program's About… dialog uses a call to *FreeMem* to list the amount of free memory available in the heap. Open several files and check the memory situation after each. You should observe that the value displayed gets smaller each time. Evidently, some process in this program is claiming heap space and not giving it back.

Failure to deallocate heap space is a quiet sort of problem and therefore especially devilish. Most of the time, it won't cause errors, because usually there's sufficient heap to keep a few bytes from being missed. Eventually, somebody, somewhere—perhaps running under Switcher or with a big disk cache or with some RAM-hog DAs open—will have this program blow up on them because of this problem.

Who's the culprit? The size reduction after each call to *DoOpen* is about 60 bytes. A heap block takes between 8 and 20 more bytes than what you ask for to maintain certain structures needed by the Memory Manager. So, we're looking for something that allocates slightly less than 60 bytes.

Where in this program did we allocate 40 to 50 bytes of heap? Right, in *DoOpen*, for the file buffer. Where in *DoOpen* do we deallocate this memory? *Nowhere*.

To fix the program, add this line to the end of *DoOpen*:

```
DisposPtr(buffer);
```

Now does the About... dialog return essentially the same value each time?

Review

The File Manager considers the data forks of files as simply a numbered sequence of bytes. Every open file has a known length and an associated position indicator, or *mark*, that indicates where the next read or write will take place.

The File Manager's routines are structured as functions returning integer error codes. A result code of zero means no error. To prepare a file for reading and/or writing, call *FSOpen*. Use *SetFPos* to set an open file's mark, and *FSRead* and *FSWrite* to read and write an open file. Call *Create* to create a new, empty file. When finished with a file, call *FSClose* and, if you've written anything to the file since opening it, call *FlushVol* at this time.

The File Manager also has auxiliary routines to rename and delete files, and to fetch their Finder information records.

An application can access files stored in the directory from which it was launched by passing 0 as the volume reference number parameter to *FSOpen*. Files in arbitrary directories can be created and read using the Standard File Package's *SFGetFile* and *SFPutFile* routines. They make it easy for programs to retrieve and store files anywhere in the user's file system. Neither reads nor writes any data, but instead they simply return the working directory reference number and name of the file to be opened or created.

40

MacTypist: A Macintosh Program

Remember the Turbo Typist program in Chapter 19? That program originated in the 25-line, 80-column world of CP/M and MS-DOS computers and was adapted to the Macintosh, essentially verbatim, for this book. Its animated cars—constructed of dashes and letters—served ably in demonstrating Turbo Pascal, but the Macintosh deserves better.

MacTypist is an advanced version of Turbo Typist. If you haven't run this program already, do so now. You'll find it in the MacTypist folder of your Turbo Tutor disk; simply compile and run the file MacTypist.Pas.

Surprisingly, MacTypist.Pas is about the same size as Typist.Pas. Both contain roughly 600 lines of source code. MacTypist is able to do more because it calls upon the talents of the Toolbox. Discounting vanilla procedures like *GotoXY* and *WriteLn*, Typist.Pas has to do everything itself.

Using MacTypist

MacTypist uses the Macintosh user interface. This makes it simple to figure out, especially for experienced Macintosh users. All the action takes place in a standard drag-able document window. Pull-down menus provide instant access to all commands. Your familiar complement of DAs are at hand. You can use the Calculator in the middle of a game to determine your words per minute average (keep track of when you start and stop) or other vital statistics.

There's a Quit option in the File menu, and, thanks to user interface consistency, you don't need to be told what it does. (The PC Typist's Quit command was *Control-C*.) Clicking the main window's close box is the same as Quit (and you probably didn't need to be told that, either).

How is this game different from the previous version? Let me count the ways. Most obviously, it simply *looks* better: The cars look like cars, the truck looks like a truck, and the street scene is straight out of a Saturday morning cartoon. Furthermore, the animation is more effective: Antennas wave and cars crumple, visibly and audibly.

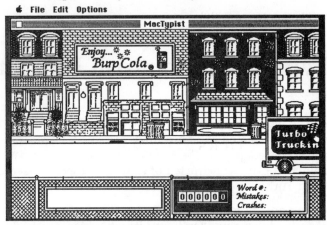

Figure 40.1: MacTypist's Main Screen

It's possible to change the speed before, during, or after a game, from a Volkswagen barely dented when it crashes to a sports car totaled when it hits the truck. The Case Sensitive option controls whether or not the program considers uppercase and lowercase distinctions when checking your words. If checked (the default), "New" doesn't match "new."

MacTypist's odometer not only looks great, it's also accurate to one tenth of a second. (**NOTE**: So far, the in-house record for this game—in the Fast option—is 00:54.6 seconds.)

Fine Points

Note how the File menu's first item changes from Start Game to Stop Game and back again, depending on whether a game is in progress.

Study the game's response to update and activate events. Open a DA and drag its window around. Whenever a system window is active, the game pauses. When the main window becomes active again, the game continues. When you drag or close a system window such that a part of the main window is uncovered, note how quickly its contents are redrawn; that's update event processing at work.

With the main window active, pull down the Edit menu. Note that each of its options are disabled. MacTypist's main window has nothing to cut, copy, or paste, so the program disables this menu's entries. Now activate a DA. When a system window is active, the situation is reversed—only the options of the Edit menu are selectable.

Try a little cutting and pasting. Open the Alarm Clock, if you have it, and copy the time and date to the clipboard. (You don't have to select anything, just click Copy.) Now, open the Scrapbook (or some other DA that supports pasting text), and paste this text in. This DA cutting and pasting is why nearly all Macintosh applications have an Edit menu, even if the concept of editing doesn't apply to them.

MacTypist's Tricks: The Background File

MacTypist's street scene and automobiles aren't created on the fly with clever *LineTo*s and *FrameRect*s. Instead, they are furnished fully formed by the MacPaint file Background.Data. MacTypist won't run if it can't find this file at run time.

Looking at file Background.Data is a little like reading a magician's instruction book. Once you know how a trick works, it's not nearly as impressive. Figure 40.2 shows the contents of this file. MacTypist could be improved by storing this graphic data inside the application itself—perhaps in its otherwise empty data fork. We'll leave that advance to you.

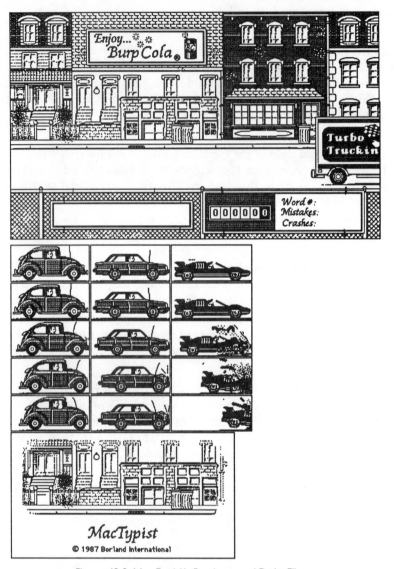

Figure 40.2: MacTypist's Background.Data File

Background.Data contains the main window's street scene, the contents of the About MacTypist... dialog, and five views of each of the three cars. Two views show unwrecked cars, differing only in antenna position and wheel highlighting, and three show progressively more severe stages of crashing.

Animation

MacTypist's main trick is moving a car while simultaneously processing keystrokes and mouse-downs. The standard Macintosh main event loop structure lends itself beautifully to this task.

At timed intervals (the faster the car, the shorter the interval), a car image is copied from an offscreen bit image (containing what used to be on disk in Background.Data) to the screen, with QuickDraw's *CopyBits* routine. Each application of *CopyBits* moves a car slightly to the right (two pixels, to be exact) of its previous position.

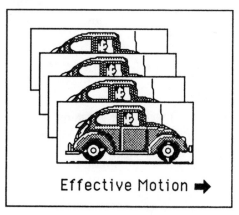

Figure 40.3: The Animation Process

As shown in Figure 40.3, each car picture has at least two columns of white pixels to the left of its leftmost black pixel. This trailing white space is central to MacTypist's animation technique: It erases the trailing edge of the previously plotted car.

A collision occurs when the rectangle enclosing the car has moved all the way to the truck's bumper. At this point, the program displays in quick succession the remaining three views of the car—all at the same place. The images themselves take care of apparent movement.

Data Structures

MacTypist.Pas's most important variable is *mainWindow*.

var

```
mainWindow: WindowPtr;
```

mainWindow, a *WindowPtr*, holds the address of the main window (the window entitled "MacTypist") throughout the duration of the program. (Well, it *will* once initialized.) Our previous demos chose not to store window pointers as global variables, but to get them as needed from such sources as *FindWindow* and *GetNextEvent*.

In this case, the main window is the only window (not counting those associated with DAs) that MacTypist will ever put on the screen. So, making *mainWindow* a global variable, at 4 bytes, isn't wasteful of memory, and it offers certain conveniences. For example, an important fact can be had at will by comparing *mainWindow* to the value returned by the Window Manager's *FrontWindow* function. If they're the same, we know that the main window is active; if they're not, we know a system window is active.

```
myBitMap: BitMap;
```

After initialization, *myBitMap*'s three fields (*baseAddr*, *rowBytes*, and *bounds*) define a large bit image in the heap containing the cars and background scene initially in file Background.Data. *MyBitMap* appears in *CopyBits* calls, sprinkled throughout the program, to move visual elements of the game to the main window. A big part of the initialization process involves getting these images from disk into the memory range defined by *myBitMap*.

```
menuApple, menuFile, menuEdit, menuOptions: MenuHandle;
```
This program declares *MenuHandle*s to each of its four menus. Unlike previous demo programs, the menu handles aren't stored in an array but as separate global variables—just for variety.

```
caseSens:              Boolean;
speed:                 Speeds;
targetWord, userWord: Str255;
wordCount, mistakeCount, crashCount: Integer;
secCount:              string[6];
```

The next cluster of data structures controls scoring and game variations. If *caseSens* is True, then the program requires exact case matches. Variable *speed*, of enumerated type *Speeds*, controls both which car is displayed and how fast (often) it moves. It can take on only the enumerated values *slow*, *medium*, and *fast*. Note that applying the *Ord* function to *speed* results in an integer between 0 and 2, where 0 equals *slow*.

String variables *targetWord* and *userWord* represent the current target word (displayed in what used to be the Burp Cola billboard) and what he or she has typed so far, respectively. Whenever the user presses *Return*, the program compares *targetWord* to *userWord*; if they're the same, it beeps the speaker and moves on to the next word. We're a little frivolous with memory here: These two Str255 variables, at 256 bytes apiece, require more storage than all the rest of the global variables put together.

WordCount, mistakeCount, crashCount, and *secCount* are responsible for the running score displayed in the lower right part of the main window. *SecCount*, the data structure behind the odometer, is defined as a character array for efficiency (that is, speed) in incrementing the odometer. The obvious way of doing it proved too slow, as we shall see.

```
var lastOdometerIncrement, lastBlink, lastMove: LongInt;
```
MacTypist declares three long integers to store time-related information. *LastMove*, for example, contains in tick form (sixtieths of a second since the system booted) the time the car was last moved. With each pass through the main event loop, this value is tested against the current time (as returned by *TickCount*) if a game is in progress. If a sufficient amount of time has gone by, the car is moved.

MacTypist's Rectangles

```
var caret,backGround,aboutFig,theCar,billboard,dragRect: Rect;
    carPix: array [0..4, slow..fast] of Rect;
```

Next are a series of rectangles. The *caret* rectangle encloses a 1-pixel wide by 15-pixel long area in the main window, which represents the blinking insertion point. (User manuals call the insertion point the insertion point; *Inside Macintosh* calls it a *caret*.)

theCar is of particular interest. During a game, this rectangle outlines the current position of the car. It's offset to the right periodically by a call to *OffsetRect*; when its right edge encounters the truck's bumper, the crash sequence is invoked. As always, changing the integers that define a rectangle doesn't have any effect on the screen. Moving the car on the screen takes a call to *CopyBits*.

The 15 car images in Background.Data are arranged as 5 rows of 3 cars each, making them suitable for a two-dimensional array. Once initialized, the *carPix* array of rectangles enclose each car's image in the offscreen bit image. For example, *carPix[4, slow]* represents the most severely crashed Volkswagen.

```
var done, gameInProgress, flipFlop: Boolean;
```

The *done* flag performs its conventional function, and boolean variable *gameInProgress* determines whether or not a game is currently in progress. If *gameInProgress* is False, then the *MyTasks* routine called in the main event loop doesn't worry about moving the car, updating the odometer, and so on. *FlipFlop* has to do with animation. If *flipFlop* equals True, then Ord(*flipFlop*) equals 1; if *flipFlop* equals False, then Ord(*flipFlop*) equals 0.

```
var soundBufferPtr: FFSynthPtr;
```

SoundBufferPtr is a pointer to a buffer that the Sound Driver interprets as sound data. Once allocated and initialized, it contains crash-radiator-steam-spewing collision sounds.

The Main Program

After some one-time initialization, program flow falls into the main event loop where it cycles repeatedly, fetching and handling *mouseDowns*, *keyDowns*, activate, and update events until the user chooses Quit.

```
begin Initialize;
  repeat
    SystemTask;
    MyTasks;
    if GetNextEvent(everyEvent,theEvent) then
      case theEvent.what of
        mouseDown:   DoMouseDown;
        keyDown:     DoKeyDown;
        autoKey:     DoKeyDown;
        updateEvt:   DoUpdate;
        activateEvt: DoActivate;
      end;
  until done;
end.
```

Initializing MacTypist

Before we're ready to process that first event, global variables must be initialized, resources read, menu bars prepared, and windows drawn. Fully a fourth of MacTypist's code is devoted to this process. Procedure *Initialize* is almost a program onto itself, with several nested procedures (which may have nested routines of their own (which may have nested routines of their own)). *IOErrTest*, for example, is nested within *LoadPackedData*, which is itself nested within *LoadMyBitMap*.

Stripped of its code, the elegantly nested structure of *Initialize* is shown here.

```
procedure Initialize;
  procedure InitManagers;
  begin
  end;
  procedure InitMenus;
  begin
  end;
  procedure InitSound;
  begin
  end;
  procedure LoadMyBitMap;
    procedure LoadPackedData;
      procedure IOErrTest(errCode: Integer);
      begin
      end;
    begin
    end;
  begin
  end;
  procedure MiscInits;
  begin
  end;
begin {initialize}
  InitManagers;
  InitMenus;
  InitSound;
  LoadMyBitMap;
  MiscInits;
end;
```

Initializing the Managers

The Toolbox can't work until it's been properly initialized. *InitManagers* touches all the bases in the right order:

```
MaxApplZone;          { Expand heap to maximum }
MoreMasters;          { 64 more master pointers }
InitGraf(@thePort);   { Initialize QuickDraw }
InitFonts;            {     "    Font Manager }
InitWindows;          {     " Window Manager }
InitMenus;            {     "   Menu Manager }
TEInit;               {     "       TextEdit }
InitDialogs(nil);     {     " Dialog Manager }
```

Initializing the Sound Buffer

For added realism, MacTypist calls on the talents of the Toolbox's Sound Driver. This routine allocates a 6K buffer in the heap and then loads it with values that will be interpreted as the sound of a car crash.

```
procedure InitSound;
var
  n : Integer;
begin
  soundBufferPtr := FFSynthPtr(NewPtr(soundBufferSize)); { allocate buffer }
  soundBufferPtr^ .mode := ffMode;                        { set FF mode }
  soundBufferPtr^ .count := FixRatio(1,1);                { always = 1.0 }
  for n := 0 to soundBufferSize - 7 do                    { load w/ random }
    soundBufferPtr^ .waveBytes[N] := Random shr 8;        { 8-bit value }
end;
```

Without wading too deeply into the deep waters of the Sound Driver, here's what's going on in *InitSound*. This program uses the so-called free-form synthesizer mode. In free-form mode, the Sound Driver creates tones by pumping bytes from a buffer (typically in the heap) to circuitry controlling the speaker. The speaker in turn generates a tiny piece of a sound corresponding to each byte's value. Collectively, the effect is music or explosion sounds or speech, depending on the values in the buffer.

Producing music requires that these bytes be carefully arranged into regular patterns. Purely random values in the buffer, on the other hand, produce "white noise" like static on the radio (or, with a little imagination, a crash).

Once activated with the *StartSound* procedure, the buffer-to-speaker pump works at the rate of 22,257 bytes per second. That means that, without repetition, one second requires a 22K buffer. This program's 6K buffer is enough for a fourth of a second of sound.

InitSound uses QuickDraw's *Random* function to load each byte of the sound buffer with a random number:

```
for n := 0 to soundBufferSize - 7 do
  soundBufferPtr^ .waveBytes[N] := Random shr 8;
```

The Sound Driver defines a *FFSynthPtr* as a pointer to a *FFSynthRec*, which is itself defined this way:

```
type FFSynthRec = record
                    mode: Integer;
                    count: Fixed;
                    waveBytes: packed array [0..30000] of Byte;
                  end;
```

You'll rarely declare a variable of type *FFSynthRec*, because each value of this type consumes more than 30,000 bytes of storage. Instead, you'll allocate a suitably sized block on the heap and access it through a pointer.

The `Random` **shr** 8 business is necessary to bring the 16-bit value returned by *Random* in line with the 8-bit value expected in each element of *waveBytes*. Shifting a random 16-bit value to the right eight times results in a random number with eight 0s in its most significant byte. We'd get the same effect with `Random` **mod** 256 but not as quickly.

If this description left your ears ringing, don't worry about it. This program's sound is secondary to its visuals. For more information, see the Sound Driver chapter in Volume II of *Inside Macintosh*.

Decoding Background.Data

Much as TEXT files are an inter-application standard for textual material, files of type PNTG (painting) are a standard for storing bit images. PNTG files are created by a number of applications, including Bill Atkinson's original classic, MacPaint, and its successors.

To understand how MacTypist decodes file Background.Data, you need to understand the structure of a file of type PNTG.

MacPaint documents contain bit images—rows and columns of bits—of a fixed size: 576 bits wide and 720 bits long. When working with a 72-bit-per-inch output device (like the Macintosh screen), this corresponds to 8 inches horizontally and 10 inches vertically—a nice fit for 8 1/2-by-11-inch paper.

A bit image with these dimensions requires

- 572/8 = 72 bytes per line
- 72 bytes per line × 720 lines = 51840 bytes of storage

Few MacPaint documents are this big, thanks to *compression*, a clever squeezing out of redundancy MacPaint performs before writing its documents to disk. MacPaint undoes the compression before displaying documents onscreen. The compression works on a line-by-line basis, turning sequences of identical bytes into codes that occupy less space. For example, 72 bytes worth of zeros (white space) is translated into 2 bytes worth of encoded data that say, in effect, "Put 72 bytes of zeros here."

The Toolbox's *PackBits* and *UnpackBits* routines perform the compressing and uncompressing, respectively.

```
procedure PackBits(var srcPtr,dstPtr; srcBytes: Integer);
procedure UnpackBits(var srcPtr,dstPtr; dstBytes: Integer);
```

They're described in the Toolbox Utilities chapter of *Inside Macintosh*, Volume I (the same place as *NewString*). Depending on the size and complexity of the image, *PackBits* can turn a 51840-byte bit image into as little as 4K or 5K. Since Background.Data is relatively complex, it compresses to about 27K.

A PNTG file results from applying *PackBits* 720 times to each line of a 576-by-720 bit image. This information is stored in the file's data fork, and the resource fork is empty. In addition, there's a 512-byte header before the compressed data containing, among other things, the various patterns MacPaint displays below its document window. Usually, this is simply ignored.

Unpacking a MacPaint file involves reading the compressed data into memory and then calling *UnpackBits* 720 times on this data (starting 512 bytes into the data to allow for the header) to reconstitute it into a 576-by-720-pixel, 51840-byte bit image.

Loading the Offscreen Bit Image

Loading and unpacking file Background.Data into an offscreen bit map defined by *myBitMap* is performed by procedure *LoadMyBitMap* and its nested assistants.

```
procedure LoadMyBitMap;
var
  packedData: Ptr;

  procedure LoadPackedData;

  procedure IOErrTest(errCode: Integer);
  var
    theStr: Str255;
  begin
    if errCode <> noErr then
    begin
      NumToString(errCode,theStr);
      ParamText(theStr,'','','');
      if StopAlert(512,nil) > 0 then ;
      ExitToShell;
    end;
  end;

  var
    refNum: Integer;
    len: LongInt;
```

```
  begin
    IOErrTest(FSOpen(PixFile,0,refNum));
    IOErrTest(GetEOF(refNum,len));
    packedData := NewPtr(len);
    IOErrTest(FSRead(refNum,len,PackedData));
    IOErrTest(FSClose(refNum));
  end;

var
  n: integer;
  srcPtr,
  dstPtr:   Ptr;
  r,r2: Rect;

begin { LoadMyBitMap }
  myBitMap.baseAddr := NewPtr(51840); { the size of a 576 by 720 bit image }
  myBitMap.rowBytes := 72;
  SetRect(myBitMap.bounds, 0,0,576,720);

  LoadPackedData;

  srcPtr := Pointer(Ord(packedData) + 512); { skip over header }
  dstPtr := myBitMap.baseAddr;
  for n := 0 to 719 do
    UnpackBits(srcPtr, dstPtr, 72);
    DisposPtr(PackedData);
      SetRect(backGround,28,4,520,300);
      SetRect(aboutFig,28,554,326,718);

      SetRect(r,28,309,133,355); { the first VW -- carPix[0,slow] }
  for n := 0 to 4 do
  begin
    r2 := r;
    for speed := slow to fast do
    begin
      carPix[n,speed] := r2;
      offsetRect(r2,108,0);
    end;
      offsetRect(r,0,49);
  end;
end;
```

The process can be summarized as follows:

- Initialize *bitMap* variable *myBitMap* to reflect the size and structure of an unpacked MacPaint document.

- Use error-trapped File Manager calls to open file Background.Data and load it into a nonrelocatable heap block.

- Unpack the image into *myBitMap* and dispose the buffer used to read the packed data.

Initializing MyBitMap

Initializing *myBitMap* requires an assignment to each of its three fields. To *baseAddr*, we assign the address of a 51840-byte, nonrelocatable block—the bit image itself. (If the target machine is low on memory, we'll die horribly at this point. A more cautious program would detect this by testing *baseAddr* against **nil** after the *NewPtr* call.)

Next, we define the structure of the bit image. Each row is 72 bytes long, and we apply a coordinate system such that (0,0) represents the top-left pixel.

Loading Background.Data

Procedure *LoadPackedData* is diligent about I/O errors. Each File Manager routine's return value is sent off for testing to procedure *IOErrTest*. Given a zero parameter (*noErr*), *IOErrTest* simply returns; for all other errors (say, `File not found`), it displays an error alert on the screen. Once the alert is dismissed, the program terminates. To see this in action, change the value of string constant *pixFile* to some file name that doesn't exist and run MacTypist again.

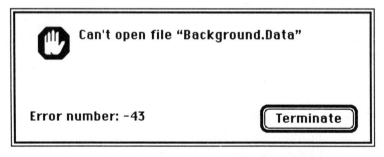

Figure 40.4: The "Can't find Background.Data" Alert

An Aside on Alerts

Alerts are modal dialogs that contain only simple buttons (usually, no more than two) and don't require ongoing interaction on the part of the program. The Dialog Manager has four calls to display alerts, differing only in the icon that appears. A single call to each performs the equivalent of *GetNewDialog*, *ModalDialog*, and *DisposDialog*.

```
function NoteAlert(alertID: Integer; filterProc: ProcPtr):Integer; { Funny man }
function CautionAlert(alertID: Integer; filterProc: ProcPtr):Integer;      { ! }
function StopAlert(alertID:Integer;filterProc:ProcPtr):Integer;{ The stop sign }
function Alert(alertID: Integer; filterProc: ProcPtr): Integer;{no icon at all }
```

Like dialogs, alerts have an associated item list and are defined in RMaker files. We'll describe the format of an ALRT template later in this chapter.

The stop alert displayed by *IOErrTest* includes the error code, so dedicated students of the game can interpret the code, resolve the problem, and live happily ever after. Without its background data, there isn't much MacTypist can do. So, after the user dismisses the alert, MacTypist simply aborts, using the Toolbox's *ExitToShell* routine.

ExitToShell returns either to the Finder or to Turbo Pascal, depending on where the program was launched from. (If you performed the renaming experiment we suggested earlier, you may have noticed that a beep accompanied this alert, even though there's not a *SysBeep* in sight. That's because of this alert's *staging word*, which we'll get into later.)

Back to *LoadPackedData*. We assume that Background.Data is going to be in the default directory, that is, either the directory MacTypist was launched from or the directory containing the System file. So, 0 is passed as *FSOpen*'s *vRefNum* parameter. After opening the file, we fetch its length with *GetEOF*, create a nonrelocatable block of that length, read the entire file into this block, and, finally, close the file.

Unpacking the File

Assuming all went well on the I/O front, a duplicate of Background.Data is now in memory: a packed 576-by-720-pixel bit image with a 512-byte header.

The next step is to uncompress the bit image. Starting at the address held in *packedData* are 720 variable-length data packets, one for each line in the original bit image. Unpacking it involves calling *UnpackBits* 720 times, each time passing pointers to the appropriate points in both the packed and unpacked buffers. *UnpackBits* takes care of advancing these pointers a suitable amount after each call. Sounds tricky, but in practice it's a two-line **for** loop:

```
for n := 0 to 719 do
```

```
UnpackBits(srcPtr, dstPtr, 72);
```

Why did we use local variables *srcPtr* and *dstPtr* here as stand-ins for *packedData* and *myBitMap.baseAddr*? Since *UnpackBits* adjusts its **var** parameters with each call, neither pointer would have its initial value after the unpacking process. As a result, *myBitMap.baseAddr* would no longer point to the start of the bit image, and any *CopyBits* call that used *myBitMap* would fail. Furthermore, since we no longer have a pointer to the first byte of the nonrelocatable block holding the compressed data, there would be no way to deallocate it.

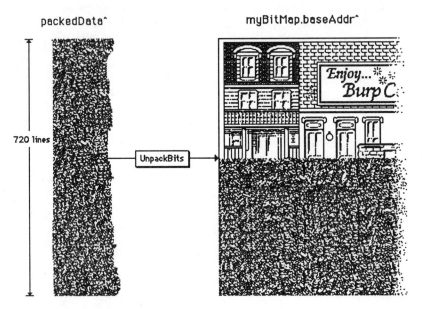

Figure 40.5: The Unpacking Process

Defining the Image Rectangles

At this point we're through with the packed data buffer, so we deallocate it. Some poor DA may need this memory.

After unpacking, the various images used by this program are down in the heap (specifically, at the address held in *myBitMap.baseAddr*). Each has a one-pixel-thick border that isn't part of the figure but that serves to guide human beings editing these images with a Paint program.

The next few statements initialize various global variables of type *Rect* that designate regions in this bit image. These coordinate values are hard-coded into the program, so if you edit Background.Data and accidentally move any of the images (perhaps with MacPaint's Show Page feature), the program won't work correctly any more. For example, the street scene is bounded by the rectangle (28,4) (520,300).

Rather than providing explicit coordinates for each of the 15 cars, we take advantage of the fact that each car's rectangle is offset a fixed amount down and to the right of its neighbor.

```
SetRect(r,28,309,133,355);
for n := 0 to 4 do                    { for each row }
begin
  r2 := r;
  for speed := slow to fast do    { for each type of car }
  begin
    carPix[n,speed] := r2;
    offsetRect(r2,108,0);
  end;
  offsetRect(r,0,49);
end;
```

The Rest of Initialization

MiscInits takes care of the rest, clearing various flag variables, initializing the drag rectangle, and miscellaneous other duties. The following statements

- set *speed* and *caseSens* to their default values,
- use the Menu Manager's *CheckItem* procedure to place a check mark next to the corresponding items of the Options menu:

```
CheckItem(MenuOptions,1,True); speed := slow;
CheckItem(MenuOptions,5,True); caseSens := True;
```

MiscInits also initializes the *billboard*, *caret*, and *theCar* rectangles. Unlike those initialized in *InitMyBitMap*, these rectangles are considered to enclose pixels in the main window (not that *SetRect* cares about this distinction). The statement

```
theCar := carPix[0,slow];
```

sets *theCar* equal to one of the car images (in particular, to the first Volkswagen, although any car would do—we're just getting the size).

When a game begins, this rectangle's coordinates are adjusted to move the car to the starting line.

The call to *GetNewWindow* puts the main window on the screen (empty—we'll draw its contents in response to the resulting update event). We set its *GrafPort* to use the Chicago font and change the cursor to an arrow. Until this point, the cursor is either a checkered flag or a watch, depending on whether the program was launched from Turbo Pascal or the Finder.

Window Processing: Activate Events

Since MacTypist has exactly one window, update and activate event processing is simplified. The Window Manager handles these event types for system (DA) windows automatically. So, we know that whenever *GetNextEvent* returns an activate or update event, it applies to the main window.

An activate event is generated at the very start of the program as a result of creating the main window in *MiscInits*. Thereafter, such events occur only as a result of DA activity. When a DA window becomes active, we receive a deactivate event for the main window. Similarly, closing that DA window generates an activate event for the main window.

Given an activate event, MacTypist

- enables the File and Options menus
- disables the Edit menu
- sets the current *GrafPort* to the main window's *GrafPort*

Similarly, a deactivate event means that a system window has become the active window. DAs have no use for this program's File and Options menus, but they may need the Edit menu. So, in response to a deactivate event, the program

- disables the File and Options menus
- enables the Edit menu
- clears the caret (according to the User Interface Guidelines, inactive windows don't have blinking insertion points)

```
procedure DoActivate;
begin
  if Odd(theEvent.modifiers) then
  begin
    EnableItem(menuFile,0);
```

```
    EnableItem(menuOptions,0);
    DisableItem(menuEdit,0);
    DrawMenuBar;
    SetPort(mainWindow);
  end
  else
  begin
    DisableItem(menuFile,0);
    DisableItem(menuOptions,0);
    EnableItem(menuEdit,0);
    DrawMenuBar;
    FillRect(caret,white);                    { turn off caret }
  end;
end;
```

The Menu Manager's *DisableItem* and *EnableItem* calls cause the indicated items of the chosen menu to become dimmed (unselectable) and vice versa, respectively.

```
procedure DisableItem(theMenu: MenuHandle; item: Integer);
procedure EnableItem(theMenu:  MenuHandle; item: Integer);
```

Passing 0 as the *item* parameter disables or enables every item of the indicated menu. *DrawMenuBar* must be called to show the newly disabled menu in dimmed form.

Update Events

Update events are generated when a window is manipulated in such a way that all or part of an application's window needs redrawing. An update event is automatically generated by the initial drawing of MacTypist's main window. (It has lower priority than the activate event created by the call to *GetNewWindow,* so the activate event happens first.)

```
procedure DoUpdate;
var
  savePort:  GrafPtr;
begin
  GetPort(savePort);
  SetPort(mainWindow);
  BeginUpdate(mainWindow);
  CopyBits(myBitMap,mainWindow^.portBits,background,
          mainWindow^.portRect,srcCopy,nil);
  if gameInProgress then
  begin
    UpdateTime;
    DisplayTargetWord;
    DisplayUserWord;
    CopyBits(myBitMap,mainWindow^.portBits,
            carPix[Ord(flipFlop),speed],theCar,srcCopy,nil)
```

```
  end;
  EndUpdate(mainWindow);
  SetPort(savePort);
end;
```

Like the update processing we performed in previous programs, *DoUpdate* goes through the motions of redrawing the entire main window. How much actually gets through the Window Manager's manipulation of the main window's *visRgn* clipping region isn't our concern.

Just what are those contents? Far and away the most important is the street scene itself, hiding in the offscreen bit image and outlined by global variable *background*. Bringing these bits to the screen takes the all-purpose bit-moving tool, *CopyBits*. Let's review what we learned about this routine back in Chapter 32.

```
procedure CopyBits (srcBits, dstBits: BitMap; srcRect, dstRect: Rect;
                    mode: Integer; maskRgn: RgnHandle);
```

CopyBits moves the bits in the bit image defined by *srcBits* and bounded by rectangle *srcRect* into the bit image defined by *dstBits* and bounded by rectangle *dstRect*. If *dstRect* and *srcRect* aren't the same size, then *CopyBits* performs scaling so that all of *dstRect* is filled with the pattern in *srcRect*.

Mode defines the transfer's boolean algebra; generally, you use *srcCopy* mode, which causes the destination bits to be totally overlaid with the source bits. *MaskRgn* defines a clipping area in the destination bit map you may choose to use: If the current *GrafPort*'s *clipRgn* is sufficient, pass **nil** for this value.

```
CopyBits(myBitMap,mainWindow^.portBits,background,
         mainWindow^.portRect,srcCopy,nil);
```

This call says to move the bits of *myBitMap* enclosed by rectangle *backGround* to the bits of the main window (*mainWindow^.portBits*) enclosed by its port rectangle (*mainWindow^.portRect*). Since these rectangles are the same size by design, no scaling is required and the operation goes quickly. (Few applications handle update events as quickly as MacTypist.)

If a game is in progress, there's more to the main window than simply the street scene. There's also a time (on the odometer), a target word on the billboard rather than a cola advertisement, a score, as much of the user's word as he or she's typed so far, and a car. The following statements add these elements to the main window:

```
UpdateTime;
DisplayTargetWord;
DisplayUserWord;
CopyBits(myBitMap,mainWindow^.portBits,
```

```
carPix[Ord(flipFlop),speed],theCar,srcCopy,nil)
```

DisplayTargetWord also refreshes the scoreboard. If an update event occurs when a game is in progress and the billboard part of the window needs redrawing, it'll first be drawn with the advertisement and then quickly replaced with the target word. If you look closely, you can see this happening. During a game, drag the main window almost completely off the screen, and then pull it back; you'll see the ad appear and then be replaced by the target word.

The car is drawn by a *CopyBits* call very much like the one used to draw the background.

```
CopyBits(myBitMap,mainWindow^.portBits,
        carPix[Ord(flipFlop),speed],theCar,srcCopy,nil);
```

This moves the bits of *myBitMap* surrounded by rectangle *carPix[ord(flipFlop),speed]* to those pixels of the main window surrounded by *theCar*. The expression *Ord(flipFlop)* selects either view #0 or view #1 of the car indicated by global variable *speed*. These first two views are identical except for subtle movements of the antenna. By changing *flipFlop* periodically, we alternate between these images and produce a more interesting animation.

A Few Passes through the Main Event Loop

Putting the main window on the screen results in both an activate and an update event, so *DoActivate* and *DoUpdate* are each called once, in that order, at the start of the program. *DoActivate* adjusts the menus appropriately and makes *mainWindow* the current *GrafPort*; *DoUpdate* draws the background scene (without a car, since a game isn't in progress yet).

Thereafter, things are quiet in the main event loop until the user does something. (*MyTasks* does nothing because *gameInProgress* is False.) Let's follow through the chain of events resulting from choosing Start Game from the File menu.

First, there's a *mouseDown* in the menu bar:

```
inMenuBar:    DoCommand(MenuSelect(theEvent.where));
```

DoCommand in turn calls *DoFileMenu*:

```
procedure DoFileMenu;
begin
```

```
case theItem of
  1: begin {Start/Stop Game}
       gameInProgress := not gameInProgress;
       if gameInProgress then
       begin
         SetItem(MenuFile,1,'Stop Game');
         secCount := '000000';
         wordCount := 1;
         mistakeCount := 0;
         crashCount := 0;
         lastBlink := TickCount;
         lastMove := lastBlink;
         lastTimeIncrement := lastBlink;
         GetIndString(targetWord, 256, 1);
         DisplayTargetWord;
         MoveCarToStart;
       end
       else
         SetItem(MenuFile,1,'Start Game')
     end;

  2: Done := True; { Quit }
  end;
end;
```

Assuming a choice of Start Game, *gameInProgress* is set to the opposite of
what it is now; in this case, to True. The program then changes the File
menu's first item to read Stop Game rather than Start Game. Key game
variables are initialized. The three time variables are set to the current tick
count.

Getting the Word to Spell

MacTypist stores its word list as a resource of type *STR#* (string list) rather
than in a discrete data file. The Toolbox utility routine *GetIndString* fetches
the *index*-th string from a *STR#* resource:

```
procedure GetIndString(var theString: Str255; strListID, index: Integer);
```

Is this one-line call easier than the *Reset/ReadLn/Close* rigamarole Typist.Pas
went through to access its word list? Yes, by a long shot. Next, we display
the word on the billboard (erasing the ad) with a call to *DisplayTargetWord*.

The car is moved to the starting line by a call to *MoveCarToStart*.

```
procedure MoveCarToStart;
begin
  FillRect(theCar,white);  { erase at current position }
  OffsetRect(theCar,-theCar.left + 8,-theCar.top + 181);
```

```
CopyBits(myBitMap,mainWindow^.portBits,
         carPix[Ord(flipFlop),speed],theCar,srcCopy,nil);
end;
```

The first statement erases the car at its current position, just in case it's still on the screen from a previous game. How do we know that this *FillRect* will draw into the main window's *GrafPort*? Because we set the current *GrafPort* to the main window in *DoActivate*. If it weren't set up that way, the user couldn't have chosen Start Game from the File menu in the first place; it would have been disabled.

Since we just started the game, *theCar* is still equal to *carPix[0,slow]*—the position of the first Volkswagen in the offscreen bit map. Applying these coordinates to the smaller main window has no effect, due to clipping. This line moves the car to the starting line:

```
OffsetRect(theCar,-theCar.left + 8,-theCar.top + 181);
```

This is easier to understand when broken down into two steps:

```
OffsetRect(theCar,-theCar.left, -theCar.top);
OffsetRect(theCar,8,181);
```

The first *OffsetRect* shifts the coordinates of the rectangle so that it retains the same length and width and takes on a top-left point of (0,0), rather than whatever it had before. The second application of *OffsetRect* moves the top-left corner to (8,181), a suitable starting point on the main window's highway.

Incidentally, most coordinate constants used in this game were determined by trial and error. Much is possible when you can go from editing to testing in three seconds flat. On a slower development system, this technique would require hours of monk-like dedication.

Procedure MyTasks

When *DoFileMenu* finally returns control to the main event loop, things are more exciting, even if the user doesn't generate any key-downs or mouse-downs. With *gameInProgress* set to True, *MyTasks* takes care of three things that must be performed at regular intervals during a game:

- blinking the insertion point
- moving the car
- incrementing the odometer

```
procedure MyTasks;
  procedure BlinkCaret;
  begin
  end;
  procedure MoveCar;
  begin
  end;
  procedure IncrementOdometer;
  begin
  end;
begin
  if gameInProgress and (FrontWindow = mainWindow) then
  begin
    if (TickCount-lastBlink) >= GetCaretTime then BlinkCaret;
    if (TickCount-lastMove) >= (3-Ord(speed)) then MoveCar;
    if (TickCount-lastOdometerIncrement) >= 6 then IncrementOdometer;
  end;
end;
```

MyTasks returns without doing anything unless there's a game in progress and the main window is active. If both conditions are met, it tests to see which (if any) of its three tasks needs to be performed.

The insertion point (caret) is blinked every *GetCaretTime* ticks. *GetCaretTime* is an obscure Event Manager routine: It returns the number of ticks the user has decided should pass before a blink of the insertion point (any insertion point, in any text-editing situation).

```
function GetCaretTime : LongInt;
```

The user sets the blinking rate with the Control Panel. A medium blinking rate corresponds to 32 ticks, so about half a second expires before the time is right for this program's first call to *BlinkCaret*, a pleasingly simple routine:

```
procedure BlinkCaret;
begin
  lastBlink := TickCount;
  InvertRect(caret);
end;
```

After first recording the time of the blink so that we do it at the right time next time, a call to QuickDraw's *InvertRect* routine is all it takes. If the pixels enclosed by the *caret* rectangle were white, now they'll be black, and vice versa. This call takes place in the main window's *GrafPort*, which is still the current *GrafPort* as a result of *DoActivate*.

Moving the Car

Procedure *MoveCar* is the heart of MacTypist. It's called every three ticks for the slow car, every two ticks for the middle car, and every tick for the fast car.

```
procedure MoveCar;

  procedure Crash];
  var
    temp: LongInt;
    n : Integer;
  begin
    StartSound(Ptr(soundBufferPtr),
             (soundBufferSize div 3) * (Ord(speed) +1), nil);
    CopyBits(myBitMap,mainWindow^.portBits,
            carPix[2,speed],theCar,srcCopy,nil);
    Delay(4 * (3-Ord(speed)),temp);
    for n := 1 to 3 do
    begin
      CopyBits(myBitMap,mainWindow^.portBits,
              carPix[3,speed],theCar,srcCopy,nil);
      Delay(10,temp);
      CopyBits(myBitMap,mainWindow^.portBits,
              carPix[4,speed],theCar,srcCopy,nil);
      Delay(10,temp);
    end;
    crashCount := crashCount + 1;
    UpdateScoreboard;
    StopSound;
    MoveCarToStart;
  end;

begin
  lastMove := TickCount;
  flipFlop := Not flipFlop;
  OffsetRect(theCar,2,0);
  if theCar.right >= 400 then
    Crash
  else
    CopyBits(myBitMap,mainWindow^.portBits,
            carPix[Ord(flipFlop),speed],theCar,srcCopy,nil)
end;
```

Like *BlinkCaret, MoveCar* first records the time of this event. By reversing the state of boolean variable *flipFlop* each time through, we alternate between views 0 and 1 of the chosen car. As described earlier, the car's enclosing rectangle is moved with a call to *OffSetRect*. After the move, we check to see if the rectangle has moved into the back of the truck (**if** theCar.right >= 400).

If it hasn't, we perform the same *CopyBits* call as in *MoveCarToStart*, which draws either view 0 or view 1 of car *speed* in its new position. Thanks to the two columns of white pixels at the left of each car's image, the rear end of the existing car image is erased. (Test this: Use MacPaint or another graphic editor to fill in the gap to the left of the first two views of the Volkswagen with black, and run the program again. Now the car leaves a trail of black as it moves.)

Crashes

The *Crash* procedure carefully displays views 2 through 4 of the chosen car. It contains no *OffsetRect* calls; the motion is built into the figures themselves. The Sound Manager's *StartSound* routine starts the white noise we stored away in the heap playing.

procedure StartSound (synthRec: Ptr; numBytes: LongInt; completionRtn: ProcPtr);

StartSound produces the sound described by the synthesizer buffer pointed to by *synthRec*, at the volume set by the user with the Control Panel desk accessory. *NumBytes* indicates the length of the buffer, and *completionRtn* points to a routine to be executed when the sound finishes. If *completionRtn* is **nil**, the sound is produced in the background.

Once started, this sound plays in the background while other statements are being executed. How long the sound lasts is a function of the car in use; it plays a third as long for the first car as it does for the third.

Next we print view #2 of the car, pause a bit (longer for the first car than for the third), then enter a loop that alternates between views #3 and #4. Finally, we increment the crash count and update the scoreboard with this new value, call the *StopSound* routine, and move the car back to the starting line so that the user can try again. With all its *Delay* calls, *Crash* takes a second or so to execute, so it's possible to store up a number of keystrokes in the Event Manager's queue at this time. Savvy MacTypist players take advantage of this characteristic to fix their words when the clock isn't running.

IncrementOdometer

Once every six ticks (every tenth of a second), *MyTasks* bumps the value of the odometer.

```
procedure IncrementOdometer;
var
  n: integer;
begin
  lastOdometerIncrement := TickCount;
  TextMode(notSrcCopy);
  MoveTo(335,267);
  for n := 6 downto 1 do
  begin
    secCount[n] := Succ(secCount[n]);
    if secCount[n] <= '9' then
    begin
      DrawChar(secCount[n]);
      TextMode(srcCopy);
      Exit;
    end;
    secCount[N] := '0';
    DrawChar('0');
    Move(-21, 0);
    TextMode(srcCopy);
  end;
end;
```

This routine is more exotic than you might expect. In early versions of this program, odometer updating was accomplished by incrementing a long integer variable, converting it to string form with *NumToString*, and then drawing that string.

This technique proved slow, largely because *NumToString* and *DrawString* took too long. The quicker way not only does away entirely with *NumToString* but also (90 percent of the time) requires only a single character to be drawn.

This is a very satisfying characteristic of programming: Routines can always be improved, often dramatically so. The *IncrementOdometer* routine you see here is fifty times faster than the first code designed for this function. The routine gains its speed by more closely modeling a real odometer. Nine increments out of ten, only the least significant digit needs changing. Of those one in ten that require two or more digit changes, nine in ten require exactly two, and so on.

Using a loop that works from the least significant digit in, digit *n* is incremented. If the increment results in the character *9* or something less, we print the character and Exit. The calls to *TextMode* take care of the white-on-black touch of the odometer's least significant digit. We have to set the text mode to *notSrcCopy* for this digit and change it before returning, lest all text put out by this program be printed like this. We also must change it before displaying the rest of the odometer's digits.

Key-Down Processing

For MacTypist, key-down events potentially represent both Command-key menu equivalents and frantic character keystrokes pressed in an effort to break the virtually unbeatable 00:54.6 world record. Key-down processing is handled by procedure *DoKeyDown* and its nested helpers, *Backspace*, *AddChar*, and *TestWord*.

```
procedure DoKeyDown;
  procedure Backspace;
  begin
  end;
  procedure AddChar(theChar: Char);
  begin
  end;
  procedure TestWord;
  begin
  end;

var
  c: Char;
begin
  c := Chr(theEvent.message and $000000FF);
  if (theEvent.modifiers and cmdKey) <> 0 then
    DoCommand(MenuKey(c))
  else
    if gameInProgress and (FrontWindow = mainWindow) then
    begin
      ObscureCursor;
      case c of
        #8        : if Length(userWord) > 0 then Backspace;
        #13       : TestWord;
        ' '..#$D8 : if Length(userWord) < Length(targetWord) then AddChar(c);
        otherwise SysBeep(1);
      end;
    end;
end;
```

If *DoKeyDown*l finds that *Command* was down, it lets *MenuKey* and *DoCommand* worry about a particular key-down event. Otherwise, it's probably a keystroke involved in the game itself.

Before a keystroke can mean anything, a game must be in progress and MacTypist's main window must be the active window. If it isn't, the program beeps. If it is, what happens next depends on the ASCII value of the keystroke:

```
case c of
  #8        : if Length(userWord) > 0 then Backspace;
  #13       : TestWord;
  ' '..#$D8 : if Length(userWord) < Length(targetWord) then AddChar(c);
```

otherwise SysBeep(1);

Backspace has the ASCII value 8. In response to it, we call the *Backspace* routine, which deletes the last character of the user's word (if it isn't empty already) from the screen and from global variable *userWord*. It erases the character from the screen by temporarily making the caret rectangle enclose the word to be deleted, then calling `FillRect(caret,white)`.

The program can display any printable character that can be generated at the keyboard, from a space (ASCII code $20) to an umlauted, lowercase *y* (ASCII code $D8). If the user's word currently has fewer letters than the target word, call *AddChar*. This puts the character on the screen and concatenates it to *userWord*. It also offsets the caret rectangle to the right an appropriate amount.

For a *Return*, call the *TestWord* routine to see if the user's word equals the target word. This procedure is more involved, because if the user's word is correct, it must get the next word or end the game.

```
procedure TestWord;
var
  uw, tw: Str255;
begin
  uw := userWord; tw := targetWord;
  if not caseSens then
  begin
    UprString(uw,True);        { an uppercase conversion utility }
    UprString(tw,True);
  end;
  if uw=tw then                                    { got it right }
  begin
    SysBeep(1);
    while length(UserWord) > 0 do Backspace;
    MoveCarToStart;
    wordCount := wordCount + 1;
    GetIndString(targetWord, 256, wordCount);
    if targetWord = '' then
    begin                                   { last word; game over }
      SysBeep(60);
      gameInProgress := False;
      SetItem(MenuFile,1,'Start Game');
      InvalRect(billboard);                     { redraw billboard }
    end
    else
      DisplayTargetWord;
  end
  else                                            { got it wrong }
  begin
    mistakeCount := mistakeCount + 1;
    UpdateScoreboard;
  end;
end;
```

If the game is currently in non-case-sensitive mode, then both the user's word and the target word are converted to uppercase by the *UprString* routine. This straightforward string conversion utility is described in the Operating System Utilities chapter of *Inside Macintosh*, Volume II:

```
procedure UprString(var theString: Str255; retainDiacriticals: Boolean);
```

Pass True for the *retainDiacriticals* parameter if you want the returned string to retain diacritical marks, such as umlauts and circumflexes. If the word isn't right, we simply increment the mistake counter and update the scoreboard. If it is, we beep the speaker, erase the user's word by calling *Backspace* as many times as the word has letters, move the car back to the starting line, and read the next word from the string list.

If this happens to be the last word in the list (we can tell by comparing the string returned by *GetIndString* to the empty string), then the game is over. Otherwise, we display the new word and the game continues.

TestWord's call to the Window Manager's *InvalRect* routine demonstrates a fine point of window management. When a game isn't in progress, the billboard contains a Burp Cola advertisement. Once a game is over, given a chance, a call to *DoUpdate* will take care of this problem automatically. But an update event that results in redrawing the billboard region of the main window isn't necessarily forthcoming, so the game's last word may stay up there instead.

The *InvalRect* routine is a way of telling the Window Manager that you want part of a window updated:

```
procedure InvalRect(badRect: Rect);
```

This forces an update event to be generated for whichever window is associated with the current *GrafPort*, just as though we had uncovered a *badRect*-sized area of the window. Because of clipping, only the pixels enclosed by the rectangle parameter are actually changed.

If you're unclear on this action, comment out the *InvalRect* call, recompile, and play a game. After the last word, note that the billboard doesn't automatically change into the ad. Manually force an update event by opening the Alarm Clock DA and moving it in front of the upper part of the billboard. Now drag it away; the part of the billboard that was covered is updated with the ad; the part that wasn't continues to hold the last target word. This is shown in the following figure.

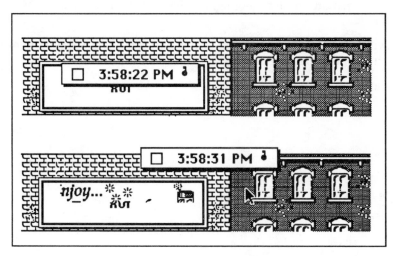

Figure 40.6: Forcing an Update Event

We could force the entire window to be redrawn after a game, by passing an appropriately large rectangle to *InvalRect*:

```
InvalRect(mainWindow^.portRect);
```

But this would have the effect of erasing the score and odometer reading, which the user may want to admire (or bemoan) after a game.

MacTypist.R

MacTypist's accompanying RMaker file contains some things we haven't seen in previous .R files. These include alert templates, string lists, icons, and Finder resources.

Defining ALRT Templates

ALRT templates consist of a resource ID, a position rectangle, an associated item list ID (of type DITL, exactly like a dialog's), and a hexadecimal "stages word." This last comprises 16 bits packed with no fewer than 12 pieces of information that determine, among other things, whether one or more beeps should accompany (or even replace) the box displayed. For more information on alert staging, see *Inside Macintosh*'s Dialog Manager chapter.

MacTypist displays this definition of the alert (and its associated item list) when it can't find Background.Data.

```
type ALRT
    ,512 (32)
60 81 180 431
512
5555

type DITL
    ,512 (32)
3
BtnItem Enabled
90 267 110 337
Terminate

StatText Disabled
10 60 70 350
Can't open file "Background.Data"

StatText Disabled
90 10 110 260
Error number: ^0
```

Defining String Lists

MacTypist's target words are stored in its resource fork as a STR# (string list) resource. The format of a string list consists of an ID number, then a count of how many strings are in the list, and the strings themselves, one per line, as shown here:

```
type STR#      ;; "string list"; i.e., the words to be spelled
    ,256 (4)
48             ;; how many
absolute
and
array
.
.
.
xor
```

Icon Resources

MacTypist.R defines two icons in an ICN# (icon list) resource. An icon is a 32-by-32 bit image. Each icon consists of 32 consecutive long integers expressed in hex. Hmmm. Let's unscramble the first icon's data and see if we can make sense of these values.

```
type ICN# = GNRL
    ,128
.H
0001 8000   -->   ...............XX................( ..= 0; X = 1)
0002 4000   -->   ..............X..X...............
0004 2000   -->   .............X....X..............
0008 1000   -->   ............X......X.............
0010 0800   -->   ...........X........X............
0020 0400   -->   ..........X..........X...........
0040 0200   -->   .........X............X..........
0080 0100   -->   ........X..............X.........
0100 0080   -->   .......X................X........
0200 0040   -->   ......X..................X.......
0400 0020   -->   .....X....................X......
0866 6610   -->   ....X....XX..XX..XX..XX....X....
1066 6608   -->   ...X....XX..XX..XX..XX....X...
2019 9804   -->   ..X........XX..XX..XX........X..
4019 9802   -->   .X........XX..XX..XX.........X.
8066 6601   -->   X........XX..XX..XX..XX........X
8066 6601   -->   X........XX..XX..XX..XX........X
4019 9802   -->   .X........XX..XX..XX.........X.
2019 9804   -->   ..X........XX..XX..XX........X..
1066 6608   -->   ...X....XX..XX..XX..XX....X...
0866 6610   -->   ....X....XX..XX..XX..XX....X....
0400 0020   -->   .....X....................X......
0200 0040   -->   ......X..................X.......
0100 0080   -->   .......X................X........
0080 0100   -->   ........X..............X.........
0040 0200   -->   .........X............X..........
0020 0400   -->   ..........X..........X...........
0010 0800   -->   ...........X........X............
0008 1000   -->   ............X......X.............
0004 2000   -->   .............X....X..............
0002 4000   -->   ..............X..X...............
0001 8000   -->   ...............XX................
```

Unlike PNTG files, icon data isn't packed but presented instead as a straightforward 32-by-32 bit image. If you compile MacTypist to disk and then exit to the Finder, you'll find this very symbol used to represent the application, as shown in the next figure.

Finder Resources

Certain resources must be present in an application's resource fork to ensure that the application receives proper treatment by the Finder.

Every application must have a *version data resource*. This consists of a resource whose type equals the application's creator signature, which in MacTypist's case is MCTY. By convention, the ID of this resource is always 0; the type of data it contains can be anything, but is usually a string containing version information. Here's MacTypist's version data resource definition:

```
type MCTY = STR
   ,0 (32)
MacTypist   Version 1.0 June 1,1987  Copyright Borland International, Inc.
```

If you want the Finder to represent your program with something other than the generic application icon, the application's resource fork must contain an icon list resource. That's the purpose of ICN# resource number 128 discussed earlier. It's a two-icon list rather than one, because the Finder requires both an icon and a mask to draw it properly against different backgrounds. Typically, the mask is like the icon, except filled in solid. MacTypist's mask (the second icon in the list) looks like this:

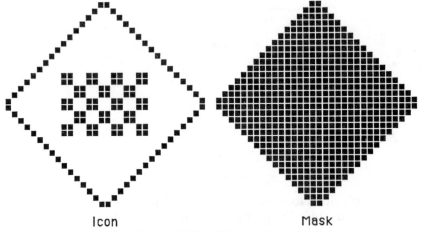

Icon   Mask

Figure 40.7: The Mask and Icon

File Reference and Bundle Resources

Finally, applications that expect the Finder to represent them (and, optionally, the files they may create) with a unique icon must have one or more FREF (file reference) resources and a single BNDL (bundle) resource. An FREF resource makes the connection between a file and the icon it should use. MacTypist declares a single FREF resource:

```
type FREF
    ,128
APPL 0
```

This defines a file reference resource of ID 128, associating the application itself (APPL) with icon list 0. 0 is a so-called local ID. The BNDL resource provides a mapping between local and actual IDs for each finder resource; in the case of this icon list, between 0 and 128.

The bundle resource ties together an application's various Finder resources and links their local and actual IDs. MacTypist's BNDL definition looks like this:

```
type BNDL
    ,128
MCTY 0
ICN#
0 128
FREF
0 128
```

This BNDL resource says that MacTypist has three Finder resources: A version resource (type MCTY, ID number 0), an ICN# resource (local ID 0, actual ID 128), and an FREF resource (local ID 0, actual ID 128). The local/actual ID code allows the Finder to arbitrate conflicts between applications that may declare the same actual IDs for a given resource type.

Finder resources must coordinate with a couple of related compiler directives in the application's source file. At the top of MacTypist.Pas, the following directives work to control what goes into the file produced when compiling this program to disk:

```
{$B+}
{$R MacTypist.Rsrc}
{$T APPLMCTY}
```

The $B+ directive causes the resulting file to have a set "bundle bit." All files maintained by the File Manager have a bundle bit, but only files with BNDL references should have this bit set. When copying a file to a volume for the first time, the Finder knows that a turned-on bundle bit means there are goodies intended for it in this file's resource fork. These resources (which are indicated by the BNDL reference) are then copied into the volume's Desktop file.

The $R *filename* directive tells Turbo that the file produced as a result of this compilation should include all of the resources in the indicated file. Upon completing a compilation, Turbo makes appropriate Resource Manager calls to copy this file's resources to the newly created application file's resource fork. If you're testing a program within Turbo Pascal, Turbo simply opens this file with the Resource Manager's *OpenResFile* call just before giving control to your program.

The $T directive sets the resulting file's type and creator. Application files must have a type of APPL, and the creator signature must match what appears in the corresponding resource file's version and bundle resources.

Review

This chapter discussed the Macintosh application MacTypist, a typing tutor program with outstanding graphics. MacTypist follows the User Interface Guidelines and so is easy for an experienced Macintosh user to understand, even without a manual.

You learned how to use the Sound Driver's free-form synthesizer mode to create a white-noise sound effect, and how to interpret compressed images in files of type PNTG (MacPaint documents). You used *CopyBits* to move images from an offscreen bit image to a window. Alerts, a convenient way to display simple dialog-box style information, were discussed, as was a way to error trap File Manager calls.

You saw how activate events can be used as a signal to enable and disable menu items, so that inappropriate menu selections are unavailable when certain windows are active.

Also, you learned that inserting a *MyTasks* call inside the main event loop gives time-oriented procedures processing time, regardless of whether or not any events need processing. An update processing routine can pick and choose what elements need to be redrawn in a window depending on the state of a program.

STR# (string list) resources and the *GetIndString* call for reading them were discussed. You also saw how to create ALRT and ICN# templates. Finder resources are version resources, file references, and bundles that make sure the Finder knows how to represent this application properly, as well as the relationship between these resources and the compiler directives $B, $R, and $T.

41

Debugging

Programs never work right the first time. What keeps them from performing as intended are bugs—flaws in logic (almost always, flaws in *your* logic) that cause the computer to do something you didn't intend. Some bugs are obvious; some are exquisitely subtle. A large part of programming is making your program work right by searching out, understanding, and fixing these errors.

Think First, Then Type

It's been said that if civil engineers built buildings like programmers build programs, the first good wind that came along would destroy civilization. Programmers, by and large, don't plan as well as they should. Given the infinitely flexible nature of programming, it's tempting to leap into a problem at some place other than its origin and worry about troublesome issues further down the road.

The best way to fix a bug is to avoid it in the first place. Don't rush into the coding phase of the software development process. Turn off the computer; go sit under a tree. Evaluate alternatives, in your head and on paper. Don't necessarily go with the first method that occurs to you. It's easier to tear up a few sheets of paper and start over than to continually patch and modify a poorly designed program.

Errors: Compile Time versus Run Time

Even with careful designing, mistakes are inevitable. Errors can be classified according to when they occur: Compile time or run time. Compile-time errors are errors of syntax caught by the compiler. Such errors include misspelled keywords, unbalanced parentheses, and unmatched parameters.

Compile-time errors usually aren't hard to find, since Turbo points out the line with the problem and takes an educated guess as to what's wrong (although unbalanced comment delimiters and **begin/end** pairs can really throw it off the track).

Run-Time Errors

Run-time errors result when a syntactically correct program does something "bad" when executing. Some can be sensed by mechanisms built into the Toolbox and the processor itself. Others can't be and usually result in a locked-up (hung) machine.

The Toolbox and the processor work together to *trap* run-time errors; that is, to first recognize that an error condition exists and then report that condition on the screen. The reporting is handled by the System Error Handler, the ROM routine behind the bomb alert.

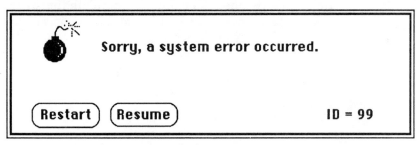

Figure 41.1: The Bomb Alert

Whenever this box appears, your application has done something so vile that, in the opinion of the Toolbox, there's no point in going on. If the program was launched from Turbo Pascal, the Resume button will be enabled, and clicking it returns control to Turbo. Depending on the type of error, Turbo Pascal then attempts to point out the statement that caused the problem.

As an example of a trapped error, consider division by zero. You may remember from a math class that the result of this operation is infinity, a value the processor has difficulty representing in its finite silicon registers. Rather than ignore this condition and let your program go its merry way, the architects of the Toolbox decreed that divide-by-zero errors be trapped. The processor is able to recognize when integer division by zero is attempted and immediately calls the System Error Handler. The following program demonstrates such an error.

```
program DivideByZero;
{$U-}
var  i,j:  Integer;
begin
   j := 0;
   i := 3 div j;
end.
```

Running this program results in system error ID 4 and the bomb alert (assuming you don't have MacsBug installed; more about that later). When you resume your way back to Turbo Pascal, it points out the offending statement.

Range Testing

Compiling a program with the range-testing switch turned on ($R+) expands run-time error trapping to cover additional error types. These include accessing non-existent array elements and inappropriate assignments to scalar and subrange variables (such as $c := 3$, where c is type $0..2$). Program *RangeErrorTrapping* demonstrates:

```
program RangeErrorTrapping;
{$R+}
var
   a: array [1..11] of Integer;
   b: Integer;
begin
   b := 12;
   a[b] := 345;
end.
```

When this program gets ready to assign to the *b*th element of array *a* at run time, testing mechanisms put in place by the compiler pop the big question: "Is the index we're about to use in the range 1 through 11?"

If the answer is no, the assignment is not performed and a trap to the error handler occurs, resulting in error ID 5. Had range-testing not been in effect, the program would simply have written to the memory address just after *a[11]*, clobbering whatever had been there previously.

Nothing comes for free: These range-testing mechanisms take up space and execution time, so programs compiled with range-testing turned on are slightly larger and slower than they would be otherwise. (Test the size effect for yourself: Compile MacTypist.Pas both ways, checking the resulting object-code size with the Compile menu's GetInfo option each time.) Typically, once a program is known to be free of range errors, you'll turn off range checking before producing a final version.

Table 41.1 lists the errors that can result in calls to the System Error Handler.

Error ID	Meaning
1	Bus error (very rare)
2	Address error (reference to word or long word at odd address)
3	Illegal instruction (undefined processor opcode)
4	Divide-by-zero exception
5	CHK exception (range-testing failed)
6	TRAPV exception (trap-on-overflow instruction failed)
7	Privilege violation (shouldn't occur)
8	Trace exception (for debuggers)
9	A-Trap dispatcher failure
10	F-Trap exception
11	Miscellaneous exception (all other processor exceptions)
12	Bad trap number
13	Spurious interrupt (no interrupt handler for an interrupt)
14	I/O System Error
15	Segment Loader error
16	SANE error
17-24	Can't load package
25	Can't allocate heap block (out of memory)
26	Segment Loader error: couldn't find CODE resource #0
27	File map destroyed
28	Stack overflow
84	Menu purged (don't make menu resources purgeable!)

Luckily, most of the errors in this table are rare. In addition to type 4 and 5 errors, buggy programs often result in error ID 2 (address error), 25 (out of heap space), and 28 (stack overflow).

Address errors are especially common, because they often result from pointer problems, a common failing of Macintosh applications. By design, a 68000-family processor doesn't permit an integer or long integer to be accessed at an odd address. For example, if you say in machine language,

"Read the long word at address 4913," system error ID 2 results. A pointer that's never been initialized may contain any value, so there's an even chance that dereferencing an uninitialized pointer will produce an address error. For example,

```
program BadPointerI;
var
  p : ^Integer;
  i : Integer;
begin
  p := Pointer(1497);
  i := p^;
end.
```

results in a system error the instant the processor tries to read the word stored at address 1497 (any odd number has the same effect). The program would be equally wrong with an arbitrary even address, but the processor won't catch the mistake.

Running Out of Heap

Insufficient heap space can put certain Toolbox routines in an untenable bind. No matter how much memory you ask for in a *NewPtr* or *NewHandle* call, a system error is never generated. Instead, the system expects you to check error codes (or a **nil** return value) and take appropriate action on your own.

Toolbox routines that need heap space don't have that option. When you call *MenuSelect* after a mouse-down in the menu bar, for example, the Menu Manager allocates memory in the heap before drawing the designated menu. This memory is for storing those bits on the screen that are about to be covered up, so they can be restored later. A big menu may require 5K or more for this purpose and, if it's not available, pow—system error ID 25. Program *NoHeap* demonstrates this effect.

```
program NoHeap;
{$U-}
uses
  MemTypes,QuickDraw,OSIntf,ToolIntf;
var
  theOnlyMenu : MenuHandle;
  theEvent    : EventRecord;
  temp        : LongInt;
  h           : Handle;

begin
  MaxApplZone;
```

```
    InitGraf(@thePort);
    InitFonts;
    InitWindows;
    InitMenus;

    theOnlyMenu := NewMenu(1,'Choose Me');
    AppendMenu(theOnlyMenu,'A Menu Item');
    InsertMenu(theOnlyMenu, 0);
    DrawMenuBar;
(*
    h := NewHandle(MaxMem(temp)); { however much heap there was, it's gone now }
*)
    repeat until GetNextEvent(mDownMask,theEvent);
    temp := MenuSelect(theEvent.Where)
end.
```

Compile and run this program. Choose from its only menu. The program ends when you release the button, allowing *MenuSelect* to return.

NoHeap works fine until you uncomment the *NewHandle* call, which allocates every single byte in the heap. *MenuSelect* needs a few hundred bytes to store the part of the screen overwritten when the menu is pulled down. It can't get it, and, since there's no error-returning provision in *MenuSelect*, it does the next best thing and generates system error 25.

Stack Overflow

It's also possible to run out of stack space. After an application calls *MaxApplZone* to fully expand its heap, it has approximately 8K of stack headroom available to it. Using more stack than this (by using large local variables, passing large variables by value, and deep nesting—especially recursive nesting) results in system error 28.

```
program StackOverflow;
{$U-}
uses
   MemTypes,QuickDraw,OSIntf;
type
   BigArray = array [1..15000] of Integer;
var
   a: BigArray;

procedure CallMe(theArray: BigArray);
begin
end;

begin
   MaxApplZone;
   CallMe(a);
end.
```

In invoking procedure *CallMe*, a copy of 30000-byte array *a* is pushed on the stack. Since the stack has only 8K of headroom after a call to *MaxApplZone*, this program promptly dies with a type 28 system error.

Common Problems

Two problems account for most run-time bugs: bad pointers and pointers that are bad. You typically use pointer *p* or handle *h* and assume you know what it points to (that is, what *p^* represents) but, sometimes, you're wrong. Perhaps you've previously deallocated the block in another part of the program and it's since been overwritten. Perhaps it was never allocated in the first place. Maybe heap compaction moved the block out from underneath your pointer (more about this later).

In any case, working with a bad pointer sooner or later produces bad results. Assigning from a dereferenced dangling pointer reads random garbage; writing to a dereferenced dangling pointer overwrites memory that may not appreciate being clobbered. As stated earlier, bad pointers often result in address errors.

A related problem concerns disposing invalid pointers and handles; that is, passing unreasonable parameters to *DisposPtr* and *DisposeHandle* (or indirectly through *DisposeWindow*, *DisposeDialog*, and so on):

```
program BadPointerII;
var
  p : ^Integer;
  i : Integer;
begin
  p := Pointer(1497);
  Dispose(p)
end.
```

A call to Turbo's *Dispose* procedure results in a call to the Memory Manager's *DiposePtr* routine. *DiposePtr*'s parameter is supposed to be the address of a nonrelocatable block in the application heap, that is, a value returned earlier by *NewPtr* when the block was first allocated. In this case, we're passing the address of something that isn't a valid block in the heap; when the deallocation routines start to work with it, they'll usually get so confused that an address error is created (or the system crashes altogether).

The Toolbox and Error Checking

Much as we might like them to, the Toolbox's routines don't perform any error checking. To illustrate, the *DisposeWindow* call

procedure DisposeWindow(theWindow: WindowPtr);

expects its parameter to be the address of a valid window record in the heap. If you pass *DisposeWindow* any old 4-byte value, it goes through the same motions: It treats what's at that address as though it really *were* a *WindowRecord* and deallocates various and sundry relocatable blocks, handles to which are supposed to be at certain fixed offsets from this address. The result of these assumptions about the contents of an undefined area of memory is almost always disastrous.

Handle Pitfalls: What Your Mother Didn't Tell You

The Mac's reputation as a difficult machine to program is due in no small part to its fancy memory-management schemes. Apparently innocent—and perfectly legal—Pascal constructs involving handles to relocatable blocks generate code that can fail, should heap movement occur at the wrong time.

For example, consider the following program:

```
program HandleProblemI;
uses
  MemTypes,QuickDraw,OSIntf;

type
  Check = record
            payee: string[40];
            date:  string[8];
            amount: Integer;
          end;
  CheckPtr = ^Check;
  CheckHdl = ^CheckPtr;

var
  theCheck: CheckHdl;
  p : Ptr;

begin
  theCheck := CheckHdl(NewHandle(Sizeof(Check)));
  with theCheck^^ do
```

```
  begin
    payee   := 'Gerald Govans';
    date    := '10/25/51';
    amount := 1234;
  end;
  Writeln(theCheck^^.amount);
  Readln;
end.
```

This program prints 1234 to the screen—no great mystery there. Now, insert the following statement just before the assignment to *amount* and run the program again:

```
p := NewPtr(10000);
```

What's printed? It probably *wasn't* 1234 and therein lies a tale.

You've probably come to think of the **with** statement as a way to write compact source code. It's that and more. Turbo Pascal's compiler keys on the **with** statement to generate faster, smaller object code, when the record variable is referenced by array or pointer notation.

Had this program's assignments been performed without the benefit of a **with** statement, like this,

```
theCheck^^.payee  := 'Gerald Govans';
theCheck^^.date   := '10/25/51';
theCheck^^.amount := 1234;
```

the resulting code would have been both longer and slower. At run time, the processor would have to perform three handle-dereferencing double reads, redundantly fetching the starting address of the check record for each field. Using the **with** form, this only has to be done once, at the start of the block. The resulting time and code savings can be significant, especially if many fields are referenced inside the **with** block. If array indexing is involved (as in **with** checkBook^^[i]), the potential savings are even greater.

So, what's the problem? Calculating the address of the check record only once—at the start of the **with** block—assumes that this address won't change for the duration of the block. Which is exactly what can happen if the block contains a statement able to trigger heap movement. The call to *NewPtr* we inserted created such an inopportune heap movement. Nonrelocatable blocks are always created low in the heap, moving relocatable blocks (check records, for instance) up and out of the way. In the process of executing the *NewPtr* call, *theCheck^^* (two of its three fields already assigned to) was moved out from under the address calculated at the start of the **with** block.

The assignment to the *amount* field writes to the address that the amount field of the check record was at before the move. It possibly clobbered something just moved there and, in any case, did not update *theCheck^^.amount*. So the *WriteLn* prints out whatever 16-bit value was in the relocatable block when it was initially allocated by *NewHandle* in the first place.

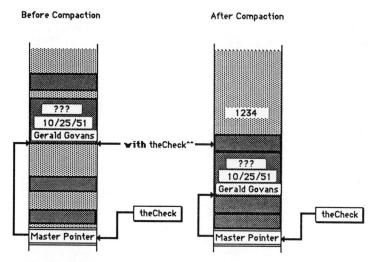

Figure 41.2: With and Relocatable Blocks

To prevent this problem, lock the relocatable object before the **with** statement and unlock it afterwards:

```
HLock(Handle(theCheck));
with theCheck^^ do
begin
  payee  := 'Gerald Govans';
  date   := '10/25/51';
  p := NewPtr(10000);
  amount := 1234;
end;
HUnlock(Handle(theCheck));
```

Now the program works fine, heap compaction or no heap compaction, because the check record's address can't change during the **with** block.

If constant locking and unlocking of a particular data structure causes your program to fill up with *HLock*s and *HUnlock*s, then change that object to a nonrelocatable block and access it with simple pointers instead—especially if the structure won't have to be enlarged as the program runs.

Handle Problems II

An even more devious way in which handles can dangle concerns passing the objects they point to as **var** parameters. Program *HandleProblemII* demonstrates:

```
program HandleProblemII;
uses
  MemTypes,QuickDraw,OSIntf;

procedure PrintValue(var i: SignedByte);
var
  p: Ptr;
begin
  p := NewPtr(30000);
  FillChar(p^,30000,0);   { write 30,000 zeros starting at the address in p }
  WriteLn(i);
  ReadLn;
end;

var
  h: Handle;
begin
  h := NewHandle(1);
  h^^ := 34;
  PrintValue(h^^);
end.
```

You'd expect this program to print *34*; instead it prints *0*. Simply deleting the **var** from *PrintValue*'s parameter list makes it work correctly. Why?

You've learned that when a **var** parameter is passed at run time to a procedure, it's the address of the object, not the object itself, that's passed on the stack. In calling *PrintValue* in this program, what goes on the stack is the 4-byte address of the byte represented by *h^^*. The problem is that this address is outdated by the time *PrintValue* gets around to executing its *WriteLn*, the call to *NewPtr* having moved *h^^* who knows where. There's a good chance it may not be overwritten at its former address, so the problem may not surface for a long time. That's why we used the *FillChar* routine to fill the newly allocated block with zeros; otherwise, the 34 may still have been there.

Code Segments and Dangling Pointers

We touched on the process of segmenting large programs in Chapter 23. To recap, no single chunk of code in a Macintosh application can exceed 32K. If a program must be larger, you have to use the $S compiler directive to break it into two or more code segments (which are stored in the application's resource fork as resources of type CODE). For example, the Turbo Tutor application is broken into 20 segments, one for each demonstration procedure and one for everything else.

Beyond adding a few $S directives into your program, there isn't much you have to do. A set of routines known as the Segment Loader takes care of automatically reading in segments from disk (into a newly allocated nonrelocatable block) whenever a procedure or function contained in one is called.

How does all this relate to dangling pointers? Well, suppose program *HeapProblemII* was large enough to require segmenting and that procedure *PrintValue* ended up in a different segment from the main program. If the segment containing *PrintValue* isn't in memory at the instant of the call, the Segment Loader will recognize that fact, allocate some heap space, and read in the segment from the application's resource fork. The act of allocation, with its ever-present potential for heap movement, means that *PrintValue* may not work even without a call to *NewPtr* or other Memory Manager routine. Simply the act of calling *PrintVal* is enough to create movement.

Avoiding Heap Problem II

Locking the object before making the call and unlocking it afterwards is a sure cure for Heap Problem II:

```
HLock(h);
PrintValue(h^^);
HUnlock(h);
```

Another fix is to use a temporary variable in place of the dereferenced handle:

```
temp := h^^;
PrintValue(temp);
```

This effect can occur on parameters that are passed by value (that is, without the **var** keyword) as well. For efficiency in passing non-**var** parameters, Turbo passes the address of the object rather than the object itself for all data objects larger than 4 bytes. It's up to the called routine to make a copy of the object given this pointer. A routine that you write and compile with Turbo Pascal will always make this copy; some smart-aleck Toolbox routines do not.

For efficiency, certain Toolbox routines passed large parameters by value don't make a copy of the object. Instead, they are simply careful not to modify the original, thus preserving the spirit—if not the letter—of Pascal's law that a copy be made of non-**var** parameters. QuickDraw's *DrawString* routine is one such renegade:

```
procedure DrawString(s: Str255);
```

Even though *s* is declared as a value parameter, it's the address of the parameter that goes on the stack when calling *DrawString*. *DrawString* has the potential to create heap movement (a font may need loading, for one thing) so, by the time it gets around to looking at this address for the characters it should output, the address may not be right anymore.

We performed such a shaky pass to *DrawString* back in Chapter 35. Remember this classic line from procedure *DoUpdate* in WindowDemo.Pas?

```
DrawString(StringHandle(WindowPeek(theWindow)^.refCon)^^);
```

Since this object (a Str255) is larger than 4 bytes, Turbo puts its address—not its content—on the stack in calling *DrawString*. If the string is moved before *DrawString* gets around to looking at its address, then anything is liable to be drawn to the screen. To be safe, we must lock this handle for the duration of the call.

```
HLock(Handle(WindowPeek(theWindow)^.refCon));
DrawString(StringHandle(WindowPeek(theWindow)^.refCon)^^);
HUnlock(Handle(WindowPeek(theWindow)^.refCon));
```

MORAL: When sending a relocatable object larger than 4 bytes to a Toolbox routine or to one of your own routines in a different code segment, *lock it down*.

Strategies in Debugging

Those of you with experience in other programming environments may have noticed that Macintosh programs are prone to sudden, lethal bugs (although a debugged Macintosh program is as dependable as any). A working Macintosh application is a little like a high-speed bottle-capping machine, whirling around its main event loop with mechanical precision many times a second. Occasionally, without warning, the machine stops. Somewhere, a spring worked loose, fell into a pulley, threw a belt, overloaded a motor, tripped a circuit breaker—all in less time than it takes to blink. In the aftermath of the crash, there are no easy clues as to what happened; the loose spring responsible for the crash has rolled out of sight.

Your job in debugging is to recreate the events that created the crash, to find the spring and figure out why it worked loose.

When a program fails with a vague system error, it's tempting to construct elaborate theories blaming everything from faulty hardware to a DA that was closed four hours ago. Usually, though, system errors result from a single bad move on your part.

Most repeatable bugs can be rooted out by a systematic determination of just how much your program is doing *right*. A strategically placed *DrawString* (displaying the value of some key variable) or a *SysBeep* can tell you that a program is getting to a certain point. With Turbo's fast compilation, it usually doesn't take long to zero in on the troublemaking procedure.

Intermittent failures are harder to figure out. One technique that often turns intermittent problems into repeatable problems is running the program under Switcher, with as little memory allocated as possible. With a smaller heap, compaction happens more often and dangling pointer problems are more likely to show themselves.

In general, don't try to outmuscle a recalcitrant bug. Instead, outsmart it. Come to the computer fresh, armed with an experiment, a new approach to the problem. When you can't remember what it was you were trying to test in the first place, you've been at the keyboard too long. Come back after lunch and try again.

MacsBug

Tracking down and exterminating tough bugs often requires a debugging program. MacsBug, documented in the Turbo Pascal manual, is the de facto standard Macintosh debugger. It's powerful and dependable (if less than a joy to use), and you'll find a copy of it in the Miscellaneous folder of your Turbo Pascal Utilities & Sample Programs Disk. (An even better debugger, TMON, is available from ICOM Simulations of Wheeling, Illinois.) How far you'll progress in MacsBug depends on how much you know (or are willing to learn) about assembly language; the "Suggested References" at the end of this book lists sources of information on the subject.

MacsBug is unusual as programs go in that it's not startable from the Finder, but instead is built into the system at startup time, where it stays until you reboot. If there's a file named MacsBug (nothing more, nothing less) in the System folder when you first turn your computer on, then this file is loaded into memory and given control early on in the booting process. MacsBug tucks itself into an out-of-the-way corner of high memory and waits quietly for a condition that requires its attention. It may never be used, in which case its only effect is to reduce the amount of memory available by about 40K.

The Programmer's Switch

If you don't have a programmer's switch, get one. The programmer's switch is a plastic widget that looks like one of the better prizes from a box of Cracker Jacks. When your Macintosh was brand new, it lay nestled next to the Guided Tour cassette—a classic "part left over."

Once installed on the left-hand side of the computer, the switch's twin prongs reach through ventilation slots to rest against two switches on the main logic board. The frontmost lever is called *Reset*: It generates, without fail, the same sequence of events as a power down/power up cycle (or clicking Restart from the System Error alert). The Reset switch doesn't assist in the debugging process, but it saves the Macintosh the shock of being turned off and on again when recovering from severe crashes.

The second (rearmost) switch generates a non-maskable *interrupt* on the processor, forcing it to execute the code at interrupt vector 31. With MacsBug installed, this code is MacsBug. MacsBug quickly saves all of screen memory but the menu bar and replaces it with a terminal-style scrolling text display.

MacsBug provides a no-nonsense, low-level view of the processor and memory. It has commands to display and alter memory locations, disassemble machine instructions, and incrementally execute a program by "single stepping" and setting *breakpoints*. You can set breakpoints anywhere in your program, or you can tell MacsBug to stop execution whenever a particular Toolbox (A-Trap) call appears. For example, you can have MacsBug get control with every call to *NewPtr*.

Getting Into MacsBug

There are three ways to enter MacsBug:

- Press the interrupt switch.
- Call MacsBug from a program.
- Create a system error.

When MacsBug is installed, the system's run-time response to errors changes. Certain problems (address and divide-by-zero errors, to name two) that used to result in the System Error alert now drop you directly into MacsBug. To invoke MacsBug from within a program, add this one-line procedure to it:

```
procedure MacsBug; inline $A9FF;
```

Calling this procedure results in the processor executing opcode $A9FF, thereby invoking MacsBug—with the processor poised to execute the very next instruction of your program. This program demonstrates. Enter and run it.

```
program MacsBugTest;

var
  a,b: Integer;

procedure MacsBug; inline $A9FF;

begin
  a := $1234;
  MacsBug;
  b := a
end.
```

The ability to activate MacsBug from within a program is a tremendous help in figuring out when, where, and why your program is going bad. Like any tool, it takes practice. When MacsBug gets control, it saves the contents of screen memory and quickly substitutes its own display. The result of running MacsBug is shown below—a program that would normally execute in a few millionths of a second frozen in time. We've caught it between its assignment to *a* and the assignment to *b*, the state of the processor and memory exposed for our study.

```
USERBREAK
023308: N:    MOVE.W $FEC8(A5),$FEC6(A5)
PC = 00023308 SR = 00002000 TM = 00028B5B
D0 = 00000000 D1 = 000231F0 D2 = FFFF0001 D3 = 00000000
D4 = 00000000 D5 = 00000000 D6 = 00000000 D7 = 00000000
A0 = 000232D6 A1 = 000ED860 A2 = 00009F82 A3 = 000ED8C0
```

```
A4 = 00023B8E A5 = 000ED89E A6 = 000ED758 A7 = 000ED758
```

(Incidentally, MacsBug will let you peek at the screen as it existed just before it took control. Simply press '(the backward apostrophe) on the top-left side of the keyboard. You can't do anything at this point except look; MacsBug is still in control. Press another key to return to the MacsBug screen.)

The 32-bit hexadecimal values printed here represent the contents of various processor registers. The processor has eight data registers (D0-D7) and eight address registers (A0-A7). Let's try to make some sense of these numbers (which came from a 1-Mb Macintosh Plus; your mileage may be different).

The most important is the value in the program counter register (PC), $23308. This is the address of the processor instruction that was about to be executed when we so rudely interrupted this program. $23308 is about 145,000 decimal—so we're talking about a point relatively low in the application heap.

Register A7 is the stack pointer. Its value ($ED758, around 970,000) puts it relatively high in RAM.

Register A5 is crucial to Macintosh applications, because it indicates the start of global variable storage. Global variables are referenced relative to the number in this register, in this case $ED89E—slightly above the stack.

The Ocean of Hex

It isn't easy navigating around this homogeneous sea of hundreds of thousands of hexadecimal numbers but, with time, you'll learn to recognize some landmarks. About 30 of these bytes are especially interesting, as they constitute the object form of the program we just wrote, compiled, and started to execute. MacsBug's DM (Display Memory) command displays the contents of a range of addresses. Enter

```
DM PC-10 30
```

MacsBug returns the following:

```
0232E6  0000 0000 4E56 0000  3B7C 1234 FEC8 A9FF  ....NV..;_.4....
0232F6  3B6D FEC8 FEC6 4E5E  4E75 4EBA F156 4EBA  ;M....N_NVN..VN.
023206  FBFA 4EBA FF86 4EBA  FFDC A9F4 8000 0012  ...N...N.......D
```

This display consists of an address, eight 16-bit values displayed in hex, and, at the end of the line, a halfhearted effort at displaying the corresponding ASCII character. Halfhearted because lowercase letters are displayed as uppercase, and all the non-ASCII values (those with codes less than 32 or greater than 127) display as dots.

The argument we supplied to the DM command (PC-10 30) describes the addresses we want to look at. PC stands for program counter; PC-10 means the address $10 less than the program counter's current value. We're backing up a bit because we want to see both a little behind and a little ahead of the current instruction. The 30 means we want to look at $30 (48) addresses.

These bytes probably don't mean much, since you're not a microprocessor, but, if you look closely, you may see a couple of familiar faces. At the end of the first line, notice $1234 and $A9FF.

MacsBug has a "disassembly" feature that makes it considerably easier to interpret byte values that happen to be 68000-family programs. Disassembly is invoked with the IL (instruction list) command. Let's disassemble these bytes instead of simply displaying them.

```
IL PC-10 30
    0232E6          ORI.B     #$00,D0
    0232EA: N:      LINK      A6,#$0000
    0232EE: N:      MOVE.W    #$1234,$FEC8(A5)
    0232F4: N:      TOOLBOX   $A9FF                    ;DEBUGGER
    0232F6: N:      MOVE.W    $FEC8(A5),$FEC6(A5)
    0232FC: N:      UNLK      A6
    0232FE: N:      RTS
```

Here MacsBug demonstrates its knowledge of the 68000 instruction set, by turning raw bytes into a textual (assembly-language) form easier for a human being to understand. Our three-line Pascal source program compiles to a compact six-line assembly language code. Let's quickly work through these six lines.

The LINK and UNLK statements bracket all Turbo Pascal-produced procedures, functions, and main programs. Their function is to allocate space on the stack for local variables, and they're called even if a routine has no local variables. Even without being 68000 assembly-language experts, the next three statements aren't too hard to understand. This statement

```
0232EE: N:      MOVE.W    #$1234,$FEC8(A5)
```

says to move the word value $1234 to the address offset $FEC8 bytes from the address stored in register A5. Without getting into the mechanics of register-relative addressing, we're referring here to the storage location for global variable *a*.

The next line is responsible for getting us into MacsBug in the first place. All 68000-family instructions that start with the hexadecimal digit *A* are Toolbox calls. $A9FF in particular is a call to wake up MacsBug.

```
0232F4: N:     TOOLBOX   $A9FF              ; DEBUGGER
```

The last line,

```
0232F6: N:     MOVE.W    $FEC8(A5), $FEC6(A5)
```

implements the assignment from global variable *a* to global variable *b*. This particular statement is the one currently pointed to by the program counter. The instructions up to this point have already been executed; for example, $1234 already resides in the address $FEC8 bytes offset from the contents of A5.

At this point, we could execute a single statement with the *T*(race) command and the remainder of the instructions in the program with the *G*(o) command, optionally setting a breakpoint or two. To return immediately to Turbo Pascal, enter *ES* (Exit to Shell).

How to Write Macintosh Software, by Scott Knaster, has an excellent discussion of debugging techniques. See the "Suggested References" at the end of this book.

Review

The process of writing a program includes fixing the errors that crop up when executing it. This fixing process is called debugging. Many errors can be avoided by carefully thinking through a problem before writing code to solve it.

Errors can be divided into those caught by the compiler (syntax errors) and those that occur when the program executes (run-time errors). The Macintosh has various built-in mechanisms able to recognize invalid conditions. These mechanisms halt program execution and call the System Error Handler, which displays an error message (the bomb alert) with a diagnostic error ID. Clicking Resume from this dialog box returns you to Turbo Pascal.

A common system error is the address error, which results from an attempt to make the microprocessor read a word or long word at an odd address. Address errors often result from dangling or uninitialized pointers.

Pointers can go dangling from a number of causes, including premature deallocation and certain Pascal constructions involving dereferenced handles. If the object of a **with** statement is a relocatable block and if the **with** block contains a statement with the indirect or direct potential for heap movement, the relocatable block referred to must be locked for the duration of the **with** statement. Similarly, when passing a relocatable object by reference (as a **var** parameter), the object must be locked if the called routine could create heap movement or if it's in another code segment. The same restriction applies when passing objects larger than 4 bytes as value (non-**var** parameters).

Most repeatable bugs can be tracked down by inserting diagnostic messages at appropriate points and recompiling, zeroing in on the problem statement(s). Intermittent bugs are harder to find and often require the assistance of MacsBug, a memory-resident debugging tool able to control and display memory and the microprocessor.

Appendixes

Turbo Pascal Tutor for the Macintosh

A

Summary of Key Toolbox Routines

This appendix is a reference to the key Toolbox routines. They are divided
into these headings:

- Memory Manager
- Resource Manager
- QuickDraw
- Font Manager
- Event Manager
- Window Manager
- Control Manager
- Desk Manager
- File Manager
- Standard File
- Miscellaneous

Memory Manager

```
type
  SignedByte  = - 128..127;
  Byte        = 0..255;
  Ptr         = ^SignedByte;
  Handle      = ^Ptr;
  ProcPtr     = Ptr;
  Fixed       = LongInt;
```

```
Str255        = string[255];
StringPtr     = ^Str255;
StringHandle  = ^StringPtr;
Size          = LongInt;
```

function NewPtr(byteCount: Size): Ptr;

NewPtr allocates a nonrelocatable block of *byteCount* bytes and returns the address of this block. If *byteCount* bytes can't be allocated, *NewPtr returns nil*.

function NewHandle(byteCount: Size); Handle;

NewHandle allocates a relocatable block of *byteCount* bytes and returns the address of a master pointer to this block. If *byteCount* bytes can't be allocated, *NewHandle* returns **nil**.

procedure DisposPtr(p: Ptr);

DisposPtr deallocates the nonrelocatable block pointed to by *p*.

procedure DisposHandle(h: Handle);

DisposHandle deallocates the relocatable block indicated by *h*.

procedure SetHandleSize(h: Handle; newSize: Size);

SetHandleSize makes the relocatable block indicated by *h newSize* bytes long.

function GetHandleSize(h: Handle): Size;

GetHandleSize returns the length of the relocatable block indicated by *h*.

procedure HPurge(h: Handle);
procedure HNoPurge(h: Handle);

HPurge and *HNoPurge* flag the relocatable block indicated by *h* as purgeable or not purgeable, respectively. By default, relocatable blocks allocated by *NewHandle* are unlocked and unpurgeable.

procedure HLock(h: Handle);
procedure HUnlock(h: Handle);

HLock and *HUnlock* flag the relocatable block indicated by *h* as not movable or movable, respectively. By default, relocatable blocks allocated by *NewHandle* are unlocked and unpurgeable.

```
procedure SetApplLimit(p: Ptr);
function GetApplLimit : Ptr;
```

SetApplLimit sets the application heap limit, the point beyond which the application heap zone can't be expanded; *GetApplLimit* returns its current value.

```
procedure MaxApplZone;
```

MaxApplZone expands the application heap zone to the application heap limit.

```
procedure MoreMasters;
```

MoreMasters allocates a nonrelocatable block of 64 master pointers. To avoid fragmentation in a program that will require more than the default block of 64 master pointers, call *MoreMasters* as necessary early on.

```
function FreeMem : LongInt;
```

FreeMem returns the total amount of free space in the current heap zone, in bytes. Due to heap fragmentation, it usually isn't possible to allocate this large a block.

```
function MaxMem(var grow: Size) : Size;
```

MaxMem compacts the current heap zone and purges all purgeable blocks from the zone. It returns the size of the largest contiguous free block in the zone after the compaction. Parameter *grow* is set to the maximum number of bytes by which the zone can grow.

Resource Manager

```
type
  ResType: packed array [1..4] of Char;
function OpenResFile(fileName: Str255): Integer;
```

OpenResFile opens the resource fork of the file indicated by *fileName* and makes it the current resource file. It returns a reference number with which to refer to the file in subsequent Resource Manager calls.

```
procedure CloseResFile(refNum: Integer);
```

CloseResFile closes open resource file *refNum*.

function CountResources(theType: ResType): Integer;

CountResources returns the total number of resources of type *theType* in all open resource files.

function GetIndResource(theType: ResType; index: Integer): Handle;

GetIndResource returns a handle to the *index*-th resource of type *theType*.

function GetResource(theType; ResType; theID: Integer): Handle;

GetResource returns a handle to the resource having the given type and ID number, reading the resource data into memory if it's not already.

procedure ReleaseResource(theResource: Handle);

ReleaseResource releases the memory occupied by *theResource^^*.

QuickDraw

```
type
  QDByte    = SignedByte;    { QD equivalents of basic types }
  QDPtr     = Ptr;
  QDHandle  = Handle;

  Pattern   = packed array [0..7] of 0..255;
  Bits16    = array [0..15] of Integer;
  VHSelect  = (v, h);
  StyleItem = (bold, italic, underline, outline, shadow, condense, extend);
  Style     = set of StyleItem;

Point = record
          case Integer of
            0:
              (v: Integer;
               h: Integer);
            1:
              (vh: array [VHSelect] of Integer);
        end;

  Rect = record
           case Integer of
             0:
```

```
                    (top:    Integer;
                     left:   Integer;
                     bottom: Integer;
                     right:  Integer);
                  1:
                     (topLeft: Point;
                      botRight: Point);
             end;

BitMap = record
             baseAddr: Ptr;
             rowBytes: Integer;
             bounds:   Rect;
          end;

Cursor = record
             data: Bits16;
             mask: Bits16;
             hotSpot: Point;
          end;

RgnHandle = ^RgnPtr;
RgnPtr = ^Region;
Region = record
             rgnSize: Integer;       { 10 for rectangular regions }
             rgnBBox: Rect;    { plus more data if not rectangular }
          end;

PicHandle = ^PicPtr;
PicPtr = ^Picture;
Picture = record
             picSize: Integer;
             picFrame: Rect;    { plus codes for picture content }
           end;

GrafPtr = ^GrafPort;
GrafPort = record
              device: Integer;
              portBits: BitMap;
              portRect: Rect;
              visRgn: RgnHandle;
              clipRgn: RgnHandle;
              bkPat: Pattern;
              fillPat: Pattern;
              pnLoc: Point;
              pnSize: Point;
              pnMode: Integer;
              pnPat: Pattern;
              pnVis: Integer;
              txFont: Integer;
```

```
          txFace: Style;
          txMode: Integer;
          txSize: Integer;
          spExtra: Fixed;
          fgColor: LongInt;
          bkColor: LongInt;
          colrBit: Integer;
          patStretch: Integer;
          picSave: Handle;
          rgnSave: Handle;
          polySave: Handle;
          grafProcs: QDProcsPtr;
       end;

var
  thePort: GrafPtr;
  white: Pattern;
  black: Pattern;
  gray: Pattern;
  ltGray: Pattern;
  dkGray: Pattern;
  arrow: Cursor;
  screenBits: BitMap;
  randSeed: LongInt;
```

procedure InitGraf(p: QDPtr);

Call *InitGraf* early in an application to initialize QuickDraw. Parameter *p* tells QuickDraw where to store its global variables, and should always be set to *@thePort*, where Turbo Pascal has allocated space for them.

procedure OpenPort(gp: GrafPtr);

OpenPort initializes the fields of *GrafPort gp^*, including allocating space for its *visRgn* and *clipRgn* fields, and makes *gp^* the current port.

procedure GetPort(**var** gp: GrafPtr);

GetPort assigns to *gp* the current value of global variable *thePort*, thus retrieving a pointer to the current *GrafPort* record.

procedure SetPort(gp: GrafPtr);

SetPort sets global variable *thePort* to *gp*, thus changing the current *GrafPort* to *gp^*.

procedure InitCursor;

InitCursor changes the cursor to the standard arrow shape.

procedure SetCursor(crsr: Cursor);

SetCursor changes the cursor to the 16 x 16 bit image passed in *crsr*.

procedure HideCursor;
procedure ShowCursor;
procedure ObscureCursor;

HideCursor removes the cursor from the screen; *ShowCursor* brings it back. *ObscureCursor* hides the cursor until the mouse is moved.

procedure GetPen(**var** pt: Point);

GetPen returns the current pen location.

procedure PenSize(width, height: Integer);

PenSize sets the dimensions of the current *GrafPort*'s pen, where *width* and *height* <= 7. Subsequent calls to *Line, LineTo,* and the procedures that draw framed shapes will use this new pen size.

procedure PenMode(mode: Integer);

PenMode sets the transfer mode through which the *GrafPort*'s *pnPat* is transferred onto the bit image when drawing lines or framed shapes.

procedure PenPat(pat: Pattern);

PenPat sets the pattern used by the pen in the current *GrafPort*.

procedure MoveTo(h,v: Integer);

MoveTo moves the pen (without drawing anything) to location (*h,v*) in the local coordinates of the current *GrafPort*.

procedure Move(dh,dv: Integer);

Move moves the pen (without drawing anything) a distance of *dh* horizontally and *dv* vertically from its current location.

procedure LineTo(h,v: Integer);

LineTo draws a line from the current pen location to the location specified by *h* and *v*. The pen location is (*h,v*) after the line is drawn.

procedure Line(dh,dv: Integer);

Line draws a line to the location a distance of *dh* horizontally and *dv* vertically from the current pen location. After the line is drawn, the pen location becomes the coordinates of the end of the line.

procedure TextFont(font:Integer);
procedure TextFace(face:Style);
procedure TextMode(mode: Integer);
procedure TextSize(size: Integer);

TextFont sets the current *GrafPort* to use font number *font* in future text drawing calls. *TextFace* sets the current *GrafPort*'s character style. *TextMode* sets the current *GrafPort*'s transfer mode for text drawing (the default mode is srcOR). *TextSize* sets the current *GrafPort*'s text size to *size* points (the default is 12).

procedure DrawChar(c: Char);

DrawChar draws the given character (in the current *GrafPort*'s text size, font, and style) at the pen location, advancing the pen a suitable amount to the right.

procedure DrawString(s: Str255);

DrawString performs calls to *DrawChar* for each character in the supplied string. No formatting (i.e., interpreting carriage returns, tabs, etc.) is performed.

function CharWidth(ch: Char) : Integer;

CharWidth returns the value that will be added to the pen horizontal coordinate were the specified character to be drawn with the current *GrafPort*'s font, size, and style.

function StringWidth(s: Str255) : Integer;

StringWidth returns the width of the given text string, which it calculates by adding the widths of all the characters in the string.

procedure SetRect(**var** r: Rect; left,top,right,bottom; Integer);

SetRect assigns coordinate values to a rectangle.

procedure OffsetRect(**var** r: Rect; dh,dv: Integer);

OffsetRect "moves" the rectangle *r* by adding *dh* to each horizontal coordinate and *dv* to each vertical coordinate. If *dh* and *dv* are positive, the movement is to the right and down; if either is negative, the change is in the opposite direction. This does not affect the screen unless you subsequently call a routine (e.g., *FrameRect*) to draw the rectangle.

procedure InsetRect(**var** r: Rect; dh,dv: Integer);

InsetRect shrinks or expands its rectangle parameter. The left and right sides are moved in by the amount specified by *dh*; the top and bottom are moved toward the center by the amount specified by *dv*. If *dh* or *dv* is negative, the corresponding pair of sides is moved outwards instead of inwards.

function PtInRect(pt: Point; r: Rect) : Boolean;

PtInRect returns True if the pixel below and to the right of the given coordinate point is enclosed in the specified rectangle, and False otherwise.

procedure FrameRect(r: Rect);

FrameRect draws a hollow outline just inside the specified rectangle using the current *GrafPort*'s pen characteristics. If a region is being formed, the outside outline of the new rectangle is added to the region's boundary.

procedure PaintRect(r: Rect);

PaintRect fills the specified rectangle with the current *GrafPort*'s pen pattern and mode. The pen location is not changed.

procedure EraseRect(r: Rect);

EraseRect paints the specified rectangle with the current *GrafPort*'s *bkPat* (background pattern) field, in *patCopy* mode. The pen location is not changed.

procedure InvertRect(r: Rect);

InvertRect inverts the pixels enclosed by the specified rectangle: white pixels become black and vice versa. The pen location is not changed.

procedure FillRect(r: Rect; pat: Pattern);

FillRect fills the specified rectangle with the given pattern (in *patCopy* mode). The pen location is not changed.

```
procedure FrameOval(r: Rect);
procedure PaintOval(r: Rect);
procedure EraseOval(r: Rect);
procedure InvertOval(r: Rect);
procedure FillOval(r: Rect; pat: Pattern);
```

The oval drawing routines are analogous to the rectangle drawing routines described above.

```
procedure FrameRoundRect(r: Rect; ovalWidth,ovalHeight: Integer);
```

FrameRoundRect draws a hollow outline just inside the specified rounded-corner rectangle, using the current *GrafPort*'s pen characteristics. The *ovalWidth* and *ovalHeight* parameters specify the diameters of curvature of the corners. The outline is as wide as the pen width and as tall as the pen height. The pen location is unchanged after this procedure.

If a region is being formed, the outside outline of the new rounded-corner rectangle is mathematically added to the region's boundary.

```
procedure PaintRoundRect(r: Rect; ovalWidth,ovalHeight: Integer);
procedure EraseRoundRect(r: Rect; ovalWidth,ovalHeight: Integer);
procedure InvertRoundRect(r: Rect; ovalWidth,ovalHeight: Integer);
procedure FillRoundRect(r: Rect; ovalWidth,ovalHeight: Integer; pat:Pattern);
```

The round rectangle routines work like their rectangle counterparts.

```
function NewRgn : RgnHandle;
```

NewRgn allocates space in the heap for a new region, initializes it to the empty region, and returns a handle to it.

```
procedure DisposeRgn(rgn: RgnHandle);
```

DisposeRgn deallocates space for the region indicated by handle *rgn*.

```
procedure OpenRgn;
```

OpenRgn tells QuickDraw to begin interpreting subsequent line and framed-shaped drawing calls as region definition information. While a region is open, all calls to *Line*, *LineTo*, and the procedures that draw framed shapes (except arcs) affect the outline of the region. *OpenRgn* calls *HidePen*, so no drawing occurs on the screen while defining the region.

```
procedure CloseRgn(dstRgn: RgnHandle);
```

CloseRgn stops the collection of lines and framed shapes, organizes them into a region definition, and saves the resulting region into *dstRgn^^*. *CloseRgn* calls *ShowPen*, balancing the *HidePen* call made by *OpenRgn*.

procedure FrameRgn(rgn: RgnHandle);

FrameRgn draws a hollow outline just inside the specified region, using the current *GrafPort*'s pen pattern, mode, and size. The pen location is not changed by this procedure. If a region is open and being formed, the outside outline of the region being framed is mathematically added to the new region's boundary.

procedure PaintRgn(rgn: RgnHandle);
procedure EraseRgn(rgn: RgnHandle);
procedure InvertRgn(rgn: RgnHandle);
procedure FillRgn(rgn: RgnHandle; pat: Pattern);

The region drawing routines function analogously to their rectangle counterparts.

procedure CopyBits(srcBits,dstBits: BitMap; srcRect,dstRect: Rect;
                  mode: Integer; maskRgn: RgnHandle);

CopyBits moves bit images between two *bitMaps*. The transfer can be performed in any of the eight source transfer modes, and is clipped to the *maskRgn* and the boundary rectangle of the destination *bitMap*; if the destination *bitMap* is the current *GrafPort*'s *portBits* (that is, if *dstBits = thePort^.portBits*), the copying operation is clipped to the intersection of the *GrafPort*'s *clipRgn* and *visRgn*. Pass **nil** for the *maskRgn* parameter if no additional clipping is required. If the rectangles are different sizes, the source bit image is expanded or shrunk as necessary to fit the destination rectangle.

function OpenPicture(picFrame: Rect) : PicHandle;

OpenPicture returns a handle to a new picture which has the given rectangle as its picture frame, and tells QuickDraw to start saving all calls to drawing routines into this picture handle.

procedure ClosePicture;

ClosePicture causes QuickDraw to stop accumulating drawing calls. You should perform one and only one *ClosePicture* for every *OpenPicture*. *ClosePicture* calls *ShowPen*, balancing the *HidePen* call made by *OpenPicture*.

```
procedure DrawPicture(myPicture: PicHandle; dstRect: Rect);
```

DrawPicture draws the picture indicated by *myPicture* in *dstRect*, expanding or shrinking it as necessary.

```
procedure SetPt(var pt: Point; h,v: Integer);
```

SetPt assigns integer coordinates to a variable of type Point.

```
procedure GlobalToLocal(var pt: Point);
procedure LocalToGlobal(var pt: Point);
```

GlobalToLocal takes a point expressed in global coordinates (i.e., with the top left corner of the *bitMap*—usually the screen—as coordinate (0,0)) and converts it into the local coordinates of the current *GrafPort*; in practice, usually a window. *LocalToGlobal* converts a point from the current *GrafPort's* local coordinate system into a global coordinate system.

```
function Random : Integer;
```

Random returns a random 16-bit value.

```
procedure StuffHex(p: QDPtr; s: Str255);
```

StuffHex pokes byte values (expressed as a string of hexadecimal digits) starting at the address in *p* and working up.

Font Manager

```
const
  systemFont = 0;    { a.k.a. chicago }
  applFont   = 1;    { a.k.a. geneva }
  newYork    = 2;
  geneva     = 3;
  monaco     = 4;
  venice     = 5;
  london     = 6;
  athens     = 7;
  sanFran    = 8;
  toronto    = 9;
  cairo      = 11;
  losAngeles = 12;
  times      = 20;
  helvetica  = 21;
```

```
courier   = 22;
symbol    = 23;
taliesin  = 24;
```

procedure InitFonts;

InitFonts initializes the Font Manager. Call this procedure before any Toolbox routine that will call the Font Manager.

Event Manager

---

const
```
nullEvent   =      0;
mouseDown   =      1;
mouseUp     =      2;
keyDown     =      3;
keyUp       =      4;
autoKey     =      5;
updateEvt   =      6;
diskEvt     =      7;
activateEvt =      8;
networkEvt  =     10;
driverEvt   =     11;
app1Evt     =     12;
app2Evt     =     13;
app3Evt     =     14;
app4Evt     =     15;
```

type
```
EventRecord = record
                what     : Integer;
                message  : LongInt;
                when     : LongInt;
                where    : Point;
                modifiers: Integer;
              end;
```

function GetNextEvent(eventMask: Integer; **var** theEvent: EventRecord): Boolean;

GetNextEvent assigns to *theEvent* the next available event of the specified type(s), as indicated by the *eventMask* parameter. If no event of the designated type(s) is available, *GetNextEvent* returns False, and *theEvent.what* is set to 0, the null event. Otherwise, *GetNextEvent* returns True, and *theEvent.what* equals the type of event being reported.

procedure GetMouse(**var** mouseLoc: Point);

GetMouse returns the current mouse location in its *mouseLoc* parameter. The location is given in the local coordinate system of the current *GrafPort*.

function Button : Boolean;

Button returns True if the mouse button is currently down, and False otherwise.

function TickCount : LongInt;

TickCount returns the current number of ticks (sixtieths of a second) since the system was booted.

function GetCaretTime : LongInt;

GetCaretTime returns the time (in ticks) between blinks of the caret in a text editing situation, as set by the user with the Control Panel DA.

function PostEvent(eventCode: Integer; eventMsg: LongInt): OSErr;

PostEvent inserts an event of type *eventCode* into the event queue read by *GetNextEvent*. The *eventMsg* parameter becomes the corresponding event record's *message* field.

Window Manager

```
type
  WindowRecord = record
                   port:           GrafPort;
                   windowKind:     Integer;
                   visible:        Boolean;
                   hilited:        Boolean;
                   goAwayFlag:     Boolean;
                   spareFlag:      Boolean;
                   strucRgn:       RgnHandle;
                   contRgn:        RgnHandle;
                   updateRgn:      RgnHandle;
                   windowDefProc:  Handle;
                   dataHandle:     Handle;
                   titleHandle:    StringHandle;
                   titleWidth:     Integer;
                   controlList:    ControlHandle;
                   nextWindow:     WindowPeek;
```

```
            windowPic:     PicHandle;
            refCon:        LongInt;
        end;

    WindowPtr  = GrafPtr;
    WindowPeek = ^WindowRecord;
```

procedure InitWindows;

InitWindows initializes the Window Manager, allocates a *GrafPort* in the heap (the "Window Manager port") and uses this port to draw the desktop and menu bar. Call *InitWindows* after *InitGraf* and *InitFonts*, and before making any other Window Manager call.

procedure GetWMgrPort(**var** wPort: GrafPtr);

GetWMgrPort returns in *wPort* a pointer to the Window Manager port.

procedure NewWindow(wStorage: Ptr; boundsRect: Rect; title: Str255;
                visible: Boolean; procID: Integer; behind: WindowPtr;
                goAwayFlag: Boolean; refCon: LongInt);

NewWindow defines and draws a window on the screen. The *wStorage* field is a pointer to the storage that's been allocated for the about-to-be created window record. Passing **nil** as the *wStorage* argument causes *NewWindow* to allocate the storage itself. The *boundsRect* parameter defines the content region of the new window, and is specified in global coordinates. The *title parameter* shows up in the title bar when the window is drawn (assuming it's a window type with a title bar, such as a document window). The *visible parameter* controls whether or not the window will initially be visible. *ProcID* defines the type of window, according to the following constants:

```
const
    documentProc  = 0;
    dBoxProc      = 1;
    plainDBox     = 2;
    altDBoxProc   = 3;
    noGrowDocProc = 4;
    zoomDocProc   = 8;
    zoomNoGrow    = 12;
    rDocProc      = 16;
```

The *behind* parameter controls the plane in which the window will appear when drawn. Use **nil** to place a new window underneath all existing windows, and *Pointer(-1)* to draw it on top. If the new window should have a close box, then pass True for the *goAwayFlag* parameter. The *refCon* parameter sets the window's initial value for the all-purpose "reference constant."

```
function GetNewWindow(ResID: Integer; wStorage: Ptr;
                      behind: WindowPtr): WindowPtr;
```

GetNewWindow creates and draws a window defined by a window template (a resource of type WIND), where *ResID* is the resource ID of that template. The *wStorage* and *behind* parameters have the same meaning as in *NewWindow*.

```
procedure DisposeWindow(theWindow: WindowPtr);
```

DisposeWindow removes a window from the screen and releases the memory occupied by its window record. Call it when you're done with a window if you caused its window record to be allocated on the heap when the window was created (by passing **nil** as the *wStorage* parameter to *NewWindow* or *GetNewWindow*).

```
function FrontWindow: WindowPtr;
```

FrontWindow returns a pointer to the frontmost (active) window on the screen.

```
procedure SelectWindow(theWindow: WindowPtr);
```

SelectWindow should be called after a mouse-down event in an inactive window; it takes a *WindowPtr* parameter and makes the window record it points to the active window. *SelectWindow* generates appropriate update events so that the application can redraw its windows in their new order.

```
function FindWindow(thePt: Point; var whichWindow: WindowPtr): Integer;
```

FindWindow is important in decoding mouse-down events. You pass *FindWindow* one fact (a point), and get back two: A numeric code that can be tested to learn more about the mouse-down (the function's return value); and, returned in *whichWindow*, a *WindowPtr* indicating the window (active or inactive) in which the mouse-down occurred. If the mouse-down wasn't in a window, then *whichWindow* returns **nil**.

```
const
  inDesk      = 0;  { missed everything }
  inMenuBar   = 1;  { somewhere in the white at the top of the screen }
  inSysWindow = 2;  { anywhere in a desk accessory window }
  inContent   = 3;  { in the content region of an application window }
```

```
inDrag      = 4;   { in the title bar of an application window }
inGrow      = 5;   { in the grow box of an application window  }
inGoAway    = 6;   { in the goAway box of an application window }
```

function TrackGoAway(theWindow: WindowPtr; thePt: Point): Boolean;

Call *TrackGoAway* if *FindWindow* indicates that the mouse-down occurred in the active window's close box. If it returns True, then the user released the button with the cursor inside the *goAway* box; otherwise, the button was released outside of the box.

procedure DragWindow(theWindow: WindowPtr; startPt: Point; boundsRect: Rect);

When there's a mouse-down event in the drag region of *theWindow*, call *DragWindow* with *startPt* equal to the point where the mouse button was pressed. *DragWindow* pulls around an outline of *theWindow*, following the mouse until the button is released. When the button is released the window is redrawn at this new location. If *theWindow* is not the active window and the Command key wasn't down during the move, it becomes the active window. If the mouse button is released when the mouse position is outside the limits of *boundsRect*, *DragWindow* simply returns without moving *theWindow* or making it active.

procedure InvalRect(badRect: Rect);

InvalRect adds the given rectangle to the update region of the window whose *GrafPort* is the current port. This causes an update event to be generated by the next call to *GetNextEvent* (assuming no higher priority events are in the queue). Upon processing that update event, the *visRgn* will include this rectangle.

procedure BeginUpdate(theWindow: WindowPtr);
procedure EndUpdate(theWindow: WindowPtr);

When redrawing the contents of *theWindow* in response to an update event, bracket the drawing calls with the *BeginUpdate* and *EndUpdate* procedures.

Control Manager

type
```
  ControlPtr    = ^ControlRecord;
  ControlHdl    = ^ControlPtr;
  ControlRecord = packed record
```

```
        nextControl:    ControlHandle;
        contrlOwner:    WindowPtr;
        contrlRect:     Rect;
        contrlVis:      Byte;
        contrlHilite:   Byte;
        contrlValue:    Integer;
        contrlMin:      Integer;
        contrlMax:      Integer
        contrlDefProc:  Handle;
        contrlData:     Handle;
        contrlAction:   ProcPtr;
        contrlRfCon:    LongInt;
        contrlTitle:    Str255;
    end;
```

function `GetNewControl(controlID:Integer;theWindow:WindowPtr): ControlHandle;`

GetNewControl allocates storage for a control, reads its template from a resource file, inserts it into the control list of *theWindow*, and returns a handle to the control.

procedure `DisposeControl(the Control: ControlHandle);`

DisposeControl erases a control from its window and frees up the memory it occupies.

procedure `DrawControls(theWindow: WindowPtr);`

DrawControls draws each control in a window's control list. Calling this procedure draws all of the visible controls (either active or inactive, depending on their *contrlHilite* field) associated with *theWindow*.

procedure `HiliteControl(theControl: ControlHandle; hiliteState: Integer);`

HiliteControl changes the status of a control from active to inactive or vice versa, and redraws the control to indicate the transition. The *hiliteState* parameter should be set as follows: 0 = no highlighting (control active); 1 – 253 represents a part code to be highlighted; 255 = highlight (control inactive).

function `FindControl(thePoint: Point; theWindow: WindowPtr;`
  var `whichControl: ControlHandle): Integer;`

When a mouse-down occurs in the active window, if that window has controls, an program checks to see if the mouse-down occurred in any of them. The *FindControl* function makes this determination, returning in *whichControl* a handle to the control, if any; the function return value is the control's part code.

```
const
  inButton     = 10;   { simple button }
  inCheckBox   = 11;   { a radio button or check box }
  inUpButton   = 20;   { scroll bar's up arrow }
  inDownButton = 21;   { scroll bar's down arrow }
  inPageUp     = 22;   { scroll bar's "page up" area }
  inPageDown   = 23;   { scroll bar's "page down" area }
  inThumb      = 129;  { scroll box }

function TrackControl(theControl: ControlHandle; startPt: Point;
                      actionProc: ProcPtr: Integer);
```

Call *TrackControl* after a mouse-down in a control. It doesn't return until the user releases the button, at which time you study the function return value to figure out what to do next. If it returns as zero, then the user moved out of the control before releasing the button, in which case you do nothing. If *TrackControl* returns the same part code that *FindControl* returned originally, then the user really intends to manipulate that control and you should take appropriate action.

```
procedure SetCtlValue(theControl: ControlHandle; theValue: Integer);
function GetCtlValue(theControl: ControlHandle): Integer;
```

Call *SetCtlValue* to set a control's value, and *GetCtlValue* to read it. *SetCtlValue* redraws the control to indicate its new value.

Menu Manager

```
procedure InitMenus;
```

InitMenus initializes the Menu Manager; call *InitMenus* once before any other Menu Manager routine.

```
function GetMenu(resourceID: Integer) : MenuHandle;
```

GetMenu returns a menu handle for the menu having the given resource ID. It calls the Resource Manager to read the menu from a resource file into a menu record in memory.

```
procedure InsertMenu(theMenu: MenuHandle; beforeID: Integer);
```

procedure DrawMenuBar;

Once an application has fetched its menus, they're inserted into the menu bar with *InsertMenu*; it inserts *theMenu* into the menu list before menu *beforeID*. If *beforeID* is 0, the new menu is added at the end. The application's menus must be drawn on the screen by the *DrawMenuBar* procedure.

procedure AddResMenu(theMenu: MenuHandle; theType: ResType);

The *AddResMenu* call adds the names of all resources of the indicated type to a MenuHandle; use type DRVR to fetch desk accessory names.

function MenuSelect(startPt: Point): LongInt;

Call *MenuSelect* after a mouse-down in the menu bar. The long integer it returns contains the number of the menu selected (1 = leftmost menu; 0 = no selection) in its most significant word and the number of the item selected (1= topmost item) in its least significant word.

function MenuKey(c: Char) : LongInt;

Call *MenuKey* to respond to keyboard events representing *Command*-key equivalents. After a key-down event with *Command* held down, pass *MenuKey* the character typed. *MenuKey* highlights the appropriate menu title, if any, and returns a long integer representing selection information in the same format returned by *MenuSelect*.

procedure HiliteMenu(menuID: Integer);

Call *HiliteMenu* with a parameter of 0 to unhighlight a menu highlighted by either *MenuSelect* or *MenuKey*.

procedure SetItem(theMenu: MenuHandle; item: Integer; itemString: Str255);
procedure GetItem(theMenu: MenuHandle; item: Integer; **var** itemString: Str255);

SetItem changes the text of the given menu item to *itemString*. *GetItem* returns the text of the given menu item in *itemString*.

procedure DisableItem(theMenu: MenuHandle; item: Integer);
procedure EnableItem(theMenu: MenuHandle; item: Integer);

Given a menu item number in the *item* parameter, *DisableItem* disables that menu item; given 0 in the *item* parameter, it disables the entire menu. Similarly, *EnableItem* enables the item and an *item* parameter of 0 enables the entire menu.

Desk Manager

```
function OpenDeskAcc(theAcc: Str255): Integer;
```

If the user chooses a desk accessory from the Apple menu, call *OpenDeskAcc*. Parameter *theAcc*—the name of the DA—is obtained with the Menu Manager's *GetItem* routine.

```
procedure SystemClick(theEvent: EventRecord; theWindow: WindowPtr);
```

Call *SystemClick* whenever *FindWindow* reports that a mouse-down occurred in a system window.

```
function SystemEdit(editCmd: Integer): Boolean;
```

Call *SystemEdit* when the user chooses one of the Edit menu's first five items. If you've arranged this menu in the standard way (Undo, separating line, Cut, Copy, Paste), this requires the expression:

```
if SystemEdit(menuItem-1) ...
```

```
procedure SystemTask;
```

SystemTask provides open DAs with periodic processing time. Call it once each time through your program's main event loop.

Dialog Manager

```
type
  DialogRecord = record
                   window: WindowRecord;
                   items: handle;
                   textH: TEHandle;
                   editField: Integer;
                   editOpen: Integer;
                   aDefItem;
                 end

  DialogPtr = WindowPtr;
  DialogPeek = ^DialogRecord;

function GetNewDialog(dialogID: Integer; dStorage: Ptr; behind: WindowPtr)
        : DialogPtr;
```

GetNewDialog fetches a DLOG template and its associated item list (DITL) resource. As with *GetNewWindow*, pass **nil** as the *dStorage* parameter and *GetNewDialog* will create storage on the heap for the dialog record for you. Pass *Pointer(-1)* to open the dialog's window on top of existing windows.

procedure DisposDialog(theDialog: DialogPtr);

When you're through with a dialog, call *DisposDialog* to erase it from the screen and free up the memory occupied by its various data structures.

procedure ModalDialog(filterProc: ProcPtr; **var** itemHit: Integer);

With a modal dialog box as the active window, call *ModalDialog* repeatedly to handle events in the dialog's window; after handling an event involving an enabled dialog item, it returns with the item number in *itemHit*.

procedure GetDItem(theDialog: DialogPtr; itemNo: Integer;
             var itemType: Integer; **var** item: Handle; **var** box: Rect);

GetDItem takes in two facts and returns three. Given the indicated dialog and item number, it returns information about that particular item: Its type (e.g., *radioButton*, *staticText*), bounding box, and a handle to its underlying data structure.

procedure GetIText(item: Handle; **var** text: Str255);
procedure SetIText(item: Handle; text: Str255);

After the user has worked with an *editText* item (as determined by *itemHit* of *ModalDialog*, use *GetIText* to see what string value it has now. To change the text (perhaps to suggest a different response), use *SetIText*. Both routines expect a handle to the structure used to store this text; you'll get this from *GetDItem*.

procedure ParamText(s1,s2,s3,s4: Str255);

ParamText provides the string data to be plugged into the ^0 through ^3 placeholders in DITL items. *S1* replaces ^0, *s2* replaces ^1, and so on. If a dialog box doesn't require four placeholders, then simply pass the null string ('') for the extras.

function NoteAlert(alertID: Integer; filterProc: ProcPtr): Integer;
function CautionAlert(alertID: Integer; filterProc: ProcPtr): Integer;
function StopAlert(alertID: Integer; filterProc: ProcPtr): Integer;
function Alert(alertID: Integer; filterProc: ProcPtr): Integer;

The four alert functions invoke the alert defined by the alert template with ID *alertID*. They function identically except for the icon displayed by the alert's window. Taking *Alert* as the example, *Alert* calls the current sound procedure, if any, passing it the sound number specified in the alert template for this stage of the alert. If no alert box is to be drawn at this stage, *Alert* returns a function result of –1; otherwise, it creates and displays the alert window, and returns the value of the button clicked to dismiss the alert.

File Manager

```
type
  OSType = packed array [1..4] of Char;
  OSErr  = Integer;
  FInfo = record                    { record of finder info }
            fdType: OSType;         { file's type }
            fdCreator: OSType;      { file's creator }
            fdFlags: Integer;       { flags ex. hasbundle,invisible,locked,etc. }
            fdLocation: Point;      { file's location in folder }
            fdFldr: Integer;        { folder containing file }
          end; { FInfo }
```

```
function FSOpen(fileName: Str255; vRefNum: Integer; var refNum: Integer): OSErr;
```

FSOpen prepares file *fileName* in volume/directory *vRefNum* for reading or writing, and sets its mark to position 0.

```
function FSRead(refNum: Integer; var count: LongInt; buffPtr: Ptr): OSErr;
```

FSRead reads *count* bytes from file *refNum*, starting at the position of its mark, and places these bytes in memory starting at address *buffPtr* and working up.

```
function SetFPos(refNum: Integer; posMode: Integer; posOff: LongInt): OSErr;
```

SetFPos sets open file *refNum*'s mark. *PosMode* controls how the *posOffset* parameter is interpreted; it must contain one of the following values:

```
const
  fsAtMark    = 0;  { at current mark -- ignore posOff }
  fsFromStart = 1;  { set mark relative to beginning of file }
  fsFromLEOF  = 2;  { set mark relative to logical end-of-file }
  fsFromMark  = 3;  { set mark relative to current mark }
```

```
function FSClose(refNum: Integer): OSErr;
```

FSClose terminates the relationship between a file and its reference number.

```
function FSWrite(refNum: Integer; var count: LongInt; buffPtr: Ptr):OSErr;
```

FSWrite writes *count* bytes from the memory buffer pointed to by *buffPtr* to file *refNum*. Writes occur at the mark of an open file and advance it an amount equal to the number of bytes written. If the file doesn't exist already, you'll need to *Create* it beforehand.

```
function Create(fileName:Str255;vRefNum:Integer;creator,fType:OSType): OSErr;
```

Create sets up a new file named *fileName* on the volume/directory combination specified by *vRefNum*. The *creator* and *fType* parameters set the corresponding Finder attributes for the new file. The new file must be opened before I/O to it can commence.

```
function FlushVol(volName: StringPtr; vRefNum: Integer): OSErr;
```

FlushVol writes out the contents of the associated volume buffer and descriptive information about the volume (if they've changed since the last *FlushVol* call).

```
function FSDelete(fileName: Str255; vRefNum: Integer): OSErr;
function Rename(oldName: Str255; vRefNum: Integer; newName: Str255): OSErr;
```

FSDelete removes file *fileName* from volume *vRefNum*. *Rename* changes the name of file *oldName* on volume/directory *vRefNum* to *newName*.

```
function GetFInfo(fileName:Str255;vRefNum:Integer; var theInfo: FInfo):OSErr;
function SetFInfo(fileName:Str255; vRefNum:Integer; theInfo: FInfo):OSErr;
```

GetFInfo and *SetFInfo* read and write Finder information about a file.

```
function GetEOF(refNum: Integer; var fileLength: LongInt): OSErr;
```

GetEOF returns the length of a file.

```
function GetFPos(refNum: Integer; var filePos: LongInt): OSErr;
```

GetFPos returns the current position of a file's mark.

Standard File

```
type
  SFReply = record
              good:    Boolean;
              copy:    Boolean;
              fType:   OSType;
              vRefNum: Integer;
              version: Integer;
              fName:   string[63];
            end;

SFTypeList = array [0..3] of OSType;

procedure SFPutFile(where: Point; prompt, origName :Str255;
                dlgHook: ProcPtr; var reply: SFReply);
```

Call *SFPutFile* to save a data file with the name and directory selected by the user. *Where* indicates the upper left corner of the PutFile dialog. *Prompt* and *origName* are a prompt string and the default file name, respectively. Pass **nil** for *dlgHook* to use default processing of this box. The user's response is stored in record variable *reply*, of type *SFReply*. No files are created or written as a result of SFPutFile; instead, you act on what returns in the *reply* record. If *reply.good* is True, then the user wants to create the file indicated by *reply.fName* in volume/directory *reply.vRefNum*.

```
procedure SFGetFile(where: Point; prompt:Str255; fileFilter: ProcPtr;
                numTypes: Integer; typeList: SFTypeList;
                dlgHook: ProcPtr; var reply: SFReply);
```

Call *SFGetFile* to let the user choose an existing file in a particular directory of a particular volume. *Where* indicates the upper left corner of the *GetFile* dialog; *prompt* is ignored. Pass **nil** for the *fileFilter* and *dlgHook* parameters to obtain default processing of this routine.

The *numTypes* and *typeList* parameters enable *SFGetFile* to include only certain file types. You invoke filtering by preparing a variable of type SFTypeList with as many as four types, and setting *numTypes* equal to the number of elements in *typeList* used. Passing –1 for *numTypes* causes all types to appear. The file is not actually read by this selection process; that's up to your program. If *reply.good* is True, then the user wants to open the file indicated by *reply.fName* in volume/directory *reply.vRefNum*.

Miscellaneous Routines

---

procedure GetSoundVol(**var** level: Integer);
procedure SetSoundVol(level: Integer);

These routines set or retrieve the current volume level, an integer between 0 and 7, inclusive.

procedure UprString(**var** theString: Str255; diacSens: BOOLEAN);

UprString converts every lowercase letter in its string parameter to its uppercase equivalent. Pass False as the *diacSens* parameter to strip diacritical marks from the string.

procedure Delay(numTicks: LongInt; **var** finalTicks: LongInt);

Delay inserts a pause of *numTicks* sixtieths of a second, and returns in *finalTicks* the total number of ticks from system startup to the end of the delay.

procedure SysBeep(duration: Integer);

SysBeep causes the speaker to beep for the number of ticks (sixtieths of a second) specified by the *duration* parameter. The volume of the beep depends on the current speaker volume setting, which the user can adjust with the Control Panel desk accessory. If the speaker volume is 0, *SysBeep* instead blinks the menu bar.

function GetString(stringID: Integer) : StringHandle;

GetString returns a handle to the string having the given resource ID, reading it from the resource file if necessary. If the resource can't be read, *GetString* returns **nil**.

procedure GetIndString(**var** theString:Str255;strListID:Integer;Index:Integer);

GetIndString returns in *theString* the *index*th entry in string list resource *strListID*. If the resource can't be read or the index is out of range, the null string is returned.

procedure PackBits(**var** srcPtr,DstPtr: Ptr; srcBytes: Integer);

PackBits compresses *srcBytes* bytes of data starting at *srcPtr* and stores the result at *dstPtr*. The value of *srcBytes* should be less than 128. After the compression, *srcPtr* is incremented by *srcBytes* and *dstPtr* is incremented by the number of bytes that the data was compressed to.

procedure UnpackBits(**var** srcPtr, dstPtr: Ptr; dstBytes: Integer);

With *srcPtr* a pointer to data compressed by *PackBits, UnpackBits* expands the data and stores the result to the address in *dstPtr. DstBytes* is the value that was passed to *PackBits* in its *srcBytes* parameter when the data was initially packed. After the data is expanded, *srcPtr* is incremented by the number of bytes that were expanded and *dstPtr* is incremented by *dstBytes*.

procedure NumToString(theNum: LongInt; **var** theString: Str255);

NumToString converts *theNum* into string form and returns the result in *theString*.

procedure StringToNum(theString: Str255; **var** theNum: LongInt);

StringToNum converts a numeric value in string form into its long integer equivalent.

function NewString(theString: Str255) : StringHandle;

NewString allocates the specified string as a relocatable object on the heap and returns a handle to it.

B

Answers to Exercises

Chapter 3

1) Identifiers:

1. user-defined constant (YourName)
2. user-defined variables (A,B,C)
3. predeclared identifiers (integer, *ReadLn*, *WriteLn*)

4) Change assignment statement to

   a) C := 2 * (A-B);
   b) C := A – 2 * B;
   c) C := 5 * A – 3 * B;
   d) C := A * B;
   e) C := A **mod** B;

5) *A* and *B* are of the type *Integer* and cannot have values of the type *Real*; trying to enter one causes a run-time error.

6) *A* and *B* are now of the type *Real* and can therefore have real values.

Chapter 6

1) 15

2) 15 (again)

3) 24

4) 15

5) 24

6) 4.8

Chapter 9

First Set

1) No (too big)

2) No (contains comma)

3) Yes (hexadecimal $b = 11 decimal)

4) Yes (predefined in Turbo)

5) Yes (smallest possible number)

6) No ("H" is not a legal hex digit)

7) No (the decimal point makes it a real number)

8) Yes

Second Set

1) 2.0E4 (or 2E4, 20E3,...)

2) −2.5E-5 (or −0.25E-4, −0.025E-3,...)

3) 4.277E1 (or 0.4277E2, etc.)

4) −5.300005E5 (and others)

Third Set

1) .00000000015

2) −5545454000000.0

3) 2.0

Chapter 10

1) One way to set Yesterday to the previous day of the week reliably would be

```
if DayOfWeek = Monday then
  Yesterday:= Sunday
else
  Yesterday := Pred (DayOfWeek);
```

Chapter 25

First Set

1) 50

2) 6188

3) 63

4) 1065

Second Set

1) 203138_5

2) $FFD

3) 101101_2

4) 1235_7

C

Help!

Do I need Turbo Pascal to be able to run programs I developed with it?

No, you can create a stand-alone (double-clickable) application by selecting the Compile To Disk command from the Compile menu.

What are the code and data limits for a Turbo Pascal program?

The Macintosh limits the code size of a program to 32K bytes. You can overcome this limitation by segmenting your program. This means you can have several 32K segments, with the total size of your program limited only by disk space. For more information on segmenting, see "Large Programs and Segmentation" (Chapter 9) and "Units and Large Programs" (Chapter 8) in the Turbo Pascal manual.

The Macintosh limits a program to 32K bytes of global data. To overcome this limitation, you can use pointers, as in the following example:

```
program SaveSpace;
type
  BigArray = array[1..10000] of Integer;
  { If we declared a variable of this type, it would }
  { occupy 20K bytes--more than half of our global data space! }
var
  SpaceSaver : ^BigArray;
  i : integer;
begin
  New(SpaceSaver);   { allocate space for array off of the heap }
  for i := 1 to 10000 do
    SpaceSaver^[i] := i; { index element by derefencing pointer }
end.
```

Are variables initialized automatically in Turbo Pascal?

Turbo Pascal doesn't initialize user-defined variables at run time. You must do so before it can be used.

What is the maximum length of a string?

Turbo Pascal allows 255 characters in a string.

I have a for loop that writes to the string position using index(str1[i]). When I write out the string, however, it has the old length.

When updating the value of an index of a string, update the length byte. We recommend using the *Insert* procedure to change the value of a particular character in a string, since all the string-manipulation routines in Turbo Pascal automatically change the length of the string.

When I use FillChar on a string, it gets messed up.

Remember that the zero-most byte of a string is used to hold the current length of the string. Immediately after using *FillChar*, set the length byte of your string to the appropriate value.

How do you raise a number to a power?

Include the following function in your program:

```
function Raise(x, y : Real) : Real;
begin
  Raise := exp(y * ln(x));
end;                        { Raise }
```

How do I get a real number printed in non-exponential notation?

You must use real formatting:

```
WriteLn(R : 14 : 3)
```

This means write the value of R, use a field width of 14 characters, and place 3 of them to the right of the decimal point.

How do I take the log base 10 of a number?

Include the following function in your program:

```
function Log(r : Real) : Real;
begin
```

```
   Log := ln(r) / ln(10);
end;
```

I tried to call one of the Macintosh Toolbox routines that takes a parameter of type PTR and got a compiler error 44 (Type Mismatch) when I passed it a StringPtr. How can I get this to compile?

Because of Pascal's strong typing rules, you can't directly assign a value of type PTR, for example, to some other pointer type. Instead, you have to coerce the pointer from one type to another with variable type casts. See "Variable-Type-Casts" at the end of Chapter 19 in the Turbo Reference manual for an example.

I am writing a program that uses a Mac-style interface. When the program starts up, a window flashes up on the screen and then disappears. How do I get rid of this window?

What you are seeing is Turbo's *PasConsole* window, which makes it easy to set up textbook programs. To eliminate *PasConsole*, set the {$U-} directive after your program statement.

WARNING: *PasConsole* initializes various Toolbox managers for you, so if you set {$U-} you must explicitly initialize these managers. Please refer to "Initialization" in Chapter 9 of the Turbo Pascal manual.

I'm trying to write a program using QuickDraw, but nothing seems to get initialized as Inside Macintosh indicates should happen. What is going wrong?

If your program does not have the {$U-} directive, the *PasConsole* unit is automatically used in your program. *PasConsole* defines and initializes its own set of *QuickDraw* global variables to support the console window.

If your program uses both *PasConsole* and *QuickDraw*, the *QuickDraw* unit's own set of global variables needs to be initialized by making the call `InitGraf(@thePort)`. Before doing this, however, you must save the pointer to the *PasConsole* window or its value will be wiped out in the *InitGraf* call, as illustrated below. Include the following procedure and call it once at the very beginning of your program.

```
procedure SetUpQuickDraw;
var
  TurboPort : GrafPtr;
begin
  GetPort(TurboPort);      { Save the PasConsole window pointer }
  InitGraf(@thePort);
  SetPort(TurboPort);      { Restore the PasConsole window pointer }
```

Help!

```
end;
```

Each time I run QuickDraw's random number generator, it generates the same sequence of numbers even though I change the value of RandSeed (the seed value used by the generator). What am I doing wrong?

RandSeed is a *QuickDraw* global variable, so you need to initialize this variable with the *SetUpQuickDraw* procedure listed in the previous answer. Below is a sample program that uses the system clock to ensure that the program generates a different sequence of numbers each time:

```
program RandomTest;
uses MemTypes, QuickDraw, OSIntf, ToolIntf;

var
  i : integer;
begin
  SetUpQuickDraw;                { Use the procedure listed above }
  RandSeed := TickCount;              { Set the seed to the time }
  for i := 1 to 20 do
    WriteLn(abs(Random) mod i);
  ReadLn;
end.
```

How do I output text from my program to the printer?

You must include the *PasPrinter* unit and *Write* to the printer logical device:

```
program PrintTest;
uses PasPrinter;

begin
  WriteLn(Printer, 'Send this to the printer');
  Close(Printer);
end.
```

NOTE: On LaserWriter printers, you *must* close the printer logical device to get output.

How do I do a screen dump to the printer? I want to print out QuickDraw graphics as well as Turbo's Turtlegraphics.

The following program demonstrates the Macintosh calls to print the top folder on the screen and/or the whole screen:

```
program ScreenDump;
uses MemTypes, QuickDraw, OSIntf, ToolIntf, MacPrint;

procedure HardCopy(TopWindowOnly : Boolean);
begin
  PrDrvOpen;
```

```
  if TopWindowOnly then
    PrtCall(iPrEvtCtl, LprEvtTop, 0, LScreenBits)
  else
    PrtCall(iPrEvtCtl, LprEvtAll, 0, LScreenBits);
  PrDrvrClose;
end;                                          { HardCopy }

begin
  HardCopy(true);          { Print Turbo's PasConsole window }
end.
```

*The Turbo Pascal manual indicates you can shift text left and right using
the Command-[] and Command- keys. I was unable to shift text in my program
using these keys. Also, these commands aren't highlighted on the Edit
menu.*

The text you highlight to be shifted must be made up of complete lines of
text. To mark a complete line, move the mouse to the leftmost column on
the screen and select the text by dragging straight down the left side. You
should see the lines highlighted all the way across the screen. You can then
shift the entire (rectangular) block.

*Is there any way to stop a Turbo program short of hitting the Reset button
and restarting the machine, which is very time consuming?*

The following procedure sets up your system, so you can break out of a
Turbo Pascal program without rebooting. The Miscellaneous folder on the
Samples & Utilities disk contains a file called MacsBug. If you put this file
in your System folder and restart your system, the MacsBug debugger will
automatically be loaded into memory.

Now, whenever you need to break out of a Turbo program, press the
Interrupt switch (the switch behind the Reset switch on the left side of your
Macintosh, assuming you have installed the switches). This puts you in the
MacsBug debugger, and you'll see a > prompt. At this prompt, type *E S* and
you'll be returned to the Turbo Environment.

*When I run my Turbo program, it bombs and brings up a Macintosh bomb
box with Error 2. After hitting the Resume Error, it goes into Turbo Pascal
and brings up an error message* Target address found in unit, *placing
the cursor at the end of my source file.*

A System Error 2 is an addressing error, because a Macintosh Toolbox
routine is being passed an invalid pointer or handle. Since the error is
happening in one of these pre-compiled units, Turbo cannot move to the
source line of the error. Make sure that your program checks all error codes

returned from Toolbox routines and that no errors have occurred before proceeding. In addition, read Chapter 14, "Debugging your Turbo Pascal Program," in the Turbo Pascal manual.

D

Error Codes

System Errors (Bomb Alert IDs)

Error ID **Meaning**

1	Bus error (very rare)
2	Address error (reference to word or long word at odd address)
3	Illegal instruction (undefined 68000 opcode)
4	Divide by zero exception
5	CHK exception (range testing failed)
6	TRAPV exception (trap-on-overflow instruction failed)
7	Privilege violation (shouldn't occur)
8	Trace exception (for debuggers)
9	A-Trap dispatcher failure
10	F-Trap exception
11	Misc. Exception (all other 68000 exceptions)
12	Bad trap number
13	Spurious interrupt (no interrupt handler for an interrupt)
14	I/O System Error
15	Segment Loader error
16	SANE error
17-24	Can't load package
25	Can't allocate heap block (out of memory)
26	Segment Loader error: couldn't find CODE resource #0
27	File map destroyed
28	Stack overflow
84	Menu purged (don't make menu resources purgeable!)

I/O Errors (File System/Memory Manager/Resource Manager)

```
const
  NoErr        =   0;  { All is well }
  DirFulErr    = -33;  { Directory full }
  DskFulErr    = -34;  { Disk full }
  NSVErr       = -35;  { No such volume }
  IOErr        = -36;  { I/O error }
  BdNamErr     = -37;  { Bad name }
  FNOpnErr     = -38;  { File not open }
  EOFErr       = -39;  { End of file }
  PosErr       = -40;  { Tried to position to before start of file (R/W) }
  MFulErr      = -41;  { Memory full (open) or file won't fit (load) }
  TMFOErr      = -42;  { Too many files open }
  FNFErr       = -43;  { File not found }
  WPrErr       = -44;  { Diskette is write protected }
  FLckdErr     = -45;  { File is locked }
  VLckdErr     = -46;  { Volume is locked }
  FBsyErr      = -47;  { File is busy (delete) }
  DupFNErr     = -48;  { Duplicate filename (rename) }
  OpWrErr      = -49;  { File already open with with write permission }
  ParamErr     = -50;  { Error in user parameter list }
  RFNumErr     = -51;  { Refnum error }
  GFPErr       = -52;  { Get file position error }
  VolOffLinErr = -53;  { Volume not on line error (was ejected) }
  PermErr      = -54;  { Permissions error (on file open) }
  VolOnLinErr  = -55;  { Drive volume already on-line at MountVol }
  NSDrvErr     = -56;  { No such drive (tried to mount a bad drive num) }
  NoMacDskErr  = -57;  { Not a mac diskette (sig bytes are wrong) }
  ExtFSErr     = -58;  { Volume in question belongs to an external fs }
  FSRnErr      = -59;  { File system rename error }
  BadMDBErr    = -60;  { Bad master directory block }
  WrPermErr    = -61;  { Write permissions error }

  lastDskErr   = -64;  { Last in a range of disk errors }
  noDriveErr   = -64;  { Drive not installed }
  offLinErr    = -65;  { R/W requested for an off-line drive }
  noNybErr     = -66;  { Couldn't find 5 nybbles in 200 tries }
  noAdrMkErr   = -67;  { Couldn't find valid addr mark }
  dataVerErr   = -68;  { Read verify compare failed }
  badCkSmErr   = -69;  { Addr mark checksum didn't check }
  badBtSlpErr  = -70;  { Bad addr mark bit slip nibbles }
  noDtaMkErr   = -71;  { Couldn't find a data mark header }
  badDCkSum    = -72;  { Bad data mark checksum }
  badDBtSlp    = -73;  { Bad data mark bit slip nibbles }
  wrUnderRun   = -74;  { Write underrun occurred }
  cantStepErr  = -75;  { Step handshake failed }
  tk0BadErr    = -76;  { Track 0 detect doesn't change }
  initIWMErr   = -77;  { Unable to initialize IWM }
  twoSideErr   = -78;  { Tried to read 2nd side on a 1-sided drive }
  spdAdjErr    = -79;  { Unable to correctly adjust disk speed }
  seekErr      = -80;  { Track number wrong on address mark }
  sectNFErr    = -81;  { Sector number never found on a track }
```

```
firstDskErr   = -84;   { First in a range of disk errors }

DirNFErr      = -120;  { Directory not found }
TMWDOErr      = -121;  { No free WDCB available }
BadMovErr     = -122;  { Move into offspring error }
WrgVolTypErr  = -123;  { Wrong volume type - operation not supported for MFS }
FSDSIntErr    = -127;  { Internal file system error }

MemFullErr    = -108;  { Not enough room in heap zone }
NilHandleErr  = -109;  { Master Pointer was nil in HandleZone or other }
MemWZErr      = -111;  { WhichZone failed (applied to free block) }
MemPurErr     = -112;  { Trying to purge a locked or non-purgeable block }
MemLockedErr  = -117;  { Block is locked }

ResNotFound   = -192;  { Resource not found }
ResFNotFound  = -193;  { Resource file not found }
AddResFailed  = -194;  { AddResource failed }
RmvResFailed  = -196;  { RmveResource failed }
ResAttrErr    = -198;  { Attribute does not permit operation }
MapReadErr    = -199;  { Map does not permit operation }
```

The Macintosh Character Set

This table shows the decimal numbers and screen representations of the Macintosh character set. Control (nonprinting) characters appear in boldface, along with their traditional abbreviations.

Some fonts may produce characters different than those shown here, which are for a typical laser printer font like Times or Helvetica. The Symbol, Dingbats, and Cairo fonts, for example, have different characters at every decimal location. A few high-ASCII decimal locations—such as numbers 252 to 255—can't be typed from the standard Macintosh keyboard.

DEC	HEX	CHAR	DEC	HEX	CHAR	DEC	HEX	CHAR	DEC	HEX	CHAR
0	00		18	12		36	24	$	54	36	6
1	01		19	13		37	25	%	55	37	7
2	02		20	14		38	26	&	56	38	8
3	03	**ETX**	21	15		39	27	'	57	39	9
4	04		22	16		40	28	(	58	3A	:
5	05		23	17		41	29	)	59	3B	;
6	06		24	18		42	2A	*	60	3C	<
7	07		25	19		43	2B	+	61	3D	=
8	08	**BS**	26	1A		44	2C	,	62	3E	>
9	09	**TAB**	27	1B	**ESC**	45	2D	-	63	3F	?
10	0A		28	1C	**FS**	46	2E	.	64	40	@
11	0B		29	1D	**GS**	47	2F	/	65	41	A
12	0C		30	1E	**RS**	48	30	0	66	42	B
13	0D	**CR**	31	1F	**US**	49	31	1	67	43	C
14	0E		32	20	*space*	50	32	2	68	44	D
15	0F		33	21	!	51	33	3	69	45	E
16	10		34	22	"	52	34	4	70	46	F
17	11		35	23	#	53	35	5	71	47	G

DEC	HEX	CHAR	DEC	HEX	CHAR	DEC	HEX	CHAR	DEC	HEX	CHAR
72	48	H	118	76	v	164	A4	§	210	D2	"
73	49	I	119	77	w	165	A5	•	211	D3	"
74	4A	J	120	78	x	166	A6	¶	212	D4	'
75	4B	K	121	79	y	167	A7	ß	213	D5	'
76	4C	L	122	7A	z	168	A8	®	214	D6	÷
77	4D	M	123	7B	{	169	A9	©	215	D7	◊
78	4E	N	124	7C	|	170	AA	™	216	D8	ÿ
79	4F	O	125	7D	}	171	AB	´	217	D9	Ÿ
80	50	P	126	7E	~	172	AC	¨	218	DA	⁄
81	51	Q	127	7F	**DEL**	173	AD	≠	219	DB	¤
82	52	R	128	80	Ä	174	AE	Æ	220	DC	‹
83	53	S	129	81	Å	175	AF	Ø	221	DD	›
84	54	T	130	82	Ç	176	B0	∞	222	DE	ﬁ
85	55	U	131	83	É	177	B1	±	223	DF	ﬂ
86	56	V	132	84	Ñ	178	B2	≤	224	E0	‡
87	57	W	133	85	Ö	179	B3	≥	225	E1	·
88	58	X	134	86	Ü	180	B4	¥	226	E2	‚
89	59	Y	135	87	á	181	B5	µ	227	E3	„
90	5A	Z	136	88	à	182	B6	∂	228	E4	‰
91	5B	[	137	89	â	183	B7	Σ	229	E5	Â
92	5C	\	138	8A	ä	184	B8	∏	230	E6	Ê
93	5D	]	139	8B	ã	185	B9	π	231	E7	Á
94	5E	^	140	8C	å	186	BA	∫	232	E8	Ë
95	5F	_	141	8D	ç	187	BB	ª	233	E9	È
96	60	`	142	8E	é	188	BC	º	234	EA	Í
97	61	a	143	8F	è	189	BD	Ω	235	EB	
98	62	b	144	90	ê	190	BE	æ	236	EC	Î
99	63	c	145	91	ë	191	BF	ø	237	ED	Ì
100	64	d	146	92	í	192	C0	¿	238	EE	Ó
101	65	e	147	93	ì	193	C1	¡	239	EF	Ô
102	66	f	148	94	î	194	C2	¬	240	F0	
103	67	g	149	95	ï	195	C3	√	241	F1	Ò
104	68	h	150	96	ñ	196	C4	ƒ	242	F2	Ú
105	69	i	151	97	ó	197	C5	≈	243	F3	Û
106	6A	j	152	98	ò	198	C6	∆	244	F4	Ù
107	6B	k	153	99	ô	199	C7	«	245	F5	
108	6C	l	154	9A	ö	200	C8	»	246	F6	^
109	6D	m	155	9B	õ	201	C9	…	247	F7	~
110	6E	n	156	9C	ú	202	CA		248	F8	¯
111	6F	o	157	9D	ù	203	CB	À	249	F9	˘
112	70	p	158	9E	û	204	CC	Ã	250	FA	˙
113	71	q	159	9F	ü	205	CD	Õ	251	FB	
114	72	r	160	A0	†	206	CE	Œ	252	FC	˝
115	73	s	161	A1	°	207	CF	œ	253	FD	˜
116	74	t	162	A2	¢	208	D0	–	254	FE	
117	75	u	163	A3	£	209	D1	—	255	FF	ˇ

Suggested References

Books

Inside Macintosh, 4 vols. (Reading, Mass.: Addison-Wesley Publishing Co., Inc., Apple Press, 1985), volumes I and II in particular.

Stephen Chernicoff, *Macintosh Revealed*, 2 vols. (Hasbrouck Heights, N.J.: Hayden Book Company, Apple Press, 1985).

R. G. Dromey, *How to Solve it by Computer* (Englewood Cliffs, N.J.: Prentice-Hall International, 1982).

E. Horowitz and S. Sahni, *Fundamentals of Data Structures in Pascal* (Rockville: Computer Science Press, Inc., 1984).

Scott Knaster, *How to Write Macintosh Software* (Hasbrouck Heights, N.J.: Hayden Book Company, Apple Press, 1986).

D. E. Knuth, *Fundamental Algorithms*, Vol. 1 of *The Art of Computer Programming*, 2d ed. (Reading, Mass.: Addison-Wesley, 1973).

D. E. Knuth, *Searching and Sorting*, Vol. 3 of *The Art of Computer Programming* (Reading, Mass.: Addison-Wesley, 1973).

R. Sedgewick, *Algorithms* (Reading: Addison-Wesley, 1984).

Dan Weston, *The Complete Book of Macintosh Assembly Language Programming*, 2 vols. (Glenview, Ill.: Scott, Foresman and Company, 1986).

Magazines

MacTutor Magazine, P.O. Box 400, Placentia, CA 92670

Information Services

SIGBOR, Borland's Special-Interest Group service on CompuServe. Type GO BOR.

Macintosh/Apple Users' Group (MAUG) on CompuServe. Type GO APPDEV.

Other

Apple Programmer's and Developer's Association (APDA), 290 SW 43rd St., Renton, WA 98055, (206) 251-6548.

Glossary

ASCII character set The American Standard Code for Information Interchange's standard set of numbers to represent the characters and control signals used by computers.

actual parameter A variable, expression, or constant that is substituted for a formal parameter in a procedure or function call.

address A specific location in memory.

allocate To reserve memory space for a particular purpose, usually from the heap.

array A sequential group of identical data elements that are arranged in a single data structure and are accessible by an index.

argument An alternative name for a parameter (see actual parameter).

assignment operator The symbol :=, which assigns a value to a variable or function of the same type.

assignment statement A statement that assigns a specific value to an identifier.

assembler A program that converts assembly-language programs into machine language.

assembly language The first language level above machine language. Assembly language is specific to the microprocessor it is running on. The major difference between assembly language and machine language is that assembly language provides mnemonics that make it more readable.

binary A method of representing numbers using base 2 notation, where 0 and 1 are the only digits.

binary-coded decimal (BCD) A method of floating-point arithmetic that prevents the normal round-off error inherent in computer-based arithmetic.

bit A binary digit with a value of either 0 or 1. The smallest unit of data in a computer.

block The associated declaration and statement parts of a program or subprogram.

boolean A data type that can have a value of True or False.

buffer An area of memory allocated as temporary storage.

byte A sequence of 8 bits.

cache A buffer storage that is constantly updated with recently accessed main-storage items.

case label A constant, or list of constants, that label a component statement in a **case** statement.

case selector An expression whose result is used to select which component statement of a **case** statement will be executed.

central processing unit (CPU) The "brain" of a computer system, which interprets and executes instructions and controls the other components of the system.

char A Pascal type that represents a single character.

code segment A portion of a compiled program up to 32,767 bytes in length.

comment A explanatory statement in the source code enclosed by the symbols (* *) or { }.

compiler A program that translates a program written in a high-level language into machine language.

compiler directive An instruction to the compiler that is embedded within the program; for example, {$R+} turns on range-checking.

compound statement A series of statements surrounded by a matching set of the reserved words **begin** and **end.**

concatenate The joining of two or more strings.

constant A fixed value in a program.

control structure A statement that manages the flow of execution of a program.

data structures Areas of related items in memory, represented as arrays, records, or linked lists.

debugger A special program that provides capabilities to start and stop execution of a program at will, as well as analyze values that the program is manipulating. *See* MacsBug.

decimal A method of representing numbers using base 10 notation, where legal digits range from 0 to 9.

declare The act of explicitly defining the name and type of an identifier in a program.

dereferencing The act of accessing a value pointed to by a pointer variable (rather than the pointer variable itself).

definition part The part of a program where constants, labels, and structured types are defined.

delimiter A boundary marker that can be a word, a character, or a symbol.

dynamic allocation The allocation and de-allocation of memory from the heap at run time.

dynamic variable A variable on the heap.

enumerated type A user-defined type that consists of a list of identifiers in which the order and identifier names are determined by the programmer.

expression Part of a statement that represents a value or can be used to calculate a value.

extension Any addition to the standard definition of a language.

external A file of one or more subprograms that have been written in assembly language and assembled to native executable code.

field list The field name and type definition of a record.

field width The number of place holders in an output statement.

file A collection of data that can be stored on and retrieved from a disk.

file pointer A pointer that tracks where the next object will be retrieved from within a file.

file variable An identifier in a program that represents a file.

fixed-point notation The representation of real numbers without decimal points.

flag A variable, usually of type Integer or Boolean, that changes value to indicate that an event has taken place.

floating-point notation The representation of real numbers using decimal points.

formal parameter An identifier in a procedure or function declaration heading that represents the arguments that will be passed to the subprogram when it is called.

forward declaration The declaration of a procedure or function and its parameters in advance of the actual definition of the subroutine.

function A subroutine that computes and returns a value.

global variable A variable declared in the main program block that can be accessed from anywhere within the program.

heap An area of memory reserved for the dynamic allocation of variables.

hexadecimal A method of representing numbers using base 16 notation, where legal digits range from 0 to 9 and A to F.

identifier A user-defined name for a specific item.

increment To increase the value of a variable.

index A position within a list of elements.

initialize The process of giving a known initial value to a variable or data structure.

input The information a program receives from some external device, such as a keyboard.

integer A numeric variable that is a whole number in the range –32768 to 32767.

interactive A program that communicates with a user through some I/O device.

interrupt The temporary halting of a program in order to process an event of higher priority.

I/O Short for Input/Output. The process of receiving or sending data.

I/O error An error that occurs while trying to input or output data.

interpreter A program that sequentially interprets each statement in a program into machine code and then immediately executes it.

islands Nonrelocatable blocks that interfere with heap compaction.

iteration The process of repetition or looping.

label An identifier that marks a place in the program text for a **goto** statement.

linked list A dynamic data structure that is made up of elements, each of which point to the next element in the list through a pointer variable.

local identifier An identifier declared within a procedure or a function.

local variable A variable declared within a procedure or a function.

long word A location in memory occupying 4 adjacent bytes; the storage required for a variable of type LongInt.

machine language A language consisting of strings of 0s and 1s that the computer interprets as instructions.

main program The main statement part of a program from which all its subprograms are executed.

module A self-contained routine or group of routines.

nesting The placement of one unit within another.

nil pointer A pointer having the special value nil; a nil pointer doesn't point to anything.

node An individual element of a tree or list.

object code The output of a compiler.

operand An argument that is combined with one or more operands and operators to form an expression.

operating system A program that manages all operations and resources of the computer.

operator A symbol, such as +, that is used to form expressions.

operator hierarchy The rules that determine the order in which operators in an expression are evaluated.

ordinal type An ordered range of values.

overflow The condition that results when an operation produces a value that is more positive or negative than the computer can represent, given the allocated space for the value or expression.

parameter A variable or value that is passed to a procedure or function.

parameter list The list of value and variable parameters declared in the heading of a procedure or function declaration.

pointer A variable that points to a specific memory location.

pop The removal of the topmost element from a stack.

predefined identifier A constant, type, file, logical device, procedure, or function that is available to the programmer without having to be defined or declared.

procedure A subprogram that can be called from various parts of a larger program.

procedure call The invocation of a procedure.

push The addition of an element to the top of a stack.

queue A data structure in which the first element placed in the data structure is the first element to be removed.

random access Directly accessing an element of a data structure without sequentially searching the entire structure for the element.

random access memory (RAM) Memory devices that can be read from and written to.

range-checking A Turbo Pascal feature that checks a value to make sure it is within the legal range defined.

read-only memory (ROM) The memory device from which data can be read but not written.

real number A number represented by decimal point and/or scientific notation.

record A structured data type referenced by one identifier that consists of several different fields.

recursion A programming technique in which a subprogram calls itself.

relational operator The operators, =, <>, <, >, <=, >=, and **in**, all of which are used to form boolean expressions.

reserved word An identifier reserved by the compiler.

SANE Standard Apple Numeric Environment; ROM-based numeric routines accessed through unit SANE.

scalar type A Pascal data type consisting of ordered components.

scope The visibility of an identifier within a program.

sequential access The ordered access of each element of a data structure, starting at the first element of the structure.

set An unordered group of elements, all of the same scalar type.

set operator The symbols, +, –, *, =, <=, >=, <>, and **in**, all of which return set-type results when used with set-type operands.

simple type A predefined or user-defined scalar type.

source code The input to a compiler.

stack A data structure in which the last element stored is the first to be removed.

stack overflow An error condition that occurs when the amount of space allocated to the computer's stack is used up.

stack segment The segment in memory allocated as the program's stack.

statement The simplest unit in a program; statements are separated by semicolons.

string A sequence of characters that can be treated as a single unit.

structured type One of the predefined types (array, set, record, file, or string) that are composed of structured data elements.

subprogram A procedure or function within a program; a subroutine.

subrange A continuous range of any scalar type.

subscript An identifier used to access a particular element of an array.

syntax error An error caused by violating the rules of a programming language.

terminal An I/O device for communication between a user and a computer.

tree A dynamic data structure in which a node (branch of a tree) may point to one or more other nodes.

type definition The specification of a type based upon other types that are already defined.

value parameter A procedure or function parameter that is passed by value; that is, the value of the parameter is passed and cannot be changed.

vanilla Programmese for standard or basic.

variable declaration A declaration that consists of the variable and its associated type.

variable parameter A procedure or function parameter that is passed by reference; that is, the address of the parameter is passed so that the value of the parameter can be accessed and modified.

variant record A record in which some fields share the same area in memory.

word A location in memory occupying 2 adjacent bytes; the storage required for a variable of type Integer.

Index

V

value parameter 598
value parameters 144
variable declaration 66
Variables 66
variant part
    syntax 188
variant records. *See also* case
    statement. 186
var vs. value parameters 176
volumes 221, 530
    reference number 535

W

while statement 85, 121
window
    terminal 50
WindowDemo.Pas 9, 474
Window Manager 463, 622
    mouse-downs and 471
Window Manager routines 470
    DisposeWindow 470
    DragWindow 471
    FrontWindow 470
    GetNewWindow 470
    InitWindows 469

    NewWindow 470
    SelectWindow 471
Windows 461, 463, 465, 467, 469, 471,
    473, 475, 477, 479, 481, 483
    active 463
    application 463
    content region 466
    document 462
    drawing 468
    goAwayFlag 466
    hilited flag 466
    inactive 463
    structure region 466
    system 463
    typing 476
    visible flag 466
    window list 470
Wirth, Niklaus 26
with statement 85, 183
pointer restrictions 186
WriteLn 48, 85
WriteLn procedure 216
Write procedure 216

X

xor 119

Borland
Software

BORLAND
I N T E R N A T I O N A L

4585 Scotts Valley Drive, Scotts Valley, CA 95066

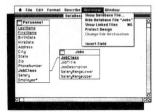
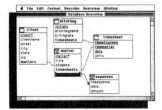
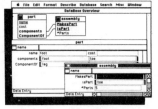

SIDEKICK®: THE DESKTOP ORGANIZER Release 2.0

Macintosh™

The most complete and comprehensive collection of desk accessories available for your Macintosh!

Thousands of users already know that SideKick is the best collection of desk accessories available for the Macintosh. With our new Release 2.0, the best just got better.

We've just added two powerful high-performance tools to SideKick—Outlook™: The Outliner and MacPlan™: The Spreadsheet. They work in perfect harmony with each other and *while* you run other programs!

Outlook: The Outliner

- It's the desk accessory with more power than a stand-alone outliner
- A great desktop publishing tool, Outlook lets you incorporate both text and graphics into your outlines
- Works hand-in-hand with MacPlan
- Allows you to work on several outlines at the same time

MacPlan: The Spreadsheet

- Integrates spreadsheets and graphs
- Does both formulas and straight numbers
- Graph types include bar charts, stacked bar charts, pie charts and line graphs
- Includes 12 example templates free!
- Pastes graphics and data right into Outlook creating professional memos and reports, complete with headers and footers.

SideKick: The Desktop Organizer, Release 2.0 now includes

- ☑ Outlook: The Outliner
- ☑ MacPlan: The Spreadsheet
- ☑ Mini word processor
- ☑ Calendar
- ☑ PhoneLog
- ☑ Analog clock
- ☑ Alarm system
- ☑ Calculator
- ☑ Report generator
- ☑ Telecommunications (new version now supports XModem file transfer protocol)

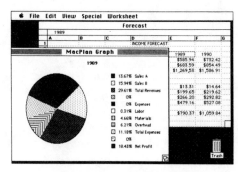

MacPlan does both spreadsheets and business graphs. Paste them into your Outlook files and generate professional reports.

Suggested Retail Price: $99.95 (not copy protected)

Minimum system configurations: Macintosh 512K or Macintosh Plus with one disk drive. One 800K or two 400K drives are recommended. With one 400K drive, a limited number of desk accessories will be installable per disk.

BORLAND
INTERNATIONAL

TURBO PASCAL MACINTOSH™

The ultimate Pascal development environment

Borland's new Turbo Pascal for the Mac is so incredibly fast that it can compile 1,420 lines of source code in the 7.1 seconds it took you to read this!

And reading the rest of this takes about *5 minutes*, which is plenty of time for Turbo Pascal for the Mac to compile at least *60,000 more lines* of source code!

Turbo Pascal for the Mac does both Windows and "Units"

The *separate* compilation of routines offered by Turbo Pascal for the Mac creates modules called "Units," which can be linked to any Turbo Pascal program. This "modular pathway" gives you "pieces" which can then be integrated into larger programs. You get a more efficient use of memory and a reduction in the time it takes to develop large programs.

Turbo Pascal for the Mac is so compatible with Lisa° that they should be living together

Routines from Macintosh Programmer's Workshop Pascal and Inside Macintosh can be compiled and run with only the subtlest changes. Turbo Pascal for the Mac is also compatible with the Hierarchical File System of the Macintosh.

The 27-second Guide to Turbo Pascal for the Mac

- Compilation speed of more than 12,000 lines per minute
- "Unit" structure lets you create programs in modular form
- Multiple editing windows—up to 8 at once
- Compilation options include compiling to disk or memory, or compile and run
- No need to switch between programs to compile or run a program
- Streamlined development and debugging
- Compatibility with Macintosh Programmer's

- Workshop Pascal (with minimal changes)
- Compatibility with Hierarchical File System of your Mac
- Ability to define default volume and folder names used in compiler directives
- Search and change features in the editor speed up and simplify alteration of routines
- Ability to use all available Macintosh memory without limit
- "Units" included to call all the routines provided by Macintosh Toolbox

---

Suggested Retail Price: $99.95* (not copy protected)

*Introductory price expires July 1, 1987

Minimum system configuration: Macintosh 512K or Macintosh Plus with one disk drive.

Turbo Pascal and SideKick are registered trademarks of Borland International, Inc. and Reflex is a registered trademark of Borland/Analytica, Inc. Macintosh is a trademark of McIntosh Laboratories, Inc. licensed to Apple Computer with its express permission. Lisa is a registered trademark of Apple Computer, Inc. Inside Macintosh is a copyright of Apple Computer, Inc.
Copyright 1987 Borland International BOR 0167A

BORLAND INTERNATIONAL

Borland Software
ORDER TODAY

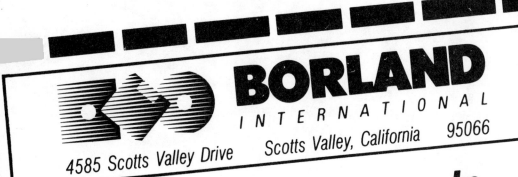

BORLAND
I N T E R N A T I O N A L

4585 Scotts Valley Drive   Scotts Valley, California   95066

To Order By Credit Card, Call (800) 255-8008

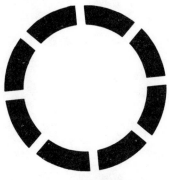

In California call (800) 742-1133

In Canada call (800) 237-1136